P9-CJX-140

DANIEL JONAH GOLDHAGEN

Hitler's Willing Executioners

Daniel Jonah Goldhagen is an Associate of Harvard University's Minda de Gunzburg Center for European Studies. His doctoral dissertation, which is the basis for this book, was awarded the American Political Science Association's 1994 Gabriel A. Almond Award for the best dissertation in the field of comparative politics. After publication of this book in Germany, in 1997 Daniel Jonah Goldhagen won the highly prestigious Democracy Prize. He is the author of *A Moral Reckoning: The Role of the Catholic Church in the Holocaust and Its Unfulfilled Duty of Repair.*

Hitler's Willing Executioners

Hitler's Willing Executioners

*Ordinary Germans and
the Holocaust*

DANIEL JONAH
GOLDHAGEN

Vintage Books

A DIVISION OF RANDOM HOUSE, INC.

NEW YORK

FIRST VINTAGE BOOKS EDITION, FEBRUARY 1997

The Library of Congress has cataloged the Knopf edition as follows:
Goldhagen, Daniel Jonah.
Hitler's willing executioners: ordinary Germans and the Holocaust / Daniel
Jonah Goldhagen.—1st ed.

p. cm.

Includes bibliographical references and index.
ISBN 0-679-44695-8
1. Holocaust, Jewish (1939–1945)—Causes. 2. Antisemitism—Germany.
3. War criminals—Germany—Psychology. 1. Title.
D804.3.G648 1996
940.53'18—dc20   95-38591
CIP

Vintage ISBN: 0-679-77268-5

Random House Web address: http://www.randomhouse.com/

Printed in the United States of America
79C86

*To Erich Goldhagen,
my father and teacher*

No man can struggle with advantage against the spirit of his age and country, and however powerful a man may be, it is hard for him to make his contemporaries share feelings and ideas which run counter to the general run of their hopes and desires.

ALEXIS DE TOCQUEVILLE
Democracy in America

CONTENTS

Maps may be found on pages 159, 205,
329, 347, 366, 367, 368, and 413.

Hitler's Willing Executioners

Introduction

RECONCEIVING CENTRAL
ASPECTS OF THE HOLOCAUST

CAPTAIN WOLFGANG HOFFMANN was a zealous executioner of Jews. As the commander of one of the three companies of Police Battalion 101, he and his fellow officers led their men, who were not SS men but ordinary Germans, in the deportation and gruesome slaughter in Poland of tens of thousands of Jewish men, women, and children. Yet this same man, in the midst of his genocidal activities, once stridently disobeyed a superior order that he deemed morally objectionable.

The order commanded that members of his company sign a declaration that had been sent to them. Hoffmann began his written refusal by saying that upon reading it, he had thought that an error had been made, "because it appeared to me a piece of impertinence to demand of a decent German soldier to sign a declaration in which he obligates himself not to steal, not to plunder, and not to buy without paying. . . ." He continued by describing how unnecessary such a demand was, since his men, of proper ideological conviction, were fully aware that such activities were punishable offenses. He also pronounced to his superiors his judgment of his men's character and actions, including, presumably, their slaughtering of Jews. He wrote that his men's adherence to German norms of morality and conduct "derives from their own free will and is not caused by a craving for advantages or fear of punishment." Hoffmann then declared defiantly: "As an officer I regret, however, that I must set my view against that of the battalion commander and am not able to carry out the order, since I feel injured in my sense of honor. I must decline to sign a general declaration."[1]

Hoffmann's letter is astonishing and instructive for a number of reasons. Here is an officer who had already led his men in the genocidal slaughter of tens of thousands of Jews, yet who deemed it an effrontery that anyone might suppose that he and his men would steal food from Poles! The genocidal killer's honor was wounded, and wounded doubly, for he was both a soldier and a German. His conception of the obligations that Germans owed the "subhuman" Poles must have been immeasurably greater than those owed Jews. Hoffmann also understood his parent institution to be so tolerant that he was willing to refuse a direct order and even to record his brazen insubordination in writing. His judgment of his men—a judgment based, no doubt, on the compass of their activities, including their genocidal ones—was that they acted not out of fear of punishment, but with willing assent; they acted from conviction, according to their inner beliefs.

Hoffmann's written refusal sets in sharp relief important, neglected aspects of the Holocaust—such as the laxness of many of the institutions of killing, the capacity of the perpetrators to refuse orders (even orders to kill), and, not least of all, their moral autonomy—and provides insight into the unusual mind-set of the perpetrators, including their motivation for killing. It should force us to ask long-ignored questions about the sort of worldview and the institutional context that could produce such a letter which, though on a tangential subject and seemingly bizarre, reveals a host of typical features of the Germans' perpetration of the Holocaust. Understanding the actions and mind-set of the tens of thousands of ordinary Germans who, like Captain Hoffmann, became genocidal killers is the subject of this book.

DURING THE HOLOCAUST, Germans extinguished the lives of six million Jews and, had Germany not been defeated, would have annihilated millions more. The Holocaust was also the defining feature of German politics and political culture during the Nazi period, the most shocking event of the twentieth century, and the most difficult event to understand in all of German history. The Germans' persecution of the Jews culminating in the Holocaust is thus the central feature of Germany during the Nazi period. It is so not because we are retrospectively shocked by the most shocking event of the century, but because of what it meant to Germans at the time and why so many of them contributed to it. It marked their departure from the community of "civilized peoples."[2] This departure needs to be explained.

Explaining the Holocaust is the central intellectual problem for understanding Germany during the Nazi period. All the other problems combined are comparatively simple. How the Nazis came to power, how they suppressed the left, how they revived the economy, how the state was structured and functioned, how they made and waged war are all more or less ordinary, "normal" events, easily enough understood. But the Holocaust and the change in sensibilities that it involved "defies" explanation. There is no comparable event in the twentieth century, indeed in modern European history. Whatever the remaining debates, every other major event of nineteenth- and twentieth-century German history and political development is, in comparison to the Holocaust, transparently clear in its genesis. Explaining how the Holocaust happened is a daunting task empirically and even more so theoretically, so much so that some have argued, in my view erroneously, that it is "inexplicable." The theoretical difficulty is shown by its utterly new nature, by the inability of social theory (or what passed for common sense) preceding it to provide a hint not only that it would happen but also that it was even possible. Retrospective theory has not done much better, shedding but modest light in the darkness.

The overall objective of this book is to explain why the Holocaust occurred, to explain how it could occur. The success of this enterprise depends upon a number of subsidiary tasks, which consist fundamentally of reconceiving three subjects: the perpetrators of the Holocaust, German antisemitism, and the nature of German society during the Nazi period.

FOREMOST AMONG the three subjects that must be reconceived are the perpetrators of the Holocaust. Few readers of this book will have failed to give some thought to the question of what impelled the perpetrators of the Holocaust to kill. Few have neglected to provide for themselves an answer to the question, an answer that necessarily derives usually not from any intimate knowledge of the perpetrators and their deeds, but greatly from the individual's conception of human nature and social life. Few would probably disagree with the notion that the perpetrators should be studied.

Yet until now the perpetrators, the most important group of people responsible for the slaughter of European Jewry, excepting the Nazi leadership itself, have received little concerted attention in the literature that describes the events and purports to explain them. Surprisingly, the vast literature on the Holocaust contains little on the people who were its executors. Little is known of who the perpetrators were, the details of their actions, the circumstances of many of their deeds, let alone their motivations. A decent estimate of how many people contributed to the genocide, of how many perpetrators there were, has never been made. Certain institutions of killing and the people who manned them have been hardly treated or not at all. As a consequence of this general lack of knowledge, all kinds of misunderstandings and myths about the perpetrators abound. These misconceptions, moreover, have broader implications for the way in which the Holocaust and Germany during the Nazi period are conceived and understood.

We must therefore refocus our attention, our intellectual energy, which has overwhelmingly been devoted elsewhere, onto the perpetrators, namely the men and women who in some intimate way knowingly contributed to the slaughter of Jews.[3] We must investigate their deeds in detail and explain their actions. It is not sufficient to treat the institutions of killing collectively or singly as internally uncomplicated instruments of the Nazi leadership's will, as well-lubricated machines that the regime activated, as if by the flick of a switch, to do its bidding, whatever it might have been. The study of the men and women who collectively gave life to the inert institutional forms, who peopled the institutions of genocidal killing must be set at the focus of scholarship on the Holocaust and become as central to investigations of the genocide as they were to its commission.

These people were overwhelmingly and most importantly Germans. While members of other national groups aided the Germans in their slaughter of Jews, the commission of the Holocaust was primarily a German undertaking. Non-Germans were not essential to the perpetration of the genocide, and they did not supply the drive and initiative that pushed it forward. To be sure, had the Germans not found European (especially, eastern European) helpers, then the Holocaust would have unfolded somewhat differently, and the Germans would likely not have succeeded in killing as many Jews. Still, this was above all a German enterprise; the decisions, plans, organizational resources, and the majority of its executors were German. Comprehension and explanation of the perpetration of the Holocaust therefore requires an explanation of the *Germans'* drive to kill Jews. Because what can be said about the Germans cannot be said about any other nationality or about all of the other nationalities combined—namely no Germans, no Holocaust—the focus here is appropriately on the German perpetrators.

The first task in restoring the perpetrators to the center of our understanding of the Holocaust is to restore to them their identities, grammatically by using not the passive but the active voice in order to ensure that they, the actors, are not absent from their own deeds (as in, "five hundred Jews were killed in city X on date Y"),[4] and by eschewing convenient, yet often inappropriate and obfuscating labels, like "Nazis" and "SS men," and calling them what they were, "Germans." The most appropriate, indeed the only appropriate *general* proper name for the Germans who perpetrated the Holocaust is "Germans."[5] They were Germans acting in the name of Germany and its highly popular leader, Adolf Hitler. Some were "Nazis," either by reason of Nazi Party membership or according to ideological conviction; some were not. Some were SS men; some were not. The perpetrators killed and made their other genocidal contributions under the auspices of many institutions other than the SS. Their chief common denominator was that they were all Germans pursuing German national political goals—in this case, the genocidal killing of Jews.[6] To be sure, it is sometimes appropriate to use institutional or occupational names or roles and the generic terms "perpetrators" or "killers" to describe the perpetrators, yet this must be done only in the understood context that these men and women were Germans first, and SS men, policemen, or camp guards second.

A second and related task is to reveal something of the perpetrators' backgrounds, to convey the character and quality of their lives as genocidal killers, to bring to life their *Lebenswelt*. What *exactly* did they do when they were killing? What did they do during their time as members of institutions of killing, while they were not undertaking killing operations? Until a great deal is known about the details of their actions and lives, neither they nor the perpetration of their crimes can be understood. The unearthing of the perpetrators' lives, the presentation of a "thick," rather than the customary paper-thin, description of their actions, as important and necessary as it is for its own sake, lays the foundation for the main task of this book's consideration of them, namely to explain their actions.[7]

It is my contention that this cannot be done unless such an analysis is embedded in an understanding of German society before and during its Nazi period, particularly of the political culture that produced the perpetrators and their actions. This has been notably absent from attempts to explain the perpetrators' actions, and has doomed these attempts to providing situational explanations, ones that focus almost exclusively on institutional and immediate social psychological influences, often conceived of as irresistible pressures. The men and women who became the Holocaust's perpetrators were shaped by and operated in a particular social and historical setting. They brought with them prior elaborate conceptions of the world, ones that were common to their society, the investigation of which is necessary for explaining their actions. This entails, most fundamentally, a reexamination of the character and development of antisemitism in Germany during its Nazi period and before, which in turn requires a theoretical reconsideration of the character of antisemitism itself.

Studies of the Holocaust have been marred by a poor understanding and an under-theorizing of antisemitism. Antisemitism is a broad, typically imprecisely used term, encompassing a wide variety of phenomena. This naturally poses enormous obstacles for explaining the perpetration of the Holocaust because a central task of any such attempt is to evaluate whether and how antisemitism produced and influenced its many aspects. In my view, our understanding of antisemitism and of the relationship of antisemitism to

the (mal)treatment of Jews is deficient. We must begin considering these subjects anew and develop a conceptual apparatus that is descriptively powerful
and analytically useful for addressing the ideational causes of social action.
The first chapter is devoted to initiating such a theoretical reconsideration.

The study of the perpetrators further demands a reconsideration, indeed
a reconceiving, of the character of German society during its Nazi period and
before. The Holocaust was the defining aspect of Nazism, but not only of
Nazism. It was also the defining feature of German society during its Nazi
period. No significant aspect of German society was untouched by anti-
Jewish policy; from the economy, to society, to politics, to culture, from cattle farmers, to merchants, to the organization of small towns, to lawyers,
doctors, physicists, and professors. No analysis of German society, no understanding or characterization of it, can be made without placing the persecution and extermination of the Jews at its center. The program's first parts,
namely the systematic exclusion of Jews from German economic and social
life, were carried out in the open, under approving eyes, and with the complicity of virtually all sectors of German society, from the legal, medical, and
teaching professions, to the churches, both Catholic and Protestant, to the
gamut of economic, social, and cultural groups and associations.[8] Hundreds
of thousands of Germans contributed to the genocide and the still larger system of subjugation that was the vast concentration camp system. Despite the
regime's half-hearted attempts to keep the genocide beyond the view of most
Germans, millions knew of the mass slaughters.[9] Hitler announced many
times, emphatically, that the war would end in the extermination of the
Jews.[10] The killings met with general understanding, if not approval. No
other policy (of similar or greater scope) was carried out with more persistence and zeal, and with fewer difficulties, than the genocide, except perhaps
the war itself. The Holocaust defines not only the history of Jews during the
middle of the twentieth century but also the history of Germans. While the
Holocaust changed Jewry and Jews irrevocably, its commission was possible,
I argue, because Germans had *already* been changed. The fate of the Jews
may have been a direct, which does not, however, mean an inexorable, outgrowth of a worldview shared by the vast majority of the German people.

Each of these reconceivings—of the perpetrators, of German antisemitism, and of German society during the Nazi period—is complex, requires difficult theoretical work and the marshaling of considerable empirical
material, and, ultimately, is deserving of a separate book in its own right.
While the undertaking of each one is justifiable on its own theoretical and empirical grounds, each, in my view, is also strengthened by the others, for they
are interrelated tasks. Together the three suggest that we must substantially
rethink important aspects of German history, the nature of Germany during

the Nazi period, and the perpetration of the Holocaust. This rethinking requires, on a number of subjects, the turning of conventional wisdom on its head, and the adoption of a new and substantially different view of essential aspects of this period, aspects which have generally been considered settled. Explaining why the Holocaust occurred requires a radical revision of what has until now been written. This book is that revision.

This revision calls for us to acknowledge what has for so long been generally denied or obscured by academic and non-academic interpreters alike: Germans' antisemitic beliefs about Jews were the central causal agent of the Holocaust. They were the central causal agent not only of Hitler's decision to annihilate European Jewry (which is accepted by many) but also of the perpetrators' willingness to kill and to brutalize Jews. The conclusion of this book is that antisemitism moved many thousands of "ordinary" Germans—and would have moved millions more, had they been appropriately positioned—to slaughter Jews. Not economic hardship, not the coercive means of a totalitarian state, not social psychological pressure, not invariable psychological propensities, but ideas about Jews that were pervasive in Germany, and had been for decades, induced ordinary Germans to kill unarmed, defenseless Jewish men, women, and children by the thousands, systematically and without pity.

FOR WHAT developments would a comprehensive explanation of the Holocaust have to account? For the extermination of the Jews to occur, four principal things were necessary:

1. The Nazis—that is, the leadership, specifically Hitler—had to decide to undertake the extermination.[11]
2. They had to gain control over the Jews, namely over the territory in which they resided.[12]
3. They had to organize the extermination and devote to it sufficient resources.[13]
4. They had to induce a large number of people to carry out the killings.

The vast literature on Nazism and the Holocaust treats in great depth the first three elements, as well as others, such as the origins and character of Hitler's genocidal beliefs, and the Nazis' ascendancy to power.[14] Yet, as I have already indicated, it has treated the last element, the focus of this book, perfunctorily and mainly by assumption. It is therefore important to discuss here some analytical and interpretive issues that are central to studying the perpetrators.

Owing to the neglect of the perpetrators in the study of the Holocaust, it is no surprise that the existing interpretations of them have been generally produced in a near empirical vacuum. Until recently, virtually no research has been done on the perpetrators, save on the leaders of the Nazi regime. In the last few years, some publications have appeared that treat one group or another, yet the state of our knowledge about the perpetrators remains deficient.[15] We know little about many of the institutions of killing, little about many aspects of the perpetration of the genocide, and still less about the perpetrators themselves. As a consequence, popular and scholarly myths and misconceptions about the perpetrators abound, including the following. It is commonly believed that the Germans slaughtered Jews by and large in the gas chambers,[16] and that without gas chambers, modern means of transportation, and efficient bureaucracies, the Germans would have been unable to kill millions of Jews. The belief persists that somehow only technology made horror on this scale possible.[17] "Assembly-line killing" is one of the stock phrases in discussions of the event. It is generally believed that gas chambers, because of their efficiency (which is itself greatly overstated), were a necessary instrument for the genocidal slaughter, and that the Germans chose to construct the gas chambers in the first place because they needed more efficient means of killing the Jews.[18] It has been generally believed by scholars (at least until very recently) and non-scholars alike that the perpetrators were primarily, overwhelmingly SS men, the most devoted and brutal Nazis.[19] It has been a widespread conviction (again until recently) that had a German refused to kill Jews, then he himself would have been killed, sent to a concentration camp, or severely punished.[20] All of these views, views that fundamentally shape people's understanding of the Holocaust, have been held unquestioningly as though they were self-evident truths. They have been virtual articles of faith (derived from sources other than historical inquiry), have substituted for knowledge, and have distorted the way in which this period is understood.

The absence of attention devoted to the perpetrators is surprising for a host of reasons, only one of which is the existence of a now over-ten-year-long debate about the genesis of the *initiation* of the Holocaust, which has come to be called by the misnomer the "intentionalist-functionalist" debate.[21] For better or worse, this debate has become the organizing debate for much of the scholarship on the Holocaust. Although it has improved our understanding of the exact chronology of the Germans' persecution and mass murder of the Jews, it has also, because of the terms in which it has been cast, confused the analysis of the causes of the Germans' policies (this is taken up in Chapter 4), and it has done next to nothing to increase our knowledge of the perpetrators. Of those who defined this debate and made its central early contributions, only one saw fit to ask the question, Why, once the killing began (however it did), did those receiving the orders to kill do so?[22] It appears that for one reason or another, all the participants in the debate assumed that executing such orders was unproblematic for the actors, and unproblematic for historians and social scientists. The limited character of our knowledge, and therefore our understanding, of this period is highlighted by the simple fact that (however the category of "perpetrator" is defined) the number of people who were perpetrators is unknown. No good estimate, virtually no estimate of any kind, exists of the number of people who knowingly contributed to the genocidal killing in some intimate way. Scholars who discuss them, inexplicably, neither attempt such an estimate nor point out that this, a topic of such great significance, is an important gap in our knowledge.[23] If ten thousand Germans were perpetrators, then the perpetration of the Holocaust, perhaps the Holocaust itself, is a phenomenon of one kind, perhaps the deed of a select, unrepresentative group. If five hundred thousand or one million Germans were perpetrators, then it is a phenomenon of another kind, perhaps best conceived as a German national project. Depending on the number and identity of the Germans who contributed to the genocidal slaughter, different sorts of questions, inquiries, and bodies of theory might be appropriate or necessary in order to explain it.

This dearth of knowledge, not only about the perpetrators but also about the functioning of their host institutions has not stopped some interpreters from making assertions about them—although the most striking fact remains how few even bother to address the subject, let alone take it up at length. Still, from the literature a number of conjectured explanations can be distilled, even if they are not always clearly specified or elaborated upon in a sustained manner. (In fact, strands of different explanations are frequently intermingled without great coherence.) Some of them have been proposed to explain the actions of the German people generally and, by extension, they would apply to the perpetrators as well. Rather than laying out what each interpreter has posited about the perpetrators, an analytical account is provided here of the major arguments, with references to leading exemplars of each one. The most important of them can be classified into five categories:

One explanation argues for external compulsion: the perpetrators were coerced. They were left, by the threat of punishment, with no choice but to follow orders. After all, they were part of military or police-like institutions, institutions with a strict chain of command, demanding subordinate compliance to orders, which should have punished insubordination severely, perhaps with death. Put a gun to anyone's head, so goes the thinking, and he will shoot others to save himself.[24]

A second explanation conceives of the perpetrators as having been blind followers of orders. A number of proposals have been made for the source or sources of this alleged propensity to obey: Hitler's charisma (the perpetrators were, so to speak, caught in his spell),[25] a general human tendency to obey authority,[26] a peculiarly German reverence for and propensity to obey authority,[27] or a totalitarian society's blunting of the individual's moral sense and its conditioning of him or her to accept all tasks as necessary.[28] So a common proposition exists, namely that people obey authority, with a variety of accounts of why this is so. Obviously, the notion that authority, particularly state authority, tends to elicit obedience merits consideration.

A third explanation holds the perpetrators to have been subject to tremendous social psychological pressure, placed upon each one by his comrades and/or by the expectations that accompany the institutional roles that individuals occupy. It is, so goes the argument, extremely difficult for individuals to resist pressures to conform, pressures which can lead individuals to participate in acts which they on their own would not do, indeed would abhor. And a variety of psychological mechanisms are available for such people to rationalize their actions.[29]

A fourth explanation sees the perpetrators as having been petty bureaucrats, or soulless technocrats, who pursued their self-interest or their technocratic goals and tasks with callous disregard for the victims. It can hold for administrators in Berlin as well as for concentration camp personnel. They all had careers to make, and because of the psychological propensity among those who are but cogs in a machine to attribute responsibility to others for overall policy, they could callously pursue their own careers or their own institutional or material interests.[30] The deadening effects of institutions upon the sense of individual responsibility, on the one hand, and the frequent willingness of people to put their interests before those of others, on the other, need hardly be belabored.

A fifth explanation asserts that because tasks were so fragmented, the perpetrators could not understand what the real nature of their actions was; they could not comprehend that their small assignments were actually part of a global extermination program. To the extent that they could, this line of thinking continues, the fragmentation of tasks allowed them to deny the importance of their own contributions and to displace responsibility for them onto others.[31] When engaged in unpleasant or morally dubious tasks, it is well known that people have a tendency to shift blame to others.

The explanations can be reconceptualized in terms of their accounts of the actors' capacity for volition: The first explanation (namely coercion) says that the killers could not say "no." The second explanation (obedience) and the third (situational pressure) maintain that Germans were psychologically incapable of saying "no." The fourth explanation (self-interest) contends that Germans had sufficient personal incentives to kill in order not to want to say "no." The fifth explanation (bureaucratic myopia) claims that it never even occurred to the perpetrators that they were engaged in an activity that might make them responsible for saying "no."

Each of these conventional explanations may sound plausible, and some of them obviously contain some truth, so what is wrong with them? While each suffers from particular defects, which are treated at length in Chapter 15, they share a number of dubious *common* assumptions and features worth mentioning here.

The conventional explanations *assume* a neutral or condemnatory attitude on the part of the perpetrators towards their actions. They therefore premise their interpretations on the assumption that it must be shown how people can be brought to commit acts to which they would not inwardly assent, acts which they would not agree are necessary or just. They either ignore, deny, or radically minimize the importance of Nazi and perhaps the perpetrators' ideology, moral values, and conception of the victims, for engendering the perpetrators' willingness to kill. Some of these conventional explanations also caricature the perpetrators, and Germans in general. The explanations treat them as if they had been people lacking a moral sense, lacking the ability to make decisions and take stances. They do not conceive of the actors as human agents, as people with wills, but as beings moved solely by external forces or by transhistorical and invariant psychological propensities, such as the slavish following of narrow "self-interest." The conventional explanations suffer from two other major conceptual failings. They do not sufficiently recognize the extraordinary nature of the deed: the mass killing of people. They *assume* and imply that inducing people to kill human beings is fundamentally no different from getting them to do any other unwanted or distasteful task. Also, none of the conventional explanations deems the *identity* of the victims to have mattered. The conventional explanations imply that the perpetrators would have treated any other group of intended victims in exactly the same way. That the victims were Jews—according to the logic of these explanations—is irrelevant.

I maintain that any explanation that fails to acknowledge the actors' capacity to know and to judge, namely to understand and to have views about the significance and the morality of their actions, that fails to hold the actors' beliefs and values as central, that fails to emphasize the autonomous motivating force of Nazi ideology, particularly its central component of antisemitism, cannot possibly succeed in telling us much about why the perpetrators acted as they did. Any explanation that ignores either the particular nature of the perpetrators' actions—the systematic, large-scale killing and brutalizing of people—or the identity of the victims is inadequate for a host of reasons. All explanations that adopt these positions, as do the conventional explanations, suffer a mirrored, double failure of recognition of the human aspect of the

Holocaust: the humanity of the perpetrators, namely their capacity to judge and to choose to act inhumanely, and the humanity of the victims, that what the perpetrators did, they did to these people with their specific identities, and not to animals or things.

My explanation—which is new to the scholarly literature on the perpetrators[32]—is that the perpetrators, "ordinary Germans," were animated by antisemitism, by a particular *type* of antisemitism that led them to conclude that the Jews *ought to die*.[33] The perpetrators' beliefs, their particular brand of antisemitism, though obviously not the sole source, was, I maintain, a most significant and indispensable source of the perpetrators' actions and must be at the center of any explanation of them. Simply put, the perpetrators, having consulted their own convictions and morality and having judged the mass annihilation of Jews to be right, did not *want* to say "no."

BECAUSE STUDYING THE perpetration of the Holocaust is a difficult task interpretively and methodologically, it is necessary to address a number of issues openly and directly. Consequently, I lay out here central features of my approach to the subject, and specify clearly the gamut of perpetrators' actions that needs to be explained. The discussion continues in Appendix 1, where I take up some related issues that might not interest the non-specialist—namely the rationale for the choice of topics and cases that are presented in this study, as well as some further items of interpretation and method.

Interpreters of this period make a grave error by refusing to believe that people could slaughter whole populations—especially populations that are by any objective evaluation not threatening—out of conviction. Why persist in the belief that "ordinary" people could not possibly sanction, let alone partake in wholesale human slaughter? The historical record, from ancient times to the present, amply testifies to the ease with which people can extinguish the lives of others, and even take joy in their deaths.[34]

No reason exists to believe that modern, western, even Christian man is incapable of holding notions which devalue human life, which call for its extinction, notions similar to those held by peoples of many religious, cultural, and political dispensations throughout history, including the crusaders and the inquisitors, to name but two relevant examples from twentieth-century Christian Europe's forebears.[35] Who doubts that the Argentine or Chilean murderers of people who opposed the recent authoritarian regimes thought that their victims deserved to die? Who doubts that the Tutsis who slaughtered Hutus in Burundi or the Hutus who slaughtered Tutsis in Rwanda, that one Lebanese militia which slaughtered the civilian supporters of another, that the Serbs who have killed Croats or Bosnian Muslims, did so out of conviction in the justice of their actions? Why do we not believe the same for the German perpetrators?

The manifold problems in writing about the Holocaust begin with the choice of assumptions that are brought to the study of Germany. This subject is taken up at greater length in Chapter 1. Perhaps the most important is whether or not it is assumed, as the rule has been for most interpreters of this period, that Germany was more or less a "normal" society, operating according to rules of "common sense" similar to our own. For people to be *willing* to slaughter others, in this view, they must be moved by a cynical lust for power or riches or they must be in the grip of a powerful ideology that is so self-evidently false that only the disturbed few could actually succumb to it (aside from those who cynically exploit it for power). The majority of modern people, simple and decent, may be pushed around by these few—but not won over.

Alternatively, this period can be approached without such assumptions, and instead with the critical eye of an anthropologist disembarking on unknown shores, open to meeting a radically different culture and conscious of the possibility that he might need to devise explanations not in keeping with, perhaps even contravening his own common-sense notions, in order to explain the culture's constitution, its idiosyncratic patterns of practice, and its collective projects and products. This would admit the possibility that large numbers of people, in this case Germans, might have killed or been willing to kill others, in this case Jews, in good conscience. Such an approach would not predetermine the task, as virtually all previous studies have done, to be the explanation of what could have forced people to act against their will (or independent of any will, namely like automatons). Instead, it might be necessary to explain how Germans came to be such potential willing mass killers and how the Nazi regime tapped this disastrous potentiality. This approach, which rejects the anthropologically and social-scientifically primitive notion of the universality of our "common sense,"[36] guides this inquiry.[37]

Central and generally unquestioned methodological and substantive assumptions that have guided virtually all scholarship on the Holocaust and its perpetrators are jettisoned here, because such assumptions are theoretically and empirically unsustainable. In contrast to previous scholarship, this book takes the actors' cognition and values seriously and investigates the perpetrators' actions in light of a model of choice. This approach, particularly with regard to the Holocaust, raises a set of social theoretical issues that, however briefly, must be addressed.

The perpetrators were working within institutions that prescribed roles for them and assigned them specific tasks, yet they individually and collectively had latitude to make choices regarding their actions. Adopting a perspective which acknowledges this requires that their choices, especially the patterns of their choices, be discerned, analyzed, and incorporated into any overall explanation or interpretation. Ideal data would answer the following questions:

What did the perpetrators actually do?

What did they do in excess of what was "necessary"?

What did they refuse to do?

What could they have refused to do?

What would they not have done?[38]

What was the manner in which they carried out their tasks?

How smoothly did the overall operations proceed?

In examining the pattern of the perpetrators' actions in light of the institutional role requirements and incentive structure, two directions beyond the simple act of killing must be explored. First, in their treatment of Jews (and other victims), the Germans subjected them to a wide range of acts other than the lethal blow. It is important to understand the *gamut* of their actions towards Jews, if the genocidal slaughter is to be explicated. This is discussed in more detail presently. Second, the perpetrators' actions when they were *not* engaged in genocidal activities also shed light on the killing; the insights that an analysis of their non-killing activities offers into their general character and disposition to action, as well as the general social psychological milieu in which they lived might be crucial for understanding the patterns of their genocidal actions.

All of this points to a fundamental question: Which of the gamut of perpetrators' acts constitute the universe of the perpetrators' actions that need to be explained? Typically, the interpreters of the perpetrators have focused on one facet of the Germans' actions: the killing. This tunnel-vision perspective must be broadened. Imagine that the Germans had not undertaken to exterminate the Jews but had still mistreated them in all the other ways that they did, in concentration camps, in ghettos, as slaves. Imagine if, in our society today, people perpetrated against Jews or Christians, Whites or Blacks anything approaching one one-hundredth of the brutality and cruelty that Germans, independent of the killing, inflicted on Jews. Everyone would recognize the need for an explanation. Had the Germans not perpetrated a genocide, then the degree of privation and cruelty to which the Germans subjected Jews would in itself have come into focus and have been deemed an historic outrage, aberration, perversion that requires explanation. Yet these same actions have been lost in the genocide's shadow and neglected by previous attempts to explain the significant aspects of this event.[39]

The fixation on the mass killing to the exclusion of the other related actions of the perpetrators has led to a radical misspecification of the explanatory task. The killing should be, for all the obvious reasons, at the center of scholarly attention. Yet it is not the only aspect of the Germans' treatment of the Jews that demands systematic scrutiny and explication. Not only the killing but also *how* the Germans killed must be explained. The "how" frequently provides great insight into the "why." A killer can endeavor to render the deaths of others—whether he thinks the killing is just or unjust—more or less painful, both physically and emotionally. The ways in which Germans, collectively and individually, sought in their actions, or merely considered, to alleviate or intensify their victims' suffering must be accounted for in any explanation. An explanation that can seemingly make sense of Germans putting Jews to death, but not of the manner in which they did it, is a faulty explanation.

If analytical clarity is to be achieved, then the actions that need to be explained must be stated clearly. A classificatory scheme that specifies four types of actions can be mapped in two dimensions. One dimension denotes whether or not a German's action was a consequence of an order to perform *that* action or was taken on his own initiative. The other dimension characterizes whether a German perpetrated cruelty.[40]

THE PERPETRATORS' ACTIONS
Ordered by Authority

	Yes	No
Cruelty Yes	Organized and "Structured" Cruelty	"Excesses" Such as Torture
Cruelty No	Killing Operations and Individual Killings	"Acts of Initiative" Such as Individually Initiated Killings

Acts committed under orders, such as rounding up, deporting, and killing Jews, which were devoid of "excess" or "surplus" cruelty, are acts that in the German context of the times were utilitarian in intent. They were the deeds that the proverbial (mythical) good German who merely slavishly "followed orders" is alleged to have committed. "Acts of initiative" and "excesses" are really both acts of initiative, not done as the mere carrying out of superior orders. Crucially, both are acts of voluntarism on the part of the individual perpetrators. They differ in the dimension of cruelty—the "acts of initiative" having been the actions of the cool executioner, the "excesses" that of the German who, presumably, took special pleasure in the suffering that he inflicted. The final category of action comprises those actions that Germans undertook under orders, the sole purpose of which was to inflict suffering on the Jews. Such actions are interesting, and some of them are discussed in the case chapters, because they cast doubt on the perpetrators' retrospective rationales for their actions which they have typically proffered after the war. Although the sorts of sham reasons that were ordinarily offered to the men at the time (and by them after the war) for killing Jews (for example, that the Jews threatened Germany, that they were "partisans" and "bandits," or that they spread disease) could perhaps have been believed by a Nazified mind in search of some utilitarian reason for the genocidal slaughter, orders to torture victims should have cast doubt on the "legality" and "reasonableness" of the alleged rationale for their overall treatment of the Jews.

The perpetrators' treatment of Jews, even the act of killing, consisted of different actions, or variables, each of which requires explanation. Any general explanation of Germans' contribution to genocidal slaughter must account for all of them. Large in number, the sorts of actions that need to be explained include those specified by the two dimensions of actions done with or without authoritative directive, and actions which were or were not cruel:

1. All perpetrator actions carried out under orders without surplus cruelty, the most important of these having been those that contributed to genocidal killing.
2. Perpetrator cruelties committed by dint of authority's directives. Institutional, structured cruelties are more important than those carried out on an *ad hoc* basis by individuals or small groups.
3. Perpetrator actions that required initiative beyond what was strictly ordered or required by authority, but which were not marked by "excessive" cruelty.
4. Perpetrator cruelties performed on the perpetrator's own initiative.

This kind of objective characterization of the perpetrators' actions, as useful as it is, remains insufficient either for adequate description and classification, or as the complete basis for explanation. Unless further qualified, this analytical scheme, like previous interpretations of the perpetrators, suggests that "order following" is an unproblematic category. Yet it must be recognized that other actions—such as an individual's disobeyal of other orders, although he carries out the lethal ones—may shed light on the meaning of "order following" in this specific context. In other words, if Germans discriminated among the orders that they chose to follow or in how well they chose to execute them, then the mere obeying of orders, as well as the manner of their execution, needs to be investigated and explained. This action classification also ignores the potential opportunities that perpetrators had to extract themselves from situations or institutions where they were likely to receive tasks that they deemed undesirable.[41] In short, these naïve character- izations of "obeying orders" or of "acting under orders" shear the perpetra- tors' actions out of their broader social, political, and institutional context. It is necessary to recapture this context if the actors' willingness to obey orders is to become intelligible.

In light of this discussion, the following must be considered: The first category of action or variable, obeying orders, is not itself unproblematic. German perpetrators had available to them the options of trying to avoid killing duty or to lessen the suffering of the victims. Why did they exercise these options as they did, not more and not less? Knowledge of the second type of action, authoritative cruelties, should lead us to pose the question of why large-scale institutions in the middle of twentieth-century Europe came to be structured in a manner that would purposely promote, to whatever ex- tent they did, enormous misery for their inhabitants. All the institutions were, for their nature and functioning, dependent upon their personnel. The third type of action, initiative or voluntarism, to the extent that it character- ized German conduct, obviously needs to be explained, for it might be sup- posed that those who opposed mass murder would have done no more than the minimum required of them. The fourth type of action, individual cruelty, must, it goes without saying, be explained.[42]

An explanation must account for two more aspects of the perpetrators' actions. The first is the manner in which the perpetrators carried out their as- signments, whether half-heartedly or zealously. Even those acts that Ger- mans undertook because of orders should be assessed for their zeal of implementation. An actor can perform a job with various degrees of dedica- tion, thoroughness, and accomplishment. When Germans were searching for hidden Jews, they could have done their utmost to uncover them or could have sought them out in a dilatory, half-hearted manner. The Germans' zeal of implementation both provides insight into their motivation and itself needs to be explained. A second additional feature that requires explanation relates to the horror of their deeds. Why did the horror, brutality, and fre- quent gruesomeness of the killing operations fail to stay the perpetrators' hands or at least substantially daunt them? The horrific nature of the opera- tions was, of course, not a type of action on the part of the perpetrators, but one of the conditions of their actions that might be thought to have been so revolting and off-putting that its failure to have affected the perpetrators sig- nificantly is itself in need of explanation.[43]

Even with these qualifications, this approach must be broadened beyond being an objective categorization of actions to include an investigation of the motives of those Germans performing acts in a given category, particularly among the "order followers." No matter what category of action a person's act is properly classified as, the person's attitude towards his act, and his motivation to undertake it, is still important, for it renders the act itself one thing or another.[44] This "objective" categorization needs to be supplemented by a subjective one of motivation. A variety of motives is compatible with acting under orders, with showing initiative, with committing "excesses," or with doing a job well or badly. Most important is the question of whether or not the perpetrators believed their treatment of the Jews to be just and, if so, why.[45]

The motivational dimension is the most crucial for explaining the perpetrators' willingness to act, and to a great extent is a product of the social construction of knowledge.[46] The types of actions that a person is willing to carry out—whether only those directly ordered, those that take initiative, those that are excessive, and those that are the product of zealousness—are derived from a person's motivation; but the person's actions do not *necessarily* correspond to his motivations, because his actions are influenced by the circumstances and opportunities for action. Obviously, without opportunity, a person's motivation to kill or to torture cannot be acted upon. But opportunity alone does not a killer or torturer make.

To say that every (socially significant) action must be motivated does not mean that all acts are merely the result of the actor's prior beliefs about the desirability and justice of the action. It simply means that a person must decide to undertake the action and that some mental calculation (even if he does not conceive of it in such terms) leads him to decide not to refrain from undertaking the action. The mental calculation can include a desire to advance one's career, not to be ridiculed by comrades, or not to be shot for insubordination. A person might kill another without believing in the justice of the death if, despite the understood injustice, he is sufficiently motivated to act by other considerations, such as his own well-being. Wanting to protect one's life is a motive. As such, structures, incentives, or sanctions, formal or informal, can themselves never be motives; they only provide inducements to act or not to act, which the actor might consider when deciding what he will do.[47] Now, of course, certain situations are such that the vast majority of people will act in the same manner, seemingly regardless of their prior beliefs and intentions. Instances of this sort have tempted many to conclude, erroneously, that "structures" cause action.[48] The structures, however, are always interpreted by the actors, who, if they share similar cognitions and values (preserving one's life is a value, as is wanting to live in a "racially pure" society, or wanting to succeed in one's career, or seeking monetary gain, or wanting to be like others at all costs), will respond to them in a like manner. Not every person will place his own well-being over principle; not every person will violate deeply held moral positions because his comrades do not share them. If people do, then the values—which are not universal values and certainly not universal social psychological dispositions—that lead them to do so must be seen as a crucial part of the explanation. Some people will risk their lives for others, renounce the advancement of their careers, dissent in word and deed from their comrades. Inanimate objects do not independently produce cognition and values; all new cognition and values depend upon a preexisting framework of cognition and value that lends meaning to the material circumstances of people's lives. And it is cognition and values, and only cognition and values, that in the last instant move someone willfully to pick up his hand and strike another.

Whatever the cognitive and value structures of individuals may be, changing the incentive structure in which they operate might, and in many cases will certainly, induce them to alter their actions, as they calculate the desired course of action in light of what they know and value, and the possibilities of realizing them in differing mixes. This, it must be emphasized, does not mean that the incentive structure itself is causing people to act, but only that it *in conjunction with the cognitive and value structures* are together producing the action.

Explaining the perpetrators' actions demands, therefore, that the perpetrators' phenomenological reality be taken seriously. We must attempt the difficult enterprise of imagining ourselves in their places, performing their deeds, acting as they did, viewing what they beheld.[49] To do so we must always bear in mind the essential nature of their actions as perpetrators: they were killing defenseless men, women, and children, people who were obviously of no martial threat to them, often emaciated and weak, in unmistakable physical and emotional agony, and sometimes begging for their lives or those of their children. Too many interpreters of this period, particularly when they are psychologizing, discuss the Germans' actions as if they were discussing the commission of mundane acts, as if they need explain little more than how a good man might occasionally shoplift.[50] They lose sight of the fundamentally different, extraordinary, and trying character of these acts. The taboo in many societies, including western ones, against killing defenseless people, against killing children, is great. The psychological mechanisms that permit "good" people to commit minor moral transgressions, or to turn a blind eye even to major ones committed by others, particularly if they are far away, cannot be applied to people's perpetration of genocidal killing, to their slaughter of hundreds of others before their own eyes—without careful consideration of such mechanisms' appropriateness for elucidating such actions.

Explaining this genocidal slaughter necessitates, therefore, that we keep two things always in mind. When writing or reading about killing operations, it is too easy to become insensitive to the numbers on the page. Ten thousand dead in one place, four hundred in another, fifteen in a third. Each of us should pause and consider that ten thousand deaths meant that Germans killed ten thousand individuals—unarmed men, women, and children, the old, the young, the healthy, and the sick—that Germans took a human life ten thousand times. Each of us should ponder what that might have meant for the Germans participating in the slaughter. When a person considers his or her own anguish, abhorrence, or revulsion, his or her own moral outrage at the murder of one person, or of a contemporary "mass murder" of, say, twenty people—whether by a serial killer, or by a semiautomatic-toting sociopath in a fast food outlet—that person gains some perspective on the reality that these Germans confronted. The Jewish victims were not the "statistics" that they appear to us on paper. To the killers whom they faced, the Jews were people who were breathing one moment and lying lifeless, often before them, the next. All of this took place independent of military operations.

The second item to bear in mind, always, is the horror of what the Germans were doing. Anyone in a killing detail who himself shot or who witnessed his comrades shoot Jews was immersed in scenes of unspeakable horror. To present mere clinical descriptions of the killing operations is to misrepresent the phenomenology of killing, to eviscerate the emotional components of the acts, and to skew any understanding of them. The proper description of the events under discussion, the re-creation of the phenomenological reality of the killers, is crucial for any explication. For this reason, I eschew the clinical approach and try to convey the horror, the gruesomeness, of the events *for the perpetrators* (which, of course, does not mean that they were always horrified). Blood, bone, and brains were flying about, often landing on the killers, smirching their faces and staining their clothes. Cries and wails of people awaiting their imminent slaughter or consumed in death throes reverberated in German ears. Such scenes—not the antiseptic descriptions that mere reportage of a killing operation presents—constituted the reality for many perpetrators. For us to comprehend the perpetrators' phenomenological world, we should describe for ourselves every gruesome image that they beheld, and every cry of anguish and pain that they heard.[51] The discussion of any killing operation, of any single death, should be replete with such descriptions. This, of course, cannot be done, because it would make any study of the Holocaust unacceptably lengthy, and also because few readers would be able to persevere in reading through the gruesome accounts—such inability itself being a powerful commentary on the extraordinary phenomenology of the perpetrators' existence and the powerful motivations that must have impelled Germans to silence such emotions so that they could kill and torture Jews, including children, as they did.

SINCE UNDERSTANDING THE BELIEFS and values common to German culture, particularly the ones that shaped Germans' attitudes towards Jews, is the most essential task for explaining the perpetration of the Holocaust, it is the first substantive topic taken up here and forms Part I of the book. The first of its three chapters proposes a framework for analyzing antisemitism. It is followed by two chapters devoted to a discussion of German antisemitism in the nineteenth and twentieth centuries, respectively. These chapters demonstrate the development in Germany well before the Nazis came to power of a virulent and violent "eliminationist" variant of antisemitism, which called for the elimination of Jewish influence or of Jews themselves from German society. When the Nazis did assume power, they found themselves the masters of a society already imbued with notions about Jews that were ready to be mobilized for the most extreme form of "elimination" imaginable.

Part II presents an overview of the measures that produced Jewish suffering and death and of the institutions that implemented the decisions. The first of its two chapters puts forward a new interpretation of the evolution of the Germans' assault on the Jews, and demonstrates that whatever the twists and turns of the policy might have been, or seem to have been, the policy conformed to the precepts of German eliminationist antisemitism. Its second chapter provides a sketch of the institutions of killing, the range of perpetrators, and a treatment of the emblematic German institution of killing: the "camp." Together, these two chapters provide the broader context in which to investigate and understand the core subjects of this study, the institutions of killing and the perpetrators.

The chapters of Parts III through V present cases from each of three institutions of mass killing: police battalions, "work" camps, and death marches. The actions of the members of each are examined in detail, as are the institutional contexts of their actions. These investigations provide the intimate knowledge of the perpetrators' actions and of the immediate settings and incentive structures of the perpetrators' lives as genocidal killers, upon which any valid analysis and interpretation of the Holocaust must depend.

Part VI contains two chapters. The first one provides a systematic analysis of the perpetrators' actions, and it demonstrates the theoretical and empirical inadequacy of the conventional explanations for the findings of the empirical studies. It shows that the perpetrators' eliminationist antisemitism explains their actions, and that the explanation is also adequate to making sense of the perpetrators' actions in a variety of comparative perspectives. The second chapter of Part VI explores further the character of eliminationist antisemitism's capacity to move the Nazi leadership, the perpetrators of the

Holocaust, and the German people to assent and, in their respective ways, to contribute to the eliminationist program. The book ends with a brief Epilogue that draws upon the lessons derived from the study of the perpetrators. It proposes that the nature of German society during the Nazi period must be reconsidered, and it suggests some features of such a revised understanding.

THIS BOOK FOCUSES on the perpetrators of the Holocaust. In explaining their actions, it integrates analyses of the micro, meso, and macro levels, of the individual, institutional, and societal. Previous studies, and almost all previous explanations of the perpetrators' actions, have been generated either in the laboratory, have been deduced purely from some philosophical or theoretical system, or have transferred conclusions (which themselves are often erroneous) from the societal or institutional levels of analysis to the individual. As such, they underdetermine the sources of the perpetrators' actions, and they fail to account for, or even to specify,[52] the varieties and variations of those actions. This is particularly the case with all non-cognitive "structural" explanations. Few interpreters have concerned themselves with the microphysics of the Holocaust's perpetration, which is where the investigation of the perpetrators' actions must begin.[53] This book, therefore, lays bare the perpetrators' actions and makes sense of them by examining them in their institutional and societal contexts, and in light of their social psychological and ideational settings.

People must be motivated to kill others, or else they would not do so. What conditions of cognition and value made genocidal motivations plausible in this period of German history? What was the structure of beliefs and values that made a genocidal onslaught against Jews intelligible and sensible to the ordinary Germans who became perpetrators? Since any explanation must account for the actions of tens of thousands of Germans of a wide variety of backgrounds working in different types of institutions, and must also account for a wide range of actions (and not merely the killing itself), a structure common to them must be found which is adequate to explaining the compass of their actions. This structure of cognition and value was located in and integral to German culture. Its nature and development form the subject of the next three chapters.

PART I

Understanding German Antisemitism: The Eliminationist Mind-set

The community of Jesus is not allowed to hear the horrible fate of the Jews other than in humility, in merciful compassion, and in holy terror. . . . For a Christian therefore there can be no indifferent attitude in this matter [of antisemitism]. . . .

> THE GERMAN PASTOR WALTER HÖCHSTÄDTER IN A FORLORN
> APPEAL TO GERMAN SOLDIERS SURREPTITIOUSLY
> DISTRIBUTED IN JUNE AND JULY 1944

How is it possible that our ears, the ears of Christians, do not ring in the presence of the . . . misery and malice [suffered by the Jews]?

> KARL BARTH, DECEMBER 1938 LECTURE IN WIPKINGEN
> (SWITZERLAND)

We do not like the Jews as a rule, it is therefore not easy for us to apply to them as well the general love for humankind. . . .

> KARL BARTH, JULY 1944 LECTURE IN ZURICH

1

RECASTING THE VIEW OF
ANTISEMITISM:
A FRAMEWORK FOR ANALYSIS

IN THINKING ABOUT German antisemitism, people have a tendency to make important, unacknowledged assumptions about Germans before and during the Nazi period that bear scrutiny and revision. The assumptions are ones that people would not adopt for investigating a preliterate group in Asia or fourteenth-century Germans, yet which they do for the study of nineteenth- and twentieth-century Germany. They can be summed up as follows: Germans were more or less like us or, rather, similar to how we represent ourselves to be: rational, sober children of the Enlightenment, who are not governed by "magical thinking," but rooted in "objective reality." They, like us, were "economic men" who, admittedly, sometimes could be moved by irrational motives, by hatreds, produced by economic frustrations or by some of the enduring human vices like the lust for power or pride. But these are all understandable; as common sources of irrationality, they seem commonsensical to us.

There are reasons to doubt the validity of such assumptions, as an American educator intimately familiar with Nazi schools and youth cautioned in 1941. Nazi schooling, he averred, "produced a generation of human beings in Nazi Germany so different from normal American youth that mere academic comparison seems inane and any sort of evaluation of the Nazi educational system is extremely difficult."[1] So what justifies the prevailing assumptions about the similarity between us and Germans during the Nazi period and before? Should we not take a fresh look and examine whether or not our notions of ourselves held for Germans in 1890, 1925, and 1941? We readily accept that preliterate peoples have believed trees to be animated by good and evil spirits, capable of transforming the material world, that the Aztecs believed human sacrifices were necessary for the sun to rise, that in the middle ages Jews were seen as agents of the Devil,[2] so why can we not believe that many Germans in the twentieth century subscribed to beliefs that appear to us to be palpably absurd, that Germans too were, at least in one realm, prone to "magical thinking"?

Why not approach Germany as an anthropologist would the world of a people about whom little is known? After all, this was a society that produced a cataclysm, the Holocaust, which people did not predict or, with rare exceptions, ever imagine to have been possible. The Holocaust was a radical break with everything known in human history, with all previous forms of political practice. It constituted a set of actions, and an imaginative orientation that was completely at odds with the intellectual foundations of modern western civilization, the Enlightenment, as well as the Christian and secular ethical and behavioral norms that had governed modern western societies. It appears, then, on the face of it, that the study of the society which produced this then unimagined, and unimaginable, event requires us to question our assumptions about that society's similarity to our own. It demands that we examine our belief that it shared the rational economic orientation that guides social scientific and popular images of our society. Such an examination would reveal that much of Germany did roughly mirror our society, but that important realms of German society were fundamentally different. Indeed, the corpus of German antisemitic literature in the nineteenth and twentieth centuries—with its wild and hallucinatory accounts of the nature of Jews, their virtually limitless power, and their responsibility for nearly every harm that has befallen the world—is so divorced from reality that anyone reading it would be hard pressed to conclude that it was anything but the product of the collective scribes of an insane asylum. No aspect of Germany is in greater need of this sort of anthropological reevaluation than is its people's antisemitism.

We know that many societies have existed in which certain cosmological and ontological beliefs were well-nigh universal. Societies have come and gone where everyone believed in God, in witches, in the supernatural, that all foreigners are not human, that an individual's race determines his moral and intellectual qualities, that men are morally superior to women, that Blacks are inferior, or that Jews are evil. The list could go on. There are two different points here. The first is that even if many of these beliefs are now considered to be absurd, people once held them dearly, as articles of faith. Because they did, such beliefs provided them with maps, considered to have been infallible, to the social world, which they used in order to apprehend the contours of the surrounding landscapes, as guides through them and, when necessary, as sources and inspiration for designs to reshape them. Second, and equally important, such beliefs, however reasonable or absurd some of them may be, could be and were subscribed to by the vast majority, if not all of the people in a given society. The beliefs seemed to be so self-evidently true that they formed part of the people's "natural world," of the "natural order" of things. In medieval Christian society, for example, fierce debates over some aspect of Christian theology or doctrine could lead to violent conflict among neighbors; yet the bedrock belief in a God and in the divinity of Jesus that made the people all Christians would, nevertheless, remain uncontested, except by some few on the mental and psychological fringe of society. Beliefs in the existence of God, in the inferiority of Blacks, in the constitutional superiority of men, in the defining quality of race, or in the evil of the Jews have served as axioms of different societies. As axioms, namely as unquestioned norms, they were embedded in the very fabric of different societies' moral orders, no more likely to have been doubted than one of the foundational notions of our own, namely that "freedom" is a good.[3]

Although most societies throughout history have been governed by absurd beliefs at the center of their cosmological and ontological notions of life, which their members have held axiomatically, the starting point for the study of Germany during the Nazi period has generally ruled out the possibility that such a state of affairs then prevailed. More specifically, the *assumptions* preponderate first that most Germans could not have shared Hitler's general characterization of Jews, presented in *Mein Kampf* and elsewhere, as being a devilishly cunning, parasitic, malevolent "race" which had harmed the German people greatly, and second that most Germans could not possibly have been so antisemitic as to countenance the Jews' mass extermination. Because this is assumed, the burden of proof has been placed on the people who would assert the opposite. Why?

In light of the obvious possibility, indeed probability, that antisemitism was an axiom of German society during the Nazi period, two reasons suggest that the prevailing interpretive approach towards German antisemitism during the Nazi period should be rejected. Germany during the Nazi period was a country in which government policies, public acts of other sorts, and the public conversation were thoroughly, almost obsessively antisemitic. Even a cursory glance at this society would suggest to the unsophisticated observer, to anyone who takes the evidence of his senses to be real, that the society was rife with antisemitism. Essentially, in Germany during the Nazi period, antisemitism was shouted from the rooftops: "The Jews are our misfortune," we must rid ourselves of them. As interpreters of this society, it is worth taking both the numbing verbal antisemitic barrage—that emanated not only from the top in what was a political dictatorship but also in large quantity from below—and also the discriminatory and violent policies as indications of the character of its members' beliefs. A society that declares antisemitism with the full power of its lungs, with apparent heart and soul, might indeed be antisemitic.

The second reason for adopting a different perspective than the prevailing one regarding German antisemitism is based on an understanding of the development of German society and culture. In the middle ages and the early modern period, without question until the Enlightenment, German society was thoroughly antisemitic.[4] That the Jews were fundamentally different and maleficent (a theme taken up in the next chapter) was at the time an axiom of German and of most of Christian culture. This evaluation of Jews was shared alike by elites and, more importantly, by the common people. Why not assume that such deeply rooted cultural beliefs, that such basic guides to the social and moral order of the world persist, unless it can be *shown* that they have changed or dissipated?

When conclusive data about the nature of a belief system are lacking, historians and social scientists interested in ascertaining its prevalence and etiology should not project the features of their own society back in time—as students of modern German antisemitism frequently do. They should instead choose a sensible starting point and work forward historically, in order to uncover what actually occurred. If we were to adopt this approach and start in the middle ages, in order to investigate if, where, when, and how Germans abandoned the then culturally ubiquitous antisemitism, our entire orientation towards this issue would change. The questions we would ask, the kinds of phenomena that would count as evidence, and the evaluation of the evidence itself would all be different. It would force us to abandon the *assumption* that, by and large, Germans in the nineteenth and twentieth centuries were not antisemitic, and instead to *demonstrate* how they freed themselves of their culture's previously ingrained antisemitism, if indeed they ever did.

If, instead of being guided by the widespread assumption of the Germans' likeness to us, we began our analysis from the opposite, more sensible position, namely that Germans during the Nazi period were generally beholden to the dominant and pervasive antisemitic creed of the time, then it would be impossible to dissuade us of this original position. Virtually no evidence exists to contradict the notion that the intense and ubiquitous public declaration of antisemitism was mirrored in people's private beliefs. Before we would change this view we would demand, in vain, that Germans' professions of dissent from the antisemitic creed be produced, that letters and diaries testifying to a conception of Jews different from the public one be unearthed. We would want reliable testimony that Germans really did look upon the Jews living in their lands as full members of the German and the human community. We would want evidence that Germans opposed and abhorred the myriad anti-Jewish measures, legislation, and persecutions, that they thought it a great crime to incarcerate Jews in concentration camps, to wrest Jews from their homes and communities, and to deport them to horrible fates from the only land that they had ever known. Isolated instances of dissenting individuals would not satisfy. We would want many cases from which it would be justifiable to generalize about significant portions or groups of German society before we would be convinced that our position is wrong. The documentary record does not even come close to meeting such a standard of evidence.

Which starting point is the appropriate one? The one that stands in stark contradiction to the record of public and private utterances and acts? Or the one in consonance with them? The one that *assumes* that a long-standing cultural orientation evaporated, or the one that demands that the subject be investigated and, before antisemitism is declared to have dissipated, that the process by which it allegedly occurred be demonstrated and explained? So why is the burden of proof not on those who maintain that German society had indeed undergone a transformation and had jettisoned its culturally borne antisemitism? With the assumption of the Germans' similarity to our ideal images of ourselves guiding us, with the assumption of the "normalcy" of the German people, the burden of proof *de facto* has lain with those who argue that tremendous antisemitism existed in Germany during the Nazi period. Methodologically, this approach is faulty and untenable. It must be abandoned.

My position is that if we knew nothing more than the character of the public discussion and governmental policies in Germany during its Nazi period, and the history of German political and cultural development, and were forced to draw conclusions about the extent of German antisemitism during the Nazi period, we could judiciously opt for believing only that it was widespread in the society, and Nazi-like in quality. Fortunately, we are not compelled to be satisfied with this state of affairs, and therefore are not wholly dependent upon the sensible assumptions that we bring to the study of Germany during the Nazi period. The conclusion that Nazi antisemitism was integral to the beliefs of ordinary Germans (as reasonable as it would be if based solely on the general historical understanding coupled with an analysis of Germany's public record during the Nazi period) finds considerable further empirical and theoretical support. So the belief in the continuation of a general, culturally shared German antisemitism into the twentieth century— which is based in part on the inability of anyone yet to demonstrate that a process producing the diminution and abandonment of antisemitism did indeed ever occur—has another foundation. As the next two chapters show, much *positive* evidence exists that antisemitism, albeit an antisemitism evolving in content with the changing times, continued to be an axiom of German culture throughout the nineteenth and twentieth centuries, and that its regnant version in Germany during its Nazi period was but a more accentuated, intensified, and elaborated form of an already broadly accepted basic model.

A general problem in uncovering lost cultural axioms and cognitive orientations of societies since gone or transformed is that they are often not articulated as clearly, frequently, or loudly as their importance for the life of a given society and its individual members might suggest. In the words of one student of German attitudes during the Nazi period, "to be an anti-Semite in Hitler's Germany was so commonplace as to go practically unnoticed."[5] Notions fundamental to the dominant worldview and operation of a society, precisely because they are taken for granted, often are not expressed in a manner commensurate with their prominence and significance or, when uttered, seen as worthy by others to be noted and recorded.[6]

Look at our own society. It is virtually an unquestioned norm that democracy (however understood) is a good thing, is the desirable form for the organization of politics. It is so unquestioned, and also uncontested in current political parlance and practice, that were we, in the evaluation of the democratic creed in this country, to adopt the approach prevalent among students of German antisemitism, then we might have to conclude that most people are not among its subscribers. We could scour the utterances, both public and private, the letters, and the diaries of Americans, and (social science research on the subject aside) we would find comparatively few professions of their democratic temper. Why? Precisely because the views are uncontested, because they are part of the "common sense" of the society. Obviously, we would find that people participate in the institutions of democracy, just as we would find that Germans massively complied with and enthusiastically lent support in a variety of ways to the antisemitic institutions, legislation, and policies of their country. The Nazi Party, a profoundly antisemitic institution, had over *eight million* members at its peak.[7] We would find among American politicians and officials professions of democratic sensibility, as we can find incessant declarations—indeed, probably far more—of the antisemitic creed among their German counterparts during and before the Nazi period. We could find expressions of the democratic creed in American books, journal and magazine articles, and newspapers, though, similarly, not nearly as frequently as we could find articulation of antisemitism in Germany of the time. The comparison could go on. The point remains that if we looked at the quality and quantity of private individuals' expressions of their attitudes towards democracy, were we already beholden to the view that Americans gave little allegiance to democratic institutions and notions, then we would be hard pressed to convince ourselves that our preconceived notion is erroneous. And it is precisely because the democratic creed is uncontested, just as (as the next two chapters show) the antisemitic creed was essentially unchallenged in Germany, that far less "evidence" as to the existence and nature of each people's beliefs on the respective subjects rises to the surface. Since the unearthing of lost cultural axioms is problematic—because the nature of the phenomenon means that they remain relatively concealed from view—pains must be taken not to rule out their existence, and not to assume that *our* cultural axioms have been shared by other peoples. To make this all too common error is to promise a fundamental misunderstanding of the society under study.[8]

A powerful way to conceive of the cognitive, cultural, and even, in part, the political life of a society is as a conversation.[9] All we know of social reality is taken from the stream of unending conversations which constitute it. How could it be otherwise, since people never hear or learn anything else? With the exception of a few strikingly original people, individuals view the world in a manner that is in consonance with their society's conversation.

Many axiomatic features of a society's conversation are not readily detectable, even to the discerning ear. They include the vast majority of culturally shared cognitive models. Cognitive models—beliefs, viewpoints, and values, which may or may not be explicitly articulated—nevertheless serve to structure every society's conversation. Cognitive models, which "typically consist of a small number of conceptual objects and their relations to each other,"[10] inform people's understanding of all aspects of their lives and the world, as well as their practices. From understanding emotions,[11] to performing mundane acts, such as buying an item in a store,[12] to negotiating face-to-face relations,[13] to conducting the most intimate of social relations,[14] to constructing a map of the social and political landscape,[15] to making choices about public institutions and politics, including matters of life and death,[16] people, in both their understanding and their actions, are guided by their culturally shared cognitive models, of which they are often but dimly or not at all aware, models such as our culturally bred conception of personal autonomy, which leads us to have a degree of personal autonomy unimaginable in cultures with different conceptions of human beings and social existence.[17]

When a conversation is monolithic or close to monolithic on certain points—and this includes the unstated, underlying cognitive models—then a society's members automatically incorporate its features into the organization of their minds, into the fundamental axioms that they use (consciously or unconsciously) in perceiving, understanding, analyzing, and responding to all social phenomena. Thus, the tenets of a society's conversation, namely the fundamental ways in which a culture conceives of and represents the order of the world and the orders and patterns of social existence, become reflected in a person's mind as it matures, because that is all that is available for a developing mind to draw on—as is the case with language. During the Nazi period, and even long before, most Germans could no more emerge with cognitive models foreign to their society—with a certain aboriginal people's model of the mind, for example—than they could speak fluent Romanian without ever having been exposed to it.

ANTISEMITISM, which often has the status and therefore the properties of cultural cognitive models, is only dimly understood. Our apprehension of what it is, how it is to be defined, what produces it, how it is to be analyzed, and how it functions, remains, despite the volumes devoted to the subject, underdeveloped. To some great extent, this is a consequence of the difficulty of studying its host domain, the mind. Our access to its data is notably difficult to win, and the yield, even under optimal conditions, is notoriously unreliable and treacherous.[18] Nevertheless, our understanding of this multifarious phenomenon can be improved. The next few pages lay out an approach that should contribute to this end.

Antisemitism—namely negative beliefs and emotions about Jews *qua* Jews—has typically been treated in an undifferentiated manner. A person is either an antisemite or not. To the extent that a more nuanced view of antisemitism is put forward, it is usually, for analytical purposes, of limited value, if not misleading. For example, "abstract" antisemitism is often distinguished from presumably "real" antisemitism.[19] The former is supposedly directed at the "idea" of Jews or of Jewry as a corporate entity, but not at live Jews, which is the putative province of the latter. This distinction, as an analysis of different kinds of antisemitism, is specious.[20]

All antisemitism is fundamentally "abstract," in the sense of not being derived from actual qualities of Jews, yet simultaneously is real and concrete in its effects. What could "abstract" antisemitism possibly mean that would make it not concrete in its consequences? That antisemitism is attached to words or to the concept of a Jew, and never to people? For such a claim to be true, the following would have to obtain: Every time an "abstract" antisemite meets a Jew, he evaluates the Jew, his personal qualities and his moral character, with as much openness, with as little prejudice, as the antisemite would any non-Jew. This is self-evidently false. "Abstract" antisemitism is actually *concrete*, because it guides perception, evaluation, and the willingness to act. It is applied to actual Jews, particularly to those who are not known by the bearer of such antisemitism. It ends up defining the nature of actual Jews for the antisemite. Antisemitism is always *abstract* in its conceptualization and its source (being divorced from actual Jews), and always concrete and *real* in its effects. Because the consequences of antisemitism are determinative for evaluating its nature and importance, all antisemitisms are "real."[21]

The moment that the meaning of such a distinction is examined, it becomes clear that it can map the social and psychological world only crudely. Composite categories, such as "dynamic, passionate hatred of Jews,"[22] although they may describe the manifest apparent quality of some antisemitic types that do exist, also cannot be the basis for analysis. Often a contradiction exists between perception and categorization on the one hand, which are often ideal-typical in nature, and the needs of analysis on the other, which are dimensional. Dimensional analysis—the breaking down of a complex phenomenon into its component parts—is imperative not only for the sake of clarity but also for elucidating various aspects of antisemitism, including its ebbs and flows, and the relationship of its various guises to the actions of antisemites. What confuses much of the discussion about antisemitism, including German antisemitism, is the failure to specify, and keep analytically separate, its various dimensions, of which there are three.[23]

The first dimension captures the type of antisemitism—that is, the antisemite's understanding of the *source* of the Jews' malefic qualities, whatever they are considered to be. What, in the antisemite's eyes, produces a Jew's unfitness or perniciousness? Is it his race, his religion, or his culture, or the alleged deformities inculcated in him by his environment? The consideration of the source of the Jews' undesirable qualities has implications for how the antisemite analyzes the "Jewish problem," as well as how his cognizance of Jews may change with other societal and cultural developments. This is partly so because each *source* is embedded in an extended metaphorical structure that automatically extends the domain of phenomena, situations, and linguistic usages relevant to the antisemitic compass in a manner paralleling the metaphorical structure itself. The analogical thinking that accompanies different metaphorical structures informs the definition of situations, the diagnoses of problems, and the prescriptions of appropriate courses of action. The biological metaphor at the heart of Nazi antisemitism, for instance (which held the Jews' evil to reside in their blood and which described them in terms of vermin and bacilli, to give but two of the images) is powerfully suggestive.[24]

The second dimension is a *latent-manifest* one that simply measures how preoccupied an antisemite is with Jews. If his antisemitic views occupy his thoughts and inform his actions only rarely, then he is at that moment a latent antisemite, or his antisemitism is in a latent state. If, on the other hand, Jews occupy a central role in his daily thinking and (perhaps) his actions as well, then his antisemitism is in a manifest state. Antisemitism can fall anywhere on the continuum, from the antisemite hardly thinking about Jews to thinking about them obsessively. The latent-manifest dimension represents the amount of time devoted to thinking about the Jews and the kind and variety of circumstances that conjure up prejudicial thoughts about Jews. It represents the centrality of the Jews in a person's consciousness.

The third dimension, which is the level or intensity of the antisemitism, is a continuum which represents the putative *perniciousness* of the Jews. Are the Jews conceived of by the antisemite to be simply clannish and stingy or to be conspiratorial and bent on dominating political and economic life? As the most casual student of antisemitism knows, the qualities that antisemites have attributed to Jews, that add up to the Jews' overall perceived perniciousness, vary greatly in content. The charges that antisemites have hurled against the Jews through the ages have been diverse and plentiful, from the mundane to the fantastic; yet there is no need to discuss them now at length, for the crucial aspect to understand is that each antisemite has some notion of how dangerous he considers the Jews to be. If an antisemite's beliefs could be measured and quantified accurately, then some index of perceived Jewish perniciousness could be calculated.[25] Although different particular accusations of Jewish malfeasance might lead to different responses by antisemites on particular issues, it is the antisemite's overall sense of the Jewish threat (and not any individual accusation) which is more important for understanding how his beliefs might inform his actions.

Antisemites who fall at similar places on this continuum can and do fall at different places on the latent-manifest continuum. Two antisemites can continually and vociferously blame many of their respective ills on the Jews, while one believes that they are due to the Jews being clannish and thus giving job opportunities to other Jews, and the second believes that the Jews are bent on conquering and destroying his society. These antisemitisms, in their different varieties, are manifest, indeed central to their holders. In the same way, each of these two beliefs about the Jews' intentions and actions can be held not only by manifest antisemites but also by latent ones, the antisemitism remaining latent, perhaps because of little contact with Jews. To take the first type, a person can believe the Jews to be clannish and discriminatory, without ever giving it much thought—for example, during economic boom times, when everyone, including the antisemite, is doing well. He can even believe the Jews to be bent upon destroying his society, but if he is preoccupied with daily affairs and is, to boot, not very political, such beliefs might simmer deep below his daily consciousness. Turning to the *source* dimension, these two different considerations of the Jews' perniciousness, whether in a relatively latent or manifest state, can be based on different understandings of the cause of the Jews' actions. An antisemite may believe that the Jews act the way that they do because their "race," namely their biology, has so programmed them, or because the tenets of their religion, including their rejection of Jesus, has so conditioned them.

Any study of antisemitism needs to specify where the antisemitism falls on each of the dimensions. The temptation should be resisted to think of the two continuous dimensions of *latent-manifest* and of *perniciousness* as dichotomies, as "either/or" propositions. Naturally, some recurring complexes of the various components of antisemitism exist. Yet their usefulness as "ideal types" derives from this dimensional analysis, which promises greater analytical clarity and precision and which in turn should yield insight into the nature and working of antisemitism.

While this dimensional analysis can usefully characterize all varieties of antisemitism, an important distinction among antisemitisms overlays and qualifies this general scheme. All antisemitisms can be divided according to one essential dissimilitude which can be usefully thought of as being dichotomous (even if, strictly speaking, this may not be the case). Some antisemitisms become woven into the moral order of society; others do not. Many aversions towards Jews—whether they be the kind of mild stereotypes that characterize much intergroup conflict, or even more conspiratorial notions about Jews controlling a country's newspapers—are aversions which, though perhaps intense, are not interwoven into the people's understanding of the moral order of society, or the cosmos. A person can assert that the Jews are bad for his country, just as he can about Blacks, Poles, or any other group, while seeing the Jews as one group, like so many others, with distasteful or harmful qualities. This is a kind of classic intergroup antipathy, which normally characterizes group conflict. In such cases, a person's understanding of the nature of the Jews does not hold them to be in violation of the moral order of society. The classic American prejudice, which takes the form "I'm Italian, or Irish, or Polish, and he's a Jew, and I don't like him," is an assertion of difference and distaste, but not one of perceived violation of the moral order by the other. Jews are sometimes just another "ethnic" group in the array of groups that make up society.

In contrast, the conception of Jews in medieval Christendom, with its uncompromising non-pluralistic and intolerant view of the moral basis of society, was one which held the Jews to violate the moral order of the world. By rejecting Jesus, by allegedly having killed him, the Jews stood in defiant opposition to the otherwise universally accepted conception of God and Man, denigrating and defiling, by their very existence, all that is sacred. As such, Jews came to represent symbolically and discursively much of the evil in the world; they not only represented it but also came to be seen by Christians as being synonymous with it, indeed as being self-willed agents of evil.[26]

The consequences of antisemites' conceiving of Jews in terms of the moral order of the world are extensive. Identifying Jews with evil, defining them as violators of the sacred and as beings opposed to the fundamental good towards which people ought to strive, demonizes them, producing a linguistic, metaphorical, and symbolic integration of Jews into the antisemites' lives. Jews are not just *evaluated* according to a culture's moral principles and norms but become *constitutive* of the moral order itself, of the cognitive building blocks that map the social and moral domains, which come partly, yet significantly, to depend for their coherence on the then prevailing conception of Jews. Conceptions of Jews, by being integrated by non-Jews into the moral order and hence the underlying symbolic and cognitive structure of society, take on ever wider ranges of meaning, meaning that accrues ever greater structural coherence and integrity. Much that is good becomes defined in opposition to Jews and, in turn, comes to depend upon maintaining this conception of Jews. It becomes difficult for non-Jews to alter the conception of Jews without altering a wide-ranging and integrated symbol structure, including important cognitive models, upon which people's understanding of society and morality rest. It becomes difficult for them to see the Jews' actions, even their existence, other than as desecration and defilement.

Certain antisemitisms conceive of Jews as being more than mere violators, however grave, of moral norms (all antisemitisms hold them to commit such transgressions), but as beings whose very existence constitutes a violation of the moral fabric of society. The fundamental nature of antisemitism of this kind is different from the great variety of antisemitisms that are not colored in this way.[27] They are more tenacious, arouse more passion, usually provoke and support a wider variety of more serious and inflammatory charges against the Jews, and inhere within them a greater potential for violent and deadly anti-Jewish action. Conceptions of Jews that hold them to be destructive of the moral order, that demonize them, can be and have been based on different understandings of the source of the Jews' perniciousness, clearly including both religious and racial understandings of Jews. The former was the case in medieval Christendom, the latter in Germany during its Nazi period.

IN ADDITION TO the *analytical approach* presented here, three major *substantive* notions about the nature of antisemitism undergird the ensuing analysis of German antisemitism. They are:

1. The existence of antisemitism and the content of antisemitic charges against Jews must be understood as an expression of the non-Jewish culture, and are fundamentally *not* a response to any objective evaluation of Jewish action, even if actual characteristics of Jews, and aspects of realistic conflicts, become incorporated into the antisemitic litany.

2. Antisemitism has been a permanent feature of Christian civilization (certainly after the beginning of the Crusades), even into the twentieth century.

3. The widely differing degree of antisemitic expression at different moments in a bounded historical time (of, say, twenty to fifty years) in a particular society is not the result of antisemitism appearing and disappearing, of larger and smaller numbers of people being or becoming antisemites, but of a generally constant antisemitism becoming more or less manifest, owing primarily to altering political and social conditions that encourage or discourage people's expression of their antisemitism.

Each of these propositions could be written about at great length, yet can be treated here only a bit more closely. The first two find support in the general literature on antisemitism. The third is new to this study.

Antisemitism tells us nothing about Jews, but much about antisemites and the culture that breeds them. Even a cursory glance at the qualities and powers that antisemites through the ages have ascribed to Jews—supernatural powers, international conspiracies, and the ability to wreck economies; using the blood of Christian children in their rituals, even murdering them for their blood; being in league with the Devil; controlling simultaneously both the levers of international capital and of Bolshevism—indicates that antisemitism draws fundamentally on cultural sources that are *independent* of the Jews' nature and actions, and the Jews themselves then become defined by the culturally derived notions which antisemites project onto them. This underlying mechanism of antisemitism is true of prejudice in general, though the impressive imaginative heights to which antisemites have repeatedly and routinely soared are rare in the vast annals of prejudice. Prejudice is not the consequence of its object's actions or attributes. It is not some objective dislike of the object's real nature. Classically, no matter what the object does, whether "X" or "not X," the bigot defames him for it. Prejudice's source is the holder of the beliefs himself, his cognitive models and his culture. Prejudice is a manifestation of people's (individual and collective) search for *meaning*.[28] It makes little sense to discuss the real nature of a bigotry's object—in this case, of Jews—when trying to understand the genesis and maintenance of the beliefs. To do so would surely be to muddle the understanding of prejudice—in this case, of antisemitism.

Because antisemitism springs from the bosom of the culture of the antisemites and not from the character of Jews' actions, it is not surprising that the nature of antisemitism in a given society tends to be in harmony with the cultural models that guide contemporary understanding of the social world. Thus, in theological times, antisemitism tends to share the prevailing religious presuppositions; in times dominated by social Darwinian notions, antisemitism tends to correspond to notions of immutability (since traits are considered to be inborn) and of nations being engaged in zero-sum conflict with each other (for the world is a struggle for survival). It is precisely because cognitive models underlie the general worldviews of those in a society and also the character of antisemitism that antisemitism mimics aspects of the regnant cultural models. Moreover, to the extent that antisemitism is central to the worldview of the people in a society, which has often been the case (especially in the Christian world), the likelihood of its congruence with the prevailing cultural models increases, because if they were in conflict, the psychological and emotional coherence of the people's worldviews would be upset, creating significant cognitive dissonance.

Antisemites typically cast their deep-seated hatreds in the prevailing terms of their era, by incorporating some actual cultural characteristics of Jews or certain elements within the Jewish community into the antisemitic litany. This is to be expected. It would be surprising were this not the case. Students of antisemitism should therefore avoid the temptation of latching on to the few incantations of a prevailing antisemitic litany which appear, if only dimly, to resonate with reality, and to see in the Jews' own actions any cause for the antisemitism; to do so is to confuse symptom with cause. A common mistake of this sort is to attribute the existence of antisemitism to the antisemites' jealousy of Jews' economic success, instead of recognizing that the economic jealousy is a consequence of an already existing antipathy towards Jews. Of the many shortcomings of the economic theory of antisemitism, two are worth mentioning here, one conceptual, one empirical. Economic hostility of this sort is necessarily predicated upon the antisemites' marking of the Jews as being different, identifying them not by the many other (more relevant) features of these people's identities, but as Jews, and then using this label as the *defining* feature of these people, rather than seeing the Jews as the antisemites see others in society, namely as fellow citizens.[29] Without this preexisting, prejudicial conception of the Jews, people would not consider their Jewishness as a relevant economic category. A second failing of the economic theory of antisemitism is that, historically, minority groups have occupied intermediary economic positions in many countries—such as Chinese in Asia and Indians in Africa—and though they have been the objects of prejudice that included economic jealousy and hostility, such prejudice does not invariably produce, indeed almost never produces, the hallucinatory charges that have been routinely directed at Jews.[30] Therefore, economic conflict could not possibly be the principal source of antisemitism, which, historically, has almost always had such hallucinatory charges at its core.

Perhaps the most telling evidence supporting the argument that anti-semitism has fundamentally nothing to do with the actions of Jews, and therefore fundamentally nothing to do with an antisemite's knowledge of the real nature of Jews, is the widespread historical and contemporary appearance of antisemitism, even in its most virulent forms, where there are no Jews, and among people who have never met Jews. This recurring phenomenon is also difficult to explain with an account of the sociology of knowledge and prejudice other than the one adopted here, namely the notion that they are each socially constructed, that they are aspects of culture and of the cognitive models integral to culture that are passed on from generation to generation. People who have never met Jews have believed that Jews were agents of the Devil, inimical to all that is good, responsible for many of the world's actual ills, and bent on the domination and destruction of their societies. England from 1290 to 1656 is a striking, but by no means rare, example of this phenomenon. During this period, it was virtually *judenrein*, purged of Jews, the English having expelled them as the culmination of the anti-Jewish campaign that began in the middle of the previous century. Still, the culture of England remained deeply and thoroughly antisemitic. "For almost four centuries the English people rarely, if ever, came into contact with flesh-and-blood Jews. Yet they considered the Jews to be an accursed group of usurers, who, in league with the Devil, were guilty of every conceivable crime that could be conjured up by the popular imagination."[31] The almost-four-hundred-year persistence of antisemitism in the folk culture of an England devoid of Jews is remarkable and, upon initial consideration, perhaps surprising. Yet when the relationship of Christianity to antisemitism is understood, coupled with an appreciation of how cognitive models and belief systems are socially transmitted, it becomes clear that it would have been surprising had antisemitism dissipated. As part of the moral system of English society, antisemitism remained integral to the standing and sway of Christianity, even when no Jews were in England, even when the people of England had never met any actual Jews.[32]

Antisemitism without Jews was the general rule of the middle ages and early modern Europe.[33] Even when Jews were permitted to live among Christians, few Christians knew Jews or had any opportunity to observe Jews at close range. Christians typically segregated Jews in ghettos, and restricted their activities through a host of oppressive laws and customs. Jews were isolated both physically and socially from Christians. Christians' antisemitism was not based on any familiarity with real Jews. It could not have been. Similarly, most virulent antisemites in Germany during Weimar and during the

Nazi period probably had little or no contact with Jews. Entire areas of Germany were practically without Jews, since Jews formed less than 1 percent of the German population and 70 percent of this small percentage of Jews lived in large urban areas.[34] The anti-Jewish beliefs and emotions of all such antisemites could not possibly have been based on any objective assessment of Jews, and must have been based only on what they had *heard* about Jews,[35] when listening to and partaking in the society's conversation, which itself was equally cavalier about representing the Jews faithfully, having a genesis, life, and shape independent of the Jews whom it purportedly described.

A second major substantive notion about antisemitism important to this study is that antisemitism has been a more or less *permanent* feature of the western world. Without a doubt, it is the all-time leading form of prejudice and hatred within Christian countries. A variety of reasons lie behind this, which are discussed in the next chapter. Briefly, until (and, to a lesser extent, even during) the modern period, with the rise of secularism, beliefs about Jews were integral to the moral order of Christian society. Christians defined themselves partly by differentiating themselves from and often in direct opposition to Jews; beliefs about Jews were intertwined with the moral system of Christianity, which in Christian societies underlies, and for much of western history has been (roughly) coterminous with, the larger moral order. Beliefs about Jews thus do not necessarily change more easily than do Christian precepts that have helped and continue to help people define and negotiate the social world. Indeed, in some ways, antisemitism has proven more durable. For much of western history, it was virtually impossible to be a Christian without being an antisemite of some stripe, without thinking ill of the people who rejected and reject Jesus and thus the moral order of the world derived from his teachings, from his revealed words. This is especially the case since Christians held the Jews responsible for Jesus' death.

That a thoroughgoing antipathy towards Jews was integral to the moral order of society explains not only why antisemitism has persisted for so long and has possessed such a great emotional charge but also why it has had its remarkably protean quality. The underlying need to think ill of Jews, to hate them, to derive meaning from this emotional stance, woven into the fabric of Christianity itself, together with the derivative notion that Jews stand in opposition to the Christian defined moral order, create a readiness, an openness, if not a disposition, to believe that the Jews are capable of all heinous acts. All charges against the Jews become plausible.[36] Of what are the Jews—the killers of Jesus and constant rejecters of his teachings—not capable? What emotion, fear, anxiety, frustration, fantasy could not believably be projected upon the Jews? And because the underlying antipathy towards the Jews has historically been bound to the definition of the moral order, when cultural, social, economic, and political forms have undergone change, robbing some of the existing charges against Jews of their resonance, new antisemitic accusations have easily replaced the old. This occurred, for example, throughout western Europe in the nineteenth century, when antisemitism shed much of its religious medieval garb and adopted new, secular clothing. Antisemitism has had an unusual adaptability, an unusual capacity to modernize itself, to keep up with the times. So when the existence of the Devil in his tangible corporeal form ceased to move ever greater numbers of people, the Jew in his guise as an agent of the Devil was easily replaced by a Jew of equal danger and malevolence wearing a secular disguise.

Without a doubt, the definition of the moral order as a Christian one, with the Jews as its sworn enemies, has been the single most powerful cause in producing an endemic antisemitism (at least until recently) in the Christian world. This has been reinforced by two other enduring causes which are only mentioned here. First, the social and psychological functions that Jew-hatred, once ensconced, comes to play in people's mental economies reinforce the antisemitism itself, for to abandon antisemitism would necessitate a discomforting reconceptualization of the social order. Second, politically and socially, Jews have historically been safe targets of hatred and verbal and physical aggression, incurring to the antisemite fewer costs than would attacks on other groups or institutions of society.[37] These two causes have buttressed the foundational Christian cause, producing a deep and enduring hatred—so out of proportion with any objective material or social conflict—of a sort that is unrivaled by any other group hatred in western history.

A third major substantive notion about antisemitism informs this study. It is distinct from the second, yet can be seen as its corollary. Over a period of years, *antisemitism*—composed of a set of beliefs and cognitive models with a stable source metaphor and understanding of the nature of the Jews' putative perniciousness—does not appear, disappear, then reappear in a given society. Always present, antisemitism becomes more or less manifest. Its cognitive salience, emotional intensity, and *expression* increases or decreases.[38] The vagaries of politics and social conditions overwhelmingly account for these swings. German and European history has seen waves of antisemitic expression. Such waves are typically described as the consequence of the growth of antisemitism—of people previously not touched by antisemitism suddenly becoming antisemites—owing to this or that cause. And when the wave subsides, the diminution of antisemitic vituperation is understood to have been caused by a decrease in, or the passing of, antisemitic belief and feeling. This account of antisemitism is wrong. Instead of *antisemitism* itself waxing and waning, it is its differential *expression* that is being observed.[39] Thus, the widespread exhibition of antisemitism *at any time* in a given historical period is properly understood as evidence of its existence, if only latent, for that entire era.

No theoretically adequate explanation for the periodic outbursts of antisemitic expression which holds antisemitism itself to appear and disappear in a society can be given. What is the evidence that the beliefs underlying the expressive and other actions vanish? Just as with the genesis of a person's action in the first place, a person might cease to act in a certain manner for many reasons, aside from the dissipation of the beliefs that prefigure it. A man who continues to believe in God may stop attending church for a variety of reasons independent of his unchanging belief. He may not like the new pastor, may have himself acted in a manner that makes him not want to show his face before his community, may need (owing to economic misfortune, for example) to use his time for other activities, and the like. Simply to assume, as so many do, that in the case of antisemitism, action and belief are synonymous, that the disappearance of the former means the disappearance of the latter, is unwarranted.

Had the antisemitic beliefs themselves truly evaporated, from where would they arise again? From thin air? Reemergent antisemitic expression typically employs images, beliefs, and accusations that were central to previous outbursts.[40] How could this be had they indeed disappeared? Particularly when the beliefs, as they so often do, contain hallucinatory elements—holding the Jews to have magical and malevolent powers imperceptible to the naked eye—could such wild beliefs rematerialize whole, in nearly identical form, had they dissipated completely? In the intervening period of months or years between outbursts of passionate hatred, do erstwhile antisemites believe the Jews to be good neighbors, citizens, people? Do they develop positive feelings for Jews? Do they learn to regard Jews favorably as their national brothers and sisters? Do they even minimally develop a strictly neutral attitude towards them, towards their Jewishness, which they still deem to be the Jews' defining feature? And, on the slim chance that the erstwhile antisemites do turn themselves around, do they then afterwards suddenly come to realize (all of them at once) that their positive views of Jews were wrong and that their initial hatreds had been correct all along? No evidence exists for these sorts of oscillations, for individuals or for collectivities.

Thus, to take the most prevalent account of antisemitism, those who argue that economic crises cause antisemitism miss the point. This is the "Jews as scapegoats" account of antisemitism. Among the many empirical and theoretical shortcomings of this account is the failure to realize that the populace could not be mobilized against just anyone or any group. It is no accident that, regardless of the real character of their economic situation or of their actions—even when the overwhelming majority of a country's Jews are poor—Jews routinely become the object of frustration and aggression owing to economic troubles. Indeed, for most people antisemitism is already integral to their worldview before the advent of a crisis, but in a latent state. Economic crises make people's antisemitism more manifest and *activate* it into open expression. People's preexisting beliefs channel their misfortune, frustration, and anxiety in the direction of the people whom they already despise: the Jews.

Antisemitism's remarkable malleability, already remarked upon, is itself evidence of its constancy. That it comes and goes, finding different forms of expression, reemerging when it seems that it no longer dwells within a society, suggests strongly that it is always there waiting to be aroused and uncovered. That it is more manifest at one point, and less at some other, should not be taken as a sign that antisemitism itself comes and goes, but, as with so many beliefs, that its *centrality* for individuals and their willingness to give it *expression* vary with social and political conditions.

By way of brief comparison, another ideology (and the emotions underlying it) that seems to appear and disappear over and over again has been nationalism. Similar to antisemitism, nationalism, namely the powerful beliefs and emotions associated with holding the nation to be the paramount political category and object of loyalty, has itself not materialized and vanished repeatedly, but its ideational centrality for people and its expression have. The nationalistic beliefs and emotions themselves lie dormant and, like antisemitism, can be activated easily, quickly, and often with devastating consequences, when social or political conditions are such as to provoke them. The rapid activation[41] of nationalistic sentiment that has occurred repeatedly, even recently, in European and German history,[42] especially during the Nazi period, is important to bear in mind, not just because it parallels the account presented here for antisemitism. Historically, the expression of nationalism, particularly in Germany, has gone hand in hand with the expression of antisemitism, since the nation was in part defined in contradistinction to the Jews. In Germany and elsewhere, nationalism and antisemitism were interwoven ideologies, fitting hand in glove.[43]

CONCLUSION

The study of Germans and their antisemitism before and during the Nazi period must be approached as an anthropologist would a previously unencountered preliterate people and their beliefs, leaving behind especially the preconception that Germans were in every ideational realm just like our ideal notions of ourselves. A primary task is thus to unearth the cognitive models that underlay and informed the Germans' thinking about the social world and politics, particularly about Jews.

Such models are primarily socially constructed, derivative of and borne by the societal conversation, linguistically and symbolically. A society's conversation defines and forms much of an individual's understanding of the world. When beliefs and images are uncontested or are even just dominant within a given society, individuals typically come to accept them as self-evident truths. Just as people today accept that the earth revolves around the sun, and once accepted that the sun revolves around the earth, so too have many people accepted culturally ubiquitous images of Jews. The capacity of an individual to diverge from prevailing cognitive models is still smaller because cognitive models are among the individual's building blocks of understanding, and are incorporated into the structures of his mind as naturally as the grammar of his language. An individual learns the cognitive models of his culture, like grammar, surely and effortlessly. They each—unless, in the case of the cultural cognitive models, the individual at some point works to reconfigure them—guide the understanding and production of forms that depend on them, contributing to the generation, in the case of grammar, of sentences and meaning, and in the case of cognitive models, of perceptions of the social world and articulated beliefs about it.

Within a society, the most important bearers of the general conversation are its institutions, including crucially the family. It is in institutions generally, and particularly in those that are prominent in socializing children and adolescents, that the belief systems and cognitive models, including those about Jews, are imparted to individuals. Without institutional support of some kind, it is extraordinarily difficult for individuals to adopt notions contrary to those that prevail in society, or to maintain them in the face of widespread, let alone near unanimous, social, symbolic, and linguistic disapproval.

Since the grinding inertia of a society reproduces its axioms and its basic cognitive models as a matter of rule,[44] the presumption here is that the absence of evidence that change occurred in Germany's cognitive models about Jews should be seen to suggest strongly that these models and the elaborated beliefs dependent upon them were reproduced and continued to exist; this perspective departs from the usual presumption that if (difficult to obtain) evidence is not found of the continuing *presence* of once obtaining cognitive models, then the cognitive models—in this case, about Jews—have been abandoned. Finally, cognitive models about Jews are seen here to have been fundamental for generating the kinds of "solutions" that Germans entertained for the "Jewish Problem" and the kinds of actions that they actually undertook.

A sociology of knowledge, an analytical framework for studying antisemitism (specifying its three dimensions of source, perniciousness, and manifestness), and some foundational substantive notions about the character of antisemitism have been presented here because these elements, whether they are articulated or not, give shape to the conclusions of any study of antisemitism. The importance in laying out the approach being employed for the study of antisemitism is greater still because the data that provide the basis for conclusions are less than ideal in a number of ways. The conclusions must be defended, therefore, not only on the basis of the data themselves, and the use to which they are put, but also on the basis of the general approach adopted for understanding beliefs and cognition, and antisemitism.

It needs to be emphasized that the analysis here cannot be definitive. The proper data simply do not exist. The data are especially deficient because the purpose here is not to trace the character of antisemitism merely among the political and cultural elites, but to gauge its nature and scope among the broad reaches of German society. Even run-of-the-mill public opinion polls, for all their shortcomings, would be an illuminating, luxurious addition to the existing record. The analysis here delineates only certain aspects of antisemitism, and indicates antisemitism's probable societal scope. It focuses on German antisemitism's central tendencies. It does so not only because the data are limited but also because of the conviction that what needs to be illuminated is the *dominant cognitive thread* from which the intricately woven yet powerfully clear and well-focused tapestry of anti-Jewish actions emerged. To focus on the exceptions to the rule—which were on the whole but secondary or tertiary aspects of Germans' views of Jews—would be a disservice, because it would shift attention from the central tendencies of German antisemitism as it developed. The analysis here also devotes less attention to a content analysis of German antisemitism than is customary, because such analyses are readily available elsewhere, and because this space is better spent delimiting antisemitism's dimensions, scope, and power as a source of action.

The next two chapters reconceive our understanding of modern German antisemitism by applying the general theoretical and methodological prescriptions enunciated here, including the dimensional framework, to a more specific analysis of the history of antisemitism in Germany prior to the Nazi period, and then to an analysis of antisemitism in Germany during the Nazi period itself. The historical account is necessary in order to clarify why the German people so easily accepted the tenets of Nazi antisemitism and supported the Nazis' anti-Jewish policies. In light of the problematic nature of the data, the discussion emerges from, among other things, the strategy of investigating "crucial" cases, namely those people or groups of people who (according to other criteria) should have been least likely to have conformed to the interpretations and explanations being presented here. If it can be shown that even the "friends" of Jews concurred with German antisemites about essential aspects of their understanding of the Jews' nature, in large measure because their thinking derived from similar cognitive models about Jews, then it would be difficult to believe anything but that antisemitism was endemic to German culture and society. When the analysis of the nature and extent of German antisemitism has been completed, the dimensional analysis is broadened, in order to demonstrate the links between antisemitism and anti-Jewish action. The discussion concludes with an analysis of the relationship of German antisemitism during the Nazi period to the measures that Germans took against Jews.

The conclusion of these chapters is that in Germany during the Nazi period an almost universally held conceptualization of the Jews existed which constituted what can be called an "eliminationist" ideology, namely the belief that Jewish influence, by nature destructive, must be eliminated irrevocably from society. During the Nazi period, all of the Germans' policy initiatives and virtually all of their important measures towards Jews, as different in nature and degree as they manifestly appear to be, were in the practical service of, and indeed were symbolically equivalent expressions of, the Germans' desire, the Germans' perceived need, to succeed in the eliminationist enterprise.

2

THE EVOLUTION OF

ELIMINATIONIST ANTISEMITISM

IN MODERN GERMANY

EUROPEAN ANTISEMITISM is a corollary of Christianity. From the earliest days of Christianity's consolidation of its hold over the Roman Empire, its leaders preached against Jews, employing explicit, powerfully worded, emotionally charged condemnations. The psychological and theological need impelling Christians to differentiate themselves from the bearers of the religion from which their own had broken off, was born anew with each generation, because as long as Jews rejected the revelation of Jesus, they unwittingly challenged the Christians' certitude in that revelation. If the Jews, the people of God, shunned the messiah that God had promised them, then something was awry. Either the messiah was false, or the people had gone profoundly astray, perhaps tempted by the Devil himself. Christians could not countenance contemplation of the former, so they opted with heart and soul for the latter: The Jews were religiously wayward in a world where religion and the moral order were coterminous, and where deviation from it was a grievous transgression.[1]

The psychological logic of this antagonism was reinforced by a second, related parallel logic. Christians conceived of their religion as superseding Judaism. Therefore, Jews as Jews ought to disappear from the earth. They ought to become Christians. But Jews adamantly would not, which meant that Christians and Jews shared a common heritage—the most important part of which was the Jewish Bible with its God-inspired words—to which Christians and Jews gave conflicting interpretations. So a never-ending antagonism over the meaning of this heritage, over the interpretation of the Bible and God's words, over many of the sacred texts of Christianity itself, produced additional pressure for Christians to disparage Jews, to impugn their understanding of the contested sacred terrain. If Jews were right, then Christians were wrong. The very understanding of the sacred order and its symbols, and of the moral order derived from them, depended upon ensuring that all Christians believed the Jews to be in error. Bernard Glassman, a historian of Christian attitudes towards Jews, writes: "The clerics believed that if Christianity was indeed the true faith and its followers were the new Israel, then Judaism had to be discredited in the eyes of the faithful. In medieval sermons, plays, and religious literature, the Jews were often portrayed as the adversaries of the church who from the time of the Crucifixion threatened good Christians."[2] Thus, the Jews came to represent much that was antithetical to the moral order of the Christian world.[3]

A third source of the abiding Christian hostility towards Jews and of their reflexive disparagement of them was the axiomatic belief that Jews were "Christ-killers." Christians held not only the Jews of Jesus' time responsible for Jesus' death but also Jews for all time. Contemporary Jews indeed rejected Jesus as messiah and the son of God no less than their forebears had, who, according to passionate and continuous Christian teaching and preaching, had killed him. All Jews, by taking this rejectionist stance, implicated themselves in the crime which had been the original consequence of their forebears' denial of Jesus' divinity. Jews became symbolic Christ-killers, were seen as having approved of the crime and, indeed, if given the chance, were considered to be capable of repeating it. And so, the Jews' continuing, daily rejection of Jesus was seen as an act of sacrilegious defiance, as an open, brazen, contemptuous gauntlet thrown in the faces of Christians.[4]

These views of Jews, fundamental to Christian theology and teaching until the modern era, were already highly articulated in the fourth century, when the Church established its suzerainty over the Roman world. John Chrysostom, a pivotal Church Father whose theology and teachings had lasting import, preached about Jews in terms that would become the stock-in-trade of Christian anti-Jewish teachings and rhetoric, which would condemn the Jews to live in a Christian Europe that despised and feared them: "Where Christ-killers gather, the cross is ridiculed, God blasphemed, the father unacknowledged, the son insulted, the grace of the Spirit rejected. . . . If the Jewish rites are holy and venerable, our way of life must be false. But if our way is true, as indeed it is, theirs is fraudulent. I am not speaking of the Scriptures. Far from it! For they lead one to Christ. I am speaking of their present impiety and madness."[5] John's diatribe expresses the just-discussed antagonisms towards Jews that were embedded in the theological and psychological fabric of Christianity. In this passage, he asserts unequivocally the essential, inexorable opposition between Christian and Jewish doctrine, and between Christians and Jews: "If the Jewish rites are holy and venerable, our way of life must be false." The unease and distemper that a Christian would have caused himself upon considering the possibility that the Jews might be right, radiate from this assertion of John's, from its either/or logic. The psychological need to deprecate the Jews is immanent in this passage, in his and the Church's view of the relationship of Christianity to Judaism. And this is not the only source of the antagonism. The gathering of Jews—of the "Christ-killers"—for prayer and worship is understood as an act of denigration against Christianity, an act of blasphemy and mockery. Obviously, to characterize the gathering of Jews in this manner is to reject Jewishness and Jews utterly (for gathering is a constitutive aspect of being Jewish) and to see their very existence as intolerable effrontery. John even makes reference to the Christian need to assert Christianity's interpretation of the Old Testament and to deprecate the Jews' understanding of it. When read properly, the books do not lead people astray. By implication, the Jews have misconstrued them. Jewish impiety, unlike the impiety of other non-Christians, was understood by John Chrysostom and those who thought as he did to be not just mere impiety, born of ignorance or the inability to recognize the true path, but a sort of madness.

John, an influential theologian, is but an early example of the Christian world's essential relationship to Jews, which was to endure well into modernity. It cannot be stressed too much that the hostility towards Jews was not of the sort that we all know so well, consisting of unflattering stereotypes and prejudices of one group towards another (which can be quite powerful) that buttress the self-esteem of the prejudiced. The Christian conception of Jews, in contrast, was interwoven into the constitution of the moral order of the Christian cosmos and society. The Jews were, by definition, inimical to it, a blight upon it. The very definition of what it meant to be a Christian entailed a thoroughgoing and visceral hostility to Jews,[6] just as it did to evil, and to the devil. It is no surprise that medieval Christians came to see Jews as agents of both.

From the time of John Chrysostom until the modern period, the attitudes and treatment of Jews in the Christian world underwent frequent adjustment, as did Christian doctrine and practice.[7] Yet while all the changes in Christians' theology and practice were taking place, the underlying belief in the divinity of Jesus remained firm. So too was antisemitism. While changes in Christians' elaborated beliefs about, and treatment of, Jews did occur, their most essential conception of the nature of Jews, as killers of Jesus and blasphemers, endured and was transmitted from generation to generation. Christians' understanding of the relationship of Christianity to Judaism, and of Christians to Jews, remained founded on the fundamental moral antagonism expressed by John Chrysostom. The conception of Jews as being violators of the moral order of the world was an axiom of Christian cultures. James Parkes, a historian of antisemitism, avers that ". . . there is no break in the line which leads from the beginning of the denigration of Judaism in the formative period of Christian history, from the exclusion of Jews from civic equality in the period of the Church's first triumph in the fourth century, through the horrors of the Middle Ages . . ."[8] Jews became embedded in the cognitive models that underlay Christians' thought. Whatever variations occurred in Christians' doctrine and practice regarding Jews—and they were substantial and significant—the Christian world's bearing towards Jews remained founded on the cognitive models of the cosmos and the moral order that had informed John's pronouncement.[9]

The account that follows of medieval and early modern Christian antisemitism and its expression is, of necessity, brief, touching on their important aspects only in order to elucidate the nature of antisemitism as it metamorphosed and also to examine the relationship of the beliefs to the Christian treatment of Jews.

THE MEDIEVAL Christian world conceived of Jews as being in binary opposition to Christianity. The Church, secure in its theological and practical hold over the dominions of Europe, was nonetheless totalitarian in aspiration. It responded to the symbolic challenge to its rule that it saw in Jews with a ferocity that was tempered or inflamed according to contextual conditions. The Jews' special status as the people that both had rejected Jesus' revelation and had "killed" him, although they, of all people, ought to have recognized and embraced him as their messiah, was the source of the enduring and bitter hatred of Jews by the Church, the Christian clergy, and the people of Europe. The intensity of the Church's hatred was thus twofold. On the one hand, it had the quality of a bitter sectarian strife: they were kindred combatants striving to establish sway over the proper interpretation of a common tradition. On the other, it had the quality of ferocious apocalyptic war, with the fate of the world, of people's souls, hanging in the balance. The Church, as Jesus' representative on earth, bore his shield in the battle. Although the Jews themselves—degraded, cowed, insignificant in numbers, and uninterested in proselytizing—were not a material threat, they became the material symbol of the agent posing the real challenge to Christian hegemony over the lives and souls of its people: the Devil.

So ran the logic of the Church Fathers and of Christian antisemitism as it gradually developed by the thirteenth century to the point where the Jew became synonymous with the Devil.[10] With its totalitarian control over European cosmology and moral culture, the Church disseminated through its representatives, its bishops, and, most important, its parish priests, its view of Jews, creating a universal and relatively uniform, pan-European cognition about Jews in which the Jews were, as creatures of the Devil, considered to be barely human, if human at all. "Really I doubt," declared Peter the Venerable of Cluny, "whether a Jew can be human for he will neither yield to human reasoning, nor find satisfaction in authoritative utterances, alike divine and Jewish."[11]

The medieval European hatred of Jews was so intense and so divorced from reality that all calamities in society could be and were attributed to the Jews' malfeasance. The Jews stood for everything that was awry, so that the reflexive reaction to a natural or social ill was to look to its supposed Jewish sources. Martin Luther's antisemitism was ferocious and influential enough to have earned him a place in the pantheon of antisemites. This did not matter to the Church that Luther was fighting, for the Church denounced him and his followers as heretics and Jews.[12] The logic of Europeans' fantastical beliefs about Jews was such that, as Jeremy Cohen concludes, "it was almost inevitable that Jews were blamed for the Black Death and many of their communities in Germany completely and permanently exterminated."[13] Attacks and expulsions of Jews were a staple of medieval history, so extensive that by the mid-1500s Christians had forcibly emptied most of western Europe of Jews.[14]

Regarding Jews, the medieval legacy to the modern world was, in Joshua Trachtenberg's words, "a hatred so vast and abysmal, so intense, that it leaves one gasping for comprehension."[15] Nevertheless, the Jews were left alive because the Church, in recognition of Christianity's and Judaism's common heritage, accepted the Jews' right to live and to practice their religion, though they were condemned to live in a degraded state, as punishment for their rejection of Jesus.[16] Ultimately, the Church wanted not to kill the Jews, for they were redeemable, but to convert them. This would reaffirm the supremacy of Christianity. Such was the *logic* of pre-modern Christian antisemitism.

THE VICISSITUDES OF antisemitism in nineteenth-century Germany were exceedingly complex. The character and content of antisemitism was in continual flux for three-quarters of a century, as it metamorphosed from its medieval religious incarnation to its modern racial one. The history of this transformation, with all of its intermediary forms, is a story of continuity and change *par excellence*. While its cognitive content was adopting new forms in the service of "modernizing" antisemitism, of harmonizing it with the new social and political landscape of Germany, the existing cultural cognitive model about Jews provided a remarkable underlying constancy to the elaborated cultural and ideological pronouncements. The cultural model pre-served or, differently conceived, was an enduring expression of the vast ma-jority of Germans' shared emotional attitude towards the Jews which was derived from the medieval animus that underlay Germans' conceptions of the Jews and relations with them. In "functional" terms, the changing mani-fest content of antisemitism could be understood, in one sense, to have been little more than the handmaiden of the pervasive anti-Jewish animus that served to maintain and give people a measure of coherence in the modern world, a world of flux that challenged existing patterns of social existence and cultural notions in a dazzling variety of ways. For hundreds of years, anti-semitism had lent coherence and esteem to the self-image of the Christian world; as many of the old certitudes about the world eroded in nineteenth-century Germany, the centrality of antisemitism as a model of cultural co-herence and eventually as a political ideology—and its balmic quality to a society losing its moorings—grew tremendously.[17]

The linguistic and cognitive transformation of the image of the Jews, and of the central metaphorical image underlying it, had already occurred by the beginning of the nineteenth century. This change can be seen by comparing the characterization of Jews in two seminal, influential antisemitic works: *Entdecktes Judentum* ("Judaism Unmasked"), by Johann Andreas Eisen-menger, which appeared at the beginning of the eighteenth century; and *Ueber die Gefährdung des Wohlstandes und des Charakters der Deutschen durch die Juden* ("On the Endangerment of the Prosperity and Character of the Germans by the Jews"), by Jakob Friedrich Fries, published during the early part of the nineteenth century. Eisenmenger, a pre-Enlightenment man, still conceived of the Jews in traditional theological terms as heretics; their per-fidy lay in their religious sensibilities, and their nature derived from the reli-gion's corrosive effects upon them. Fries, writing a century later, had already adopted in 1816 the secularized vocabulary of modern antisemitism, which replaced theologically informed and elaborated notions of Jews with a social and political outlook emphasizing the debased moral character of the Jews. The Jews, in Fries' view, were a group of fundamentally immoral "asocials" who were bent upon undermining the order of society and upon wresting control of Germany away from the Germans. He conceived of Jews not fore-most as a religious group (although he acknowledged this dimension of their identity), but as a nation and a political association.[18]

Much of the discussion in Germany about Jews over the first three-quarters of the nineteenth century was devoted, though not by conscious in-tent, to the hammering out of a common conception of the constitution of the Jews' identity. The religious definition of Jews progressively held less sway, though it continued to resonate and to find sympathy with the populace.

Notions of Jews being a "nation" or some corporate political group were bandied about in the antisemitic literature. The definition of the Jews that was to emerge in the second half of the nineteenth century from the confusing fray of conceptualizations, namely that the Jews were a "race," was given voice already in the first half of the nineteenth century.[19] How Germans conceived of Jews mattered a great deal, because in the conceptualizations inhered different consequences for their potential treatment of Jews. Nevertheless, although in the welter of the German definitional and polemical fray an evident lack of consensus existed on what made the Jews what they were, on what imbued them with their putative noxious qualities, consensus did reign on the fundamental belief that they were noxious.[20] Virtually all participants in the voluminous and protracted discussion of Jews and of the Jews' proper place in German society—and this includes even those who defended the Jews' emancipation and their right to reside within Germany—agreed that Jewishness and Germanness (however each was defined) were incompatible with each other; more pointedly, Jewishness was inimical and deleterious, if not life-threatening, to all things German.[21] One liberal "friend" of the Jews opined, "The Jew appears . . . as a distortion, a shadow, the dark side of human nature."[22]

The underlying German cultural model of "the Jew" (*der Jude*) was composed of three notions: that the Jew was different from the German, that he was a binary opposite of the German, and that he was not just benignly different but malevolent and corrosive. Whether conceived of as religion, nation, political group, or race, the Jew was always a *Fremdkörper*, an alien body within Germany.[23] The centrality and power of this conception of Jews was such that antisemites came to see everything that was awry in society, from social organization, to political movements, to economic troubles as being linked to, if not derived from, the Jews. An identification of Jews with social dysfunctions came to obtain. As such, the symbolic understanding of the Jew could be summed up by the notion that the Jew was everything that was awry, and that he was intentionally so.[24] These, it must be emphasized, were not merely the views of prominent antisemitic polemicists but also the views that were dominant throughout German society.

Given the ubiquitous and profound hatred of the ghettoized Jews that was integral to German culture as Germany emerged from the middle ages and early modern times, a new elaboration on the dangerous nature of Jewry was almost a natural reaction to the proposals for Jewish emancipation that began at the end of the eighteenth century, to the nineteenth century's piecemeal and progressive measures of emancipation, and to the accompanying society-wide discussion regarding the wisdom of granting Jews any civil rights in the first place and then of expanding them. As the status quo was threatened and then subverted, those opposed to the civil integration of Jews into German society mustered their energies, intellects, and considerable polemical talents to sway their countrymen to resist and to turn back the tide of perceived Jewish infiltration that threatened to break the moorings of Germans' social and cultural identities. The result was a societal conversation of ever-increasing emotion that focused ever more on the definition, character, and valuation of Jews, all in terms of their relations to Germans, who were, as an assumption of the conversation, different from, if not incompatible with, Jews.[25] No minority group's image would fare well in a discussion taking place under these conditions and cast in these terms, where it is defined as being by far the most consequential group that is different from the otherwise homogeneous societal majority, and where so much emotion is discharged against it. The Jews fared particularly badly in this discussion because the cultural model of Jews, inherited from Germany's medieval Christian constitution, was the substratum of the entire discussion. The discussion was kept alive—from the first German state's emancipation of the Jews in 1807[26] to the extension of total civil equality during 1869 to 1871 to all of German Jewry—to a great extent owing to the political mobilization of antisemitic sentiment in the continual legislative and parliamentary battles throughout Germany over the civil status of Jews. Whether it was in Berlin, Baden, Frankfurt, or Bavaria, bitter political fights accompanied attempts to confer upon the Jews the status of German subjects or citizens.[27] This discussion was, of course, not only about the Jews but equally about the identity of Germans and about the character of the German nation and the political form in which it should find its expression. German antisemitism and German nationalism became and remained—until after the Second World War—inextricably intertwined.[28]

The formal strife over the acceptance of Jews as Germans inflamed and all but guaranteed an ever-growing political character to the ever-elaborating deadly image of Jews that was an axiom of German culture. There cannot be any doubt that conservatives and Volkish nationalists in Germany, who formed the vast majority of the population, were, from the beginning of the nineteenth century onward, thoroughly antisemitic. The evidence for this is overwhelming, as the literature on the period persuasively demonstrates.[29] The most powerful evidence, however, for the ubiquitousness of antisemitism in the nineteenth century is its existence even among the "friends" of Jews, among "liberals," "philosemites," among the most "progressive" strata of German society. The most influential book urging the emancipation of the Jews and, more generally, written in Germany on the Jews' behalf, Christian Wilhelm von Dohm's *On the Civic Improvement of the Jews*, published in 1781,[30] accepted the need for the Jews to be remade, not just politically but also morally. For Dohm, emancipation was a bargain to be struck: the Jews would receive political equality in exchange for their willing reformation of their ways, especially of their moral outlook and their underhanded economic practices. The Jews, he believed, freed from the debilitating cocoon of their social and legal isolation, would, under conditions of freedom, naturally accept the bargain: "When the oppression which he [the Jew] experienced for centuries has made him morally corrupt, then a more equitable treatment will again restore him."[31] Dohm, the Jews' greatest "friend," agreed with their greatest enemies that the Jews were "morally corrupt," that as "Jews" they were not fit for citizenship, for taking a place in the bosom of German society. He departed from the uncompromising antisemites by embracing the universal potential of *Bildung*, thus rendering the Jews educable; he could believe this, in large measure, because of his understanding of the source of the Jews' putative perniciousness. His was an ecological conception of the Jews' nature, leading him to conclude that the "solution" to the "Jewish Problem" was to alter the environment.

Dohm's self-conceived, well-intentioned defense of the Jews, "the Jew is more a man [human] than a Jew,"[32] betrayed his acceptance of the German cultural cognitive model: "Jewishness" stood in opposition to desirable qualities, to "human" qualities, and for a Jew to be laudable, his Jewishness must be denied. The notion that the Jewishness had to be eradicated was enshrined in liberal thought following the appearance of Dohm's work, and even in the "terms" of emancipation itself. The 1809 emancipation edict of Baden, for example, included ominous words for a people being granted "equality": "This legal equality can become fully operative only when you [the Jews] in general exert yourselves to match it in your political and moral formation. In order that we may be certain of this effort, and in the meantime your legal equality does not rebound to the disadvantage of the other citizens, we legislate in this regard the following. . . ."[33] The Jews were put on probation, not just in Baden and not just because of the demands of their enemies but also all over Germany and according to the terms derived from their staunchest proponents' conception of them and of their potential rehabilitation.[34] It was a probation that, even in the eyes of their friends, would never end and that the Jews would inevitably break, unless they were to renounce their Jewishness completely.

The "liberals," those "friends" of the Jews, shared the central tenets of the antisemites' image of Jewishness. Even while arguing for Jewish emancipation and then for full civil equality of Jews, they too believed and explicitly argued that Jews were different from, opposed to, and deleterious to Germans, that the Jews were alien to Germany and, essentially, that they should disappear. They differed from the self-conceived antisemites in that they believed the source of the Jews' differentness was corrigible, that the Jews could be reformed, that they, the liberals, would be able to persuade emancipated Jews, tempted by the prospect of full integration into German society, to renounce their Jewishness, to efface their origins and their identity and to become Germans. As David Sorkin writes: "Underlying the discussions of emancipation was an image of a corrupt and debased Jewish people. Because of this image, emancipation was to become linked to the notion of the Jews' moral regeneration. The emancipation debate essentially turned on whether this regeneration was possible, who was to be responsible for it, and when and under what conditions it was to take place."[35] The major difference between the liberal proponents of Jewish emancipation and that of their opponents was the Enlightenment's rationalist social theory that convinced the Jews' "friends" that the Jews could be educated, reformed, and regenerated, and thereby become moral human beings. They also differed, and this is implied in their stance, in the degree of perniciousness that they ascribed to the Jews; their view of the corrosiveness of Jews for Germany was less frightening, their emotional aversion to the Jews was less profound. So a period of transition during which the Jews would gradually divest themselves of their Jewishness could be contemplated. The liberals, whatever their self-conception, were antisemites in sheep's clothing. Towards the end of the century, they would by and large strip themselves of their ill-fitting garb and reveal themselves to be not much different from their erstwhile opponents, the conservative, unabashed antisemites.[36]

Liberals continued to defend Jews in the first half of the nineteenth century on the ominous basis of affirming the Jews' capacity for moral and social regeneration. Their conception of the harmful nature of the Jews *qua* Jews remained in important ways similar to that of the antisemites.[37] Their hope was to humanize the Jews, to revolutionize the Jews' nature. Their support for Jewish rights and defense of Jews were therefore of bad faith. "We will defend you, so long as you stop being yourselves" was their essential message. And the way in which Jews could renounce their Jewishness was to renounce their Judaism, because even those Germans who were secularly oriented understood the unwholesomeness of Jews to derive at least in large part from the tenets of Judaism, a religion asserted to be devoid of love and humanity by the German cultural judgment. The Jews must "cease being Jews" and convert to a "religion of reason" (*Vernunftreligion*). They would be admitted to the German nation when they lived up to Christian standards, when they acted according to "Christian virtues," and when they renounced their "conceited and selfish conception of God."[38]

By the end of the nineteenth century, the Jews' greatest friends, the liberals, had by and large abandoned them. The liberals' social theory promising Jewish "regeneration"—which was summed up by a forward-looking churchman in 1831 who declaimed that one "will want to be just towards the Jews, only when they are no more"[39]—had been proven wrong.[40] This social theory was what had differentiated the liberals from the antisemites, was what had led them to draw conclusions about the future of Jewry different from those of the majority of Germans, with whom the liberals shared the cultural model of the Jews that held them to be alien and corrosive to German existence. They had believed the Jews to be rational beings who, when freed of the debilitations produced by their environment, namely the social and legal restrictions, would naturally reform themselves by, among other things, renouncing the second source of their putative asociability, the Jewish religion. As Uriel Tal, the historian of Christian-Jewish relations in Germany, writes, "the insistence of German Jewry on retaining its identity was contrary to the liberal view of material progress, spiritual enlightenment, and the goals of national destiny; the liberals therefore began to regard the Jews, the prototype of particularism, as the chief impediment to national and spiritual unity."[41] The Jews, by now modern in every other way, confounded liberals by not responding to their new environmental conditions, as the liberals' redemptive social theory had promised. Liberals, shorn of their optimism, were left with the cultural model of Jews as aliens, and more and more fell prey to the only convincing explanation of the source of the Jews' perniciousness, now considered to be unalterable: The Jews were a race.[42] Thus, the liberals' transformation from a "philosemitism" with "benign" eliminationist intent to an antisemitism which tended to less benign eliminationist "solutions" occurred. The major shift constituted a changed conceptualization of the *source* of the Jews' nature.

If the small intellectual and political elite of liberals, which was the group in Germany with the most "positive" attitudes towards Jews, could be aptly characterized as having been philosemitic antisemites—philosemitic so long as they maintained faith in a "redemptive" social theory—if the Jews' best friends held them to be alien agents within the German body social, then this is already powerful evidence for the existence of a German cultural model of Jews that was antisemitic. And it is hardly the only evidence that German society, both in the first and the second half of the nineteenth century, was axiomatically antisemitic.

The array of institutions and groups beholden to and even preaching antisemitism in nineteenth-century Germany touched virtually every sector of the society. The vast majority of the lower classes, whether they lived in cities or the countryside, continued to subscribe to the cultural cognitive model of the Jews. The Pollyannaish sentiment concerning the potential of the German people expressed in 1845 by the progressive democratic newspaper the *Mannheimer Abendzeitung* was touchingly naïve. The current "voice of the people," the newspaper ventured, is not the people's true voice; if enlightened, the people would abjure their thoroughgoing Jew-hatred and their view that the Jews are the source of all harm. Stripped of its optimism, this evaluation reveals the contemporary cultural attitude towards the Jews. Similarly, in 1849 the District President of Lower Bavaria deemed that "the antipathy against the equal rights of the Israelites" is "quite widespread." In the cities and towns, antisemitic preaching and agitation was a regular feature of social life and institutions.

From the university fraternities (those incubators of the German elite, professional classes, and civil servants), to their adult analogues, the patriotic societies, to the economic associations of small businessmen and artisans, to the loci of social life, the hostelers and taverns, antisemitism formed part of the framework of social perception and discussion, and more, for it was actively preached and spread. Such preaching corresponded to the vituperation against Jews that emanated from the pulpit, especially in the countryside, which was so virulent that in the middle part of the nineteenth century government authorities and, naturally, Jewish groups, across Germany, from Prussia to the Rhineland to Bavaria, saw the agitation as a cause for concern. Elected officials, down to the level of town Mayor, were intent upon keeping antisemitic agitation confined to the realm of discussion, since they wanted to maintain public order. This did not prevent many of them from themselves agitating against the Jews. Through the countryside, existing antisemitism was kept aroused by artisans and Christian guild members.[43]

What were ordinary Germans to think? They had been weaned and fed on an existing antisemitic culture, still heavily informed by the traditional Christian conception of Jews. This was now overlaid with a set of new charges—that the Jews, identified with the French, whose conquest of Germany had in some areas directly and in others indirectly led to the Jews' emancipation,[44] worked against German national goals, that they were undoing the social order, that they were the source of the dislocations of the changing economy and society, to name but a few. All the institutions of society, moreover, continued to preach the antisemitic litany. Their churches, still a formidable source of authority and guidance, reinforced the animus against the Jews.[45] Professional and economic organizations were institutionally antisemitic.[46] The main loci of recreation and of moral and political discussion—clubs, leagues, and taverns—were hothouses for antisemitic speech and emotion.[47] And against the overwhelming verbal barrage, who agitated on behalf of the Jews? Some liberal newspapers which, even while arguing for granting the Jews equal rights, often mimicked the antisemitic sentiments at the root of the cultural antipathy. How and from what source were the people of Germany—the vast majority of whom had never met a Jew or, if they had, had had little intimate contact with Jews—supposed to have developed a different conception of them? Especially since even educated Germans, the intellectual and cultural elite of Germany, were by and large as unenlightened regarding Jews as were the "unenlightened."[48] The pressure on Jews of substantial cultural attainments to renounce their Judaism, a pressure that came from the wider German milieu, was so great that, during the middle part of the nineteenth century, two-thirds of culturally prominent Jews are estimated to have converted to Christianity.[49] Social and professional acceptance by their peers and by the "enlightened" public that consumed high culture appeared to so many Jews to be closed off to them, as long as they remained Jews. Such was the inhospitableness of Germany even to the most cultured, most western, most accomplished, most admirable, most "German" of Jews.

Most of this brief survey has viewed the state of German society in the first half of the nineteenth century. In comparison to the outpouring of antisemitism that was to inflame the last two decades of the century, during this earlier period, antisemitism, as pronounced as it already was, was generally a simmering hatred, a cultural norm that was given social expression as a matter of routine, but that was not yet turned into the organized, powerful political force that it was to become. In fact, for the two decades or so after the revolution of 1848, antisemitism simmered on a still lower flame than it had before, exploding into outbursts less frequently and generally not playing as conspicuous a role in the public life of German society. Its shattering eruption in the 1870s took many, Jews among them, by surprise.[50]

One of the many threads weaving together the social and political history of nineteenth-century German antisemitism was the series of petition campaigns against Jewish emancipation and rights. On December 14, 1849, the lower house of the Bavarian Parliament passed a bill to grant Bavarian Jews full equality. Immediately, throughout Bavaria, press and popular opposition erupted, and a petition campaign that was "spontaneous, extremely broad-based, and genuine" sprang up against the bill. In "a remarkable feat of political action," during the difficult conditions of a harsh winter, petitions from over 1,700 (that is, nearly one-quarter) of the communities in Bavaria containing the signatures, by conservative estimate, of between 10 and 20 percent of all adult male citizens of the entire Bavarian population, were collected within just three months.[51] The popular forces favoring Jewish emancipation, in contrast, were effectively practically non-existent. In all of Bavaria, only three communities sent petitions supporting the emancipation bill, two of which contained sizable Jewish populations.[52] James Harris' study of the petition campaign concludes that, in one region of Bavaria, five to six times more Germans opposed than favored Jewish emancipation.[53] This outpouring of anti-Jewish sentiment and of outrage at the notion that Jews should be treated not as dangerous aliens, but as Germans, occurred during a period of the nineteenth century when antisemitic expression was relatively low compared to other, especially later periods. According to Harris, the petitions make clear that "many Christian Bavarians feared Jews. They disliked the Jewish religion, respected Jewish talents and success, and regarded Jews as unalterably different." Invoking the range of antisemitic charges that were the common sense of contemporary German culture, many petitions maintained that Jews were predatory, that Jews, because they were talented, posed an acute danger to the well-being of Germans, and that they would never assimilate. Many petitions asserted the unalterable, alien character of the Jews with various formulations, including the oft recurring phrase "Jews remain Jews." Petition after petition, by presupposing that any law that would benefit Jews would necessarily harm Christians, gave expression to the Manichaean model that undergirded much of Germans' thinking about Jews.[54] The petitioners did not hesitate to convey their expectations of the dire consequences of Jewish evil if it were to be fully unleashed. According to Harris:

> A few [petitions] merely expressed doubts about the good effects of emancipation upon the Jews, but most of those making a forecast were decidedly pessimistic. Conditions were bad, a petition from Swabia read; if emancipation occurred, they would be worse. The same point was made by several petitions: if Jews were emancipated, Bavaria would serve Jews; if emancipated, Jews will "have us by the throat"; if they are emancipated, we will become slaves; if emancipated, this "refined" people will fill all offices; and if Jews are emancipated, they will dominate. Several petitions stated that the future was not the issue. Bavarians needed immediate emancipation from Jews rather than Jews from Christians. Control and domination of Christians by Jews in general, and not just economically, was a recurring motif in the petitions.[55]

One petition summed up the folly of the emancipation bill by asserting that to grant the Jews full equality would be like putting the fox in a chicken coop.[56]

Thirty years later, Germans around the country indicated that they believed that this mid-century Bavarian anti-Jewish grass-roots effort had been prescient and wise. In 1880, a nationwide campaign calling for the rescission of Jewish rights in the now united Germany gained 265,000 petition signatures, and led the national parliament, the Reichstag, to consider the demand in full debate that lasted two days. Significantly, the petition signatures came mainly not from the unwashed, "unenlightened" lower classes, but from landowners, priests, teachers, and civil servants.[57]

THAT GERMANS WERE fundamentally antisemitic is, in light of how knowledge is socially constructed, less astonishing than was the cultural and political centrality of Jews in their minds and emotions. Perhaps the most striking feature of the discussion of the Jews' place in Germany was the obsessive attention paid to the subject, the avalanche of words devoted to it, the passion expended on it. After all, during the most explosive period of antisemitic vituperation, Jews formed but around 1 percent of the German population. Many entire regions of Germany were virtually without Jews.[58] Why the fuss at all, and why such a fuss indeed?

Ludwig Börne, a noted baptized Jewish writer who was still considered by himself and others to be a Jew, commented in a letter of 1832 on the German obsession with Jews: "It is like a wonder! I have experienced it thousands of times and yet it remains ever new to me. Some blame me for being a Jew; others forgive me; the third [*sic*] even praises me for it; but all think about it. It is as though they were spellbound in this magical Jewish circle, no one can get out."[59] No German could extricate himself from the magical spell that riveted his attention on Jews. Börne's inability to provide an explanation adequate to account for this German obsession no doubt intensified the marvel that he felt when contemplating this German "spell." Börne's testimony does not reflect some idiosyncratic experience; discussion of Jews swirled not only around him but also around Germany. Throughout the nineteenth century, groups with broad popular support continually attempted to roll back the gains that Jews had made through emancipation and during its aftermath. Such attempts had no parallels in other western countries, which is in itself powerful testimony to the singular character and deep cultural sources of German antisemitism. The *Judenfrage*, the "Jewish Problem," was of central concern particularly to nineteenth-century German theologians and politicians, who inflated the significance of the Jews to such fantastical proportions that during the debates of the Rhineland State Parliament over the emancipation of the Jews (to give but one example), it could in all seriousness be stated that the "Jewish Problem" touched the "entire world."[60]

The rupture in the German cultural fabric that Jews represented to Germans—and that they indeed constituted as a consequence of Germans' conception and treatment of them—was such that cultural taboos failed to hold sway when Germans discussed the Jews. The calls for their annihilation during the nineteenth century (discussed below) present an obvious, though not often recognized, example. Also striking was the frequent broaching of the topic of sexuality, in the form of linking the Jews with prostitution and all forms of sexual depravity, and particularly by charging the Jews with defiling unsuspecting German virgins.[61] Ritual murder accusations, the age-old antisemitic canard, and trials continued to haunt the Jewish community; in Germany and the Austrian Empire, twelve such trials took place between 1867 and 1914.[62] Even liberal newspapers took to printing all manner of rumors and accusations against Jews, including ritual murder charges, as if they had been proven facts.[63]

As telling as the content of the antisemitism that Germans expressed was the sheer volume of ink devoted to the "Jewish Problem." Eleonore Sterling, one of the foremost students of antisemitism in Germany during the first half of the nineteenth century, writes: "This doctrine of hatred is disseminated among the people through innumerable leaflets, posters, and newspaper articles. In the streets and in the taverns 'rabble-rousers' deliver hateful speeches and distribute inflammatory petitions among the population . . . the agitation continues to be conducted not only by street and tavern orators, but even by those who fancy themselves to be the 'most Christian.' "[64] The antisemitic barrage grew still more fearsome in the last quarter of the nineteenth century, when the "Jewish Problem" was written about in Germany with a passion and frequency unmatched by any other political subject. In the last three decades of the nineteenth century, according to one estimate, 1,200 publications devoted themselves to examining the "Jewish Problem," the vast majority of which belonged to the overtly antisemitic camp. The number of publications during this period that focused on the relationship between the nation and minorities (in which Jews necessarily figured prominently), according to another tabulation, exceeded the number of "political-polemical publications" devoted to *all other topics* combined.[65] If judged solely by the volume and character of the society's verbal and literary production, then the conclusion would be unavoidable that German society was focused on an urgent mortal threat of the first order. Such was the centrality of this objectively insignificant issue in the public discussion of German society.

AXIOMATIC AS THE EMOTIONAL and cognitive animus towards the Jews was, the exact *content* of nineteenth-century German antisemitism was in a state of continuous evolution. At any moment, not to mention over the course of decades, the antisemitic litany was composed of a wide variety of notions, not all of which were in harmony. Nevertheless, some central tendencies and features are discernible. The prevailing general image of the Jews held them to be malevolent, powerful, and dangerous. They were parasitic, contributing nothing to society—a central, obsessively intoned notion being that Jews shirked work, performing no productive labor—yet living off that same society, nourishing themselves at their hosts' expense. The Jews' unwholesomeness contained yet another dimension: Jews were considered to be still more caustic than parasites, which, however deleterious they may be, restrict themselves to taking without returning in kind; the Jews willfully, actively under-mined the order of society, corroding its mores and cohesion, and introduc-ing disorder and disharmony into an otherwise well-integrated whole. They were spoilers; wherever Jews spread their influence, depredation followed.[66]

And they were organized. The prevailing German view held Jews to be not just a collection of individual nodes of decomposition but a corporate group, acting in concert, as if with one will. The danger that they posed, their capacity to inflict harm, was believed by Germans to be colossal, especially be-cause of their particular talent for economic infiltration, which would eventu-ally accrue power to them through economic domination; the effect of this, in the words of an early nineteenth-century liberal and "friend" of the Jews (cast in the naturalistic, organic metaphorical language so favored by antisemites of all stripes) was fearsome. The Jews were "a rapidly growing parasitic plant that winds round the still healthy tree to suck up the life juice until the trunk, ema-ciated and eaten up from within, falls moldering into decay."[67] Conceiving of the Jews in such organic terms, each as part of one interconnected alien body invasively occupying Germany, tended to constrain Germans from seeing in-dividual Jews as individuals, and to prevent many from allowing individual Jews to meet the German requirements (whatever they were) for full accep-tance and incorporation into German society. The more that Germans con-ceived of Jews in corporate terms, the less likely they were to accept individual Jews' adoption of a Germanic cast, including Christianity, as proof of their al-legiance to Germany and of their membership in the German nation.

As the nineteenth century proceeded, a number of related changes in the character of German antisemitism could be discerned.[68] German antisemites increasingly adopted a naturalistic metaphor for Jews, of the kind just dis-cussed; their diagnosis of the Jewish-German social situation changed from the early nineteenth-century notion that the Jews were invading the Ger-mans' houses to the belief that they had already captured them; the pre-emancipation sentiment, "Keep them out," became "Expel them";[69] the Jews became conceived of more as a nation instead of a religious community;[70] this, of course, went hand in hand with a fusion of Germanism and Chris-tianity, whereby the very notion of "German" included in it a Christian ele-ment.[71] So a contemporaneous, interrelated fusion of Judaism with a newly conceived belief in Jews as a nation on the one hand, and Christianity with Germanness on the other, bespoke the creation of a virtually insuperable cog-nitive and consequent social barrier for Jews to overcome were they ever to be accepted as Germans. As if this cognitive obstacle had not been imposing enough, German antisemitism in the latter part of the century coalesced around a new master concept: race. Race, an immutable quality, dictated that a Jew could never become a German.[72]

The concept of race gave coherence to the various changing strands of antisemitism that vied to map the place of the Jews in the evolving social and political landscape of nineteenth-century Germany. It can also be seen as having been the ideological culmination of one line of argumentation that antisemites offered against the Jews' emancipation. Antisemites undercut the liberal position's conceptual foundation that the Jews were corrigible and redeemable by declaiming the Jews' nature to be unchangeable. The claims of *Bildung* were powerful; now an equally potent rejoinder was hurled against them. Even when acknowledging that the rationalist, humanist, and universalist positions of the Enlightenment were valid, antisemites asserted that because of the Jews' peculiar nature, these qualities did not pertain to Jews.[73] Already before the emancipation, in response to Dohm's book on behalf of the Jews, arguments grounded in notions about the "innate" character of Jews appeared.[74] Those holding essentialist notions about Jews began to adopt the vocabulary and the conceptual foundation of "race" as early as the 1840s.[75]

The Volkish ideology that served as the surrogate national cement, as a poor but potent substitute for a united polity, gained an ever greater ideational hold in the nineteenth century. With the "discovery" of the Germanic and Jewish "races" in the middle of the century, the conceptualization of the *Volk*'s basis as being linguistic and national itself underwent a transformation with the adoption of the essentialist, and seemingly scientific, foundation of race. In 1847, one of the most popular, influential Volkish and antisemitic polemicists captured this metamorphosis; he explained that "sense of vigor" and "love of Fatherland" were founded upon the "Germanic Christian spirit" and the "Germanic racial unity" (*germanische Blutseinheit*). The Jews, in keeping with the image of blood that was the elixir of German racial thinking, were the "eternal thoroughbred of foreignness."[76]

The concept of "race" provided an as yet unachieved coherence to modern German antisemitism. Previously, a welter of antisemitic charges and understandings of the source of the Jews' perniciousness had characterized the outpouring of anti-Jewish sentiment since the "Jewish Problem" had become a central political theme as a reaction to the movement for their emancipation. Now, with race, a unifying, easily comprehended, and metaphorically powerful concept at last appeared to integrate those various and inconsistent strands into a comprehensive, consistent explanation of Jewry and its relation to Germany.[77] The cognitive model underlying the notion of race had a number of properties that were particularly suited to antisemites, and dangerous for Jews, and which made it easy to graft onto the ancient antisemitic base.[78] By pitting Germanness and Jewishness against one another, the cognitive model underlying the notion of race recapitulated the absolute and binary opposition that traditional antisemites had always believed to exist between Christianity and

Judaism. Like medieval Christian antisemitism, this new Manichaean division transformed people, the Jews, into a central cultural symbol, the symbol of all that was awry in the world. In both conceptions, the Jews were not, however, mere inanimate symbols, but active agents, who willfully threatened the natural, the sacred order of the world. The German antisemites' evil and malevolent image of Jews was sufficient to cast the Jews as this secular worldview's Devil, no less, if not as explicitly articulated, than medieval Christian minds had identified Jews with the Devil, sorcery, and witchcraft. Race-based antisemitism appropriated and reproduced the *form* of Christian antisemitism's cognitive model while injecting it with new *content*. Because of this, the transformation was performed and accepted by Germany's enormous antisemitic constituency with remarkable ease. The new antisemitism was a "natural" modern successor to the age-old, enduring animus, the Christian cognitive elaboration of which resonated in the emerging, ever more secular era with but diminished power. This new, politically different era required contemporary justifications that mapped the changing social conditions if the animus against the Jews was to remain central.[79] Its cognitive model needed to be refurbished somewhat, so that it would not conflict with other fundamental notions in society. The new elaboration of the old animus also served to transform it; with antisemitism's new content, especially with Germans' new understanding of the *source* of the Jews' perniciousness and unfitness to be neighbors, came a new conceptualization of the "Jewish Problem" that, in turn, implied different kinds of potential "solutions."[80]

The language and accusations of racist antisemitism leave no doubt that the Jew was the source of, and was more or less identified with, everything awry in society. As it had in medieval times, the antisemitic litany included virtually every social, political, and economic ill in Germany.[81] Yet in its modern form, German antisemitism attributed to Jews a new and still greater cosmological centrality. In medieval times, to be sure, the Jews were seen to be responsible for many ills, but they remained always somewhat peripheral, on the fringes, spatially and theologically, of the Christian world, not central to its understanding of the world's troubles. Because modern German antisemites believed that the Jews were the prime source of disorder and decay, they could assert that until the Jews were vanquished, the world would never see peace. Medieval Christians could not say this, for even if the Jews were to disappear, the Devil, the ultimate source of evil, would remain. Because modern German antisemites had transformed the Jew from being an agent of the Devil to being the Devil himself, the descriptions and depictions of the Jews and the harm that they putatively wrought in Germany were fearsome. From the descriptions of Jews, abounding in organic metaphors of decomposition, it would be hard to recognize that human beings were at issue. Simply put,

Jews were poison. And, as discussed above, these accusations were hurled with enormous frequency and obsessiveness throughout German society, and so widespread were they that they were increasingly held to be true even by those in Germany who had once been the Jews' allies.

In the latter half of the nineteenth century, it became impossible to discuss the German *Volk* without conjuring up notions of race, and hence of Jewish exclusion from Germany. The concepts of *"Volk"* and "race" overlapped and became intertwined, so that it would be hard to define precisely the differences between the contemporary usage and meaning of the two terms. The fusion of Germanness and Christianity, moreover, also stripped away from the ideational repertoire of religious antisemitism the old baptismal standby—the means by which Jews could wash away their imputed sins and renounce their putative nature. The animus derived from Christianity against the "Christ-killers" remained, the capacity of the old canards to mobilize hatred against the Jews endured, but Germans' changed understanding of the source of the alleged deicides' nature no longer made the Jews redeemable. The symbolic power and metaphorical implications of the new master concept of race gave antisemitism an explosive new charge.

The pervasiveness and power of the new racially informed Volkish conception of Germanness was so great that it undermined a fundamental precept of Christianity which was unable to maintain itself under this new hegemonic outlook. The cognitive model of ontology that underlay the essentialist, racist Volkish worldview contradicted and did not admit the Christian one that had held sway for centuries. Racist antisemites denied the dated Christian notion that all souls could be saved through baptism, and the notion that conversion would remove the only difference between Jewish Germans and Christian Germans. Johannes Nordmann, a popular, influential pamphleteering antisemite, expressed this putative physiological barrier to the Jews' assumption of Christianity during the height of one antisemitic wave in 1881 in unmistakable terms: The conversion to Christianity could no more transform the Jews into Germans than the skin of Blacks could be turned white.[82] Germans came to see conversion to Christianity as a deceptive Jewish maneuver, a sham. Because of the constitution of Jews, it could not have been otherwise. And so conversion became irrelevant to the designation of who was Jewish, and to a person's moral evaluation. Even some Christian theologians began to hedge on the reach of baptism's power, agreeing that a "Volkish consciousness" (*völkisches Bewusstsein*), which by definition was alien to Jews, was a requirement of being German.[83]

The ineluctability of the conflict between Jews and German, the ceaseless attempts by Jews to dominate and destroy Germany, was inherent in this racial Volkish conceptualization of Jews that coalesced in the latter part of the nineteenth century. The absence of any option other than facing down the Jews was implicit in an archetypical description of this antisemitic ideology, penned in 1877. The Germans must recognize "that even the most honest Jew, under the inescapable influence of his blood, the carrier of his Semitic morality (*Semitenmoral*) which is fully opposed to your [German morality], must work everywhere only towards the subversion and destruction of the German nature, German morality, German civilization."[84] The essential thrust of this statement could be agreed to by all late-nineteenth-century, and for that matter twentieth-century, German antisemites, whether they conceived of themselves explicitly as racial Volkish antisemites, (with some exceptions) Christian antisemites, or, as the atheoretical majority likely did, simply as fearful haters of Jews, their hatred based upon the belief that Jews were, and were doing, precisely what the quoted statement maintained. The urgent Jewish danger was clear to all. How it should be met was less clear.

The eliminationist mind-set that characterized virtually all who spoke out on the "Jewish Problem" from the end of the eighteenth century onward was another constant in Germans' thinking about Jews.[85] For Germany to be properly ordered, regulated, and, for many, safeguarded, Jewishness had to be *eliminated* from German society. What "elimination"—in the sense of successfully ridding Germany of Jewishness—meant, and the manner in which this was to be done, was unclear and hazy to many, and found no consensus during the period of modern German antisemitism.[86] But the necessity of the elimination of Jewishness was clear to all. It followed from the conception of the Jews as alien invaders of the German body social. If two peoples are conceived of as binary opposites, with the qualities of goodness inhering in one people, and those of evil in the other, then the exorcism of that evil from the shared social and temporal space, by whatever means, would be urgent, an imperative. "The German *Volk*," asserted one antisemite before the midpoint of the century, "needs only to topple the Jews" in order to become "united and free."[87]

The nineteenth-century elaborations of antisemites' responses to the Jewish threat are interesting in a variety of ways. Given that antisemites believed the "Jewish Problem" to be the most serious and pressing one in Germany, it is not surprising that calls to action were often issued with great force. What is astonishing, however, is that a large percentage of the antisemites proposed no action at all, despite their belief that the Jews were dreaded and powerful enemies. About half of the pamphlets and speeches in the latter part of the nineteenth century presented no recommendations for how the "Jewish Problem" should be solved.[88] By the latter part of the nineteenth century, when Jews had already integrated themselves into the economic and professional life of Germany, some, like Wilhelm Marr, who coined the term "antisemitism" and was one of the most prominent antisemitic writers, no doubt believed the cause of purifying Germany to have been already lost: "We Germans, have, with the year 1848, completed our official abdication in favour of Judaism. . . . The Thirty Years' War which Jewry has officially waged against us since 1848 . . . does not even leave open the hope of some rotten Peace of Westphalia."[89] The Jews had occupied their homes and the Germans would never be able to expel them. The Jews had already won. Some likely saw no use in suggesting "solutions" that were not remotely possible. Still others, in this pre-Holocaust age, likely dared not utter what they thought to be the only "solution" to the "Jewish Problem" adequate for their conception of the Jews. Since no middle ground would suffice, why propose anything? The sometimes mild proposals of those who did offer "solutions" stood in such glaring contrast to the mortal danger that they asserted the Jews to be posing that it must be considered that some antisemites, as rabid as their hatred for Jews was, either were not able to make the imaginative and moral leap to contemplating large-scale violence or remained ethically inhibited in this era that had not yet loosened all expressive imaginative restraints. Or perhaps, constrained by the limited real possibilities for action, boundaries imposed by the German state, they—as Hitler would in his initial years of power—bowed to pragmatism, offering prescriptions far less radical than those that they truly desired.

The "solutions" that antisemites did propose in the latter part of the nineteenth century ran the gamut from the old liberal hope of causing the Jews to disappear through their total assimilation, to creating new legal constraints on the Jews, including a rollback of the emancipation, to forcible and violent expulsion, and even to total annihilation. All these "solutions" are but variations, enormously different as they may be, on the eliminationist mind-set. From the antisemites' perspective, though not from that of the Jews, these "solutions" were, with their remaining differences, rough functional equivalents. They emanated from the common belief that German society must be de-Jewified, made *judenrein*, one way or another. The eliminationist mind-set was the logical and actual product of this belief. The exact "solutions" deemed to be appropriate depended on the particular nature and variant of the antisemitism moving the person who was agitating for social restructuring, as well as the broader social and ethical theories that guided him. As the content of antisemitism coalesced around the beliefs that the Jews were a race and that the danger that they posed was mortal, in the latter part of the nineteenth century the most prominent antisemitic writers increasingly accepted the logic of their beliefs, calling for nothing less than the Jews' extermination:

The voices which, in accordance with the absolutely negative verdict on the Jewish being, urged merciless persecution and annihilation, were by far in the majority and their appeal increased from decade to decade. In their eyes the Jews were parasites and vermin that had to be exterminated. The wealth that they had amassed through thieving and cheating must be wrested from them and they themselves exported for a good profit to a remote corner of the earth, say to Guinea. Some advocated the simplest solution, to kill the Jews; since the duty to defend . . . "morals, humanity and culture" demanded a pitiless struggle against the evil . . . The annihilation of the Jews meant for most antisemites the salvation of Germany. They were apparently convinced that the elimination of a minority would bring an end to all the miseries and make the German people again the master in its own house.[90]

Klemens Felden, the author of the above passage, has done a content analysis of fifty-one prominent antisemitic writers and publications that appeared between 1861 and 1895 in Germany. The findings are startling.[91] Twenty-eight of them proposed "solutions" to the "Jewish Problem." Of those, nineteen called for the *physical extermination of the Jews*. During this pre-genocidal era of European civilization—when consciousness of the mass human slaughter of the First and Second World Wars, let alone of genocide as an instrument of national policy, did not exist—fully two-thirds of these prominent antisemites took their beliefs to their extreme logical consequences and uttered, indeed called for, a genocidal response. Of the forty who wrote about and explicated their understanding of the corporate basis of the Jews' unity, only one considered them to be purely a religious community, and just six others mentioned religion along with other attributes as a unifying feature of Jewishness. In contrast, thirty-two conceptualized the Jews' nature as *unchanging*. Twenty-three of these presented the Jews as a race. The elective affinity between the development of the notion of the unchanging and unchangeable nature of the Jews, conceptualized primarily in explicitly racial terms, and seeing the "solution" to the "Jewish Problem" to be their physical annihilation, is unmistakable. *The eliminationist mind-set tended towards an exterminationist one.*[92] And it did so already in the nineteenth century, prior to the political birth of Hitler. Indeed, already at the end of the eighteenth century, Dohm recognized that the antisemites' characterization of Jews logically implied that "one must wipe the Jews from the face of the earth."[93] Only two of those who called for the extermination of the Jews (and who declared their understanding of the Jews' nature) failed to conceptualize the Jews in the explicit language of race, and these two called the Jews a nation. Racial antisemites were indeed convinced, as Felden observes, that the extermination of the Jews was the salvation of Germany, and, not surprisingly, the frequency and intensity of such demands grew consistently during the latter part of the century. The 1899 political program of the Hamburg branch of the united antisemitic parties illustrated this with its prophetic and hortatory words: "Thanks to the development of our modern means of communication, the Jewish Problem would become in the course of the twentieth century a global problem and as such, it would be jointly and decisively solved by the other nations through total segregation and (if self-defense should demand it) finally through the annihilation of the Jewish people."[94] In their "redemptive" proposals, nineteenth- and early-twentieth-century racial antisemites were true to the implication of their conceptualization of Jews.

By the end of the nineteenth century, the view that Jews posed extreme danger to Germany and that the source of their perniciousness was immutable, namely their race, and the consequential belief that the Jews had to be *eliminated* from Germany were extremely widespread in German society. The tendency to consider and propose the most radical form of elimination—that is, extermination—was already strong and had been given much voice. German society continued to be thoroughly antisemitic, as it had been at the beginning of the nineteenth century, yet the nature of the transformed, modernized racial antisemitism suggested more comprehensive, radical, even deadly "solutions" to the perceived "Jewish Problem." With the arrival of the twentieth century, the seeds for Nazi antisemitism and Nazi anti-Jewish policies had been widely sown, had already sprouted, and had flourished considerably. The antisemitism found expression mainly through talk and individual discriminatory actions, and also through intense political activity. As powerful and potentially violent as the antisemitism was, it nevertheless failed to erupt during this period into concerted and sustained violence because the conditions to transform it into a program of physical assault did not obtain; the state would not allow it to become the basis of collective social action of this sort. Wilhelmine Germany would not tolerate the organized violence for which antisemites appeared to long.[95] Without political mobilization, antisemitism remained for Jews an extremely unpleasant, prominent feature of German culture and politics, resulting in continuous verbal assaults, social discrimination, and incessant psychological wounds, but it did not generally threaten the physical security of German Jews.

Throughout the nineteenth century, particularly in its second half, no non-antisemitic alternative image of the Jews found *institutional* support (the Social Democratic Party partially excepted), certainly not widespread institutional support in Germany. This was true not only of political institutions but also of the Tocquevillian substructure of society, the associations that provided the staging ground for people's political education and activity. As the historian of German antisemitism Werner Jochmann writes, "a wealth of examples shows how, in the [18]90's, anti-Semitism infiltrated in this way into *every last* citizens' association, penetrating folk clubs and cultural societies [my emphasis]." By this time it was the reigning ideology of most middle-class organizations, including economic ones. So powerful was antisemitism that in 1893, at the first general meeting of the *Deutschnationaler Handlungsgehilfenverband*, an association of clerks that described itself as having been "born of antisemitism," the governing board averred: "We cannot escape this [antisemitic] wave, and would be well advised to let ourselves be carried along by it."[96] This and other economic and non-economic organizations declared themselves to be *judenrein*, prohibiting Jews from becoming members no matter their common economic position.[97] Indeed, antisemitism was so widespread and so powerful an energizing force that it was used as a matter of course by the widest spectrum of groups trying to mobilize supporters. When the Farmers' Association sought in the 1890s to organize disparate agricultural interests, from large landowners to small farmers and agriculturally dependent artisans, "antisemitism appeared to be almost the only means of recruiting and holding them." Catholics, locked in battle with the anti-Catholic central government, attacked it as Prussianized and Judaized.[98] Declaring the Jews to be one's enemy or declaring one's enemy to be beholden to the Jews was so effective for winning adherents that it became a standard part of the political and social repertoire of late nineteenth-century Germany.

A powerful subterranean anti-Jewish animus had already been a part of Germans' cultural cognitive model of Jews as they had embarked upon and struggled through the industrial revolution and the political process of creating a unified Germany, the basis of the latter process having been the exclusionary concept of the *Volk*. To the large extent that the subject of the Jews was part of the public conversation of society, German writers and speakers discussed them overwhelmingly in a sinister, if not demonic, light, in the racist, dehumanizing idiom of the day. In the words of Ludwig Bamberger, the leader of the National Liberals, penned in 1882, "the organs that are the actual life blood of the nation—army, schools, the scholarly world—are filled to the brim with it [antisemitism] . . ." so it was no surprise that "it has become an obsession that does not leave one untouched."[99] Despite their "emancipation," Jews furthermore continued to suffer all sorts of public, prominent, and highly meaningful disabilities that suggested to all in Germany that Jews were not really Germans, that they could not be trusted to be full members of society. The Germans' well-known and effective continuing exclusion of Jews from the institution most identified with German patriotism, the army's officer corps, and from the institutions that collectively guided, served, cared for, and governed the people, the civil service, especially the judiciary (even if Jews were formally admitted to this),[100] sent a continuous, unmistakable signal to the German people that Jews were really not Germans, but outsiders, not fit to take part in the sharing of power. Indeed, these disabilities were so widespread and debilitating, enforced and even

often actively promoted by civil servants, judges, and teachers, that one leading jurist described what effectively amounted to a partial rescission of emancipation as "the reversal of the Constitution by the administration."[101]

The ubiquitous antisemitism that existed in 1800 and in 1850 became, if
anything, more intense and certainly more deadly as the century was drawing
to a close, as Germany became more economically and technologically advanced. Antisemitism and modernity were perfectly compatible in Germany,
because the foundational conception of political community constituting
modern Germany was the *Volk*, and this conception was also given a pseudo-
scientific modern basis in the racist and social Darwinian theories that were
the common currency of much of late nineteenth-century European culture.[102] As has already been argued, by the end of the century the Jews' best
friends during the first half of the century, the liberals, had by and large renounced their philosemitic antisemitism, their assimilationist version of the
eliminationist mind-set, and adopted the antisemitic model, idiom, and outlook of modern German antisemitism, with its less benign eliminationist proposals. This was not true only of the ever-shrinking core of left-liberals, who
remained faithful to Enlightenment principles. Yet their adherence to these
anti-antisemitic principles meant that they became politically irrelevant in
such an antisemitic country, continuously losing the erstwhile liberal voters.
In some areas of Germany, a majority of middle-class voters cast their lots
with antisemitic political parties.[103] German conservatives (to be distinguished from those who defined themselves almost exclusively by their antisemitism) had always been thoroughly antisemitic. In the 1884 national
election campaign, the Conservative Party avowedly declared Jews to be in binary opposition to Germans. Jews' allegiance was to "international, non-
German powers," the fact of which "must finally convince every truly
German man" that Jews "would never accord precedence to the interests of
the German fatherland."[104] Racial antisemitism was already *de rigueur* in
Protestant circles. And it had made inroads even among Catholics.[105] The
only significant, identifiable groups in Germany which formally abjured and
were relatively protected against the prevailing antisemitic views were the
core of the socialist movement, its intellectuals and leaders, and the politically
ineffectual left-liberal elite. These small groups were moved by a counter-
ideology that denied the premises underlying antisemitism.[106]

It is thus incontestable that the fundamentals of Nazi antisemitism, the
antisemitic brew that spawned Nazi thinking about the Jews, had deep roots
in Germany, was part of the cultural cognitive model of German society, and
was integral to German political culture. It is incontestable that racial antisemitism was the salient form of antisemitism in Germany and that it was
broadly part of the public conversation of German society. It is incontestable

that it had enormously wide and solid institutional and political support in Germany at various times (as evidenced in voting, petitions, and associational life).[107] It is incontestable that this racial antisemitism which held the Jews to pose a mortal threat to Germany was pregnant with murder. The only matter that cannot be ascertained is, broadly held though this view of Jews was, precisely how many Germans subscribed to it in 1900, 1920, 1933, or 1941.

The "Jewish Problem" had, since the end of the eighteenth century, always been a political issue in Germany, as Germans' agitation for this or that "solution" to the "problem" was aimed always finally at the political authorities who, in the end, made the legal decisions. The "Jewish Problem," while in the eyes of the antisemites also an economic and a social problem, was primarily a political issue that required a political response. Whether it was to be the legal rescission of the emancipation, the expulsion of the Jews, or their extermination, the state would have to be the primary agent of change. With the mass political mobilization that accompanied the development of parliamentary politics in Wilhelmine Germany, it is therefore no surprise that antisemitism came to be central in electoral and parliamentary politics.

The rise and (as is discussed presently) even the decline of antisemitic political parties in Germany and Austria confirm two notions. Antisemitism was, in the beginning decades of the twentieth century, broadly part of German and Austrian societies, and constitutive of their political cultures. It was also a powerful political force, decisive for the political fortunes of parties and regimes. In the 1880s, antisemitic political parties were founded to contest German parliamentary elections. These parties were not just hospitable to antisemitism. They explicitly defined themselves above all as antisemitic parties.[108] Even more important than their founding and subsequent electoral success was the *formal declaration* by the Conservative Party—the main parliamentary supporter of Bismarck and of the Wilhelmine Reich—that it was antisemitic in its Tivoli Program of December 1892: "We combat the widely obtruding and decomposing Jewish influence on our popular life. We demand a Christian authority for the Christian people and Christian teachers for Christian children."[109] The Conservative Party had long been thoroughly antisemitic and recognized as such, as the *Preussische Jahrbücher* commented: "Basically the conservatives have always been anti-Semitic . . . By becoming anti-Semitic, the Conservative Party has turned into . . . nothing new in its content, but it has become demagogic . . ."[110] The electoral appeal of the antisemitic parties—that is, of the parties that declared antisemitism as their reason for being—finally necessitated the Conservatives' formal adoption of an antisemitic identity and program lest they lose more of their support. In the election of 1893, parties avowedly antisemitic gained a *majority* in the Reichstag, the vast majority of the votes having been cast for the Conservative Party. In Saxony, where the Jewish population was as of 1880 an infinitesimal one-quarter of 1 percent, the Conservative and antisemitic parties together polled 42.6 percent of the vote, with the antisemitic parties garnering for themselves 19.6 percent of the ballots cast.[111]

The electoral fortunes of the antisemitic parties, other than the Conservative Party, declined in the first decade of the twentieth century. Their lack of staying power resulted mainly from two developments: the co-optation of their message by the Conservative Party and the temporary reorienting of attention to foreign policy. By this time antisemitism had become such a mainstay in the non-socialist parties' outlooks that the thunder of the antisemitic parties had been stolen. Since these parties had little else to offer by way of a program, they faded from the horizon. Also, because of the tremendous focus during these years on Germany's foreign-policy adventures and conflicts, Germans' political attention was diverted from their antisemitic concerns and aspirations, so the antisemitism receded, becoming less manifest, and less a basis for political mobilization.[112]

The rise of antisemitic political parties and the conversion of the established parties either to overt antisemitism or to its tacit acceptance indicate how powerful a force antisemitism had become in German society. The decline of the antisemitic parties was therefore not symptomatic of a decline in antisemitism, for these particular parties had already performed their historic role of moving antisemitism from the street and the beer hall's *Stammtisch* into the electoral booth and the seat of parliament, into, in Max Weber's formulation, the house of power. The antisemitic parties had rendered themselves moot.[113] They could quietly disappear, leaving the political terrain to more potent successors who were fit for the next upsurge in antisemitic expression and activity. The decline of these parties also coincided with a temporary cognitive and political submergence of antisemitism as other spectacular issues of foreign affairs became more pressing. Again, this meant not that antisemitism was dissipating, but that it was merely less articulated and therefore partly disappeared from view. It would erupt again with great force only a few years hence.

This brief history of antisemitism's evolution and character is obviously not meant to be definitive, in the sense of presenting full substantiation for its every assertion, as well as the qualifications and nuances that a longer treatment would include. Owing to the limited space available for treating this vast subject, it could not be otherwise. The purpose here has been to redraw our understanding of the development of modern German antisemitism by bringing together known developments from different periods that have generally been treated as distinct, and to reconceptualize them in the light of the new analytical and interpretive framework that was enunciated in the previous chapter. This approach yields a new understanding of antisemitism that holds it to have had greater continuity and to have been more ubiquitous in German society during the modern period than others have maintained.

This brief history, moreover, has concentrated on establishing the existence, extent, and content of German antisemitism—because this is what is relevant to and necessary for the upcoming analysis—and not on providing a full historical sociology that analyzes the phenomenon against the variety of political, social, and economic developments that occurred in Germany. The treatment here is also, obviously, not a *comparative* historical sociology, because the extent and nature of antisemitism in other countries is not at issue here.[114] The purpose of the discussion has been to establish and focus on the *central features* of antisemitism in nineteenth-century Germany (and not on the exceptional divergences from the norm), because the central features were the ones that would shape the history of twentieth-century Germany:

1. From the beginning of the nineteenth century, antisemitism was ubiquitous in Germany. It was its "common sense."
2. The preoccupation with Jews had an obsessive quality.
3. Jews came to be identified with and symbolic of anything and everything which was deemed awry in German society.
4. The central image of the Jews held them to be malevolent, powerful, a principal, if not the principal, source of the ills that beset Germany, and therefore dangerous to the welfare of Germans. This was different from the medieval Christian view, which deemed the Jews to be evil and the source of great harm, but in which the Jews always remained somewhat peripheral. Modern German antisemites, unlike their medieval forebears, could say that there would be no peace on earth until the Jews were destroyed.
5. This cultural model in the second half of the nineteenth century coalesced around the concept of "race."
6. This brand of antisemitism was unusually violent in its imagery, and it tended towards violence.
7. Its logic was to promote the "elimination" of Jews by whatever means necessary and possible, given the prevailing ethical constraints.

The purpose of this account more generally is to demonstrate two points: that the cognitive model of Nazi antisemitism had taken shape well before the Nazis came to power, and that this model, throughout the nineteenth and early twentieth centuries, was also extremely widespread in all social classes and sectors of German society, for it was deeply embedded in German cultural and political life and conversation, as well as integrated into the moral structure of society.[115] The foundational concept for German popular political thought, the *Volk*, was conceptually linked to, and partly dependent upon, a definition of Jews as the *Volk*'s antithesis. Built into the concept of *Volk* was a deprecation of Jews, who embodied all the negative qualities and ideals which were absent from the *Volk*, including moral ones. Thus, the conceptual and moral foundation of German political existence incorporated the perniciousness of the Jews, which guaranteed still greater staying power and political potency to the antisemitic cultural cognitive model.

The discussion here further illustrates the argument put forward in the previous chapter that antisemitism, while undergoing important changes in its character during the nineteenth century and while always having been widely present in German society, became more or less *manifest*, in response to varying developments in German society, especially to the fortunes of the economy.[116] In light of this history—which, despite cycles of great antisemitic agitation, quiescence, and then renewed agitation, was characterized by a continuity of cognitions and accusations about Jews—it would be false to believe that the changes in the degree of German antisemitic expression indicate that Germans became antisemites, then rejected antisemitism, only to adopt its precepts whole again, etc. The evidence, moreover, of a public discussion which was overwhelmingly antisemitic, presenting for the German people's consideration virtually only negative images of Jews, and negative images that portrayed the Jews as poisonous, evil, eternally strange, as subversive infiltrators, destroyers, and demon-like in their aims and powers—a discussion in which the German people were *active participants*—can leave little doubt that the cognitions and emotions about Jews dominant in society were given no reason during the course of the nineteenth century to evaporate. Since the vast majority of Germans had little or no contact with Jews, and certainly did not know Jews well, the only Jews whom they actually met and came to know were the ones represented in the antisemitic speeches, writings, caricatures, and discussions on which they were nurtured. Folktales, literature, the popular press, and political pamphlets and cartoons, the bearers of potent antisemitic images, provided the poisonous *Bildung* about Jews that was at the core of German culture.[117]

In the nineteenth century, those who agitated for the emancipation of the Jews hardly spoke for the majority of Germans; they won their battle but barely.[118] Built into emancipation itself—an emancipation that proceeded upon a cultural model of Jews derived from hostile Christianity—was the belief that Jews would disappear; since Jews refused to do so, the false promises of emancipation created all but a structural guarantee that antisemitism would develop new virulence (as Jews, to use the idiom of the day, invaded the Germans' home and became the objects of great envy because of their meteoric rise from pariah status), would metamorphose itself cognitively to account for the changing conditions of German society and the position of Jews within it, and, since economic troubles and social dislocations were bound to occur, would intensify and become activated politically. This was the nineteenth-century antisemitic legacy that was to inform twentieth-century German society and politics.

It is no wonder that in light of this evidence, no one has yet been able to *demonstrate* that the vast majority of Germans, or even significant minorities (save for small elite groups), had at any time renounced their cultural heritage of an anti-Jewish animus, had freed themselves of the cognitive model of Jews that governed Germany. It is not enough to assume and assert it, or to trace the writings of a few liberal intellectuals, as other interpreters of German antisemitism have done. As I have argued, demonstrating this—namely providing *evidence* that the scope and intensity of antisemitism had atrophied—should be the analytical burden when discussing the degree to which Germans were antisemitic. It remains unmet. The fact was that as the 1920s and then the Nazi takeover approached, the German people were more dangerously oriented towards Jews than they had been during any other time since the dawn of modernity.

3

ELIMINATIONIST ANTISEMITISM:
THE "COMMON SENSE" OF
GERMAN SOCIETY DURING
THE NAZI PERIOD

BY THE EVE of the First World War, a discourse—namely a discussion structured by a stable framework with widely accepted reference points, images, and explicit elaborations—had for over thirty years been in place with regard to the Jews. The consolidation of this discourse, the forging of a common set of assumptions and beliefs about Jews, the solidifying of the Jews as a cultural and political symbol, one of decomposition, malignancy, and willful evil, meant that it was well-nigh impossible to discuss Jews except in its frame of reference. In the antisemitic publications of the late nineteenth century, when some new accusation against, or argument about, the Jews would appear, the construction would then be incorporated into subsequent editions of other antisemites' works that had initially been published prior to the novel contribution to the corpus of anti-Jewish thought.[1] The German discourse in some sense had as its foundation the extremely widespread, virtually axiomatic notion that a *"Judenfrage,"* a "Jewish Problem," existed.[2] The term *"Judenfrage"* presupposed and inhered within it a set of interrelated notions. Jewish Germans were essentially different from non-Jewish Germans. Because of the Jews' presence, a serious problem existed in Germany. Responsibility for the problem lay with the Jews, not the Germans. As a consequence of these "facts," some fundamental change in the nature of Jews or in their position in Germany was necessary and urgent. Everyone who accepted the existence of a "Jewish Problem"—even those who were not passionately hostile to the Jews—subscribed to these notions, for they were constitutive of the concept's cognitive model. Every time the word *"Judenfrage"* (or any word or phrase associated with it) was uttered, heard, or read, those partaking in the conversation activated the cognitive model necessary to understand it.[3]

Change of some sort was seen as necessary, yet the Jews' nature, because of their "race," was understood by Germans to be unchangeable, since the prevailing German conception of the Jews posited them to be a race inexorably alien to the Germanic race. Also, the "evidence" of their senses told Germans that the majority of Jews had already assimilated, in the sense of having taken on the manners, dress, and idiom of modern Germany, and so the Jews had already been given every possible chance to become good Germans—and failed.[4] This axiomatic belief in the existence of the "Jewish Problem," more or less promised an axiomatic belief in the need to "eliminate" Jewishness from Germany as the "problem's" only "solution."

The toll of these decades of verbal, literary, institutionally organized, and political antisemitism was wearing down even those who, true to Enlightenment principles, had resisted the demonization of the Jews. The eliminationist mind-set was so prevalent that the inveterate antisemite and founder of the Pan-German League, Friedrich Lange, could with verity declaim the universal belief in the "Jewish Problem," rightly pointing out that the means to the "solution," and not the existence of the "problem" itself, was the only remaining subject of doubt and disagreement: "I assert that the attitude of the educated Germans towards Judaism has become totally different from what it was only a few years ago . . . The Jewish Problem is today no longer a question of 'whether'? but only one of 'how'?"[5] The axiom that Jews were harmful and that they must be eliminated from Germany found renewed, intense expression in an unexpected context, during a time when national solidarity is typically forged and hardened, and social conflicts are dampened and deferred—namely the national emergency of full-scale war.

During World War I, Germans accused the Jews of not serving in the military, of not defending the Fatherland. Instead, Jews were alleged to have been staying safe at home and using the wartime conditions to exploit and immiserate the Germans for their own profit on the black market. The upsurge against the Jews was so extreme that in 1916 the Prussian authorities conducted a census of Jews in the armed forces in order to assess the Jews' martial contribution—a humiliating measure providing stunning testament to the Jews' precarious social position and to the ongoing belief in the centrality of the "Jewish Problem."[6] It is precisely because Jews had long been considered dangerous aliens that the closing of Germans' ranks in social solidarity produced not a diminution of social animosity towards the Jews, but an upsurge in antisemitic expression and attacks. The more perilous the times, so drove the antisemitic logic, the more dangerous and injurious the Jews must be. Franz Oppenheimer summarized the attitudes of Germans towards Jews, attitudes that Jews could not favorably alter no matter how fervently they might dedicate themselves to the German cause: "Don't fool yourselves, you are and will remain Germany's pariahs."[7] German antisemites had always been somewhat autistic in their conception of Jews. The autism was to grow worse.

THE WEIMAR REPUBLIC was founded in 1919 in the wake of the military defeat, the abdication of the German monarch, and the crumbling of the Second German Empire. With the exception of a few prominent figures, Jews were not central in the founding and governance of Weimar, yet like all things hated in Germany, Weimar's many enemies, as a matter of faith, identified it with the Jews, the purpose and effect of which was to help to delegitimize the democracy.

The economic privations of Weimar's first few years, including food shortages and inflation, were enormous. Germans, as a matter of course, routinely and widely blamed their individual and collective suffering on the Jews. A large number of government reports from around Germany attest to this, portraying a virulent hatred of Jews that was assessed by public officials to be explosive. The President of the Swabian district government, for instance, reported in March 1920: "I must not fail to point out with emphasis again and again the extraordinary agitation and discord that has taken hold of the population in the cities and in the country as a result of steadily-rising prices. . . . One hears everywhere that 'our government is delivering us over to the Jews.'" A Munich report on the political climate from October 1919 warned that the mood of the people was such that pogroms against Jews appeared "quite possible." Two years later, in August 1921, another police situation summary described Germans' attitudes towards Jews as being, if anything, more ominous: "Reports agree that the mood for Jewish pogroms is spreading systematically in *all parts* of the country [my emphasis]."[8]

A survey of the political and social life of Weimar reveals that virtually every major institution and group in Germany—including schools and universities, the military, bureaucracy, and judiciary, professional associations, the churches, and political parties—was permeated by antisemitism. Many had gone so far as to declare themselves openly and proudly to be antisemitic. A look at what is perhaps the most revealing of them all, the educational institutions, indicates that the youth and young adults of Weimar Germany provided large, willing cadres for the coming Nazi dispensation. Schools had become so rife with the words and symbols of antisemitism, on the part of both teachers and pupils, that between 1919 and 1922 the ministries of culture of a number of German states issued prohibitions against the dissemination of antisemitic literature and the wearing of the swastika and other antisemitic symbols. Yet many teachers continued to preach aspects of the antisemitic litany, which included the foundational notion that a "Jewish Problem" existed in Germany, with all of its implicit and explicit warnings of the danger that Jews posed to the well-being of Germans.[9]

The universities were still more swept along by the antisemitic wave that engulfed them and German society. During Weimar, student organizations and student bodies throughout the country showed themselves to be virulently antisemitic. In one university after the next, governing student associations were already, in the first years of the Weimar Republic, captured by nationalist, *völkisch*, and antisemitic forces, often by electoral majorities of two-thirds to three-quarters. Many of them, with little opposition, subsequently adopted "Aryan paragraphs," clauses that called for the exclusion of Jews or for their severe restriction, both from student organizations and from study at universities. In 1920, for example, two-thirds of the student assembly at the Technical University of Hannover endorsed the call for "students of Jewish descent" to be excluded from the Union of German Students. The hostility to Jews, by both students and professors, and the many accompanying discriminatory acts were alarmingly described by the Prussian Minister of Science, Art, and Popular Education in 1920 as a "massive swelling of antisemitic tendencies at our universities." Max Weber, a few months earlier, commented in a letter that "the academic atmosphere has become extremely reactionary, and in addition radically antisemitic."[10] All of this was to grow only worse ten years later, when many of these same organizations would wholeheartedly accept the leadership of Nazi students, and the National Socialist German Student League would win the allegiance of the majority of students in Germany and Austria. Professors, themselves anything but immune to the prevailing cultural models about Jews, rarely criticized the racist antisemitism that was the widespread norm on campuses. Even the great historian Friedrich Meinecke, a political liberal and a democrat, was an antisemite.[11]

Antisemitism was endemic to Weimar Germany, so widespread that nearly every political group in the country shunned the Jews. Jews, though ferociously attacked, found virtually no defenders in German society. The public conversation about Jews was almost wholly negative. So convinced of the hopelessness of the position of Jews in Germany was Albert Einstein—who, prior to his arrival in Germany a few years earlier, had been neither particularly conscious of his Jewishness nor sensitive to antisemitism—that already in 1921 he averred that he would "be forced to leave Germany within 10 years."[12] A police situation report from October of the following year predicted a bright future for the Nazi Party because its central focus on the danger of the Jews was broadly subscribed to in Germany, and not only by some restricted groups: "The fact cannot be denied that the antisemitic idea has penetrated the widest levels of the middle class, even far into the working class."[13] Werner Jochmann concludes, after surveying the period of 1914 to 1924, "that already in the first years of the republic the antisemitic flood had inundated all the dams of legality. Still greater was the devastation in the spiritual realm. Even the democratic parties and the governments of the republic believed that they could escape the pressure being exerted on them if they recommended to the Jews restraint in political and social life, and deported or interned the East European Jews."[14] What was so at the advent of Weimar became ever more the case as the Republic's life unfolded. Not just words but riotous attacks were also unleashed by Germans upon Jews throughout Weimar, beginning already in 1918 in Munich and Berlin, where enraged mobs attacked Jews during the revolution. Another wave of mob attacks, which erupted around Germany in 1923–1924, led to the death of some Jews.[15] Given the ubiquity and intensity of anti-Jewish feeling in Germany, sentiments that would later be activated and channeled by the Nazi regime into violent and murderous assaults, the restraints imposed by the Weimar government certainly prevented Germans' steady verbal assaults upon Jews from escalating still more frequently into physical ones.

The simple fact was that in a society that so continuously and vocally defined Jews and Germans as polar beings, that made the status of Jews within Germany a preeminent *political* question (and not just a theme of "civil society"), it was virtually impossible not to take sides, not to have an opinion about the "solving" of the "Jewish Problem," and, when doing so, to avoid adopting the prevailing Manichaean idiom of Germany. Because the party leaders knew that antisemitism permeated their constituencies, including the working class, at the end of Weimar the political parties did not attack Hitler's antisemitism, although they attacked him on many other grounds.[16] The correlation of forces that existed at the end of Weimar has been summed up as follows: "For antisemitism hundreds of thousands were ready to ascend the barricades, to fight brawls in public halls, to demonstrate in the streets; against antisemitism hardly a hand stirred. Insofar as slogans were in those days raised against Hitler, they put forward other things, but not the revulsion against antisemitism."[17] The groups that were most likely to have harbored favorable, or at least different, conceptions of Jews in Germany either did not or perhaps felt compelled to keep their counsel in the face of the thoroughgoing antisemitism that permeated the society, its institutions and its politics. The Jews stood abandoned and alone, as Germany in 1933 was about to make unequivocal what had been true already for a while, that it had, in the words of Max

Warburg, the prominent Jewish banker, "disqualified itself from the ranks of the civilized peoples [*Kulturvölker*] and taken its place among the ranks of the pogrom lands [*Pogromländer*]."[18]

THE NAZI PARTY was the most radical political party to gain control of a government in European history. Significantly, its openly murderous radicality notwithstanding, it did so through electoral means. The National Socialist German Workers' Party, as the Nazi Party was formally named, was founded as the German Workers' Party in Munich on January 5, 1919, during the turbulent period of defeat, revolution, and reconstruction after World War I. The twenty-nine-year-old Adolf Hitler, who, after having served as a corporal during the war, was living in Munich, gravitated to it in September of that year as its seventh member. He soon was put in charge of the Party's propaganda, and by 1921 he became its political as well as its intellectual and ideological leader. Hitler, in possession of great oratorical skills, was the Party's most forceful public speaker.

Like Hitler, the Party from its earliest days was devoted to the destruction of Weimar democracy, a revision of Versailles, revanchism, anti-Bolshevism, militarism, and, most especially and relentlessly, antisemitism. The Jews, as Hitler and the Nazis intoned obsessively, were seen to be the root cause of all of Germany's other afflictions, including the loss of the First World War, the evisceration of Germany's strength by the imposition of democracy, the threat posed by Bolshevism, the discontinuities and disorientations of modernity, and more. The twenty-five-point Party program, promulgated in February 1920 (and never altered), included in many of its points attacks on the Jews and the call for their exclusion from membership in and influence on German society and institutions. Point Four declared: "Only members of the nation may be citizens of the State. Only those of German blood, whatever their creed, may be members of the nation. Accordingly no Jew may be a member of the nation." The program, written by Hitler and Anton Drexler, the Party's founder, was explicitly racist in its understanding of Jews. It dedicated the Party to combating "the Jewish-materialist spirit," effectively to an eliminationist project.[19] The Nazi Party became Hitler's Party, obsessively antisemitic and apocalyptic in its rhetoric about its enemies. The centrality of antisemitism in the Party's worldview, program, and rhetoric—if in a more elaborated and avowedly violent form—mirrored the sentiments of German culture. The Party's rise in Germany at the end of the decade was to be meteoric.

In its first years, the Nazis remained a small, grass-roots organization. During its formative years, its main appearance on the national political scene was Hitler's Beer Hall Putsch of November 8–9, 1923, when he and two to three thousand followers attempted to overthrow the Weimar Republic, an attempt that was immediately quashed. But for Nazism's eventual triumph, this quixotic, almost comical "revolution" would barely be remembered. Hitler's subsequent trial won for him further national exposure (the sympathetic court allowed him to use the trial as his soapbox), and his nine months in prison brought him the time to write his "memoirs," which set forth more systematically the views about politics, Germany, and the Jews that he had so frequently proclaimed in his tireless and popular speech-giving. *Mein Kampf* was an effective blueprint for his major undertakings later as Germany's leader. With terrifying and murderous language, Hitler revealed himself to be a visionary leader, offering Germans a future of a racially harmonious society, purged of class conflict and, especially, of Jews. Hitler brazenly put forward racist antisemitism as his first principle. In a characteristic passage, he explained why his understanding of history and the contemporary world meant that national salvation was possible only with lethal measures:

> *Today it is not princes and princes' mistresses who haggle and bargain over state borders; it is the inexorable Jew who struggles for his domination over the nations.* No nation can remove this hand from its throat except by the sword. Only the assembled and concentrated might of a national passion rearing up in its strength can defy the international enslavement of peoples. Such a process is and remains a bloody one.[20]

Looking back on the role of German Jews during the First World War, he mused in a typically murderous fashion: "If at the beginning of the War and during the War twelve or fifteen thousand of these Hebrew corrupters of the people had been held under poison gas," then millions of "real Germans" would not have died.[21] In his writings, speeches, and conversation, Hitler was direct and clear. Germany's enemies at home and abroad were to be destroyed or rendered inert. No one who heard or read Hitler could have missed this clarion message.

Within a few short years of Hitler's release from prison and the Party's resuscitation, the Nazi Party was to become the dominant political party in Weimar. The Nazis first began to have some small success in national and regional elections starting in 1925, and became a substantial electoral force in the national election of September 14, 1930. They collected 6.4 million votes, totaling 18.3 percent of all votes cast, which won for them 107 of the 577 seats in the Reichstag. The Nazis were suddenly the second largest political party in Germany. The Weimar Republic, never having been accepted as legitimate by a large portion of the German people, soon came under siege, owing to an economic depression that saw fully 30.8 percent of the work force unemployed in 1932. Hitler, the charismatic figure, and the Nazis' anti-Weimar, anti-Bolshevik, anti-international, and antisemitic message gained ever greater appeal during these difficult times. In the election of July 31, 1932, almost *fourteen million* Germans, 37.4 percent of the voters, cast their lots for Hitler, crowning the Nazis the largest, most powerful political party in Germany, with 230 seats in the Reichstag. At the beginning of 1933, Weimar's President, Paul von Hindenburg, after another election in November which actually saw the Nazi percentage of the vote dip four percentage points, asked Hitler to become Chancellor and form a government.

The Nazis came to power, owing to a confluence of factors, including the economic depression, the yearning in Germany for an end to the disorder and organized street violence that had plagued Weimar's final years, the widespread hatred of democratic Weimar more generally, the seeming threat of a leftist takeover, the Nazis' visionary ideology, and Hitler's own personality, which, his burning hatreds open for all to see, was attractive, even compelling, to so many Germans. The catastrophic political and economic disorder was clearly the proximate cause for the Nazis' final victory. Many Germans voted for the Nazis as the only political force in the country that appeared to them capable of restoring order and social peace—and of vanquishing Germany's enemies at home and of restoring Germany's status as a great power abroad.[22]

Upon assuming the Chancellorship, Hitler held one final national election on March 5, 1933. It was hardly a free and fair election (the Communist Party was outlawed and intimidation of the opposition was extensive), yet these undemocratic tactics, and the violence that the Nazis had already unleashed upon Jews and leftists, did not deter voters, but increased the Nazi vote to over seventeen million people, namely 43.9 percent of those who cast ballots.[23] By this time, Hitler had effectively abolished civil liberties in Germany, the Weimar Republic, and any mechanism to depose him short of using violence. The Nazis were in power. They could begin pursuing Hitler's revolutionary program, some of which Germans would oppose and much of which they would embrace as their own.

WHEN THE FATEFUL day of Hitler's assumption of the office of German Chancellor came on January 30, 1933, the Nazis found that they did not have to remake Germans at least on one central issue—arguably the most important one from their point of view—the nature of Jewry. Whatever else Germans thought about Hitler and the Nazi movement, however much they might have detested aspects of Nazism, the vast majority of them subscribed to the underlying Nazi model of Jews and in this sense (as the Nazis themselves understood) were "Nazified" in their views of Jews. It is, to risk understatement, no surprise that under the Nazi dispensation the vast majority of Germans continued to remain antisemitic, that their antisemitism continued to be virulent and racially grounded, and that their socially shared "solution" to the "Jewish Problem" continued to be eliminationist. *Nothing* occurred in Nazi Germany to undermine or erode the cultural cognitive model of Jews that had for decades underlain German attitudes and emotions towards the despised minority among them. Everything publicly said or done worked to reinforce the model.[24]

In Germany during the Nazi period, putative Jewish evil permeated the air. It was discussed incessantly. It was said to be the source of every ill that had befallen Germany and of every continuing threat. The Jew, *der Jude*, was both a metaphysical and an existential threat, as real to Germans as that of a powerful enemy army poised on Germany's borders for the attack. The character, ubiquity, and logic of action of German antisemitism during the Nazi period is captured brilliantly by Melita Maschmann in a confessional memoir written to her lost, former childhood Jewish friend. A devoted member of the girls' division of the Hitler youth, Maschmann was not the progeny of country bumpkins, being the daughter of a university-educated man and a woman who had grown up in a prosperous business family. She begins telling of her youthful understanding of Jews by observing that the regnant conception of "the Jews" had no empirical basis.

> *Those* Jews were and remained something mysteriously menacing and anonymous. They were not the sum of all Jewish individuals . . . They were an evil power, something with the attributes of a spook. One could not see it, but it was there, an active force for evil.
>
> As children we had been told fairy stories which sought to make us believe in witches and wizards. Now we were too grown up to take this witchcraft seriously, but we still went on believing in the "wicked Jews." They had never appeared to us in bodily form, but it was our daily experience that adults believed in them. After all, we could not check to see if the earth was round rather than flat—or, to be more precise, it was not a proposition we thought it necessary to check. The grownups "knew" it and one took over this knowledge without mistrust. They also "knew" that the Jews were wicked. The wickedness was directed against the prosperity, unity and prestige of the German nation, which we had learned to love from an early age. The anti-semitism of my parents was a part of their outlook which was taken for granted. . . .
>
> For as long as we could remember, the adults had lived in this contradictory way with complete unconcern. One was friendly with individual Jews whom one liked, just as one was friendly as a Protestant with individual Catholics. But while it occurred to nobody to be ideologically hostile to *the* Catholics, one was, utterly, to *the* Jews. In all this no one seemed to

worry about the fact that they had no clear idea of who "*the* Jews" were. They included the baptized and the orthodox, yiddish [*sic*] speaking second hand dealers and professors of German literature, Communist agents and First World War officers decorated with high orders, enthusiasts for Zionism and chauvinistic German nationalists. . . . I had learned from my parents' example that one could have anti-semitic opinions without this interfering in one's personal relations with individual Jews. There may appear to be a vestige of tolerance in this attitude, but it is really just this confusion which I blame for the fact that I later contrived to dedicate body and soul to an inhuman political system, without this giving me doubts about my own individual decency. In preaching that all the misery of the nations was due to the Jews or that the Jewish spirit was seditious and Jewish blood was corrupting, I was not compelled to think of you or old Herr Lewy or Rosel Cohen: I thought only of the bogeyman, "*the* Jew." And when I heard that the Jews were being driven from their professions and homes and imprisoned in ghettos, the points switched automatically in my mind to steer me round the thought that such a fate could also overtake you or old Lewy. It was only *the* Jew who was being persecuted and "made harmless."[25]

Maschmann's account conveys, better than any scholarly analysis of which I know, the central qualities of German antisemitism: its hallucinatory image of the Jews; the specter of evil that they appeared to Germans to be casting over Germany; Germans' virulent hatred of them; the "abstract" character of the beliefs that informed the treatment which its bearers accorded *real* Jews; the unquestioned nature of these beliefs; and the eliminationist logic that led Germans to approve of the persecution, ghettoization, and extermination of Jews (the evident meaning of the euphemism "made harmless"). Maschmann leaves no doubt that antisemitism in Germany was, for many, like mother's milk, part of the Durkheimian collective consciousness; it was, in this woman's astute account, "a part of their outlook which was taken for granted." The consequences of these views, of this ideological map, can be seen in the wild success of the unfolding eliminationist antisemitic persecution that began with the Nazis' assumption of power.

DURING ITS NAZI period, German antisemitism took predictable turns. Harnessed now to a state occupied by the most virulent and dedicated antisemites ever to assume the leadership of a modern nation,[26] anti-Jewish hatreds and yearnings previously confined to civil society by states that would not organize the burning sentiments into systemic persecution became during the Nazi period the guiding principles of state policy, with a number of unsurprising results:

1. The enactment of extensive, severe legal restrictions upon Jewish existence in Germany.
2. Physical and increased verbal attacks upon Jews, both spontaneous ones from ordinary Germans and ones orchestrated by governmental and party institutions.
3. A further intensification of antisemitism within society.
4. The transformation of Jews into "socially dead" beings.[27]
5. A society-wide consensus on the need to eliminate Jewish influence from Germany.

All of these characterized not just the Nazi leadership but the vast majority of the German people, who were aware of what their government and their countrymen were doing to Jews, assented to the measures, and, when the opportunity presented itself, lent their active support to them.

The litany of German anti-Jewish policies and legal measures began with the almost instantaneous, yet sporadic, physical attacks upon Jews, their property, burial sites, and houses of worship, and with the establishment of "wild" concentration camps for them and for the political left.[28] The regime's and the public's highly injurious verbal attacks aside, the first large-scale and potently symbolic organized assault upon German Jewry came just two months after Hitler's assumption of power. The nationwide boycott of Jewish businesses on April 1, 1933, was a signal event, announcing to all Germans that the Nazis were resolute.[29] The Jews would be treated in accordance with the oft-stated conception of them: as aliens within the German body social, inimical to its well-being. Rhetoric was to be turned into reality. How did Germans react to the boycott? One Jew recounts that a few Germans defiantly expressed their solidarity with the beleaguered Jews. Yet "such protests were not very common. The general attitude of the public was reflected in an incident which occurred at a chemist's shop. A lady, accompanied by two uniformed Nazis, had entered. She brought with her some goods she had purchased a few days before, and demanded that the chemist should return her money. 'I did not know that you were a Jew,' she declared, 'I don't want to buy anything of Jews.' "[30] Here was the sight of the German *Volk*, organized by the German state, collectively boycotting an entire group of German citizens, because this group allegedly, in cahoots with racial brethren abroad, was harming Germany.[31] The Nazis signaled repeatedly and clearly, the boycott having been but one instance, that the era of Jews in Germany would soon come to a close.

Following upon this boycott, which was devastating to the social position of Jews, who were now publicly, officially proclaimed to be, and treated as, a pariah people, was a series of anti-Jewish legal measures that began what was to become the systematic elimination of Jews from German economic, social, and cultural life, from a public and social existence in Germany.[32] The Nazis passed the Law for the Restoration of the Professional Civil Service just a few days after the boycott, which led to the immediate dismissal of thousands of Jews, because it mandated "race" as a qualification for civil service employment.[33] Again, the symbolism was quite clear. This law, one of the first that the Nazis promulgated on any matter, was directed at the Jews, producing a "purification" of the state, an elimination of the Jewish presence in the institution perhaps most identified with the common and collective welfare of the people, most identified with serving the people. By definition, Jews could not serve (because serving implies helping) the German people. Although there were Germans who voiced criticism towards the open violence against Jews and towards the boycott (which was deemed to hurt Germany's standing abroad and was accompanied by great brutality), the criticism generally betrayed neither dissent from the conception of Jews underlying these measures nor solidarity with the beleaguered Jews.[34] The law excluding Jews from the civil service, being unaccompanied by public displays of brutality, was, not surprisingly, widely popular in Germany.[35] It was especially popular among the Jews' civil service colleagues. Working closely for years with the Jews did not, as would have ordinarily been expected, engender among the Germans feelings of camaraderie and sympathy.[36] Thomas Mann, who had already long been an outspoken opponent of Nazism, could nevertheless find some common ground with the Nazis when it came to eliminating Jewish influence in Germany: ". . . it is no great misfortune after all that . . . the Jewish presence in the judiciary has been ended."[37] The dominant cultural cognitive model of Jews and the eliminationist mind-set that it spawned was dominant in Germany.

For the next two years, Germans inside and outside the government succeeded in making life for Jews in Germany—who suffered under a plethora of laws, measures, and assaults upon their livelihoods, social positions, and persons—all but unbearable.[38] During this period, the society-wide attack upon the Jews proceeded in an uncoordinated manner. Some of its aspects were mandated from above, some initiated from below, the latter generally, though not always, by avowed Nazis. The main, though not sole, initiators of assaults upon Jews were the men of the SA, the brown shirt shock troops of the regime. During the middle part of 1933, they unleashed physically destructive and symbolic attacks against Jews all across Germany. The assaults ran the gamut of what was to become the standard German repertoire. Verbal assaults were so common as to be "normal" actions, unworthy of special notice. The Jews' pariah status was publicly declared in Germany on explicit, unequivocal public signs. For example, all over Franconia, at the entrances to many villages and in restaurants and hotels, Germans posted signs with

Sign in Braunschweig in 1935 warns: "Jews enter this place at their own risk."

proclamations like "Jews Not Wanted Here" or "Entry Forbidden to Jews."[39] Munich, already in May 1933, also boasted signs on its outskirts that declared "Jews Not Wanted."[40]

During the 1930s, towns throughout Germany issued official prohibitions on Jews entering them, and such signs were a near ubiquitous feature of the German landscape. One historian and observer of Germany described them in 1938:

> Where formal decrees [banning Jews from a locale] are lacking, placards on the highways leading to the towns have the desired effect. "Jews Enter This Place at Their Risk," "Jews Strictly Forbidden in This Town," "Warning to Pickpockets and Jews" are favorites. Poets have been encouraged to make these announcements rhyme with "sow," "garlic," and "stink." Artists have been given an opportunity to depict on the placard the fate of any Jews incautious enough to disregard the warning. These placards are universal throughout Hessia, East Prussia, Pomerania, and Mecklenburg, and can be found in about one-half of the towns elsewhere. (None, however, will be found in such tourist resorts as Baden-Baden, Kissingen, or Nauheim.) Railway stations, government buildings, and all important highways take up the refrain. In the neighborhood of Ludwigshaven, a dangerous bend in the road

bears the following advice to motorists: "Drive Carefully, Sharp Curve—Jews, 75 miles an hour!"[41]

Such "public defamation"[42] and humiliation expressed the Germans' eliminationist intent.

Supplementing the verbal assaults were physical attacks of fearsome symbolic content that began in the first months of the Nazi period and continued until its end. They included Germans forcibly cutting Jews' beards and hair.

A German cuts a Jew's beard in Warsaw in 1939, while others look on in laughter.

One Jewish refugee recalls having seen, in a Berlin hospital in early 1933, an old Jewish man with unusual facial wounds: "He was a poor rabbi from Galicia, who had been stopped in the street by two men in uniform. One of them gripped him by the shoulders, the other held his long beard. Then the second man took a knife from his pocket, and cut off the old man's beard. To remove it thoroughly, he had cut off several pieces of skin." Upon being asked by the physician whether or not the perpetrator had said anything, the man responded, "I don't know. He screamed at me: 'Death to the Jews!' "[43] Attacks upon Jewish businesses, synagogues, and cemeteries were perpetrated both by individuals and by organized groups. In Munich in 1934, for example, a man who had no Nazi affiliation provoked crowds of Germans to demonstrate against Jewish store owners, a demonstration that eventually erupted in violence. Beatings, maimings, and killings of Jews also became an all too "normal" occurrence during these years.[44] An illustrative episode was recounted by the daughter of an unsuspecting cattle dealer from a small town in East Prussia, who was set upon by five heavily armed SA men in the middle of the night in March 1933. The "SA-man first beat my father, then my mother, and finally myself with a rubber truncheon. My mother received a deep cut on her head, and my forehead was also lacerated. . . . Outside the front door all of my father's competitors had gathered, and they behaved in such an indecent manner that I, as a young girl, cannot relate of this to you . . ."[45] Attacks against Jews during this period were by no means confined to cities. Jews living in the countryside and in small towns throughout Germany were so persecuted by their non-Jewish neighbors and were subjected to so much violence in the first years of the regime that they by and large fled their homes to larger and more anonymous cities or abroad.[46] Such neighborly attacks, coming from people who had lived, worked, given birth, and buried parents, side by side with them, were intense. What took place in two nearby small towns in Hesse was by no means out of the ordinary.[47]

Forty Jewish families were living in one of the Hessen towns, Gedern, upon the Nazis' assumption of power. Already, less than two months into the Nazi era, on the night of March 12, 1933, Germans broke into the houses of the town's Jews and brutalized them. They bludgeoned one Jew so badly that he had to spend a year in a hospital. When, on the occasion of the one national election that took place during the Nazi period, graffiti urging a vote for the (forbidden) leader of the Communist Party was discovered, Germans of the town marched some Jews in drill step to the bridge and forced them to wash it clean. They then beat the Jews. During this period, one Jewish boy was assaulted on the street, losing his eye to his assailant. A little while later, the Germans forced two Jewish men to parade in front of the town, beating them with whips which they had procured from a prosperous farmer. They communicated their desire to be rid of Jews with another unmistakably symbolic act, common to Germany at the time—the overturning of the gravestones in the Jewish cemetery. All of the Jews fled their intolerable existence in this town well before *Kristallnacht*, the last Jew leaving on April 19, 1937. Upon his departure, this apparently destitute man was denied food by his erstwhile neighbors.[48]

A second town, Bindsachen, was yet another home to an early assault on Jewish existence. On the evening of the attack, March 27, 1933, immediately before it commenced, a large part of the town assembled in order to witness SA men bludgeon the chosen Jewish victim, who was known to everyone in the town. The townspeople, enthusiastic at the sight of their suffering neighbor, urged on the SA man with cheers.[49]

A chronicle of Germans' attacks of all varieties upon Jews during this period (uncoordinated by state or Party offices) would fill many volumes. The instances recounted here were anything but atypical. Attacks of these sorts were a "normal," quotidian part of Germany once Nazism was in a position to unleash the pent-up antisemitic passion.[50] The SA's rank and file, eager at last to give regular expression to their hatred of Jews, initiated much of the violence on their own. The state had implicitly declared the Jews to be "fair game"—beings who were to be eliminated from German society, by whatever means necessary, including violence.

The SA has typically been characterized as an organization of the rabble in uniform, of brutal men from the fringes of society, seething with resentment and bursting with violent urges.[51] To a great extent this characterization is apt. Yet it must be emphasized that the membership of the SA was about *two million* men, which was approximately 10 percent of the German civilian male population of the age cohorts on which the SA drew.[52] As the numbers indicate, the SA was representative of a significant percentage of the German people. Moreover, as with any radical, martial organization of this sort, many Germans outside the organization could be counted on to sympathize with the brutal antisemites in the SA who were willing to participate in attacks on Jews. The example of the savagely beaten and tormented Jew of Bindsachen illustrates this common phenomenon. The SA men took the initiative and were cheered on and aided by people from their town, who were presumably not SA members.

The attacks upon Jews during these first years of Nazi governance of Germany were so widespread—and broad-based—that it would be grievously wrong to attribute them solely to the toughs of the SA, as if the wider German public had no influence over, or part in, the violence. A Gestapo report in August 1935 from Osnabrück belies the notion of an innocent German public. Robert Gellately writes:

> In that city and surrounding area there were "massive demonstrations" against Jewish businesses, which were publicly branded and surrounded by mobs; people who frequented Jewish businesses were photographed and the pictures were displayed in public. The streets were alive with action—parades and so on. . . . The "high point of the struggle against the Jews," as the report went, was a meeting on 20 August, which brought together 25,000 people to hear Kreisleiter Münzer on the theme of "Osnabrück and the Jewish Problem." The situation was so inflamed, however, that the Gestapo and other state officials had to call on Münzer to put a stop to the "individual actions," and he did so by publishing a warning in all the local newspapers; these actions were officially outlawed on 27 August.[53]

The attacks upon Jews during this period, the attempts to hasten the eliminationist program, came by no means only from the "rabble" of German society, that 10 percent at the lower end of the socioeconomic scale, all too blithely dismissed by interpreters of this period as immoral or amoral people from whom one could not expect better conduct. The initiative to eliminate Jews from social contact with Germans was also taken by municipalities and heterogeneous groups of Germans of all classes well before the state demanded such action, such as when, on their own, cities and towns began to bar Jews as early as 1933 from using swimming pools or public bathing facilities.[54] So many measures and assaults against Jews were initiated by small businessmen during this early period that this social stratum appears to have been the font of the majority of attacks originating from private German citizens.[55] Yet the initiative to eliminate Jewish influence from society was also taken by the most prestigious and best-educated professionals. German medical institutions and groups, for example, giving expression to their hatred of Jews, on their own began to exclude their Jewish colleagues, even before the government mandated the measures.[56] University administrators, faculty, and students across Germany similarly applauded and contributed to driving their Jewish colleagues out from their ranks.[57]

Thousands of Germans gather at a mass rally on August 15, 1935, in Berlin, in order to listen to antisemitic speeches and to hear of a future Germany "cleansed" of Jews. The two banners read: "The Jews Are Our Misfortune" and "Women and Girls, the Jews Are Your Ruin."

Judges and members of the legal profession were so eager to purge their institutions and their country of Jewish influence that they, beginning already in the first few months of Nazi governance, often outran the legal mandates that the regime promulgated. In October 1933, one Berlin court upheld the dismissal of a Jew from administering an estate, ruling that the people's pervasive hatred of Jews "made it seem inadvisable to retain a Jew in office, even in the absence of a special law to this effect." Earlier that year, in July, another Berlin court provided a more sweeping justification for judges taking such initiative in the battle against Jewry. According to *Die Juristische Wochenschrift*, the most important German legal periodical, the court, writing with obvious approval, pointed out "that a revolutionary legislature [the Nazis had been in office but six months] naturally leaves loopholes which ought to be filled by the Court in applying the principles of the National Socialist *Weltanschauung*."[58] The German judiciary—almost all of whom had taken the bench during Weimar and therefore were, at least formally, not "Nazi judges"—was composed of such ardent racial antisemites that leading Nazis (bound to the belief that the eliminationist program should be legally governed) chastised judges for having violated the law in their rampant eliminationist ardor. Interior Minister Wilhelm Frick similarly tried to rein in all those under his jurisdiction, including many holdovers from Weimar, from extending the eliminationist measures beyond the laws that the regime had made.[59] The judiciary's extensive contribution to the persecution of the Jews during the Nazi period reveals its members to have been zealous implementers and initiators of eliminationist measures. The judges composed a group that was obviously bristling with anti-Jewish hatred during Weimar, and then, when Hitler took power, was freed to act upon these beliefs.[60] In this sense, the judges, all their education and training in law notwithstanding, were like so many other groups in Germany. With the judges, this transformation is simply that much more glaring.

THE UNSYSTEMATIC NATURE of the legal measures taken against the Jews during the first few years of Nazism, and particularly the uncoordinated and often wild attacks upon Jews which, according to the government's own reports, occurred in every administrative district and in almost every locality,[61] did cause many Germans to feel unsettled. Some objected to the wanton violence, and many, in and out of government and the Party, were unsure what sorts of action against the Jews were to be taken or tolerated. The Nuremberg Laws of September 1935 and subsequent legislation brought order to the uncoordinated state of affairs, defining precisely who was to be considered a Jew, or a partial Jew, and enacting a broad set of prohibitions that provided a good measure of coherence to the eliminationist program. Above all else, the Nuremberg Laws made explicit and to a great extent codified the elimination of Jews from a civil or social existence in Germany, going a long way towards creating an insuperable separation between Jews and members of the *Volk*. Its two measures, the Reich Citizenship Law and the Law for the Protection of German Blood and German Honor, stripped Jews of their citizenship and forbade new marriages and sexual relations outside of existing marriages between Jews and Germans.[62] The laws were very popular among the German people. Germans welcomed the laws because of the coherence that they imposed in this most pressing of spheres, and more so because of the content of the measures. A Gestapo report from Magdeburg captured well the popular mood when it noted that "the population regards the regulation of the relationships of the Jews as an emancipatory act, which brings clarity and simultaneously greater firmness in the protection of the racial interests of the German people."[63] The eliminationist program had received at once its most coherent statement and its most powerful push forward. The Nuremberg Laws promised to accomplish what had heretofore for decades been but discussed and urged on *ad nauseam*. With this codifying moment of the Nazi German "religion," the regime held up the eliminationist writing on the Nazi tablets for every German to read. All were literate in its language. And many wanted the implementation of its program to be hastened, as a Gestapo report from Hildesheim covering February 1936, a few months after the laws' promulgation, conveys: "It is said by many that the Jews in Germany are still treated much too humanely."[64]

After the Nuremberg Laws, Germans' attacks upon Jews declined and remained at a reduced level through 1937. During this period, Germans continued to assault Jews verbally and physically, and the ongoing legal, economic, social, and professional exclusion of Jews from Germany's life proceeded, yet the sheer volume of violence diminished. The comparative quiet, however, gave way in 1938 to renewed attacks of all kinds upon Jews, with both state and Party institutions working hard to "solve" the "Jewish Problem." To give an illustration of the intensity of antisemitic activity, during one two-week period, as part of a concerted Party campaign under the slogan "A *Volk* breaks its chains," 1,350 antisemitic meetings took place in Saxony alone.[65] An upsurge of Germans' attacks on Jews, destruction of their property, public humiliations, and arrests followed by incarceration in concentration camps characterized this year. The hostility of ordinary Germans was so great that by this time Jewish life outside the big cities, the only places where Jews could hope for some anonymity, became untenable. According to a July 1938 Social Democratic Party summary report: "In consequence of the steady antisemitic barrage, German Jews can scarcely stay in the smaller provincial localities. More and more, localities announce themselves to be "Jew-free" [*judenrein*] . . ."[66] Not only did rural areas become practically empty of Jews, but as a welcome consequence of how unbearable both the regime and ordinary Germans were making the lives of Jews, Jewish emigration from Germany also increased. The reaction of the populace at large was one of general approval of the eliminationist goals and measures, though it was accompanied by significant disapproval of the licentious brutality. Sometimes excepting acquaintances, Germans showed little sympathy for the plight of the Jews.[67]

However much the renewed violence of 1938 signaled to everyone that the relative peace of the previous two years had been a passing, aberrant phase, any notion of a continuing Jewish presence within Germany was shattered by the country-wide violence, unprecedented in modern German history, of *Kristallnacht*. In light of the widespread persecution and violence that had occurred throughout (especially rural) Germany, *Kristallnacht* was, in one sense, but the crowning moment in the wild domestic terror that Germans perpetrated upon Jews. Propaganda Minister Joseph Goebbels orchestrated the assault as putative retribution for the killing of a German diplomat by a distraught Jew whose parents the Germans had deported earlier in the year to Poland along with fifteen thousand other Polish Jews.[68] On the night of November 9–10, Germans in cities, towns, and vil-

Germans watch the Börneplatz Synagogue of Frankfurt in flames during Kristallnacht.

lages across the country were awakened to the sounds of shattering glass, the light and smell of burning synagogues, and the cries of agony emitted by Jews whom their countrymen were beating to a pulp. The magnitude of the violence and destruction, the (by the still embryonic standards of the time) enormity of the Rubicon night, is reflected in the statistics. The perpetrators, principally SA men, killed approximately one hundred Jews and hauled off thirty thousand more to concentration camps. They burned down and demolished hundreds of synagogues, almost all of those that they and their countrymen had not destroyed earlier. They shattered the storefront glass of about 7,500 Jewish stores and businesses, hence the appellation *Kristallnacht* (Crystal Night).[69]

How did the German people react? In small towns, the SA men were greeted by many willing locals who availed themselves of the opportunity to join the assault on the Jews. "The realization that on that day the Jews were 'fair game' [*vogelfrei*] was communicated to the inhabitants who did not at all belong to the task force [*Einsatztrupps*] and were not even members of the Party . . . And as a result . . . some allowed themselves to be carried away, beating down on the harried and defenceless Jews."[70] Ordinary Germans

Spectators line the streets of Regensburg on the morning after Kristallnacht, *in order to watch the deportation of Jewish men to Dachau. The placard announces the "Exodus of the Jews."*

spontaneously, without provocation or encouragement, participated in the brutalities. Even youths and children contributed to the attacks, some undoubtedly with their parents' blessings. Hundreds and thousands more watched the night's assault, as well as the next day, when the perpetrators ceremoniously marched Jews off to concentration camps.[71]

The SA men, with or without the aid of such volunteers, produced a fearsome sight of wantonness and brutality that was lethal to the Jews and unsettling to many Germans. Much criticism of the authoritatively directed, wild violence was voiced by Germans of all stations, including those in the Party. Of course, some Germans did feel sympathy at the sight of the beaten and terrorized victims. Yet the evidence suggests that the criticism of the violence was overwhelmingly a result not of a principled disapproval of the sufferings inflicted on the Jews, not of a belief that an injustice had been done them.

By and large, the criticism, even sometimes outrage, that Germans expressed at *Kristallnacht* had three sources. Many abhorred the licentious violence in their midst. So unsettling was the sight of the SA men and others bursting with savagery, wreaking destruction and death in the streets of their communities, that for the first time some non-Jewish and non-leftist Germans began to wonder whether this radical movement might yet turn on them too.[72] Many, interpreting the events in terms of their hallucinatory understanding of the all-powerful Jews, also felt anxiety at the prospect of the Jews eventually revenging themselves upon Germany.[73] One German memoirist remembers his aunt greeting him on the day after *Kristallnacht* with "solemn words": " 'We Germans will pay dearly for what was done to the Jews last night. Our churches, our houses, and our stores will be destroyed. You can be sure of that.' "[74] Finally, Germans abhorred the destruction of so much property.[75] Even if Germans wanted the Jews to reap what they believed the Jews to have sown, it was still unnecessary to lay waste to so much of value.[76] Estimates total the damage in the hundreds of millions of Reichsmarks.[77] The national focus on the profligate material destruction was so great even among the working class—whose members are, with little evidence, commonly *assumed* to have been among the least antisemitic groups in Germany—that, in the wake of *Kristallnacht*, the Communist underground tried to win their sympathies primarily by addressing the material costs of *Kristallnacht*. In their appeal, the Communists hopefully dissociated the "German people" from the deeds, saying that the violence and destruction are in no sense "due to the 'rage of the German people' . . ." How could the Communists be sure of this? Not because they believed that the people felt sympathy for and solidarity with their fellow Jewish citizens, but because "workers are calculating the number of extra hours they will need to work to repair the damage done to German national property. Workers' wives . . . watched the waste of much property with bitterness. . . ."[78]

The criticism of *Kristallnacht*'s licentious violence and wasteful destruction that could be heard around Germany should be understood as the limited criticism of an eliminationist path that the overwhelming majority of Germans considered to be fundamentally sound, but which, in this case, had taken a momentary wrong turn. Against this bounded criticism stood the Germans' enthusiasm for the eliminationist enterprise that continued unabated after *Kristallnacht*, as well as the enormous satisfaction with which many Germans openly greeted *Kristallnacht* itself. Nuremberg, for example, the day after *Kristallnacht*, saw a rally, which was attended by close to 100,000 people who came voluntarily in order to hear the anti-Jewish invective of Julius Streicher, the publisher of *Der Stürmer* and the man known to be the most rabid antisemite in Germany. Photographs of the rally show relatively few men in uniform. Instead, the faces of ordinary Germans—that is, the collective face of Nuremberg and of Germany—can be seen there conveying their ardent support for their government and the eliminationist program. In the words of one commentator reflecting back on this rally after the war, "The overwhelming majority of the men and women of Nuremberg could have stayed away without risking reprisal; instead, they acclaimed the criminals in government."[79]

Not just all of Germany but the entire western world beheld *Kristallnacht*, and the world reacted with moral revulsion and outrage. The German people failed to exhibit equivalent revulsion and outrage—and principled dissent from the antisemitic model that underlay the night's depredation—even though what had occurred was done in their name, in their midst, to defenseless people, and to *their* countrymen. This was the moment when it was apparent for all Germans to see that their government would not recoil from using the most radical means in order to ensure the elimination of Jews and Jewish influence from Germany. As Alfons Heck, an erstwhile member of the Hitler Youth, put it, "after *Kristallnacht*, no German old enough to walk could ever plead ignorance of the persecution of the Jews, and no Jews could harbor any delusion that Hitler wanted Germany anything but *judenrein*, clean of Jews."[80] Criticism of *Kristallnacht* was indeed possible, and Germans did express openly and volubly their disenchantment with the wastefulness and the naked brutality of the nationwide assault. It is therefore significant that Germans did not cry out against the enormity of the injustice, which appears not to have moved them. Among Bavarian religious instructors there was moral outrage, but not for what their countrymen had done to Jews, of which they obviously approved. Fully 84 percent of Protestant and 75 percent of Catholic religious instructors in Middle and Upper Franconia protested the assassination of the German diplomat—not the immense suffering of the innocent Jews—by not teaching religious classes.[81]

This, perhaps the most revealing day of the entire Nazi era, the day on which an opportunity presented itself for the German people to rise up in solidarity with fellow citizens, was the day on which the German people sealed the fate of the Jews by letting the authorities know that they concurred in the unfolding eliminationist enterprise, even if they objected, sometimes vociferously, to some of its measures. Melita Maschmann once again conveys the thinking that guided Germans as they tried to make sense of the manifest horror that wakened Germany that night:

> For the space of a second I was clearly aware that something terrible had happened there. Something frighteningly brutal. But almost at once I switched over to accepting what had happened as over and done with and avoiding critical reflection. I said to myself: The Jews are the enemies of the new Germany. Last night they had a taste of what this means. Let us hope that World Jewry, which has resolved to hinder Germany's "new steps towards greatness," will take the events of last night as a warning. If the Jews sow hatred against us all over the world, they must learn that we have hostages for them in our hands.[82]

Clearly, whatever condemnation Germans expressed at the nature of the sentence and the means by which the perpetrators had carried it out, they, with few exceptions, agreed that the Jews collectively were guilty.

The progressive exclusion of Jews from German society that had been proceeding since the Nazis' assumption of power gained greater momentum with *Kristallnacht*. The Germans had by now transformed those Jews who had not fled for their lives from Germany into a "leprous community," a community shunned and reviled, as if its members were medieval lepers.[83] Contact with Jews, reduced to a minimum by virtually all Germans, was seen in the public ideology, and generally mirrored in personal action, as polluting—dangerous to Germans' well-being. Why else have a "Law for the Protection of German Blood and Honor," a law that was promulgated after many Germans called for it, and that was immensely popular in Germany, and not only because it had finally codified which relations with Jews were permissible? Charges of "race defilement" (*Rassenschande*), namely of extramarital sexual relations between Jews and Germans, which were utterly prohibited, were, not surprisingly, frequently leveled by ordinary Germans against Jews.[84]

The story of Emma Becker, recounted by David Bankier, is particularly illustrative of Germans' implacable hostility towards Jews. Becker was a "Jew" in a situation that might be supposed to have been unusually propitious for her to have received decent treatment from her fellow Germans. Married to a Catholic, she had herself converted to her husband's faith, thus renouncing her Jewish identity and severing formal ties to Judaism. Nevertheless, in 1940, her neighbors made it clear that they did not wish to live next to her, she evidently being, in their racially oriented minds, still a Jew. The only person who visited her was her own priest. For his kindness, for carrying out his religious duties, he himself was abused by her neighbors. She tells of other open expressions of hatred directed at her, and her complete ostracism from the "Christian" community, to the point where she became a leprous outcast in her own church. Forced by others to retire from the church choir, for they did not want to sing praise to God alongside this "Jew," her "coreligionists" refused to kneel beside her or take communion with her. Even priests, these men of God, who ostensibly believed in the power of baptism, shunned her in church. These ordinary Germans, who also included educated civil servants, went far beyond what the regime mandated; as a convert married to a Catholic, Becker was legally *protected* from the general persecution.[85] By law, Becker was allowed to live where she did, to carry on normal social intercourse, and, certainly, to attend church. These Germans were expressing in no uncertain terms their hatred for Jews, a hatred grounded in a racial conception that treated a person as a Jew regardless of her religion, her self-identity, or her renunciation of all ties to things Jewish. Catholics, moreover, were among the Germans who, steeped in the time-honored conception of Jewish evil as derived from their religion, should have been more resistant to the racial cognitive model of Jews. Yet the widespread persecution among Catholics of converted Jews indicates that they too had accepted the tenets of racist antisemitism.[86] Becker's treatment is by no means an isolated case, for throughout Germany, Protestant and Catholic churches tried to find ways to separate converts from the larger congregations, attempts which were generally responses to ordinary Germans' vocal objections to having "Jews" among them praying to God and taking communion.[87] The German people had strayed so far from Christian precepts that the Confessing Church in Breslau, in leaflets distributed throughout Germany, urged Germans not to discriminate against converted Jews, and suggested measures to prevent Germans from attacking the converts while in church![88] This suggests how beholden to eliminationist racist antisemitism the church hierarchy—that part of it which was still allegiant to the Christian doctrine of baptismal salvation—knew its flock to be.

The final installment in the "final solution," as it was played out for German Jews within Germany proper, was the Germans' deportation of the Jews to their deaths in the East, which began in October 1941 and lasted through the beginning of 1943.[89] The deportations, the most visible and unequivocal eliminationist measure yet taken within Germany itself, were, with some exceptions, greatly popular among the populace. During this period, when Germans had already hounded or deported the majority of German Jews from the country and were killing millions of Jews throughout Europe, an illustrative episode occurred, which a non-Jewish woman recorded in her diary. It was October 1942 in Stuttgart: "I rode on a tram. It was overcrowded. An old lady got on. Her feet were so swollen that they bulged out of the top of her shoes. She wore the star of David on her dress. I stood up so that the old lady could sit. By this I provoked—how else could it be?—the so well practiced 'popular fury'. Someone yelled 'Get out!' Soon a whole chorus yelled 'Get out!' Amidst the din of voices, I heard the outraged words: 'Jew-slave! Person without dignity!' The tram stopped between stations [*auf offener Strecke*]. The conductor ordered: 'Both of you get out!' "[90] Such was the spontaneously expressed hatred for a forlorn member of a people who were then being slaughtered. The depth of ordinary Germans' antisemitic passion was such that scenes of open, enthusiastic reveling in the Jews' expected fate occurred in Berlin as the Jews were assembled for deportation. One German woman witnessed this: "Unfortunately, I must also report that many people stood in their doorways and in the face of this procession of misery, gave expression to their joy. 'Look at the impudent Jews!' shouted one. 'Now they are still laughing, but their final short hour has rung.' "[91]

A few Germans, as others had after *Kristallnacht* and after other instances of wanton violence in the streets, objected to the brutality, the obviously unnecessary brutality, of their countrymen who conducted the deportations. The editor of *Das Schwarze Korps*, the official newspaper of the SS, a man who was no friend of the Jews, himself wrote to Heinrich Himmler, the head of the SS, complaining that, despite the worthiness of the enterprise and its goals, it was unfortunate that such brutality had been perpetrated in full view of civilians, women, and even foreigners, for, "after all, we do not want to look like frenzied sadists."[92] During the course of the Germans' deportation of German Jewry, few could have had illusions about the fate of the Jews, since reports of mass killings in the East abounded in Germany. On December 15, 1941, one schoolteacher recorded in his diary the obvious meaning of these deportations: "It is as clear as daylight that this spells destruction. They will be taken to an uninhabited, devastated region in Russia and there they will be left to starve and freeze to death. He who is dead says nothing more."[93] A woman who worked to save Jews in Berlin noted in her diary on December 2, 1942: "The Jews are disappearing in throngs. Ghastly rumors are current about the fate of the evacuees—mass shootings and death by starvation, tortures, and gassings."[94] No one could believe that anything but a dire fate awaited the Jewish men and women, the elderly and the children, whom, in the midst of this war, the German government was forcibly sending, often with open brutality, to the East. The degree of enthusiasm that Germans did express, Germans' evident lack of sympathy for these forlorn people who had once lived among them, and the absence of widespread disapproval of and opposition to the deportations, indicate that Germans assented to these measures to make Germany *judenrein*, free of Jews, the probable slaughter of these last Jews notwithstanding.[95]

AFTER JANUARY 1933, no public institutionalized support existed in Germany for any view of Jews other than the one already long dominant in Germany, now given extreme expression in its obsessive Nazi elaboration. Every important national institution and forum of expression promoted the notion that the Jews were unalterably hostile and dangerous for Germany. The conception of Jews as a *race* apart, and a thoroughgoing racist interpretation of human differences and history, was the common sense of the political culture, with the sometime exception of the Catholic Church. And even in the Catholic Church—despite its powerful, coherent view of the world at odds with Nazi German racism—so many, as was demonstrated by their own abandonment and persecution of Jewish converts, succumbed to the racist cognitions and idiom of the day.[96] Indeed, so powerful was the racial cognitive cultural model of humanity in Germany that the German Catholic Church by and large accepted and disseminated it in its own teachings. The German episcopate's February 1936 official guidelines for religious instruction declared: "Race, soil, blood and people are precious natural values which God the Lord has created and the care of which he has entrusted to us Germans."[97] The overlay of official and obsessive public racial antisemitism onto the antisemitism that had more or less governed the ideational life of German civil society in its recent pre-Nazi history cemented into place the hegemonic racist antisemitic ideology, from which few dissented.

This can most easily be demonstrated by looking at those groups who, it might be thought, would have been the least disposed to concur with this conception of Jews. As has already been mentioned, virtually every high-status professional group—namely those with education, characterized by the habit of thinking independently, and possessing the greatest training to see bunk for what it was—demonstrated itself to be beholden to antisemitism. Workers, many of whom had been adherents of Marxism and were thus ideological opponents of Nazism, were, on the issue of the Jews, in general accord with the Nazis, as many of the intelligence agents of the Social Democratic Party (who were on the whole reluctant to find signs pointing to the hopelessness of their own cause) themselves acknowledged despairingly.

In Saxony, a notably antisemitic region of Germany, a report from January 1936 concluded:

> Antisemitism has no doubt taken root in wide circles of the population. If people nevertheless buy from Jews, then it is not in order to help the Jews but to annoy the Nazis. The general antisemitic psychosis affects even thoughtful people, our comrades as well. All are decided opponents of violence, one is however in favor of breaking once and for all the supremacy of the Jews and of restricting them to certain fields of activity. [Julius] Streicher [the publisher of *Der Stürmer*] is universally rejected, but fundamentally one agrees to a large extent with Hitler. The workers say: in the [Weimar] [R]epublic and in the [Social Democratic] Party the Jews have grown too big.[98]

The editors of the volume of intelligence reports concluded, even though some of the reports paint a rosier picture of the German workers' attitudes towards the Jews, that "it is a common opinion that there exists a 'Jewish Problem.' "[99] The near universality of this belief, and therefore of the acceptance of its underlying cognitive model discussed above, can hardly be doubted.[100]

The moral bankruptcy of the German churches, Protestant and Catholic alike, regarding Jews was so extensive and abject that it warrants far more attention than can be devoted to it here. Already during Weimar, the antisemitism of the churches as institutions, of their national and local clergy as well as their acolytes, was widespread and ominous. During Weimar, 70 to 80 percent of Protestant pastors had allied themselves with the antisemitic German National People's Party, and their antisemitism had permeated the Protestant press even before the Nazis were voted into power.[101] The Protestant press, with its millions of readers, was extremely influential, and provides us insight into both the mind and temper of the religious officials and the fare on which their flock was nourished. In the twenties, the amount and intensity of the antisemitic agitation issuing from Protestant sources increased enormously. This increase paralleled the general proliferation and heightening of antisemitism in the politically turbulent atmosphere of Weimar. The most prominent and most influential religious vehicles for the diffusion of anti-Jewish sentiments in the Protestant world were the *Sonntagsblätter*, the weekly Sunday newspapers, whose combined circulation numbered over 1.8 million copies and whose readership has been conservatively estimated at three times that number.[102] By reason of their great volume, they had a considerable share in shaping the collective opinions of the Protestant laity that composed almost 63 percent of the German population in 1933.[103] A survey of sixty-eight *Sonntagsblätter* printed between 1918 and 1933 revealed that Jews and Jewry were themes "of great topicality" in them.

The press's treatment of these themes was almost invariably hostile. These religious weeklies, which were devoted to the edification of their readers and to the cultivation of Christian piety, preached that the Jews were "the natural enemies of the Christian-national tradition," that they had caused "the collapse of the Christian and monarchical order," and that they were the authors of a variety of other evils. Ino Arndt, the author of this study, concludes that the ceaseless defamation of the Jews in the Protestant Sunday papers must have blunted in millions of their readers "the human and finally also the Christian feelings" for the Jews.[104] Small wonder that these Christian readers would look with unpitying eyes upon the Jews as they were being attacked, tormented, degraded, and reduced to social lepers during the Nazi period.

From the end of 1930 until the Nazi assumption of power and beyond, the anti-Jewish "diction" of "nearly all the *Sonntagsblätter*" grew "by far sharper" than it had been hitherto. Emboldened and influenced by the intensifying antisemitic atmosphere, the papers emulated the vituperative force and strident tone of the antisemitic rhetoric of the Nazi Party, whose victory was in prospect. Upon coming to power, the Nazis would work to synchronize the beliefs and conduct of all Germans with the edicts of the new dispensation. The Christian churches and bodies would not execute this Nazi demand with soldier-like obedience. On the contrary, they resisted "synchronization" in all weighty matters in which their values clashed with those of the Nazis. But when it came to fundamental beliefs and attitudes regarding the Jews, the Nazis and the Protestant Sunday papers were not far apart. They were qualitatively kindred. "Synchronization" in this realm therefore proceeded smoothly. Even before Hitler came to power, as his ascendancy became increasingly probable, the editors of these pious Christian papers brought their already virulently antisemitic rhetoric into closer concord with that of the Nazis. They did so unbidden, entirely voluntarily, and with unmistakable passion and alacrity.

The Protestant press, of course, could not have offered such vituperative, Nazi-like, antisemitic fare to the people of Germany so relentlessly had the Church's religious leadership not approved. Indeed, the Protestant leadership conceived of the Jews as Christianity's and Germany's bitter enemies before Hitler came to power.[105] One of the moral pastors of the nation, for example, the General Superintendent of the Kurmark Diocese of the Evangelical (Lutheran) Church in Prussia, Bishop Otto Dibelius, declared in a letter shortly after the April 1933 Boycott that he has been "always an antisemite." "One cannot fail to appreciate," he continued, "that in all of the corrosive manifestations of modern civilization Jewry plays a leading role."[106] In 1928, five years before Hitler came to power, Dibelius had even expressed the logic of the reigning eliminationist antisemitism when he offered the following "solution" to the "Jewish Problem": All Jewish immigration from eastern Europe should be prohibited. As soon as this prohibition takes effect, the decline of Jewry would set in. "The number of children of the Jewish families is small. The process of dying out occurs surprisingly rapidly."[107] Unlike Hitler, who wanted to kill the Jews, the Lutheran bishop wished them to die out peaceably, bloodlessly. Wolfgang Gerlach, a German Evangelical pastor and historian of the Christian churches during the Nazi period, observes that Bishop Dibelius' antisemitic sentiments were "well nigh representative of German Christendom [*deutsche Christenheit*] in the beginning of 1933."[108] This retrospective judgment is confirmed by the contemporaneous judgment of the eminent Protestant theologian Dietrich Bonhoeffer, who despaired at the flood tide of antisemitism that even his colleagues were then expressing. Shortly after Hitler came to power, Bonhoeffer wrote to a theologian friend that regarding the Jews "the most sensible people have lost their heads and their entire Bible."[109]

Although there was more private dissent at the highest levels of the German Catholic Church from some aspects of Nazi doctrine about Jews and from the lethal aspects of the eliminationist enterprise—which but reflected its greater, more general conflict with a regime that was bent upon breaking its power—the Catholic Church as an institution remained thoroughly and publicly antisemitic. Cardinal Michael Faulhaber of Munich expressed this in his Advent sermons at the end of 1933, in which he might well have been speaking for Catholics in general. Although Faulhaber defended the Jewish religion and the Jews who lived prior to Jesus, he made it clear that those Jews were to be distinguished from the Jews who lived after Jesus, a group which, of course, included contemporary Jews. When, the following year, foreigners misrepresented his words by asserting that Faulhaber had championed German Jews, Faulhaber emphatically denied this.[110] Before and during the Nazi period, Catholic publications, whether written for the laity, clerics, or theologians, disseminated the contemporary antisemitic litany in ways that were often indistinguishable from the Nazis', and justified the desire to eliminate the Jewish "alien bodies" (*Fremdkörper*) from Germany. Taking action against the Jews, according to the body of these publications, was "justifiable self-defense to prevent the harmful characteristics and influences of the Jewish race."[111] In March 1941, by which time Germans had already inflicted enormous harm on the Jews of Germany and Europe, Archbishop Konrad Gröber published a pastoral letter replete with antisemitism. He placed the blame upon the Jews for the death of Jesus, which he implied justified what Germans were then doing to the Jews: "The self-imposed curse of the Jews, 'His blood be upon us and upon our children,' has come true terribly until the present time, until today."[112] Gröber was anything but a solitary anti-Jewish figure in the Catholic Church. Although the Catholic Church's leadership openly condemned many aspects of Nazi policy, it issued no official condemnation of the regime's eliminationist persecution of the Jews, or of the signal events of the program. It did not officially protest the April 1933 boycott, the Nuremberg Laws, the depredations of *Kristallnacht*, or even the Nazis' deportation of German Jews to their deaths.[113]

It is, therefore, no surprise that although the Catholic bishops did make a few public statements that decried the treatment or killing of foreigners, they did not speak out explicitly against the extermination of the Jews (of which they had full knowledge), remaining content with vague formulations that could apply to many people, including Christian Slavs, in war-torn and German-barbarized Europe. The Protestant hierarchy was even less forthcoming regarding the fate of the Jews.[114] Never once did any German bishop, Catholic or Protestant, speak out publicly on behalf of the Jews, as did the French Catholic Archbishop of Toulouse, Jules-Gérard Saliège: "It has been reserved to our time to witness the sad spectacle of children, of women, of fathers and mothers, being treated like a herd of beasts; to see members of the same family separated one from another and shipped away to an unknown destination. . . . Jews are men. Jewesses are women. . . . They cannot be maltreated at will. . . . They are part of the human race. They are our brethren as much as are so many others. A Christian cannot forget that."[115] Although the German churches spoke out forcefully against the regime on many issues, they forsook the Jews of Germany utterly; in this sense, the religious leaders of Germany were men of God second and Germans first—so powerful was the antisemitic model—for these German men of God could not bring themselves to utter that Jews "are part of the human race" and to declare to their flocks that the moral laws were not suspended for the treatment of Jews.

Thoroughly antisemitic, not only did these German men of God not stand up for Jews as they watched them being hounded, beaten, forced from their homes and country, and then murdered by their own parishioners, but they also actively aided the eliminationist enterprise. By this is meant not just the many antisemitic sermons with which they—the German nation's pastors of morality—reinforced and consecrated the hatreds of ordinary Germans. The foundational element of the Nuremberg Laws was the regime's capacity to distinguish and demonstrate the extent of a person's Jewish ancestry, to know who was a Jew. Enforcement therefore depended upon the use of the genealogical records in the possession of local churches. The historian of the Catholic Church Guenther Lewy, writes:

> The very question of whether the [Catholic] Church should lend its help to the Nazi state in sorting out people of Jewish descent was never debated. On

the contrary. "We have always unselfishly worked for the people without regard to gratitude or ingratitude," a priest wrote in the *Klerusblatt* in September 1934. "We shall also do our best to help in this service to the people."
And the co-operation of the Church in this matter continued right through
the war years, when the price of being Jewish was no longer dismissal from
a government job and loss of livelihood, but deportation and outright physical destruction.[116]

The German churches cooperated wholeheartedly in this obviously eliminationist and often lethal measure. If the moral beacons and consciences of Germany willingly worked to serve the antisemitic policies, could less have been
expected from their acolytes? These religious leaders were the men who
earnestly and openly fought the so-called Euthanasia killings, as well as other
governmental measures, such as governmental tolerance of dueling and crema-
tion (but not the crematoria of Auschwitz, of which they knew).[117] While
Church leaders across other European countries, including German-occupied
Denmark, the Netherlands, Norway, and Vichy, as well as occupied France,
openly condemned the persecution and slaughter of the Jews and urged their
countrymen (sometimes in vain) not to take part in it,[118] the German religious
leadership left the Jews (with the only sometime exception of converts to Christianity) to their fates, or even contributed to the eliminationist persecution.[119]

Bishop Dibelius' 1928 hopeful musings about the Jews' eventual bloodless extinction were but a prelude to the open endorsements that a significant
number of German Church leaders gave during the Nazi period to the
most radical and violent eliminationist measures while the regime was pursuing them. One leading Protestant churchman, Bishop Martin Sasse of
Thuringia, published a compendium of Martin Luther's antisemitic vitriol
shortly after *Kristallnacht*'s orgy of anti-Jewish violence. In the foreword to
the volume, he applauded the burning of the synagogues and the coincidence
of the day: "On November 10, 1938, on Luther's birthday, the synagogues are
burning in Germany." The German people, he urged, ought to heed these
words "of the greatest antisemite of his time, the warner of his people against
the Jews."[120] In light of the eliminationist antisemitism that pervaded the
Protestant churches, it is no great surprise that even many prominent Church
leaders threw their moral weight behind anti-Jewish measures that were still
more radical than those of *Kristallnacht*.

The Germans' systematic extermination of European Jewry began in
June 1941 in the Soviet Union. By the end of the year, the slaughter was well
under way and had become widely known among the millions of Germans
serving as soldiers or colonizers in the East, as well as among the German people at home, as the Minister of the American Church in Berlin, Stewart Her-

man, who remained in Germany until December 1941, attested: "It became definitely known through the soldiers returning from the front that in occupied Russia, especially at Kiev [the site of the Babi Yar massacre of more than thirty-three thousand Jews at the end of September], Jewish civilians—men, women, and babies—were being lined up and machine-gunned by the thousands."[121] Knowledge of the killings spread, not least of all among the Church leadership, as the Protestant bishop Theophil Wurm made clear when he wrote in December 1941 to the Reich Minister for Church Affairs Hanns Kerrl of "rumors about the mass killings in the East" that had reached the populace.[122] But even such knowledge did not temper much of the Church leadership's hostility towards Jews and its support for the regime's policies. That same month, on December 17, 1941, Protestant Evangelical Church leaders of Mecklenburg, Thuringia, Saxony, Nassau-Hesse, Schleswig-Holstein, Anhalt, and Lübeck collectively issued an official proclamation which declared the Jews to be incapable of being saved by baptism, owing to their racial constitution, to be responsible for the war, and to be "born enemies of the world and Germany" (*geborene Welt- und Reichsfeinde*). They therefore urged that the "severest measures against the Jews be adopted and that they be banished from German lands."[123] The superlative, the "severest measures," logically implies that any penalty, however extreme, could be applied to the Jews, including the death penalty. And with the context of the apocalyptic war with the Soviet Union and of the Germans' already ongoing extermination of Soviet Jewry, it could have meant only one thing. With these words, the Protestant Church leadership of a good part of Germany—collectively, as a corporate group, and with the authority of their offices—on their own initiative implicitly endorsed the mass slaughter of Jews.[124]

Even the most prominent churchmen who resisted and worked against the regime could be deeply antisemitic, sharing central elements of the Nazis' portrait of the Jews. This is strikingly conveyed in the following antisemitic oration: "We speak of the 'eternal Jew' and conjure up the picture of a restless wanderer who has no home and who cannot find peace. We see a highly gifted people which produces idea after idea for the benefit of the world, but whatever it takes up becomes poisoned, and all that it ever reaps is contempt and hatred because ever and anon the world notices the deception and avenges itself in its own way."[125] These are the words not of a Nazi ideologue, but of one of the great and celebrated opponents of Nazism, the Protestant minister Martin Niemöller. He delivered them in a sermon to his flock during the early years of Nazi rule. As did many who were opponents of Nazism, despite his hatred of the regime, he concurred with the Nazi view of the world in one foundational respect: the Jews were eternally evil.[126]

The justly admired and revered Pastor Heinrich Grüber—a deeply humane, compassionate, and charitable clergyman, who was the head of a bureau created by the Protestant Church to aid Jewish converts to Christianity and who in 1940 was imprisoned for having protested the deportation of Jews—even someone no less than this heroic German held beliefs about Jews which were akin to those of the Nazis. In an interview with a Dutch newspaper on February 1, 1939, he criticized the Dutch for their refusal to accept the notion of "rootless Jewry," a notion of which, as he put it approvingly, "one gladly speaks in National Socialist Germany." Grüber professed to be "convinced" that "most of the Jews who had lived in Germany were rootless. They performed no productive labor, but did 'business' [meaning shady dealings]." The Jews' perniciousness was greater than mere rootlessness. "It was these Jews who from 1919 until 1932 ruled Germany financially, economically, politically, culturally, and journalistically. There was indeed a Jewish predominance." Although Grüber believed that "there were numerous better Israelites who remained faithful to the laws of Moses," the Dutch needed to recognize that there is indeed a worldwide "Jewish Problem" and to refrain from criticizing Germany, which had given an "example" of how that problem is to be tackled. "Whoever wants to contribute to the solution [of the "Jewish Problem"] should not allow himself to be ruled by feelings of sympathy or antipathy," but collaborate with other people of good will in facilitating the emigration of Jews to countries "where they are needed."[127] Grüber was a typical German in that he, a product of their common culture, essentially shared the antisemitic convictions of his countrymen, but he was a rare German because he adhered to an authentic Christian ethic which led him to devote himself to relieving the plight of the Jews, even though he believed that they had done enormous harm to Germany. So commonsensical was antisemitism in Germany that this great self-sacrificing German helper of Jews harbored and espoused Nazi-like beliefs about them.

Karl Barth, the great theologian, leader of the Protestant Confessing Church, and bitter opponent of Nazism, was also an antisemite. As the 1930s progressed, he became for theological reasons a defender of the Jews, despite his own deep-seated antisemitism, which had moved him, in his Advent sermon of 1933, to denounce the Jews as "an obstinate and evil people."[128]

It should be said that—as these and many other Church leaders, whether opponents or supporters of Nazism, showed by their statements—it was not the antisemites who were the exceptions among the Christian leadership in Germany. The rarities were those who remained untouched by antisemitism. Those few within the churches who took up the Jews' cause found, if anyone, but a few others to stand with them. Grüber, who did aid the Jews, recalled that "in a few meetings of the Confessing Church a call to protest was given.

But protests were made by the few, in comparison with the millions who co-operated or kept silent, who, at best, played the ostrich or clenched their fists in their pockets."[129] Indeed, regarding the Jews, there was but little difference between the mainstream Protestant churches and the breakaway, avowedly racist and antisemitic "German Christians" who sought to merge Christian theology with racism and the other principles of Nazism. In the many letters that mainstream Protestant pastors wrote explaining their rejection of the German Christian movement, they emphasized the German Christians' impermissible mixing of religion and politics, but not a single one criticized the ongoing persecution of the Jews, which was central to the German Christians' politics and theology.[130] As one historian writes, "the fearless statements and deeds of individuals [on behalf of Jews] should not obscure the fact that the Church became a compliant helper of Nazi Jewish Policy."[131] After the war, Martin Niemöller, having by then apprehended the evil that German antisemitism was, concurred with this devastating judgment. In a March 1946 lecture in Zurich, he declaimed: "Christianity in Germany bears a greater responsibility before God than the National Socialists, the SS and the Gestapo. We ought to have recognized the Lord Jesus in the brother who suffered and was persecuted despite him being a communist or a Jew. . . . Are not we Christians much more to blame, am I not much more guilty, than many who bathed their hands in blood?" The hyperbole aside, Niemöller spoke the harsh truth: "Christianity in Germany" had failed to see the radical eliminationist persecution as a moral transgression. At root, the problem had clearly been a cognitive one, namely the failure of Church pastors and Germans in general to have recognized that the Jews by nature are not an evil tribe.[132]

The members of the fabled resistance to Hitler, who were articulate and vehement in their objections to Nazism, were also the people who should have been among the most likely to reject the dominant cultural cognitive model of Jews and the eliminationist program. Yet, like Niemöller and Barth, they too were, by and large, animated by the common conception of the Jews. The pre-genocidal eliminationist measures of the 1930s, the stripping of Jews' citizenship and rights, their immiseration, the violence that Germans perpetrated against them, the regime's incarceration of them in concentration camps, and the hounding of them to emigrate from Germany—the sum of these radical measures did not incense, or produce substantial opposition among, those who would eventually form the major resistance groups. Indeed, in the view of the foremost expert on the subject, Christof Dipper, the Gestapo's evaluation of the captured July 20 conspirators (based on the conspirators' own statements during interrogation), accurately depicts them as having fundamentally shared the regime's conception of the Jews, even if they differed on how the Jews ought to have been treated: " '. . . The conspirators, while agreeing in principle with antisemitism, rejected the methods of implementation. In part, humanitarian motives were being stressed; the measures were not humane enough, and they were not in keeping with the German character. In part, questions of expediency were being raised, pointing to the strained relations with the rest of the world as a result of the rigorous short-term removal of the Jews.' "¹³³

By and large, those in the opposition and resistance to the Nazis were not moved to opposition by a principled disapproval of the elimination of the Jews from German society. The brother of someone no less than Claus von Stauffenberg, the man who on July 20, 1944, placed the bomb that was intended to kill Hitler, testified: "In the sphere of internal politics we had welcomed the basic tenets of National Socialism for the most part . . . The concept of race seemed sound and very promising . . ."; their objection was merely that its "implementation was exaggerated and carried too far."¹³⁴ Speaking for most of the members of the non-communist and non-socialist resistance, the uncle of Stauffenberg, Count Uxküll, summarized the intentions of the largest and most influential resistance group, the conservative and military opposition which was organized around Stauffenberg and Carl Goerdeler: "We should hold on to the concept of race as far as possible."¹³⁵ In Nazi Germany, affirmation of "race" as an organizing principle of social and political life was to accept the foundation of the regnant cultural cognitive model of Jews, since the two were intertwined. One of the central documents of the resistance to Hitler—prepared at the beginning of 1943 at Dietrich Bonhoeffer's initiative by the Freiburg Circle, consisting of leading Protestant theologians and university professors, and with the knowledge of Goerdeler—contained an appendix called "Proposals for a Solution to the Jewish Problem in Germany." It affirmed that the post-Nazi state would be justified in taking steps "to ward off the calamitous influence of one race on the national community [*Volksgemeinschaft*]." Although it explicitly condemned the genocide, the document's debt to eliminationist antisemitism is unmistakable. Wherever they were, Jews caused trouble for the host nation. The document accepted that a "Jewish Problem" existed, that the Jews had harmed Germany, and that a "solution" was necessary that would prevent future harm to Germans. The proposal ventured that in the future perhaps it would be possible to allow Jews back into Germany with full rights. Why? Because the Nazis had killed so many Jews: "The number of Jews surviving and returning to Germany will not be so large that they could still be regarded as a danger to the German Nation."¹³⁶ The resistance groups' own, often antisemitic pronouncements and programs typically envisaged a future Germany without Jews or with a Jewry denied fundamental rights, like citizenship.¹³⁷ Their disenchantment with the regime's murderous practice was owing to ethical inhibitions and pragmatic considerations, and not to a dissenting, benign view of the Jews. The eliminationist persecution and, by and large, even the extermination of the Jews failed to mobilize not only the conservative and religious conspirators against Hitler but also the working-class resistance to the Nazis.[138]

The curious phenomenon that the Nazis' greatest crimes failed to excite even many of those who were predisposed to oppose Nazism appears less curious in light of the history and ubiquity of antisemitism in Germany. It is persuasive evidence of the disjunction of realms, whereby bitter opponents of Nazism could concur and applaud the elimination, even the extermination, of the Jews.[139] If a favorable, or at least a neutral, view of Jews was not to be found either among the Christian moral pastors of Germany or among Hitler's mortal enemies—whose hatred of him and habit of independence made them the most likely dissenters from the antisemitic creed—then where was it to be found in Germany? The cultural cognitive model of Jews was the property of Nazis and non-Nazis alike.

The glaring absence of significant protest or privately expressed dissent, especially principled dissent, with respect to the treatment and eventual genocidal slaughter of the Jews should be seen as being a result neither of Nazi "brainwashing" of Germans nor of the inability of Germans to express their dissatisfaction with the regime or its policies, because the record of this period does not in any way support either contention. In many different spheres and on many different issues, the Nazis failed to "indoctrinate" the German people—put differently, failed to convince them of the wisdom or justice of their positions or policies—and Germans spoke out, expressing dissent and opposition to many of those same policies. The differing responses by Germans—accepting and supporting the eliminationist program while dissenting from and even working against other Nazi policies—make unequivocally clear that the German people should not be regarded as having been passive pawns or terrorized victims of their own government. As Germans' actions regarding a variety of Nazi policies show, they were willful agents, making conscious choices in accord with their preexisting, if evolving, values and beliefs. Of course, they operated within the constraints that the regime imposed, yet similar constraints applied to spheres and issues other than the Jews without having influenced Germans' actions in the same manner.

Most revealing in this regard is the Germans' treatment of non-Jewish foreigners. Germans treated other peoples whom the Nazis and most Germans deemed to be inferior, even "subhuman," such as Poles, far differently and better than Jews.[140] The perpetrators' comparatively far better treatment of non-Jews than of Jews in concentration camps and other settings, not surprisingly, mirrored that of the German civilian population, and is discussed at length in the coming chapters. Within German society, enforcement of "racial" laws and regulations depended greatly on voluntary information supplied to the Gestapo, since—contrary to the mythological image of it—it was a terribly undermanned institution, incapable of policing German society on its own. The selective aid that Germans gave to the Gestapo in prosecuting various victim groups reveals both that Germans' actions in this sphere was voluntaristic and that they were moved by greatly different conceptions of the groups. Germans helped the Gestapo to police Jews—who were longtime residents of Germany—with more alacrity and diligence than they did foreigners, including the "subhuman" Slavs.[141] The German people, who had helped so much in the eliminationist measures against Jews, were by and large recalcitrant in aiding the authorities in the enforcement of racial policy towards the "subhuman" Poles.[142] They not only chose to comply with and aid the policies in a consistently differentiated manner, but they themselves also treated Jews and non-Jews differently, often violating the law by treating non-Jewish foreigners decently. Prohibition of sexual contact with the millions of foreigners, most of whom were Slavs, employed as slave laborers in Germany was as stringent as it had been with Jews since 1935. Yet, while Germans kept the leprous Jews at arm's length, in their actions towards foreign workers, they gave the Gestapo much to do. Between May and August 1942, for example, the Gestapo dealt with 4,960 cases of forbidden relations between Germans and foreign workers. The following year, from July to September, the Gestapo arrested 4,637 Germans for socializing with such foreigners.[143] These figures, wholly unimaginable for Germans and Jews, reflect only those cases that the Gestapo uncovered, which can be assumed to have been only a fraction of those that existed.

Germans also stood up for Poles as they did not do for Jews. Priests often spoke out on behalf of Poles but not of Jews.[144] Poles, of course, were Catholics, yet the Jews' condition and fate, far worse than that of Poles, made them by far the more needy of help. Justice authorities in Bamberg by late 1944 were so impressed by the futility of their task of getting Germans to abide by the laws against "blood-mixing" with non-Jewish foreigners that they more or less gave up hope. In a fanciful characterization of Germans which no Jew could have imagined pertained to him, they wrote: "The racially foreign person in many cases lives with the German national comrade—especially in the country-side—under the same roof; the national comrade does not see in him the member of a foreign or enemy state, but a valuable fellow worker at a time of labour shortage. Pity and charity are the products of this false point of view and German sentimentalism."[145] "They are people too!" was an oft-heard remark, critical of the regime, that testified to Germans' conception of Poles who were being hanged for offenses that they considered to be insufficiently grave to warrant such a punishment.[146] Statements of the Jews' humanity, or genuine and authentic expressions of sympathy for Jews, were so rarely heard in the Germany that had given itself to Nazism that they stood out. In openly speaking their minds in the variety of ways that they did, Germans once again showed that they were not "brain-washed," that they held views contrary to those of the regime, and that they were often willing to voice them. It is no wonder that the Nazi *Gauleiter* of Würzburg, writing in December 1939 about the treatment accorded Polish laborers and prisoners of war, concluded that "the attitude of the population leaves much to be desired."[147] Germans' antisemitism was not merely a prejudice against a vilified minority group. If Germans had been so pliable and indiscriminate as to consume with alacrity whatever the regime's ideological menu offered them, then they would have adopted similar uncompromising attitudes against Poles. No simplifying social psychological explanation that ignores the highly elaborate, long-existing, hallucinatory, particular German conception of *Jews* can account for Germans' attitudes and actions.

The evidence of the Germans' capacity to oppose policies with which they disagreed extends to many other realms of social and political life. The Nazis' public assaults on Christianity, for example, created much dissatisfaction among the German people. This was especially so in Catholic regions. Local attempts by Nazi officials to restrict religious practices and to remove crucifixes from schools in Bavaria led to such outrage, such an outcry, and such fierce protest that the officials generally rescinded their orders.[148] It is noteworthy that this occurred at the same time that attacks on Jews were taking place all over the region, with Bavarians expressing hardly a word of dissent, let alone protest. Already in 1934, the Party's repeated attempts to mobilize the populace for political rallies and parades began to meet with concerted criticism and opposition from the populace. Even if they approved of the general direction in which Nazi Germany was moving, Germans vocally resisted the exhortations of the regime to greater participation, as a 1934 report from the Governor of the Koblenz District attests: "The farming public claims that so long as no significant changes have actually been instituted, despite the party's tales of constant improvements, there is no point in attending its meetings."[149] The disaffection with many of the regime's policies and propaganda was by no means restricted to the rural population. Industrial workers expressed much discontent with the Nazis' attempts to indoctrinate them, and especially with Nazi economic policies.[150] Moreover, they frequently acted on their discontent by going out on strike. Between February 1936 and July 1937, for example, an incomplete government tabulation recorded 192 strikes as having taken place in Germany.[151] These were open protests against regime policies that workers deemed to be unfair—and the regime often acquiesced to the workers' demands. More generally, the continuing desire of the German people to get news from foreign sources indicated a degree of reserve, even distrust of the regime.[152]

The regime's placement of thousands of agents around the country to report on the mood of the people—and not to effect arrests—itself strongly suggests that the regime was well aware that people had more than minor disaffection with the country's policies and were willing to voice them. And the content of the reports themselves bore out the regime's suspicions—in spades.[153] Ian Kershaw remarks in astonishment at "how many people *were* ready to express open criticism in spite of the climate of intimidation, and how often the reports record such critical comments in evidently faithful fashion."[154]

The best-known case of protest that took place in Nazi Germany was an outgrowth of the widespread outrage at the government's so-called Euthanasia program (referred to as T4, after its Berlin headquarters at *Tiergarten Strasse 4*), which saw German physicians take the lives of more than seventy thousand people whom they deemed to have a "life unworthy of living" because of mental infirmity and congenital physical defects. The outcry, initially from relatives of the murdered people, spread throughout the country and found leadership among priests and bishops. Germans (1) recognized this slaughter to be wrong, (2) expressed their views about it, (3) openly protested for an end to the killing, (4) suffered no retribution for having expressed their views and for pressing their demands, and (5) succeeded in producing a formal cessation of the killing program, and saving German lives.[155] Here was a model—put into practice by the same Germans who would continue to stand by as the eliminationist program unfolded—for a response to the persecution and genocide of the Jews: moral evaluation and recognition, expression, protest, and, perhaps, success. These German steps, so easy to discern as having occurred in the face of the slaughter of the congenitally or mentally infirm, should be just as easy, in fact easier (owing to the greater enormity and duration of the Holocaust) to uncover had they ever been taken on behalf of Jewish Germans. Yet they are, with rare exceptions, not to be found.[156] Only once was there large-scale protest by Germans on behalf of Jews, namely when German women massed in Berlin and demonstrated for three days for the release of their recently incarcerated Jewish husbands. How did the regime respond in the face of this popular opposition? It backed down. The six thousand Jewish men were freed. The women suffered no disabilities.[157] Clearly, had Germans cared about the welfare of Germany's Jews, then not only would we know of it, but also the capacity of the regime to pursue its eliminationist program would have been greatly restricted.[158]

The long and impressive record of Germans' dissent from *particular* Nazi policies did not by any means translate into *general* opposition to the regime itself,[159] to the Nazi German system and its primary goals of a racially purified

Germany and a militarized, resurgent Germany within Europe. The regime was very popular in its first years, becoming still more enthusiastically supported towards the end of the 1930s, with Hitler's foreign policy and initial military success.[160] As Ian Kershaw has observed, even the Catholics of Bavaria, who despised the regime's attacks upon their church, were mainly ardent supporters of the Nazis' central goals: "This same area [Bavaria] where popular opposition to Nazi Church policy was so vigorous continued, in fact, to prove itself a hotbed of vicious popular anti-Semitism, provided no indication of anything but wholehearted support for the regime's chauvinistic and aggressive foreign policy, and remained a bastion of intense pro-Hitler feeling. The opposition in the Church conflict was overwhelmingly leveled not at the regime itself but merely at one unattractive and—it was felt—wholly unnecessary aspect of its policy."[161] Even the most bitter conflicts, which produced long-lasting, determined popular protests against the regime, did not substantially dent the solid German support that existed for Nazism and especially for its eliminationist program.

Similarly, episodic distemper with aspects of the regime's assault on the Jews should not be understood as being indicative of a widespread, general rejection of the eliminationist ideal and program. It is not surprising that expressions of dissent and discomfort with the unprecedented eliminationist policies, though almost never with the ideational foundation from which they sprang, were to be heard in Germany during the 1930s. Many interpreters of this period have proffered such criticism as evidence that a sizable portion of the German people was not antisemitic or that many Germans disapproved in principle of the persecution of the Jews. This view is mistaken.[162] It is erroneous not only because the character and overwhelming plenitude of the counter-evidence (only a small fraction of which can be presented here) is vastly greater than Germans' numerically paltry expressions of disapproval of what, upon closer examination, can be seen to have been generally only *specific aspects* of the larger eliminationist program—and not of its governing principles. When examined for their content, those critical expressions also, and most significantly, reveal that the dissatisfaction was almost never born of a rejection of antisemitism, a rejection of the beliefs that Jews had willfully, grievously injured and were a source of continuing harm to Germany, and that Germans would and should profit enormously by the elimination of the Jews and their influence from Germany. The dissatisfaction that Germans did feel almost always emanated from one of a variety of other sources.

One source of Germans' displeasure was a reluctance to undergo financial hardship by severing crucial economic ties to Jews. This was seen during the 1930s in the general failure of the regime's call for Germans not to frequent Jewish businesses, many of which offered goods and services at favorable prices, and was also especially to be seen in some rural areas, where German farmers were often dependent on their commercial relations with Jews.[163] Another source of dissatisfaction was Germans' condemnation of pogrom-like, wanton brutality in the streets of their neighborhoods, which many Germans recoiled against instinctively as something unlawful, unseemly, unnecessary, and, in its naked, atavistic savagery, unworthy of a civilized society. A Gestapo report from August 1935 in Hannover records that in recent weeks "the antisemitic mood has increased considerably among the broad masses of the population. Except for a few unteachable exceptions, the drastic repulsion of the Jews' inroads is everywhere and generally welcomed. By far the greater part of the population, however, does not understand the senseless individual acts of violence and terror [against Jews] which have been observed of late, unfortunately, in Hannover of all places."[164] The report goes on to describe how, in order to put an end to such attacks, the police were compelled to intervene in the name of law and order, and it expresses its author's fear that, because members of the populace had witnessed the terrorizers of Jews calling the police "Jew-slave" (*Judenhöriger*) and "Jew-friend" (*Judenfreund*), state authority was undermined. This report provides but one illustration of how the condemnation of "senseless acts of terror" was voiced by antisemites. The Gestapo man himself exemplifies the absence of contradiction between these two positions. He was such an antisemite, and knew how antisemitic the populace was, that he worried that the mere suggestion that the police might be helping Jews would make them suspect and diminish their authority. Yet he, like the people whom he described, also clearly disapproved of the "senseless acts of terror."[165]

Anxiety over the revenge that Germans, in their antisemitic stupor, fantasized that the Jews would exact upon them for the persecution also made some ambivalent about their country's eliminationist assault on the Jews. This was expressed repeatedly during the 1930s and then after the war began, especially with regard to the bombing of Germany. So in November 1943, the president of the State Supreme Court in Braunschweig reported that there were many people who blamed the Nazi Party for the terror bombing, which it had caused by its treatment of the Jews.[166] The fear of reprisals from the all-powerful Jews, even in the 1930s, and then the destruction of Germany that Germans believed the Jews to be causing with the war, were of sufficient magnitude to prompt even dedicated antisemites to reconsider the wisdom of the national assault on the Jews. Their attribution of responsibility for the leveling of German cities to the objectively impotent Jews is, by itself, proof positive of their adherence to a Nazified view of Jews.[167]

Another source of Germans' criticism of aspects of the eliminationist program was a wish on the part of some to make exceptions for personal acquaintances. This is a well-known phenomenon among the prejudiced that easily coexists, as it did in Germany, with the same people's profound hatred for the group as a whole. A 1938 report from a Saxon region illustrates well this attitude and reveals how insignificant a qualification such objections were to the Germans' near-axiomatic endorsement of the eliminationist enterprise and its underlying principles: "In our district there are only a few Jews. When the people read of the measures taken against the Jews in the big cities, then they approve of them. But when a Jew of their circle of close acquaintances is affected, then the very same people moan about the terror of the regime. Then compassion stirs in them again."[168] It is the Germans' attitudes towards the Jews in the big cities, namely towards Jews in general, that is fundamental. Against them the Germans applaud the eliminationist measures. Such testimony is evidence not of Germans' departure from the essence of Nazi precept and practice, but of their endorsement of it.

The final source of some Germans' dissent, in this case only with respect to the most radical aspect of the eliminationist program, was either pragmatic or ethical objections to the implementation of a corporate death sentence, to genocide as a policy of state. Pragmatic objections could be found, as has already been discussed, among the conservative opposition to Hitler. Ethical objections to genocide were most prominent among members of the religious leadership.[169] In July 1943, when the Germans had already slaughtered most of their Jewish victims, Bishop Wurm finally wrote to Hitler a private letter of protest against the extermination, though he did not mention the Jews explicitly. Yet Wurm himself made it clear in many statements that he shared essential features of the Nazis' view of Jews. Wurm's objection was not to the thrust and goal of the Nazis' policies, but to the inhuman manner in which the regime was putting them into practice. Three months earlier, he had explained to Interior Minister Frick that his and other Christians' criticism of the regime's policies was, of course, not the result of any "partiality towards the Jews whose disproportionately huge influence on cultural, economic, and political life in the time [of Weimar] . . . Christians almost alone recognized as disastrous."[170] Indeed, Wurm, in a letter to the head of Hitler's Chancellery, Hans Lammers, at the end of 1943, articulated explicitly that ethical objections to genocide should in no sense be understood by Lammers (or by us) to be indicative of dissent from the regnant demonizing conception of Jewry, which, as he said, was shared by Christians. Wurm declared that he and like-minded Christians were not moved "by any philosemitic inclinations, but simply by religious and ethical feelings."[171]

The different kinds of qualms, to the extent that they even existed, were perfectly understandable reactions to various features of such a radical eliminationist program. Aspects of Nazi antisemitic practice met opposition from even some practitioners of the Holocaust. At a November 12, 1938, meeting after *Kristallnacht*, for example, Hermann Göring, who was charged by Hitler with coordinating the eliminationist program, reproached some of those who were present for the enormous material destruction that they had helped cause, but not for the attack upon German Jews: "I would have rather you had killed 200 Jews and not destroyed such valuable assets."[172] Such reproaches on the part of those who persecuted and even killed Jews did not mean that they were not antisemites or opponents of the Holocaust. People who support the principles underlying even non-radical governmental programs, and this is not specific to Germany during the Nazi period, are often critical of the manner in which a program is being executed. In light of this, it can be said that most significant for the fate of the Jews and for our understanding of the character of Germans' attitudes towards Jews is that the misgivings about certain eliminationist measures that did exist among some Germans cannot, by and large, rightly be interpreted as having been expressions of principled disapproval of the eliminationist project and especially of the beliefs that gave birth to it.[173] The principal exception to this is to be found among those Germans who, for various reasons, gave aid to the approximately ten thousand German Jews who tried to escape deportation by hiding. The isolation of these Germans and of others who stood by their Jewish spouses indicates how exceptional they were among the larger German populace.[174] Indeed, with the exception of these people, almost all Germans' criticism of the persecution—and the criticism was overwhelmingly directed at but certain aspects of the persecution—was epiphenomenal. It was epiphenomenal, as these paradigmatic examples show, in the sense that the criticism did not emanate from (and therefore does not signify) Germans' departure from the two fundamental, bedrock features relevant to the fate of the Jews at the hands of Germans during the Nazi period, namely eliminationist antisemitism and its practical consequence, the program to eliminate all Jewish influence from Germany. Those misgivings that Germans did express typically betray their authors' acceptance of the essence of the Nazified view of Jews. If many Germans had dissented from the cognitive model of Jews described here, then there can be no doubt that we would know about it, because we, in fact, do know about their dissent regarding the treatment of other groups. During the war, the regime's own security service recorded substantial public sympathy for foreign forced laborers and prisoners of war despite the severe penalties that existed for all manner of support or intercourse with them, but virtually none was in evidence for the Jews, even though the extermination was widely known.[175] The entire record of Germany during its Nazi period reveals that Germans' expressions of principled agreement with antisemitism and the eliminationist enterprise was practically limitless, but expressions of principled dissent from either one were but isolated, unusual examples—the voices of lonely criers in a desolate night.

The physical assaults aside, during the 1930s German Jews were subjected probably to more frequent and intensive verbal attacks, more concentrated verbal violence, than any group has ever been by its own society.[176] Given the horrors that were to come, the significance of the verbal violence is easily, though wrongly, neglected. Yet its effect, the toll that it took on the Jews, and also on Germans, was enormous.

Graffiti on the wall of a Jewish cemetery in Saarbrücken from May 1933 proclaims: "The Jews' death will eliminate the Saarland's misery."

The quantity and intensity of verbal violence, which included the widespread posting of signs (which Germans and Jews saw daily) that forbade Jews' physical and social existence among Germans of given locales and institutions, should be seen as an assault in its own right, having been intended to produce profound damage—emotional, psychological, and social—to the dignity and honor of the Jews. The wounds that people suffer by having to listen publicly (particularly, in front of their children) to such vituperation and by not being able to respond—can be as bad as the humiliation of a public beating.[177] Germans of the time understood this, just as Germans or Americans today do when they confront even a tiny fraction of it around them. All those engaging in or watching these assaults (with any emotions except horror) affirmed their views of the Jews as fit for the most abject humiliations. In an important sense (this is taken up in the next chapter), deportation and physical violence were not a radical break with, but a corollary of, the monumental intended harm that Germans, through the medium of language, perpetrated upon the Jews *constantly*.[178]

Inherent in this barrage of verbal violence and the view of Jews which it expressed was its lethal potential. Some acute observers correctly predicted in the 1930s that the Germans would seek to exterminate the Jews. Already in 1932—before the Nazis came to power, and there was no guarantee that they ever would—the German Jewish writer Theodor Lessing articulated the eliminationist logic that gripped much of Germany. Germans, he predicted, would solve the "Jewish Problem" with violence: "We always seek the easiest way. It is easiest to deny or to eliminate that which is uncomfortable. It would be simplest to kill the 12 or 14 million Jews."[179] It was not, in every sense of the word, the "simplest" solution, but it was the most "final," which is what Lessing actually might have meant here. In 1932, all Lessing could observe was that the Germans' animus towards Jews was such that it could motivate genocidal killing.

The American Jewish literary critic Ludwig Lewisohn was able to grasp the essence of the Nazi project from its initial measures. He dubbed Nazism to be "The Revolt Against Civilization," the title that he gave to his penetrating, prophetic article of 1934. Among many other things, he pointed to the "stabbed in the back" myth which attributed the loss of the First World War to the Jews: "Incredible as it may appear to sane people elsewhere in the world, this myth is *believed*." In light of this and their many other fantasies, he asked, how would Germans tolerate such people to live among them? He concluded: "The whole thing would be more like a ghastly farce if it did not constitute so grave a danger for human civilization, if it were not corrupting the souls and hopelessly addling the brains of a whole generation of the German people. For it is clear today that they will act according to their myths. They have begun. The scapegoat is being slain; the Jew is crucified."[180] In another essay in the same volume, the journalist Dorothy Thompson, having grasped the nature of the eliminationist continuum, suggested that only pragmatic constraints would prevent the Nazis from exterminating the Jews.[181] Thompson understood the eliminationist continuum; she prophesied that forced emigration was, from the Germans' perspective, but the best eliminationist program realistically thinkable under the conditions of the 1930s. She and Lewisohn, unlike most others who refused to believe the evidence of their senses, took the Nazi pronouncements seriously and recognized the eliminationist and genocidal thrust of German racial antisemitism and practice for what they were. Lessing, even though he had not yet seen the post-Weimar persecution of the Jews, understood that a genocidal potential already resided in Germans before Hitler came to power and was able to channel it.

The pre-existing genocidal potential that inhered in Germans' eliminationist antisemitism, and therefore in Germans themselves, can be seen not only in the evaluations of people like Lessing, Lewisohn, Thompson, and the mid-1939 congressional testimony of the American journalist Quentin Reynolds, who predicted the "annihilation" of the Jews in "a complete pogrom."[182] Other sources suggest how broad and deep was the lethality of the antisemitic ideational current. On June 1, 1933, the leading Protestant theologian and biblical scholar, Gerhard Kittel, gave in Tübingen a public lecture, *"Die Judenfrage"* ("The Jewish Problem"), which was subsequently published. In it, he etches clearly the fundamentals of the German cultural cognitive model of Jews that had developed in the nineteenth century and that had now come to power with the Nazis. The Jews, he states as a well-known matter of common sense, are a racially constituted, alien body within Germany. Emancipation and assimilation, rather than rendering the Jews more fit for German society, allowed the Jews to infect the German people with their blood and spirit, with calamitous consequences. What might be the "solution" to the "Jewish Problem"? Kittel considers four. He rejects Zionism, the creation of a Jewish state in Palestine, as impractical. He rejects assimilation, because assimilation is itself a great evil which, by constitution, promotes the pollution of the racial stock. Most significantly, he explicitly considers extermination as a potential "solution": "One can try to exterminate [*auszurotten*] the Jews [pogroms]." Being not yet able to conceive of a state-organized systematic extermination, Kittel considers this "solution" in the light of the model of the pogrom, which leads him to reject extermination as impractical, as a policy that did not and could not work. Kittel therefore settles on the eliminationist "solution" of "guest status" (*Fremdlingschaft*), namely the separation of Jews from their host peoples.[183] That this eminent theologian would publicly contemplate the extermination of the Jews already in June 1933—almost in passing, without any great elaboration or justification, and as a normal, easily discussed option when trying to fashion a "solution" to the "Jewish Problem"—reveals the lethality of the regnant eliminationist antisemitism, and how ordinary its discussion must have seemed to ordinary Germans in the Germany of the early 1930s.

From the same early period of the Nazi ascendancy came statements even more chilling and instructive than Kittel's contemplation of genocidal possibility. A letter of protest from the American chairman of The Universal Christian Council for Life and Work to a high official in the German Protestant Church's foreign office reveals that

colleagues of mine were assured this summer in Berlin by official representatives of the churches that the (German) policy could be described as one
of "humane extermination" . . . Frankly speaking, the Christians of America cannot conceive of any extermination of human beings as "humane".
They find it even more difficult to understand how churchmen in any land
at any time can deliberately lend their influence to the carrying on of such
policy . . . Yet we have been forced to observe, that even before the revolution, when freedom of speech was still a reality in Germany, there were no
protests which reached us from churchmen in Germany against the violent
anti-Semitism of the National Socialists. Since then we have had apologies
for the situation in great number, but no official and few personal statements
which seem to recognize the moral factors involved.[184]

So far gone were these antisemitic, unnamed "official representatives of the
churches" that they did not hesitate to reveal their and their society's exterminatory impulse to visiting prominent American Christians. They appear to
have believed that their American colleagues would understand and approve
of "humane extermination" as a "solution" to the "Jewish Problem," a policy
(at least the extermination part of it) which they rightly knew to be entirely in
keeping with the eliminationist core of the Nazi program. There can be no
mistaking that these locutions had not been meant metaphorically or had been
misunderstood by the Americans. The letter of protest makes it clear what was
at issue, as does the response to the American's letter. If the American's account of the Germans' position had resulted from some confusion or misunderstanding, then the responsible German Church authorities would have
undoubtedly sought to clarify their position, to persuade their American colleagues that these German men of God did not endorse a policy of "humane
extermination." It would have been shaming, alarming, and painful for anyone
who did not advocate such a policy to think that his views and intentions had
been so misrepresented. Instead of penning such a clarification, the German
board member of the High Church Council who dealt with this letter notes,
with obvious contempt for the ineducable Americans, that further correspondence with the American chairman was "no longer practical." The revelation
contained in the American's letter, and in the response to it, provides a further
glimpse into the lethal potential of German eliminationist antisemitism as it
existed in Germany prior to and during the initial months of the Nazi period,
and well before the regime began to implement its exterminatory policies.

The eliminationist ideology, derived from the German cultural cognitive
model of Jews, was at the root of the policies of the 1930s which the German
people supported. The genocidal program of the war was grounded in the
same ideology and set of cognitions. It was a more extreme "solution" to a
problem, the diagnosis of which had long been agreed upon in Germany.
Seen in this light, the leap from supporting the eliminationist policies of the

1930s to supporting a genocidal "solution" is not as great as it has been almost universally supposed to have been.[185] Overcoming the ethical inhibitions to wholesale slaughter of this kind was for some a substantial task. Yet the motivational foundation for such a radical "solution" had long been in place, requiring Germans to have the courage of their convictions and to place their trust in Hitler, their *Führer*, that he indeed would solve the "problem" while ensuring Germany's long-term welfare. It is thus no surprise that as knowledge of mass and systematic killings of Jews spread widely throughout Germany, Germans expressed little more than unease—born of the residual fear that such a frightening measure would be bound to provoke in a people brought up on the commandment "Thou shalt not kill," and of dread at the thought of what those putatively powerful beings, the Jews, would do to them should the Germans fail.[186] The alternative to victory on the battlefield, according to the hallucinatory understanding of the world that the former Hitler Youth, Heck, shared with his countrymen, was "the endless night of Bolshevik-Jewish slavery, [which] was too horrible to contemplate."[187] Equally fearful for Germans to contemplate were the consequences should their nation fail in its program to exterminate the Jews.

These unsurprising yet comparatively slight misgivings aside, ordinary Germans were poised in 1939 to have their racial antisemitism channeled in a genocidal direction and *activated* for a genocidal enterprise. Did their antisemitism and eliminationist ideology prepare them to take their convictions to their logical, most radical extreme? Would they, when finally confronted with the "evil" that most of them had known only from afar, be willing to expurgate it in the only manner that would be "final"? The theoretical framework elucidated here for understanding antisemitism suggests that they would have, because such a "solution" had as its ideational foundation the same demonized view of the Jews that underlay the various highly popular measures of the 1930s which the regime and ordinary Germans in all walks of life had already taken in order to degrade and immiserate Jews and to exclude them from German society. Yet the theoretical assessment alone is not sufficient. An empirical investigation is also necessary. That is why, after an analysis of how eliminationist antisemitism informed the evolution of Nazi anti-Jewish policy, a detailed examination is undertaken of the actions of such ordinary Germans when they were thrust into the exterminationist enterprise. That ordinary Germans were possessed of racial, demonological antisemitism cannot be doubted. How powerful a motive force was this common property? How would it induce them to act when they would be asked to become willing genocidal killers?

PART II

The Eliminationist Program
and Institutions

This people must disappear from the face of the earth.
HEINRICH HIMMLER, "SPEECH TO THE LEADERS OF THE NAZI PARTY,"
POSEN, OCTOBER 6, 1943

4

THE NAZIS' ASSAULT ON THE JEWS:
ITS CHARACTER AND EVOLUTION

ALTHOUGH HITLER and the Nazis' eliminationist desire was, even
before their ascension to power, clear and constant, the evolution of
their immediate intentions and actual policies towards the Jews was
not linear and unambiguous. This is not surprising. A regime had come to
power determined to undertake a task—the elimination not only of Jews
from all spheres of social life in Germany but also of their putative capacity
to harm Germany—that was enormously complex and difficult, and that was
without precedent in modern times. It was a task, no less, that had to be carried out under a variety of constraints and concurrently with competing, if
not conflicting, goals. The Nazis had assumed power under trying circumstances in the middle of a depression, beset by hostile outside powers and
with a number of revanchist and revolutionary goals in mind. To expect any
regime, especially when operating in this setting, to have pursued the goal of
eliminating Jewry from Germany, from Europe, from the world, without any
twists and turns of policy, without any tactical compromises, without pragmatic adjustments, without deferring long-term goals in favor of short- or
medium-term gains in other areas, is to have unrealistic expectations of the
nature of governance. It is to attribute to the Nazis a prodigious capacity to
carry their ideals into practice, their preferences into policy outcomes.

The course of the Nazis' assault on the Jews inevitably did not conform to
this idealized, caricatured view of how preferences are turned into policy.
Their anti-Jewish policy was indeed characterized by seeming inconsistencies

and by conflicts among competing loci of deliberation and of power. Focusing on the manifest policies, however, has led some to conclude that the evolution of the Nazis' policy was incoherent, that no one was in control, that the decision to annihilate the Jews was but the outgrowth of unwanted, contingent exigencies, had little to do with the intentions of the Nazi leadership or of Hitler, and was not organic to the Nazis' worldview. These views are erroneous. Nazi policy towards the Jews was eminently coherent and goal-directed.

The Nazis based their intentions and policies throughout on an articulated, shared understanding of Jews, namely their eliminationist, racial anti-semitism. When it is recognized that the eliminationist ideology—which provided a diagnosis of the perceived problem and which implied a variety of possible practical "solutions" to it—underlay the Nazis' thinking and actions, then the contours of their policies towards Jews appear far less enigmatic, far more deliberate, far easier to understand for what they were: *a concerted yet flexible and necessarily experimental attempt, born of conscious intent, to eliminate putative Jewish power and influence as thoroughly and finally as possible.* It was conscious because it was openly and frequently articulated, concerted because it was pursued consistently and devotedly by so many people, experimental and flexible because of the unmapped territory within which, and the practical constraints under which, the Germans had to conceive, forge, and execute the policy. In fact, in light of all of the constraints and uncertainties governing the policies, the Nazis were *remarkably consistent*, more consistent than it has generally been recognized in recent scholarship, more consistent than might reasonably have been expected.

Demonstrating this *and* making sense of the Nazis' anti-Jewish policies require that some issues be reconceived and a new interpretive framework be used.[1] So before examining the evolution of Nazi policy towards Jews, some conceptual and analytical issues need to be addressed briefly. The notion of "intentionality," the relationship of Hitler to his followers, and the manner of assessing the degree to which a set of actions are consistent—important matters all—have been, and are likely to continue to be, subjects of explicit and implicit dispute, so it is worth pausing over them for clarification.

Germany during the Nazi period had a political system that was both dictatorial and consensual, dictatorial in that no formal mechanisms—such as elections—existed to check Hitler's power or to remove him from office, consensual in that the people who staffed the institutions of the political system, as well as the broader German public by and large, accepted the system and Hitler's authority as desirable and legitimate.[2] Within this broad consensus, differences and conflicts over many issues, including Jewish policy, existed within the political system, for three principal reasons. First, constraints were real, leading to compromise steps and the deferral of policy preferences until propitious circumstances appeared or could be created. Second, Hitler's often non-interventionist leadership style created a great deal of leeway for subordinates, often in different institutions and with somewhat different ideas, to design the policies.[3] The third reason was the natural tensions and inconsistencies that emerge whenever a new, difficult, nationwide enterprise is undertaken in which competitive institutions (in this case, with confused and overlapping jurisdictions) within the political system participate without a central (let alone powerful) organ of control.[4]

Finally, regarding Nazi Jewish policy, as if these three features of the political system did not already promise to produce inconsistency, the eliminationist ideology was compatible with a variety of "solutions," and virtually all of them were unprecedented and difficult to implement. All of this led the people fashioning and executing the anti-Jewish policy, the central tenets of which they agreed upon, to vary on the details of the policy, on how the policy was to be pursued in light of other policy goals, on which aspects of it were to be treated as short-, medium-, or long-term features, and on the speed with which each such portion ought to be introduced. It is no wonder that the Nazis groped towards the "solution" to their "Jewish Problem."

These features of the Nazi system complicate the attempt to understand what the Nazis' intentions were for disposing of German and European Jews and, whatever their intentions were, what considerations moved them to adopt the actual policies and measures that they chose. The current prevailing analytical strategy for addressing these issues has been to build a plausible developmental sequence, not only of policies but also of intentions, which is based on the measures that were being pursued *at each moment*, and at what the various protagonists seemed to have known about the intentions behind the measures. Every stage of this sequence is then explained by the political, institutional, territorial, and military configurations of the moment, which are understood to have been shaping the intentions and actions of the relevant actors. This method reveals much about the micro- and meso-level conceptualizations and deeds of the actors, yet when not supplemented by a broader interpretive framework, it produces conclusions that are biased towards situational and material factors, that tend greatly to overplay the significance of tertiary deviations from the general thrust of policy, and that lose sight of the overall character of Nazism and the Nazis' eliminationist Jewish policy. Ground-level perspectives are highly instructive—and necessary—but they are only a supplement to, not a substitute for, the aerial overview.

Keeping these interpretive and explanatory difficulties in mind, the approach here is grounded in the following:

Any evaluation of these events must begin with Hitler. However much more we would like to know about Hitler's deliberations and role, it is nonetheless clear that Hitler, having made the crucial decisions himself, was the prime mover of the persecution that culminated in genocide.[5] Moreover, two things can be said with certainty. First, Hitler *never* wavered from his eliminationist precepts and intent, which he articulated publicly already on August 13, 1920, in a speech, "Why Are We Antisemites?" To his listeners he proclaimed that the first step is to recognize the Jews' nature, following upon which an organization must arise "which one day will proceed with the deed; and our resolve to execute that deed is unshakably firm. It is called: The removal of the Jews from our *Volk*."[6] Second, Hitler's "unshakable" constancy provided the framework for German policy towards the Jews. (He never seriously considered or proposed that Germans could live together in harmonious peace with Jews.) The constancy of Hitler's eliminationist resolve is not surprising in light of his early and unchanging evaluation of the severity of the Jewish threat. The danger was so great—as he declared in 1920 at a public meeting before 1,200 people—that he would shrink from nothing in order to get rid of the Jews. He declared ominously, ". . . we are animated with an inexorable resolve to seize the Evil [the Jews] by the roots and to exterminate (*auszurotten*) it root and branch. To attain our aim we should stop at nothing, even if we must join forces with the Devil."[7] Hitler was proclaiming, in stating his willingness to "join forces with the Devil," that he would do whatever was necessary, even adopt highly unconventional and tabooed means, in his quest to eliminate the Jews. Hitler's use of the idiom of total extermination was anything but a slip of the tongue. The central question, then, is: How did Hitler give his constant eliminationist intent concrete formulations for action in light of changing opportunities and constraints and of his own competing values and goals?

If the issues at hand are to be fathomed, then a set of distinctions must be made and kept in mind. "Ideals" are the optimal images a person has of what is desirable in a world unencumbered by the constraints of social and physical existence. "Intentions" are the real-world plans that people formulate under a variety of real or possible conditions and constraints. "Policies" are the courses of action that a person actually decides upon at a specific moment for a given set of existing conditions and constraints. None necessarily reflects either of the others perfectly. Unless blocked by barriers, a person's intentions tend to follow his ideals, and his actions, namely the policies he pursues, tend to be formulated in order to achieve his intentions. Nevertheless, ideals often are wildly at odds with any achievable reality. Intentions, therefore, often approximate the ideals on which they are based but poorly, because a person makes reasonable concessions to reality. And policies often barely reflect intentions, not to mention ideals, because the formulation of courses of action must make still greater concessions to reality than even the formulation of prudential intentions. Moreover, policies may be formulated with a variety of competing ideals and intentions in mind, in which case it might *seem* that certain existing, even determined intentions might not be held by the person. It is thus possible for someone to have an ideal of a world free of Jewish influence, to have the fervent intention of bringing about such a world when propitious conditions develop, yet to pursue policies, even changing policies, that do not promise to effect such change because he judges the achievement of the ideal, the fulfillment of the intention, as simply not feasible for the moment. For a person to bide his time, while pursuing a set of interim or less than wholly satisfactory policies, is a rational, prudent response to insurmountable obstacles. Such a course of action is not incompatible with holding such ideals and ultimate intentions. It thus fails to constitute evidence for the absence of either.

In light of this, the following can be said about the overall course of the Germans' persecution and slaughter of the Jews: Hitler was the driving force behind the anti-Jewish policy. In the first few years of his rule, he settled for compromise "solutions" to the "Jewish problem" because of the apparent immediate or even long-term impossibility of "solving" it as he might have wished. All of the "solutions" that he and his subordinates pursued derived directly and immediately from the same diagnosis of the problem, as articulated by his eliminationist racial antisemitism in one of the most frequently intoned slogans of any kind during the Nazi years: "Jew perish." The Germans' policies towards Jews were but variations on the common eliminationist theme. Although the variations produced enormously different consequences for the victims, they were rough functional equivalents from the vantage point of the perpetrators: They had the same meaning for the perpetrators and sprang from the same motive, which is the crucial element for explaining the course of the persecution. The same cultural cognitive model of Jews informed them all, and this model provided the rationale, the fearsome energy, and the essential direction for all of the measures.

Distilling the essence from the broad array of the Germans' policies towards German and European Jews reveals that the policies shared two important features and objectives:

1. To turn the Jews into "socially dead" beings—beings that were violently dominated, natally alienated, and generally dishonored—and, once they were, to treat them as such.[8]
2. To remove the Jews as thoroughly and permanently from social and, as far as possible, from physical contact with the German people, and thereby to neutralize them as a factor in German life.

These two features were constant components of the Germans' Jewish policy, whatever the actual measures were. The belief in the desirability of these goals composed the anti-Jewish policy's axioms, its underlying cognitive model.

The implementation of these objectives included a number of changing policies and measures, some of which overlapped temporally. They included:

1. Verbal assault.
2. Physical assault.
3. Legal and administrative measures to isolate Jews from non-Jews.
4. Driving them to emigrate.
5. Forced deportation and "resettlement."
6. Physical separation in ghettos.
7. Killing through starvation, debilitation, and disease (prior to the formal genocidal program).
8. Slave labor as a surrogate for death.
9. Genocide, primarily by means of mass shootings, calculated starvation, and gassing.
10. Death marches.

None of the Germans' major policies towards the Jews was divorced from either of the two central objectives of the anti-Jewish policy: producing the "social death" of Jews and removing their presence and influence from the German dominion. Nevertheless, three policies stand out as having contributed simultaneously and symbiotically to both objectives: the verbal assault on Jews, the physical assault upon them, and the legal and administrative restrictions placed upon them. Certainly, by 1939 the Germans had succeeded in rendering the Jews socially dead within German society.

The most consistent, frequently acted upon, and pervasive German governmental policy was one which, although recognized and discussed, is rarely analyzed as having been an integral feature of the Germans' anti-Jewish policy. Constant, ubiquitous, antisemitic vituperation issued from Germany's public organs, ranging from Hitler's own speeches, to never-ending installments in Germany's radio, newspapers, magazines, and journals, to films, to public signage and verbal fusillades, to schoolbooks. The effect of this incessant antisemitic barrage upon Germans' cognitions about Jews has already been discussed in the previous chapter. Here it is worth pausing to emphasize its political and social purpose. It was above all an expressive act, the statement of Hitler's and his followers' innermost beliefs, which included a declaration of their intent to free Germany from the Jews' putative destructive yoke. This verbal violence was meant to be heard not only by Germans but also by Jews. Its intent was to buttress the Germans' beliefs and to terrorize the Jews. These terrorizing measures served the emotionally satisfying purpose of plunging the Jews into fear and the programmatic goal of inducing them to leave Germany and, it was hoped, once gone, to leave it alone. The verbal assault contributed, as much as any other policy, to transforming the

Jews into socially dead beings, beings who were seen to be owed few if any moral obligations by Germans and who were conceived of as being thoroughly dishonorable, indeed incapable of bearing honor. One Jewish survivor records this aspect of Nazi policy during the aftermath of the April 1 boycott: "The barrage of propaganda was directed against the Jews with undiminished vehemence and intensity. In ceaseless repetitions, it was hammered into the heads of the readers and listening audience that the Jews were subhuman creatures and the source of all evil. . . ."[9] Perpetrating verbal violence upon the Jews was an integral part of both of the major Hitlerian objectives of rendering the Jews socially dead (thus preparing Germans for still more drastic eliminationist measures) and, by inducing them to emigrate, of reducing their influence over Germany.

A second policy pursued throughout the life of Nazism, though in the 1930s only intermittently, was the assault upon the Jews' bodies. The regime perpetrated, encouraged, or tolerated violence against Jews, which in the 1940s became part of the Jews' everyday existence, could erupt at any moment even during the 1930s. It took the form sometimes of impromptu physical attacks and ritualistic degradation by local officials, and sometimes of centrally organized campaigns of violence, terror, and incarceration in concentration camps. As has already been discussed, the physical assaults, similar to the verbal violence, announced to everyone that the Jews were beyond the moral community, and that they would best absent themselves from Germany. The assaults also suggested the dire fate that might await the Jews.

A third German policy towards the Jews was the ever-increasing, legally and administratively promulgated social separation of Jews from Germans. Of all of the policies, this was the most closely related non-verbal analogue to the verbal violence; unlike most of the anti-Jewish measures that they eventually adopted, Germans put this into effect almost from the moment of the Nazis' assumption of power and never relented from this program, which they intensified as the 1930s and 1940s wore on. The progress of the gradual, systematic exclusion of Jews from all spheres of society—the political, social, economic, and cultural—was as grinding as the hardship that it created for Jews was punishing.[10] The Germans began to exclude Jews from governmental service one week after the April 1, 1933, boycott, with the Law for the Restoration of the Professional Civil Service of April 7, and from many of the professions in the ensuing weeks.[11] The Germans' exclusion of Jews from the economy proceeded throughout the first years of the regime as the economic health of the country permitted, and then with increased vigor in 1938.[12] On September 22, 1933, the Germans removed Jews from the cultural spheres and the press, which many deemed to be especially "poisoned" by Jews. During the life of the regime, the Germans proscribed virtually all aspects of general Jewish intercourse with Germans, as well as important Jewish religious practices, publishing a deluge of restrictive laws regulating what Jews might or might not do. They prohibited Jewish ritual slaughter soon after the Nazi era began on April 21, 1933, which, because it was a defining practice of Jewry, could be understood only as a declaration that Jewishness itself was a violation of the order and moral norms of society. All told, Germans witnessed the promulgation of almost two thousand laws and administrative regulations that degraded and immiserated the country's Jews, in a manner and degree that no minority in Europe had suffered for hundreds of years.[13]

The signal legal event in this tightening chain of restrictions was the announcement of the Nuremberg Laws of September 1935, which together with subsequent decrees defined legally who was a Jew, providing for the first time a clear national understanding of which people were to be subject to the laws and decrees regulating Jews. Faithful to the racial foundation of the dominant worldview and understanding of Jews, the definitional criteria relied essentially upon bloodlines and not religious identity. Thus, the laws of Germany deemed to be Jews those people who (owing to their or their parents' conversions) were Christians if a requisite portion of their ancestry was Jewish—no matter that they might have no psychological or other social identification with things Jewish.[14] The Nuremberg Laws also stripped Jews of citizenship and, with enormous symbolic as well as practical import, proscribed new marriages and extramarital sexual relations between Jews and non-Jews. All of the laws, regulations, and measures of the 1930s served to rob Jews of their livelihoods, to sink them into a state of hopelessness, and to isolate them from the larger society in which they had moved freely but a few years earlier. They made Jews socially dead.

Starting on September 1, 1941, the social isolation of the Jews within Germany, the marking of them as socially dead beings, was further intensified and symbolized by the government regulation compelling German Jews to wear in public a sizable yellow star of David inscribed in black with the word *"Jude."* The effects of this were obvious. Branding Jews publicly in this manner furthered their already great humiliation; wearing such a visible target among such a hostile populace also caused Jews to feel acute insecurity, and, because any German passerby could now identify them easily, Jews, especially Jewish children, suffered increased verbal and physical assaults. One Jewish woman from Stuttgart recalls: "Wearing the yellow star, with which we were branded from 1941 onwards as if we were criminals, was a form of torture. Every day when I went out in the street I had to struggle to maintain my composure."[15] The introduction of the yellow star also meant that all Germans could now better recognize, monitor, and shun those bearing the

mark of the social dead. Not surprisingly, a standard feature of German occupation policy around Europe was to force Jews to wear the degrading yellow stars and badges.[16]

This social separation, with all of its contributing components, and the
verbal (and also the physical) violence were complementary and mutually reinforcing in their effects. While the verbal violence proclaimed to Germans
and Jews alike the moral caesura separating them, the laws and regulations
declared and enforced a physical and social gulf. Together, they turned the
Jews into socially dead beings, into *de facto* inhabitants of a leprous community, a community against which anything might and could be done. Together, they also made Jewish practical and existential life in Germany so
inhospitable, difficult, and degrading that German Jews fled the country in
droves. Of the 525,000 Jews living in Germany in January 1933, almost
130,000 emigrated during the next five years. By 1938, even the most self-
delusionary of Jews had to admit to themselves that Jews could not live in
Germany; the pace of emigration picked up during 1938–1939, when an additional 118,000 emigrated, choosing to go by this time to any country that
would admit them. Slightly over 30,000 Jews managed to flee Germany after
the war began.[17] The Germans thus succeeded in forcing over half of the
Jews of Germany to leave—usually forfeiting virtually all of their property,
belongings, and wealth—what had been to them a beloved homeland.

While Hitler's *ideal* throughout the 1930s remained the elimination of all
Jewish power, his immediate *intentions*, reflected in the Germans' policies,
were scaled down to the more modest goal of making Germany *judenrein*, free
of Jews. It was the most effective, even if ultimately unsatisfying, policy that
could have been pursued under the international conditions of the 1930s.
The encircled, weak Germany of this period could not have undertaken more
radical measures without risking a war that it could not yet hope to win. Germany, during the 1930s, was pulling itself out of an economic depression,
rearming itself, and, through diplomacy and force of arms in the second part
of the decade, winning territorial and foreign policy victories—the *de facto*
abrogation of the restrictions of the Versailles Treaty, the remilitarization of
the Rhineland in 1936, the annexation of Austria in March 1938, and the dis-
memberment of Czechoslovakia in 1938 and 1939. A systematic, all-out
physical assault upon the Jews of Germany threatened to prevent Germany
from rebuilding its strength, the most essential precondition for Hitler to realize his various apocalyptic aims, including the vanquishing of world Jewry.
Even had Hitler and his compatriots decided to ignore these formidable constraints in pursuit of the annihilation of German Jewry, the victory would
have been pyrrhic. It would not have provided a "final solution" to the "Jewish Problem," for it would have left world Jewry barely weakened. Paul Zapp,

who was to become the commander of *Sonderkommando 11a*, which slaughtered Jews in the southern Ukraine and Crimea, articulated this self-evident "truth": "One can first conceive of the absolute cleansing of the Jewish question when one succeeds in striking decisively at world Jewry. The political and diplomatic leadership of Adolf Hitler has built the foundation for the European solution of the Jewish question. From this vantage point the solution to the world Jewish question will be tackled."[18] "International Jewry," believed to be manipulating both the Soviet Union and the western democracies, especially the United States, could have been expected to mobilize itself and the rest of the world to defeat and destroy Germany.[19] Hitler expected that an ultimate reckoning with the Jews would eventually take place; yet the time and conditions for it should be of the Germans' choosing.

Killing the Jews of Germany in the 1930s, even if it had been possible, would, given the compass of Hitler's goals, have been premature and ultimately self-defeating. Hitler and the Nazis were firmly in the grip of a hallucinatory ideology, but they were not madmen. They were extraordinarily adept at achieving their goals, at reconstructing German society and the international environment to conform with their ideals. Had Hitler and his compatriots wanted with all their hearts to slaughter every last Jew at the moment of their ascension to power, everything about the calculating manner in which they proceeded in the 1930s, and even during the war, regarding matters other than the Jews suggests that they would not have done so, choosing instead to bide their time, until the time was ripe.

So the German government coolly settled temporarily for the complementary eliminationist policies of legally and administratively isolating the Jews within Germany and of pressuring them to emigrate. The policies, coordinated from above, proceeded apace, restrained only by the domestic considerations of maintaining the appearance of legality and ensuring as non-injurious an extraction as possible of Jews from the economy, and by the constraints of world opinion and its effects upon Germany's standing and prospects.[20]

Kristallnacht, the nationwide pogrom of November 9–10, 1938, was an event of enormous significance. The Germans' measures taken until then had not succeeded in completely removing the Jews from their country, so it was time to become more severe, to send an unmistakable message and warning: Leave, or else. In this sense, *Kristallnacht*—the nationwide assault on the Jews' persons, on their livelihoods, and on the central symbols and structures of their community—was an unsurprising next step for the Nazi regime.[21] It was also an ominous portent of the future. With *Kristallnacht*, the Germans made clearer than ever two things that everyone could discern: the Jews had no place in Germany, and the Nazis wanted to spill Jewish blood. To destroy a community's institutions is psychologically almost the same and almost as satisfying as destroying its people. As a general "cleansing" of Germany of Jewish synagogues, *Kristallnacht* was a proto-genocidal assault.

After *Kristallnacht*, the Germans' eliminationist enterprise steadily evolved more comprehensive and deadly immediate intentions and corresponding policy measures. Yet at many steps along the way, Hitler and his compatriots were not entirely sure how best to implement their eliminationist intentions, and to develop appropriate policies and plans. The changing strategic situation on the traditional battlefield and on the one with the Jews, and the uncertainty and difficulties of having to implement what was becoming a continent-wide eliminationist program, the likes of which had never been seriously conceived or attempted, made planning difficult. How, then, can the course of the Germans' anti-Jewish policy after *Kristallnacht* best be understood?

The policies that the Germans subsequently implemented were articulated by *Das Schwarze Korps* two weeks after this nationwide orgy of violence, after this psychic equivalent of genocide.[22] In an editorial, this official newspaper of the SS, the institution which more than any other organized and implemented the eliminationist and exterminationist measures, declared ominously: "The Jews must be driven from our residential districts and segregated where they will be among themselves, having as little contact with Germans as possible. . . . Confined to themselves, these parasites will be . . . reduced to poverty. . . ." Yet, according to this organ of the SS, this would not be enough. There was to be a next stage. The editorial continued:

> Let no one fancy, however, that we shall then stand idly by, merely watching the process. The German people are not in the least inclined to tolerate in their country hundreds of thousands of criminals, who not only secure their existence through crime, but also want to exact revenge. . . . These hundreds of thousands of impoverished Jews [would create] a breeding ground for Bolshevism and a collection of the politically criminal subhuman elements. . . . In such a situation we would be faced with the hard necessity of exterminating the Jewish underworld in the same way as, under our government of law and order, we are accustomed to exterminating any other criminals—that is, by fire and sword. The result would be the actual and final end of Jewry in Germany, its absolute annihilation.[23]

It is not known whether or not this was the Germans' actual long-range policy at this moment, even though the first part of *Das Schwarze Korps'* editorial was clearly expressing the sense of a high-level meeting of November 12, 1938, where the assembled considered how they ought to dispose of Germany's Jews. Göring, who, on Hitler's orders, had convened this meeting, in which Reinhard Heydrich played a prominent role, himself indicated that war would be calamitous for the Jews: "If the German Reich should in any foreseeable future get involved in a foreign conflict, it goes without question that we in Germany also will in the first place think of carrying out a great reckoning with the Jews."[24] *Das Schwarze Korps* was enunciating a framework that extrapolated from known intentions and from current measures to a plausible, desirable future; it was delineating a conceivable, measured, step-wise escalation of the unquestioned eliminationist program, each step being but a different measure in consonance with the reigning eliminationist anti-semitism.[25] That it bespoke the Nazis' fundamental intentions was attested to by the British consul in Germany. A few days prior to *Das Schwarze Korps'* editorial, a senior member of Hitler's Chancellery, in discussion with the British consul, "had 'made it clear that Germany intended to get rid of her Jews, either by emigration or if necessary by starving or killing them, since she would not risk having such a hostile minority in the country in the event of war.' The official had added that Germany 'intended to expel or kill off the Jews in Poland, Hungary and the Ukraine when she took control of those countries.' "[26] A few days after *Kristallnacht*, on November 21, Hitler told the South African Economics and Defense Minister that in the event of war, the Jews would be killed.[27] Less than three months later, on the anniversary of his assumption of power, Hitler echoed these more elaborated genocidal warnings with a pithy prophecy. On January 30, 1939, in a speech before the Reichstag which was subsequently published in the Party's principal newspaper, *Völkischer Beobachter*, and in a special pamphlet, he first explained how the Jews had laughed at his previous "prophecies" only to watch them come true. Then he declared: "Today I will once more be a prophet: if the international Jewish financiers in and outside Europe should succeed in plunging the nations once more into a world war, then the result will not be the Bol-shevizing of the earth, and thus the victory of Jewry, but the annihilation of the Jewish race in Europe!"[28]

It must be emphasized that, like the editorial in *Das Schwarze Korps*, this was not the announcement of a program which was immediately to be made operational and implemented. It was a clear declaration of Hitler's ideal and, given the opportunity, his intent, a declaration that he was willing to make not only to his inner circle but also in a speech to the German nation and in seri-ous discussion with foreign leaders. The relationship between a general war and the extermination of the Jews was sealed in Hitler's mind.[29] Yet, with the outbreak of the war, other developments had to occur for his firm intention to become feasible. Still, it was obvious that military conflict would lead Hitler to adopt policies towards the Jews that were still more dire than those of the 1930s. That Hitler and other Nazis were at the very least bandying about the idea of a genocidal "final solution" at that time is as clear as their unmistakable words. That wholesale killing of those deemed unfit for human cohabitation was or would shortly already be part of their policy repertoire became evident with the initiation of the so-called Euthanasia program in October 1939.[30]

It is highly implausible to maintain that Hitler and those who implemented the so-called Euthanasia program set out to kill, by the tens of thousands, non-Jewish Germans with mental illness but did not consider, let alone believe with religious-like certitude, that the Jews—conceived of as being far more malignant and dangerous—ought to share this fate. Those whom the Nazis marked for slaughter in the "Euthanasia" program (aside from the small percentage of Jews among the victims), if conceived of as being "life unworthy of living," were nevertheless thought to be far less of a threat to Germany than were the Jews. The congenitally infirm and insane imperiled the health of the nation in two ways: by their potential for passing on their maladies to new generations through propagation and, second, by consuming food and other resources.[31] But this was child's play compared to the putative threat of the Jews, who—unlike the "Euthanasia" program's victims—were considered to be willfully malignant, powerful, bent upon and perhaps capable of destroying the German people *in toto*. Until the Jews were stamped out, Germany would be afflicted by their plague. As Hitler put it, "countless illnesses are caused by one bacillus: the Jews!" It followed that "we will become healthy when we eliminate the Jews."[32] To believe that Hitler and other Nazi leaders would have undertaken the "Euthanasia" program and not want to have done the same to the Jews is to believe that the same person who would kill a bedbug would prefer not to kill the black widow, but to let it continue to live somewhere in his house—or within striking distance next door.[33]

Hitler's and other Germans' bold warnings and prophecies notwithstanding, September 1939 was not yet a propitious time to undertake a program of exterminating the Jews. So they searched, indeed groped for the best possible interim "solutions" under constantly changing geostrategic conditions. Until they began to execute a program of systematic extermination in the summer of 1941, this search was an uncertain one, conducted simultaneously by uncoordinated and often competing institutions.[34] It consisted in the main of various considerations and measures to isolate, ghettoize, "resettle," and let the Jews diminish in number through starvation and its associated maladies—essentially the first of the two phases that had authoritatively been mapped out by *Das Schwarze Korps* after Göring's meeting.

While legal isolation within Germany and emigration abroad were both the maximal feasible and the actual eliminationist strategies in the 1930s, the conquest of Poland presented still greater eliminationist opportunities, of which Hitler and his followers were happy to take advantage. In two senses, more "final" solutions could now be hatched: Germans controlled or expected soon to conquer various territories that could be used as a dumping ground for a vast number of Jews, and they now had within their physical grasp not just hundreds of thousands of Jews but millions.

No doubt, not everyone in the German leadership saw their suzerainty over so many Jews purely in terms of "opportunity," for the disposal of so many Jews posed enormous practical problems and created day-to-day difficulties for those charged with Jewish affairs.[35] Nevertheless, the prospect of ridding Europe of the millions of Jews under German control was not an unwanted burden but a redemptive chance to be seized. The opportunities inflamed the imaginations of those fashioning proposed "solutions" to consider more extreme and permanent policy measures, measures that were actually in greater harmony with their antisemitic eliminationist ideals. Omnipotent musings and policy proposals to move vast populations around the European landmass, to transform peoples into Helotic masses, and to decimate threatening or unwanted peoples came naturally and easily to the Nazified mind.[36] The Jews, the central demonic figures in the Nazi eschatology, inevitably fared badly when Germans gave free rein to their eliminationist sensibilities, to their dreams of reconstructing the social landscape and "human substance" of Europe, and to their "problem"-solving inventiveness.

Yet how could the Germans eliminate the nearly two million Jews in the German-occupied part of Poland as well as the more than one million additional Jews living under German domination?[37] Only two possibilities existed: to deport all of them to some designated region, or to kill them. In 1939 and 1940, genocide was not a feasible undertaking. The killing of German and Polish Jews would not have "solved" the problem, as the Nazis conceived of it. Yet even if Hitler had wanted to opt for such a risky partial "solution," other compelling reasons cautioned against it. Hitler had an uneasy live-and-let-live non-aggression pact with the Soviet Union. Soviet troops were stationed in the heart of Poland and would have immediately become aware of a genocidal assault upon Polish Jewry. Given Hitler's belief that the Jews were all-powerful in the Soviet Union, that Bolshevism was more aptly called "Jewish-Bolshevism"—because Bolshevism was, in Hitler's words, "a monstrous product of the Jews"[38] and but a tool in their hands—a genocidal onslaught against Polish Jewry would, given Hitler's worldview, likely have sparked a war with the Soviet Union before Hitler was prepared for it. Moreover, to the extent that Hitler was still considering a separate peace with England, he could expect such plans to have been scuttled were Germany to undertake the mass extermination of Jewish civilians.[39] As long as Germany had to reckon with the responses of other powerful countries, genocide was not a practical policy.

Immediately upon Poland's capitulation, Heydrich issued on September 21, 1939, an ominous order authorizing the ghettoization of Polish Jewry. Heydrich began the order by distinguishing between long-term goals and interim measures:

> A distinction must be made between.
>   1. the final goal (which will require a lengthy period) and
>   2. the stages towards the achievement of this final goal (which can be carried out on a short-term basis).
> The measures envisaged require the most thorough preparation both in the technical and in the economic sense.

Heydrich then declared:

> I. The first preliminary measure for achieving the final goal is the concentration of the Jews from the countryside in the larger cities. It must be speedily implemented.[40]

It was not so speedily implemented; yet ghettoization did take place broadly throughout Poland in 1940 and the spring of 1941.[41] Whatever the unstated "final goal" was, this order, together with the barrage of legal restrictions that the German occupation authorities placed on the Jews, signaled the resolute German intention that the Jews soon would no longer be permitted to dwell within the society of German-occupied Poland.[42] Whatever the "final goal" would be—which could have meant only mass deportation or extermination—concentrating the Jews was to have been a preliminary step that would facilitate the implementation of any of the conceivable future German eliminationist policies. The top civil administrator of the Łódź District, Friedrich Übelhör, in discussing in December 1939 the planned ghetto in Łódź, articulated the general understanding that existed regarding the relationship between short- and long-term goals, and the pre-genocidal nature of Heydrich's order: "The creation of the ghetto is, of course, only a transition measure. I shall determine at what time and with what means the ghetto—and thereby also the city of Łódź—will be cleansed of Jews. The final goal, at any rate, must be that we burn out this bubonic plague utterly."[43]

Given that in 1939 and 1940 genocide was not yet practical (and might not have been for the foreseeable future because of the geostrategic situation), Hitler and his subordinates turned to the next best "solution": plans of mass deportation. A few plans for transferring the Jews out of these regions, especially out of the Warthegau, the Polish territory now incorporated into the

Reich, were proposed, entertained for a while, and even begun to be implemented before the Germans abandoned them. The two most comprehensive proposals that received some serious consideration were, first, to create a "reservation," a dumping ground, for the Jews in the Lublin region of eastern Poland and, second, to ship them all to Madagascar. None of the proposals for mass deportation, including these two, was anything but, in Leni Yahil's phrase, a "phantom of a solution," namely an interim step on the road to genocide or, put differently, a form of bloodless genocide. Those fashioning these schemes did not conceive of these prospective dumping grounds as habitable environments where Jews could make new lives for themselves. Their temper of mind was revealed by the then District Governor of Lublin in November 1939, who suggested that the "district with its very marshy character could . . . serve as a Jew-reservation [*Judenreservat*], a measure which could possibly lead to a widespread decimation [*starke Dezimierung*] of the Jews."[44] The proposed reservations were to be, at best, enormous prisons—like the walled-in ghettos that the Germans were to construct for Polish Jewry— consisting of economically unsustainable territory, in which the Jews, cut off from the rest of the world, would slowly die off. Those hatching the plans, by and large, were well aware that the proposed destinations were woefully insufficient in resources for the Jews that they expected to cram into them. There is, furthermore, especially in the case of Lublin, no evidence that such deportations would have been anything but a way station for the Jews, until the Germans were ready for their final disposal.

September 1939 through the beginning of 1941 was not an interlude in the prosecution of the eliminationist enterprise,[45] but a period of eliminationist *experimentation* that produced a series of measures ultimately unsatisfactory to the Germans; they were not feasible as "final" solutions. The central eliminationist policies of this period included the initial systematic killing of some Jews in the fall of 1939, the establishment of ghettos, especially the two largest ones in Warsaw in November 1940 and in Łódź earlier that year in April, the decimation of Jewish health and life through calculated starvation,[46] and the groping around for a more comprehensive relocation of the Jews into some distant area that would be an enormous ghetto that could eventually be transformed into an enormous cemetery.

Already in the 1939–1941 period, the Germans had no long-term intention of keeping the Jews within their dominion alive—either where the Jews then lived or in some distant land—and in many ways they were already eagerly treating the socially dead Jews more apocalyptically, as if a collective death sentence had been passed. This period sealed the fate of the Jews in the sense that Hitler's subordinates began to fashion concrete plans for a "final solution," a "solution" that admitted no place for Jews not just within the

German Reich but within an expanded and ever-expanding German dominion. Before this, the elimination of the Jews from the European landmass had been an ideal to be discussed in programmatic, though wishful, terms; now, with the new opportunities, the Germans immediately began more concrete planning: during this period, the *best* intended fate for the Jews was that they would be placed in hermetically sealed, economically unviable leper colonies that would not receive adequate food supplies—which was psychologically and ideologically the functional, if not the eventual actual, equivalent of genocide.

With the planning of the war against the Soviet Union in the first half of 1941, Hitler's thinking about the immediate disposition of the Jews changed. Unlike in the previous twelve to fifteen months, when all kinds of proposals for "solving" the "Jewish Problem" were floated, during early 1941 this inventive eliminationist search came to a halt. All these earlier ruminations regarding less final "solutions" were now rendered moot by Hitler's turn to the most "final solution" imaginable.[47] By this time, Hitler had given up on invading or striking a separate peace with Britain, and was turning eastward for a final accounting with the Soviet Union and Jewry. After all this time, the opportunity existed for Hitler to fulfill his prophecy, to make good on his promise that a war would result in the annihilation of the Jews of Europe. Sometime either at the end of 1940 or in early 1941, Hitler resolved finally to turn his ideal into reality, and made the *decision* to kill all of European Jewry.[48] The evidence indicates that by the end of January 1941, Heydrich, having been charged by Hitler to develop a suitable plan, submitted his proposal for the Europe-wide "Final Solution project" (*Endlösungsprojekt*).[49]

It is no coincidence that during this time Hitler referred publicly to his January 30, 1939 prophecy. Yet for the first time, his reference took the form not of a prediction of some development in some indefinite future, but of a firm intention that would be carried out shortly. On January 30, 1941, the eighth anniversary of his assumption of power and precisely two years after enunciating his apocalyptic "prophecy," he reminded the nation that he had "pointed out that should the other [*sic*] world be plunged into war by Jewry, the whole of Jewry will have played out its role in Europe. They [the Jews] may also laugh about it even today, just as they laughed earlier about my prophecies. *The coming months and years* will prove that I have been right [my emphasis]."[50] Just less than three months earlier, on November 8, 1940, Hitler had referred to his "prophecy" as something that was still off on the horizon.[51] Yet now, on January 30, 1941, he could say that he would begin to play it out in "the coming months." He also, at this time, stated for the first time something that he had not said before, and that he was to repeat during later references to his prophecy while the Germans were in the process of exterminating European Jewry. Now that he had decided to implement his genocidal wish, he could taunt the Jews, just as he would later do while his followers were killing them *en masse*. He was now confident of the outcome: Let the Jews laugh, he declared publicly, just as they had laughed at his earlier prophecies. Hitler had taken the decision. He was sure that he would be laughing last.[52]

With Hitler having finally decided upon the only policy that was fully satisfactory to his eliminationist ideal, new eliminationist institutions soon became prominent. While verbal assaults, legal restrictions, and ghettos—the central institutions of the anti-Jewish policy through 1941—all remained part of the Germans' policy repertoire, they were now superseded in importance by the execution squad, concentration and "work" camps, and the gas chamber.

During the spring of 1941, the Germans planned and prepared for a dual assault on the Soviet Union. Greatly different in the scope, complexity, and the number of men and resources to be used, the vastly larger military campaign and the smaller exterminatory one were intertwined, parallel operations in Hitler's planning. The institutions charged with the execution of the two—the armed forces having been primarily responsible for the former, and the SS having been chiefly responsible for the latter—signed, prior to the invasion, a jurisdictional and operational agreement, and then cooperated closely in the field.[53] Units of each were assigned to the four geographical areas into which the Germans divided the conquered Soviet territory from north to south. The armed forces, the *Einsatzgruppen* (see below), and the other security forces all understood that this war was not to be a war like other wars; it was not to be a war of mere military conquest, but one in which the opponents—for the armed forces, the Soviet army and state; for the *Einsatzgruppen*, the Jewish people—were to be vanquished utterly, destroyed, obliterated from the face of the earth.

In order to conduct the genocidal campaign against the Jews, Himmler, as the chief of staff of the genocidal cohort, set up four mobile *Einsatzgruppen* that would spearhead the wholesale slaughter. Each was subdivided into a number of smaller units, called *Einsatzkommandos* and *Sonderkommandos*. The organized mass killing of Jews, initially conducted mainly by them, although other police and security units also participated, began in the first few days of Operation Barbarossa, the Germans' code name for the assault on the Soviet Union. Although the evidence regarding the *Einsatzgruppen*'s initial orders and how these orders subsequently changed is ambiguous, the best interpretation of the evidence indicates the following developments.

In the days before the attack, Heydrich and his direct subordinates addressed the officers of the *Einsatzgruppen* on two different occasions, first in

Berlin and then at the *Einsatzgruppen*'s staging ground for the upcoming campaign in Pretzsch.[54] The *Einsatzgruppen* officers were told of their duties, which consisted broadly of securing the conquered rear areas behind the ever-advancing army. This job required that they identify and kill leading representatives of the Communist regime, anyone who might foment and organize resistance against the German occupation.[55] They also learned of Hitler's decision to exterminate Soviet Jewry.[56] Walter Blume, the commander of *Sonderkommando 7a*, describes the momentous scene: "Heydrich himself explained that the Russian campaign was imminent, that partisan war was to be expected, and that in this region many Jews lived who had to be exterminated through liquidation. When one of those assembled called out: 'How are we supposed to do this?' he said, 'You will find out.' He explained further that Eastern Jewry, as the breeding ground [*Keimzelle*] of World Jewry, was to be annihilated. There was no mistaking it that all Jews were supposed to be exterminated, without regard to age or sex."[57] This decision was a *strategic* one with an open-ended, still-to-be-hammered-out battle plan, the tactical details of which would be transmitted to the *Einsatzkommandos* in accord with the demands of the unfolding events.[58] As the reservations of Otto Ohlendorf, the commander of *Einsatzgruppe D*, about the planned mass shootings indicate, he and other *Einsatzgruppen* officers were leery that their men would not have the stomachs to carry out such gruesome orders, and that the deed would also brutalize them, rendering them unfit for human society.[59]

For this reason, it made sense for *Einsatzkommando* leaders to have discretion in the initial phase of implementing the genocidal order. They could, as one tack, try to enlist local Lithuanians, Latvians, or Ukrainians to do the dirty work. This spared the Germans from carrying out such gruesome tasks, and it served to strengthen the resolve of the Germans to kill so many unarmed people by letting them witness the "just" revenge of the local peoples, who ostensibly had suffered at the hands of these Jews. Using local henchmen was encouraged by Heydrich in written orders to the *Einsatzgruppen*,[60] for, as the perpetrators themselves understood it, "the purpose of this measure was to preserve the psychological equilibrium of our own people. . . ."[61] The *Einsatzgruppen* officers also could habituate their men into their new vocation as genocidal executioners through a stepwise escalation of the killing. First, by shooting primarily teenage and adult Jewish males, they would be able to acclimate themselves to mass executions without the shock of killing women, young children, and the infirm. According to Alfred Filbert, the commander of *Einsatzkommando 9*, the order from Heydrich "quite clearly" "included also women and children." Yet, "in the first instance, without a doubt, the executions were limited generally to Jewish males."[62] By generally keeping units' initial massacres to smallish numbers (by German standards) of a few hundred or even a thousand or so, instead of many thousands, the perpetrators would be less likely to become over-whelmed by the enormity of the gargantuan bloodbaths that were to follow. They also could believe that they were selectively killing the most dangerous Jews, which was a measure that they could conceive to be reasonable for this apocalyptic war. Once the men became used to slaughtering Jews on this sex-selective and smaller scale, the officers could more easily expand the scope and size of the killing operations.[63]

Another, probably more important determinant of the stepwise imple-mentation of the genocidal order was two related considerations. The Ger-mans were expecting to vanquish the Soviet Union in short order, so there was no immediate rush to destroy the Jews. For this reason, Himmler was content to leave the scaled-down, early implementation of the policy to a force sufficient in size to this task, though undermanned for the larger geno-cidal undertaking. The *Einsatzgruppen* were initially composed of about three thousand men. As Himmler, Heydrich, and the *Einsatzgruppen* lead-ers themselves well knew, these mobile killing squads were too small to suc-ceed in an immediate all-out slaughter of Soviet Jewry.[64] Thus, at the beginning of July, on the occasion of the first killing operation of *Ein-satzkommando 8* in Białystok, its commander, Otto Bradfisch, told one of his subordinates that although the *Kommando* had to "pacify" the conquered areas, it "did not have to do it so thoroughly, because larger units would fol-low that would take care of the rest."[65] Second, the program of utter anni-hilation was a novel enterprise which required that the Germans feel their way, that they learn through experimentation how to organize the killing operations logistically and what the most effective techniques were. After all, no models existed for the unprecedented undertaking. It is no wonder, therefore, that they began with a smaller than ultimately desirable and nec-essary force, which would blaze the way for the soon-to-be-expanded geno-cidal cohorts in the form of additional SS and police units. In the first few weeks, the *Einsatzkommandos* were the equivalent of genocidal scouting par-ties, developing the methods of killing, habituating the perpetrators to their new vocation and, generally speaking, working out the feasibility of the overall enterprise.[66]

The first *Einsatzkommando* killing operation occurred on the third day of Barbarossa, when a *Kommando* of *Einsatzgruppe A* shot 201 people in the Lithuanian border town of Garsden, most of whom were Jews. In the next days and weeks, the *Einsatzkommandos* orchestrated a host of mass slaughters of Jews. Some they perpetrated themselves; some they perpetrated in conjunction with locally organized auxiliaries; and for some they allowed such locals, especially in Lithuania and the Ukraine (with German guidance) to slaughter Jews by the hundreds and thousands in pogrom-like rampages and massacres.[67]

Under the eyes of German soldiers, Lithuanians beat Jews to death in Kovno at the end of June 1941.

The Germans, together with their Lithuanian henchmen, slaughtered thousands of Jews in Kovno (Kaunas) in the last days of June and first days of July; in Lvov, the Germans, together with Ukrainians, killed a few thousand

Jews.[68] The first large mass shooting that the *Einsatzkommandos* carried out by themselves was probably in the Ukrainian city of Lutsk on July 2, where the men of *Sonderkommando 4a* shot over 1,100 Jews, although this was preceded by an orgy of killing perpetrated by the German Police Battalion 309 in Bia-łystok on June 27.[69] A great deal of variation characterized the technique of these early killing forays because the Germans were experimenting, seeking to devise an ever better exterminationist formula. Himmler, like a good commanding general, traveled around the killing fields in order to inspect the troops. He consulted with his officers and even once observed a killing operation in Minsk.[70] The reports that Himmler received from the *Einsatzgruppen* and his own inspection trips to the area provided him with evidence that the initial genocidal forays had been successful insofar as they demonstrated that the men could bring themselves to kill Jews *en masse* and that the techniques for such killing were sufficient. He thus ordered an expansion of the embryonic genocidal killing to unrestrained genocidal slaughter.[71]

A remarkable aspect of this transition to wholesale slaughter was how "normal" it was to the men of the *Einsatzkommandos* and the other units that were contributing to the genocide. In their postwar testimony, the killers hardly remark upon the expansion of the scope of the killing to include women, children, and the aged, or the increased size and speed of the slaughter. The perpetrators in these units certainly did not see either of these changes—the increased scope and tempo of their killing operations—as being a fundamental alteration in their task, as constituting a qualitatively different assignment. These Germans do not say: "At first we were killing only 'Jewish Bolsheviks,' 'saboteurs,' or 'partisans,' and then all of a sudden we were told to annihilate entire communities, including women and children." Although some speak of their unease upon receiving their initial orders to kill and realizing what they were being asked to do, or of the shock of their initial killings, as a rule the Germans report this escalation and expansion of the slaughter—if at all—in neutral tones, which is not surprising, for, though it was a new, somewhat different task, it did not fundamentally alter the Germans' understanding of what they were doing. For this reason, the change is typically not even mentioned by the perpetrators at all.[72] Himmler, ever the pragmatist, had initially detailed the *Einsatzkommandos*, as a prelude to the full battle, to engage in probing forays in order to test their mettle and hone their tactics against the enemy; when this baptismal phase was over, he sent them on the all-out, full-frontal assault, an assault whose essential outline and purpose they had known would be soon in coming. The transformation was as little noticed and as little worthy of comment as the reception by army soldiers of orders to launch a new offensive action in a war that they had already been fighting.

One man who does mention the expansion of the killing was the chief of personnel of *Einsatzkommando 9*. He maintains that at first the *Kommando*'s killing of Jews was restricted to males, and was expanded to include women and children in the second half of July. He is sure that Filbert, the commander, had informed them of their execution orders *before* the attack on the Soviet Union. Yet, he is unsure whether Filbert "had spoken of 'all Jews' or only of the 'male Jews.' "[73] The subsequent inclusion of women and children among the slaughtered was obviously but an *operational* development, not a fundamental alteration in the understanding of the men of *Einsatzkommando 9* of what they were doing. Had it been otherwise, then this man and others would surely have remembered whether the initial order had meant that they were contributing to the extermination of all of Soviet Jewry or just of the Jewish men. That this man and men in other *Einsatzkommandos* and police battalions which killed Jews in the Soviet Union testify that their commanders had informed them of the order to exterminate Soviet Jewry, *either before the attack on the Soviet Union or during its first few days*, is conclusive evidence that such a general order was given, and that Hitler had taken the genocidal decision before Barbarossa commenced.[74]

Even if the interpretation put forward here of the *Einsatzgruppen*'s exact initial order is wrong—even if those who doubt that an order for the total extermination of Soviet Jewry was at first issued are correct, and the initial order was to kill "only" teenage and adult Jewish males—the order was still genocidal and clearly was understood by the perpetrators as such. The men of Police Battalion 307, for instance, already in the first half of July, received the order to round up Jewish males in Brest-Litovsk between the ages of sixteen to sixty. They managed to assemble between six thousand and ten thousand Jews, whom they then shot because of their "race."[75] The killing of the adult males of a community is nothing less than the destruction of that community, especially when the women are forbidden to bear children (in the unlikely event that the Germans would not have also shortly slaughtered them). With the preparation for the military attack on the Soviet Union, Hitler and his subordinates had crossed the psychological and moral Rubicon to genocide—and the die was cast for all of European Jewry. All that was left was for the Germans to devise the operational plans, organize the resources, and implement the genocide on a full scale.[76]

The second stage of operationalizing the genocidal plan required additional manpower, which Himmler assigned to the various Higher SS and Police Leaders (*HSSPF*) in the Soviet Union under whose jurisdiction the *Einsatzgruppen* operated. With Himmler's alteration of their operational orders, the *Einsatzkommandos*, together with SS, police, and even army units, began to perpetrate gargantuan massacres, which systematically decimated entire Jewish

154   HITLER'S WILLING EXECUTIONERS

communities. The photographs below show two scenes of the Germans' annihilation of the Jews from the ghetto Mizoč on October 14, 1942. In the first
photograph, Jewish women and children huddle together naked as they await
their execution. In the second photograph, two Germans wade among some of
the dead in order to administer another bullet to anyone still alive after the initial salvos, such as the woman who is raising her head and upper body.

A sample of the Germans' slaughters included 23,600 Jews in Kamenets-
Podolski on August 27–28, 1941; 19,000 in Minsk, divided during two different massacres in November 1941; 21,000 in Rovno on November 7–8, 1941;
a total of over 25,000 Jews near Riga on November 30 and December 8–9,
1941; 10,000 to 20,000 in Kharkov in January 1942; and, in the largest single
shooting massacre, more than 33,000 over two days at Babi Yar on the outskirts of Kiev at the end of September 1941.

While conceiving or preparing the attack on the Soviet Union, Hitler finally made the transition to the genocidal policy variant of the eliminationist
ideology, which had long lurked in his mind. During the actual assault, it became clear to the involved Germans, officers and enlisted men alike, that the
eliminationist ideology was finally to be implemented in its most uncompromising, logical form. Although it is not known for sure, it is most unlikely that
Hitler decided to annihilate Soviet Jewry without at the same time deciding

Einsatzkommandos *force Jewish women from the Mizoč Ghetto to undress
before executing them.*

Their corpses after the execution. Two of the German killers finish off the women who survived the initial shooting with individual shots to the head.

The execution ravine at Babi Yar

that the moment had come to exterminate all of European Jewry as well. Given his conception of the "Jewish Problem," it would have made no sense whatsoever to do the job only halfway. The time had come for making good on his prophecy and promise for the destruction of European Jewry; moving to an exterminationist "solution" for Soviet Jewry entailed the same "solution" for all Jews.[77]

Not surprisingly, the actual *operational* planning for the Europe-wide expansion of the extermination program began at the very latest around the time, in mid to late July, that Himmler changed the *operational* orders of the *Einsatzgruppen* by increasing the tempo of the Germans' killing of Jews in the Soviet Union.[78] At this point, after a few weeks into the genocidal onslaught against Soviet Jewry, after the *Einsatzgruppen* had demonstrated the feasibility of systematic mass slaughters, and after the *planning* for the attack on Soviet Jews had been completed, Himmler, the Nazi leadership, and the SS could turn their attention to the implementation of the genocidal decision across the continent, to the bringing of Nazi reality closer to Nazi ideals. Until then their energies and attention had been taken up in the planning, organizing, and implementing of the genocide in the most important and first operational area. Once the mass slaughter began in the Soviet Union, attention could be diverted to the rest of Europe, and the extension of the killing elsewhere was but a matter of operational detail, logistics, and timing. The Germans had to concern themselves only with practical matters of organizing the genocide and with doing so in a manner that would be harmonious with their other strategic, economic, and transformative objectives (even if this would not always be easy). Drawing on the experience that they were accumulating in the Soviet Union, they realized that they needed to consider some changes in their mode of operating.

Himmler's assessment that the institutions and the men were up to the genocidal task was proving to be correct, for they were killing Jews and effacing Jewish communities in the Soviet Union at a furious pace. Yet the officers in the field and also the higher leadership were becoming dissatisfied with the method of slaughter; however dedicated to their goal the Germans manning the killing squads were, the seemingly ceaseless slaughtering of unarmed men, women, and children was taking a psychological toll on some of them. Ohlendorf's intuitive apprehension, upon learning of the genocidal decision, that perpetrating such slaughter would not be good for the Germans involved was partly being borne out.[79] Himmler, ever solicitous of the welfare of those who were turning his and Hitler's apocalyptic visions into deed, began to search about for a means of killing that would be less burdensome to the executioners. In the spirit of their initial, then rejected attempts to kill Soviet Jews by engineering "pogroms," and of their stepwise escalation of the slaughter of Soviet Jews, the Nazi leaders, as they always had, continued to be willing to employ tactical flexibility in pursuit of their strategic objective. After some experimentation with other means of killing and the development of mobile gas vans, which the *Einsatzkommandos* and other Germans used to kill tens of thousands of Jews, the Germans constructed permanent gassing installations.[80] The move to gassing, whether in mobile or fixed installations—contrary to the widely accepted belief—was prompted not by considerations of efficiency, but by the search for a method that would ease the psychological burden of killing for the Germans.[81] Permanent gassing installations were preferable to mobile ones because they had a greater killing capacity, they allowed the Germans to conduct the killings out of sight of the unwanted onlookers that had routinely watched the *Einsatzkommando* slaughters in the Soviet Union, and they could house installations for the disposal of the bodies—a task that had been a problem for the two itinerant institutions of killing: shooting commandos and gas vans.

The preparations for the next operational phase of the genocidal program took place from the summer of 1941 into the first months of 1942.[82] The most significant developments were the erection of death camps. The Germans experimented with Auschwitz's initial "small" gas chamber on September 3, 1941, using Zyklon B (hydrogen cyanide) to kill about 850 people, 600 of whom were Soviet prisoners of war. Systematic gassing of Jews began at Auschwitz-Birkenau in March 1942. The first fixed gassing institution to become operational on more than an experimental basis was Chełmno, in which, using gas vans, the Germans began killing Jews from Łódź on December 8, 1941. Gassing began at the *Aktion Reinhard* death camps in 1942, in Bełżec on March 17, in Sobibór in early May, and in Treblinka on July 23. The Germans located the death camps in Poland primarily because Poland was the demographic center of European Jewry, which made it logistically the most practical site for these mass extermination facilities.[83] They also situated each of the death camps strategically, intending that each would consume the Jews of designated regions. The Germans killed the Jews of the Warthegau at Chełmno, the two million Jews of the *Generalgouvernement* at the three *Aktion Reinhard* camps of Bełżec, Sobibór, and Treblinka, and the Jews of western, southern, and southeastern Europe at Auschwitz.

With the plans and the installations already well in development, and after many preparatory meetings and measures, Heydrich finally assembled representatives of the relevant administrations together in Berlin at the Wannsee Conference of January 20, 1942, where he informed them of their duties in the ongoing extermination of European Jewry, which would total eleven million. For the same reason that Hitler had not been content to re-strict the genocidal killing to the Soviet Union, the apocalyptic intentions re-vealed by Heydrich to the others were not confined to Jews currently within the Nazi dominion. On the itemized list of the intended German victims were the Jews of Turkey, Switzerland, England, and Ireland. No half mea-sures were acceptable once this apocalyptic enterprise became realizable.[84]

Within a year after the initiation of the *Aktion Reinhard* slaughter of Pol-ish Jewry living in the *Generalgouvernement*, the Germans had killed 75 to 80 percent of their eventual Jewish victims. *Aktion Reinhard* itself consumed the lives of approximately two million Polish Jews, through *Einsatzgruppen*-style mass shootings and mainly in the gas chambers of Bełżec, Sobibór, and Tre-blinka, the last having been the destination of the Warsaw ghetto's inhabitants. By this time, Auschwitz had claimed hundreds of thousands of victims from around German-occupied Europe. All told, the Germans had slaughtered, mainly by shooting and gassing (in gas vans), over two million Jews in territo-ries that they had seized from the Soviet Union. During this period, the ex-terminationist option of the eliminationist anti-Jewish program was given priority over other German goals. The Germans, both the leadership and those implementing the plans, pursued the Jews' destruction with a single-mindedness that, as a rule, shunted other objectives aside. Now that the pri-mary achievement of a Germania free of the putative timeless Jewish threat was in sight, the tactical compromises that had previously been made to other important goals were no longer deemed necessary and occurred ever less fre-quently. Annihilating European Jewry became, with the war and at times even of higher priority than the war, the central mission of the German juggernaut.

Coincidental to the rising exterminationist tempo was the great expan-sion of the camp system and the number of Jews and non-Jews condemned to its horrors. The Germans began to employ slave labor, mainly non-Jews, in greater numbers as the war economy's labor shortage became ever more acute. In contrast, the employment of Jews in economic production, never an important part of the Germans' disposition of Jews, counted ever less weightily in their deliberations, although the growing acuity of the labor shortage made it ever more *economically* essential that they be used for pro-duction. This is significant because it demonstrates unequivocally that the priority given to the extermination of the Jews, both by Hitler and the Nazi leadership, as well as to those commanding and staffing the concentration camp and "work" camp system, was so great that the Germans willfully de-stroyed irreplaceable and desperately needed Jewish labor and production, and thereby further imperiled their prospects of military victory. The de-struction of the Jews, once it had become achievable, took priority even over safeguarding Nazism's very existence.[85]

Nazis' Master Plan for the Extermination of European Jewry

(1942 borders are shown)

Arctic Ocean

Norwegian Sea

North Atlantic Ocean

FINLAND 2,300

SWEDEN 8,000

NORWAY 1,300
Oslo

Helsinki

Leningrad

Stockholm

ESTONIA "Free of Jews"

USSR* 5,000,000
*Includes White Russia and the Ukraine

Moscow

North Sea

DENMARK 5,600
Copenhagen

Baltic Sea

Riga

LATVIA 3,500

WHITE RUSSIA 446,484

IRELAND 4,000

UNITED KINGDOM 330,000
London

NETHERLANDS 160,000

LITHUANIA 34,000

Minsk

BIAŁYSTOK DISTRICT 400,000

GERMANY 131,800
Berlin

Warsaw

EASTERN TERRITORIES 420,000

English Channel

BELGIUM 43,000

Paris

FRANCE Occupied Territory 165,000

BOHEMIA AND MORAVIA 74,200
Prague

Vienna

GENERAL-GOUVERNEMENT 2,284,000

UKRAINE 2,994,684

88,000

SLOVAKIA

AUSTRIA 43,700

Budapest

HUNGARY 742,800

FRANCE Unoccupied Territory 700,000

18,000

SWITZERLAND

Zagreb

CROATIA 40,000

Sarajevo

Belgrade

SERBIA 10,000

ROMANIA 342,000

Bucharest

Black Sea

PORTUGAL 3,000

Madrid

SPAIN 6,000

Marseilles

ITALY 58,000

Rome

Adriatic Sea

BULGARIA 48,000
Sofia

TURKEY (European Part) 55,500
Istanbul

ALBANIA 200

GREECE 69,600

Athens

Aegean Sea

Mediterranean Sea

0 miles 400
0 kilometers 600

N W E S

© Mark Stein Studios, 1995

The priority of the extermination was so great that it continued to the dying gasps of the regime. Its appropriateness and necessity as *the* "solution" to the "Jewish Problem" was so accepted, internalized, by Germans at all levels who perpetrated the slaughters, that they by and large naturally continued to pursue its goals even as their Nazified world was disintegrating around them. The last major national community of Jews that the Germans decimated was the Hungarian, a good portion of which they deported to Auschwitz in the summer of 1944. The war was clearly already lost, yet between May 15 and July 9 the Germans crammed 437,000 Hungarian Jews into 147 transports of scarce rolling stock, diverted from essential war activities. In the single most concentrated killing orgy at Auschwitz, the Germans immediately killed most of these Jews in the gas chambers, with many more subsequently dying in other German camps and on death marches.[86] The death marches, which are treated in depth in subsequent chapters, were an even greater testament to the will of Germans—of all ranks serving in a range of institutions—to bring about the destruction of the Jews. Beginning with the need to vacate areas imperiled by the Soviet advance in the last months of 1944, and then within Germany itself during the last weeks and days of the war, the Germans sent Jews and non-Jews on forced marches under brutal conditions while depriving them of nourishment. Thousands of Jews died on these marches, both from the Germans' shots and blows and from starvation, exhaustion, and the ravages that they produced on the body. Perhaps nothing illustrates better the fanatical devotion of Hitler and all those engaged in implementing the exterminationist "solution" to the "Jewish Problem" than do the death marches.[87]

Just as Hitler began his suzerainty with verbal tirades and a symbolic eliminationist assault on the Jewish community of Germany in the form of the April 1, 1933, boycott, he ended his rule and his life while his faithful followers slaughtered Jews up to the last moment, proclaiming on April 29, 1945, his testament to the German people, which concluded with the concern that had always been central to Hitler's worldview and his governing project, namely

the true culprit behind this murderous struggle: Jewry! I have also not left anybody in the dark about the fact that this time it would not only be millions of children of Europeans from the Aryan nations who will die of hunger, not only millions of grown men who will suffer death, and not only hundreds of thousands of women and children who will burn to death in the cities and be permitted to be bombarded to death, without holding the true culprit responsible for his crime, even though it be by more humane methods. Above all I pledge the leadership of the nation and its followers to the scrupulous observation of the racial laws and to an implacable opposition against the universal poisoner of all peoples, international Jewry.[88]

Whatever they sound like to us, it would be a mistake to dismiss these as the words of a desperate madman facing death. In fact, they reveal Hitler's long-standing ideals, his hopeful intentions, and the foundation of every feature of his eliminationist program, whatever its momentary policy measures were. They were words that expressed the beliefs that had infused a country and its people with energy and guidance during a twelve-year pursuit of the expurgation of the Jewish people from any influence over Germany. They were the most significant words that Hitler believed that he could bequeath to the German people so that, as the words had in the past, they might command, guide, and inspire Germans for future action.

CONCLUSION

The moment that the opportunity existed for the only "final solution" that was "final," Hitler seized the opportunity to begin to bring about his *ideal* of a world forever freed of Jewry and made the leap to genocide. This occurred when the prospect appeared of conquering what the Germans considered to be, together with Poland, the wellspring of Jewry, the Soviet Union. When the correlations are made of the Germans' anti-Jewish measures with their deduced or imputed intentions, Hitler's hypothesized psychological states and moods, and the Germans' military fortunes, the correlation that stands out, that jumps out, as having been more significant than any other (than *all* of the others) is that Hitler opted for genocide at the first moment that the policy became practical. That the Nazis implemented and considered other policies up to this point in no sense indicates that they deemed any of these policies to be preferable or superior. They decided upon these policies under conditions that did not lend themselves to a final genocidal accounting with world Jewry. Before 1941, Hitler and the Nazi leadership did, however, consistently seek out and implement extreme, utterly radical eliminationist measures, consistently taking advantage of new opportunities to fashion more comprehensive and more "final" plans. Explaining the course of the Hitlerian anti-Jewish policy can best be done not by focusing on the structure of the system or by giving enormous weight to Hitler's and other Nazis' alleged moods allegedly deriving from the successes or failures of their attempts to conquer and reshape Europe, but by taking Hitler's stated ideals and ultimate intentions seriously.[89] The unfolding of the Germans' eliminationist enterprise—in which every major German measure against the Jews conformed to its assumptions and goals—can be explained in the most obvious of ways, as the product of Hitler's and the socially shared, deeply held antisemitic eliminationist convictions and ideals, operationalized in light of changing opportunities and strategic considerations. The essence of the eliminationist program and its development can be encapsulated by a simple statement of the four causally interrelated aspects of Hitler's, and therefore of Germany's, anti-Jewish policy:

1. Hitler expressed his obsessive eliminationist racial antisemitism from his earliest days in public life. Indeed, his first published political writing was devoted to antisemitism,[90] as was his final testament to the German people. Eliminationist antisemitism was the linchpin of his worldview, as stated in *Mein Kampf* and repeatedly elsewhere. It was the single most consistent and passionately held aspect of Hitler's political thought and expression.

2. Upon assuming office, Hitler and his regime, in keeping with Hitler's prior pronouncements, turned the eliminationist antisemitism into unprecedented radical measures and pursued them with unceasing vigor.

3. Before the outbreak of the war, Hitler announced, and then during the war repeated many times, his prophecy, indeed his promise: the war would provide him with the opportunity to exterminate European Jewry.[91]

4. When the moment was ripe, when the opportunity appeared, Hitler carried out his intention and succeeded in slaying approximately six million Jews.

The genocide was the outgrowth not of Hitler's moods, not of local initiative, not of the impersonal hand of structural obstacles, but of Hitler's ideal to eliminate all Jewish power, an ideal which was broadly shared in Germany. Rarely has a national leader so openly, frequently, and emphatically announced an apocalyptic intention—in this case, to destroy Jewish power and even the Jews themselves—and made good on his promise. It is remarkable and, indeed, almost inexplicable that interpreters today could construe Hitler's prophecy, his oft-stated intention to destroy the Jews, to have been meant but metaphorically or to have been but meaningless verbiage. Hitler himself clearly looked back on his January 30, 1939, "prophecy" as having been a firm statement of intention, and repeatedly said so, as if to make sure that he would not be misunderstood. Contrary to those who would dismiss Hitler's words, there is every reason to privilege Hitler's understanding of his own intentions, to take the congruence between stated annihilationist intentions and consummated deed at face value.[92]

Hitler had, in fact, indicated prior to the outbreak of war that there were two groups whom he would destroy if war should come: the Jews and the congenitally infirm. Already in 1935, he informed the Chief Physician of the Reich that "the euthanasia problem would be taken up and solved" under the cloak of war.[93] This parallelism between a statement of intention and the subsequent action that was faithful to the pronouncement should be seen as convincing evidence for the existence—on both counts—of Hitler's annihilationist intent *and* of his patience to wait for the opportune moment for the implementation of his pre-existing will. What more evidence of premeditation can reasonably be expected?

The will to kill the Jews was not infused into Hitler and his followers by external conditions, but, embedded deep in their beliefs about Jews, it welled up from within them, driving them forward to action when the opportunity presented itself. Demonological racial antisemitism was the motive force of the eliminationist program, pushing it to its logical genocidal conclusion once German military prowess succeeded in creating appropriate conditions. When examining the contours of the course of the Germans' anti-Jewish policy, we should not lose sight of this fundamental truth. Nazi common sense—that the Jews must disappear forever were the millennium to come—was at the root of the genocidal impulse. It energized the sustained, twelve-year attempt to bring about this fevered vision of a Germany and the world freed of all Jewish influence. Not only was it the source of the exterminationist impulse, but Nazi common sense also made genocide the most preferable of all eliminationist options.

5

THE AGENTS AND MACHINERY
OF DESTRUCTION

WHAT DEFINES AN INSTITUTION of genocidal killing? What defines a perpetrator? An institution of genocidal killing is any institution that was part of the system of destruction. A perpetrator is anyone who knowingly contributed in some intimate way to the mass slaughter of Jews,[1] generally anyone who worked in an institution of genocidal killing. This includes all people who themselves took the lives of Jews, and all those who set the scene for the final lethal act, whose help was instrumental in bringing about the deaths of Jews. So anyone who shot Jews as part of a killing squad was a perpetrator. Those who rounded up these same Jews, deported them (with knowledge of their fate) to a killing location, or cordoned off the area where their compatriots shot them were also perpetrators, even if they themselves did not do the actual killing. Perpetrators include railroad engineers and administrators who knew that they were transporting Jews to their deaths. They include any Church officials who knew that their participation in the identification of Jews as non-Christians would lead to the deaths of the Jews. They include the by now proverbial "desk-murderer" (*Schreibtischtäter*), who himself may not have seen the victims yet whose paperwork lubricated the wheels of deportation and destruction.

In most cases, it is easy to decide whether or not certain individuals or categories of people are to be deemed perpetrators. Anyone who worked at a death camp, who was a member of an *Einsatzkommando*, a police battalion, or some other police or civil institution that slaughtered Jews or deported them to death camps, who was in an army unit that undertook genocidal operations, anyone who on his own killed a Jew, knowing that Germany had decided upon a policy of genocidal slaughter, was a perpetrator. What about Germans, police or civilian, who guarded or administered ghettos, those German holding tanks for Jews consigned to extinction? The conditions in many ghettos were themselves deadly, yet they were not formally institutions of genocidal killing. What about the Germans who used Jewish slave labor, knowing (as virtually all of them after 1941 must have) that their work was but a temporary respite before death, particularly those who treated the Jews with great brutality? Even the guards in some German camps, some of which were "work" camps, as brutal as they might have been to Jews, may not have contributed to the deaths of Jews in a direct manner. So how should they be classified? This can obviously be debated. The definition adopted here holds anyone who worked in an institution that was part of the system of brutal, lethal domination, a system that had at its apogee the institutions of direct mass slaughter, to have been a perpetrator, for he knew that by his actions he was sustaining institutions of genocidal killing.[2] The question "Why was he willing to partake in actions that were part of this genocidal program, and to act in a manner that could only hasten the death of these Jews?" or the question "How was this person able to do what he did, knowing that his acts brought Germany closer to the goal of killing the Jewish people?" is as appropriate for those who were the sovereigns and petty tyrants of ghettos as for those who worked in Treblinka. Even though the psychological differences attending these two roles may have been great, they do not make one person a perpetrator and the other not. The differences need only to be accounted for when explaining each person's actions.[3]

The perpetrators operated in an impressive array of institutions and made their contributions to genocidal slaughter in a variety of ways. The gas chambers in the death camps have been the overwhelming focus of popular and even scholarly attention.[4] As horrific as these houses of slaughter devoted to "assembly-line" killing were, the focus on these physical installations has been, from the perspective of analysis, deleterious to understanding in two ways. It has siphoned attention away from the other institutions of killing, the study of which would reveal more about the central questions of the period, and it has also helped to deemphasize the importance of the perpetrators themselves. The monstrous gas chambers and crematoria, together with the "monsters" Hitler, Himmler, Eichmann, and a few others, have become the star villains of this mid-twentieth-century horror. The people who worked in the vast network of camps other than those death camps that were outfitted with mass extermination facilities and, more so, the people who worked the less notorious institutions of killing have largely fallen from view.

This book does not focus on the Germans who worked in the death camps, who were the "desk murderers," or who are on the fringe of the category of perpetrator because, as the ensuing treatment makes clear, such people are not of burning *analytical* importance, their enormous historical importance notwithstanding. The concentration camps, though rarely their personnel, have been the object of a large literature.[5] Unfortunately, the other institutions of killing have received, until recently, little analytical attention.[6] Not until 1981 did a good monograph appear on the *Einsatzgruppen*.[7] It reveals, however, little about the men who served in them. Concerted study of the Germans controlling ghettos has been wanting, the ghettos remaining the province of the memoirists and of those who write about the life of their Jewish inhabitants.[8] Until very recently, the Order Police (*Ordnungspolizei*) has hardly been mentioned in the literature, although its men contributed to the deaths of millions of Jews. The first monograph on one branch of the Order Police, the police battalions, has recently appeared, yet it focuses overwhelmingly on one battalion.[9] Of the other branch of the Order Police, the *Gendarmerie*, which itself was in the thick of the genocide, almost nothing can be learned from the existing literature. Men and women in the various German civil administrations and institutions operating in different countries, especially Poland, contributed substantially to the genocidal slaughter, yet they too have been overlooked. German economic concerns and their personnel also need to be studied in far greater depth than they have been.[10] Only in the last few years have we begun to learn more than the outlines of the genocidal exploits of the German army, yet this too has remained at a too general level.[11] The men and women who were the Jews' masters in "work" camps have remained almost completely faceless. Even the personnel of the SS and its various security forces need to be studied more extensively and in greater depth.[12]

This brief account of the institutions that need to be studied suggests not just how little we know about the perpetrators of the Holocaust. It also suggests that so many institutions and people were involved in the genocidal slaughter. With some hyperbole, it can be said that virtually every German institution in occupied eastern Europe, especially Poland, gave at least a helping hand to the genocidal killing. The number of people who were in these institutions, if the complicit members of the German army are included, ran into the millions, although not all of them contributed directly to the mass killing. This was a huge operation.

The number of people who were actual perpetrators was also enormous.[13] Many hundreds of thousands of Germans were part of the vast system of violent domination in which Jews and non-Jews lived and died. If the men and women using and dragooning slave laborers are included (over 7.6 million in the German Reich in August 1944),[14] then the number of Germans who perpetrated grievous crimes might run into the millions. Of these, the number who became perpetrators of the Holocaust (in the sense that it is meant here) was certainly over one hundred thousand. It would not be surprising if the number turned out to be five hundred thousand or more.

Some figures on the institutions of killing and their personnel, incomplete as they are, convey the magnitude of the German system of destruction. A recent study of all varieties of German "camps" (including ghettos) has identified a total of 10,005 positively, with the full knowledge that many more existed which have not yet been uncovered.[15] Among the ten thousand camps (not all of which housed Jews), 941 forced labor camps designated specially for Jews were within the borders of just (today's) Poland. An additional 230 special camps for Hungarian Jews were set up on the Austrian border. The Germans created 399 ghettos in Poland, 34 in East Galicia, 16 in small Lithuania. So just the known forced labor camps and ghettos reserved for Jews totaled over 1,600. In addition to these, there were 52 main concentration camps, which had a total of 1,202 satellite camps (*Aussenlager*).[16] It is not known how many Germans staffed each of these camps and ghettos. Auschwitz, by itself, with its 50 satellite camps, had 7,000 guards among its personnel at various times.[17] In April 1945, 4,100 guards and administrators were stationed in Dachau alone. At the same time, the Germans had over 5,700 people staffing Mauthausen and its satellite camps.[18] One estimate concludes that 50 guards were necessary for every 500 prisoners in a satellite camp, a ratio of one to ten.[19] If anything resembling this ratio is applied to the more than 10,000 German camps with its millions of prisoners, or even to the smaller number of these camps which housed Jews, it becomes obvious that the number of people manning the system of destruction was enormous.

Turning to itinerant killing institutions, the *Einsatzgruppen* started out with 3,000 men,[20] and people rotated in and out of them. The unit catalogue in Zentrale Stelle der Landesjustizverwaltungen zur Aufklärung nationalsozialistischer Verbrechen in Ludwigsburg (ZStL), includes over 6,000 people among the *Einsatzgruppen*. The thirty-eight police battalions that I have identified as having participated in the genocidal slaughter of European Jews had a minimum of 19,000 men in them, and probably more, because they also had personnel rotations.[21] Three SS brigades, totaling 25,000 men, under Himmler's direct command, slaughtered Jews in the Soviet Union from 1941 to 1943.[22] Unknown thousands of other Germans contributed to the genocide in their roles as administrators of many varieties: railroad officials; army soldiers; police and other security forces who deported Jews from, among other places, Germany and western Europe; and the many who contributed to the slaughter of Jewish slave laborers working under them in production facilities. The ZStL has over 333,000 entries in its catalogue (*Einheitskartei*), which lists the members of the various institutions of killing. It has information on 4,105 institutions involved or suspected of having been involved in Nazi crimes (not only against Jews).

When the number of people who were parties to the genocidal enterprise, who must have staffed these institutions and occupied these roles, is considered, and when the still far larger number who worked in the larger system of domination—the enormous extent of which is only suggested by the 10,000 camps so far identified—is also taken into account, the inescapable conclusion is that the number of Germans who contributed to and, more broadly, had knowledge of this regime's fundamental criminality was staggering. Yet so little is known about them.

THE INSTITUTIONS OF KILLING were organized differently and performed their tasks with different procedures, so the perpetrators operated in a variety of milieus, with different degrees of contact with their victims and by varying routines. It is thus difficult to characterize generally the institutions of killing. Although they differed in a host of ways, they did share one crucial feature, namely that they were institutions that handled (and sometimes housed) beings who were socially dead and considered by the Germans to be evil, powerful, and dangerous. These two German facts about Jews—the first a formal status, the second a social theory that suggested what ought to be done with them—structured the character of the institutions of killing as much as architectural plans did their physical plants.

Social death is a formal status. According to Orlando Patterson, it is the violent domination of natally alienated and generally dishonored people. It is at once a culturally shared conception of the socially dead people and a set of practices towards them. The two are intertwined and mutually dependent. Members of a society conceive of the socially dead as being bereft of some essential human attributes and undeserving of essential social, civil, and legal protections. They do not believe that the socially dead are capable of being honorable. They thus deny them honor, and treat them in a manner that denies them even the *possibility* of receiving social honor, which is a requisite for becoming a recognized and full member of a social community. Since they are socially dishonored beings, the oppressors do not understand them to have many elemental communal rights, including, and most fundamentally, the right to have their kinship ties acknowledged and respected. This is what is meant by natal alienation. In effect, in the eyes of the oppressors, they have forfeited this right. In practice, such ties are not recognized so that, whenever it suits them, the oppressors have the right to, and indeed do, separate families permanently as easily as they would job seekers who happen to be stand-ing on the same street corner. To maintain the socially dead as socially dead, as generally dishonored and natally alienated people, the oppressors must subject them to extreme violence or to the threat of it. Thus, social death is a formal status, denoting any people who suffer these three extreme social dis-abilities. The most well-known category of people who have been socially dead, for whom the term was coined, are slaves, though the universe of the social dead has been inhabited by people other than slaves.[23]

Slaves are socially dead people who, in most slave societies, are conceived of as human and who have utilitarian value, indeed great utilitarian value. In Germany during the Nazi period, Jews were socially dead people—they were violently dominated, natally alienated, and deemed incapable of bearing honor—who were not thought to be a part of the human race, and who were seen to have virtually no utilitarian value. Historically, slaves have not neces-sarily been considered to be evil or to be moral blights. Indeed, it has usually been the opposite. To the majority of Germans, Jews were both. Slaves, gen-erally understood to be useful and morally neutral, are supposed to obey and work. Jews, conceived of in Germany as being evil and destructive to the moral and social order, were supposed to suffer and die. Slaves are to be fed adequately and kept healthy, so that they can produce. Jews were purposely starved, so that they would weaken and die. Each group has been socially dead, yet their oppressors conceived of them very differently and therefore treated them very differently.

In a most fundamental sense, slaves did not suffer complete "social death" (even if the concept was created to account for the character of slavery), be-cause slave societies depend upon slaves for production and even honor. More-over, slaves have often lived within the societies, and some, if not many, of them have had ongoing social relations and ties to the oppressors, including in-timate and even loving sexual relations. Jews were really socially dead. The Germans wanted nothing from them but their suffering and their deaths. They refused to depend on them for production; they would not let the Jews live among them; and they endeavored to sunder all social relations between Germans and Jews (and even between most other "inferior" peoples, such as Poles, and Jews). The difference between slaves throughout history and Jews during the Nazi period was not the formal status of social death, which they shared, but the cognitions which the oppressors had of each. The oppressor's cognition determined the socially dead person's being.

That some people are considered by others to be socially dead, therefore, tells us much, but still very little about how the oppressors treat them. The cultural cognitive models that the oppressors apply to the social dead shape their practices most fundamentally. Given the predominant German cultural cognitive model of Jews, the institutions that they used to house and handle Jews were almost guaranteed to become places of unremitting misery and, when the time came, of death.

The variety of such institutions was large. They therefore cannot all be examined here in detail. However, one of the institutions, the "camp," is worth discussing in general terms because, in many ways, it was the paradigmatic institution of destruction and genocide. Not coincidentally, it was also the emblematic institution of Germany during its Nazi period. The "camp," often called generically, if not entirely precisely, the "concentration camp," had no serious rival for this distinction. It was emblematic because manifold features of camps represented and symbolized distinctive central aspects of Germany during its Nazi period. It was also in the camps that essential aspects of the Nazi German revolution were being carried out and where the character of the future Nazi-dominated Europe could most clearly be seen.

What was a "camp" and what constituted the universe of the camps? A "camp" (to be distinguished from a prison) was any institution of incarceration that housed Jews or non-Jews on a permanent or semi-permanent basis, and which was not fundamentally subject to legal restraint. As ordinary Germans knew, camps were the special new institutions of the regime being put to the special ends described below, ends which were as different from those of prisons as the SS was from the Wilhelmine army. This essential quality was the common feature of the variety of camps that the Germans created, although camps differed in purpose and in the identities of their denizens. These included camps with extermination facilities, concentration camps, work camps, transit camps, and ghettos, to name a few of the varieties.[24]

The camp was the first major distinctively new institution that Nazism founded after Hitler's ascension to power. The camp was Nazism's symbolic act of creation, the first instance of the Nazis' great capacity for destructiveness. In March 1933, on the heels of the fire that destroyed the Reichstag, the regime established a variety of provisional camps to help house the twenty-five thousand people whom they rounded up, mainly Communists, Social Democrats, and trade unionists. On March 20, 1933, Himmler convened a press conference at which he announced the establishment of the first formal concentration camp, in Dachau, to incarcerate five thousand prisoners. The regime, anything but bashful about its violent measures, made no secret of the founding of this novel institution.[25]

The camp was not only the first major, distinctively new institution of Germany during the Nazi period but also—and more significantly—Germany's largest and most important institutional innovation during its Nazi period. The number of camps (more than 10,000) which the Germans established, maintained, and staffed was staggering. They were strewn around the European continent, with the majority located in eastern Europe. Poland alone, the primary site for the vast genocidal slaughter of the Jews, as well as the area which the Germans were transforming into a vast slave plantation, contained over 5,800 camps. Yet, contrary to what much of the scholarly literature suggests, the regime made no serious effort to spare the German people from exposure to these institutions of violence, subjugation, and death. Within Germany itself, within sight of the German people, the regime created an enormous network of camps that saturated the country; this network was a criminal infrastructure of suffering as constitutive and essential to the nature of Germany during the 1940s as was any other aspect of the country's infrastructure—and it did not serve to delegitimize the regime. It is not known how many camps existed in Germany, because the research has not been done. In the small state of Hesse alone, it is known that at least 606 camps—one for every five-by-seven-mile area—gave an apocalyptic shape to the physical and social landscape.[26] Berlin, the country's capital and showpiece, was itself the home to 645 camps just for forced laborers.[27] It would be interesting to ascertain what the mean physical distance was between Germans and a camp, and how little removed the most distant spot in Germany was from a camp.

This mind-staggering network of camps—housing, handling, immiserating, exploiting, and killing millions of innocent, martially and physically unthreatening people—was the largest institutional creation of Germany during its Nazi period. It was the largest not just because of the enormous number of installations, not just because of the millions of people who suffered within its confines, not just because of the vast number of Germans and German minions who worked in and for these camps, but also because it constituted an entirely new subsystem of society.

Modern industrial societies can, according to a variety of schemes, be conceived of as being composed of different "systems."[28] Commonly, society is thought to be constituted of distinct political, social, economic, and cultural systems. The boundaries among these systems are sometimes difficult to determine exactly, and they all interact with one another, yet each contains its own institutions, mode of overall organization, governing rules (formal and informal), and patterns of practice. Each of these systems can also usefully be conceived of as having subsystems of its own. During the Nazi period, Germany, for the first time in western Europe (the Soviet Union had the Gulag), created a distinct, new system in society: the "camp system." It was distinct from the other systems of society insofar as it had its own institutions, its own singular mode of organization, its own highly distinctive governing rules, and its own highly distinctive practices.

The camp system was not subsumed under any of the other systems of society and cannot usefully be thought of as being anything but distinct. During the 1940s, it was at once integral to the working of Germany and yet fundamentally separate from the other systems of the society, in large measure because it housed a violently dominated population which had no place in the other systems' spheres (except, for some, as economically productive slaves). The camp system was so different from the institutions of any of the other spheres of German society, the assumptions on which it rested and which governed its practices were so at odds with those of what passed for the "ordinary" in Germany, that the camp system, while integral to the nature and functioning of Germany during its Nazi period, was a world unto itself. The "camp world" was the largest, most novel, and most significant institutional creation in Germany during its Nazi years. Its dissimilarities were so pronounced and thoroughgoing that its inhabitants might as well have been living on another planet.

The camp system was an ever-expanding world, becoming ever more important, more integral to the workings of the new Germany, ever more its defining trait. If the defining feature of a democracy is often the political system—with its institutions of political representation and its guarantees of certain fundamental liberties—and not, say, the cultural system, then at least one of the defining features of Germany during its Nazi period increasingly became its camp system. It defined Germany because it was within the camp system that many of Germany's most singular and essential practices were carried out and where the true nature of the evolving regime and society was, to a great extent, being forged and could be observed.

The scholarly writing about camps has generally treated them in narrow terms, focusing on their instrumental sides, particularly in their roles as instruments of violence and as sites of economic production.[29] If, instead, the "camp world" is conceived of as having been a *system* of German society, then it becomes evident that a more multifaceted conceptualization of camps is necessary. The essential nature of the camp world needs to be considered, as well as the variety of instrumental practices to which it was put and the expressive practices that took place within it. The camp system had four essential features:

1. It was a world in which Germans carried out certain violent tasks and pursued a set of concrete goals.
2. It was a site of the freest self-expression, where Germans could become masters who were not hemmed in by the bourgeois restraints which Nazism was rapidly superseding with a new anti-Christian morality.
3. It was a world in which the Germans refashioned their victims to conform to their own image of them, thus validating their own worldview.

4. It was a revolutionary world, in which the social transformation and value transmutation that were at the heart of Nazism's program were being most assiduously implemented.

The first three features are discussed below. The fourth is treated in the Epilogue.

THE FIRST FACET of the camp system consisted of the obvious instrumental ends for which camps were used. These were the ends which were understood by all of the Germans participating in the camp system (and millions outside it), and they are the features of camps that are most discussed in the literature: the systematic slaughter of designated enemies, principally of Jews, the enslavement of people, primarily "subhumans," for economic benefit, and the incarceration and punishment of the enemies of the new Germany.

At the apogee of the camp system were the extermination camps of Auschwitz, Bełżec, Chełmno, Sobibór, and Treblinka. In them the Germans constructed extermination facilities for the annihilation of European Jews who composed the overwhelming majority of the victims, and slaughtered them by the hundreds of thousands. The workings of the gas chambers and crematoria are well known, so they do not have to be elaborated upon here.[30] Yet the Germans slaughtered people wholesale in camps other than those which have come to be known as "death camps." After the beginning of 1942, the camp system in general was lethal for Jews. Whether the Germans were killing them immediately and directly in the gas chambers of an extermination camp or working and starving them to death in camps that they had not constructed for the express purpose of extermination (namely in concentration or "work" camps), the mortality rates of Jews in camps was at exterminatory, genocidal levels and typically far exceeded the mortality rates of other groups living side by side with them. Once the German genocidal program was under way, the distinction between extermination camps (which the Germans had constructed expressly for the killing of *Jews*) and non-extermination camps can be seen as having been specious for Jews—though not for other peoples. The monthly death rate for Jews in Mauthausen was, from the end of 1942 to 1943, 100 percent. Mauthausen was not formally an extermination camp and, indeed, it was not for non-Jews, who at the end of 1943 all had a mortality rate below 2 percent.[31] Camps housing Jews did so on a *temporary* basis, because the Germans had consigned all Jews to death. Only the rate of extermination, not the goal, might vary.

If the most arresting major task of camps was the killing of designated groups, this was by no means the only or even the central purpose of the camp system. In a labor-starved war economy, the camp system became above all a world for the economic exploitation of millions of slaves. Slavery accorded perfectly well with the prevailing cosmology and model of humanity in Germany, which held peoples to be unequal in moral worth and capacities. Most of the slave laborers were Slavs, people who, according to Nazi ideology and widespread belief in Germany, were "subhumans," inferior beings fit for such exploitation. Most of them the Germans enslaved in the camp system (many also lived on farms in the German countryside), though the portion of the camp system formally called "concentration camps" housed but a small percentage, at its peak about 750,000, of the millions whom the Germans kidnapped, kept prisoner, and forced to work, under at best difficult and at worst murderous conditions.[32]

If mass annihilation and enslavement for economic exploitation were the camp system's primary ends, it had others. The Germans used the camp system for the incarceration of individuals who worked to defeat them, namely German opponents of Nazism and non-Germans who fought their occupation. It served, both within Germany and in the occupied countries, as a terror institution; everyone knew of the horrific fate that awaited those who, by reason of their deeds or identities, would be thrust into it. The specter of being sent to a "concentration camp" instilled paralyzing fear into many of the small minority of Germans who would have been active opponents of Nazi German domination. Independent of its genocidal and exploitive aspects, the camp system was thus an institution of incarceration, punishment, and terror, used to maintain German domination over subject peoples and over the *small minority* of Germans who, after the initial few years, wished to overthrow the Nazi regime.

The camp system was for its German masters not just a tool for achieving these well-understood ends. It was also—and this is the second feature of the camp system, even if it was not openly described, or by many, probably most, even conceptualized in this manner—a world without restraint, a world in which the master could express in word and deed every barbaric desire, could gain any psychological satisfaction and pleasure that dominion over others might bring. Every German guard was an unquestioned, untrammeled, absolute lord over the camp's inmates. He or she could indulge any urge by degrading, torturing, or killing a camp prisoner at a whim, without fearing or suffering repercussions. He or she could indulge in orgiastic displays of cruelty and gratify whatever aggressive and sadistic impulses that he or she might harbor. The camps thus became institutions in which Germans could indulge and give expression to any ideologically suggested practice, any psychological impetus, by using the minds and bodies of the inmates as instruments of work and objects for every gratification. It was a world without restraint, where the new Germans could express their deeply held hatreds, could practice their mastery over their "inferiors" and their enemies, could give free rein to the Nazi German morality of pitilessness in the application of violence to "subhumans."

Yet the freedom from expressive constraints and the gratification that Germans derived from this freedom were not merely the expression of whatever base impulses that humans may harbor. To be sure, the camp system not only allowed but also promoted the expression of any such tendencies. Yet the Germans' differing conceptions of the victim groups fundamentally shaped their handling of the inmates, providing the underlying framework for the expression of whatever aggressive and sadistic impulses that they might have had. Not surprisingly, the Germans' treatment of the inmates of the camp system varied greatly, roughly according in harshness and brutality with the official and unofficial beliefs about the relative worth of different "races." They treated west Europeans the best, southern Europeans less well, Poles much worse, Russians and other eastern Slavs still worse, and, of the non-Jews, Gypsies most murderously.[33] The Germans' treatment of Jews—who were seen as the secular incarnation of the Devil—was so horrific that it can hardly be compared to that of other peoples. No matter what the purpose, organization, and general practices of a given camp were, Jews, structurally in the same situation as other prisoners, were always made to suffer the most—a fact regularly noted by survivors of the camp world, Jews and non-Jews alike.[34]

The camp system was a world in which the moral rules and practices that governed "ordinary" German society did not apply. In this new world—governed by the Nazi German morality of pitilessness in the application of violence to "subhumans"—Nazi German man and Nazi German woman could treat non-Germans as they saw fit, according to their ideologically informed understanding of their victims and according to their innermost base personal wishes. Nazism, in the location of the camp system, gave them full freedom to so.

The third central feature of the camp system was its transformation of the victims to conform to the Nazi image of them. Since the Germans were helotizing the denizens of the camp world, they, not surprisingly, took many measures to dehumanize them. They robbed the prisoners of their individuality, both because this made it easier to treat them brutally and because they thought it appropriate, in conformity with the moral order of the world—for the Germans did not conceive of the prisoners as meriting the fundamental respect that the recognition of individual personalities confers. Not surprisingly, the Germans typically sheared the inmates' hair, making them more of an indistinguishable mass. Indeed, when robbed of their hair and subjected

to extreme undernourishment, men and women look almost indistinguishable. The Germans almost never took pains to learn the names of a camp's inmates; in Auschwitz, they denied the very existence of a prisoner's name—
this mark of humanity—tattooing each with a number which, with the exception of some privileged prisoners, was the only identifying label used by
the camp's staff. In Auschwitz, there were no Moshes, Ivans, or Lechs, but
only prisoners with numbers like 10431 or 69771.

Dehumanizing each person by robbing him of his individuality, by rendering each, to the German eye, but another body in an undifferentiated
mass, was but the first step towards fashioning their "subhumans." The Germans plunged the camp system's inhabitants into deprived and desperate
physical, mental, and emotional conditions far worse than anything Europe
had seen for centuries. By denying the camp system's populace adequate nutrition, indeed by subjecting many to starvation, by forcing them to perform
backbreaking labor for unmanageably long hours, by providing them with
grossly inadequate clothing and shelter, not to mention medical care, and by
perpetrating steady violence on their bodies and minds, the Germans succeeded in making many of the camp system's inhabitants take on the appearance—including festering, open wounds, and the marks of disease and
illness—and behavioral attributes of the "subhumans" that the Germans
imagined them to be.[35]

The camp world's unrestrained violence served two main purposes. The
first, discussed above, was its nature as an expressive outlet, as a means of
gratification, for the new German. The second was its contribution to the recreation of the prisoners. The violence which the Germans perpetrated
upon the prisoners served to confirm the Germans' view of their "subhumanity" in a variety of ways. By injuring them, the violence marked the prisoners' bodies with constant reminders of their abject state; it weakened them
greatly, producing still more of the "subhumanizing" effects engendered
by malnutrition, exposure, and overwork. A bevy of psychological consequences also ensued from the violence. It created terror among the prisoners, leading them to cower in the presence of their German overlords, to
cower as no people would before equals. The sight—in the camp world a frequent sight—of someone submitting to a brutal beating without raising a
hand in self-defense (which was the rule for prisoners) could only confirm
in the Germans' minds how devoid of dignity these creatures were, how far
removed they were from being humans worthy of respect and full moral
consideration.

Germans thus refashioned the names, the bodies, the spirit, the social
conduct, the entire conditions of life of those in the camp world. They
turned them into beings who essentially labored, suffered, and, with varia-

tions among different groups, died. They, as ongoing self-ratification, created beings who did seem to them to be "subhuman," lacking a variety of essential human attributes, not the least of which was even a minimally healthy human appearance. The camp world was thus a world in which not only the new German could be seen, but also the future new "subhumans" into which the Germans, had they won the war, would have fashioned most of the people of eastern Europe.

CONCLUSION

The transformation of the camp system from its modest yet portentous beginnings into a new system of German society mirrored the evolution of the Nazis' implementation of their central ideological prescriptions, especially the eliminationist antisemitism. At first, the camps were sites of torture and episodic killing, conducted at the whims and for the pleasure of its guards. They remained insignificant in size (less than twenty-five thousand were in the camp system in 1939) and overall effect, except to instill fear into opponents of the regime and Jews. The implementation of the eliminationist antisemitic ideology was initially similarly modest, consisting of generally non-murderous measures, punctuated by gratifying outbursts of violence and killing, the main purpose of which was to make life difficult and frightening enough so that the Jews would leave Germany. The camps were important tools in this eliminationist project.

Like the eliminationist measures, the camps in the beginning killed only episodically. Like the eliminationist ideology, when the conditions were ripe, the Germans activated camps for killing. The camp system's size grew in conjunction with the implementation of the most apocalyptic portions of the Nazi German creed. Thus, parallel logics characterized the evolution of the eliminationist policy and the development of camps. In this sense as well, the camp was the emblematic institution of Germany during its Nazi period, just as the extermination of the Jews was its emblematic national project.

As the emblematic institution of Germany during its Nazi period and the paradigmatic institution of the Holocaust, the camp serves as a backdrop for studying other killing institutions in more detail. Police battalions, "work" camps, and death marches highlight in different ways *general features* of the Holocaust that were also to be found in the camp world.

The huge number of camps, for example, necessitated that they be staffed by an even larger number of Germans. This was especially true of the camps in Germany proper. An enormous number of ordinary Germans, Germans who had no particular affiliation with Nazi institutions like the Party and the SS, provided personnel for the camp system. Together with other or-dinary Germans in the SS and the Party, they killed, tortured, and immiser-ated the camps' unwilling denizens. Yet, as revealing as the camps are on this subject, the role of ordinary Germans in the Holocaust, and the significance of their participation, can best be understood by investigating other genoci-dal institutions, those made up often overwhelmingly of ordinary Germans, such as police battalions.

PART III

Police Battalions:
Ordinary Germans,
Willing Killers

I would also like to say that it did not at all occur to me that these orders could be unjust. It is true that I know that it is also the duty of the police to protect the innocent, but I was then of the conviction that the Jews were not innocent but guilty. I believed the propaganda that all Jews were criminals and subhumans and that they were the cause of Germany's decline after the First World War. The thought that one should disobey or evade the order to participate in the extermination of the Jews did not therefore enter my mind at all.

KURT MÖBIUS, FORMER POLICE BATTALION
MEMBER WHO SERVED IN CHEŁMNO, TESTIFYING ON
NOVEMBER 8, 1961

6

POLICE BATTALIONS:

AGENTS OF GENOCIDE

THE ORDER POLICE (*Ordnungspolizei*) was as integral to the commission of the Holocaust as the *Einsatzgruppen* and the SS were. It was composed of the Uniformed Police (*Schutzpolizei*), under which police battalions operated, and the *Gendarmerie* (Rural Police).[1] Police battalions were the branch of the Order Police most intimately involved in the genocide. Their mobility made them, unlike other parts of the Order Police, a flexible, general instrument for implementing genocidal policies. The character of these units and the deeds that they performed provide an unusually clear window onto some of the central issues of the Holocaust.

An analysis of the role and significance of police battalions' contribution to the slaughter of Jews does not depend upon a thorough comprehension of the institutional development of the Order Police or of police battalions during the Nazi period. It requires only that three features of police battalions be understood:

1. A large percentage of the Germans who were their members were an inauspicious lot, not selected for them because of military or ideological fitness. In fact, the men were often chosen for service in a haphazard manner and were frequently the least desirable of the manpower pool, even considered unfit for military service. Moreover, no ideological screening to speak of was performed on these men.

2. Once in police battalions, these unpromising men often received below par training in weapons, logistics, and procedures, and the ideological training

or indoctrination to which they were subjected was minimal, at times laugh-
ably perfunctory and ineffective.

3. Police battalions were not "Nazi" institutions. Their men were not particularly Nazified in any significant sense save that they were, loosely speaking,
representative of the Nazified German society.

The Order Police grew from a total of 131,000 officers and men on the
eve of the war[2] to 310,000 men and officers by the beginning of 1943, of
whom 132,000 (42 percent) were reservists.[3] It was a security organization of
considerable dimension and importance. With increased size and the new demands of policing territories populated by "inferior races" came added duties, such as fighting partisans, transferring populations, and, though
unmentioned in these organizational reports, killing civilians, especially and
overwhelmingly Jews. These developments produced an institution that by
1942 was radically different from its prewar incarnation. Although its institutional structure remained essentially unchanged, it had quadrupled in size
(since 1938) and had gone from being a relatively decentralized professional
police force whose men were stationed primarily in their hometowns or na-
tive regions, to an organization staffed ever more by non-professionals, devoted to colonial domination, with its men strewn about the European
landmass among hostile peoples of different languages, customs, and aspirations. By 1942, the Order Police had become, compared to its character in
1938, unrecognizable in size, composition, activities, and ethos.

Police battalions and reserve police battalions were the organizational
home of a large number of Germans.[4] They were units averaging more than
five hundred men, performing a wide range of duties in the occupied areas
and in Germany itself. Initially, they were composed of four companies and a
battalion staff, led by a captain or a major. (They were subsequently reduced
to three companies.) Each company was subdivided into three platoons,
which were further subdivided into groups of ten to fifteen men. As they
were conceived of in 1939, they policed, garrisoned, regulated traffic flow,
guarded installations, and helped to transfer populations in occupied areas
such as the Poland of 1940.[5] Also, owing to an agreement with the German
army, they were, in times of need, to fight in traditional military operations
(and to combat partisans behind the lines). Police battalions did participate in
the 1939 campaign against Poland, the 1940 campaign in the west, and the
battles in the Soviet Union during the German onslaught. Except possibly
for the fighting, these were the normal wartime duties of policemen in occupied areas. The low priority given to their manpower needs, their light armaments, and especially their often inadequate training reflected these modest
expectations of police "normality." There is no indication from any record,

utterance, or act that in 1939 any preparation was being made for the men of the police battalions to take part in genocidal slaughter.

Police battalions were raised and trained in a haphazard manner, reflecting the low status of the Order Police within the array of German security and military forces[6] as well as its continuous manpower problems throughout the war. The Order Police estimated in November 1941 that its manpower shortage was approaching 100,000 men (its strength at the time was less than 300,000) and that it urgently needed an infusion of 43,000.[7] Its ability to recruit the most able men having been restricted, the Order Police had to rely to a great extent on the drafting of men less soldierly in profile in order to meet its increasing, and increasingly unmet, manpower needs,[8] including many who were older than the normal military age and others who had failed to meet the standard of physical qualification for police duty. Such compromises were explained by "the current difficult personnel situation in the Order Police."[9] The Order Police, in scraping together anyone it could, was depleting the last available reserves. Police Battalion 83, for example, had completely exhausted the manpower of the eastern German city of Gleiwitz, where it was raised, so it had to forgo filling one of its units completely.[10]

Not only was there little attempt on the part of the regime to stock the Order Police and its police battalions with especially able men or with men who had demonstrated fidelity to Nazism beyond that of any randomly selected group of Germans, but also the training given these men indicated the low expectations that the regime had of them.

The Order Police's draftees were not auspicious recruits; most had had no military training, many were marginal physical fodder, and their ages and already established family and professional lives made them less pliable than the youngsters whom military and police organizations typically seek. They desire young men for good reason; the experience of millennia teaches that young people are more malleable, more easily turned into integrated bearers of an institution's ethos and practices. So, even with its low operational expectations, the Order Police faced a formidable training task, which was made still more difficult by the paucity of training time, owing to the pressing need to get the men into the field.

The Order Police's training of its new inductees was nevertheless inattentive, and perfunctory to the point of being negligent. Even when the men of reserve police battalions received it in full (which many did not), the training lasted only about three months, an inadequate period for units of this kind, which before the war had been allotted a year of training.[11] The overall inadequacy of the actual training is borne out by an inspector's conclusion that almost six months after their creation, one-third of the reservists of Police Battalions 65 and 67 were not yet sufficiently trained.[12] The inattention to training is corroborated by the men of police battalions themselves, many of whom mention its perfunctory nature.

During their training period, usually a paltry two hours a week were devoted to ideological training. The weeks covered different topics (with more than one topic being treated each week), which were laid out in the educational guidelines. Many of Nazism's staple ideological themes were included (Versailles, "the preservation of the blood," "the leadership of the Reich") but were allotted insufficient time to allow for in-depth treatment.[13] This superficial ideological education, which actually did little more than familiarize the new inductees with the laws that codified ideological principles, was unlikely to have had much more of an effect upon them than did listening to a couple of Hitler's speeches, something that these men undoubtedly had already done. During the weeks of intensive and tiring training, the meager sessions devoted to ideological pronouncements were probably more effective as rest periods than as indoctrination sessions.[14]

There was to be continuing ideological training during the war, with planned daily, weekly, and monthly instruction of the men in police battalions. The "daily instruction" (to take place at least every other day) informed the men of political and military developments. The weekly instruction was intended to shape their ideological views and build their character. Once a month, the men were instructed in a designated theme supplied by Himmler's office, the purpose of which was to treat thoroughly a topic of contemporary ideological importance. Although at first glance all of this may seem to add up to considerable ideological inundation, it amounted to little time each week and—even when carried out to the full extent of the orders—likely had little effect on the men. The "daily instruction" was meant only to convey and interpret the news, and therefore probably focused on military fortunes. The weekly instruction was to present material so that "the educational goals of National Socialism are clearly presented." Three types of presentations were suggested as appropriate: (1) a brief lecture about experiences in the war, or about the exploits of men of the Order Police; (2) the reading of passages from an appropriate book, such as *Pflichten des deutschen Soldaten* ("Duties of the German Soldier"); or (3) discussing material from SS educational pamphlets. The impression of casualness that these instructions convey, and hence the sessions' ineffectiveness in indoctrinating the men, is further reinforced by the directive's declaration that no special preparation is necessary for conducting these sessions. Moreover, all educational meetings were to be conducted by the pedagogically innocent officers of the police battalions themselves and not by trained teachers. The once-a-week "weekly" instructional sessions, the central forum of the continuing ideological education efforts, was to last an anemic thirty to forty-five minutes, and could be omitted if they "disturb[ed] or hamper[ed] concentration and spiritual receptivity."[15]

THE ORDER POLICE, as a whole, and particularly the police reserve, which stocked the police battalions, were not elite institutions. The age profile was highly unmilitary; the men were unusually old for military institutions. The training was insufficient. A large proportion of the men that it chose had managed to stave off more "military" military service (whether in the SS or in the army), indicating certainly no great disposition for military discipline and activities, including killing. They were likely to have a large number of fathers among them. They were as far away from eighteen-year-old youths, with no life experience, easily molded to the needs of an army, as an effective military institution is likely to be. They did not share the bravado of youth, and they were used to thinking for themselves. By age, family situation, and disposition, the Order Police, and especially the police reserve, were likely to be composed of men who were more personally independent than whatever the norm was in Germany during its Nazi incarnation.

The Order Police was also not a *Nazi* institution, in the sense of being molded by the regime in its own image. Its officers were not especially Nazified by German standards of the day, and the rank and file even less so. It made little effort to fill its ranks with people especially beholden to Nazism. Except for mild regard paid to an officer's ideology in promotion, ideological stance was almost an absent criterion for the daily workings of the Order Police.[16] The institution did not screen its enlisted men for their ideological views, and the paltry ideological training it gave them was unlikely to have intensified anyone's existing Nazi views perceptibly, let alone to have converted the unconvinced. Compared to the daily ideological fare of German society itself, the institution's ideological instruction was meager gruel. The Order Police accepted into its ranks whomever it could get. Owing to the selection process and the available pool of applicants, it got men who were less than ideal as policemen and, if anything, were, as a group, less Nazified than average for German society. The Order Police was populated by neither martial spirits nor Nazi supermen.

The men in police battalions could not have been expected to be particularly Nazified, and their institution had not prepared them in any purposive way to become more Nazified, let alone genocidal killers. Yet the regime would soon send them to kill, and would discover, as expected, that the ordinary Germans who composed the Order Police, equipped with little more than the cultural notions current in Germany, would easily become genocidal executioners.

OUR KNOWLEDGE OF police battalion activities during the war is fragmented and partial. No survey—systematic or otherwise—of their contribution to mass murder has appeared. An overview of police battalion activities in the occupied areas can, however, be constructed.[17] Administratively, they were subordinate to the *Higher SS and Police Leader* (*HSSPF*) of the region in which they were operating. The *HSSPF* were responsible for all SS, police, and security forces (aside from army units) within their jurisdictions.[18] Orders for *killing operations* were transmitted almost always orally (either face to face or over the telephone). Depending on the nature of the operation and on the identity of other institutions that might also have been involved, the officers and men of German police battalions had varying degrees of autonomy in the manner of executing their orders.

A police battalion undertook operations of all sorts, sometimes in battalion strength, sometimes in company strength, sometimes employing just a few men. Since a police battalion's primary task was to police and ensure order in an assigned (often hostile) area, it was typically garrisoned in a city, or its companies were garrisoned separately in various cities or towns in a region, which were used as bases for their forays into the surrounding areas. The men of police battalions operated both alone and frequently in conjunction with forces from other institutions, including the army, the *Einsatzkommandos*, the SS Security Service (SD), concentration camp personnel, the *Gendarmerie*, and the German civilian administration—in short, with just about any German governmental or security institution that was to be found in the occupied areas. Police battalions might stay garrisoned in one place for quite a while; however, because a shortage of German police manpower was the rule, their general existence, especially in eastern Europe, was peripatetic; when extra forces were needed in a particular locale, men of a nearby police battalion would often be shifted into the breach.

Police battalion activities ranged widely. The majority of time spent by the men of police battalions was devoted to non-genocidal activities. They undertook ordinary police duties. They guarded installations and buildings. They engaged in anti-partisan warfare. Some even fought beside the army on the front. Yet they also rounded people up. They deported people from their homes for resettlement, to perform slave labor in Germany, or to a camp of some kind, often a death camp. They regularly killed people in cold blood, often *en masse*.

Whatever the duties of a given day were, the police battalion men were off duty a good portion of the time. This is an aspect of their lives that—though little is known about it—should not be ignored. Understanding them and their deeds requires that we investigate the fullness of their lives and avoid viewing them wrested from their social relations, a view which tends to caricature them. These men were not isolated individuals or oppressed. While in the field, the Germans who served in police battalions went to church and to movies, had sports competitions, enjoyed furloughs, and wrote letters home. They went to night spots and bars, drank, sang, had sex, and talked. Like all people, they had opinions about the character of their lives and what they were doing. Like all men serving in military and police institutions, they talked—in groups, in intimate circles, privately one on one. They talked among themselves about all the topics of the day, which naturally included the war, as well as their lethal activities, which they knew—whether they won or lost the war—would become the hallmark of this period of history, of their country, of this regime, of their lives. In reality, while they were genocidal executioners, the Germans in police battalions, except perhaps for the small percentage of the time when they were on killing operations, led relatively easy, and often easygoing, lives.

POLICE BATTALION PARTICIPATION in large-scale killing operations, in genocide, began with the German attack on the Soviet Union. The killings that some police battalions had perpetrated earlier in Poland were not systematic and not part of a formal genocidal program. The men of Police Battalion 9 filled out the ranks of three of the four *Einsatzgruppen*, the German killing squads serving as the main agents of genocide in the Soviet Union. One of the battalion's companies was attached to each of these *Einsatzgruppen*. The companies were further subdivided among the various *Einsatzkommandos* and *Sonderkommandos*, so that the police contingent portion of the 100-to-150-man-strong *Kommandos* was a platoon of about 30 to 40 men. In December 1941, Police Battalion 9 was transferred from the *Einsatzgruppen*, and was replaced by Police Battalion 3. The men of each police battalion were operationally subordinate to the *Einsatzgruppen*, and in their duties and actions were barely distinguishable from them.[19] The *Einsatzgruppen* killed over one million Jews in territories conquered from the Soviet Union. The police battalion men among them, most of whom were reservists, fully contributed to this toll.

The two police battalions assigned to the *Einsatzgruppen* were not the only ones who slaughtered Jews in the Soviet Union. Other police battalions contributed to the deaths of tens of thousands, at times killing in conjunction with the units of the *Einsatzgruppen*, at times on their own. The three battalions of Police Regiment 10 (Police Battalions 45, 303, and 314) and of Police Regiment 11 (Police Battalions 304, 315, and 320), all operating under the aegis of the *HSSPF* Russia-South, helped to decimate Ukrainian Jewry.[20] The three police battalions of Police Regiment Russia-Center (Police Battalions 307, 316, and 322) marched through Belorussia with great destructiveness.[21]

One of the first slaughters of the genocidal campaign unleashed against Soviet Jewry was perpetrated by yet another police battalion, Police Battalion 309. A few days after Operation Barbarossa began, the Germans of Police Battalion 309 ignited a portentous, symbolic fiery inferno in the city of Białystok.

The officers and the men of at least one company of Police Battalion 309 knew from the moment of their entry into territory taken from the Soviet Union that they were to play a role in the planned destruction of Jewry.[22] After entering Białystok on the twenty-seventh of June, a city which the Germans had captured, like many others, without a fight, the battalion commander, Major Ernst Weis, ordered his men to round up male Jews by combing through Jewish residential areas. Although the purpose of congregating the Jews was to kill them, instructions about the manner in which the Germans would extinguish their lives were not given at that time. The entire battalion participated in the ensuing roundup, which itself proceeded with great brutality and wanton murderousness. These Germans could finally unleash themselves without restraint upon the Jews. One Jew recalls that "the unit had barely driven into the city when the soldiers swarmed out and, without any sensible cause, shot up the entire city, apparently also in order to frighten the people. The incessant shooting was utterly horrible. They shot blindly, in fact, into houses and windows, without regard for whether they hit anyone. The shooting (*Schiesserei*) lasted the entire day."[23] The Germans of this battalion broke into people's homes who had not lifted a finger in hostility, dragged them out, kicked them, beat them with their rifle butts, and shot them. The streets were strewn with corpses.[24] These individually, autonomously initiated brutalities and killings were by any standard of utility, unnecessary. Why did they occur? The Germans themselves, in their postwar testimony, are mute on this point. Yet some episodes are suggestive. During the roundup, one nameless Jew opened his door a crack in order to assess the unfolding, perilous scene. A lieutenant in the battalion, having noticed the slit, seized the opportunity and shot him through the small opening.[25] In order to fulfill his orders, the German only had to bring the Jew to the assembly point. Yet he chose to shoot him. It is hard to imagine that this German felt moral qualms when the target fell to his splendid shot.

Another scene saw some of the Germans in this battalion compel old Jewish men to dance before them. In addition to the amusement that they evidently derived from their choreography, the Germans were mocking, denigrating, and asserting their mastery over these Jews, particularly since the selected Jews were their elders, people of an age to whom normally regard and respect are due. Apparently, and to their great misfortune, the Jews failed to dance to a sufficiently brisk and pleasing tempo, so the Germans set the Jews' beards on fire.[26]

Elsewhere, near the Jewish district, two desperate Jews fell to their knees begging a German general for protection. One member of Police Battalion 309, who observed these entreaties, decided to intervene with what he must have thought to be a fitting commentary: He unzipped his pants and urinated upon them. The antisemitic atmosphere and practice among the Germans was such that this man brazenly exposed himself in front of a general in order to perform a rare public act of virtually unsurpassable disdain. Indeed, the man had nothing to fear for his breach of military discipline and decorum. Neither the general nor anyone else sought to stop him.[27]

Still other deeds of this battalion's slaughter in Białystok are revealing. At one point the Germans combed through a hospital in search of Jewish patients to kill. In doing so, they demonstrated zeal and fidelity to their task, seeking to slaughter people who obviously posed no conceivable physical threat. They were not, moreover, out to kill any enemy of Germany, just the figmental Jewish enemy. Indeed, they showed no interest in the Soviet Uzbeki soldiers lying wounded in the hospital. They were thirsting for the blood only of Jews.[28]

The men of Police Battalion 309 used the marketplace near the Jewish districts to assemble the Jews. During the afternoon, a German army officer appalled by the licentious killing of unarmed civilians appeared and argued heatedly with the captain who commanded First Company. The captain refused to comply with the officer's order to allow the Jews to go free, maintaining that the officer had no command authority over him and his men. The captain had his orders, and he was determined to carry them out.[29] Subsequently, the Germans took hundreds of Jews from the marketplace to nearby sites, where they shot them.[30] Yet the killing was proceeding too slowly for the Germans' taste. The men were bringing more Jews to the assembly points in the marketplace and the area in front of the city's main synagogue faster than they could kill them. The number of Jews was swelling. So another "solution" was improvised on the spot.

The Germans, without precise orders about the methods by which to achieve their ends, took their own initiative (as they so often were to do during the Holocaust) in devising a new course of action. The main synagogue of Białystok was a towering symbol of Jewish life. An impressive squarish stone structure crowned with a dome, it was the largest synagogue in Poland. Casting about for a way to dispose of the mass of assembled Jews under the shadow of this looming testament to the life of the Jewish enemy, the Germans adopted a plan to destroy both simultaneously—the Jews as well as their spiritual and symbolic home—which was a natural conclusion for their anti-semitically inflamed minds.[31] The burning of synagogues, especially during *Kristallnacht*, had already become a motif of German anti-Jewish action, and, once established, it was available to be drawn upon anew as a guide to action. Transubstantiating a house of worship into a charnel house was an ironic beginning to the campaign that these men knew was supposed to end with Jewry's extinction.

The men of Police Battalion 309's First and Third Companies drove their victims into the synagogue, the less compliant Jews receiving from the Germans liberal blows of encouragement. The Germans packed the large synagogue full. The fearful Jews began to chant and pray loudly. After spreading gasoline around the building, the Germans set it ablaze; one of the men tossed an explosive through a window, to ignite the holocaust. The Jews' prayers turned into screams. A battalion member later described the scene that he witnessed: "I saw . . . smoke, that came out of the synagogue and heard there how the incarcerated people cried loudly for help. I was about 70 meters' distance from the synagogue. I could see the building and observed that people tried to escape through the windows. One shot at them. Circling the synagogue stood the police members who were apparently supposed to cordon it off, in order to ensure that no one emerged."[32] Between 100 and 150 men of the battalion surrounded the burning synagogue. They collectively ensured that none of the appointed Jews escaped the inferno. They watched as over seven hundred people died this hideous and painful death, listening to screams of agony. Most of the victims were men, though some women and children were among them.[33] Not surprisingly, some of the Jews within spared themselves the fiery death by hanging themselves or severing their arteries. At least six Jews came running out of the synagogue, their clothes and bodies aflame. The Germans shot each one down, only to watch these human torches burn themselves out.[34]

With what emotions did the men of Police Battalion 309 gaze upon this sacrificial pyre to the exterminationist creed? One exclaimed: "Let it burn, it's a nice little fire [*schönes Feuerlein*], it's great fun." Another exulted: "Splendid, the entire city should burn down."[35]

The men of this police battalion, many of whom were not even professional policemen, having opted for service with the police as a means of avoiding army service when they were called up to duty,[36] became instantaneous *Weltanschauungskrieger*, or ideological warriors, killing that day between 2,000 and 2,200 Jewish men, women, and children.[37] The manner in which they rounded up Jews, the wanton beatings and killings, the turning of the streets of Białystok into corpse- and blood-bestrewn pathways, and their own improvised solution of a cleansing conflagration, are indeed acts of *Weltan-schauungskrieger*—more specifically, of antisemitic warriors. They carried out an order, embellished upon it, acted not with disgust and hesitation but with apparent relish and excess. Their major had ordered them to round up Jewish men, yet knowing that Hitler had slated the Jews of the Soviet Union for total extermination, the men themselves expanded the order to include some women and children. These Germans were willful in their killing and brutality, for they did more than their specific orders had required of them; they chose to act according to the spirit of the more general order, according to the spirit of their times. The men of Police Battalion 309 performed what can be seen as the emblematic initial killing operation of the formal genocide. They were "ordinary" Germans who, when faced with Germany's deadly foe, when given a chance to have a free hand with the Jews, acted with license, and sent many of their victims to the unnecessarily gruesome death of being burned alive.

ANOTHER ITINERANT UNIT that saw action in the initial genocidal onslaught was Police Battalion 65, which was raised in Recklinghausen, a medium-sized city in the Ruhr area, the industrial heartland of Germany, and was mainly composed of reservists.[38] Initially, it served in the west. On May 26, 1941, when the preparations for Operation Barbarossa were already far advanced, Police Battalion 65 was positioned in Heilsberg, East Prussia, which was its jumping-off point for the campaign. On June 22, it marched over Tilsit with the 285th Security Division into the Baltics. Its task was to mop up Soviet stragglers and to secure the rear areas behind the advancing German troops. On June 26, the First and Second Companies of the battalion set up quarters in Kovno, while the Third Company was stationed in Šiauliai. Before resuming its advance deeper into Soviet territory, Police Battalion 65 received its baptism in genocidal slaughter.

Kovno was the site of incredible butchery of Jews, open for all, Germans and Lithuanians alike, to see. The initial assault upon the unsuspecting, unarmed, and obviously unthreatening Jewish community occurred immediately after the German army marched into Kovno on the heels of the Soviet retreat. With German encouragement and support, Lithuanians, in a frenzied orgy of bludgeoning, slashing, and shooting, slaughtered 3,800 Jews in the city's streets. Two companies of Police Battalion 65 were among the many Germans witnessing these slaughters. In the first week in July, Lithuanian units operating under German command shot another 3,000 Jews in Kovno. The killings, whether wild or systematic, had a circus-like quality, with bystanders observing at their pleasure the slaying, the cudgeling to death of

Jews, watching with approval as crowds once watched the gladiators slaying their beasts.[39] A number of the men of Police Battalion 65 have related what they observed during the Kovno massacres, including Lithuanian handiwork on one leisurely Sunday, when "we stood on a hill and in a low-lying area near the citadel, about a hundred people (men and women) were shot by machine-gun and rifle fire."[40] While some of the men of First and Second Companies had to wait a while yet before they themselves would have a hand in what they had only watched in Kovno, other members of these companies participated in the killings by cordoning off the area around the citadel where the Lithuanians shot the Jews.[41] The men of Third Company, similarly, had no such gradual initiation into genocidal slaughter.

Šiauliai was a medium-size Lithuanian city seventy-five miles north of Kovno. The men of Third Company repeatedly perpetrated massacres in Šiauliai and the surrounding area. Beginning already at the end of June 1941, they killed a considerable number of Jews, including, it seems, women, in what was part of the initial phase of the Germans' genocidal campaign against Soviet Jews. The details of their many killings are murky, yet the general outlines are clear.[42] The men of Third Company, at least some of the time, themselves rounded up the Jews from their houses.[43] They then transported the Jews on the company's trucks to nearby woods where they shot them.

Already in this early stage of genocidal killing, an impulse of the Germans that was to repeat itself again and again—though it did not become an iron rule—found expression: Exterminating Germany's deadly foes, though imperative, would be carried out by those Germans who wanted to do it. One reservist relates: "I can still remember with certainty that our Sergeant S. two or three times (2 times for sure) assembled the execution squads. . . . I would like to say that this sort of squad was composed *only* of volunteers [emphasis in original]."[44] The gruesomeness of mass shootings at close range was such that even some of the volunteers, indisputably willing killers, at first found it physically disgusting. One volunteer executioner, who was a reservist, is remembered to have returned from a killing foray shaken: " 'I've done it once, never again, I won't be able to eat for three days.' "[45] Whatever the visceral reactions were to the initiation in genocidal slaughter, the killing went on smoothly. A few days after Third Company's arrival, posters appeared in Šiauliai proclaiming: "This City Is Jew-free!!" (*Diese Stadt ist judenfrei!!*).[46] Such celebratory declarations were often given occasion to appear shortly after the Germans arrived in a Soviet city.

Throughout the summer and fall of 1941, all three companies of Police Battalion 65 contributed to the extermination of the Jews of the Baltics, sometimes killing the Jews themselves, sometimes leaving the actual killing to other units, while they contributed by rounding up, guarding, or transporting the victims. The killing squads were not always formed only with men who specifically had volunteered for killing assignments. Yet the evidence does not suggest that the men killed unwillingly, or that coercion was necessary in order to guarantee their compliance with orders.[47] They killed in Raseiniai, in Pskov, and in many other locales about which detailed accounts no longer exist, as they advanced northeastward into the Soviet Union.[48] After describing a killing in Šiauliai, one reservist summed up their fall vocation: "Similar shooting operations took place repeatedly during the march to Luga."[49] The volume of killings blurred the Germans' memories about individual massacres.

Arriving in Luga, a city seventy-five miles south of Leningrad, in September, Police Battalion 65 settled into winter quarters. For four months, its energies were devoted to guarding installations and to fighting partisans, in Luga and its environs. Its men also helped to guard a prisoner-of-war camp that housed captured Soviet troops. True to the character of their new lives, they participated in at least one massacre of Jewish men, women, and children, and the killing of those Soviet prisoners who were identified as Jews.[50]

The Germans employed Soviet prisoners of war for their own use, bringing them to their living quarters, where they performed menial tasks in their workshops and kitchens.[51] They regularly maltreated the Jewish prisoners, and when they discovered that a "houseboy" was Jewish or a Soviet commissar, they shot him. By Luga, the men of Police Battalion 65, or at least some of the men, had internalized the need to kill Jews. They accepted that Jews were fundamentally different from other Soviet citizens, that this difference resided not in any demonstrated actions or character traits of the Jews, but in their "race," in the simple fact that a person had Jewish parents, Jewish blood. During their encampment in Luga, they killed Jews whom they easily could have spared. One killer even tells of a time he was sent alone with a Jew to the woods. He was under absolutely no supervision, so it was a perfect opportunity to let a victim flee, had he opposed the existing war of racist purgation. But he shot him.[52] Similarly, it would have been easy for the Germans not to have "discovered" that their houseboys were Jewish; no pressure existed in the quiet of their quarters to do so. But they did, and with regularity. And their beating of their victims was gratuitous. One particular Jew was not only battered (*misshandelt*) by the men of Police Battalion 65, but he was also mocked and degraded, having been forced to dance with a stuffed bear which the Germans had found in their lodgings. Only then did the Germans shoot him.[53]

These Germans were treating the Jews according to their own inwardly held standards, which they could apply as they wished, for they clearly had been granted the autonomy to make life-and-death decisions. It had already become axiomatic to the members of Police Battalion 65 that all Jews (and Soviet commissars) were to disappear from the face of the earth. They needed neither prompting nor permission in order to kill any Jew whom they discovered.[54] This autonomy is remarkable, since military and police institutions are generally loath to allow enlisted men to make the capital decisions normally reserved for officers. Regarding Jews, the normal rules did not hold. Every German was inquisitor, judge, and executioner.

EVEN MORE SO than their contribution to the annihilation of Soviet Jewry, the efforts of police battalions were integral to the success of *Aktion Reinhard*, the Germans' name for the systematic killing of Jews living in the area of Poland that the Germans called the *Generalgouvernement*.[55] In the course of less than two years, from March 1942 to November 1943, the Germans killed around two million Polish Jews. The vast majority of them met their deaths in the gas chambers of Treblinka, Belżec, and Sobibór, camps that the Germans constructed especially to dry up this vast reservoir of Jewry. Many thousands never made it to the camps, because the Germans did not bother to transport them, choosing instead to kill them in or near the cities where they were living. Whether the Germans transported them over the rail system to a death camp or shot them on the outskirts of cities and towns, they required substantial manpower to collect the Jews and to ensure that they reached their designated end, whether a pit in the ground or the crematoria's ovens. Various units of the Order Police, chief among them police battalions, frequently supplied the men.[56]

Focusing on the activities of the Order Police generally and of police battalions in particular in one of the *Generalgouvernement*'s five districts, Lublin, reveals a collective portrait of institutions immersed in genocidal slaughter.

In charge of the Order Police's units operating in the Lublin District was the commander of the Order Police in Lublin (*KdO* Lublin). The units can be grouped into three categories. In the first were the regimental staff and units of police directly attached to it. The second category included seven different battalions of police: the three battalions composing Police Regiment 25—numbered 65, 67, and 101—Police Battalion 41, and Police Battalion 316, as well as two other mobile battalion-strength units, Mounted Police Third Squadron (a police cavalry unit) and Motorized Gendarme Battalion. These latter two performed tasks similar to police battalions, were by membership, composition, and function comparable to police battalions, and contributed to the slaughter of tens of thousands of Jews. They are thus included in the ensuing analysis as if they had been police battalions. Finally, auxiliary mobile police battalions (*Schutzmannschaft-Bataillone*), composed of volunteers from the occupied countries (in this case, from eastern Europe), also acted at the *KdO* Lublin's behest. In the third category were the *Gendarmerie* and the Uniformed Police, which were stationary units of police assigned to particular cities, towns, and installations for garrison and guard duty.[57]

As was characteristic of some German institutions during the Nazi period, there was no single command structure governing the units of the Order Police in Lublin.[58] The irregular command structure, combined with the orders for killing operations having been transmitted orally and not in writing, frequently makes it difficult to ascertain how and from whom the units of the Order Police received orders for the various killing operations. The Order Police units, particularly its police battalions, received two different kinds of orders for genocidal activities. Assignments to carry out deportations or shooting massacres in a particular city or town on a specific day accounted for most of their victims. "I can say the following about the content of these orders," remembers a former clerk on the staff of the *KdO* Lublin: "A day was designated on which the Jewish populace of a certain locality was to be deported. A particular battalion was assigned to carry it out. . . . The orders further stipulated that in case of flight or resistance, one should shoot immediately."[59] In addition to these large-scale, organized killing operations, a general unspecified enabling order, called the *Schiessbefehl* ("shoot-to-kill order"), mandated the shooting of all Jews found outside of ghettos and camps—on country roads, in woods, hiding in homes or on farms. The *Schiessbefehl* made the Jews, including Jewish children, *vogelfrei*, outlaws facing an automatic death sentence. The order communicated unequivocally to the men of the Order Police that no Jew was to be permitted to be free, that the punishment for a Jew's attempt to gain freedom was death, and that the social landscape was to be purged of even the most infinitesimal Jewish presence. This order, for all its symbolic importance, was not merely symbolic. All units under the *KdO*'s command acted upon it.[60] Indeed, the men of the Order Police, especially of police battalions, put it into effect so frequently that killing stray Jews became a regular part of their lives.

The *KdO* received regular reports from its units about their general activities, including the genocidal ones. Weekly and monthly reports could be augmented by immediate reports for special occurrences. The individual unit reports would then be collated and synthesized by the operations officer into a monthly report sent to the *KdO*'s superiors.[61] The reports came in different forms and are themselves revealing. Written reports contained tallies of the people whom the Germans killed: of Jews, under the *Schiessbefehl*'s mandate; and of non-Jews, generally as a consequence of their attempts to stamp out partisan activity and other resistance. As a rule, the reports kept the Germans' slaughter of Jews distinct from their killing of non-Jews. Naturally, the Germans routinely employed their linguistic camouflage, conveying often, for example, that Jews were "dealt with according to orders" (*befehlsgemäss behandelt*). Mass killings and deportations were generally not included in the written reports, having been communicated to the *KdO* orally or in such veiled language that it was difficult to discern whether the Germans had shot the Jews on the spot or deported them to a death camp.[62] No matter: as everyone knew, they were functional equivalents.

The weekly reports from July 25 to December 12 of 1942 of Police Battalion 133's First Company have survived. At the time, First Company was operating in East Galicia around Kolomyia, leaving a swath of corpses in its wake. Its reports, the same kind that were received by the *KdO* Lublin from its own subordinate units,[63] demonstrate a number of points. The number of Jews that Police Battalion 133's First Company killed owing to its men's initiative on search-and-destroy missions, and as a result of their general enabling orders to kill Jews, was impressive. It reported that its men managed to hunt down, uncover, and kill 780 Jews, roughly six Jews per man. Between November 1 and December 12, it reported that its men killed 481 Jews. This averaged out to 80 Jews a week, or 11 a day. They had, moreover, singled out Jews for slaughter. They always reported the number of Jews whom they killed separately from the other categories of victims, which included bandits, accomplices, beggars, thieves, vagabonds, the mentally ill, and asocials. And the "reasons" given for the killing of Jews were shams, having no more to do with why the Germans killed them than had Hitler's protestations of his peaceful desires to do with the German designs for carving up Czechoslovakia. Among the reasons First Company reported for killing Jews were: "work-shirkers," "epidemic threats," "was without armband," "bribery," "leaped from transport," "vagabondage," "unauthorized departure from place of residence," "deportation," and "hidden after deportation." In many cases, no reason whatsoever was proffered, save the word "Jews," which was obviously a sufficient reason in itself.[64] Since this was so, all of the aforementioned "reasons" were superfluous, because a Jew, whether he or she was a putative "epidemic threat" or not, could and would be killed if encountered by this police company's men. Since Jewishness was a sufficient cause, all the "reasons" given were clearly not necessary, and were window dressing of one kind or another.

The strikingly unpraetorian institution, the Order Police, had become an institution immersed in genocidal activities and the discussion of them. Repeatedly, orders went down the chain of command calling for the slaughter of one community after another, the individual operations coalescing into the annihilation of Jews of entire regions. Regular reports came back up the chain of command telling of the men's accomplishments and successes. The Order Police's relations and cooperation with the other security institutions, the Security Police and the SS and Police Leaders (*SSPF*), were close. The members of these kindred institutions worked hand in hand towards the fulfillment of this national project. Genocidal slaughter and its attendant activities (of filling out reports, requisitioning ammunition, assigning trucks from the motor pool) had become a constituent part of the Order Police and of the lives of its men.

The battalions of Police Regiment 25 were in the thick of the genocide. The three battalions had varied histories up to their respective transfers to the *Generalgouvernement*. Two of them are discussed here at some length, first Police Battalion 65 and then, in greater depth, Police Battalion 101.[65]

POLICE BATTALION 65 is one unit which formed a bridge between two of the main loci of the Holocaust, the Soviet Union and the *Generalgouvernement*. After its murderous 1941 advance through northern Soviet territory, described above, the new year greeted the men of Police Battalion 65 with more hazardous duty than bringing unarmed people to slaughter. In January 1942, most of its men joined group "Scheerer," which was engaged in the bitter battles around Cholm in northern Russia, more than one hundred miles southeast of the battalion's headquarters in Luga. Their engagement in battle lasted over three months, during which they fought alongside army troops in fierce encounters with the Soviet army. For a while, the entire battalion was in peril as Soviet units encircled it completely. The battalion suffered extremely heavy casualties at the front and was rotated back when other German forces fought through the Soviet encirclement to free them at the beginning of May.[66] In recognition of its performance in battle, the battalion's official designation was forthwith changed to Police Battalion 65 "Cholm," and the survivors of the battles each received a "Cholm-badge" (*Cholm-Schild*).

Such intensive combat was not the norm for police battalions engaged in the genocide. At the beginning of June, the depleted battalion moved from Luga to Brunowice, near Cracow. Those who had seen battle received leave to visit their homes, and then, as a group, they went for recuperation and ski instruction courses in Zakopane, on the southern border of Poland. Altogether their rest lasted about eight weeks.[67] While its seasoned personnel was elsewhere, the battalion's green replacements, who restored the battalion close to its normal strength, were trained in Brunowice.

From June 1942 until May 1943, Police Battalion 65 served its second, and more significant, stint as an institution of genocidal killing, by contributing to the decimation of Polish Jewry, first in the Cracow region, and then around Lublin. During this period, the death camps were burning overtime, consuming the Jewish arrivals from one community after another. Police Battalion 65 fed the furnaces of both Auschwitz and Bełżec.

Shortly after their arrival in Brunowice, the battalion's commander made an announcement to the battalion. According to one man from First Company, he said: "We have here in Cracow a special task to perform. But the responsibility for it lies with the higher authorities." Although the message was cryptic, the meaning was certainly not lost on this battalion's seasoned killers. The witness to this announcement admitted that he immediately thought that this meant that they would be killing Jews.[68] The Germans of this police battalion knew that, after a five-month interlude of soldiering and rest, they were to resume their slaughter of Jews.

In the Cracow region, Police Battalion 65 was involved repeatedly in killing operations of various kinds. About many of them there is little or no evidence. Still, enough material exists for the character of their stay in Poland to be clear. The first sort of contribution that they made to the fulfillment of *Aktion Reinhard*'s goal was rounding up ghetto-dwelling Jews, loading them onto freight cars, and depositing them before the gates of a death factory. The battalion did this repeatedly, its three companies taking turns at bringing the Jews of Cracow to the city's freight depot, or the Jews from surrounding cities to their local train stations. They then crammed the Jews into freight cars, in the typical German manner of these years, so that there was not even enough room for people to sit down. A smaller, thirty-strong detachment of its men then accompanied the transport to its destination, to either Auschwitz or Bełżec, a journey normally lasting about five hours.[69] A reservist, then thirty-four years old, sketchily describes one such deportation from Cracow:

> It was in November 1942, when all available company members were assigned to a transport of Jews [*Judentransport*]. We had to report to the ghetto and there we took charge of a column of Jewish people, who were being led out of the ghetto. We had to accompany these people to the waiting freight cars, in which a multitude of people were already to be found. These Jews (men, women, and children) were crammed in the most inhumane manner into the available cars. We then had to ride guard on the train. I cannot remember very well the place of destination. I am sure it was not Auschwitz. The name Bełżec has been mentioned. This sounds more likely. At least the name means something to me. We had to leave the train at the final destination, and SS took charge. The train stopped by a fence or a lattice, and with the locomotive, the SS guided the train inside. In the area we noticed a distinct smell of corpses. We could imagine what these people had to look forward to, and above all, that it was an extermination camp. We had previously been told that these people were being resettled.[70]

Many, killers and bystanders, who came to the environs of a death camp have commented on the unmistakable odor of death hanging in the air for miles.

The policemen all knew of the Jews' final destination well before they reached the gates of the inferno. The Germans' various euphemisms for killing were known to all engaged in the business. The men of Police Battalion 65 were particularly wise to the nature of Jewish "resettlement," having been among the first Germans in the Soviet Union to perpetrate genocidal massacres of Jews, well over a year before this particular deportation.[71]

After descending from a different transport immediately outside Auschwitz, which they handed over to the camp's personnel, who brought it inside, the men of Police Battalion 65 rested before their return journey. They were in repose before the gates of a death factory, of an institution like no other in human history—built, refined, and continually modernized for the explicit purpose of consuming human lives. This rest time afforded the Germans almost an irresistible opportunity for reflection. They had just unburdened themselves of their human cargo destined for the furnaces inside. In turning their backs on Auschwitz, they were closing another chapter in their nation's unfolding blood-written chronicle. These men had just contributed to a small yet palpable alteration of the world. They had just completed a deed of great moral magnitude. Not one of them, especially the first time he stood before these gates, could fail to have been aware of this. How did they evaluate the morality of what they had just done? With what emotions did they gaze upon the transport disappearing into the death camp? What did they say among themselves as they saw the smoke rise, as the unmistakable smell of burning flesh assaulted their senses?

One battalion member, a thirty-four-year-old reservist, who had been drafted in 1940 on the Saturday before Pentecost, recalls the moment:

> It stank terribly all around; when we took a rest in a restaurant nearby a drunken SS man (he spoke broken German) came over and told us that the Jews had to undress and they were then told that they would go for a delousing. In reality, one was in fact gassing these people and later burning them. The people who did not go along were continuously driven on with whips. I still remember this discussion very clearly. From this moment on I knew that extermination camps for Jews [*Judenvernichtungslager*] existed.[72]

This reservist had already known that the Germans were killing Jews *en masse;* before the gates of Auschwitz he finally learned of the death factories' workings, down to the ruse used for filling the gas chambers. Through both direct experience and discussion, the perpetrators' knowledge of the scope and methods of Germany's slaughter of Jews increased, and they incrementally expanded their understanding of their own place in this larger, national enterprise. In this restaurant, the killers openly talked about the techniques of their trade. Discussion of genocidal slaughter among its perpetrators was an aspect of the vocation. It was shop talk.

It is not at all surprising that this man and others describe Auschwitz as a "Jewish extermination camp" (*Judenvernichtungslager*), even though non-Jews perished in Auschwitz as well. The killers understood that the Germans were annihilating all Jews, cleansing the world of the putative Jewish blight, so that the institutions devoted to death were in their mental world devoted to the death of the Jewish people. The deaths of non-Jews were understood to have been incidental to the major enterprise, mere tactical operations. Their image of the camp was fundamentally correct, all the more so because, in a real sense, Auschwitz was a "Jewish extermination camp," not only because the vast majority of its victims was Jewish but also because its continually expanding extermination facilities would not have been erected and improved upon had the Germans not been engaged in a genocidal slaughter of the Jews.

Not all the Jews that Police Battalion 65 wrested from ghettos in the fall of 1942 met their deaths in extermination camps. Its men frequently finished off the job themselves. There is scant information about most of their massacres, though it is likely that they conformed to the general pattern of one of the mass killings about which there is testimony, since typically, at the latest after the initial massacres, units would settle upon standardized procedures for the operations. One dawn that autumn, the men of Police Battalion 65 rounded up the Jews of a ghetto near Cracow, after having surrounded the ghetto in order to prevent escapes. They took the Jews to woods outside the city, where they shot them. The Jewish men, women, and children had to undress themselves by the edge of the pit that would become their mass grave. An execution squad of ten Germans, using rifles, shot the Jews in installments until the job was finished. After each batch of Jews had fallen into the pit, one of the men delivered a final shot to the head of anyone who still appeared to be alive. This day's work consumed the lives of eight hundred people.[73]

This killing operation seems to have been organized by SS and SD men. Police battalions, this one as well, typically (though not as a rule) performed their jobs according to the planning and sometimes under the supervision of the local SS and SD commanders. This was the case during a series of mass shootings that took place during the fall of 1942, when the men of Police Battalion 65 killed the patients of a Jewish hospital. One of the participants, who was at the time thirty-nine years old, relates that the killings were spread out over five or six occasions. In each instance, a commando of about twenty-five men from First Company drove to woods on the outskirts of Cracow. There the Germans separated into two groups, one to secure the area and the other to kill the Jewish patients, who were brought to the killing site by ten SS and

SD men. During every one of these operations, they shot up to 150 Jews, who were aged or sick; some of the latter were children. This killer had been assigned to each of these commandos, though he claims that he was always in the group that did not kill. Nevertheless, at least five different times, this man went with his comrades to massacre hospital patients, people who obviously posed no threat to the Germans, people whose condition would in others arouse instincts of nurturance. But not in these men.[74]

The men of Police Battalion 65 learned of this and other genocidal assignments from notices on a bulletin board in their quarters; killing Jews was so routine, so part of the "natural" world of the perpetrators, who served in this and in other police battalions, that notices of genocidal operations often simply got posted in their quarters. Friends within this battalion undoubtedly walked by the bulletin board in order to apprise themselves of their upcoming activities. What did they say to each other upon reading that another operation in the ongoing destruction of the Jews was in the offing, and upon going down the roster of those who would be carrying it out? Did they mutter curses? Did they bemoan that their fate was to be mass murderers? Did they lament the fate of the Jews? They have given no testimony of such reactions, no testimony that recounts the men's hatred of reading the information posted on that genocidal board. Surely, such thoughts and emotions would have stuck in their memories had they conceived of them as the distribution point for cataclysmic news.[75]

In addition to rounding up Jews in ghettos, sitting ducks to be either transported to death camps or shot immediately, the men of Police Battalion 65 repeatedly went into the countryside on search-and-destroy missions, both in the area around Cracow and during the early months of 1943 around Lublin. Their job was to comb the woods for hidden Jews, and then to kill them.[76] Since large numbers of Jews had fled the ghettos of the *Generalgouvernement*, many police battalions and other SS and police units devoted a great deal of time to hunting down Jews—and with great success.[77] The prodigious killing on these missions perpetrated by Police Battalion 133's First Company has already been mentioned. The Germans discovered so many Jews because of the zeal they brought to their jobs. When people are sent to look for a needle in a haystack that they do not wish to uncover, the easiest thing for them to do is not to find it.

In May 1943, Police Battalion 65 was sent to Copenhagen, where its men engaged in a variety of genocide-abetting undertakings, rounding up Jews, deporting them, and trying to prevent their escape.[78] February 1944 saw the battalion transferred to Yugoslavia, where it was occupied for the remainder of the year in warfare against partisans and in shooting hostages. It suffered heavy losses. In spring 1945, the battalion retreated towards Germany, and was captured near the end of the war by British forces in the area around Klagenfurt in Austria.[79]

Police battalions and other units of the Order Police commenced slaughtering Jews *en masse* with the beginning of the simultaneous onslaught against the Soviet Union and its Jews, and continued as long as Germans continued to kill Jews systematically. It cannot be said precisely in how many deaths police battalions were complicit. The number is certainly over one million, and could be three times as high.[80]

7

POLICE BATTALION 101:
THE MEN'S DEEDS

LIKE POLICE BATTALION 65 and the other units of Police Regiment 25, Police Battalion 101 engaged wholeheartedly in the German extermination of European Jewry.[1] The battalion had two lives. The early one lasted until May 1941, when the battalion was remade as its initial personnel of professional policemen were replaced almost completely by raw draftees. Before its first life came to a close, Police Battalion 101 participated in lethal activities, but, in comparison to its later life, only sporadically. Its second life lasted from that May until its dissolution, and was marked by the overwhelming bulk of its killing activities. Because a personnel change demarcates the battalion's two instantiations, its first life had little relevance for the deeds that shaped the identity of the battalion's second life as a *Völkermordkohorte*, or genocidal cohort.

Police Battalion 101's pre-genocidal life course was essentially uneventful.[2] Police Battalion 101 was established in September 1939 and was then composed exclusively of active policemen (*Polizeibeamter*). Sent immediately to Poland, it operated there until December 1939, securing conquered areas and guarding POWs and military installations. Upon returning to Hamburg, it took part in general police duties. In May 1940, the battalion was sent again to Poland, for the second of its three turns at "pacifying" and restructuring the subjugated territory. Its most important activities were the forced evacuation of Poles from the region around Posen, so that ethnic Germans from the Baltics and the Soviet Union could be resettled there, and providing guards for the Łódź ghetto. There the men of Police Battalion 101 participated in the immiseration, brutalizing, and even killing of Jews. During this stay in Poland, which lasted until April 1941, the battalion's men occasionally shot Polish "hostages."[3]

Upon returning to its home base of Hamburg, Police Battalion 101 was broken up when its men were distributed among three other recently established police battalions from Hamburg, numbered 102, 103, and 104. Its ranks were replenished with draftees, and like these three other police battalions, it received the designation of being a reserve battalion, so its official name became "Reserve Police Battalion 101." Remaining for the time being garrisoned in Hamburg, Police Battalion 101 engaged in activities that were the normal, unremarkable duties of policemen. The exceptions to this were the three separate deportations that its men conducted of Jews from Hamburg to conquered areas of the Soviet Union. The Jews were massacred there, at least one time by some of the men of the battalion. Obviously, deporting the Jews to their deaths was not opposed by many in the battalion, because, as some men report, the deportation duty was coveted. One man testifies that only a small circle of "favored comrades" got to go.[4]

In June 1942, the battalion's third tour of duty began in Poland, which lasted until the beginning of 1944. Stationed the entire time in the Lublin region, the battalion's headquarters moved from Biłgoraj in June 1942, to Radzyń the next month, to Łuków in October, back to Radzyń in April 1943, and then to Międzyrzec at the beginning of 1944. Its companies and their platoons were sometimes stationed in the city of the battalion headquarters, though they were generally assigned to surrounding cities and towns.[5] In February 1943, the older members of the battalion (those born before 1900), like those of other police battalions, were transferred home, to be replaced by younger men. During this period, Police Battalion 101's officers and men were principally and fully engaged in *Aktion Reinhard*, undertaking numerous killing operations against Jews, sometimes shooting the Jews themselves, even by the thousands, and at other times deporting thousands more to the gas chambers.

Police Battalion 101 was divided into a battalion staff and three companies, with a total strength, if a gradually changing membership, of about five hundred men. The battalion was led by Major Wilhelm Trapp. Two of the companies were commanded by captains, the third by a lieutenant. In addition to the small company staffs, each company was composed of three platoons. Generally, two of the three platoons were led by lieutenants and the third by a non-commissioned officer. The platoons were further divided into groups of about ten men, with a non-commissioned officer in charge. The battalion was lightly armed, having only four machine guns per company to augment the rifles that its men carried. The battalion had its own transport, which included trucks and, for conducting patrols, bicycles.[6]

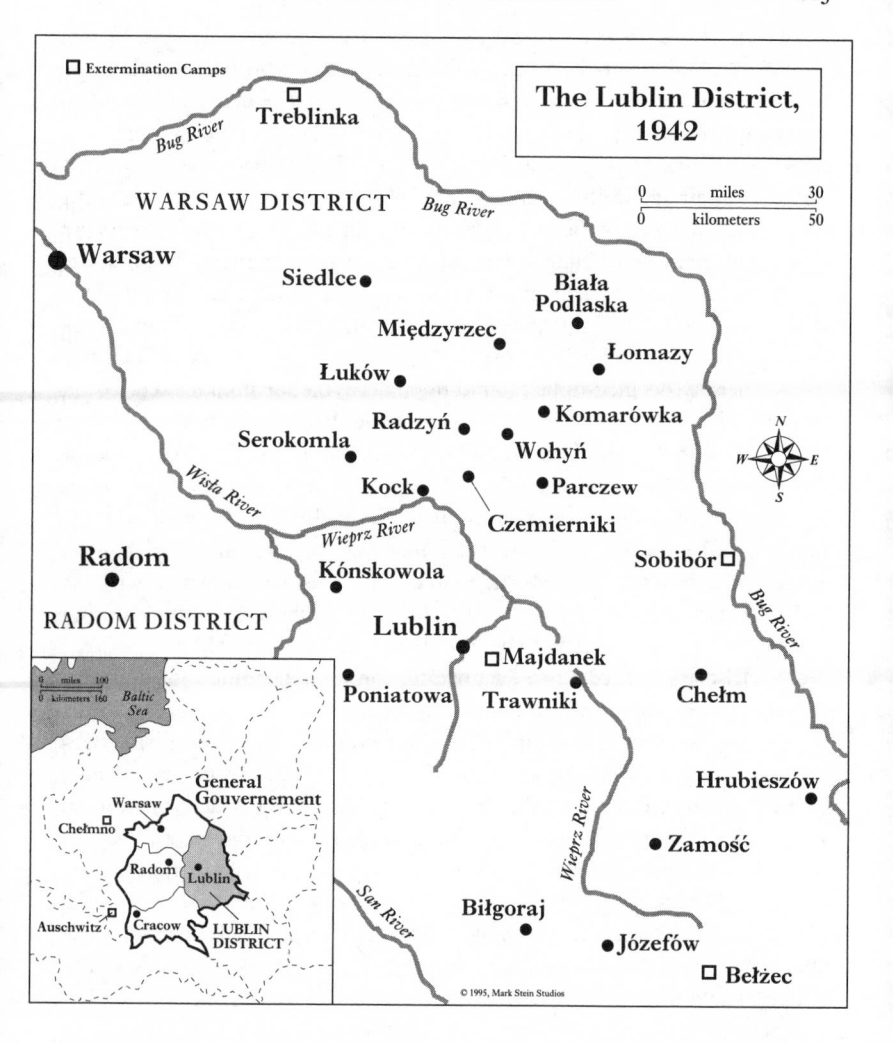

The Lublin District, 1942

□ Extermination Camps

WARSAW DISTRICT

Bug River

Treblinka □

Warsaw ●

Siedlce ●

Biała Podlaska ●

Międzyrzec ●

Łomazy ●

Łuków ●

Radzyń ●

Komarówka ●

Serokomla ●

Wohyń ●

Kock ●

Parczew ●

Czemierniki

Radom ●

RADOM DISTRICT

Kónskowola ●

Wieprz River

Sobibór □

Bug River

Lublin

□ Majdanek

Poniatowa ●

Trawniki ●

Chełm ●

Hrubieszów ●

Zamość ●

Wieprz River

San River

Biłgoraj ●

Józefów ●

□ Bełżec

General Gouvernement

Warsaw ●

Chełmno □

Baltic Sea

Radom ● Lublin ●

Auschwitz □ Cracow ● LUBLIN DISTRICT

© 1995, Mark Stein Studios

Who were the men of Police Battalion 101? The biographical data that exist on these men are scanty, so only a partial portrait of the battalion can be drawn.[7] This turns out not to be a crucial problem, because enough of the relevant data do exist to suffice for the primary task of drawing this portrait. Since the men did not choose to join an institution known to be devoted to mass slaughter, the purpose here is not to seek the elements of their backgrounds that might explain their participation. Rather, assessing their backgrounds allows us to gauge how representative the men of Police Battalion 101 were of other Germans, and whether or not the conclusions drawn about them might also apply to their countrymen.

Police Battalion 101 was manned overwhelmingly by reservists, by men who were called to duty between 1939 and 1941, men who were not yet in any military or security institution, the men least likely to be martial in spirit and temperament. Of the 550 men who are known to have served in Police Battalion 101 during its genocidal stay in Poland, the birthdays of 519 are known.[8] Their age profile was extremely old for a military or police institution. Their mean age, when their genocidal killing began, was 36.5 years old. Only 42 of them were younger than thirty, a measly 8.1 percent. One hundred fifty-three of them, a shade under 30 percent, were older than forty. Nine of them were over fifty. Fully 382 of them, or almost three-quarters (73.6 percent) came from the birth cohorts of 1900–1909, the cohorts of men who were generally deemed to be too old to be desirable for military service and from which most reservists who served in police battalions were raised. That they were older is significant. They were not the impressionable, malleable eighteen-year-olds that armies love to mold according to the institution's specified needs. These were mature men who had life experience, who had families and children. The overwhelming majority of them had reached adulthood before the Nazis ascended to power. They had known other political dispensations, had lived in other ideological climates. They were not wide-eyed youngsters ready to believe whatever they were told.

Social class, according to occupation, can be determined for 291 (52.9 percent) of the members of Police Battalion 101.[9] They were distributed widely among all of the occupational groups in Germany, except for those forming the elite. Following a variant of the standard occupational classification system for Germany of this era, German society is divided according to a tripartite scheme of lower class, lower middle class, and elite. The elite formed a tiny upper crust in the society of less than 3 percent, with the overwhelming bulk of the people being divided between the lower and lower middle classes. Each class is further subdivided into occupational subgroups. The table below gives the occupational breakdown for Germany as a whole and for Police Battalion 101.[10]

CLASS

Occupational Subgroup	Percent of Total		
		Police	
	Germany	*Battalion 101*	
	%	(n)	%
LOWER			
1. Unskilled workers	37.3	(64)	22.0
2. Skilled workers	17.3	(38)	13.1
Subtotal	54.6	(102)	35.1

LOWER MIDDLE

3. Master craftsmen (independent)	9.6	(22)	7.6
4. Nonacademic professionals	1.8	(9)	3.1
5. Lower and intermediate employees	12.4	(66)	22.7
6. Lower and intermediate civil servants	5.2	(59)	20.3
7. Merchants (self-employed)	6.0	(22)	7.6
8. Farmers (self-employed)	7.7	(2)	0.7
Subtotal	42.6	(180)	61.9

ELITE

9. Managers	0.5	(1)	0.3
10. Higher civil servants	0.5	(1)	0.3
11. Academic professionals	1.0	(1)	0.3
12. Students (university and upper school)	0.5	(0)	0
13. Entrepreneurs	0.3	(6)	2.1
Subtotal	2.8	(9)	3.1
Total	100.0	(291)	100.0

Part of this graph is based on information from Michael H. Kater's *The Nazi Party*.

Compared to the German population as a whole, the men of Police Battalion 101 came more from the lower middle class and less from the lower class. This imbalance was due mainly to the unit's shortage, on the one hand, of unskilled workers compared to the general population, and its overabundance, on the other, of lower and intermediate employees from business and the government. Within the lower middle strata, the battalion was particularly lacking in farmers, which is not surprising, since the battalion was raised primarily from an urban environment. Its representatives of the elite, all nine of them, were in virtually identical proportion (3.1 percent) to that existing in the general population. All in all, the differences between the occupational profiles of Police Battalion 101 and Germany as a whole were not of great significance.[11] A smaller percentage of blue-collar workers and farmers, and a greater percentage of lower-level white-collar workers populated the battalion than German society as a whole, but significant numbers of each nonetheless were to be found in its ranks.

The most important characteristic of the battalion's men for assessing their actions and the degree to which they were, as a group, representative of German society—that is, ordinary Germans—is their degree of Nazification. This can be appraised by looking at their institutional affiliation, which, if imprecise, is the best indicator of Nazification beyond the degree to which most Germans were generally Nazified (particularly on the independent dimension of antisemitism). In short, how many men in Police Battalion 101 were members of the Nazi Party and of the SS? Of the 550 men, 179 were Party members, composing 32.5 percent of the battalion, which was not much greater than the national average. Seventeen of the Party members were also in the SS. An additional 4 were SS men who were not Party members. So, in sum, only 21, but 3.8 percent of the men, mainly reservists, were in the SS—a tiny percentage—which, though higher than the national average, is of no great significance for understanding this battalion's actions.

The major issue here, anyway, is not the percentage of these men who were Nazified according to institutional affiliation in comparison to the national average, and therefore how *representative* a sample these men form in this respect. It is those who had no Nazi or SS affiliation who are analytically the most significant people, because they (and the thousands like them in other police battalions) provide insight into the likely conduct of other ordinary Germans, had they too been asked to become genocidal killers. In this battalion, *379 men had no affiliation whatsoever with the major Nazi institutions.* And it cannot even be concluded that Nazi Party membership meant for each person a higher degree of ideological Nazification than that which existed in the general populace, because many non-ideological reasons induced people to join the Party. Obviously, whether or not people were members of the Nazi Party did differentiate Germans from each other. Still, the Party members who were Nazified beyond the standard existing in Germany was a subset of all Party members. Moreover, at the time of Police Battalion 101's major killings, about seven million Germans could boast of membership in the Party, over 20 percent of the adult male German population. Being a member of the Party was a rather ordinary distinction in Germany. Being a Nazi was "ordinary" in Germany. Thus, the most remarkable and significant fact is that 96 percent of these men were not in the SS, the association of the true believers. As a group, the men of Police Battalion 101 were not an unusually Nazified lot for German society. Overwhelmingly, they consisted of ordinary Germans—of both kinds—those who were in the Party and, especially, those who were not.

A comparison of the age and occupational profiles between Party and non-Party members reveals that they were remarkably alike. Party members were on average about one year older than non-Party members (37.1 to 36.2 years). The occupational breakdowns of the two groups are remarkably parallel.

CLASS

Occupational Subgroup	Percent of Total	
	Party	*Non-Party*
LOWER		
1. Unskilled workers	23.3	20.6
2. Skilled workers	10.2	16.3
Subtotal	33.5	36.9

LOWER MIDDLE

3. Master craftsmen (independent)	5.8	9.2
4. Nonacademic professionals	4.7	1.4
5. Lower and intermediate employees	19.3	26.2
6. Lower and intermediate civil servants	22.7	17.7
7. Merchants (self-employed)	8.7	6.4
8. Farmers (self-employed)	0.7	0.7
Subtotal	61.8	61.7

ELITE

9. Managers	0.7	0
10. Higher civil servants	0.7	0
11. Academic professionals	0.7	0
12. Students (university and upper school)	0.0	0
13. Entrepreneurs	2.7	1.4
Subtotal	4.7	1.4
Total	(150) 100.0	(141) 100.0

Part of this graph is based on information from Michael H. Kater's *The Nazi Party*.

The men of Police Battalion 101 came predominantly from Hamburg and the surrounding region. A small contingent of around a dozen men from Luxembourg was also in the battalion.[12] Since the Hamburg region of Germany was overwhelmingly Evangelical Protestant, so too most of them must have been. The smattering of data on their religious affiliation indicates that some percentage of them had renounced the Church and declared themselves "*gottgläubig*," the Nazi-approved term for having a proper religious attitude without being a member of one of the traditional churches. Their geographic origins and religious affiliations almost certainly had nothing to do with their participation in genocidal slaughter, as police battalions and other killing units were raised from all regions of Germany and drew on Protestants, Catholics, and the *gottgläubig* alike.

The relatively advanced age of these men is of significance. Many of them headed families and had children. Unfortunately, the data on their family status are partial and difficult to interpret. There are data on the marital status of only ninety-six of them. All but one, 99 percent, of them had wives. Almost three-quarters of them, seventy-two of the ninety-eight for whom data exist, had children at the time of the killings. It is safe to surmise that these percentages are higher than was true for the entire battalion. In their irregular biographical self-reporting, those who were married and, particularly, those who had children were probably more likely to offer these tidbits about themselves. How much the existing sample overrepresents the contingent of husbands and fathers among the battalion is impossible to say. It is safe, however, to assume that many of the battalion's men were married and had children, similar to a large majority of Germans of their ages. Nothing about their histories suggests that they would have been anomalous in these matters.

The political views and previous political affiliations of these men cannot be determined. Only the most paltry of evidence exists about them in the available sources. Because they were mainly from Hamburg, a city that supported the Nazis somewhat less enthusiastically than the nation as a whole and that was a traditional bastion of support for the left, it might be presumed that among these men were more former Social Democrats and Communists than in Germany as a whole. Also, that the men had not signed up for other military institutions might suggest a certain coolness to Nazism, though they might have kept themselves free because of family responsibilities. In any case, as was discussed earlier, by the time of the battalion's genocidal activity, the enterprise of national aggrandizement was greatly popular among the German people generally, whatever their previous politics had been. That a smaller percentage of lower-class men made up their ranks, from whom the left drew its traditional strength, might have worked to counterbalance this presumed relative coolness to Nazism that its Hamburg origins might have bequeathed to the battalion. All of this, however, is educated guesswork. What is safe to assume is that within the battalion were men who had been and were political supporters of the regime (as were most Germans), and some who were not. Much more on this subject cannot be said.

In forming this battalion, the Order Police drew on an ordinary population, distinguished chiefly by its advanced age and its status of not being enrolled in military service. Some of the men had been previously declared unfit for duty because of age or physical infirmities.[13] In so doing, the regime was employing men who were among the least fit able-bodied men that it could find (both physically and by disposition) for staffing its roving police battalion. The men's advanced age brought with it longer histories of personal independence as adults, knowledge of other political orders, and the experience derived from having and heading families. Their Nazi Party and SS membership was somewhat higher than the national average, though the large majority among them were free of Nazi institutional affiliation. These men form anything but the portrait of hand-selected *Weltanschauungskrieger*, of men that would have been selected had a search been conducted to find the "right" men to carry out an apocalyptic deed like the wholesale mass slaughter of civilians.

The Order Police filled out Police Battalion 101 with an inauspicious group. It nevertheless made little effort to hone these men, through physical or ideological training, into men bearing a more soldierly and Nazi attitude. In chorus, the men testify to the perfunctory nature of their training. Some men were drafted but weeks or days ahead of the beginning of the battalion's killing life, and were thrown directly into the genocidal fray. One such man was a dairy farmer until April 1942. He was called up, given brief training prior to being sent to Police Battalion 101, and, before he knew it, found himself engaged in genocidal slaughter.[14] Nothing whatsoever indicates that any attempt was made to examine the "fitness" of these men for their future genocidal activities by investigating their views on crucial ideological subjects, particularly the Jews. Although no reason exists to believe that the Order Police was aware of it, some of the men in this police battalion had previously shown hostility to the regime. One had been declared untrustworthy by the Gestapo, and others had been active opponents of Nazi rule in the SPD or trade unions.[15] This simply did not matter. The manpower shortage dictated that the Order Police would take anyone it could find—and it had to pick from the leftovers.

ON JUNE 20, 1942 Police Battalion 101 received the order to embark on its third tour of duty in Poland. Setting out for Poland were 11 officers, 5 administrators, and 486 men.[16] They traveled by truck over five hundred miles, arriving a few days later in Biłgoraj, a city to the south of Lublin. At this time, its men had not received word that they would soon be committing genocidal slaughter. Yet perhaps some, especially the officers, suspected what might have lain before them. After all, the battalion had already escorted Jews from Hamburg to their deaths; its officers, during the battalion's second tour in Poland, had been in the thick of executing the anti-Jewish policy of the time; and many, if not most, undoubtedly knew of their brethren's mass killing of the Jews in the Soviet Union and Poland.

The first order to kill Jews was communicated to the battalion's commander, Major Trapp, some short time before the operation's designated day. The day before the foray, he gathered his officers for a briefing and divulged to them their orders.[17] Presumably, the company commanders were not supposed to inform their men of the anticipated event. Some evidence suggests that not all of them kept quiet. Captain Julius Wohlauf, the commander of First Company, who was to become an enthusiastic killer of Jews, apparently could not keep his anticipation to himself. One of his men remembers Wohlauf having characterized their upcoming mission in Józefów as an "extremely interesting task" (*hochinteressante Aufgabe*).[18] Without stating explicitly whether he then learned of the upcoming massacre, another man recounts having learned of an aspect of the preparations that presaged the character of their entire stay. "I can still remember clearly that on the evening before the killing [*Aktion*] in Józefów whips were handed out. I personally did not witness it because I was in town making purchases. I learned it, however, from my comrades after my return to our quarters. In the meantime, we got wind of what kind of operation lay ahead of us the next day. The whips were to be used in driving the Jews out of their homes. The whips were made of genuine ox hide."[19] The men thus outfitted for the upcoming massacre were those assigned to drive the Jews out from their homes and to the assembly point. Exactly which companies they were from, he says he cannot remember.

The battalion's companies rode in trucks to Józefów, which was less than twenty miles away. They departed after midnight and rode for about two hours. Those among them who had learned of the nature of their operation, had time, as the trucks jolted them up and down over the bumpy roads, to contemplate their tasks' meaning and appeal. The others were to discover only moments before the Dantesque production would commence that they had been chosen to help bring about their *Führer*'s dream, frequently articulated by him and those close to him—the dream of exterminating the Jews.

Major Trapp assembled his battalion. The men formed three sides of a square around Trapp in order to hear his address.

> He announced that in the locality before us we were to carry out a mass killing by shooting and he brought out clearly that those whom we were supposed to shoot were Jews. During his address he bid us to think of our women and children in our homeland who had to endure aerial bombardments. In particular, we were supposed to bear in mind that many women and children lose their lives in these attacks. Thinking of these facts would make it easier for us to carry out the order during the upcoming [killing] action. Major Trapp remarked that the action was entirely not in his spirit, but that he had received this order from higher authority.[20]

The unequivocal communication to these ordinary Germans that they were expected to take part in genocidal slaughter was made to them that morning, as they stood near a sleeping small Polish city about to be awakened to scenes that were nightmarish beyond its inhabitants' imagination. Some of the men testify that Trapp justified the killing with the transparently weak argument that the Jews were supporting the partisans.[21] Why the partisans' fortunes, which at this point were actually meager to non-existent, bore any relationship to their task of killing infants, small children, the elderly, and the incapacitated was not explained. The appeal to the Jews' alleged partisan activity was intended to place a gloss, however thin, of military normality on the large massacre, for the slaughtering of an entire community as its members slept in their beds might have been expected to give pause to the Germans the first time around. Similarly, Trapp's appeal to superior orders likely had two sources. It needed to be made clear to the men that an order of such gravity came from the highest of authorities and was therefore consecrated by the state and Hitler. Trapp also seemed to be expressing his genuine emotions.

He was shaken by the order. Trapp was later heard to have exclaimed, upon seeing the battalion's doctor: "My God, why must I do this."[22]

Yet Trapp's reservations appear not to have been born of a view of Jews that diverged from the dominant antisemitic model. His explanation to the men that the killing of the Jews, including the Jewish women and children, was a response to the bombing of German cities betrays his Nazified conception of the Jews. How could such a statement make sense to him and to all those who heard and understood it?[23] It is not clear what the exact logic of the comparison was, yet it suggested that the slaughter of the Jews was either just retribution for the bombing of German cities or perhaps a retaliatory act that would have some salutary effect on the bombing, or both. To the Germans who were on the verge of utterly effacing this remote and prostrate Jewish community, the connection between the Jews in this sleepy city in Poland and the Allies' bombing of Germany appears to have been real. In fact, the men in the police battalion do not comment on the ludicrousness of Trapp's central justification, spoken to them at their baptismal moment as genocidal executioners. The perversity of the Nazified German mind was such that thinking of their own children was not intended to, calculated to, and evidently did not—except in the case of a few—arouse sympathy for other children who happened to be Jewish. Instead, thinking of their children spurred the Germans to kill Jewish children.[24]

Trapp's address to his men included general instructions for the conduct of the operation. The assembled Germans—whether they had learned on that morning or the night before about the phase in their lives that they were then initiating—understood that they were embarking on a momentous undertaking, not some routine police operation. They received explicit orders to shoot the most helpless Jews—the old, the young, and the sick, women and children—but not men capable of doing work, who would be spared.[25] Did these ordinary Germans want to do it? Did any of them mutter to themselves, as men, including those in uniform, often do when they receive onerous, disagreeable, or unpalatable orders, that they wished they were elsewhere? If they had, then the continuation of Trapp's address was for them a godsend. Their beloved commander, their "Papa" Trapp, gave them a way out, at least initially to the older battalion men. He made a remarkable offer: "As the conclusion of his address, the major put the question to the older battalion members of whether there were among them those who did not feel up to the task. At first no one had the courage to come forward. I was then the first to step forward and stated that I was one of those who was not fit for the task. Only then did others come forward. We were then about ten to twelve men, who were kept at the major's disposal."[26]

Those who were a party to the scene must have felt some uncertainty. The Germans were at the staging ground for the wholesale slaughter of a community. They were entering a new moral world. Who among them had ever imagined, say, three years before, that he would be standing in eastern Poland with such a charge, to kill all the women and children he would find? Yet the *Führer* had ordered the killing, the killing of these Jews. And now their commander was giving at least some of them the option not to kill. He was a genuine man who was, by all accounts, solicitous of them.[27] Some of the men stepped forward. If they were hesitant, however, their uncertainty must have been further intensified by Captain Hoffmann's reaction. The man who first took advantage of Trapp's offer continues: "In this connection, I remember that the chief of my company, Hoffmann, became very agitated at my having stepped forward. I remember that he said something to the effect: 'This fellow ought to be shot!' But Major Trapp cut him off. . . ."[28] Hoffmann, who was to prove himself a zealous, if fainthearted killer, was publicly silenced and put in his place by Trapp. Trapp's way was to be the battalion's way. That was unequivocal. The men who had stepped forward were all excused from the killing operation. Yet it must be noted, as it was undoubtedly noted by the assembled men, that Hoffmann's willingness to object so openly and vociferously to the acceptance of Trapp's offer was publicly to call into question a superior order. It was hardly the picture of obedience.

Another man, Alois Weber, agrees that Trapp made the offer to excuse those who did not want to kill, yet he maintains that the offer was made not just to the older men but to the entire battalion: "Trapp's request was not intended as a trap. It did not require much courage to step forward. One man of my company stepped forward. An angry exchange of words between Hoffmann and Papen developed. . . . It is possible that twelve stepped forward. I did not hear that only older men could step forward. Younger ones also stepped forward. Everyone must have heard that one may step forward, because I heard it too."[29] It is difficult to know which account is correct. To my mind, the assertion of a more inclusive offer of reassignment is the more plausible of the two. In addition to it simply sounding more credible, three further items support this conclusion. During the unfolding of the killing operation that day, men of all ages, and not just the older men, were easily able to excuse themselves from the killing. Second, Weber testifies that younger men also stepped forward when Trapp made his offer, which is unlikely to have occurred had Trapp not addressed them as well. Finally, Weber indicts himself by admitting that he did not choose to avoid becoming a genocidal killer of Jews even though he knew that he had that option and saw others who chose not to contribute in this way to genocide.[30] In some sense, it does not matter very much which account is correct; even if Trapp's initial offer had been directed only to the older men, it soon became clear to the others that it was not only the older men who had the option to avoid killing. Once the killing began, moreover, when the full horror of the enterprise engulfed them, the emotional incentive to opt out of the killing grew enormously, but had little discernible effect on the men's choices.

The battalion assembly was followed by a series of smaller meetings. Trapp gave assignments to the company commanders, who then informed their men of their tasks (a sergeant did the briefing for First Company), which included the shooting of those who could not so easily be brought to the assembly point—the old, the young, and the sick—on the spot, namely in their homes, even in their beds.[31] Initially, First Company was detailed first to help out in clearing the Jews out of the ghetto and then to man the execution squads. Second Company received the main responsibility of clearing the ghetto, of going door to door and compelling the Jews to assemble at the specified gathering place, Józefów's market square. The majority of Third Company was supposed to secure the city by cordoning it off. One of its platoons was assigned to help Second Company.[32] As the operation unfolded, the logistical arrangements were modified, so members of the various companies took part in the duties originally assigned to other companies.

When dawn arrived, the Germans began rounding up the Jews from the ghetto of Józefów. They combed through the ghetto in small groups, generally of two or three, driving Jews from their homes. The men of Third Company had received, directly from their company commander, the same instructions as the others, "that during the evacuation, the old and the sick as well as infants and small children and Jews, who put up resistance, are to be shot on the spot."[33] The Germans were incredibly brutal, carrying out with abandon their orders not to bother transporting the non-ambulatory to the roundup point and instead to kill them on the spot. "I saw about six Jewish corpses, who had, according to orders, been shot by my comrades where they found them. Among others I saw an old woman, who lay dead in her bed."[34] When the Germans' work was completed, Jewish corpses lay strewn throughout the ghetto, as one of the Germans put it, in the "front yards, doorways, and streets all the way to the market square."[35] A member of Third Company describes the handiwork: ". . . I also know that this order was carried out, because as I walked through the Jewish district during the evacuation, I saw dead old people and infants. I also know that during the evacuation all patients of a Jewish hospital were shot by the troops combing the district."[36]

It is easy to read these two sentences, shudder for a moment, and continue on. But consider how intense the psychological pressure not to slaughter such people would have been had these men indeed been opposed to the slaughter, had they indeed not seen the Jews as deserving this fate. They had just heard from their commander that he was willing to excuse those who wanted to demur. Instead of accepting his offer, they chose to walk into a hospital, a house of healing, and to shoot the sick, who must have been cowering, begging, and screaming for mercy. They killed babies.[37] None of the Germans has seen fit to recount details of such killings. In all probability, a killer either shot a baby in its mother's arms, and perhaps the mother for good measure, or, as was sometimes the habit during these years, held it at arm's length by the leg, shooting it with a pistol. Perhaps the mother looked on in horror. The tiny corpse was then dropped like so much trash and left to rot. A life extinguished. The horror of killing just one baby, or of taking part in the massacre of the Jewish hospital patients, let alone all of the other killing that was then or later that day to occur, ought to have induced those who saw Jews as part of the human family to investigate whether Trapp's offer might yet be taken up by them as well. As far as it is known, none did.

After the initial roundup was finished, the Germans combed through the ghetto to ensure that no Jews would escape their appointed fate. By mid-1942, Jews all over Poland, having learned through individual and the collective Jewish experience what the Germans intended for them, had constructed hiding places, often ingenious, in the hope that they might escape detection. The Germans, aware of the Jews' attempts to cheat the hangmen's nooses, assiduously applied themselves to uncovering the concealed places. Aided by eager local Poles, these Germans left no wall untapped and no stone unturned: "The residential district was searched again. In many cases, with the aid of Poles, numerous Jews were found hiding in blockaded rooms and alcoves. I remember that a Pole drew my attention to a so-called dead space between two walls of adjoining rooms. In another case, a Pole drew attention to a subterranean hideout. The Jews found in two hideouts were not killed in accordance with the order but upon my instructions were brought to the marketplace."[38] This man, if he is to be believed, preferred to let others do the dirty work. He chose to disobey his orders to kill all resisters, and to bring about the same end in a more palatable manner (by letting others do the killing). Had he been opposed to the killing of Jews, rather than merely finding it distasteful to do it himself, it would have been easy not to find Jews who had done their utmost to remain hidden; yet in his extensive testimony, he gives no indication that he or others made an effort to turn a blind eye to concealed Jews.[39]

The Germans assembled the Jews at the market square. The driving of the Jews from their homes had taken a long time. It was Police Battalion 101's first killing operation, and they had not yet streamlined their routine. Some of the officers were dissatisfied with the progress of the operation. They went around spurring their men onward: "We're not making headway! It's not going fast enough!"[40] Finally, around 10 a.m., the Germans sorted out the so-called able-bodied (*Arbeitsfähigen*), about four hundred men, and sent them to a "work" camp near Lublin.[41] The men of Police Battalion 101 were now ready to enter into the climactic stage of their first genocidal enterprise. New assignments were given to the men, and so they were set to begin the systematic slaughter. They had already been instructed in the recommended shooting technique during the initial assemblage around Trapp. "About Dr. Schoenfelder I recall with certainty. . . . We stood, as I said, in a semicircle round Dr. Schoenfelder and the other officers. Dr. Schoenfelder sketched on the ground—so that we could all see—the outline of the upper part of a human body and marked on the neck the spot at which we should fire. This picture stands clearly before my eyes. Of one thing I am not sure, whether in drawing on the ground, he used a stick or something else."[42] The battalion's doctor, their healer, who tutored the men on the best way to kill, obviously did not deem his Hippocratic oath to apply to Jews.[43] Further discussions on refining the killing technique took place. "It was discussed how the shooting should be carried out. The question was whether [to shoot] with or without a bayonet mounted on the rifle. . . . The mounted bayonet would avoid misfirings and the man need not come too close to the victims."[44]

From the market square the Germans trucked the Jews, one group at a time, to woods on the outskirts of Józefów, whereupon "the Jews were ordered by the policemen in escort to jump down from the trucks, and were naturally, as circumstances warranted, given a 'helping hand' ['*nachgeholfen*' *wurde*] to speed things up."[45] Even though this was their first killing operation, it was already, according to this killer, "natural" for the men of Police Battalion 101 to strike Jews (the obvious meaning of the euphemistic "helping hand," which appears in his testimony in quotation marks). So "natural" was it that the killer mentions it in an offhand, passing manner, not deeming it worthy of any further attention or elaboration.

The men of First Company, who were initially assigned to shoot the Jews, were joined around noon by members of Second Company because Major Trapp anticipated that they would not otherwise finish the slaughter before nightfall.[46] The actual killing duties ended up being shared by more of the battalion than Trapp had originally planned. The exact manner of transport and procedure of execution differed a bit from unit to unit and also evolved during the course of the day. The platoons of First Company, to focus on it, had broken down into killing squads of about eight. The initial procedure was some variation on the following. A squad would approach the group of Jews who had just arrived, from which each member would choose his victim—a man, a woman, or a child.[47] The Jews and Germans would then walk in parallel single file so that each killer moved in step with his victim, until they reached a clearing for the killing where they would position themselves and await the firing order from their squad leader.[48]

The walk into the woods afforded each perpetrator an opportunity for re-flection. Walking side by side with his victim, he was able to imbue the human form beside him with the projections of his mind. Some of the Germans, of course, had children walking beside them. It is highly likely that, back in Ger-many, these men had previously walked through woods with their own chil-dren by their sides, marching gaily and inquisitively along. With what thoughts and emotions did each of these men march, gazing sidelong at the form of, say, an eight- or twelve-year-old girl, who to the unideologized mind would have looked like any other girl? In these moments, each killer had a per-sonalized, face-to-face relationship to his victim, to his little girl. Did he see a little girl, and ask himself why he was about to kill this little, delicate human being who, if seen as a little girl by him, would normally have received his compassion, protection, and nurturance? Or did he see a Jew, a young one, but a Jew nonetheless? Did he wonder incredulously what could possibly justify his blowing a vulnerable little girl's brains out? Or did he understand the rea-sonableness of the order, the necessity of nipping the believed-in Jewish blight in the bud? The "Jew-child," after all, was mother to the Jew.

The killing itself was a gruesome affair. After the walk through the woods, each of the Germans had to raise his gun to the back of the head, now face down on the ground, that had bobbed along beside him, pull the trigger, and watch the person, sometimes a little girl, twitch and then move no more. The Germans had to remain hardened to the crying of the victims, to the cry-ing of women, to the whimpering of children.[49] At such close range, the Ger-mans often became spattered with human gore. In the words of one man, "the supplementary shot struck the skull with such force that the entire back of the skull was torn off and blood, bone splinters, and brain matter soiled the marksmen."[50] Sergeant Anton Bentheim indicates that this was not an iso-lated episode, but rather the general condition: "The executioners were grue-somely soiled with blood, brain matter, and bone splinters. It stuck to their clothes."[51] Although this is obviously viscerally unsettling, capable of dis-turbing even the most hardened of executioners, these German initiates re-turned to fetch new victims, new little girls, and to begin the journey back into the woods. They sought unstained locations in the woods for each new batch of Jews.[52]

In this personalized, individual manner, each of the men who took part in the shooting generally killed between five and ten Jews, most of whom were elderly, women, and children. The approximately thirty men of Lieutenant Kurt Drucker's platoon of Second Company, for example, shot between two hundred and three hundred Jews in three to four hours.[53] They took breaks during the killing, for rest, for relief, and for smoking cigarettes.[54] Uncharac-teristically for German killing operations, the men of Police Battalion 101 neither forced the Jews to undress nor collected valuables from them. They had one single-minded mission that day. In total, between the wild slaughter in the ghetto itself and the methodical executions in the woods, the Germans killed that day somewhere over 1,200 Jews, perhaps a few hundred more. The Germans abandoned the bodies where they lay, whether in the streets of Józefów or in the surrounding woods, having left the burial for Józefów's Polish Mayor to arrange.[55]

Among the victims was a considerable number of German Jews from the northern part of Germany, who spoke German in an accent similar to that of the men in Police Battalion 101. The linguistic strangeness of Polish Jews (who were the majority of the victims) and their alien Polish Jewish customs served to buttress the monumental cognitive and psychological barrier that effectively prevented the Germans from recognizing the Jews' humanity. However much the Germans could dissociate the Polish Jews from themselves, the Jews from their own region of Germany, who addressed the killers in the cadences of their mother tongue, might nevertheless have shocked the Germans into considering the humanity of these Jews. Two members of Second Company remember a Jew from Bremen, who was a veteran of the First World War, having begged for his life to be spared. It did the Jew no good,[56] just as the rest of the German Jews' Germanness yielded them nothing but the Germans' egalitarian bullets, which—in the Germans' eyes and in reality—leveled all Jews, German or Polish, male or female, young or old.

What was the effect of the killing on the killers? Their assiduousness in killing is not to be doubted. They applied themselves diligently to their task with telling effect. The gruesomeness of it revolted some, but not all, of them. One killer describes a vivid memory from that day:

> These Jews were brought into the woods on the instruction of [Sergeant] Steinmetz. We went with the Jews. After about 220 yards Steinmetz directed that the Jews had to lay themselves next to each other in a row on the ground. I would like to mention now that only women and children were there. They were largely women and children around twelve years old. . . . I had to shoot an old woman, who was over sixty years old. I can still remember, that the old woman said to me, will you make it short or about the same. . . . Next to me was the Policeman Koch. . . . He had to shoot a small boy of perhaps twelve years. We had been expressly told that we should hold the gun's barrel eight inches from the head. Koch had apparently not done this, because while leaving the execution site, the other comrades laughed at me, because pieces of the child's brains had spattered onto my sidearm and had stuck there. I first asked, why are you laughing, whereupon Koch, pointing to the brains on my sidearm, said: That's from mine, he has stopped twitching. He said this in an obviously boastful tone. . . .[57]

This kind of jocularity, this kind of boyish, open joy being taken in the mass slaughter, was not a singular occurrence, never to be repeated. After describing the mocker's tone as boastful, the killer remarks: "I have experienced more obscenities [*Schweinereien*] of this kind. . . ."

The ghastliness of the killing scene did disturb some of the killers. Of this, there can be no doubt. Some were shaken badly. Entering an ordinary animal slaughterhouse is unpleasant for many, even for some avid meat eaters. Not surprisingly, a few of the killers felt the need to excuse themselves from the killing or to take a breather during its course. One squad leader, Sergeant Ernst Hergert, reports that within his platoon two to five men asked to be exempted from the killing after these men had already begun, because they found it too burdensome to shoot women and children. The men were excused by him or by their lieutenant and given either guard or transport duties for the duration of the killing.[58] Two other sergeants, Bentheim and Arthur Kammer, also excused a few men under their commands.[59] A third sergeant, Heinrich Steinmetz, explicitly told his men before the killings that they did not have to kill. "I would like also to mention that before the beginning of the execution, Sergeant Steinmetz said to the members of the platoon that those who did not feel up to the upcoming task could come forward. No one, to be sure, exempted himself."[60] Significantly, these men had already participated in the brutal ghetto clearing, so by the time of his offer they had had the opportunity to confront the gruesome reality of the genocidal enterprise. Yet not even one of them took up the ready offer to avoid further killing at the time. According to one of his men, Steinmetz repeated the offer after the killing had gotten under way. This man admitted to having killed six or eight Jews before asking the sergeant to excuse him. His request was granted.[61] Sergeant Steinmetz was not a superior who was unfeeling towards his men.

A particularly noteworthy refusal to kill was that of one of the battalion's officers, Lieutenant Heinz Buchmann. Beginning with the killing in Józefów and in subsequent killings, he avoided participating directly in the executions, having managed to get himself assigned other duties. At Józefów, he led the escort of the so-called able-bodied Jews to a "work camp" near Lublin. Everyone in the battalion knew that this lieutenant avoided killing duty. His wish not to participate in the killings was so accepted in the hierarchy of command that his company commander circumvented him when killing operations were at hand, and gave orders directly to the lieutenant's subordinates.[62]

Obviously, at least some of the men felt no hesitation to ask out. The fact was that they easily got themselves excused from the killing and that others saw that extricating themselves from the gruesome task was possible. Trapp's offer had been made before the entire battalion. At least one sergeant in charge of a contingent of executioners explicitly made the same offer to his men, and the lieutenant and sergeant running another squad easily acceded to requests by men that they be excused. Offers and opportunities for removal from direct killing were accepted, both in front of the assembled battalion and in the intimacy of the platoons and squads. Even one reluctant officer served as an example to the battalion's rank and file that extricating oneself from the gruesome killing was possible—and not dishonorable. Up and down Police Battalion 101's hierarchy, there was what appears to have been a partly formal and partly informal understanding that men who did not want to kill should not be forced to do so.[63] That mere sergeants, and not only the battalion commander, were exercising discretion to excuse men from killing demonstrates how accepted the men's opting out was. It also makes unequivocal that those who slaughtered Jews, including Jewish children, did so voluntarily.[64]

After the day's work, the men had the chance to digest what they had done, to talk it over among themselves. The company clerk, for example, who had remained behind in Biłgoraj, was informed by the others of their deeds upon their return.[65] Clearly, they talked. And it is unimaginable that these ordinary Germans spoke in value-neutral terms when discussing their anything-but-value-neutral deeds. Many of the men were shaken, even momentarily depressed, by the killings: "No comrades participated in these things with joy. Afterwards, they were all very depressed."[66] They lost their appetites that day: "I still remember that upon their return none of my comrades could enjoy the meal. They did, however, enjoy the alcohol which was available as a special supplementary ration."[67] Clearly, many did not have a neutral reaction to their deeds. In their postwar testimonies, some of the men speak with great passion of their and their comrades' distressed feelings after their first massacre. That some were initially unhappy, disturbed, perhaps even incensed to have been thrust into such gruesome duty is clear.[68] Yet the men's postwar self-reporting of their own afflictions should be viewed with some circumspection; the temptation to read more into them than they warrant should be resisted.[69] The men were sickened by the exploded skulls, the flying blood and bone, the sight of so many freshly killed corpses of their own making,[70] and they were given pause, even shaken by having plunged into mass slaughter and committing deeds that would change and forever define them socially and morally. Their reaction was similar to that of many soldiers after sampling for the first time the grisly offerings of real battle. They too often feel sickened, throw up, and lose their appetites. That it happened to these Germans upon their initiation into killing in such a gruesome manner is understandable. But it is hard to believe that the reaction was born from anything but the shock and gruesomeness of the moment, as their soon-thereafter-renewed, assiduous efforts in mass slaughter indicate. Despite their disgust and shock, as the battalion medical corpsman testifies, no one suffered any significant emotional difficulties after the Józefów communal slaying. The corpsman knows of no man who "because of the experience got sick or by any stretch of the imagination had a nervous breakdown."[71]

The portrait of this battalion is one of verbal give-and-take, of men discussing their views and emotions, of disagreements, even to some extent between people at different levels of the battalion hierarchy. In the midst of the afternoon's executions, a heated argument broke out between Lieutenant Hartwig Gnade, the commander of First Company, and one of his junior lieutenants over where they should have been shooting a batch of Jews. Gnade was heard to have screamed at the recalcitrant subordinate that he could not work with him if he would not obey orders.[72] This insubordination—an officer arguing with his commander (in front of the men, no less) over such an insignificant operational matter, and the evident unwillingness or inability on the part of the superior to assert his prerogative of absolute authority—reveals a great deal about the undraconian, lax character of this police battalion. It was not characterized by the submissive holding of one's tongue in the face of a superior's order, let alone by unthinking obedience to any order.

Despite the evident difficulty displayed by some of these Germans in this, their initial mass slaughter, despite their having found the byproducts of their shots to the backs of Jewish heads revolting, and despite their having had the opportunity to extricate themselves from the killing, from the grisly, disgusting duty, almost all of them chose to carry out their lethal tasks. Had anyone disapproved of the killing of the Jews, of the killing of Jewish children and infants, especially when even the toughest stomach would have been sorely tested by the blood, bone, and brains that spattered them, then it is difficult to understand not only why he killed, but also how he could have managed to bring himself to kill and to continue to kill. He had a way out. Even some who in principle did not disapprove of the killing of Jews, but who were unnerved by the gruesomeness, got themselves temporarily excused.[73]

THE RESPITE FROM their contribution to the "solving" of the "Jewish Problem" lasted only a few days for the men of Police Battalion 101, as they embarked immediately on a number of small operations in the area around Biłgoraj and Zamość, in which they removed Jews from small villages and locales to larger concentrations. Although the operations appear to have been frequent, few details are known of them, because the perpetrators have said little about them.[74]

A major communal extermination, this time in nearby Łomazy, was entered in Police Battalion 101's ledger shortly after the Józefów slaughter. Unlike in Józefów, where the entire battalion participated in the genocidal slaughter, in Łomazy the killing was left to Second Company to perform on its own. The day before the operation, the company commander called his platoon leaders together in Biała-Podlaska, where the company staff was headquartered. The company's platoons were at that time distributed among various nearby locations, with a portion of one of the platoons, under the command of Sergeant Heinrich Bekemeier, having been stationed in Łomazy since August 9. The company commander, Lieutenant Gnade, informed them of the planned killing operation, and told them to have their men in Łomazy the next morning, August 19, around 4 or 5 a.m.

Łomazy was a town of less than 3,000, more than half of whom were at this time Jews. Of the 1,600 to 1,700 Jews whom the Germans found in Łomazy, most were not local Polish Jews, but from elsewhere, including from Germany, some even from Hamburg.[75] The Germans had deported these Jews over the previous months to Łomazy as a first step in the two-stage process of killing them. Although a walled-in ghetto did not constrain them, the Jews were concentrated in their own section of the city. It took the men of Second Company about two hours to round up their victims and to bring them to the designated assembly point, the athletic area neighboring the town's school. The roundup proceeded without pity. The Germans, as Gnade had instructed in the pre-operation meeting, killed those on the spot who on their own could not make it to the assembly point. The dedication of the men to their task is summarized in the court judgment:

> The scouring of the houses was carried out with extraordinary thoroughness. The available forces were divided into search parties of 2 to 3 policemen. The witness H. has reported that it was one of their tasks to search also the cellars and the attics of the houses. The Jews were no longer unsuspecting. They had learned of what was happening to the members of their race in the whole of the *Generalgouvernement*. They therefore attempted to hide and thus to escape annihilation. Everywhere in the Jewish quarter there was shooting. The witness H. counted in his sector alone, in a bloc of houses, about 15 Jews shot to death. After 2 hours or so the easily surveyed Jewish quarter was cleared.[76]

The Germans shot the old, the infirm, and the young, on the streets, in their homes, in their beds.[77]

That the Germans proceeded with such murderousness in the Łomazy roundup is noteworthy, since the overall plan for the massacre was intended to spare them from shooting the victims themselves. Gnade had announced in the briefing preceding the operation that a unit of "Trawnikis," sometimes known as "Hiwis"[78]—eastern Europeans, mainly Ukrainians who worked as German auxiliaries in the mass extermination—would be doing the actual killing under German supervision. Every Jew whom each of the Germans could bring to the gathering point would be a Jew whom that German would himself not have to shoot at close range. He would spare himself the ordeal, if indeed it was an ordeal, of having to shoot cowering Jews attempting to conceal themselves, an old man in his bed, or an infant. As a group, the Germans rounding up the Jews did not take advantage of this opportunity to forgo close-range, personalized killing.[79]

At the athletic area, the Germans separated the men from the women. They lingered on the field for hours waiting for the final preparations for the kill to be completed. The following three photos show portions of the assemblage, the first two from up close and the third from a distance.

Men of Police Battalion 101 guard Jews on the athletic field of Łomazy before executing them.

This first photograph shows a German standing in front of the second row of Jews holding a folded whip in his hand. That he stood momentarily with his back to the Jews under his guard, squarely facing the photographer, suggests

Close-up of the Jews on the athletic field of Łomazy

View of the assembled Jews of Łomazy from edge of the town

that he was proud of his actions, wanting not to conceal the image of him participating in a genocidal operation but to preserve it for posterity.

The reverse side of the third photograph was inscribed by the photographer as reproduced on the next page.

Vorurteilte Juden

Lomartzie 18. Aug 42,

1600

It says:

Condemned Jews / Lomartzie 18 Aug 42 / 1600

This man wrote down the pertinent information, made sure that years later he would not confuse or forget the accomplishments of the day. By his count, they killed 1,600 Jews.[80]

Men of Police Battalion 101 compel Jews to dig their own mass grave on the outskirts of Łomazy.

From the field, a detail of First Platoon led a group of about fifty to sixty Jews outfitted with spades and shovels to a wooded area more than a thousand yards away, where the execution would take place. The Germans compelled the Jews to excavate a large pit for the execution, which can be seen in the previous photograph filling with water.[81] The inscription on the back of this photograph also identifies the scene for posterity:

Jews constructing a mass grave / Lomartczy 18 Aug 1942 / 1600

The overdue Hiwis finally arrived, and promptly sat down for breakfast. In full sight of their imminent victims, the Hiwis, between forty and fifty strong,[82] satisfied their hunger and slaked their thirst, the latter with vodka, which would make them still more brutal. Gnade and the German commander of the Hiwis also began to drink.[83] The Jews, who could not but be strongly suspicious of what awaited them, watched their killers feast in their presence before the kill. The Germans, despite the intense heat of the day, let the Jews have no food or water.

The trek to the execution site then commenced. The bulk of the Jews began their journey only after Polish peasants brought a long rope which they had knotted together for the march. For some inexplicable reason, perhaps according to some bizarre Nazi logic, the Germans ringed the assembled Jews with the rope, with the expectation that this would ensure that they trudge along in an orderly manner in a column of six or eight abreast on the death march.[84] The Germans shot any Jew who strayed, generally by falling behind, outside the confines of the moving ring of rope. Because the pace set by the Germans was brisk, the less fit had trouble keeping up, the effect of which was severe bunching at the back of the ring. The fear produced among the Jews by the shooting of the stragglers was such that at one point they surged forward, knocking some of their brethren down. The fallen were first trampled by others and then, in the words of one of the perpetrators, Sergeant Bentheim, were "brutally driven forward and also shot" by the Germans.[85] Before reaching the execution staging ground, the Germans finally dispensed with the ill-conceived and functionally purposeless rope.

When the column neared the execution site, the Germans separated the men and the women, depositing them at different locations, around fifty yards from the killing pit. The Germans forced all of the Jews to shed their outer clothing. The men had to bare their upper bodies completely. Some ended up naked. The Germans also divested their victims of whatever valuables they possessed.[86] The ignominy of having to disrobe in public was nothing compared to what awaited the Jews, but it was an ignominy nonetheless. It had another consequence, for this occurred in the middle of August. "I recall vividly the picture of these Jews, most of whom were undressed to the waist, lying for several hours in the glare of the sun and getting severely sunburnt. For, after undressing, the Jews had to lie prostrate in a rather confined area and were not permitted to move."[87] When the killing was finally ready to commence, the men of Second Platoon formed a gauntlet running between the staging ground for the killing and the killing site itself. Successive groups of fifteen to twenty Jews were forced to run to the killing site's pit, to run the German gauntlet, with the Germans shouting at them and beating them with rifle butts (*Kolbenhiebe*) as they passed by.[88] As if this general terrorizing and torturing of the victims during their final moments of life were not satisfying enough, Gnade selected Jews of heightened symbolic value for special treatment. The memory of this, not surprisingly, was indelibly etched in the mind of one of Gnade's men.

> During these executions I observed still something else which I will never forget. Even before the executions began, Lieutenant Gnade himself had selected about twenty to twenty-five elderly Jews. They were exclusively men with full beards. Gnade made these old men crawl on the ground before the grave. Before he gave them the command to crawl, they had to undress. While the now completely naked Jews were crawling, Lieutenant Gnade screamed to those around, "Where are my NCOs, don't you yet have any clubs?" Thereupon the NCOs went to the edge of the forest, got themselves clubs, and then with these clubs rained mighty blows on the Jews . . . it is my opinion that all of the NCOs of our company complied with the Lieutenant Gnade's order and rained blows on the Jews. . . .[89]

Having beaten them badly, but not to death, the Germans subsequently shot these old Jewish men, these, in the Nazified German mind, archetypical Jews. Why degrade and torture the Jews and especially these old Jews? Was the extinction of more than a legion of Jews not satisfying enough for these Germans? Cold, mechanical executioners would have just killed their victims. Men opposed to the killing would not have first tortured these old, suffering Jewish men, would not have created more misery before ending their misery. These Germans were not such emotionless or reluctant functionaries.

The killing site itself presented an unspeakable scene. The pit, seen being excavated in the photo above, was between 1.6 and 2 yards deep, and about 30 yards wide by 55 yards long.[90] It sloped down at one end. The Jews were forced to clamber down the incline and lay themselves face down. The Hiwis, standing in the pit and using rifles, put a bullet into the back of each Jew's head. The next wave of Jews had to lay themselves down on top of their bloodied and skull-bursted predecessors. Using this method, the pit gradually filled up. The Hiwis, who had continued to drink steadily, were drunk, and therefore aimed errantly. This caused them to aim badly, even at close range. The bad marksmanship produced a hair-raising scene, the ghastliness of which is difficult to imagine and comprehend. Many of the Jews were not killed by the bullets. Because the Germans chose this day not to administer "mercy shots" (*Gnadenschüsse*) to those still alive after the initial volley, successive groups of Jews had to lay themselves down not just on bloodied bodies, but some of them on bloodied bodies in their death throes, writhing and emitting human screams articulating their inarticulatable pain. As if this were not gruesome enough, the pit had been dug below the water table. The rising water mixed with blood and the bodies floated about a bit. The Hiwis doing the killing had descended into the pit and stood up to their knees in the bloodied water.[91]

Many of the Germans were witnesses to the unfolding horror as they formed a cordon thirty yards around the pit. The Hiwis eventually became so drunk that it was impossible to let them continue. "I feared that they would shoot us too,"[92] recounts one German. When Gnade ordered his two lieutenants to have their men replace the Hiwis,[93] the Germans already knew what was expected of them. The lieutenants, according to one of the men,

> . . . informed us that Gnade had ordered that the company be now employed as executioners [*Schützen*]. They further said that we should carry out the execution in the same manner as the Hiwis. We rebelled against it, as the groundwater in the pit had stood above half a meter. Moreover, corpses lay or rather floated about the whole area of the pit. I remember with particular horror that also during the execution a great number of the Jews who were shot had not been fatally hit and nonetheless, without being put out of their misery [*ohne Abgabe von Gnadenschüssen*], were covered by the victims that followed.

As this man remembers, he and his comrades decided among themselves to adopt a different killing stance. "At this conference we agreed that the execution should be carried out by two groups, each numbering 8 to 10 men. In contrast to the *modus operandi* of the Hiwis, these two execution squads should put themselves on opposite sides of the earth walls of the pit and from these positions kill by cross fire." The men on each side shot the Jews who lined up at the base of the pit's wall opposite them. The execution commandos shot for perhaps half an hour before being relieved by comrades. First Platoon manned one side of the pit, while either Second or Third Platoon hailed bullets down from the other.

> Also, during this operation the members of the platoon were frequently changed. I mean the roughly ten to twelve shooters were exchanged after five to six executions. When all the members of the platoon had taken their turns, one began anew with the first groups, so that each group had to carry out for a second time five to six executions. . . . I am further of the opinion that apart from a few indispensable men doing guard duty, no one was spared from participating in the execution with the exception of some who beat it into the country. This was entirely possible, as the platoons of the groups in part performed different tasks.

This killer remembers that the Germans shot for about two hours. The Hiwis, who in the meantime had sobered themselves up, some of them having fallen asleep on the grass, replaced the Germans and continued killing for at least another hour. They too now killed from above the pit, though some of them again descended into the body- and blood-filled cavity.[94] The pit eventually was overflowing with corpses. "I can still picture the scene," remarks one German, "and thought at the time, that one would simply not be able to cover the corpses with dirt."[95]

Approximately 1,700 Jewish men, women, and children died in this horrible manner, a significant number of whom, by chance, were German Jews from, among other places, the battalion's home, Hamburg.[96] Some endured what was twelve hours of mental and physical torture before receiving a bullet in the head. Starting with the shock of having been wrested from sleep and driven from their houses by the marauding Germans, they had to endure the hours at the assembly field, followed by the murderous march to the execution staging place. Except for the first batch of victims, all of them heard the agonies of their fellow Jews as they were first driven with blows from the Germans to the pit and then forced to descend into a version of hell. After hearing the screams and the salvos announcing the Jews' final disposition (some of the victims had to listen to them for hours), each Jew made the same journey. Late in the afternoon, the Germans and their Hiwis finally finished the gruesome slaughter, except for one final detail. A group of about twenty Jews had been left alive to shovel dirt atop the execution pit, now a mass grave. Some of the Jews, writhing below, were thereby buried alive. No matter to the Germans, who promptly killed these momentarily spared, grave-sealing Jews.

Second Company's massacre in Łomazy is instructive on a number of matters. Its intended logistics and character differed markedly from those of the Józefów slaughter; it was supposed to have followed more closely the pattern of an *Einsatzkommando* killing.[97] The Germans had planned it to be less individualized, to place less of a psychological burden on the killers, by delegating the dirty work to the Hiwis and by using more of an assembly-line method instead of the piecework manner of Józefów. Reflecting back to Józefów, it appears that the green, untutored police battalion had improvised the first time around, and only later had learned of a more appropriate technique, the one that distanced the killers somewhat from the victims and the gore of the work. Their ill-preparedness for the Józefów killing illustrates how cavalier the German command was about these things. Returning to Łomazy, though, it is clear that the procedures taken to render the killing easier for the men were, in fact, not necessary and were violated as the day unfolded. The men of this company had already acclimated themselves to their vocation.[98]

The Łomazy killing is illuminating for reasons other than those suggested by comparison with its predecessor in Józefów. First, the Germans did not here sort out, spare, and husband for work the so-called able-bodied Łomazy Jews. Their objective was to kill Jews without regard to other possible objectives. Second, the Germans' cruelty throughout the day bespoke their attitudes towards their victims and their task. And the cruelty that they allowed their minions to perpetrate was incessant; as one of the Germans describes it, "the cruelties occurred from the staging ground [*Abladeplatz*] to the pit."[99] Third, when Gnade ordered the Germans to replace the Hiwis, they balked at his order for them to enter the gruesome pit, but not at the order itself. They did disobey a part of his order, the part that they found unsavory. And they had their way. Fourth, it is curious that the Germans would tolerate such licentious, unprofessional, and even dangerous conduct on the part of their Hiwis, who by no means seemed unwilling—quite the contrary—to kill their share of Jews. Fifth, there was no pretense on virtually anyone's part at this massacre that any military rationale was motivating the killing. The Germans knew that their country's policy in Poland was genocidal, and that genocide, the desire to rid the earth of the putative Jewish scourge, was its own rationale, in need of no other. It was thus a day for each in his own way to have his fun with the Jews, even if it got too messy for the taste of some.

After the Germans had made Łomazy *judenrein*, the men of Second Company returned to their various garrisons elsewhere. Sergeant Bekemeier's group remained in Łomazy, having arrived there over a week before the killing. Their stay in Łomazy appears, from the photographic record, to have agreed with them. They took formal group portraits in front of the school adjacent to the athletic field, which served as the assembly point for the slaughter of the Jews.[100] They also took less formal photographs, including one in which the Germans are assembled somewhat informally for their portrait, looking rather happy. Others captured the men in unguarded moments, and posing in a friendly manner with some of the presumably Polish residents of Łomazy, including children. Although it is not known whether such candid shots were taken before or after the gruesome massacre that reduced the population of Łomazy by more than half, Bekemeier's men posed for another photograph right before their final departure from Łomazy, days after the mass slaughter. The Germans' desire to have a photographic testament to their stay in Łomazy, with their obvious good cheer displayed for the camera, was their own contemporary final commentary on the time they passed in this town, its defining feature having been their transformation of a half-Jewish town to a *judenrein* one. Theirs was a profound social revolution. And few social revolutionaries gaze with unhappiness on those whom they have expropriated. In this case, the expropriated lost their lives.

These two early major killing operations of Police Battalion 101 are described here at some length, in order to convey what they were like *for the perpetrators*. The questions of how the Germans could have brought themselves to act in the manner that they did, and why they did not seek to avoid participating in the slaughters take on a different light when the details of their actions and the choices that they made are considered. The men of Police Battalion 101 rounded up, deported, and slaughtered Jews on many other occasions. These killing operations could also be described in horrific detail, the accounts based mainly on the perpetrators' own testimony, but, owing to space limitations, only some of them are even fleetingly discussed. With variations, they were on a par for cruelty and gruesomeness with the killing operations of Józefów and Łomazy. Their description would provide only more evidence to substantiate the portrait of the battalion being drawn here.

During the fall of 1942, the men of Police Battalion 101 conducted numerous additional major killing and other operations against the Jews of the Lublin region. In some they shot the Jews themselves; in others they deported the Jews to extermination camps. Whether characterized by mass shootings or deportations to the gas chambers, the killing operations followed a similar structure. They began with roundups of the kind described, during which the Germans shot the old, sick, and young in their homes and on the streets. The Germans brought the Jews to some central location, like a market square, where they typically, though not always, separated the so-called able-bodied Jews and sent them to a "work" camp. The Jews also frequently spent some time waiting at the assembly point until the arrangements were completed for their final disposition. Typically, the waiting time was used to degrade and torture the victims, whether at the hands of the battalion men themselves or at the hands of the Hiwis or the other German security forces who sometimes worked in conjunction with Police Battalion 101. When they were finally ready, the Germans marched the Jews either to the waiting railway cars, cramming them in with kicks, blows, and lashes, or to the chosen killing location, where they shot one group of Jews after another. Their major killing operations against the Jews that fall were:[101]

Location	Date	Victims	Operation
Józefów	July 1942	1,500 Jews	shooting
Lublin District	from July 1942	Jews, 100s	repeated small roundups
Łomazy	August 1942	1,700 Jews	shooting
Parczew	August 1942	5,000 Jews	deportation to death camp
Międzyrzec	August 1942	11,000 Jews	deportation to death camp[102]
Serokomla	September 1942	200 Jews	shooting
Talcyn/Kock	September 1942	200 Jews, 79 Poles	shooting
Radzyń	October 1942	2,000 Jews	deportation to death camp
Łuków	October 1942	7,000 Jews	deportation to death camp

Parczew	October 1942	100 Jews	shooting
Kónskowola	October 1942	1,100 Jews	shooting
Międzyrzec	October and November, 1942		
Biała		4,800 Jews	deportation to death camp
Biała Podlaska county		6,000 Jews	deportation to death camp
Komarówka		600 Jews	deportation to death camp
Wohyn		800 Jews	deportation to death camp
Czemierniki		1,000 Jews	deportation to death camp
Radzyń		2,000 Jews	deportation to death camp
Lublin District	from October 1942	Jews, many 100s	"Jew-hunts"
Łuków	November 1943	3,000 Jews	deportation to death camp

Because the Germans managed to kill most of the region's Jews by the new year, Police Battalion 101 engaged in fewer large-scale killing operations in 1943, concentrating during that year on smaller ones. The large ones were:

Location	Date	Victims	Operation
Międzyrzec	May 1943	3,000 Jews	deportation to death camp
Majdanek	November 1943	16,500 Jews	shooting
Poniatowa	November 1943	14,000 Jews	shooting

The year's killing culminated in the November 1943 immense slaughter in Majdanek and Poniatowa, which was part of the German-dubbed *Operation Erntefest* (Operation Harvest Festival). All told, the men in Police Battalion 101 participated in killing operations in which they, alone or together with others, shot or deported to their deaths well over eighty thousand Jews.

The large-scale massacres and deportations that were the signal events of Police Battalion 101's existence in Poland were not the only contribution its men made to the fulfillment of Hitler's genocidal scheme. Wherever they were stationed, they were continuously engaged in killing smaller groupings of Jews that were to be found in their areas.

> Our main task consisted in the annihilation of Jews. At these "actions" Jews living in small localities, villages, and estates were liquidated. From time to time under the leadership of Sergeant Steinmetz, the platoon would set out on lorries. . . . In the localities the houses were searched for Jews. Again, the infirm and the sick were shot in the houses and the rest of the Jews at the outskirts of the locality. In each of these operations ten to forty persons were liquidated, the number varying with the size of the locality. The Jews had to lie down and were killed by bullets in the back of the neck. In no case were graves dug. The commando did not concern itself with burial. Altogether about ten operations of this kind might have been done, which dealt exclusively with the annihilation of the Jews . . .

There were always adventurers and volunteers who together with
Sergeant Steinmetz took these buildings [*sic*] first and shot the Jews.[103]

The Germans' killing of Jews found living in small communities or estates resembled in procedure the large ones, except in scale. Yet if the large killing operations made the deepest impression on the killers, suggesting the historic
importance of their activities, the frequent small ones made the killing of Jews
a normal constituent feature of their days and lives. That this man and others
understood the extermination of the Jews to have been their primary activity
is due, to a large extent, to the great frequency of their engagement in it. Contributing to the sense that the perpetrators had of themselves as being above
all else genocidal agents were the regular patrols they went on, in order to
search out Jews hiding in the countryside and kill them. These "search-and-
destroy" missions (this is my appellation) differed in character from the large
killings that have been described. They differed in scale, not just in the number of victims, which could be as few as one or two people, but also in the number of Germans who manned them. The search-and-destroy missions also
demanded a degree of individual initiative that during the destruction of
ghettos was required generally only of those (though this was often a large
number) who searched through the Jews' homes for the hidden. "Today I still
remember exactly that we were already right before the bunker when a five-
year-old boy came out crawling. He was immediately grabbed by a policeman
and led aside. This policeman then set the pistol to his neck and shot him. He
was an active policeman [*Beamter*] who when with us was employed as a medical orderly. He was the only medical orderly of the platoon."[104]

Police Battalion 101, like other German forces, had received the *Schiessbefehl*,[105] mandating that they shoot all Jews found outside the ghettos and approved areas in Poland. Essentially, it bestowed upon the most junior men of
Police Battalion 101 executive power over capital decisions regarding Jews.
Each was deemed to be a fit judge and executioner. The men of Police Battalion 101 proved the trust in them to have been well placed.

Whenever the men of Police Battalion 101 learned (often from Polish informers) or suspected that Jews were living or hiding in a certain area, they
formed a detachment of a size sufficient for the expected task, sought out the
Jews, and, if found, killed them.[106] Sometimes the Germans' information regarding the Jews' whereabouts was very specific, sometimes vague. The
forces assembled for search-and-destroy missions varied in size from company strength to a few men. These variations, however, were but tertiary factors in the ongoing, coordinated German sweeping of the countryside, which
was necessary if Poland were indeed to become *judenrein*, free of Jews.

The search-and-destroy missions, which began in the fall of 1942 and continued throughout 1943, together with the slaughter of Jews living in small groups in towns and on estates, became the main operational activity of the men of Police Battalion 101. Many of them have testified to the great frequency of these missions. In fact, so many of the men went on so many search-and-destroy missions that after the war they had difficulty recollecting the details of them. The missions blur together.[107] A member of Second Company recalls: "From the diverse locations of our platoon, every week several operations were started. They were aimed at the so-called pacification of the area entrusted to us. It goes without saying that in the course of the general patrolling we were alert to the presence of Jews and if we met any we shot them on the spot."[108] A member of Third Company relates that "it is entirely true that after the completion of a [killing] action, operations against Jews were frequently undertaken. . . . It may be true of me as well that I participated in ten to twelve such operations. The number of victims ranged from two to twenty. The number of times Herr Nehring and I participated applies also to the other members of the platoon."[109] These missions were so frequent and so successful, according to another man of Third Company, that from the beginning of August 1942 until the end of August 1943, "almost daily stray Jews who had been chanced upon by any squad in the field were shot on the spot."[110]

The men of Police Battalion 101 undertook both mop-up operations after large killings and search-and-destroy missions in the surrounding region. This was true of the group under Sergeant Bekemeier which remained in Łomazy after the August 19 extermination of the city's Jews. A few days after the massacre, the rest of Second Company having already returned to the garrison locations, Bekemeier's men combed through the ghetto that had a few days earlier been teeming with life, and found about twenty Jews—men, women, and children. They took them to the woods, forced them to lay themselves on the ground without undressing, and shot them in the back of their heads (*Genickschuss*) with pistols.[111] The small detachment of around twenty men who were under Bekemeier's command were acting independent of the supervision of superiors. Whether they found a few more or a few fewer Jews made no difference vis-à-vis the battalion command. The command had no way of knowing how many Jews were really on the loose. Even if it had, the locally stationed men could have conjured up any numbers that they wanted, since no evidence of killings was requested or provided. Such killings were so routine and so expected that the Germans treated them as part of the normal fabric of life and therefore did not see them as noteworthy. When Bekemeier's men did find Jews, they not only killed them but, in one instance that has been described, they, or at least Bekemeier, also had fun with them beforehand:

One episode has been preserved in my memory to this day. Under the command of Sergeant Bekemeier we had to convey a transport of Jews to some place. He had the Jews crawl through a water hole and sing as they did it. When an old man could not walk anymore, which was when the crawling episode was finished, he shot him at close range in the mouth. . . .[112]

After Bekemeier had shot the Jew, the latter raised his hand as if to appeal to God and then collapsed. The corpse of the Jew was simply left lying. We did not concern ourselves with it.[113]

One photograph that was available for the photo albums of these executioners shows Bekemeier and his men holding their bicycles and posing with evident pride as they prepare to embark on the sort of patrol that led so frequently to their slaughter of Jews. The following photograph shows Lieutenant Gnade with his men on a search-and-destroy mission.

Lieutenant Gnade and his men hunting through the countryside for hidden Jews

These photographic mementos, so innocent-looking to the uninitiated, were replete with significance for the Germans of Police Battalion 101.

A search-and-destroy mission that harvested among the greatest number of Jewish corpses occurred near Kónskowola. Members of Third Company had been ordered by Hoffmann to an area where reports indicated Jews to be hiding. They came across a series of underground bunkers, whereupon they yelled for the Jews to come out. Silence greeted them. The Germans threw in tear-gas grenades, which revealed to them something of their victims:

". . . from the bunkers rang out the cries and whimpers of women and children." The Germans again ordered them to come out, to no effect. "And when no one emerged, hand grenades were thrown into the bunker. I remember that hand grenades were thrown again and again until it had become completely lifeless inside the bunker in question. . . . I cannot state the exact number of victims because we did not excavate the bunker after finishing the operation. Nor did we verify the deaths of the occupants."[114]

In the organized ghetto liquidations, the Germans operated in large formation, in a situation structured according to their commander's design, which did constrain their actions, even if they were always able to find opportunities for personal expression in the form of gratuitous brutality. On search-and-destroy missions, in contrast, small groups of comrades, with minimal supervision, leisurely riding or walking through the countryside, were free to search zealously or lethargically, with keenness or inattentively. When finding Jews, they had a free hand to treat them as they wanted to, whether their innermost wishes were to kill them or not. They could degrade and torture the Jews before killing them, or just kill them. They could try to kill them while inflicting as little additional suffering as possible, be unconcerned about such matters, or perpetrate gratuitous degradations and brutalities on the victims. The killers' own testimony about the search-and-destroy missions reveals men who acted with zeal, and at the very least with disregard for the suffering of their Jewish victims, who were frequently women and children. These Germans do not claim that they purposely failed to find Jews or that they tried their best to inflict as little suffering on them. Indeed, in a matter-of-fact manner, they report on their routine success in uncovering and killing Jews, and on the cavalier fashion in which they did so. It is not surprising that these Germans failed to spare Jews; they undertook the avowedly genocidal patrols— which were so frequent that one man describes them and therefore the killing of Jews as having been "more or less our daily bread"[115]—with unmistakable alacrity. The killers admit that it was the norm for men to volunteer for missions to find, ferret out, and annihilate more Jews. The killers also tell us that, typically, more men volunteered than was required to fill out a given mission.[116] It is safe to say that these ordinary Germans wanted to kill the Jews.

The only rationale for the search-and-destroy missions was genocide, and it was understood as such. The Germans in this police battalion did not encounter one single case of armed resistance from the Jews on all the search-and-destroy missions that they undertook.[117] Many of the men went on many such missions. For them it was a hunt, pure and simple, the purpose of which was to denude the countryside of the offending beasts. The Germans themselves conceived of these missions in this manner. Among themselves, they tellingly called a search-and-destroy mission a "Jew-hunt" (*Judenjagd*):[118]

The Germans' use of the term "Jew-hunt" was not casual. It expressed the killers' conception of the nature of their activity and the attendant emotion. Theirs was the exterminatory pursuit of the remnants of a particularly pernicious species that needed to be destroyed in its entirety. Moreover, the word *"Jagd"* has a positive *Gefühlswert*, a positive emotive valence. Hunting is a pleasurable pursuit, rich in adventure, involving no danger to the hunter, and its reward is a record of animals slain—in the case of the men of this police battalion and other German "Jew-hunters," a record of Jews ferreted out and killed.

BASED ON THEIR activities and on the revelations contained in their own testimony, the men of Police Battalion 101 can be aptly described as members of a "genocidal cohort" (*Völkermordkohorte*), and it cannot be doubted that they conceived of themselves as such: "Our main task continued to consist, however, in the annihilation of the Jews."[119] Their devotion to annihilating the Jews was such that they would even postpone operations against real partisans, against the people who posed a real military threat to them, in order to undertake search-and-destroy missions against the Jews.[120] The descriptions and analyses of their actions here suggest that these Germans viewed the genocidal killing, their primary activity in Poland, and themselves favorably. They repeatedly showed initiative in killing and did not shirk their assigned tasks, though they could have without punishment. They gave priority to the killing of Jews and even acted with cruel abandon. Their dedication to the genocidal slaughter was such that they persisted in it despite the gruesomeness which, though conveyed here at times graphically and in some detail, is difficult, perhaps impossible, to imagine and comprehend for anyone who has not been a party to similar scenes. Much of the killing was also personalized, in that the men often faced their victims one on one. Frequently, they were facing children.

8

POLICE BATTALION 101:
ASSESSING THE MEN'S MOTIVES

OW SHOULD WE understand the Germans in Police Battalion 101, whose deeds encompass not only the killings and deportations but also the manner in which the men conducted them? On the face of it, these Germans' actions appear to have been incompatible with a principled disapproval of the genocidal slaughter of Jews. Actions sometimes do express their own motivation, at least approximately. Still, the perpetrators' understanding of their actions, and the motivations for their actions, becomes still clearer when certain specific issues and their lives in Poland are investigated in greater depth.

Casting a comparative glance at the other national group whose members Police Battalion 101 slaughtered is instructive. In addition to having been assigned an important role in the extermination of Polish Jewry, the men of Police Battalion 101 were charged with "pacifying" their region. As a consequence, they sometimes massacred Poles. Partisans were active, even if not nearly as troublesome at this time as some have claimed, and they inflicted damage on German forces and installations, eventually on Police Battalion 101 itself. In Poland, as elsewhere, the Germans practiced draconian occupation policies. Casualties suffered by Germans were multiplied fifty- or one-hundred-fold when the Germans revenged themselves on innocent Polish civilians.

On September 25, 1942, a detachment of Third Company was ambushed in Talcyn during an operation to trap two resistance fighters. One of the Germans, a sergeant, was killed. Even though Police Battalion 101 was already complicit in the killing of around twenty thousand Jews, this may have been the first casualty suffered by its men during the three months that they had then completed in Poland, which may shed some light on their staggeringly violent reaction to it. Major Trapp submitted a report of over two and a half single-space pages, recounting in great detail the events preceding, during, and following the ambush—all because of the death of one sergeant in an occupied, hostile territory. More significantly, the Germans exacted retribution for what Trapp—in an unwitting testament to selective compassion and to a stunning lack of self-reflectiveness—called in his report the "cowardly murder" (*feige Mordtat*). Four platoons, led by Trapp himself, first combed the area around Talcyn for partisans, without success. They had been instructed to take two hundred lives in retribution for the German's death. So they assembled the three hundred Polish inhabitants of the village, choosing, however, only seventy-eight (there may have been some women and children among them), and shot them at the cemetery.[1] What was Trapp's attitude towards the killing of Poles? One of his men was struck by it: "I can still recall very vividly that our battalion commander was very shaken after this action. He even wept. He was what one would call a fine human being and I deem it impossible that it was he who had ordered the shooting of the hostages."[2] Trapp—who years later, despite having led his men in mass murder, is remarkably pronounced "a fine human being"—was not content to inflict the full toll of two hundred deaths on the village where his man had been ambushed and killed, a village which he himself reported was "known for a long time as a notorious nest of [bandit] accomplices."[3] So the men of Police Battalion 101 traveled five miles to where they could lay their hands on some Jews in Kock's Jewish quarter. They proceeded to slaughter 180 Jews "as a further retributive measure."[4] This man does not say that Trapp became unsettled and agitated after they killed the Jews.

This illustrative episode juxtaposes the Germans' attitudes towards Poles and Jews. They did indeed kill the Poles, according to a punitive military rationale that was, if normal for German occupation forces, a crime against the victims. Yet they chose to spare an additional 122 Poles whom they ought to have killed according to their orders. Trapp, who had in the last two and one half months led his men on killing operations claiming about twenty thousand Jewish lives, was "shaken" at having killed fewer than one hundred Poles! He cried. And it was not just Trapp who was disturbed by the killing of Poles. Some of the men expressed afterwards their desire not to undertake any more missions of this sort.[5] Trapp also, in an act of solicitude never shown towards Jewish victims, sent one of his men to calm the women, holed up in a schoolroom, whose husbands the Germans were shooting.[6] The Germans acted that day as if some Nazi rule of thumb guided them, namely that no mass slaughter should be visited on a population without available Jews falling lifeless as well—in this case, by a better than two-to-one ratio to the Poles. The men of Police Battalion 101 went to a city that was not proximate to the scene of the crime, where they slaked their Jewish blood-lust by killing Jews, and by killing a significantly greater number of them than their quota even required. Trapp, moved to tears by the killing of Poles, turned around and *initiated* the killing of Jews, Jews whose relationship to the offending act was non-existent, except in the Nazified German mind, in which the Jews were considered to be a metaphysical enemy.[7]

After this "retributive killing," Police Battalion 101 participated in a large-scale retributive slaughter of Poles, following the killing in Biała Podlaska of a Nazi Party official. Police Battalion 101 was ordered into action together with Wehrmacht units and eastern European SS auxiliary troops. Trapp tried to keep his men out of the thick of things, succeeding in having them do no more than comb the woods, leaving the killing and the burning of the villages to the Hiwis.[8]

When compared to the obvious distaste and reluctance shown by Police Battalion 101 in its comparatively small-scale revenge killings of Poles, the men's zealous and dedicated slaughtering of Jews stands in sharp relief. The killing of Poles was a regrettable necessity. Towards Jews all inhibitions had fallen from them. Yet the men's comparative gusto in killing Jews is not all that distinguishes it. Their willingness to be seen by others, including loved ones, as genocidal executioners also reveals their approval of the deeds. Among others, at least two of the officers, Lieutenant Paul Brand and Captain Wohlauf, the commander of First Company, had their wives by their sides while they were killing in Poland. Wohlauf had earlier returned to Hamburg shortly after Police Battalion 101 arrived in Poland, in order to go through with an already scheduled wedding, which took place on June 29, 1942. He then caught up with his comrades, while his wife delayed a bit, joining him and the battalion shortly after their first major killing in Józefów. She stayed with the battalion for at least several weeks and several killing operations, and participated in one, if not two, of the large ones.[9]

Wohlauf's wife attended the day-long killing operation that the entire battalion conducted at Międzyrzec on August 25. The roundup, the driving of the Jews from their homes to the market square, was perhaps the most brutal and licentious of all those that Police Battalion 101 conducted. The men left hundreds of dead Jews strewn about the streets. The scene at the market square was also among the most gruesome. Some of the notable features included the Germans forcing the Jews to squat for hours in the burning sun so that many fainted, and shooting any Jew who did nothing more than stand up.

The market square became littered with the dead.[10] Such shootings naturally included many children, who found it particularly difficult to remain immobile in such discomfort for hours on end. The Hiwis and some of the Germans in the Międzyrzec's German *Gendarmerie* also used the occasion to satisfy their lust for cruelty. They entertained themselves by flogging Jews with whips.[11] Not only was Frau Wohlauf a party to all of this, but so were the wives of some of the locally stationed Germans, as well as a group of German Red Cross nurses.[12] Frau Wohlauf, if conforming to her usual practice, probably carried that symbol of domination, a riding whip, with her.[13] That day, she and the other German women got to observe firsthand how their men were purging the world of the putative Jewish menace, by killing around one thousand and deporting ten thousand more to their deaths. This is how the pregnant Frau Wohlauf spent her honeymoon.

If Wohlauf and the other officers did not care that their labors were observed by his wife, by other German women, even by Red Cross nurses, many of the men of Police Battalion 101 thought that at least the presence of Frau Wohlauf was inappropriate. One man tells of his reaction: "On the day of the 'action,' I myself saw Frau Wohlauf dressed in normal clothes on the market place of Międzyrzec. Not just once, but frequently over a long period of time. I too was astonished at the behavior of our Company Commander and his spouse, and it made me angry all the more so, since our Company Commander knew full well before an 'action' what was going to happen."[14] Another man tells of the general reaction in the battalion: "Moreover, my comrades told me of their anger that the wife of our Company Commander watched the evacuation, although she was pregnant."[15] Their objections bespeak no shame at what they were doing, no desire to conceal from others their contribution to mass annihilation and torture, but rather a sense of chivalry and propriety that Frau Wohlauf's presence violated, particularly since this ghetto clearing was, even by their standards, unusually brutal and gruesome.[16] That it was this woman in particular who was not supposed to see such things is clear because they did not object to the presence of other women, including Lieutenant Brand's wife, who at one point apparently also observed them in action. Although they may have generally believed that women should not be exposed to such horrors, it was this woman, because she was pregnant, whose presence aroused them. The emphasis on her pregnancy makes it clear that the men were agitated because of possible damage to her sensibilities and person. Living with the battalion, Frau Wohlauf already knew of their genocidal killing; by having been in Międzyrzec she was acquiring no fundamentally new knowledge, except perhaps of the details of such an operation. That it was her "condition" and her welfare that was the cause of the men's agitation is testified to by the wife of Lieutenant Brand: "I remember exactly that a

*Vera Wohlauf and
Captain Julius Wohlauf*

short while later Major Trapp denounced this incident publicly and declared
something to the effect that he thought it outrageous that women who are in
a state of pregnancy should witness such a thing." Trapp chose to inform the
women of his anger while many of his men were in attendance. Frau Brand
explains: "By public denunciation I mean that Major Trapp delivered his
statements before a rather large gathering of officers and NCOs, and in the
presence of various wives who were staying with their husbands as visitors,
including also me."[17] The men of Police Battalion 101 voiced no general objection to having had Frau Wohlauf, Frau Brand, and other women living
with their battalion in Poland, fully knowledgeable of their genocidal killing
of Jews that was, as two of the men put it, their "daily bread."[18] Indeed,
Trapp was comfortable enough with what they were doing that he was willing to discuss it openly with the women in front of many of his men. He
merely wanted to make it clear that their killing operations were scenes to
which the women, especially the pregnant Frau Wohlauf, would not be directly exposed any further. Their killing operations were, after all, usually violent and gruesome.

More generally, beyond Police Battalion 101, the perpetrators who operated in Poland and elsewhere also voiced no objection to having their deeds known to those beyond their immediate genocidal cohort, including to women and to loved ones. German women—the perpetrators' wives and girl-friends, as well as secretaries, nurses, employees of economic enterprises, and entertainers—were everywhere in Poland, which meant that they learned of the genocidal slaughter; the Germans' extermination of Polish Jewry, comprising around 10 percent of the entire Polish population, was, after all, common knowledge. The German security police's own reports on the mood of the people in the Lublin District tell again and again that the Germans' and Poles' knowledge of the mass extermination of the Jews was extensive. According to one member of the security police, the fate of the Jews was discussed in all German offices, including in post offices and on trains. That the Germans were gassing the Jews was, according to him, an open secret.[19] Another German who had been stationed in Lublin admits in a memorable phrase how open and widespread discussion of the systematic slaughter of Jews had been: "The sparrows sang about it from the roofs."[20] Lieutenant Brand's wife—in recounting an incident in which one German was brazen about his lust for Jewish blood—also indicates the temper of the free and unconcealed discussion about the genocidal enterprise:

> I was sitting one morning at breakfast with my husband in the garden of his lodgings when an ordinary policeman of his platoon came up to us, snapped to attention, and declared: "Lieutenant, I have not yet had breakfast." When my husband looked at him quizzically, he declared further: "I have not yet bumped off any Jews." The whole thing sounded so cynical that I indignantly reprimanded the man in harsh words and also called him, I believe, a scoundrel [*Lumpen*]. My husband sent the policeman away and, to boot, then reproached me, explaining that by my statements I would bring great trouble down onto my head.[21]

For the perpetrators in general and the men of Police Battalion 101 in particular, it was fine for women to possess knowledge of their genocidal operations. Otherwise, the Germans would not have allowed so many women, if only as witnesses, to have been a party to the brutal persecution and killing of Jews. But, for some, the direct exposure of women to the gruesomeness, to the visual horrors, of the campaign of extermination was deemed to be improper. Like soldiers from many eras, who would have become incensed had women been allowed beside them in battle, the men of Police Battalion 101 thought it a job fit only for men, or at least not for pregnant women. They, like soldiers, could at once have objected to the presence of women, without being ashamed of their own activities as warriors in the service of their nation.

The Germans' openness about their genocidal slaughtering—making it available to the view of so many other German men and women who happened to be stationed in Poland—is but an indication of the perpetrators' *obvious* approval of their historic deeds. Yet nothing betrays the falseness of their routine postwar denials of their approval of, indeed their pride in, the killings, more than the photographs that the Germans in Police Battalion 101 took memorializing their time in Poland, of which only some unknown percentage has come to light. These Germans' willingness to make an extensive photographic record of their deeds, including their killing operations, in which they appear with cheerful and proud demeanors as men entirely comfortable with their environment, their vocation, and with the images that are being preserved, is compelling evidence that they did not conceive of themselves as having been engaged in crime, let alone in one of the greatest crimes of the century. The following photograph illustrates to us, as it celebrated for the Germans, their active disregard for the dignity of Jews, their denial that Jews possessed dignity. It is an example of the Germans' use of the socially dead Jews as playthings for their own satisfaction.[22]

A man from Police Battalion 101 amuses himself and the beaming German onlookers with their Jewish playthings.

Photographic evidence, as the cliché tells us, often conveys more than do many words of testimony. Yet few words can intensify the communicative power of the visual evidence of a photograph as do those that this preening German penned on the reverse side of this revealing image. "He should work, but he must be clean-shaven" (*Arbeiten soll er, aber Rasirt* [sic] *muss er sein*). The German was not merely recording the event but giving his ironic commentary on it.[23] Degrading Jews in this manner, namely by cutting off their beards, was a common practice among Germans of the time. It was doubly symbolic. It represented the absolute mastery of the photographed German over the Jew. The Jew, a grown man, had no choice but to stand by as another abridged his sovereignty over his own body by cutting away his beard, a symbol of his manhood. The personal desecration was done, moreover, in front of the camera's recording eye, ensuring that the victim's shame would be displayed to people for years to come. This simple act conveyed unequivocally—to the German, to the Jew, and to all who watched, contemporaneously or later—the virtually limitless power of the shearer over his victim. The act, and its enjoyment by others, bespeaks a mind-set found among "masters" dealing with the socially dead, particularly during those moments when they mark them physically in order to convey to them that they possess no honor.[24] What better way for a man to display to his children and grandchildren his heroics during the war for the German *Volk*'s survival than to have such a testament? The second symbolic aspect of the deed was the choice of the beard, which was not haphazard. Just as Gnade selected bearded, old Jewish men to beat at the killing of Łomazy, just as the Police Battalion 309 men in Białystok set the beards of Jews on fire, and just as Germans frequently and spontaneously cut Jews' beards during the Holocaust, so too did this man create a record of his separating this Jew from the luxuriant growth that Germans identified with Jewry.

The photographs that the Germans in Police Battalion 101 made as keepsakes of their work in Poland were generously shared among the entire battalion. They were not private mementos, furtively taken, guarded, and husbanded by individuals. The affirmative atmosphere that reigned within the battalion regarding their work took on an almost celebratory, festive quality in the public displaying and sharing of the photographs. "I would like to remark on these photographs. They were laid out hanging on the wall and anyone, as he pleased, could order copies of them. I too acquired these photographs through such an order, even though I had not always participated in the events that the photographs depict. If my memory serves me right, most of the photographs had been taken by a member of the company's office."[25] It is as if they were saying: "Here is a great event. Anyone who wants to preserve for himself images of the heroic accomplishments can order copies." It is reminiscent of travelers purchasing postcards or asking for duplicates of friends' snapshots that have captured favorite vistas and scenes from an enjoyable and memorable trip.

The photographs serve as two kinds of evidence. Not only did the men want to adorn their photo albums with images from their genocidal operations. The images themselves are also revealing. Photographs taken in Łomazy and elsewhere remind us to question the prevailing views that hold these Germans to have been frightened, coerced, unwilling, disapproving, or horrified killers of people whom they considered to be innocent. Indeed, some of the photos capture men who look tranquil and happy, and others show them in poses of pride and joy as they undertake their dealings with their Jewish victims. It is difficult to see in the photographs men who viewed the killing to be a crime. Yet, as eloquent as they are, the photographs described and reproduced to this point seem almost mute compared to two others. The first one was taken in Radzyń, likely sometime between late August and October 1942. From a period when the battalion was carrying out several of its large mass killings and brutal deportations, it memorializes a group of officers from the battalion staff and First Company sitting outdoors around a long table with the wives of two of the officers, Frau Brand and Frau Wohlauf. They are drinking in what appears to be a convivial atmosphere. Frau Wohlauf, who can be seen displaying a big smile, is evidently having a good time.

A second photograph, from Czermierniki sometime during the second half of 1942, is truly festive. It captures more than fifteen men of Lieutenant Oscar Peters' Third Company platoon celebrating. The Germans are holding drinks, grinning broadly, and appear to be singing to the accompaniment of violin playing. Hanging on the wall behind them is a hand-lettered ditty which they obviously composed themselves:

> *The watchword for today*
> *Now the light-stepped fun begins*
> *And all feels well.*
>
> (*Parole für Heute*
> *Jetzt gehts los im Trapp*
> *Und alles fühlt sich Wohlauf.*)

Punning on their leaders' names (Trapp means "clip-clop" and Wohlauf, the name of First Company's commander, means "well" or "in good health"), the men described their state of mind. These Germans were celebrating, not cursing, the names of the men who repeatedly sent them to kill Jews. These men—whose lives were then dedicated to mass slaughter, who, in addition to the large company- and battalion-strength killings taking place during this period, were conducting numerous search-and-destroy missions in their own area—were feeling great.[26]

The perpetrators' places of congregation not only housed photographs but were also filled with conversation of the mass slaughter. The men of Police Battalion 101 reveal little of their own contemporary intimate conversations of their deeds. A side glance at their brethren in Police Regiment 25, who were engaged in the same enterprise and perpetrated their mass slaughters in a manner indistinguishable from that of Police Battalion 101, is suggestive on this point. Its officers talked frequently and approvingly of the genocidal slaughter: ". . . I know that the Company Commander, as well as the other officers of Police Regiment 25, which was then stationed in Lublin, spoke in the officers' club of the killings that had been executed. . . . the younger officers spoke very much of these things. They deemed themselves to be at war in Poland and to have accomplished feats of heroism by these killings."[27] These Germans were so in the grip of antisemitic fantasies that they conceived of the manifestly inert, unarmed Jewish population of the Lublin region, which was destitute, prostrate, and compliant in the face of German demands, as being at war with Germany. In slaughtering Jews, the ideological warriors believed themselves to be performing heroic deeds. The postwar testimony refers not to the men of Police Battalion 101 specifically, but to the officers of the regiment to which it and Police Battalion 65 belonged. Nevertheless, it conveys the atmosphere of approval that permeated this police regiment and its battalions. As this man, who was the commander of the Order Police in Lublin from July 1940 to July 1944, put it, the officers "always discussed the shootings and were also pretty proud of them."[28]

It cannot be doubted that the men of Police Battalion 101 discussed their wholesale slaughtering among themselves. The clerk of First Company recounts, for example, how the men, upon returning from killing operations, regularly filled him in on their handiwork in detail.[29] Many have testified that they complained vociferously to each other of Frau Wohlauf's presence at the killing in Międzyrzec, which is an instance of such discussion, of moral evaluation, and of the expression of severe criticism of their superiors.[30] While the men's postwar testimony does not announce explicitly that they had generally approved of the genocide and its attendant cruelties (this is not surprising, since such announcements could have put them in legal jeopardy), its thousands of pages also do not warrant the conclusion that these men disapproved of it in principle. On the contrary, the men's accounts of the conversations that they had while in the killing fields suggest the opposite, namely that these men in principle approved of the genocide and of their own deeds.[31] One of the men, for example, reports of the good spirits and jocularity that reigned during a meal after one killing operation: "At lunch a few of my comrades made merry [*machten lustig*] over the experiences that they had had during the operation. From their stories, I could gather that they had been involved in a shooting operation. So I remember as a particularly crass case that one of the men remarked with aplomb that now we eat 'Jew-brains.' This remark was so disgusting to me that I reprimanded the man, who then indeed stopped. The other comrades who had laughed at this, to me, 'grue-some joke' also stopped."[32] The testimony of one former member of Police Battalion 101's Second Company makes clear that such talk was common, that the men did indeed routinely discuss the killings and the brutalities: "Evenings, in quarters, stories were often told of the terrible abuses against Jews, by which First Company was supposed to have especially distinguished itself. In that company there was 'Big Raeder,' who was referred to as 'Slug-ger' [*Schläger*] and who treated Jews and Poles very ruthlessly."[33]

The question, of course, is in what tone and with what emotions did the speakers and listeners contemplate the tales. The evidence suggests that these regular public tellings were occasions to swap stories for entertainment, in the spirit of general approval. Even if First Company was prominent in cruelty, its men are presented here as but having "distinguished" themselves in an ac-tivity that engaged the others as well. This would mean that some of Second Company's perpetrators of such "excesses" were themselves likely to gather around and share in their own accomplishments as well as in those of others. Furthermore, the men of Second Company must themselves have perpe-trated many of the deeds under discussion, for the three companies were typ-ically stationed apart from one another, so each company had to rely primarily on its own activities for conversational material. Obviously, many of the men of Police Battalion 101 were committing many brutalities. If a spirit of ap-proval had not animated such evening discussions, if some of the men had in-deed responded to the stories by indicating their principled opposition to the brutalizing and killing of Jews, then they undoubtedly would have said so after the war. The men's silence on this point is almost as revealing as self-indicting admissions would be.[34]

What do the men of Police Battalion 101 say of their attitudes towards the genocidal slaughter? The lieutenant, Buchmann, who did refuse to kill explains what led him to demur when his fellow officers did not. "I was then a little older and, moreover, a reserve officer. I was not intent on being promoted or other-wise to advance, because I had at home my prosperous business. The Company Commanders, Wohlauf and Hoffmann, by contrast, were young people on ac-tive duty who aspired to become somebody. Through my business experience, which especially extended also abroad, I had a better comprehension of things. Moreover, I already knew from before, through my business activity, many Jews."[35] Although the lieutenant speaks of the importance of the other officers' career ambitions, he—despite his stated heartfelt intention not to incriminate others[36]—unwittingly betrays their operative motivation and the crucial difference between him and them when he gives this brief account of why he viewed the killings differently from the others. His "better comprehension of these matters" consisted of his recognition that they were committing crimes. The basis for his view, which he implies was exceptional for the times, was his different experience abroad and with Jews. Simply put, he viewed Jews differently. With this comparison, he acknowledges by implication that his fellow officers were beholden to the regnant German antisemitism that was the basis for and had engendered the policy of total extermination.

The lieutenant's depiction of himself as having been fundamentally different in attitude towards the mass slaughter is confirmed by others in the battalion. The reservist who served as the clerk of First Company portrays this lieutenant as the exception in his company, saying that neither he nor his comrades had the sense that the officers, particularly their commander, Wohlauf, killed Jews unwillingly. While the lieutenant was objecting to the killings and complaining about them openly and frequently, the other officers evinced no sympathy with his views, though they tolerated and accepted his inaction.[37] One time, when the lieutenant found himself under the command not of Trapp, but of the security police in Łuków, he apparently felt pressured enough, his opposition to the killing notwithstanding, to lead his men in a killing operation, in which they marched Jews to a killing site and shot them.[38] But, fortunately for him, these circumstances were extraordinary for Police Battalion 101. Under the indulgent Trapp, he and the others were not pressured to kill. Lieutenant Buchmann did not kill because pressure was not applied; the others killed anyway, because pressure was unnecessary.

Two of the most significant and revealing actions of the men of Police Battalion 101 are, on the one hand, the men's incessant volunteering to kill and, on the other, the failure of the men to avail themselves of the opportunities to avoid killing. One of the Germans in Second Company states the simple truth: "It is also perfectly possible that one could keep away from the executions if one wanted to."[39] This was, moreover, not just a presumption on their part. Lieutenant Buchmann explains: "I can remember that from time to time before operations it was asked whether anyone did not feel up to the impending task. If anyone answered affirmatively . . . he was entrusted with other tasks."[40] When discussing the Józefów slaughter, Erwin Grafmann, a member of Second Company, states: "In any case, as matters stood, one could either volunteer or avail oneself of the opportunity to abstain from participation if one did not feel up to the task."[41] The disinclination to kill that the Germans did have and occasionally acted upon was a visceral, and not an ethical, one. The reason that some would and did opt out of the killing was because the duty was at times unpleasant. Not everyone always "felt up to it." As such, the decision to kill or not to kill was a matter of taste and not of principle.

The testimony of another killer inadvertently confirms that neither he nor the others considered a comrade's acceptance of the option not to kill as an ideological or ethical rejection of the genocidal enterprise. "When the question is put to me why did I at all participate in the shooting, I must say that one does not want to be considered a coward."[42] He is saying here that it was the threat of being considered a coward that might have inhibited some men from excusing themselves from the killing. This can only mean that an essentially unquestioned consensus on the justice of the extermination existed. For conceiving of someone as a coward, as a psychological weakling with an inferior constitution, presupposes agreement by everyone that the deed being asked of the actor meets his own as well as general approval. And so, right before their initial killing in Józefów, Gnade's final words during his address to his company, according to the testimony of one of his men, was an admonition to the effect of "Do not therefore go soft."[43] A person can be a coward, he can fail to act owing to being "soft," only because he is not courageous enough or not made of sufficient mettle to carry out a task that he wants to see accomplished. If a person is not in favor of the deed, then the failure to carry it out is an indication of his opposition to it, not of cowardice or weakness.[44] Pacifists—those who as a matter of principle oppose war—are not cowards. It is noteworthy that the men of Police Battalion 101 do not say that those who chose to avoid killing ran the risk of being seen as "Jew-lovers" (*Judenbegünstiger*), namely as principled opponents of the deed. This censorious possibility evidently did not occur to the individuals, either at the time or after the war. And it certainly would have if solidarity with the Jews had indeed existed and been an operative motivation within the battalion, or if it had been even remotely possible that the men of Police Battalion 101 suspected that principled opposition to the killing was the source of a person's disinclination to kill Jews. The tenor within the battalion was such that, in the men's testimony, the charge of being "Jew-lovers" is not discussed.

It is also revealing that the "pep talk" given to Police Battalion 101 before the Józefów massacre was, as has been noted, a transparently thin justification for the huge slaughter of civilian Jews. The justification—namely that German women and children dying in air raids should motivate the annihilation of destitute Polish Jewish communities *in toto*, prostrate, unarmed communities in a defeated country hundreds of miles away—would not have made sense, would have sounded and been received like the "logic" of a madman to anyone who did not share the Nazi eliminationist antisemitic creed, of which an article of faith was that the Jews' demonic capacities reached far, with powerful destructive effects. The reminder of the civilian losses at home was meant to activate Germans' culturally shared cognitive model of Jewry, and thereby merely to remind the men of what Jews by nature were—and not to win dissenters over to a conception of Jewry that they did not already share. The notion that the justification made sense to the men of Police Battalion 101 finds further substantiation in their silence about it. Not one of them has testified that he thought it was crazy, that he did not at the time see some causal relationship between the deaths of Germans and the need to kill Jews, some organic connection between the bombing and the genocide.

The rule for search-and-destroy missions and for forming the shooting commando for the large-scale killing operations was odd for a security organization of this sort and is therefore significant. It was to staff them with volunteers. The officers knew that this was unpleasant duty, and so it made sense to let each man decide for himself if he felt up to it. The officers could do so for two reasons. The first was that they understood that any reluctance to participate in executions was a reaction to the real gruesomeness of such killings and not the result of any moral opposition to them. The officers were being solicitous of their men. No evidence exists to suggest that in Police Battalion 101 a man's desire to forgo a killing operation was perceived as a challenge to the German moral order, or as a principled repudiation of the regime or of this, one of its most important projects. Had it been so, then the officers would likely have been less willing to countenance their men's selectivity in deciding to take part in what was their principal activity while stationed in Poland.

The second reason that the officers could rely upon volunteers was that letting the men decide for themselves who would kill posed no difficulty for getting the job done. "It is, moreover, true," testifies one man from Second Company, "that there were always enough volunteers for the executions. I too volunteered once or twice for executions, specifically for small-scale operations of the platoon."[45] A number of his comrades confirm the voluntarism that pervaded their ranks. One relates: "I must first and foremost state categorically that whenever the superior requested them, there were enough volunteers for execution squads. This was the case also in Józefów. I must add that, in fact, so many volunteered that some had to be left behind."[46] The first of these two men, Grafmann, is one of the small number of men who, in the midst of the killing operation of Józefów, asked to be excused because of their disgust at the gruesomeness of the face-to-face killing during this, their baptismal genocidal operation. Obviously, as Grafmann's own testimony indicates and his later volunteering to be an executioner demonstrates, Grafmann's request was not born of a moral antipathy to the slaughtering of Jews.[47] Grafmann may have been a paradigmatic killer of the type who had difficulty at first because of the gruesomeness, yet who freely chose to resume killing even after having been excused. Volunteering for killing, as in many police battalions, was the battalion norm.[48]

THE OPPORTUNITIES GIVEN to the men to avoid killing have already been touched upon. In addition to the men who chose not to kill, the recalcitrant lieutenant served as a powerful example to the entire battalion that the men could refuse to kill without suffering tangible hardships. Furthermore, from the battalion commander down to its non-commissioned officers, those in command positions showed understanding for the disinclination that their subordinates might have had in performing their unsavory tasks. As one of the men puts it when discussing Trapp's initial offer, "it did not take special courage for someone to step forward."[49] But let us imagine that despite the opportunities to avoid killing, despite the possibilities that existed not to volunteer to shoot Jews, some of the men were hesitant to declare their disinclination to kill, either by asking to be excused from killing or by repeatedly and perhaps conspicuously failing to volunteer for killing operations. Let us imagine that they were of such weak will that, although they perceived the genocide to be a monumental crime, they nevertheless preferred to be genocidal executioners, to witness and produce the gruesome scenes that were the roundups and the executions. They still could have done what the disapproving lieutenant did: apply for a transfer. The lieutenant wrote to the police president of Hamburg stating his opposition to the killing and asking to be returned to Hamburg for duty there. His request was granted.[50] Indeed, his refusal was not held against him. He was subsequently promoted to a higher rank and installed in the trusted position of adjutant to the Police President of Hamburg.[51]

As generally is the case in military and police institutions, procedures did exist within the Order Police for men to request transfers. Men of the Order Police did avail themselves of the transfer mechanism. In February 1940, for example, two men of Police Battalion 102, also a Hamburg battalion, submitted requests to be transferred to their home garrisons that were approved. The father of one had died, leaving his elderly mother alone to manage their two-and-a-half-acre property. The serious heart condition of the second man's wife was deemed an acceptable reason. In August of that year, another man was granted his request to be transferred from the battalion, because of a troublesome leg that swelled and pained him on long marches.[52] General transfer procedures did exist within the Order Police. Men took advantage of them, and the institution appears to have been, if anything, rather liberal in granting them. Furthermore, when assessing the men's opportunities to remove themselves from killing operations, the transfer offers made to the men must also be taken into account. One that has survived in documentary form was a request which was submitted to all three battalions of Police Regiment

25 and to Police Battalion 53 for young, active policemen from the communications platoons to volunteer for training for a "communications replacement company" in Cracow. The request came in December 1942, when all the units were already steeped in mass slaughter. Two men of Police Battalion 101 did apply and were transferred.[53] Why did all the qualified men in these battalions not apply? Aside from these two men, no evidence exists that any of the men of Police Battalion 101 applied for transfers, either on their own or in response to officially posted transfer opportunities, during the period of their genocidal killings. Despite all of their easy protestations that they did not look favorably on the killing, that they would have liked to have avoided killing but could not, virtually none of the men of Police Battalion 101 has even *claimed* that he put in for a transfer.[54]

Another facet of these men's lives needs to be considered. During their time as genocidal killers, the men of Police Battalion 101 went home on furloughs, lasting weeks.[55] Some of the men say that they were instructed not to discuss their genocidal activities; others deny that they received any such injunction. Lieutenant Kurt Drucker, for example, admits that he, "on the occasion of a furlough, spoke with friends about the events."[56] Whatever their instructions were (and they might have varied from company to company), the battalion members have been practically mute regarding what they did or talked about while at home with friends and loved ones. Had the perpetrators believed the genocidal slaughter to be a crime, had they therefore seen while at home the prospect of returning to the brutalities and blood of the killings as being as uninviting a prospect as a principled opponent of them would have beheld them to be, then how could they bear to bring themselves to return to Poland? Once back home in Hamburg or Bremen, how could opponents of the killings not have cringed with horror at returning to the gruesomeness of the mass murdering? The point is not that they could have been expected to desert (although it is noteworthy that no evidence exists of any who did), with all the real dangers that desertion entailed. It is that the respite from genocidal operations ought to have given opponents of it, namely those who actually considered it to be mass *murder* (and not justified extermination), the opportunity and time to reflect even more on their situation and options. They were in the bosom of their families, away from whatever social psychological pressures living in an institution of genocidal slaughter created for individuals. And they knew the horrors that awaited their return to Poland. So why did they not resolve to apply for a transfer? Why did they not appeal to whatever resources they had at home—family, friends, or acquaintances who might have had contacts or themselves have been in government agencies—to help them escape their horrible assignment? Had the men of Police Battalion 101 made any effort to extricate themselves from the genocidal killing, then they would have asserted as much after the war. They reflexively say that they wish they had not had to kill—hardly convincing testimony from those who are being interrogated for their mass murdering. Yet, despite their powerful desire to exculpate themselves, only one man in the entire battalion, aside from Lieutenant Buchmann, tells of having done precisely what would be expected of opponents of mass murder, namely attempt to extricate themselves from the killing institution. This man got his wife to write to the Hamburg police authorities that she was unable to raise their (at the time) eight children without his assistance. His transfer back to Hamburg followed a few months later.[57] The rest of the battalion's men do not claim, let alone corroborate the claim, that while on furlough they either expressed to friends and family a wish to extricate themselves from the killing, or actually attempted to liberate themselves from the job of mass murdering, which further reinforces the notion that they did not disapprove of the genocidal slaughter.

The German culture of cruelty that existed towards Jews cannot be documented for this battalion to the extent that it can for many other institutions of killing. Few survivors have emerged, and so it is often up to the Germans to report their own brutality—however much there was—and thereby to incriminate themselves, which they are naturally reluctant to do. Moreover, the Federal Republic of Germany's investigating authorities were generally not interested in learning about instances of cruelty, since by the time of these investigations, all crimes, except murder, had passed the time limit for prosecution that is specified in the statute of limitations. No matter how much a German in a police battalion had beaten, tortured, or maimed a Jew, if he did not kill his victim, then he could not be prosecuted for his actions. Still, enough evidence has emerged to suggest that the culture of cruelty was also part of Police Battalion 101's constitution.

These Germans expended no effort to spare the victims any unnecessary suffering. Moreover, the evidence does not suggest that they gave any thought to the matter. The entire course of the destruction of a Jewish community— from the brutality of the roundups, to the suffering inflicted upon the Jews at the assembly points (by forcing them to sit, crouch, or lie motionless for hours on end in the midsummer heat without water), to the manner of execution, in Łomazy, for example—bespeaks a tolerance, if not a willful administration of suffering upon the victims. The roundups did not have to be such licentious affairs. The Germans did not have to instill terror in the victims and leave scores, sometimes hundreds of dead in the streets. When the Jews were waiting for the Germans to march them to the city's outskirts or to load them onto freight cars, it would have been easy for the Germans to distribute some water to them, and to let them move around a bit, rather than to shoot any who stood up. As a number of the battalion members have testified, it was evident to the Germans that the Jews suffered greatly and needlessly as they waited. Finally, the cruelty of the Germans' manner of shooting Jews or of using clubs and whips to drive them from their houses or into the freight cars speaks for itself. Because such brutality and cruelty became integral to the practice of ghetto clearings and annihilations, and also because the goal itself of mass extermination is so horrific and tends to overwhelm the consideration of "lesser" crimes, when compiling the ledger of German brutality and cruelty—in the endeavor to assess the actions and attitudes of the killers—it is easy to overlook these practices, as cruel as they were. Why did they not have "orderly" killing operations, without the public killing of children, the beatings, without the symbolic degradation?

In addition to the willfully and unnecessarily brutal manner in which the Germans and their helpers conducted the various stages of a ghetto annihilation—namely the routinized roundup and execution procedures—they also gratuitously brutalized and tortured the Jews. Sometimes the agents inflicting suffering on the Jews were the Germans' eastern European Hiwis, such as during one of the Międzyrzec deportations, when the Hiwis, obviously influenced by the Germans' own brutality, lashed Jews with whips. Any brutality that the Hiwis publicly perpetrated upon the Jews was permitted, if not promoted, by the Germans, who had absolute control over them, and such brutality should be taken into account when evaluating the Germans' treatment of the Jews. The scene at the marketplace during the last large deportation from Międzyrzec is such an instance. The Germans forced the Jews to sit or squat huddled together. The following photograph depicts a similar scene from another of these Germans' deportations from Międzyrzec.

The Jews were praying and crying, and therefore making much noise. This disturbed their German masters: "Intermittently, Hiwis beat the people with their rifle-butts, in order to enforce silence. The SD men had knotted whips, similar to horse whips. They walked along the rows of the squatting people, sometimes beating them vehemently."[58] The men of Police Battalion 101 themselves were not to be outdone by their eastern European minions. Although they also degraded and tortured Jews at Międzyrzec in the most gratuitous, willful manner, their deeds are entirely absent from their testimony. The accounts of survivors tell a different, more accurate, and revealing story. Survivors are adamant that the Germans were indeed incredibly brutal, that their cruelty that day was wanton, at times turning into sadistic sport. At the marketplace, the Jews, who had been forced to squat for hours, were "mocked" (*khoyzek gemacht*) and "kicked," and some of the Germans organized "a game" (*shpil*) of "tossing apples and whoever was struck by the apple was then killed." This sport was continued at the railway station, this

*Men of Police Battalion 101 guard Jews of Międzyrzec on May 26, 1943.
The Germans deported them to Majdanek, where the men of Police Battal-
ion 101 and others slaughtered them in the November 1943 "Operation
Harvest Festival."*

time with empty liquor bottles. "Bottles were tossed over Jewish heads and
whoever was struck by a bottle was dragged out of the crowd and beaten murderously amid roaring laughter. Then some of those who were thus mangled
[*tseharget*] were shot." Afterwards, they loaded the dead together with the living onto freight cars bound for Treblinka. One photograph documenting the
final stage of what may be this deportation has survived (see next page).

Frightened Jewish women, urged on by the Germans (one can but guess
how), are running with their children into a dark interior from which they
will emerge only to be gassed. The German closest to them, whose identity
is unknown, can be seen walking menacingly with a whip grasped firmly in
hand.

Small wonder that to the eyes of the victims—but not in the self-serving
testimony of the perpetrators—these ordinary Germans appeared not as
mere murderers, certainly not as reluctant killers dragged to their task against
their inner opposition to the genocide, but as "two-legged beasts" filled with
"bloodthirstiness."[59]

The Germans report but rarely on their torturing of victims, on every
unnecessary rifle-butt blow to a Jewish head, yet the evidence suggests that

*Germans cramming Jewish women and children of Międzyrzec into freight
cars.*

the tortures which they inflicted in Międzyrzec and Łomazy (where they beat
the bearded Jewish men whom they compelled to crawl to their execution)
were not rare exceptions. Although the men of Police Battalion 101 do not tell
of their cruelties in the mass deportation of Jews that they conducted from
Łuków, one of the *Gendarmerie* stationed in Łuków recounts what he saw as
he gazed out of his office window: "[The Jews] were driven on by the German policemen [*Polizeibeamter*]. I could see the way the policemen beat with
clubs Jews who had collapsed. It was for me a shattering sight. People who
could not rise to their feet by themselves were pulled up by the policemen.
The beating was constant and the driving [of the Jews] was accompanied by
yelling [*lautstark angetrieben*]. . . ."[60]

The men of Police Battalion 101 report the cruelties of others, as of the
Germans in the SD and of the Hiwis in Międzyrzec, while remaining reticent
about their own. They fail to mention the clubs that they themselves used in this
deportation and to what devastating effect they wielded them, although many
of them were engaged in driving the Jews from this ghetto. Presumably, they
used them for all their ghetto clearings and in other killing operations, though
but scant indications of their use of clubs are to be found in the testimony. We
learn of the whips in Józefów, the clubs in Łomazy (only because someone
thought to recount the incident where the Germans beat the bearded Jews), and
the whips in Międzyrzec, in each case from only one or two men. None of the
Germans reveals that any of them used a whip in Łomazy. All we know of is the

one whip that was captured in one of the photographs that has surfaced from that day. The men of Police Battalion 101 similarly fail to volunteer accounts of the scene from Łuków documented in the two photographs on the next page.

Members of Police Battalion 101 mocked these Jews in Łuków before dispatching them and seven thousand others to the gas chambers of Treblinka. They forced them to wear prayer shawls, to kneel as if in prayer, and, perhaps, to chant prayers. The sight of Jewish religious objects and rituals evoked in the German "solvers of the Jewish Problem" derisive laughter and incited them to cruelty. In their eyes, these were undoubtedly the bizarre accouterments, the grotesque ceremonies, and the mysterious implements of a demonic brood. The Holocaust was one of the rare mass slaughters in which perpetrators, like these and other men of Police Battalion 101, routinely mocked their victims and forced them to perform antics before sending them to their deaths. These proud, joyous poses of German masters (note the beaming face in the first photo) degrading men who were for them archetypical Jews wearing prayer shawls (note the absent hat, presumably knocked off, in the second photo), are undoubtedly representative of many such scenes of degradation and others of cruelty about which the men of Police Battalion 101 remain silent, and about which the Jews did not survive to give witness. If we relied upon the specific and precise accounts of the battalion's members themselves, then we would have a skewed portrait of their actions, grossly underestimating the gratuitous suffering that they inflicted on the Jews, not to mention the evident gusto with which they at times visited cruelties upon their defenseless victims. Major Trapp, who was a killer with mixed emotions, at least once rebuked the men for their cruelty. One of his men tells of the disapproval Trapp expressed to the assembled battalion after the licentiousness of the initial killing operation in Józefów: "According to my memory he mentioned something to the effect that he could not agree with the maltreatment of the Jews *which he had observed* [my emphasis]. We had the task to shoot the Jews, but not to beat and torture them."[61] It is significant that the battalion member remembers not a categorical prohibition, but an expression of disapproval (Trapp was *nicht einverstanden*). Here is the voice of authority in the person of an atypical German commanding officer seeking to restrain the cruelty that had already welled up unbidden in his men. Trapp—unwittingly paraphrasing a line from Shakespeare: "We shall be call'd purgers, not murderers"[62]— was saying to his men: Let us be killers, not torturers. But in vain, for his men persisted in their cruelties, as is evidenced by those which they perpetrated at Międzyrzec and elsewhere, and by the subsequent discussion and boasting among the men of the "awful excesses against Jews."[63]

It cannot be doubted that a variety of attitudes towards the genocidal slaughter existed within Police Battalion 101. Even if general, principled ap-

Shortly before deporting the Jews of Łuków to their deaths in Treblinka, men of Police Battalion 101 take time out to force a group of Jews to pose for photographic mementos.

proval reigned, the men approached their destructive tasks with a range of stances and emotions. Some "types" are the reveling, sadistic slayers of Jews, like Gnade and Bekemeier, the zealous but faint-of-heart killers, like Hoffmann,[64] the dedicated but non-celebratory executioners, like Grafmann, and the approving but uneasy and conflicted killers, like Trapp. These types differed in the amount of pleasure they took in the killing, without differing on the justice of the enterprise. Given the existing data, it is hard to know what the distribution of the various types was within the battalion. The information that exists about most of the individual men is insufficient for conclusions of this sort to be drawn. For the same reason, it is impossible to say how many men killed with what frequency. It is even harder to know how many men perpetrated what kinds of gratuitous cruelties and how often they did so. And it is impossible to know the exact emotions with which they gazed upon their labor's product, whether it was a pit filled or a street strewn with Jewish corpses, including those of the old and the young. It would have been surprising had any of the killers in the 1960s reported to the legal authorities, or to the world at large, feelings of joy and triumph that might have moved them while beholding these scenes. It is equally difficult to believe that these men looked upon the Jews whom they were slaughtering with fond or even neutral feelings, with sympathy for fellow human beings.

The evidence is, however, unequivocal that the overwhelming majority of the men in Police Battalion 101 rounded up and then killed or deported Jews to their deaths—and not just once, but repeatedly. Furthermore, it is noteworthy that only at the first mass slaughter of Józefów were the men shaken by their handiwork to the point where they asked to be excused, to the point where they also manifested signs of emotional difficulty. Had this reaction been the consequence of principled opposition and not mere disgust, the psychological and emotional strain would, with subsequent killings, have likely increased and not subsided completely, particularly since the men had repeatedly been offered a way out. But like medical students who might initially be shaken by their exposure to blood and guts yet who view their work as ethically laudable, these men easily adjusted to the unpleasant aspect of their calling. The moral approbation that the work met explains why only a small minority of Police Battalion 101's men asked to be excused from killing, and why the officers could rely upon volunteers to fill out the killing squads.[65] In this battalion, killing Jews was the norm in both senses of the word. Even the medical personnel killed. In First Company, in keeping with the all too familiar German perversion of medicine during the Nazi period, the two medical corpsmen inspected the Jews after they were shot, in order to ascertain whether or not they were dead. "It happened repeatedly that both finished them off with bullets [*Gnadenschüsse*] when the victims were still alive."[66] Not only did virtually all the men of this battalion kill, but they killed with dedication and zeal, which is not surprising, since, as one of the men testifies, "it is true, that among my comrades there were many fanatics."[67] Their unflagging contribution to the destruction of what was considered to be Germany's foremost enemy, international Jewry, was substantial, and worthy of recognition by higher authorities. Conrad Mehler, a member of First Company, received the Distinguished Service Cross (*Kriegsverdienstkreuz*), Second Class, its citation lauding him, among other reasons, because he "distinguished himself during the operations, evacuations, and deportations of Jews with hard and intrepid conduct."[68] The men of Police Battalion 101, together with those in their brother battalions of Police Regiment 25, received a final evaluation of their collective work from their commander, who, observing the purposely deceptive German language rules, did not explicitly mention the genocide, though he knew that their main task for much of their time in Lublin had been to slaughter Jews.

> On the occasion of . . . leaving SS-Police-Regiment 25, I feel bound sincerely to thank you all, officers, non-commissioned officers, and men for your indefatigable work, as well as your proven loyalty to me and willingness to sacrifice. You have all given your best for *Führer, Volk,* and Fatherland in the tenacious, hard, and bloody partisan fighting.
>   Carry on in the same spirit, and forward to victory![69]

Though the men of Police Battalion 101 may not, after the war, have publicly expressed pride in the collective and individual commendations that they had earned—over twenty of them received individual commendations—their citations (as evaluations of their devotion and effectiveness) were wholly deserved.[70] These accolades, of which they undoubtedly were not ashamed at the time, and the deeds that they rewarded—not the men's postwar denials— should be the final word on the actions and attitudes of the men of Police Battalion 101. They did not just do their job. In service to the German nation, they killed with distinction.

9

POLICE BATTALIONS:

LIVES, KILLINGS, AND MOTIVES

IN SURVEYING THE genocidal contributions of Police Battalion 101 and other police battalions, it becomes easy to view the perpetrators only through the prism of their murderous deeds. This produces some distortion. The extraordinary character of the killing operations, not surprisingly, leads many to consider the perpetrators and their deeds in isolation, sequestered from the rest of human social activity, from the "normal" workings of society, in part because the genocidal deeds seem not to inhabit the same social or moral universe but to belong to a special sub-universe of reality. This can lead to caricature of the perpetrators and their lives. These Germans partook in activities other than genocidal slaughter, and they lived a social existence. Understanding them and their deeds requires that the non-killing aspects of their lives be acknowledged and investigated.

Police battalions did not kill in a social or cultural vacuum. The Germans had rapidly constructed for themselves an institutional network and cultural existence in Poland that was, in its essence, autonomous from Poles (not to mention Jews), as befitting self-conceived *Übermenschen* who had come to displace "subhumans" and to remake conquered territory in their own image. In fact, an elaborate German cultural life in Poland was the locus for police battalion existence in Poland. After slaughtering unarmed Jews by the thousands, the police battalion men returned to the more conventional type of German cultural life. Their cultural activities—the police's "clubs, recreation centers, and canteens,"[1] the sporting events, movies and plays, religious activities, emotional attachments, and moral discussion and injunction—present a stark, even jarring, contrast to their apocalyptic deeds.

Even the routine orders that were circulated by the various institutional commanders, as incomplete and schematic as they were, convey that these genocidal executioners were not the clichéd, atomized individuals that they are often asserted to have been—and that virtually all people today probably conceive them to have been. "Regimental Order No. 25" of Police Regiment 25, which was distributed to its subordinate units, including Police Battalion 65 and Police Battalion 101, gives some sense of the character of the non-killing life that the men of police battalions led. Six items are contained in the order's two pages. The first item reports the results of a race: "On Sunday, October 18, 1942, and October 25, 1942, a team of the Motorized Gendarme Battalion participated in the autumn track meet in Radom." It names the four team members who "in the 'open class' beat the Radom Luftwaffe in both 4,000 meter races, achieving the day's best times." Another man in the Motorized Gendarme Battalion took second place in a different event. The regimental commander adds: "I extend to the winners my congratulations on their achievements."

The second item of the "Regimental Order" lists, as a matter of routine, the officer and enlisted man who would be on duty for each day of the coming week. The third item tells of the resumption of train service from Cracow to Krynica, "for the promotion of the spa Krynica." It gives the winter train schedule to this recreational destination, which was hours away. The fourth item, entitled "A play for the men," announces another recreational opportunity:

> On November 3 and 4 at 8 PM in the House of the NSDAP [Nazi Party] in Lublin the theater troupe of the police
> "Ostermänn"—better known as "Berlin Youth"
> will perform for the members of the Order Police and their families.
> —Admission is free.—

The fifth and sixth items concern health measures, one ordering that infectious diseases be reported immediately and the other alerting the units of upcoming notices about typhus, which are supposed to be posted.

"Regimental Order 25," which is one unremarkable example of the weekly orders that went out to all of the regiment's units, presents a picture at odds with the one-dimensional image that is easy to develop of the perpetrators and of the institutions in which they operated. The regimental commander is naturally proud of his men's athletic achievements against the Luftwaffe, which took place in distant Radom. He informs his men of their recreational opportunity in Krynica, a noted southern Polish resort famous for its mineral baths. He invites them with their families, at no charge, to an evening of entertainment, to be provided by the police's own theater troupe.

"Regimental Order 25" emanated from Lublin on October 30, 1942, radiating outward to the regiment's units strewn about the district.[2] What were these units undertaking in the war against the Jews around the time when they received this notice of leisure activities?

Police Battalion 101 was in the middle of its methodical genocidal decimation of the Jews in its region, having just three days before completed one of its deportations of Jews from Międzyrzec to a death camp. Police Battalion 65 was in high gear, shooting and deporting to Auschwitz the Jews of Cracow and its environs. Police Battalion 67 was decimating the Jewish communities around Biłgoraj and Zamość. Around this time, Police Battalion 316 was slaughtering two thousand Jews of Bobruisk.

The "Regimental Order" of October 25, 1942, was in no sense out of the ordinary. Notices of athletic events,[3] cultural opportunities,[4] and other leisure activities were normal items for the genocidal killers to receive. At the end of June 1942, for instance, the men learned of the swimming pool's operating hours in Lublin, and of the tennis opportunities open to them. Although, the men had to furnish their own rackets, "a small number of tennis balls are available at the SS and Police Sports society, Ostlandstr. 8c, Room 2. They can be borrowed for a fee. On account of the difficulty in obtaining them, tennis uniforms are not obligatory. However, the tennis court can be entered only in sports shoes with rubber soles."[5] The circulars sent to the men of police units informed them of all kinds of routine matters, such as when and where coal for winter heating would be distributed,[6] as well as of new administrative procedures. They communicated the latest instructions for the treatment, including killing, of "hostages" and for operations against Jews. It is in itself noteworthy and telling that such "normal" lethal matters were discussed in paragraphs sitting side by side with discussions of leisure activities.

The orders also contained all sorts of instructions about the men's conduct both in their duty and in their leisure time, often admonishing them for breaking regulations or for not living up to expectations. In one order, the commander informed his men that it had come to his attention that "large quantities of wrapping material, mineral water and other bottles lie about." The profligacy of the men incensed him: "It is irresponsible," he wrote, "that in the present raw material and supply conditions, the responsible persons do not endeavor to make immediate renewed use of the empty containers and the wrapping material." He promised to hold responsible all those who continued to waste such materials.[7] It appears from this and the many other admonitions that were responses to breaches of superior orders or decorum that these Germans were hardly automatons, hardly perfectly obedient subordinates; but like others, they were inconstant and selectively inattentive to duty, regulations, and social norms.

The Germans in the police units stationed in Lublin had many opportunities to attend not only police cultural functions but also those of the armed forces. The men of Police Regiment 25 did not always conduct themselves in a satisfactory manner when in attendance, as this reprimand from the regimental commander attests:

> By issuing free tickets to theater performances, concerts, movie showings, the armed forces performances are attended also by members of the Uniformed Police, who find no pleasure in them and who manifest their displeasure by loud remarks, laughter, and disorderly conduct. Such behavior bespeaks a disregard for other spectators as well as for the artists, and is apt to lower the reputation of the Uniformed Police. It is incumbent upon the unit commanders and office managers to issue pedagogical instructions to the effect that everyone should behave correctly and wait quietly for the end of the performance or for the next intermission.[8]

Although present in institutions where people routinely conducted themselves decently, where no external authority was as a rule needed for the normal decorum of minimal civility to prevail, the Germans of Police Regiment 25, living by the supposedly strict norms of a police institution, violated the social rules of everyday existence in a gross manner. What does this tell us about these men, about their devotion to rule-following, about the nature of their parent institution, which they clearly did not fear? In the same "Regimental Order," another reprimand is conveyed, this time not just for inconsiderate, anti-social activity but for illegal acts: "Members of the Order Police who were assigned to the protection of the harvest unlawfully hunted wild boars. I must point out that every kind of illegal hunting will be treated as poaching. Repeaters will be called to account."[9]

These institutional orders, even with the scanty information that they contain—so paltry in volume and variety in comparison to the reality of the stream of the Germans' daily actions while on duty and at leisure—are still sufficient to suggest a number of conclusions: The stereotypes about the perpetrators that have emerged whole out of thin air exist, to a great extent, in an empirical vacuum. Little attempt has been made by those who have created or countenanced such erroneous stereotypes to confront the institutional and social context of the perpetrators' actions or the fullness of their lives.[10]

The perpetrators were not robotic killing machines. They were human beings who lived "thick" lives, not the thin, one-dimensional ones that the lit-

erature on the Holocaust generally suggests. They had many and complex social relations, and performed a relatively wide variety of daily tasks. They had
family at home, friends within their units—some of whom could undoubtedly be classified as buddies—and, in the areas where they were stationed,
contacts with Germans in other institutions and with non-Germans as well.
Although they were living in the shadows of genocidal slaughter, some significant number of perpetrators must have had their family members with
them, as the invitation to the evening with the theater troupe suggests, by explicitly stating that families were welcome. Clearly, Wohlauf and Lieutenant
Brand were by no means exceptional in having their wives by their sides. The
perpetrators also had love affairs. One of the men of Police Regiment 25
began a relationship with the woman who was to become his wife, while he
served as a regimental clerk, recording, among other items, the progress of
the regiment's genocidal killing. She was working in the office of the commander of the Order Police in Lublin, first as a telephone operator and then
as a secretary for the operations unit where they planned the genocidal operations.[11] Theirs was not a society devoid of women. The men of Police Battalion 101 had, for example, frequent "social evenings" (*geselligen Abenden*),
where one of the men, a violinist, remembers that Dr. Schoenfelder, the
healer of Germans who had given instructions in the technique of killing
Jews, played "the accordion marvelously and did so with us frequently."[12]
They had musical afternoons, like one that Second Company enjoyed in
Międzyrzec, the site of their most frequent and largest killing operations.
Four surviving photographs show a small group of musicians playing from a
second-story porch before a yard filled with the company's men, who are sitting or milling about. For their further recreation, the men of Police Battalion 101 had a bowling alley, which they fashioned in their own workshop. The
game that they played, *Kegeln*, like bowling, is a quintessentially social game,
where a small group of men, typically from two to six, congregate at one end
of the alley and match their skills, amid rooting and cheering, against the pins
and one another.[13]

The perpetrators had free time which they could use, depending on
where they were stationed, for a variety of activities that allowed, even
prompted, them to activate their moral faculties and to take a personal, individual stance. Whether they were in church, at a play, or in a small group, say,
drinking in a bar and surveying the terrain of their lives, the perpetrators
lived in a moral world of contemplation, discussion, and argument. They
could not but react, have opinions, and pass judgment on the events large and
small unfolding before them daily. Some of the men went to church, prayed
to God, contemplated the eternal questions, and recited prayers which reminded them of their obligations to other humans; the Catholics among them

took communion and went to confession.[14] And when they went at night to their wives and girlfriends, how many of the killers discussed their genocidal activities?

The Germans in police battalions were also not slavishly devoted to orders, as their superiors' frequent reprimands concerning both their inattentiveness and outright transgressions indicate. Their penchant for recording photographic images of their heroics against Jews was combated by a stream of orders prohibiting such activity, but to little avail.[15] These were not robotic Germans; they had their opinions about the rules that governed them, and these views obviously informed their preferences and the choices that they actually made about whether or not to adhere to the rules and, if so, in what manner.

In their postwar testimony, the perpetrators say next to nothing about their leisure activities; their interrogators were interested in querying them about their crimes, not the frequency of their theater visits, the number of goals which they scored in their soccer matches, or what they talked about when relaxing in their social clubs. So the perpetrators are relatively mute on the array of subjects and activities that need to be examined, if the full character of their lives as ideological warriors is to be reconstructed.

Particularly interesting to know would be their reaction to certain orders which they received regarding animals, orders that would have struck any but those beholden to the Nazi antisemitic creed as deeply ironic and disturbing. One regimental order, from August 1942, informs the men that the *Generalgouvernement* has been declared to be an "animal epidemic region" (*Tierseuchengebiet*). In light of this, certain procedures for the care of police dogs were prescribed, mainly the mandate to provide strict veterinary examination of the dogs, especially when they traveled to and from different areas. "During the whole time the dog manager must observe his dog extremely closely and bring him to the local police veterinarian upon the slightest symptom of illness or change in the behavior of the animal."[16] Concern for the health of police dogs (they were, after all, useful for, among other tasks, the brutalizing of Jews) and for preventing contagious illnesses from spreading is understandable. Did the killers, upon reading this, not reflect on the difference in treatment they were meting out to dogs and Jews? At the slightest hint of illness or irregular behavior exhibited by the dogs, the Germans were directed to whisk the dogs to a veterinarian for care. Jews who were sick, especially the gravely ill, or those who gave the slightest indication of having contagious illnesses, like typhus, made no visits to the doctor. As a rule, the Germans fought Jewish illnesses with a bullet or a social-biologically "sanitizing" trip to the gas chamber. Not only did Germans respond to sickness in dogs and in Jews in diametrically opposed ways, but they also killed healthy Jews, using the pretext of sickness as a formal justification, as a deceptive verbal locution for genocidal killings. In fact, to the Germans, Jews became synonymous with illness, and illness of this sort was seen and treated as cancerous, to be excised from the body social. The transvaluation of values was expressed with pride by one German doctor working in Auschwitz: "Of course I am a doctor and I want to preserve life. And out of respect for human life, I would remove a gangrenous appendix from a diseased body. The Jew is the gangrenous appendix in the body of mankind."[17]

The desire to prevent illness in police dogs can be seen as having been purely a utilitarian measure. The ties of affection binding one SS general to his dog, however, were also capable of moving genocidal agents to action. In October 1942, the men of Police Regiment 25 learned in a postscript to a regimental order that "a fourteen-month-old yellow German shepherd, answering to the name Harry" had, weeks earlier, jumped from a train near Lublin, and had not yet been recovered. "All stations," the order continued, "are requested to look for the German shepherd so that he be returned to his master."[18] The regimental headquarters was to be notified upon the dog's capture. Owing to their missions in search of hidden Jews, most of the men receiving this order were already acclimated to scouring the countryside. Perhaps each kept an eye peeled for the dog, as he combed the terrain for every last Jew. The dog's fate, if indeed he ever was found, was greatly preferable to that of the Jews. In every respect, the Germans would have agreed, it was better to be a dog.

The orders concerning dogs might have provoked the Germans to think about their vocation if their sensibilities had remotely approximated our own; the comparison in their expected treatment of dogs and their actual treatment of Jews might have fostered in the Germans self-examination and knowledge. Yet, however much the reading of these orders about dogs would have evoked disturbing comparisons in non-Nazified people, the effect of the series of orders sent out regarding "cruelty to animals" (*Tierquälerei*) would have likely been to the non-Nazified psychologically gripping, even devastating.

On June 11, 1943, the commander of Police Regiment 25 reprimanded the regiment for not having met regulations in posting the information sheets regarding animal protection (*Tierschutz*). In light of this negligence, he had concluded that "no attention is paid to the protection of animals." He continued:

One should with renewed strength take measures against cruelty to animals (*Tierquälereien*) and to report it to the regiment.

Special attention is to be devoted to the beef cattle, since through overcrowding in the railway cars great losses of the animals have occurred, and the food supply has thereby been severely endangered.

The enclosed notices are to be used as a subject for instruction.[19]

Genocidal executioners and torturers promulgated and received orders, obviously heartfelt ones, enjoining consideration for animals. The order then discussed the problem of packing cows too tightly into cattle cars! Contrast this with an account from a member of Police Battalion 101 of their cattle car treatment of Jews in Międzyrzec: "As particularly cruel, I remember that the Jews were jammed into the cars. The cars were stuffed so full that one had to labor in order to close the sliding doors. Not seldom did one have to lend aid with one's feet."[20]

The bizarre world of Germany during the Nazi period produced this telling juxtaposition between the solicitude owed animals and the pitilessness and cruelty shown Jews.[21] Orders not to cram Jews too tightly into cattle cars never came the way of the Germans in Poland who deported Jews to their deaths, typically by using kicks and blows to force as many Jews into the railway cars as was possible. The freight cars carried both cattle and Jews. Which of the two was to be handled more decently, more humanely, was clear to all involved. The cows were not to be crushed in the cars because of the food that they produced. But this was not the only reason. The Germans, throughout this period, took great pains to ensure that animals were treated decently. In their minds, it was a moral imperative.[22]

However arresting this contrast of cattle cars might be to us, as well as the stream of orders commanding decent, "humane" treatment of animals, they likely were hardly noted as remarkable by the Germans involved. What appear to be ironies, so obvious that they could be missed by none, so cruel that they should have shaken any involved, were undoubtedly lost on the perpetrators. They were too far gone. Their cognitive framework was such that the juxtaposition could not register. With regard to Jews, the perpetrators were each, to quote the title of one of the plays that was performed for their entertainment, a "Man Without Heart" (*Mann ohne Herz*).[23] It is safe to assume that the irony of the title was also lost on them.

THE HISTORIES PRESENTED here of certain police battalions—of these itinerant, genocidal cohorts of ideological warriors going from one Jewish community to the next in order to obliterate each one's existence—are not isolated or singular examples. Their tales of horrors and willfulness could, in their essential features, be written for a host of other police battalions. The police battalions discussed here (Police Battalions 309, 133, 65, and 101) were not the most murderous of battalions (see the table below), and their men's actions were not exceptional by the brutal and murderous standards that the German police set during the Holocaust. This being the case, what can be said more generally about the overall complicity of police battalions in the Holocaust?

Obviously, not all police battalions perpetrated genocidal slaughter. Many simply never received the orders to participate in killing operations. So the *percentage* of police battalions that were complicit in genocide is not an illuminating figure, for such tasks were not voluntary in the sense that the regime sent out recruitment notices giving particularly bloodthirsty battalions and men the opportunity to sign up to become genocidal executioners. By chance, some police battalions ended up in killing operations and others did not. No evidence suggests that the regime either hesitated to use police battalions at all for mass killings of Jews or discriminated among police battalions in making such assignments, by screening them according to some criteria of fitness and willingness, or by using any other means that took the character of battalions and their men into account.[24] Happenstance accounts for much of why the men of one police battalion killed Jews while those of another did not. Relevant to an analysis of police battalions' role in the genocide, therefore, are the actions of the men only of those police battalions that were ordered to deport Jews to their deaths or to kill them with their own hands.

On this point some general things can be said. A large enough number of police battalions contributed to the Holocaust that their participation in the perpetration of the Holocaust was seen as, and indeed was, absolutely ordinary. The regime *routinely* turned to police battalions as implementers of the genocidal will. As far as my (considerable but not exhaustive) research has determined, at least thirty-eight police battalions killed or deported Jews to death camps in the stock manner of Police Battalions 65 and 101. (Undoubtedly, more will be uncovered.) The material that exists on some of these battalions is so sketchy that little can be said of the extent and character of their actions, except that they perpetrated mass slaughter of Jews. Of these thirty-eight battalions, at least thirty perpetrated *large-scale* slaughters or deportations. The following table contains only some of the major killing operations (over one thousand victims) of these thirty battalions. They and other police battalions carried out an enormous number of other killing operations, large and small, that are not listed.[25]

Police Battalion	Location	Date	Number of Victims
3	Soviet Union	December 1941–	100,000s
9	Soviet Union	June–December 1941	100,000s
11	Slutsk	Fall 1941	1,000s
13	Mława District	November, December 1942	12,000
	Plöhnen	End of 1942	5,000

Police Battalion	Location	Date	Number of Victims
22	Riga	November, December 1941	25,000
	Slutsk	February 8–9, 1943	3,000
32	Lvov	September 1941	1,000s
41	Warsaw ghetto	Early 1943	10,000s
	Majdanek	November 3, 1943	16,000
	Poniatowa	November 3, 1943	14,000
45	Berdichev	September 12, 1941	1,000
	Babi Yar	September 29–30, 1941	33,000
53	Warsaw ghetto	Early 1943	10,000s
64	Sajmište	September 26, 1941	6,000
65	Šiauliai	Summer 1941	3,000
	Cracow	Summer and Fall 1942	1,000s
67	Szczebrzeszyn	Fall 1941	1,000
	near Zamość	Summer or Fall 1942	2,000
	Biłgoraj	Fall 1942	1,200
96	Rovno	November 7–8, 1941	21,000
101	Parczew	August 1942	5,000
	Międzyrzec	August 25, 1942	10,000
	Majdanek	November 3, 1943	16,000
	Poniatowa	November 3, 1943	14,000
133	Stanisławów	October 12, 1941	12,000
	Nadvornaya	October 16, 1941	2,000
	Delatyn	2 killings, Fall 1941	2,000
251	Białystok	August 16–20, 1943	25,000–30,000
255	Białystok	August 16–20, 1943	25,000–30,000
256	Białystok	August 16–20, 1943	25,000–30,000
303	Babi Yar	September 29–30, 1941	33,000
	Zhitomir	September 1941	18,000
306	Luninets	September 4, 1942	2,800
	Wysokie	September 9, 1942	1,400
	David Gorodok	September 10, 1942	1,100
	Stolin	September 11, 1942	6,500
	Janów Podlaski	September 25, 1942,	2,500
	Pinsk	October 29– November 1, 1942	16,200
307	Brest-Litovsk	early July 1941	6,000–10,000
	Tarnów	June 1942	16,000
	Neu Sandau	August 1942	18,000
309	Białystok	June 27, 1941	2,000

Police Battalion	Location	Date	Number of Victims
314	Dnepropetrovsk	November 1941	1,000s
	Kharkov	January 1942	10,000–20,000
316	Białystok	July 12–13, 1941	3,000
	Mogilev	November 1941	3,700
	Bobruisk	End of 1942	2,000
320	Kamenets-Podolski	August 27–28, 1941	23,600
	Rovno	November 7–8, 1941	21,000
	Kostopol	July 14, 1942	5,000
	Pinsk	October 29–November 1, 1942	16,200
322	Białystok	July 12–13, 1941	3,000
	Mogilev	October 19, 1941	3,700
	Minsk	November 1941	19,000
	Minsk	July 28–30, 1942	9,000
Mounted Police Third Squadron	Majdanek	November 3, 1943	16,000
	Poniatowa	November 3, 1943	14,000
	Trawniki	November 3, 1943	12,000
Motorized Gendarme Battalion	Majdanek	November 3, 1943	16,000
	Poniatowa	November 3, 1943	14,000
Police Guard Battalion I (Posen)	Stry	Summer 1943	1,000
	Drogobych	1943	1,000
	Rogatin	1943	cleared ghetto
	Tarnopol	Summer 1943	cleared ghetto
Police Reserve Company Cologne	Kielce	August 20–24, 1942	20,000
	Warsaw ghetto	May 1943	1,000s

The men of these police battalions had unequivocal proof that they were being asked to take part not just in some harsh military measure, however just or unjust, such as the killing of one hundred "hostages" from a town in retribution against the local population for having allegedly aided partisans. When slaughtering thousands of people or sending entire communities packed in freight cars to death factories, these Germans did not and could not have had illusions that they were members of something other than a genocidal cohort, even if they might not have articulated it in so many words.

It is hard to say how many Germans were involved in the killing operations of just these police battalions. The precise size of each battalion is not known, and it is not always possible to ascertain how many men of each battalion participated directly in the deportations and killings. Moreover, police battalions had shifting memberships because of transfers and casualties, which certainly increased the number of Germans under the aegis of police battalions complicit in the genocide. Some rough estimates, each of which is undoubtedly low, would be as follows. If the average strength of police battalions is taken to have been five hundred men (which is probably an underestimate), it would mean that nineteen thousand men were members of the thirty-eight police battalions known to have been engaged in the mass slaughter of Jews. In the thirty police battalions known to have carried out large-scale killings, the number of Germans was, by this calculation, fifteen thousand. It cannot be said for sure what percentage of each battalion took part in killings. It is known that battalions that engaged in large-scale killings typically deployed high percentages of their men in the operations. Testimony from many police battalions indicates that everyone in those battalions was so employed.[26] So even if the number of Germans who can be counted as perpetrators is somewhat smaller than the estimates of the number of men in the genocide-abetting police battalions, the numbers are still large. Many of them were "ordinary" Germans.

The composition of individual police battalions made no difference for their performance. Whether battalions were populated mainly by reservists, mainly by professional policemen, or with various admixtures of the two, they carried out their tasks with little variation, and to deadly effect. Whatever the percentage of Party members or SS men among them, the battalions as a whole performed their genocidal jobs in a manner that would have made Hitler proud. In fact, the postwar testimony of the Germans in police battalions reveals little consciousness of differences in attitude or action between those who were either Party or SS members and those who were not. For the men it seems to have been a non-issue, in all likelihood because when it came to their most important activity no difference, certainly no systematic difference, existed between those who belonged to these two leading Nazi institutions and those who did not. Killing Jews was a great leveler, a great equalizer, in Germany during the Nazi period, effacing differences that in other realms of activity normally marked Germans of different backgrounds, professions, and outlooks as being distinct from one another.

The institutional histories of police battalions also were immaterial to their men's effectiveness and willingness as genocidal killers. Whether or not they had seen front-line fighting, whether or not they themselves had confronted the horrors of war and feared for their lives, cannot be discerned from their performances as genocidal killers. Police Battalion 65 killed Jews before it was ordered to the front, where it became encircled, fought for its life, and sustained heavy casualties in the northern part of the Soviet Union. It killed Jews in the *Generalgouvernement* after its baptism in the sufferings of war. The "brutalization" that the men underwent during the fighting had no appreciable effect on their treatment of Jews. Similarly, none of the evidence suggests that prolonged engagement in genocidal slaughter altered the treatment that the men of police battalions meted out to Jews. Except sometimes for the killers' baptismal massacre, owing to the shock that the killings' gruesomeness administered to the Germans, the Germans' demeanor, their zeal in performing their duty, and the high quality of their apocalyptic product appear to have remained constant throughout their lives in a genocidal cohort. So notions that during the course of the killing the men became progressively disinhibited towards Jews, or more brutish because of the psychological effects on them of repeatedly slaughtering Jews, and that these developments (if they actually occurred) *caused* them to act towards Jews as they did, are not borne out—indeed, are falsified—by the record.[27] Police battalions—the most innocent and most experienced, the most sheltered and the most exposed to privation and danger—killed Jews proficiently, in a manner that would have satisfied the most virulent and pathological antisemites. Hitler and Himmler were pleased.

The Germans in police battalions slaughtered Jews in a variety of formations and settings. They conducted killing operations in battalion strength, in company strength, or sometimes just a platoon at a time. In the very large massacres, they killed in conjunction with other police and non-police units, together with Germans and non-German auxiliaries. In the small ones, they killed in small groups. Sometimes they were supervised by officers; sometimes the enlisted men assigned to the killing operation acted without supervision. No evidence suggests that the size of the killing detail or the degree of officer oversight for a given operation was determined by any consideration other than practical ones, mainly the number of men which they considered necessary for accomplishing the task. The Germans in police battalions just as easily worked in large concert, in medium-size groups, or in groups of two, three, or five. They brought off their assignments whether they were ghetto clearings, deportations, mass shootings, or search-and-destroy missions. These Germans were flexible, versatile, and accomplished in their vocation.

The absence of significant variation in actions among the Germans of different police battalions, either owing to the battalions' membership composition, their histories, or the immediate setting of their deeds, is paralleled by a similar absence of difference between the actions of their men on the one hand, and of the men in the *Einsatzkommandos* and other SS units on the other. Police battalions and *Einsatzkommandos*, for example, in addition to their different membership composition, had different corporate identities. Police battalions were formally and mainly devoted to policing and maintaining order. Like the *Einsatzkommandos*, they also had to secure their assigned areas, which meant fighting the enemies of the regime, but their entire (even if often perfunctory) training and their ethos were that of policemen, if perhaps that of colonial policemen. The *Einsatzkommandos*, by contrast, were ideological warriors by stated vocation, whose understood reason for being was to exterminate Jews. They also performed other duties, but their prime directive was to kill enemies of the regime. Despite their divergent identities and orientation, police battalions and *Einsatzkommandos*—in their manner of operating and their treatment of Jews—look very much alike.

In two important respects, police battalions differed from the *Einsatzkommandos*. The *Einsatzkommandos* were typically eased into genocidal slaughters by having initially killed Jewish men, sparing them the psychologically more difficult task of killing women and children so as to give them time to become acclimated to their new vocation. This was the case as well for the Germans of a few police battalions that killed during the first phase of the assault on Soviet Jewry. But the Germans of many other battalions received no such stepwise initiation into genocidal annihilation. Considerable numbers of women and children were among their first victims, testing their dedication and their nerves more strenuously. The Germans appear to have learned that, contrary to their original expectations, easing the men into genocidal killing was not necessary. Even if some were initially shocked, most adjusted quickly and easily to the killing. With Police Battalion 101, however, the opposite was the case. At first, they killed mainly women, children, and the aged and infirm, because they sorted out many of the more healthy men for transport to "work" camps. Also, by this time the genocidal enterprise was in full swing and had become such a normal affair that selective killing would have gone against the grain of *Aktion Reinhard*'s spirit and procedures.

Second, police battalions typically, and similarly from the very beginning of their contribution to the genocide, annihilated Jewish ghettos—those German-perceived blights on the social landscape—in the dual sense of killing a ghetto's inhabitants and destroying the social institution. The Germans ferreted out hidden Jews and killed the old and the infirm on the spot, sometimes in their beds. The ghetto clearings, as described above, turned into licentious affairs that bore no resemblance to military activities. From the start, it was clear to everyone involved that no real military rationale was behind these horrific, Dantesque scenes. The ghetto clearings required a willfulness and a degree of initiative that the more orderly, more (if only in appearance) military *Einsatzkommando* killings of the initial phase did not.[28]

If anything, then, on the margins, the men in some of the police battalions had a more demanding, more psychologically difficult road to travel. Unlike the *Einsatzkommandos,* they were not eased into the genocidal killing, and integral to their operations was the emptying of ghettos of all life, with all the brutalities that it entailed. These differences, it is worth emphasizing, did not exist in all cases, and are, in the end, but marginal, if meaningful, differences in degree. Both their significance and their psychological effects upon the perpetrators can be debated. Certainly, however, in light of the genocidal slaughter that was the Germans' essential activity, the differences are eclipsed in importance by the similarities; overall, the convergence in action between police battalions and *Einsatzkommandos* is remarkable.

The study of police battalions, finally, yields two fundamental facts: First, ordinary Germans easily became genocidal killers. Second, they did so even though they did not have to.

The haphazard method by which the regime filled the ranks of many police battalions was extremely likely to produce battalions stocked with ordinary Germans, people who were, by important measures, broadly representative of German society. The biographical data on the men of Police Battalion 101 confirm that this was indeed the case. Still, an additional sample was taken from two other reserve police battalions that conducted a great deal of killing, Police Battalion 65 and Police Battalion 67, in order to ensure that the composition of Police Battalion 101 was not idiosyncratic. A combined sample of 220 men yielded 49 Nazi Party members, which is 22.3 percent, and 13 SS men, or 6.0 percent. The Party membership percentage for these two battalions was lower than for Police Battalion 101, while the percentage of SS men was slightly higher. Of the 770 men in the total sample from the three battalions, 228 (29.6 percent) had Nazi Party membership and a paltry 34 (4.4 percent) had SS membership. Thus, the degree of Nazification of Police Battalion 101 was, by the measure of these two other battalions, not high for police battalions.

The Germans in police battalions were—by their prior institutional affiliation, their social background, and, with some minor differences, even by their degree of ideological preparation—ordinary members of German society. At least seventeen of the thirty-eight police battalions that perpetrated genocidal killings and fourteen of the thirty that perpetrated large-scale massacres had a significant number of members who were not professional policemen, whose profiles in all likelihood resembled those of the sample, because the manner in which they were recruited was similar.[29] Most of them, as the training schedules show, also had very little training, because the Nazi regime and the Order Police did not conceive of the possibility that much further ideological preparation would be necessary in order to gain these men's accedence and willing cooperation in Jew-killing.

Finally, opportunities existed for the men in police battalions individually to avoid killing altogether or at least to remove themselves from continuing as genocidal executioners. It is a demonstrable fact that such opportunities were available to the men of many police battalions, and it is probable—though it is not known—that such opportunities were available to the vast majority of them. Evidence exists for at least eight different police battalions and a ninth similar unit, the Motorized Gendarme Battalion, that the men had been informed that they would not be punished for refusing to kill.[30] For Police Battalion 101, the evidence on this point is unequivocal and arresting. The general solicitude that many individual commanders showed their men, by making it possible for so many to extract themselves easily from the killing, was likely reinforced by another source; in light of testimony, it appears that Himmler issued a general order giving dispensation for members of police and security forces to opt out of killing.[31] In all probability, the men of police battalions other than these nine were similarly informed about the possibilities to excuse themselves, although they have not revealed this in postwar testimony. Such admissions would be self-indicting. The major who was in charge of the Operations Division of Police Regiment 25 tells of one colonel who requested to be relieved of his duty in Lemberg because his conscience would not permit him to continue with the killing. This colonel was given an important job back in Berlin. The major, who would certainly have become aware if any such instance had occurred in Police Regiment 25, because he was the officer responsible for dealing with such matters, states unequivocally that he knows of no case in the Order Police in which a man who refused to take part in the genocide was punished.[32]

But even if no announcement had been made to them, the men of police battalions could have taken steps that had some chance of freeing them from these onerous tasks. They could have requested transfers. They could have indicated that they were not capable of this duty. The men of a number of police battalions describe their commanders as having been fatherly, understanding, or kind.[33] Surely, they could have approached such a commander and explained to him that the killing of children was just too difficult for them. If worse came to worst, they could have feigned breakdowns. To be sure, isolated attempts to avoid killing were made, yet the evidence suggests that they were few indeed.[34]

The Germans in police battalions were thinking beings who had moral faculties and who could not fail to have an opinion about the mass slaughters that they were perpetrating. It is significant that, in the voluminous self-exculpating postwar testimony, the former perpetrators' denials of their own participation and approval of the killings are almost exclusively made by the testifying individual with respect to himself. If these numbingly frequent individual denials reflected the true prevailing state of affairs while the killing was taking place, then it would mean that widespread opposition to the killings had existed, and that the men had shared their condemnation among themselves. It could be expected, then, that legions of individual perpetrators, each corroborating the other, would have given testimony about how they and their comrades had discussed the criminality of the mass murder, about how each voiced to the other his lamentation at having been bound to this crime—had such discussions indeed taken place. Yet these sorts of assertions—of the principled opposition by the testifier's comrades to killing—appear hardly at all in the testimony of the men of police battalions. This is true for the battalions for which evidence exists that the men knew that they did not have to kill, and for battalions for which such evidence is absent.

In the end, whether or not it was known in more than nine police battalions that it was possible for the Germans who served in them to refuse to kill without suffering seriously is in itself not of great importance for drawing conclusions about police battalion contribution to the genocide, because those Germans who were informed that they could be excused from genocidal duties killed anyway. The Germans in nine police battalions, totaling 4,500 men or more, did indeed know that they did not have to take part in genocidal killing, yet they, with virtual unanimity, chose to kill and to continue to kill. Significantly, of these nine battalions, all but one were composed predominantly or substantially of reservists. This suggests that the men of other police battalions would have killed no matter what they might have known about the possibility of opting out. No evidence or reason exists to conclude the opposite. The men of these nine battalions form a sample sufficient to generalize with confidence about other police battalions. By choosing not to excuse themselves from the genocide of the Jews, the Germans in police battalions themselves indicated that they wanted to be genocidal executioners.

Why would they have done otherwise, given that they conceived of the Jews as being powerfully evil? Erwin Grafmann, in significant respects the most forthcoming and honest of all the men in Police Battalion 101,[35] was asked why he and the other men had not taken up his sergeant's offer before their first killing foray and excused themselves from the execution squad. He responded that, "at the time, we did not give it any second thoughts at all."[36] Despite the offer, it simply never occurred to him and his comrades to accept it. Why not? Because they wanted to do it. Speaking of the Józefów killing,

Grafmann asserts unequivocally: "I did not witness that a single one of my comrades said that he did not want to participate."[37] Grafmann, in suggesting the degree to which they had assented to their actions, confirms that they had been in the grip of an ideology powerful enough to induce them to kill Jews willingly: "Only in later years did one actually become fully cognizant of what had taken place at the time." He had been so Nazified that only years later (presumably when, sobered, he began to perceive the world through non-Nazi eyes) did he first comprehend what they had committed—a monstrous crime. That what Grafmann meant here was that he and, as he was speaking for them, his comrades were not morally opposed to killing Jews is made clear by his next sentences, in which he explains why he got himself excused from the further killing that day, after he had already shot "between about ten to twenty" Jews: "I requested to be relieved particularly because my neighbor shot so ineptly. Apparently, he always held the barrel of the rifle too high because horrible wounds were inflicted on the victims. In some cases, the entire rear skull of a victim was so shattered that brain matter spattered about. I simply could not look at it any longer."[38] Grafmann explicitly emphasizes that it was merely disgust that made him want to take a breather, and utters not a word to indicate that either he or the other killers thought the killing to be immoral. As Grafmann said later, at his trial, it was only afterwards that the thought first "occurred to me that it [the killing] was not right."[39]

Another member of the battalion, in the middle of discussing "bandits," explains why they (presumably also Grafmann) did not have any moral qualms about what they were doing. As he himself says—and this was true not only for the men of this police battalion but for Germans serving throughout eastern Europe—Jews were axiomatically identified with "bandits" and their anti-German activities. How did this German and his comrades conceive of them? "The category of human being was not applicable . . ."[40] Another genocidal executioner, a member of one of the mobile police units subordinated to the commander of the Order Police in Lublin, confirms this. His is a candid, confessional sentence that brings out, in sharp relief, the motivational mainspring of the Germans who—uncoerced, willingly, zealously, and with extraordinary brutality—participated in the destruction of European Jewry. Simply put, "The Jew was not acknowledged by us to be a human being."[41]

PART IV

Jewish "Work" Is Annihilation

Work [for Jews] consisted once of plundering traveling caravans, and today it consists of plundering indebted farmers, industrialists, middle-class people, etc. The forms did change, all right, but the principle remained the same. We do not call it work, but robbery.

ADOLF HITLER, AUGUST 13, 1920, SPEECH IN MUNICH

10

THE SOURCES AND PATTERN OF
JEWISH "WORK"
DURING THE NAZI PERIOD

WHY DID THE Germans put Jews to work? Why did they not simply kill them? Why did certain idiosyncratic patterns and practices emerge when the Germans did employ Jews in labor settings? The complex answers to these questions defy our common sense to such a degree that influential interpreters of the Germans' use of Jewish labor have been thoroughly misled. Two such interpreters write that the experts helping to plan the extermination of the Jews "did not revel in myths of blood and race, but thought in categories of large-scale economic spaces, structural renewal, and overpopulation with its attendant food problems."[1] Interpreters who share this perspective have typically described the Germans' use of Jewish labor as having accorded with rational, if brutal, economic principles. Some have gone so far as to say that German policies of labor mobilization, and more generally of economic exploitation, were the central feature of their policies towards the Jews, the deaths of Jews having been but a secondary phenomenon and not in itself a goal motivating the policies.[2]

The Germans' slaughter of Jews was not a byproduct of other undertakings and, by the standards of anyone not imbued with an exterminationist ideology, the Germans' use of Jewish labor was manifestly irrational. The self-injurious destruction of a large, talented, and irreplaceable labor force during total war is anything but a means towards bringing about more "rational methods of production." But *given the Nazis' goals*, and only in light of those goals, the pattern of the Germans' utilization of Jewish labor was, surprising as it may sound, mainly rational, being the product of an evolving set of compromises among incompatible goals.

The Germans' pattern of use and non-use of Jewish labor had three central sources. The first was to eliminate and then, certainly no later than June 1941, to exterminate them. The second, born of pragmatism yet often standing in conflict with the first and therefore largely ignored by the Germans disposing of Jews, was the need to extract from Jews the greatest possible economic contribution to the winning of the war. The third is less obvious but was no less important. It consisted of numerous purposes to which they put the Jews, and from which the Germans derived emotional satisfaction. This included the need to put them to "work."[3]

Since the industrial revolution, work, although sometimes understood as an intrinsically moral activity,[4] has usually been conceived of as an instrumental activity the purpose of which is to fashion useful goods and services. Its efficacy is judged in a non-sentimental way: how much and what quality of what kind of good is produced at what cost. This was the case in German society generally and for the Nazis as well, but there was one significant exception to this: Jewish work.

A widespread, deeply rooted, though little-remarked-upon notion in the German and, more generally, in the European antisemitic tradition,[5] possessing an intense quality in the Nazified German mind, was that Jews shirk physical work, and, more generally, that they do not do *honest* work. Four hundred years before Hitler, Luther expressed this cultural axiom about the Jews: "They hold us captive in our country. They let us work in the sweat of our noses, to earn money and property for them, while they sit behind the oven, lazy, let off gas, bake pears, eat, drink, live softly and well from our wealth. They . . . mock us and spit on us, because we work and permit them to be lazy squires who own us and our realm."[6] The petitions of the enormous grass-roots Bavarian anti-emancipation campaign of 1849–1850 asserted with regularity that Jews would not engage in wholesome labor.[7] During the second half of the nineteenth century, the theme of Jewish parasitism was so prominent that almost every antisemite leveled the charge: "Exploitation as the antithesis of productive work became a notion that [was] absolutely identical with the activity of the Jews."[8] The writer Friedrich Rühs anticipating the Nazis' use of labor punitively for Jews, asserted in 1816 that "Jews regard all labor as punishment."[9]

The theme of Jewish parasitism was also central to the societal conversation about Jews in Weimar and during the Nazi period. Statements such as "Jews do not work," or "The Jew is the person who hucksters with the work and industry of others" could be read or heard with great frequency in Germany, especially during its Nazi period.[10] Hitler himself echoed this theme repeatedly, declaring in *Mein Kampf* that although the Jews are a nomadic group, they are unlike nomads, who "had a definite [positive] attitude toward the concept of work . . . In the Jew, however, this attitude is not at all present; for that reason he was never a nomad, but only and always a *parasite* in the body of other peoples." The "Jew" could not conceivably do honest, productive work, which was antithetical to his life's work, for "he destroys more and more thoroughly the foundations of any economy that will really benefit the people."[11] The swastika—the central, ubiquitous symbol of the new Germany—expressed this view. It was emblazoned on the Nazi flag, which, according to Hitler, told the following tale: "As National Socialists, we see our program in our flag. In *red* we see the social idea of the movement, in *white* the nationalistic idea, in the *swastika* the mission of the struggle for the victory of the Aryan man, and, by the same token, the victory of the idea of creative work, which as such always has been and always will be anti-Semitic."[12] So fundamental was the belief in the binary opposition of Jews to "creative work," to productive, honest work, that of all of the meanings that Hitler could conceivably have lent to the central symbols of his movement and the new Germany, he chose to emphasize this.

The depth of Germans' belief in the Jews' actual and real—and not just symbolic—incapacity to engage in productive work was expressed by Hans Frank, the German Governor of occupied Poland, in a speech given in November 1941 at the University of Berlin. Frank, faced by an audience of ordinary Germans, was none too confident of his ability to disabuse them of an axiom of their culturally shared antisemitism. He declared: "But these Jews [in the *Generalgouvernement*] are not that parasite gang alone, from our point of view, but *strangely enough*—we only realized it over there—there is another category of Jews, *something one would never have thought possible.* There are laboring Jews over there who work in transport, in building, in factories, and others are skilled workers such as tailors, shoemakers, etc. [my emphasis]."[13]

The common view in Germany echoed Hitler's: The Jews were parasites whose working lives were devoted to feeding on the blood of the industrious German people.[14] Because of this cultural cognitive model of Jews, German discussions of Jews and work, and all policies of putting Jews to work were imbued with a symbolic and moral dimension. Getting a Jew to work, for those beholden to the prevailing German model of Jews, was an expressive act, was, to use Weber's term, value rational.[15] It was an achievement in itself, regardless of the worth of the product, regardless of whether or not the work was at all productive. Jewish work was to be done for its own sake.

Getting a Jew to work, aside from the material instrumentality, appears to have sprung from two related, antisemitically derived motives: First, since the Jew's putative disposition eschewed work, all honest labor was to him a taxing burden. Work "punished" the Jew physically, and thus wreaked vengeance upon him for his centuries, indeed millennia, of exploitation. A poem from an illustrated educational book of the Nazi period conveys this feature of the German cultural cognitive model of Jews, namely that work was a form of punishment. According to the poem, entitled "The Father of the Jews Is the Devil," immediately after the creation of the world, "the Jew-boy went on strike," because "cheating, not working, was his aim." Confronted with the Jews, the Egyptian Pharaoh decided, " 'I'll torment the lazy blighters/These people shall make bricks for me!' "[16] The Pharaoh, the hero of this 1936 poem, expresses clearly the Germans' conception of work as a means to "torment" Jews; he is also a harbinger of the Germans' future enslavement of Jews and of their purposeful use of "work" as an instrument of Jewish suffering. The second non-material motive for getting a Jew to work was the satisfaction it gave his German masters, by providing them with the pleasing sight of a laboring Jew and by demonstrating their ability to subdue the Jew to such a degree that he acts contrary to his nature, namely like an honest man (even if he never could become one). It fulfilled the psychological need, expressed again and again in Germans' treatment of Jews, to have total power over Jews.

Because the ideological and psychological impulses to put Jews to work were so great, Germans often compelled Jews to work for working's sake. The phenomenon of "non-instrumental" labor, namely labor without any productive purpose, was widespread in the Germans' treatment of Jews, and needs to be at the core of any analysis of the subject. Eugen Kogon, without accounting for its source, describes non-instrumental labor as a regular feature of the Buchenwald landscape: "Some of the work in camp was useful but some of it was utterly senseless, intended only as a form of torture, a diversion engaged in by the SS 'for fun'. The Jews especially, often had to build walls, only to tear them down the next day, rebuild them again, and so on."[17]

The antisemitically derived ideological impulse to force Jews to "work" for its own sake was given expression throughout the German dominion. Nowhere, however, was it more striking than in Austria in March 1938, where it welled up spontaneously during the euphoria accompanying its annexation by Germany. The Austrians' hearty celebrations included immediate symbolic acts of revenge upon the Jews, who in Austria, no less than in Germany, were believed to have exploited and injured the larger society. As seen here, again and again, the circus of Jewish men, women, and children—commanded to don their finest clothes, being forced to wash streets, sidewalks, and buildings of Vienna (frequently with small brushes and water mixed with burning acid)—was met by the cheers and jeers of crowds of Austrian onlookers. "In Währing, one of Vienna's wealthier sections, Nazis, after order-

In celebration of Germany's annexation of Austria, a gleeful crowd watches Jews scrub a Viennese street with small brushes.

ing Jewish women to scrub streets in their fur coats, then stood over them and urinated on their heads."[18] This was the purest form of "non-instrumental" labor, and the purest expression of its ideational and psychological sources.

GERMAN POLICIES TOWARDS Jews and work, because they emerged from competing sources—the independent desires to exterminate them, to extract economic benefit from them, and to put them to work for working's sake—formed a thicket of inconsistent and, ultimately, self-injurious measures. It was not at all clear *a priori* how each of the sources of German action would influence the formation and implementation of policy regarding Jews and work. To what degree would the compelling rationale, during the acute labor shortage of total war, for using Jewish labor productively prevail over the exterminationist and other expressive impulses to destroy or debilitate Jews? Would the Germans' use of Jewish productive labor turn out to be more than a detail, if a significant one, in influencing the fate of European Jewry during the Nazi period?

The most salient fact about Germans' employment of Jews is that it had *nothing* to do with the creation of the Germans' overall design for European Jews. Wide-scale mobilization of Jews for *productive* labor was an afterthought, coming late in the war, well after Hitler had decided the Jews' fate. Similarly, the camp system was originally constructed as a penal system, evolving only later, during the war, after the Germans had already killed most of their Jewish victims, into its large industrial role.[19]

During the late 1930s, even as labor shortages were developing, Germans were driving Jews from the economy, and from the country itself. It was during this period that the main eliminationist thrust consisted of turning the Jews into socially dead beings, a part of the process having been the severing of all social ties between Jews and Germans, and of ridding Germany of Jews through emigration. So the dominant policy was not to put Jews to work, but to prevent them from working. Indeed, the German economy's achievement of full employment in 1936, when there was no longer a reserve army of labor but an incipient labor shortage, did not derail the eliminationist imperative; it was at that time that the Nazis began planning the *Entjudung der deutschen Wirtschaft*, the full exclusion of Jews from the German economy. The process began the following year and gathered speed in 1938.[20] This was the first instance of what became a general pattern: Despite pressing economic needs, Germans failed to use Jews to fill those needs, only to let them go unmet by closing down enterprises or substituting for the Jews other "inferior" peoples (who were often not as skilled).[21] From the German perspective, what was "rational" in the treatment of other peoples was not "rational" when formulating policy for Jews. Jews, even in the economy, even when toiling over identical machines, when serving as mute appendages to the German war effort, remained in the Germans' eyes beings apart.

The conquest of Poland and then of France led the Germans to mobilize Poles and French civilians and prisoners of war in order to offset, only somewhat, the ever-growing labor shortage in the German economy. All told, in the fall of 1940, they compelled more than two million foreign civilians and POWs to work in the German Reich, who formed almost 10 percent of its work force.[22] Yet the Germans failed to tap another abundant labor source in their dominion: Polish Jews. Hans Frank, the German Governor of Poland, did issue on October 26, 1939, an order for the compulsory labor of Jews, which led to the forming of Jewish labor gangs.[23] But this was more an ideological reflex than a rational economic measure; for, despite an acute consciousness of their production needs, from the beginning the Germans by and large dissipated Polish Jewry's economic productiveness. Not only did they abstain from organizing Jewish labor efficiently—having been so blinded by their ideology that they first began to recognize only in the middle of 1940 that Jewish workers might indeed be capable of contributing economically, and even then employed Jewish labor power in half-hearted ways[24]—but they also took measures which debilitated Jewish workers, leading to the deaths of thousands, even before they formally instituted the policy of extermination.

The Warsaw ghetto was a prime example of this. At its most swollen, the ghetto housed 445,000 Jews, and was the largest concentration of Jews and Jewish workers in Poland. The ghetto's living conditions would have been irrational if the Germans' designs for Polish Jews had accorded any significant place for them to work productively; the Germans' policies, in fact, form a textbook plan of how to turn healthy, able workers quickly into shadows of human beings, into decrepit living skeletons, or real ones. The Warsaw ghetto contained 30 percent of Warsaw's population in 2.4 percent of its area, making for a population density of 200,000 per square mile. It had a housing density of over 9 people per *room* in every apartment. Water, heating, and sewage were catastrophically inadequate. The unbearable overpopulation of the ghetto together with the unhealthful hygienic conditions were alone bound to produce illness and disease. Yet the food situation, which amounted to a policy of planned starvation, made these other inhuman conditions, by comparison, seem livable.[25] The official daily food ration for the Jews of the Warsaw ghetto was 300 calories. For Poles it was 634 calories, and for Germans it was 2,310.[26] The Jews did not even receive all of this pitiful, official allotment.[27] The predictable, expected consequences of this policy occurred. The inhabitants of the ghetto quickly reached a permanent state of semi-starvation, producing a dangerously weakened population unsuitable for sustained work, let alone for physically taxing employment. The number of deaths in the ghetto, mainly due to starvation and its attendant afflictions, was staggering, averaging about 4,650 Jews per month between May 1941 and May 1942, which was over 1 percent of the population each month, or 12 percent a year.[28]

The Germans' policies for the Jews of Warsaw, which characterized how they treated Polish Jews generally, were calculated to destroy the Jews, not to use their labor power.[29] That the Germans purposely failed to maintain the Jews' health at a work-functioning level *already in 1940*—well before the competing goal of extermination was formally decided upon and then, a few months later in June 1941, begun to be implemented—is in itself eloquent testimony to the marginal place that economic considerations had in forming the Germans' Jewish policy, as well as to the exterminationist tendency inherent to their racial antisemitism.[30]

In Poland during 1940 and 1941, the Germans continued their practice of sacrificing Jewish economic productiveness while simultaneously marshaling workers of "inferior" peoples in order to help combat an ever-growing labor shortage, which in September 1941 stood at 2.6 million workers.[31] In

1942, according to German statistics, there were over 1.4 million Jewish workers in the *Generalgouvernement*. About 450,000 were working full time, and "980,000 were employed for a short period." So in the face of this labor shortage, the Germans failed to use *one million* Jewish workers.[32]

While the Germans' more intensive labor mobilization of non-Jewish subject peoples began in the fall of 1941 and 1942, leading to a number of important changes in their labor policies, the contrast in the nature of the Germans' "rationality" for the disposing of non-Jews compared with that for Jews became still starker. Despite the ardent and until then decisive ideological opposition to the employment of Russian "subhumans" within Germany—a purely ideological stance that had led the Germans to kill, mainly by starvation, 2.8 million young, healthy Soviet POWs in less than eight months[33]—the policy was reversed during this period. In 1942, owing to ever more pressing economic need, the Germans stopped the decimation of Soviet POWs through starvation and began to use them as laborers, leading by 1944 to the presence of over 2.7 million Soviet citizens (many were not POWs) working in the German economy.[34] Yet it was precisely during this period that the Germans erected death camps and began to wipe out, systematically, the Jews of Europe, this large reservoir of useful, and often irreplaceable, laborers, necessitating the closing of defense-related enterprises.[35] This meant that by the time that the Germans implemented their economic plans for the camp system—and established large concentration camp complexes with industrial enterprises at, among others, Auschwitz, Gross-Rosen, and Majdanek in Poland, Mauthausen in Austria, and Buchenwald and Dachau in Germany[36]—they had already killed the majority of their Jewish victims.

TO THE EXTENT that the Germans did employ Jews in economic activity after 1942, the work was understood to be a form of temporary exploitation of the Jews before their deaths, if not itself a means of killing them. The death rates were staggering, so high as to suggest that, with regard to Jews, the conventional distinction between concentration camps and death camps needs to be rethought.[37] Nevertheless, despite the ongoing policies of extermination, some wholesale, some piecemeal, the Germans were making a greater effort, starting in late 1942, to extract some productive labor from Jews before killing them. During this latter period of *partial* labor extraction, the Germans typically kept Jews alive or at "work" only until the local military situation became perilous or their exterminationist drive became irrepressible. The former was the case with the Łódź ghetto in western Poland. At its founding in April 1940, the ghetto housed 164,000 people. With over 40,000 new additions in 1941 and 1942, the total number of ghetto dwellers was over 200,000. During the first part of 1942, the Germans deported 55,000 of its Jews to the gas vans of Chełmno, after which slightly over 100,000 Jews remained. Through further deportations and attrition owing to calculated starvation (43,500 people—fully 21 percent of all those who entered the ghetto—died of starvation and disease), the Germans reduced the ghetto's population to 77,000 by May 1944, most of whom were engaged in productive enterprises. With the approach of the Soviet army, in August 1944 the Germans liquidated the ghetto, deporting all but a rump group to Auschwitz.[38] Productive labor had brought the Jews a temporary stay of execution. The Nazi worldview dictated that the postponement could never become permanent.

Even during this period of more assiduous exploitation of Jewish labor power, Jewish workers could be killed *en masse* at any moment, with utter disregard of their product, closing down industrial enterprises overnight. After *Aktion Reinhard* was officially brought to a close, the only Jews officially allowed to remain alive in the *Generalgouvernement* were those employed in SS-run "work" camps.[39] All of the Jews in these camps had been "selected" as "fit for work," and they were engaged in defense-related industrial enterprises. Yet, suddenly (even the camp commanders were not forewarned), on November 3–4, 1943, the Germans shot 43,000 Jews in these camps, in *Operation Erntefest* (Operation Harvest Festival), the largest single shooting massacre of the war.[40] Aptly named in keeping with the Germans' customary love of irony, *Erntefest* was their festive harvest of Jewish labor.

Only in 1944, when the economic and military crisis became even more acute, did an important reversal take place in German labor usage of Jews. German policy towards Jews had always been to free German soil of their contaminating presence. Even in the face of pressing labor needs, Hitler had refused to allow Himmler and Albert Speer to bring Jewish camp prisoners into Germany in September 1942, since Germany had to remain *judenrein*, free of Jews.[41] In April 1944, a year and a half after Hitler had ordered Germany finally to be made *judenrein* by deporting the last Jewish armament workers in Berlin, he agreed to permit 100,000 Hungarian Jews, who were otherwise slated for imminent extermination, to be brought to Germany, where they worked in the excavation of huge underground bunkers and in defense enterprises. Despite the terrible treatment that the Jews received and the high mortality rate that they suffered, especially in the underground construction facilities, the Germans' decision to exploit their labor potential inadvertently saved many of their lives. The other 350,000 Hungarian Jews deported with them during 1944 were gassed in Auschwitz.[42] Significantly, despite the dire economic need, many able-bodied Jews were among those whom the Germans killed.[43]

The general contours of German labor policies suggest that for Jews, work was a way station to death. Enormous labor shortages led Germans, if reluctantly, to use non-Jewish foreigners on a massive scale, so that in 1942 there were over 4 million, in 1943 over 6 million, and by 1944 over 7.5 million foreign civilians and POWs employed in virtually every sector of the German economy.[44] Yet, despite the acute labor shortfall that was never closed, the Germans' treatment of Jewish workers was markedly different.

The fundamental irrelevance of labor needs and economic logic in shaping the overall German treatment of Jews was expressed again and again by German authorities, in word and in deed—perhaps most pithily in the following exchange. In response to an inquiry on November 15, 1941, from the Reich Commissar for the Ostland about whether they were "to liquidate all Jews in the East . . . without regard to age and sex and armaments interests (of the Wehrmacht, for instance in specialists in the armament industry)," the Eastern Ministry responded: "Economic considerations should fundamentally remain unconsidered in the settlement of the problem."[45] The dead Jews were replaced, if at all, by other "subhumans." A gulf between the Germans' policies towards Jews and other peoples, including the least valued of the "subhuman" Slavs, was so large, even with regard to work, as to suggest that the Germans employed a completely different calculus for each.[46]

The negligible importance of economic production in shaping the Germans' treatment of Jews characterized not only their overall policy. It was in the nature of everyday "work" and of life in "work" camps that the fundamental irrelevance of economic considerations for engendering the Germans' desire to put Jews to "work" is so striking.

11

LIFE IN THE "WORK" CAMPS

BY THE BEGINNING of 1943, the campaign of extermination known as *Aktion Reinhard* had already claimed the lives of the bulk of the Jews living in the *Generalgouvernement,* principally in the death camps, Treblinka, Bełżec, and Sobibór. The only Jews whom the Germans now permitted to remain alive in the *Generalgouvernement* were those engaged in defense-related work in SS-run camps. During this period of Jewish work utilization *par excellence,* by definition, all the Jews in the camps were deemed by the Germans to be capable workers. Such pure "work" camps, which formally had no mission other than production, are therefore likely to reveal much about the nature of Jewish "work" in Nazi Germany.

Most such camps were in the District of Lublin.[1] The largest and by far the best known among them was Majdanek. Majdanek, ordered on July 21, 1941, by Himmler to be constructed on the southeastern edge of the city of Lublin, was a camp, on a smaller scale than Auschwitz, which housed a complex of work installations as well as gas chambers. Its population was heterogeneous, with the largest groups being Poles, Jews, and Soviets. Of the close to 500,000 people who were at some time in Majdanek, around 360,000 died (most of the others were transferred to other camps), though according to rhythms that differed from those at the classical extermination camps. In Auschwitz, Chełmno, and the three *Aktion Reinhard* death camps, the Germans gassed the overwhelming majority of the almost exclusively Jewish victims upon their arrival. In Majdanek, they gassed or shot 40 percent of the victims. The other 60 percent died from conditions to which the Germans subjected them (including gross physical maltreatment), which weakened them so that the proximate causes of death were starvation, starvation-induced work exhaustion, and disease.[2]

Although a "work" camp, Majdanek had a mortality rate that was the highest of any camp, except for Auschwitz and the other four mass extermination camps.[3] Although a "work" camp, Majdanek did not have productive labor for many of its inmates, so its German masters resorted to forcing the Jews to labor in a manner intended to generate mainly suffering and death. Many former prisoners comment on their purposeless toil. One Jewish survivor, who arrived in Majdanek in April 1943, during the "height" of Jewish labor utilization in the Lublin District, characterizes Majdanek as a "pure extermination camp, devoted solely to tormenting and killing." The inmates were not put to useful labor. Every day commenced with a roll call that might last hours and where many were beaten until they were "half-dead."

> Then we went to "work."[4] In our wooden shoes we were chased by blows from rods into a corner of the field and had to fill sometimes our caps, at other times our jackets, with stones, wet sand or mud, and, holding them with both hands and running under a hail of blows, bring them to the opposite corner of the field, empty the stuff, refill it and bring it back to the opposite corner, and so on. A gauntlet of screaming SS men and privileged prisoners [*Häftlingsprominenz*], armed with rods and whips, let loose on us a hail of blows. It was hell.[5]

The consequences of such treatment were obvious, and are described by another survivor: "On their way back to the camp, the commandos dragged heaps of corpses on sledges; the living were led by the arms; left to themselves inside the gate, they would crawl to the blocks, using their hands and feet to cross the ice-covered assembly area; those who managed to reach the barracks, tried to get up with the help of the wall, but they could not keep standing for long."[6] And if they could, they had the evening's brutal roll call to look forward to. Many more testimonies exist as to the exterminationist nature of "work" in one of the Germans' greatest "work" camps.[7]

Not surprisingly, even though there were large numbers of non-Jews in the camps, the gas chambers' victims were almost exclusively Jews. The Germans in Majdanek treated the camp's Jews throughout fundamentally differently and worse than its non-Jewish prisoners. At its peak, Majdanek incarcerated between 35,000 to 40,000 people, remaining far below its projected 150,000 capacity because of its lack of equipment and materiel. Its extant Jewish population of 18,000 was utterly decimated during the Germans' wholesale slaughter of *Erntefest*. The Germans here, as elsewhere, were not, however, indiscriminate killers. They left the non-Jews alive, and the camp continued to operate until Soviet troops liberated it on July 22, 1944.[8]

While Majdanek was a large facility of mixed purposes and mixed population, the area's other post–*Aktion Reinhard* camps were smaller, were ostensibly devoted solely to work, and were populated almost exclusively by Jews. They therefore provide a still clearer picture of the character of Jewish "work." Two of these were Lipowa Camp (*Lipowa Lager*) and the *Flughafenlager*.[9]

Lipowa Camp, founded in December 1939 at a former riding ring in Lublin's Lipowa Street, evolved gradually from its early function primarily as an assembly point, into a typical concentration camp with an incarcerated prisoner population.[10] Two developments impelled this transformation during 1940–1941. The German authorities found that Jews from Lublin were evading their conscription in work units, and so they began to imprison recalcitrant Jews on the square. Also, the expectation of large transports of Jews from the Reich, who were to remain in the camp at least temporarily, and of Jewish Polish POWs necessitated facilities to hold them. During the winter of 1940–1941, at least two thousand POWs arrived, making them the dominant prisoner group in the camp.[11] The population of the camp was further augmented by periodic roundups in the Lublin ghetto. By April 1942, Lipowa was completely at the disposal of the chief of all SS and police forces in Lublin, the *SS- und Polizeiführer* (*SSPF*) Lublin. Its production was devoted to SS enterprises. The camp's inmates also helped sort the belongings of the Jews whom the Germans had killed during *Aktion Reinhard;* Lipowa specialized in shoes.[12] The brief lease on life given by the Germans to the camp's 3,000 or more Jews ran out in November 1943.[13] They perished in the Germans' *Erntefest* mass shootings.

In the first two years of Lipowa's existence, the production and productivity of its Jewish workers was minimal. This is particularly significant, since the camp's initial and continuing purpose ostensibly was to put Jews from Lublin to work. Starting in December 1939, the *Judenrat* of Lublin each day had to supply 800 to 1,000 workers, many of whom were skilled craftsmen. Yet until Lipowa's production came under the jurisdiction of the SS Deutsche Ausrüstungs-Werke (DAW) in the fall of 1941, the camp's workshops were incompetently outfitted and run.[14] The *skills* of skilled laborers went for the most part unused, meaning that the Germans squandered a great portion of the labor power of these workers, who under normal circumstances would have been highly valued and very productive.

With the DAW's assumption of production and the December arrival of Hermann Moering, who was to manage the camp, an energetic building spree began. New barracks and workshops were erected, and DAW machinery began to arrive. As the capacity to utilize the skills of the Jews increased, the Germans progressively employed more of the Jews in the camp's workshops, and the number sent to work outside of the camp (previously, almost one-third) declined in the spring of 1943 to one 50-man commando.[15] According to Moering, the number of Jewish craftsmen employed increased from 280 (when he arrived) to 1,590 (in the fall of 1943). The high point of Lipowa's productivity, from the summer of 1942 until its destruction in November 1943, saw the camp become the DAW's most important enterprise outside of Germany (*Reichsgebiet*) itself,[16] and an important supply source of shoes and clothing for the *SSPF* Lublin, as well as for the army, the SS, the police, and the civil administration. On the DAW's books, the camp seems to have been profitable.[17]

When, after two years of non-productivity and economic wastefulness, serious work finally got under way, Lipowa, seen in the narrow light of strict accounting terms, might seem to have been a rationally conducted economic enterprise. But when evaluated in the broader context of the enormously counterproductive manner of the German's labor utilization of Jews, the piddling profit of its final, brief productive period, belies the impression of profitability—as do the camp's first two years of general economic inactivity. The products of fewer than 16,000 Jewish prisoners in all of the DAW's enterprises in 1943, and of another 16,000 in the enterprises of the SS company Ostindustrie GbmM (Osti), can hardly be seen to have been economically rational in light of the approximately two million Polish Jews who had already perished.[18] And when, in November 1943, the Germans slaughtered this labor force for which there was no substitute, they condemned the camp's production facilities to remain virtually unused for the rest of the war.[19]

The Germans ran the camp itself, moreover, in an absolutely irrational manner from the viewpoint of production. Their handling of the Jews in Lipowa was brutal, and severely undermined economic production, which was the ostensible purpose of the camp. Both the overall regime—that is, the general rules and punishments—and the non-codified conduct of the individual guards, made daily existence perilous, full of mortal danger and suffering for the Jews. As in the camps in general, there appears to have been no limitations on what the Germans could and did do to Jews with impunity.

Starting certainly by the beginning of 1941, the Germans punished attempts to escape from Lipowa with death. Death—a staple, virtually reflexive German reaction to all manner of Jews' infractions, pseudo-infractions, and displeasing acts—was also meted out with ease by the Germans in Lipowa. The Germans punished theft with death. Overseers interested in maintaining the health and work capabilities of their laborers might have welcomed attempts by their workers to acquire for themselves through the underground economy an extra crust of bread, in order to supplement their in-adequate, debilitating rations, or some additional clothing, in order to help buttress their existing meager protection against the penetrating cold. But the Germans did everything in their power to prevent Jews from staving off enervation and disease.

The Germans' brutality in Lipowa did not develop as a deterrent for the protection of valuable goods. All Jewish violations, no matter how insignifi-cant, of German established norms, no matter how counterproductive or eco-nomically irrational, were met with massive retaliation. One Jew, for example, was shot point-blank with a pistol for having stolen woolen mittens during 1941.[20] The worth of stolen items was not the issue, since the severity of Ger-man actions bore no relation to their value. In Lipowa, the Germans penal-ized with death even Jews who took valueless industrial scraps.[21] The Germans were reacting not to palpable injuries done to materiel or output, but to the act of violation itself; therefore insignificant violations and truly in-jurious ones brought upon the transgressing Jew similar sentences.

With death sentences or other brutal "punishments," which were noth-ing else but acts of torture, awaiting the Jews for many necessary acts of sur-vival under conditions of acute privation, the need for Jews to engage in such acts multiplied with the German blows that they absorbed. Virtually all of Lipowa's personnel carried whips or some functional equivalent, and they used them frequently and with energy, striking out at the Jews often arbitrar-ily and without any apparent cause, even by the Germans' liberal notions of causality. In addition to the Germans' quotidian exercise of their whips, their routine cruelty took particular forms which included:

1. Brutal beatings with whips into which small iron balls had been wrought (*eingearbeitet*).
2. Incarceration in a bunker for an indeterminate length of time.
3. Beatings in a bunker on a special whipping table (*Auspeitschtisch*) invented by one of the Germans specifically for such occasions.
4. The forcing of Jews to run the gauntlet.
5. Torturing Jews with electric shocks.
6. Compelling Jews to stand for hours barefoot in the snow, after waking them with blows.
7. Public hangings, which terrorized the Jews still more than unseen execu-tions.

Some Jews died from their tormentors' self-expression; the "fortunate" ones suffered serious physical debilitation.[22]

In Lipowa, as in the Germans' camp and exterminationist empire gener-ally, the Germans' cruel treatment of Jews was no secret. It was done openly, and the participation of the guards was general and routine. Visiting cruelties upon the Jews was both the semi-official policy of the camp, and the unwritten, unpromulgated norm that developed among its personnel. Although the kind of brutal, daily torturing that took place in this camp was, by German standards, unexceptional, even for "work" camps, two unusual, particularly illustrative incidents did occur.[23]

Although the German army treated Jewish Polish POWs as POWs,[24] if second-class ones, the SS refused to respect this status. For them, Jewish Polish POWs were simply Jews. The Jewish POWs who came to Lipowa had previously been under the army's jurisdiction, and had been treated relatively decently. The Germans in Lipowa knew this, so in order to drive the point home to the POWs that for them a Jew was but a Jew, they conducted an unannounced nocturnal ceremony shortly after these Jews arrived in the camp, for the bestowing of the new status, for the social transformation of the POWs. One survivor recalls: "At night we were driven out of the barracks, half naked and barefoot. We had to stay for a long time in the snow, lying down on the snow-covered ground. We were told that we were not prisoners of war but only interned Jews. On this occasion we were beaten . . . We were then ordered to run back to the barracks, and as we did so, we were beaten and dogs were set upon us."[25] Other surviving former POWs provide similar descriptions of the several hours they spent during this unforgettable midwinter night, adding that many of them fell ill from the exposure (and the beatings) and died. The camp's leading officers and "many others" participated in this night's activity.[26]

The symbolic component of this "renaming ceremony" is reminiscent of the rituals performed upon free people being transformed into slaves, into socially dead beings. Accompanying the announcement of the new social status, typically, are actions which make the meaning of that status clear, which imprint in everyone's mind the social valuation of the transformed individual's new place in society.[27] The Germans did not merely impart verbally to the POWs that, in their eyes, they were from then on mere Jewish prisoners and thus no longer to be afforded the protections of international conventions. This would not do. Additionally, the Germans naturally adopted and replicated, certainly without conscious knowledge of such practices, a recurring feature of the process of changing people into slaves—in this case, by translating their announcement into the idiom that best communicated what being a Jew denoted in their world: the language of pain. And through this ritual-like renaming of the Jews, they spoke their special language with their own special elocutionary flair: Jews were creatures to be wrested from any repose, meant to suffer, to be beaten and tortured, to be attacked by dogs, to die at the whim of his German *Übermensch*. The Germans had to infuse the Jews' souls irrevocably, through the medium of their bodies, with the knowledge that they were no more than playthings for Germans, living at German sufferance. The Germans were here operating on their communicative principle that a lash is worth a thousand words; and the Jewish prisoners quickly learned the idiom of the new order.[28]

A second ceremony that took place was one of pure festivity, though the meaning that it conveyed about the attitudes of the Germans towards their overall enterprise is just as eloquent as the physically debilitating, gratuitous cruelty that they perpetrated upon the Jewish POWs. The ceremony was a party thrown by Odilo Globocnik, the head of *Aktion Reinhard*, for a particularly brutal figure in the camp, the commandant of Lipowa, Alfred Dressler. A Jewish survivor relates that one day, "when I was working at Globocnik's, a celebration took place there in honor of Dressler on the occasion of his murder of the fifty-thousandth Jew. In the house of Globocnik, the reason for the celebration was the common topic of conversation. During it Globocnik summoned me into the hall and, threatening me with a gun, forced me to down a bottle of vodka."[29] Such was the "production" milestone that the Germans celebrated in the life of this "work" camp.

Supplementing the German personnel who ran and staffed the camp were, successively, contingents of ethnic German paramilitary units, ethnic Germans in the Waffen-SS, members of the Kommando Dirlewanger, and finally Ukrainians, who generally lived outside the camp, coming to the camp primarily to man its perimeter and guard groups of Jews who toiled beyond its fences.[30] These contingents ranged in size from thirty to forty men at a time. The Germans themselves consisted mainly of SS men, subordinate to the *SSPF* Lublin. From the limited information available about forty-six of the Germans, identified in postwar investigations, who ran the camp, they appear to have been an unextraordinary lot, by the German standards of the time.[31] Among them were also some non-SS men who were in the camp in technical capacities, and women clerical workers.

As in all German-run camps, some individual Germans departed from the base-line level of pervasive brutality, usually by making the already inhuman norm seem lenient. Some stood out by having been less brutal towards the Jews. Not surprisingly, an individual's personality influenced the substance and style of the cruelty that he visited upon the Jews, though almost all could be counted upon consistently to produce a substantial amount of Jewish pain. In Lipowa, virtually all of the personnel appear to have made good use of their whips. Some, like the commandant himself, who helped set the tone of conduct for the camp, were heavy hitters. The prisoners, among themselves, altered his name slightly to include the word "death" (*Mord*) in his appellation. The pervasiveness of the cruelty was such that social pressure among the Germans to conform was great; survivors describe one guard as having been particularly decent, yet he nevertheless beat them when under the watchful eyes of superiors.[32] This reveals in two ways the camp personnel's norm in treating the Jews. The Jews expected that this German would hit them, and, despite his beating of them, they considered him to have been the most upstanding German in the camp; the other Germans were worse than he. Second, had the others not really have wanted to inflict pain upon the Jews, then they too could have hit only when under observation, and hit in a manner calculated to cause as little pain and damage as possible. Yet, as the testimony of survivors makes clear, they *chose* not to minimize Jewish suffering. Of the forty-six members of the German camp staff discussed in the legal investigation, survivors give positive evaluations of this man and only two others.[33]

Another "work" camp, nearby in Lublin, provides a tale of German cruelty and of murderous, uneconomic action that casts still greater doubt on the notion that productive criteria guided the Germans in their treatment of Jews in any but tertiary, transitory ways. The camp complex, which went under various names in German documents, including "Work Camp Lublin" and "*Flughafen* Lublin" (Airport Lublin), is referred to here by one of its appellations, the "*Flughafenlager*" (the Airport Camp).[34] Its primary economic activities were the sorting of booty taken from the Jews who perished in *Aktion Reinhard* and also, late in its existence, the production of brushes. Planned armaments production for the camp never got under way. This output, although of some economic importance, was but a byproduct of its major activity. The camp was most prodigious in producing corpses out of its "workers."

The *Flughafenlager*, founded in the fall of 1941, was located in Lublin on the route leading to Zamość about halfway out to Majdanek. Unlike the other "work" camps which were allegedly devoted to economic production in and around Lublin, the *Flughafenlager* actually had work for its Jews more or less from the beginning. Each of the main subdivisions of the camp was a camp in itself, a relatively distinct entity with its own tasks, personnel, prisoners, and history of cruelty and death. The main subdivisions were the relatively small Main Supply Camp (*Hauptnachschublager*) Russia-South, the central SS Clothing Works (*Bekleidungswerk*), a work of the DAW, and the late-developing Osti enterprises.[35] Its main enterprise, the Clothing Works was an establishment of the SS Economic-Administrative Main Office yet functioned above all as an instrument of the *SSPF* Lublin, as part of its *Aktion Reinhard* genocidal undertaking.[36]

Tens of thousands of Jews, males and females of all ages, passed through the *Flughafenlager*. Large transports of Jews deported from Warsaw, Białystok, and Belzyce alighted there temporarily, so that the Germans could decide to allocate the Jews either to the ovens of Treblinka or to the nearby camps of Majdanek, Budzyń, Poniatowa, Trawniki, and Lipowa. The *Flughafenlager*'s own population of Jews averaged between 7,500 and 8,500 men and women during its existence, with the continually dying Jews being replaced by new arrivals.[37] Of the many thousands who spent part of their lives as prisoners in the *Flughafenlager*, a figurative handful, only forty to fifty, survived.[38]

The Main Supply Camp was throughout its history a small enterprise, with a core prisoner population of twenty-five Jews and labor crews arriving daily from another camp of up to one hundred more.[39] They were engaged in loading and unloading freight cars and in constructing barracks.

Few details are known about the Jews' life within the Main Supply Camp and the entire *Flughafenlager* prior to autumn 1942, because, as far as can be ascertained, only one person from this "work" camp survived this period of its existence, a woman who was briefly in the Clothing Works. So for the climate of life in one part of the *Flughafenlager*, the Main Supply Camp, we must rely on the testimony of Albert Fischer, one of the German personnel who, unlike his confreres, is forthcoming about the nature of their treatment of the Jews.[40] He relates only the string of horrors which *he* witnessed that occurred only during a three-month period in the camp starting in March 1942. His is but an extremely partial view, circumscribed by his brief stay there and by the natural limitation of his having been able to observe only those acts of cruelty which occurred in his presence. What he relates, which cannot be assumed to be coextensive even with what he saw, should be multiplied by some large factor if the scale of suffering that the Main Supply Camp's Germans willfully inflicted on its Jews is to be imagined and comprehended.

Even though little is known of the Main Supply Camp,[41] one thing is clear: Brutality and savagery were the air that the Jews breathed. Fischer summarizes life in the camp definitively, by saying that "beating was the camp's invariable daily fare" (*Schlägereien waren im Lager an der Tagesordnung*). Despite this overall characterization, Fischer in his testimony focuses almost exclusively on one particularly cruel and brutal sergeant, Max Dietrich, who clearly may be seen as the paragon of the camp's brutality, as but an accentuated example of the ordinary German way of acting in the camp. An SS man since February 1, 1933, Dietrich was twenty-nine years old when Fischer knew him, and was already well versed in the handling of prisoners, having cut his teeth, starting at the age of twenty-one, as a guard in Dachau, where he served from 1934 to 1938. In 1941, he was a commander of Jewish work details, including of Polish Jewish POWs from Lipowa, for the *SSPF* Lublin. In the Main Supply Camp, he was similarly in charge of the Jewish work details from May 1942 until sometime in 1943.[42]

Already on Fischer's second or third day in camp, he became acquainted with Dietrich's manner, witnessing how Dietrich "with a leather whip flogged Jews fearfully." A day or two later, he witnessed another display. This time, Dietrich chose an iron rod to communicate his conception of the worth of a Jewish "worker," in the unmistakable idiom of the German pep talk: "I approached when Dietrich struck the Jew, just about how one strikes a rabbit in the back of the neck if one is going to kill it. He used an iron rod of about the length and thickness of a baby carriage's axle. The Jew collapsed and lay there lifeless."[43]

Dietrich did not confine himself to old-fashioned cudgelings, however brutal and fatal they might have been. Fischer, with another German, one day followed the trail of ghastly screams, to discover Dietrich "once again in one of his tantrums," and to witness a scene of this "work" leader's making that is hard to fathom could occur in an institution devoted to economic productivity: "There I saw that Dietrich beat the Jew so long until he lay unconscious on the ground. Then Dietrich ordered other Jews fully to undress the unconscious Jew and to pour water on him. When the Jew regained consciousness, Dietrich grabbed the hands of the Jew, who had defecated all over himself, dunked them in the excrement and forced him to eat the excrement. I walked away, as the spectacle sickened me." Fischer found out that evening that this Jewish worker, nourished on his own excrement, was dead.[44]

Dietrich, despite his pronounced sadism, illustrates a great deal about the nature of his colleagues. Dietrich was the most outstanding of the camp's free-swingers, a man who was merely more remarkable than his comrades in vigor and gusto when wielding his whip and other implements of expression. Fischer presents an incisive summary of Dietrich's character and actions, and the relationship between them and the camp's norms: "Beating was the camp's invariable daily fare. Dietrich was especially active as a hitter. It started first thing in the morning when the Jews arrived. Dietrich beat a few Jews and was then contented. Only then did he enjoy his coffee. When we spoke to him about these incidents, he became very agitated and threatened [us] with a pistol." Beating was the applied ethical rule of the camp. It was the grammar of expression and communication. Dietrich was but a type whose compulsive need to subject the Jews to pain and degradation gave pause to the others who were merely dedicated, but not obsessive dispensers of blows. It was Dietrich's psychological dependence upon marking Jewish bodies that disturbed his colleagues,[45] for licentious brutality tends to unnerve even the extremely brutal who are able to maintain control of themselves. But it was certainly not the camp's invariable daily fare itself that bothered Dietrich's comrades, for with the rising sun they themselves arose and willingly dispensed it. They meted it out every single day.

That Fischer himself saw nothing wrong with the general treatment of the Jews, he all but admits. He joined the Waffen-SS in 1940 as an eager, Nazi-besotted sixteen-year-old, or, as he describes it, "because I was at the time for the cause with my heart and soul" (*weil ich damals Feuer and Flamme für die Sache war*). In this regard, he might as well have been speaking for his entire generation. He fought on the Russian front and was wounded in November 1941. After a convalescence, he served in different posts, ending up in the Main Supply Camp in March 1942, where his Nazi zeal came up against its logical consequence, the most brutal Nazi reality. In a fleeting reference to the slow process by which some humanity awakened within him, which produced in him the need to give this confessional testimony, he explains: "It was only in the later years that I gradually came to recognize that much was rotten. And afterwards, my eyes were opened." He gave evidence because "I wanted to make a clean breast of it and to unburden myself of all that had happened." He speaks as a man with much on his conscience.

Unlike the small Main Supply Camp, the part of the *Flughafenlager* that was the Clothing Works was a camp of considerable size. It was the central productive portion of the *Flughafenlager* over the course of its life, with a prisoner population made up *exclusively* of Jews, averaging somewhere between 3,500 and 5,500, of whom 2,000 to 3,000 were women.[46] The women came from Poland, Czechoslovakia, the Netherlands, and some considerable number from Germany, particularly from Aachen and Koblenz.[47]

Only the bare outlines of the early life of the Clothing Works are discernible—of its development, the kind of work its prisoners performed, and the treatment of its prisoners. Although the SS initially brought Jews to the site for construction purposes in July 1940 at the latest (and perhaps earlier), the *Flughafenlager* was first established as a camp in autumn 1941. Erection of the installations of the Clothing Works itself began in the winter of 1941–42.[48] The Clothing Works' establishment and expansion had two sources. The first was Globocnik's desire, which he began to act upon in 1942, to create an economic empire under his control for the SS in Lublin, where he was *SSPF*.[49] The second was a need that arose with the onset of *Aktion Reinhard*, to sort the belongings of the slain Jews.[50]

The Clothing Works was a "work" camp, avowedly meant to exploit Jewish labor power for economic product and profit, meant to put Jews "to work." Yet until it received the infusion of Jewish clothing and belongings from *Aktion Reinhard*, a fortuitous development which had not been foreseen during the camp's founding, the Clothing Works, a "work" camp, did not have enough real work to employ more than a fraction of its Jewish population in productive activities.[51] Its inmates, as with Jews throughout the camp world, had been wrested from the various economies in which they had labored productively; thus, the founding of the Clothing Works and its early period can be seen only as having had little to do with any real economic rationality or desire to make use of Jewish labor power.

The Germans, however, did not permit the Jews to be idle. Indeed, they endeavored, as the next chapter discusses, to ensure that the Jews should never be in a painless state. The Germans put the Jews to work, though in no rational economic sense, in no normal lexicon, would it have been called "work," or the people so occupied, "workers." Forcing them to perform backbreaking, senseless activity calculated to exhaust and shatter the health of even the strongest,[52] the Germans also fed them miserably. One Jewish woman describes their fare: "The bread was hard and barely palatable. At noon there was a soup which we called 'sand soup.' They made it with potatoes and carrots which they did not bother to clean. Into this soup they threw one or two cow heads with teeth, hair, and eyes."[53] The hygienic conditions were miserable. The only running water in the camp available to the prisoners was in the infirmary.[54] The prisoners had to carry it in pails to the barracks. Not surprisingly—in fact, for the Germans it was expected—the once healthy and productive Jews of this "work" camp produced little, and died at a rapid rate, including from repeated outbreaks of diseases, like typhus and dysentery, caused by the severe undernourishment and unhygienic conditions.[55] Since this one Jewish woman is the only survivor of the Clothing Works from before the fall of 1942 (she was in the camp for only three weeks in April 1942), details about the senseless "work" that was performed are unavailable. A contemporaneous, typical instance of non-productive labor from the sibling institution, the Main Supply Camp, provides some idea of the meaning of "work" in the Clothing Works and the *Flughafenlager* in general. Dietrich, once again, was the prime mover. On a Sunday, the one day during which the Germans normally allowed their camp prisoners to rest, he assembled a commando of Jews in order to put them to "work":

> One of the barracks at the rail siding was filled with straw mattresses. On the other side of the track there was a barracks that was empty at the time. Dietrich had the Jews carry the mattresses running from the first barracks to the empty one, and after the latter was filled, back again to the barracks where they had at first been. The Jews had to perform the work on the run, and Dietrich beat them with a whip until a portion of the Jews collapsed and were unable to continue. Then Dietrich was at peace. He sat down in his quarters and got drunk.[56]

During this first period, the Clothing Works was, no matter what the Germans called it, a camp of extermination, where the means employed—of exhausting activity combined with severe undernourishment, and punishing brutality—differentiated it from other extermination camps only in that these exterminatory means took somewhat longer.

The second period of the Clothing Works' history commenced in the fall of 1942 with the arrival of large quantities of clothes and possessions that had belonged to Jews consumed in *Aktion Reinhard*'s flames. Finally, the Germans had enough work to keep the labor force in this "work" camp, otherwise poorly appointed for work, in productive motion. The prisoner population, having been around two thousand, grew quickly beginning at the end of 1942, and the physical plant of the camp was commensurately expanded during a rapid building program.[57]

The prisoners sorted a prodigious amount of booty. According to Globocnik, 1,901 boxcars of clothes, linen, feathers for bedding, and rags confiscated from Jews were delivered to German industry. The Germans also accumulated 103,614 watches (in need of repair), 29,391 pairs of glasses, many jewels, as well as large sums of money. The total take was calculated to be worth over 178 million Reichsmarks.[58] Much (though it is unknown how much) of this was sorted at the Clothing Works.

Knowing full well that the conditions of life that he and his underlings had heretofore created for the Jews were antithetical to their performance of even the relatively light work of sorting clothing, Christian Wirth, the Clothing Works' commander, now increased the rations and instituted a somewhat less brutal regime of treatment. During this period, at the beginning of 1943, the camp first got sewage and more adequate supplies of running water.[59] The alterations, as significant and slight as they at once were, merely highlight that the Germans' policy in the Clothing Works had until then been "extermination through 'work.'"

The health of the prisoners had by then been so damaged by the conditions at this "work" camp as to render them actually unfit for productive labor. In the spring of 1943, Osti established manufacturing installations in the *Flughafenlager*, and initially drew on the population of the Clothing Works for its laborers. Unlike the rulers and staff of the camp empire, the Osti, an economic institution, really was interested in productive labor. The manager of one of the Osti plants was appalled when he discovered the condition of the workers who were to have been his labor reservoir. They were dangerously undernourished and physically ruined. Before putting them to work, he had to let them rest and recuperate for two weeks in order to bring them up to minimal working strength.[60] Still, like the Osti's other plants relying on debilitated Jewish workers, the brush factory and the iron foundry in the *Flughafenlager* were economic failures.[61]

During this period, Wirth not only increased the rations but also took other steps to sustain the prisoners. He reestablished the abandoned infirmary, which nevertheless remained a place for Germans to go when in the mood to kill Jews,[62] and even decreased the number of Jews that they weeded out for killing. Still, Jewish life in the camp was a bitter fight for temporary survival. Undernourishment remained a constant companion and undermined the Jews' ability to persevere. The Germans drove the Jews at work, and themselves killed or sent to Majdanek for slaughter any Jew who was too weakened or wounded to perform at the merciless pace.[63]

Complementing and reinforcing the effects of the general life conditions in the Clothing Works was the Germans' own treatment of the Jewish prisoners. Together, they reveal the Germans' conception of their institution's real genocidal purpose. As in Lipowa, the Germans killed Jews on the slightest of pretexts. Any Jew who stole even worthless objects, including potato peelings and used undergarments, was deemed by the Germans a "saboteur" and killed. Even a Jew's unauthorized acceptance of *freely given* bread from German personnel or from Poles with whom they happened to come into contact was seen as "sabotage." It did not matter that the unauthorized possessions might be the bare necessities of existence, minimum prerequisites for maintaining the productive capacity of workers; if they were unauthorized, the Jew who had them was subject to a death sentence, to be executed in a variety of ways, depending on the Germans' disposition; if in the mood for the emotional jolt that bullets provided, they shot the Jews on the spot; if preferring to feel flesh split and bone crush under the lash or the cudgel, to see blood flow, and to hear the whimpering and agonies of the victims, they pummeled them to death; if in a more ceremonious mood, they opted for a hanging. Such hangings, also *de rigueur* for attempted escapes, were public spectacles,[64] and like all public spectacles, they were intended to impress the audience, which, aside from the Germans who went to it for its circus-like appeal, included all the Jewish prisoners of the camp. The Germans took pains to make sure not only that the Jews were present, but also that they gave their full attention to the spectacle before them. One survivor tells of having been beaten for averting her eyes during one of the hangings.[65] As a part of the Clothing Works' hangings, the Germans made the victims complicit in their own deaths, a favorite Teutonic technique of the era, meant to degrade and imprint upon the victims the abject state of their servile condition. The Germans forced the victims to construct the gallows from which they would hang and to slip the nooses around their own necks.[66] A member of the "world Jewish conspiracy" dying, in part, by his own hand was a delectable irony. It was especially enjoyable when accompanied by yet additional forms of symbolic degradation.[67]

Insufficiently speedy or competent work, unlike the "sabotage" of possessing bread, was met with "light" whippings, transfer to a punishment detail, or, if the SS man or woman felt like having a workout, fifty lashes might be counted out on a Jew's denuded body. The Germans also killed prisoners on the spot. The Jews, moreover, always labored under the threat of being sent to nearby Majdanek for gassing should they arouse a German's displeasure,[68] which could be done just by drawing a German's attention. Given the feeble physical condition of most of the prisoners, less than stellar work could only have been expected, so the Germans' torture and killing of their "workers" was an integral and structured part of the Clothing Works' workaday world. Cruelty was embedded in the fabric of "work."

The fact is that the German personnel's beating of the prisoners was so routine that a survivor, when describing one of the more outstanding torturers in camp, can remark upon the camp's routine cruelty in passing, as if it had been an ordinary expectation: "Wagner was a sadist. He would not only beat the women; that was done by all the SS men."[69] Elsewhere, she provides a fuller description of Wagner's singularity: "He was active not with a gun, but with a whip, and he frequently beat women so terribly that they died of the effects . . . In his sadism towards women, Wagner appeared to us to be absolutely abnormal; the other SS men, who held total power over us, were of course also very cruel, but were not sadistic in the same way as Wagner."[70] The standard of normality for the German personnel of this camp did not include the obvious sexual gratification Karl Wagner derived from the sadistic beatings that he administered to the women, whom he sometimes first forced to undress.[71] Wagner stood out, seemed "absolutely abnormal," not because he was brutal to the women, not because he beat them, but because of the unusual, clear sadistic sexual component of his brutality. The general norm of brutality and violence in the Clothing Works was such that mere floggings hardly merit a mention. It was a constitutive activity of the camp's ordinary Germans.

The Germans' freedom to torture Jews at will and the inventiveness that they brought to this vocationally related avocation make it not at all surprising that in the propitious climate of the Clothing Works, some distinguished contributions to the German cornucopia of cruelty emerged, which included Wirth riding his horse, at his pleasure, into large assemblages of Jews, the horse's hind hooves sending Jews flying, badly injuring some and killing others. The Germans of the camp saw fit to amuse themselves with experimental gassings in a barracks,[72] even though functioning and adequate gassing installations were but a stone's throw away in Majdanek, rendering this enterprise instrumentally pointless. This was not so surprising, since, before joining the Clothing Works, Wirth and others in its administration had had distinguished personal histories with gassing Jews.[73] Wirth had been in charge of gassing both in the so-called Euthanasia program and then in the *Aktion Reinhard* death camps. He and his underlings, at once professional and avocational executioners, brought old habits to their new posts, where killing remained one of their tasks. They took initiative and employed their energy in recreating what they knew well. These men were not mere executioners. They were engaged, enthusiastic killers alive with a tinkering, inventive spirit.

In the Clothing Works, the Germans sometimes hanged Jews from the camp gate, an atypical practice for camps, since the corpse could be seen by anyone on the outside.[74] Apparently, Wirth did not care to be guided by the sham norm of maintaining secrecy about such camps, since it was common knowledge in Lublin and the region—including among the large number of Germans there, whether in the military, police, civilian administration, or the economy—that the Germans were exterminating the Jews. The hanging of Jews on the camp gate sent a number of obvious symbolic messages. Doors and gates often indicate the nature of the institution whose entrance from the outside world they regulate. The hanging corpse proclaimed visually, for all to see, the real business of the Clothing Works. It also announced, with a degree of accuracy which few such markers approach, the manner in which its Jewish inhabitants would leave this institution, for gates are also the passageway of return to the outside world.[75] The hanging Jew elaborated on the infamous camp emblem, *"Arbeit Macht Frei,"* intended both as irony and deception, but which bespoke more subjective truth than the Germans themselves always understood. For Jews, the hanging corpse was the sort of freedom that "work" was. It defined one important usage and meaning of the word "work" in the special lexicon that the Germans had developed for Jews.

The vast and varied German repertoire of cruelty, the voluminous, bloodbespattered history of their treatment of the Jews, is so numbing in its enormity that it is difficult to see many particular incidents as extraordinary. Still, few instances rival one unforgettable part of the Clothing Works' landscape in its pathological, shocking, and depressing quality—affecting even the numbed Jewish victims themselves—and in revealing the Germans' state of mind: the sadistic transformation of a Jewish boy into a German henchman.

Children, as a rule, were not allowed to stay alive in German camps (except ghettos) because, among other reasons, they symbolized the renewal and continuation of the Jewish people, a future which the Germans sought to obliterate emotionally and in deed. This prohibition, in force in the Clothing Works, dictated that the Clothing Works would also be a landscape devoid of the element by which a community can best imagine its future and can judge its own health. There was one noticeable exception to the barrenness of the Clothing Works' terrain: a little Jewish boy, around ten years of age, whom Wirth treated with solicitude, feeding him sweets and giving him every little boy's dream, a pony. But Wirth's kindness was in the service of his cruelty. One survivor recalls:

I have personally seen that this SS commander led a Jewish boy, who was about 10 years old, whom he kept and whom he fed chocolate and other goodies, to kill with a machine gun here and there 2 or 3 Jews at a time. I myself stood about 10 meters away when this boy carried out such shootings. The SS commander, who rode a white horse and who had given a horse to the boy, joined in the shooting. These two human beings together killed— in my presence—among the several occasions some 50 to 60 Jews. Among the victims were also women.[76]

In keeping with the German attentiveness to symbolic expression when dealing with Jews, this boy was furnished with appropriate accouterments for his transformation into a slayer of his people. The Germans clothed him in a specially tailored, miniature SS uniform, which he wore when spraying bullets from his lordly perch on his pony. And, if the disclosures of the Clothing Works' denizens are correct, it was not just faceless Jews he killed: he is said to have shot and killed his own mother.[77]

The only visible Jewish child in the camp,[78] who might otherwise have provided a little hope, a spark of joy, in the grim lives of the despondent Jews, was transformed by Wirth into the negation of hope, into a symbol of hopelessness, into a little SS man. Adults in the Clothing Works had to cower in fear before a child—a bizarre, infantilizing, and dehumanizing situation itself—a Jewish child no less, who was barely old enough to comprehend what he was doing, a child whom Wirth had so warped that he cut down his figurative and literal parents, all the time bouncing joyfully on his pony. Nothing could have driven home the point more painfully: the world had been turned upside down, and this was for the Jews a surreal place of pain and misery from which they were unlikely to emerge alive. Wirth and his comrades certainly understood this. The Germans' inauguration of the new world order, their stripping of power from the corrosive Jews, their transvaluation of values— all of these could be read in the symbolism of this Jewish child's transformation. The Germans induced a ten-year-old boy to kill his own mother.

The second period of the Clothing Works was marked by still another alteration in camp life. Its Jewish population, now treated somewhat better, was expanding, so Wirth decided to enlist Jews in keeping the other Jews in order by getting them to perform some of the Germans' dirty work. He created a hierarchy among the Jews, whereas before they had been an undifferentiated mass. Emulating the classical camp model, with which he was all too familiar, he appointed Jewish Kapos and established other privileged positions for Jews. He induced their cooperation with promises of freedom and the prospect of a portion of the *Aktion Reinhard* booty. He also organized an event which may be unique in the history of German camps: a German-organized Jewish wedding, which the camp's Germans, accompanied by a large number of invited guests, celebrated together with these Jewish "co-workers," together totaling an estimated 1,100 people. Its extraordinary nature was intended to deceive the privileged Jews into concluding, against their better judgment, that the Germans were acting in good faith. It accorded with Wirth's policy, during the Clothing Works' second period, of gaining Jewish compliance "with the carrot and the whip" (*mit Zuckerbrot und Peitsche*).[79] Wirth, and the others, could revel in this Jewish celebration, all the time celebrating not the marriage, but the ruse. They were toasting a symbolic final Jewish marriage, a marriage doomed at birth, destined, if ever one was, to be barren. The Germans must have been so amused while carousing at this farcical pageant. Wirth's love of cruel irony, his titillation at mocking and subverting the hallowed bonds of Jewish relationships—that found such exquisite expression in his Jewish SS boy—was motivation enough for this wedding, whatever utilitarian purposes of duplicity it might also have served.[80]

In its second period, the Clothing Works was conceived of as being mainly an adjunct institution of *Aktion Reinhard*, where Jews would "work" temporarily, until the time when they would no longer be needed to sort the belongings of their exterminated brethren. These Jews would then perish, having been destined to outlast but fleetingly the Jews whom the Germans killed immediately in *Aktion Reinhard*. Even during this period of useful employment (sometimes, there was so much work that the women would be sorting belongings night and day)[81] and improved conditions, which was also the period, in Wirth's words, of the "extermination of Jews with the help of Jews," the Clothing Works reveals the second aspect of the prevailing German conception of Jewish "work"—work as temporary exploitation, as a brief detour on the inexorable road to the crematoria or the pits. In the Clothing Works, the real relationship between "work" and death was explicit, and undeniable.

The conditions and character of "work" in Lipowa and the *Flughafen-lager* were reproduced for Jews generally throughout the camp system, in Auschwitz, Buchenwald, Mauthausen, Płaszów, Budzyń, Kraśnik, Poniatowa, Trawniki, and many others.[82] Lipowa and the *Flughafenlager* do not stand out as unusually brutal or mild, as unusually rational or irrational in their work policies. They are typical cases which accurately convey the nature of Jewish "work" and existence during the final phase of the Holocaust.

The destructive nature of Lipowa, the *Flughafenlager*, and the other camps in which Jews "worked"—their common pattern of destruction, structured debilitation, and widespread, personally motivated acts of cruelty—accords well with the general inattention to productive rationality in the Germans' *overall policies* towards Jewish labor. An unusual consonance of the macro, meso, and the micro existed in disposing of Jewish labor power. From Hitler and the Nazi leadership's consistent subordination of economic needs to the ideologically prior desire to rid Germany and the world of Jews, to the lethal conditions and routines of "work" camps, to the individual German overseer's continual unprovoked beating, crippling, or killing of Jewish workers in "work" camps, a faithful adherence was shown to an unspoken principle: that matters of economy would not dictate German "rationality" in their treatment of Jews. Economic self-injury generally worried or deterred neither Hitler nor the lowliest camp guard.

JEWISH "WORK" IN COMPARATIVE PERSPECTIVE

There is no doubt that in the *employment* of Jews and non-Jews, namely in the simple act of deciding whether or not (and where) to take advantage of each one's labor power, the Germans consistently demonstrated an unwillingness to employ Jews in enterprises for which they were ably suited, either substituting for them the often less competent workers of other subject peoples or letting their jobs remain unfilled and their lost production lost. Politics took precedence over economics. Did this ideologically derived and self-injurious discriminatory pattern find analogous expression in the *conditions* of employment when the Germans did employ Jews? Did they routinely treat Jewish workers differently from the workers of other subject peoples? Did their notions of rationality differ for the utilization of Jews and non-Jews?

The first and perhaps best measure of relative treatment are comparative death rates. At all institutional levels, Jewish death rates were substantially higher than that of other peoples. In Poland, the Baltics, the occupied portions of the Soviet Union, Czechoslovakia, Yugoslavia, and Greece, the Germans killed between 80 and 90 percent (for the occupied Soviet Union, the percentage may be even higher) of each country's Jews. No other people suffered losses approaching these.[83]

Another telling difference is that the only groups of currently employed workers whom the Germans killed *en masse*, necessitating the closing down of manufacturing installations, were Jews. *Operation Erntefest*, just one example of such a self-inflicted German economic wound, took the lives of 43,000 Jewish workers for whom they had no substitutes. Even Auschwitz suffered from a labor shortage by the end of 1942, one easily averted had the exterminationist ethic not dominated the camp's life, not led the Germans to slaughter immediately the majority of work-age Jews who arrived.[84] Overall, the number of Jews employed by the Germans in Poland (and many of them not very productively) plummeted from 700,000 in 1940 to 500,000 in 1942 to somewhat over 100,000 in mid-1943. This precipitous decline, which was a consequence of the extermination, appears to have been even more self-injurious when it is compared to the total number of *available* Jewish workers, which in the *Generalgouvernement* alone was 1.4 million in 1942.[85] Never, in the history of German rule, did the Germans act irrationally and close down factories in order to kill *non-Jewish* workers. Never for Poles, never for Russians, never for Serbs, never for Greeks, never for French, never for Danes, never for Germans. Only for Jews.

Finally, the levels of attrition (through starvation, disease, and individual killings) during the *course* of "normal" work were much higher for Jewish than for non-Jewish workers. Had productivity been the guiding criterion, or even an important one, for the Germans' treatment of Jews, then the Jewish death rates would not have differed significantly from that of other subject peoples, such as Poles. Yet they did,[86] as the monthly death rates for different categories of prisoners in the Mauthausen camp show:[87]

	November–December 1942	January–February 1943	November–December 1943
Jews	100%	100%	100%
Political prisoners	3%	1%	2%
Criminals	1%	0%	1%
Preventive detainees	35%	29%	2%
Asocials	0%	0%	0%
Poles	4%	3%	1%
Soviet civilian workers	—	—	2%

The Jewish *monthly* mortality rate was 100 percent. That of Poles was below 5 percent. The figures for November and December 1943 are particularly illustrative, because by the fall of 1943 full-scale mobilization of the Mauthausen prison population for armaments production had taken place. There was a consequent precipitous fall in the death rate of the "preventive detainees," from 35 percent to 2 percent. Yet the new priority placed on the economic use of the camp's prisoners for the urgent task of supporting the war effort did not reduce the death rate of Jewish prisoners, which remained at 100 percent.[88] German production concerns altered the general pace of their extermination of European Jewry only on the margins.[89]

Not just the death rate but also the *conditions* of work for Jews and non-Jews were substantially different. As a rule, Germans employed "racial" criteria in determining the general treatment, the amount and nutritional value of food, and the job assignments that they gave to Jews and non-Jews. In every respect, the Jews fared the worst; within a given camp or institution, Germans treated Jews far more harshly, fed them more miserably, and assigned them the most exhausting and demeaning jobs.[90] This systematic and deadly discrimination existed both in camps and at the end of the war, when Jews were employed in the huge construction projects in Germany itself.[91] It mirrored faithfully the systematic discrimination that Jews suffered throughout the German camp system, discussed in Chapter 5.

The Germans, moreover, gave senseless work almost exclusively to Jews. The ideological compulsion to put Jews to work was absent in the Germans' treatment of other subject peoples, even of Gypsies, a people whom Germans dehumanized thoroughly and exterminated in large numbers. This aspect of Jewish "work" represents a significant departure from the criteria that the Germans applied to other peoples, and in itself is enough to suggest that this radical alteration of German sensibility and rationality occurred for Jews—and only for Jews.

Not only camp guards but also the German people generally reacted differently to the presence of Jews and non-Jewish foreigners working among them. The millions of ordinary Germans who supervised or worked with foreigners were the ones—as much as the regime itself—who in their individual actions determined what life would be like for foreign workers. Unfortunately for the workers, a high percentage of the German people demonstrated in their attitudes and in their maltreatment of non-German workers that they had become imbued with the Nazi racist doctrines, particularly those about Slavic "subhumanity."[92] At first, Germans' widespread, serious abuse of foreign workers caused their productivity to fall below expected levels. This spontaneous expression of Germans' innermost beliefs was so injurious that the regime, in the first part of 1943, undertook a campaign to persuade Germans to treat the foreign workers better.[93] The degree of inhumanity and cruelty that Germans showed the various foreign workers accorded with the "racial" hierarchy at the foundation of the Nazi order, of German society, and of German thought during the Nazi period. The French were treated far better than Poles, whose existence under German rule was, in turn, preferable to that of Russians,[94] who suffered in the early stages of their employment tremendously and died at a staggering rate.[95] Nonetheless, cracks in the ideological armor developed when Germans came into contact with non-Jewish "subhumans," even with Russians and other Soviet peoples.

The component of Nazi ideology and of the German cultural code that held the Slavs to be subhuman, for example, had neither the near universal acceptance nor as tenacious a hold on Germans' minds as had antisemitism. The *substance* of the beliefs about the Slavs was also not as fear-inspiring to the Germans (see Appendix 2). These beliefs failed to place before the Germans the same sort of psychological and perceptual barriers for Slavs that their hallucinatory antisemitism did for Jews. Many Germans were still capable of perceiving the reality of the foreign workers for what it was. Such Germans who had contact with Poles and Russians were able to readjust the relevant part of their cognitive framework to take into account the obvious humanity of these "subhumans." Their beliefs about them, and the relative superficiality of the beliefs (compared to those about Jews), produced a cognitive framework that retained a measure of flexibility.

German workers and farmers saw and *acknowledged* that the Poles and the Russians worked hard and well, and they interpreted this as evidence of their humanity. A Bayreuth worker commented: "Our propaganda always represents the Russians as unthinking and stupid. I have found here just the opposite. The Russians think while they work and do not at all appear to be so stupid."[96] The Russians and Poles had loved ones, and these familial ties were *recognized* and fundamentally accorded respect by Germans. A Security Service report from Liegnitz, after giving some examples, concluded that "the population thinks of the Bolsheviks' sense of family the opposite of what our propaganda conveys. The Russians are very worried about their family members, and there exists among them an ordered family life. They visit one another on every occasion. There are strong ties among parents, children, and grandparents."[97] Such eye-opening realizations led Germans to express themselves and act in ways that departed from, and indicated a concomitant reassessment of their general preexisting cultural beliefs about *these* "subhumans."[98] Many Germans recognized Russians, not to mention Poles and other foreigners, as being valuable and dignified workers. Frequent love affairs developed between Germans and foreign workers. In 1942 and 1943, close to five thousand Germans were arrested per month for forbidden relations with foreigners. Although there was assiduous enforcement of the prohibition backed up by draconian penalties, this willful, massive violation of the racial law occurred.[99] The Germans allowed foreign workers to write letters home, and permitted many to take vacations. They often heeded the workers' complaints, and German industrialists lobbied for better provisions for them with a vigor and a frame of reference that they did not display for Jews.[100] Polish workers who became pregnant were not killed by the Germans, as Jewish women typically were, but were sent home by the sixth month, as were the physically and mentally ill.[101] Most significant, on a broad scale, relations developed between Germans and their non-German workers that, though remaining a relationship of dominance, were based on many Germans' recognition of their common humanity and were sometimes even characterized by friendliness.[102] This almost never happened between Germans and Jews.

Overall, although Germans' treatment of foreign workers was deplorable, and shows how thoroughly racist a good part of the German people were,[103] their treatment of foreign workers was still incommensurately better than that of Jews. So while the regime was imploring German peasants to cease letting their foreign workers eat with them at the same table and attend their festive occasions, it was making Germany *judenrein*, to the celebration of some of the "cleansed" communities, and it was "quarantining" Jews in ghettos as "immune bacillus-carrier[s] of the plagues."[104] In each case, action dovetailed with belief.[105]

Germans were murderous and cruel towards Jewish workers, and murderous and cruel in ways that they reserved especially for Jews. Higher death rates, lower rations, more brutality and symbolic degradation, a unique inability to alter beliefs—all of the differences that existed in camps—were the lot of Jews compared to other subject peoples employed in work. Although Germans were generally brutal and murderous in the use of other peoples (the level of cruelty, violence, and killing far outstripped that of many slave societies), their policies for non-Jews were guided much more by calculations of material rationality. By the beginning of 1943, at the latest, the Germans' use of most non-Jewish foreign labor was organized according to reasonably rational economic principles.[106] Germans treated non-Jews well enough that their productivity levels were respectable, particularly after the public education campaigns designed to temper the hatred of the populace. The following figures from the Rhineland and Westphalia represent the average productivity of different peoples as a percentage of German workers in similar jobs:[107]

Easterners	80–100%
Eastern women	50–75%
compared to German women	90–100%
Poles	60–80%
Belgians	80–100%
Dutch	60–80%
Italians, Yugoslavians, and Croats	70–80%
POWs in mining	50%
POWs in metal industries	70%

The kind of rational labor use that produced this work was not adopted for Jews, except on a small scale in local circumstances. And these differences in the treatment of Jews and non-Jews in work existed throughout the German hierarchy, from the level of high policy, to the middle-level executors of its policies, to ordinary Germans whose workaday existence brought them into contact with the various subject peoples, and who, in the accumulation of their discrete actions, greatly molded the character of the subject peoples' lives. Had the Germans been guided to any significant degree by considerations of economic rationality, then their use of Jewish labor power—both the overall policies and the personalized treatment—would have been at least as rational as their use of Polish labor power,[108] not to mention French, Dutch, or even German. The discriminating actions of Germans of all stations and from all walks of life reinforce the already considerable evidence that they viewed and treated the Jews as beings apart, as beings—whatever else was to be done with and to them—ultimately fit only to suffer and die.

12

WORK AND DEATH

W HY DID THE GERMANS persist in the staggering economic irrationality of destroying a talented, unusually productive labor
force? Why did they willfully create debilitating conditions and
treat the Jews so cruelly when they put them to "work"? What kind of political and social context and in light of what cognitive framework did the Germans' treatment of Jewish labor power *make sense* to them?

The Germans' essential failure to engage untapped Jewish labor power
throughout Europe and their treatment of Jewish "workers" within institutions of "work," such as Majdanek, Lipowa, the *Flughafenlager,* and many
other camps, provide an empirical starting point for answering these questions. Together, they indicate that the central objective features of Jewish
"work" were pathological, a stark departure from the character of normal
work:

1. The potential usefulness of Jewish work was essentially disregarded in the
   Germans' treatment of Jews. The Germans demonstrated this again and
   again by their willingness to kill the Jews of entire communities and work
   installations, and thus to put a sudden end to irreplaceable and essential production.
2. Even when Jews were "working," the "work" was characterized by the Germans' systematic underutilization of their productive abilities: Germans
   wrested Jews away from productive machinery and locations and sent them
   to other locations without similar facilities, so that they typically worked

with primitive or decrepit equipment. Jews were, moreover, often assigned jobs that did not match their skills. The consequence of this was that,

3. Jewish "work" was characterized by abysmal productivity, on two different levels: the overall productivity of Jews in Europe, and the productivity of a given work force in a particular location.

4. Jewish "work" had at least some purely "retributive" aspect (aside from its debilitating consequences), as the phenomenon of non-instrumental labor indicates.

5. Jewish "work" was characterized above all by the Germans' severe debilitation of the Jews. The Germans drove them at an inhuman, physically unsustainable pace. This, together with woefully inadequate nourishment and purposely unhygienic conditions, plunged the Jews into a catastrophic state of health.

6. Jewish "work" was characterized by its fatal consequences. The only reason that more Jews did not drop dead from starvation, physical exhaustion, and disease was that the Germans regularly killed them shortly before their health had reached the bottom of its free fall. The debilitation of the Jewish workers moved them well along on the road to death. While the Jews were on the road to death, the Germans exploited them for some production and for deriving various kinds of psychological gratification. All kinds of imagined and real infractions (against the inhuman camp order) provided occasions for Germans to kill Jews.

7. Jewish "work" was characterized by the continual cruelty of the German personnel.

8. Though not at all times or in every feature, Jewish "work" in its essence was fundamentally, qualitatively different from the work of non-Jewish subject peoples.

In no sense did Germans treat Jewish "workers" in keeping with the common understanding of what a "worker" is, or even in keeping with the common understanding of what a "slave" is. The Germans did not use Jews rationally in production, did not value and husband their productive capacities, and forbade them to reproduce.[1] Within a society, both workers and slaves are evaluated by what they produce through work. The Jews were not; their product was irrelevant to their fate, except possibly in the very short term. The Germans treated Jews like criminals condemned to death, who were forced to break a few stones before their date with the gallows. For workers and slaves, work is a means to life and reproduction (and for workers, a source of dignity). For Jews, "work" was a means to death. Their fate, like that of condemned criminals, was sealed. In fact, they were worse off than mere criminals, for their captors felt the compulsion to be cruel to them.

Objectively, Jewish "work" during the Nazi period was a gross violation of rational notions and forms of work—without parallel in the history of modern industrial society, and indeed with few parallels even in slave societies. It was a constituent part of the destructive enterprise. Principally, Jewish "work" was destruction itself.

WHAT, THEN, were the cognitive framework, the assumptions, the general political and social context in which work could take on the character of destruction and develop the various central, aberrant features that marked Jewish work? In other words, what was the Germans' *subjective* conception, of Jews and of their fate, that induced them to turn work—a normally instrumental activity of efficient and rational production—into destruction, and led them, even in the workplace, to treat Jews not like workers, but worse than criminals condemned to death?

This metamorphosis of the meaning and practice of work depended upon the Germans' antisemitic cognitive framework, the most important element of which was that Jewish lives were "lives unworthy of living." They were socially dead beings who could justly be killed in the dual sense that it was morally correct and *de facto* legally allowable. Because of the Jews' putatively satanic nature, not only were the Jews not to be accorded the most minimal rights that safeguard life, but their deaths were also seen as morally laudable. This understanding existed within the camp system, including the ghettos, among those supervising Jewish "work" *even before the explicit policy of genocide had begun.* When the German leadership decided upon genocide and the various institutions and its members began to carry out the policy, this existing annihilationist cultural orientation, which had roughly corresponded to implied and vague official policies, came to mesh perfectly with the new policy of total extermination. In fact, the new policy transformed the moral valuation of causing Jewish deaths through "work" from a non-obligatory positive occurrence to a moral norm. The killing of Jews, previously but a good deed, now took on an urgent quality.

Without this knowledge, without the moral approbation bestowed upon killing Jews, the Germans' general debilitation of a work force, the individual German's arbitrary killings of individual Jews, and the astronomical death rates within work camps could not have occurred and would not have been tolerated at all levels of administrative oversight. Without this orientation, the destruction of desperately needed laborers and their desperately needed production would otherwise simply not have made sense to the perpetrators.

A second element of the subjective framework was that the Jews must suffer. It was not just that Jews had "lives unworthy of living," and were therefore fit to die. While alive, they also had to be punished and degraded, so the practice of degrading and inflicting pain upon Jews acquired a normative force. The unwritten commandment to beat Jews, to mock them, to make their lives miserable was at the root of the Germans' pervasive cruelty in "work" camps. In the "work" camps, the Germans debased and inflicted pain upon Jews with a regularity calculated not just to cripple their bodies but also to plunge them into a state of perpetual terror. And it was not merely the cruelties of individual Germans or the collective cruelties of all the individuals; Jewish suffering was woven into the fabric of camp life, from the lack of sewage and water, to the structurally induced beatings for the inevitably below-par work, to the constant fear of "selections."

The assumption that the Jews must suffer was a cognitive prerequisite for the incessant, economically irrational cruelty (both of the debilitating camp conditions and of the individual perpetrators) that Germans visited upon Jewish workers. It should be underscored, when considering the cognitive framework that shaped the Germans' actions, that whenever individual Germans killed or were cruel to Jews without orders, the acts were *voluntaristic*. Since the perpetration of suffering was action that was, with some exceptions, common to the entire German personnel of these camps (such as the rampant, persistent floggings), a generally shared, though uncodified, understanding among the Germans appears to have been that the production of Jewish misery was an essential feature of their jobs. Without a subjective attitude that placed premium value upon Jewish suffering, the actions that produced not only the suffering but also considerable economic self-injury neither would have made sense to the actors nor would have been undertaken by them. It would also never have been tolerated, let alone institutionally promoted. The obvious joy and the frequent spirit of inventiveness with which Germans inflicted suffering, psychological and physical, upon the Jews was yet another ideologically produced perversion of the role of foreman.

A third element in the cognitive framework, related to the second, was the belief that Jews were parasitic work shirkers. In the Germans' minds, to compel Jews to do manual work, or indeed any honest work, was to make them suffer, because it was antithetical to their natures. This element was less influential than the others in shaping the Germans' *general* treatment of the Jews, though it governed many particular instances of German action. So it deserves special mention for two reasons. Germans often put the Jews to "work" in non-instrumental labor. When analyzing the sources of Germans' treatment of Jews as "workers," this important and telling phenomenon, unlike the other forms of cruelty, cannot be adequately explained by the belief of Germans that the Jews must suffer. Also, in order to understand the ways in which Germans talked about Jewish "work," which, in turn, influenced how they treated Jewish workers, the notion, ingrained in German culture, that Jews do not work must be at the center of the analysis.

The final relevant element of the cognitive framework was that economically rational means of treating Jewish workers would occur only within the local context of a particular camp or workshop, and even then could be sub-ordinated to the other elements. That is to say that within the parameters set by grossly economically irrational policies affecting the Jewish work force of Europe (general extermination, general debilitation, general degradation), particular installations, with all of their own particular irrationalities, might nonetheless see Germans employ Jews according to some seemingly rational economic criteria. But these kinds of economies failed to take precedence over the exterminationist drive and urges, or over the general need to make Jews exist in misery. The brush factory of the *Flughafenlager*'s Osti enter-prises is a good example of this kind of local productive rationality. The Ger-mans wrested the Jews from any normal production environment. The machinery that the Jews had been using had been destroyed or lay elsewhere. The Jews had hardly any tools at their disposal. So the Germans "worked" them at a brutal pace. Knowing that the Jews were going to die and failing to have sufficient plant and machinery for normal production methods made it sensible, made it locally "rational," for Germans to "work" the "workers," figuratively and literally, to death.

Germans often did pursue increased production and profit under these, from an economic perspective, irrational conditions of Jewish labor employ-ment. However, this local rationality could not supersede in importance, could not take priority over, extermination and Jewish suffering more than on a temporary basis.[2] As Oswald Pohl, the man in charge of all concentration camp labor, expressed it to Himmler in a classic euphemistic formulation of the period, "the able-bodied Jews, destined for eastward migration [extermi-nation] must therefore interrupt their journey and do armaments labor."[3] The journey would then continue. This knowledge—namely that a program of extermination was the political and social context for the employment of Jews—was the single most important condition for this kind of brutal, nor-mally irrational treatment of "workers" to gain the appearance of economic rationality to local German administrators, and for them to treat these "work-ers" in this way. Since the Germans "worked" Jews to death when they could not employ them in gainful production, it is no surprise that they would do the same when using them in production.

The framework that made the Germans' overall utilization of Jewish labor power and their general treatment of Jewish workers intelligible to *Ger-mans* was thus structured by the iron principles of extermination and immis-eration, and adorned by the notions that Jews must labor in some way and that Germany might exploit them economically before they die.[4] This cogni-tive framework, this model of Jewish "work," and only this one, accounts for the broad pattern of German action. Only within the general parameters of treatment derived from the principles of extermination and immiseration could some considerations of economic rationality be followed—and only for a limited time. The substance, moreover, of the concrete policies that came to be situationally rational within the thoroughly economically irrational over-all context—such as a health-destroying pace of "work" under primitive con-ditions of production, for workers that did not need to be kept alive and, in fact, were destined to die soon anyway—turned out, principally, to further the exterminationist program itself. The assumption of extermination and immiseration transformed economic production itself into the handmaiden of the genocidal destruction of the workers. Even the profit sheets of partic-ular enterprises do not tell a story of economic rationality; they hide the gar-gantuan hidden economic cost of the German exterminationist policies. Getting a young, healthy, skilled worker to weave the rope and build the gal-lows (with bloodied, swollen, stiffened hands and substandard tools) from which he will hang can be seen as an economically rational use of his labor power only by those who want him to hang and who do not care about the loss of his valuable productivity.

As so many of the Germans' statements make clear, it cannot be doubted that they understood that their policies were, economically, catastrophically self-injurious, harming above all the war effort. Arguments, when they were offered, against killing the Jews typically invoked a utilitarian calculus, and not a moral one. As an armaments inspector in Ukraine wrote in a December 1941 report: "Who in all the world is then supposed to produce economic val-ues here?" But this sort of perspective, even when it was expressed, failed to persuade minds in the grip of the genocidal eliminationist antisemitism, for, as the report itself noted when discussing the "150,000 to 200,000 Jews" whom the Germans had already killed in the region, the policy towards the Jews was "obviously . . . based on the ideological theories as a matter of prin-ciple."[5] According to the guiding values, represented at all levels of the Ger-man institutions which regulated Jewish labor, economic rationality was a consideration, but ultimately a subsidiary one.

THE REAL MEANING of Jewish "work" was announced by Heydrich when, at the Wannsee Conference of January 20, 1942, he informed the assembled representatives of the various ministries and bureaucracies of their respective responsibilities in the "Final Solution of the Jewish Problem," which was al-ready under way: "The Jews will be conscripted for labor . . . and undoubt-edly a large number of them will drop out through natural wastage." The rest would be killed.[6] At this meeting Heydrich communicated the most funda-mental of the alterations in the cognitive framework that would be applied and lend meaning to the word "work" when employed for Jews. It was this meeting which, in a sense, formalized the meaning of Jewish "work" within the Nazi German empire as a means of destruction, as a partial synonym for killing. It was at this meeting that representatives of most of the major institutions handling Jews and Jewish "work" were instructed about what that "work" should above all accomplish. Thus, Himmler concluded his October 1942 order for the temporary concentration of the Jews of the Warsaw and Lublin regions in a "few large concentration camp factories" by stating: "Of course, there too, the Jews shall some day disappear in accordance with the Führer's wishes."[7] Of course. It was *selbstverständlich*.

The phenomenon of Jewish "work" was such a triumph of politics and ideology over economic self-interest not only because the Germans killed irreplaceable workers, but also in the more profound sense that even when they were not killing them, Germans, owing to the character of their racial anti-semitism, had great difficulties in employing Jews rationally in the economy. The words and deeds of Heydrich, Himmler, and countless others reveal the real relationship between Jewish "work" and Jewish death in Germany. Killing Jews did not merely take priority over putting them to work. Work put into motion beings whom the Germans themselves had already condemned to death, socially dead beings with a temporary lease on socially dead life. In its essence, Jewish "work" was not work in any ordinary sense of "work," but a suspended form of death—in other words, it was death itself.

PART V

Death Marches:
To the Final Days

The hearts of men, they must perforce have melted,
And barbarism itself have pitied him.
WILLIAM SHAKESPEARE, *RICHARD II*

13

THE DEADLY WAY

THE LONG-DISTANCE marching of Jews and other victims began (as early as late 1939 and ended only a day or two after the war had formally come to an end. These marches were appropriately dubbed by the victims "death marches" (*Todesmärsche*).[1] Most such marches took place in the last year, particularly in the last half year, of Nazi German suzerainty. For this and other reasons, this final phase of marches is the focus of this chapter.

The marches can be broken up into three distinct periods. The first period, in which few marches occurred, extends from the onset of the war to the beginning of the Germans' systematic extermination of the Jews in June 1941. The second covers the years of extermination until the summer of 1944. The third covers the time of the Reich's denouement, when its doom was understood to be near, when all that the Germans could do was to hold on and stave off the end for a while longer, and when the extermination program was winding down.[2]

The logic behind this periodization of death marches is simple. The first period preceded the formal policy of extermination. It should therefore have produced few deaths when Jews were marching—that is, had the Germans overseeing the marches not themselves been animated by a set of beliefs that made them desire the Jews' deaths. The second period coincides with the time of full-scale extermination, when killing Jews on the march would have been but a natural component of genocidal slaughter. In light of the prevailing norms and treatment of Jews during this time of feverish killing, marches, like the camps, would likely have been replete with cruelty and death. The third span constitutes a distinct historical time, when the Germans' prospects had become bleak, rendering their efforts vain. Germany and Germans were facing a new, different mix of considerations, and the Nazi regime itself began to practice different politics. Moreover, the institutions and locales of extermination underwent significant change; the death camps had been or were being shut down, and in the German-controlled areas, only remnants of European Jewry survived—and they in skeletal condition. It is not at all clear how the circumstances of this period would have affected the Germans' victims, given the acute labor shortage that the German economy faced, and given the need for local German commanders and their subordinates to think about their own futures in the coming, yet undefined new order, where proof of their decent treatment of their prisoners might buy them some protection, might save their hides. Because the extermination camps had been closed down, because the Nazi era was drawing to a close, the actions of the Germans might not have been easily predicted: Would the marches be used as means to continue the camps' genocidal work, or would a more humane policy be instituted, if not from above, then from below?

In the three periods of death marches, the institution of the march itself does not change significantly. Its structure remains more or less the same, with Jews and other peoples marching through the countryside from one place to another, guarded by a contingent of Germans, sometimes supplemented by non-German auxiliaries. Although the marches were embedded in distinctly different policy environments regarding the Jews, the character of the marches, namely how the Germans treated the Jews, varied only somewhat with the changing circumstances and policies of each period. Indeed, the marches in the different periods look remarkably alike; they share the same essential lethal character.[3]

The death marches were the ambulatory analogue to the cattle car. Or, conversely, the cattle car was the rolling equivalent of the death march. The cattle car presaged the nature of the final death marches. The Germans showed no concern on either one for the Jews' comfort, dignity, or even for keeping them alive. The Germans let the cars sit sometimes for days, without allowing the Jews out, even though this could easily have been done. They afforded the Jews no food, no water, no latrines, hardly enough air-holes, not even enough room to sit down. During the Nazi period, Germans structured different forms of the "normal" mass transportation for Jews in the same way.

During the third and most significant death march period, unlike in the first two periods, the Germans did not decide, according to their own autonomous designs, when to transport and kill Jews and non-Jews. Rather, the marches commenced and proliferated because approaching enemy armies threatened to overrun the institutions housing Jews and other prisoners. The

Germans found themselves in the position of either having to move the prisoners or losing them. They were no longer the logistical masters of events. This period itself should be seen as having had three different phases. The first began in the summer of 1944, when the Soviet army was nearing the camps in the western part of the Soviet Union and eastern Poland. The second phase of marches covered January to March 1945, when the great westward migration back to Germany of camp prisoners was under way, when the prisoners and German guards were returning to the bosom of their respective dispensations. Auschwitz, Gross-Rosen, and other large camp complexes in western Poland and eastern Germany were emptied of their surviving prisoners, who trudged (and sometimes rode) through the frozen countryside to some new hellish holding pen temporarily beyond the Allies' reach. The third

The Red Army Advance and the Auschwitz Region Evacuations of January 18, 1945

0 miles 120
0 kilometers 200

Baltic Sea

North Sea

DENMARK
Rostock
Neuengamme
Hamburg
GERMANY (East)
Bremen
Bergen-Belsen
Ravensbrück
Sachsenhausen
Hannover
Salzwedel
Gardelegen
Berlin
GERMANY (West)
Dora-Mittelbau
Elbe
Nordhausen
Leipzig
Cologne
Buchenwald
Rhemsdorf
Dresden
Gross Rosen
Ohrdruf
Wroclaw (Breslau)
Fulda
Frankfurt
Flossenbürg
Prague
Nürnberg
Plzeň
CZECHOSLOVAKIA
FRANCE
Schömberg
Stuttgart
French Forces
Schörzingen
Dachau
Spaichingen
Gusen
Mauthausen
Tuttlingen
Munich
Gunskirchen
Zürich
Schlier
Ebensee
Salzburg
Vienna
SWITZERLAND
AUSTRIA
HUNGARY

Danzig
Stutthof

POLAND

Poznań
Warsaw

Soviet Forces on
Jan. 23, 1945

Częstochowa
6,000 Evacuated

Cracow

Loslau

4,200 Shot
Jan. 20
Birkenau

Auschwitz
98,000 Evacuated

Danube

Budapest

NETHERLANDS
BELGIUM
U.S. and British Forces
Rhine

□ camps
Borders are postwar, 1945.

© Mark Stein Studios, 1995

phase began in March 1945 and ended with the war. During this phase—when virtually no one could believe any longer that the war would still be won—the Germans shuffled prisoners around Germany aimlessly, from place to place to place. The Germans guarding them were not returning homeward (and therefore had no incentive to take part in the journey), as they had been during the second phase's return to Germany from Poland. They could not have believed that keeping the prisoners one step ahead of the Allies served any sensible purpose.

The various estimates about the death rates and the total number of deaths during the third period's death marches suggest that between one-third and one-half of the 750,000 current inmates of the formal concentration camp—between 250,000 and 375,000 people—fell victim to them.[4] Many of these were not Jews, since not only Jews inhabited the concentration camp system.[5] Nevertheless, the evidence suggests that the mortality rate of Jews in this final period of destruction was, as in the camps themselves, significantly higher than that of non-Jews. Jews were generally in worse health before setting out on the marches, so under comparable conditions of privation they would have undoubtedly died from malnutrition, wounds, exhaustion, exposure, and disease at a faster rate than non-Jews. The Germans also regularly treated Jews worse than non-Jews and massacred Jews with far greater frequency. Much of this became known to the world only in the final days of the war, which is when one march came to an end near the border between southern Germany and Czechoslovakia.

ON MAY 7, 1945, a captain of the 5th Medical Battalion, 5th Infantry Division of the U.S. Army, received orders to take along six men for the delousing of a group of displaced persons who, it was suspected, might also need medical care. Two days later, the captain described in oral testimony to the American officer investigating the case what he had discovered after his arrival in Volary, Czechoslovakia:

> I contacted Captain Wi. at Lohora and drove to Volary where I was told a group of emaciated, eachetic [sic], and debili[t]ated women were being brought to a school house, used as a hospital for treatment, from an old barn, which was a short distance away. . . . At the barn I met Capt. Wa. and asked him what he had. He replied that he had a group of 118 Jewish women and said that it was the most horrible sight he ever laid eyes on. He asked that I go into this barn and look the situation over and this I did. The barn was a one story wooden shack. The interior was extremely dark and filled with filth of all sorts. My first glance at these individuals was one of extreme shock not ever believing that a human being can be degraded, can be

starved, can be so skinny and even live under such circumstances. My view at this time was very cursory in nature. What I ultimately did see about this small room was like mice on top of one another to[o] weak to as much as raise an arm. In addition to their clothes being dirty, worn out, ill fitting, tattered and torn they were covered for the most part with human stool which was spread for the most part all over the floor. The explanation for this was that these women had severe diarrhea with an evacuation about every two to five minutes. They were too weak to walk to evacuate their bowels. One thing that surprised me when I entered this barn is that I thought that we had a group of old men lying and spread about and would at this time have judged that their ages ranged between fifty and sixty years. I was surprised and shocked when I asked one of these girls how old she was and she said seventeen, when to me she appeared to be no less than fifty. I then returned to the Ortslazarett [hospital] in Volary and at this time was given complete charge of the evacuation, housing, feeding and treatment of these individuals from the old barn to the Ortslazarett and during their stay in the Ortslazarett. The hospital was made ready to receive these patients immediately when these patients arrived at the hospital and were for the most part litter cases. I would estimate about seventy-five per cent had to be carried in by litters. The other twenty-five per cent were able with the help of others to drag their weary bodies from the shack to the ambulance into the hospital. Our first task was to get these women into something that resembled a bed and to begin the immediate life-saving measures which at this time amounted to for the most part intravenous administration of whole blood, intravenous administration of plasma and in a few of the more healthy ones the introduction of intravenous fluids. During this initial period of treatment the patients were critically ill for the most part and still are today two days later. As a medical officer of the Army of the United States it is my opinion that at least fifty per cent of these 118 women would have died within twenty-four hours were they not located and given the best of care. Upon examining these patients I found that they suffered from the following symptoms and diseases; 1. extreme malnutrition 2. vitamin deficiency diseases were present in ninety percent of these 118 women 3. for the most part all of their feet were edemat[o]us with a four plus pitting edema 4. severe frostbite of the toes with dry gangerine [*sic*] present; in one patient in particular this gangerine extents [*sic*] to the legs bi-laterally which will undoubtedly necessitate a bi-lateral amputation in the lower one-third of the legs in the very near future. A good percentage of these women have severe decubitious ulcers. Approximately fifty percent have severe persistent productive coughs with underlined pulmonary pathology. Approximately ten percent of these women have been wounded by shell fragments at a place near here from one to two weeks ago and have never received any treatment for these wounds. The wounds at the present time are angry looking, very possibly with localized gangerine [*sic*] in many cases. At the hospital it was noted that many of these with diarrhea were associated with melena and

high temperatures. During the first few hours after admit[t]ing these patients to the hospital two died. Within the next forty-eight hours one more
died. At the present time many are critically ill and offer a poor prognosis.[6]

These Jewish women were survivors of a death march that had just three
weeks earlier departed the Helmbrechts camp, which followed an earlier death
march that had brought them from the Schlesiersee camp to Helmbrechts.[7]
These women were among the lucky ones, if they can be called lucky, for many
of their compatriots did not live to see liberation. The events and treatment
that plunged these women into a condition so abysmal that a physician found
it difficult to believe that bodily organs could continue to function constituted
an unsurprising denouement of the Germans' war against the Jews.

AMONG THE DEATH marches that moved Jews westward during January
1945 were those that emptied the satellite camps of the Gross-Rosen camp.
Schlesiersee, one of the four Gross-Rosen satellite camps for women erected
in October and November 1944 along the northeast border of Lower Silesia,
was a small camp housing about one thousand Jewish women who, like the
prisoners of the other three, had come from Auschwitz. The largest group
among them was from Hungary and the Hungarian-speaking border regions
of Czechoslovakia. The next largest group was from Poland. All of the women
were young.[8] The main work that they performed while in Schlesiersee was
the digging of anti-tank ditches. The conditions were cruel: "During our stay
in this camp, we had to dig anti-tank ditches in freezing weather and while
standing in deep snow. The legs of many of the girls became frozen, since we
had received no shoes and many were barefoot."[9] The cruelty of Schlesiersee
was not confined to the women's exposure to the elements while at work. The
guards whipped them for attempting to keep themselves a little warmer.

> It was bitter cold at Schlesiersee and we were only lightly dressed; some of
> the women took the only blanket they possessed and took them with them
> to work. Three or four times, all women who returned from work were in-
> spected. All those who had wrapped themselves in their blankets were pun-
> ished with twenty-five whip lashes. I myself saw this punishment. The
> women with whom I worked together once received 30 of this kind of pun-
> ishment. We were as a rule also beaten if our clothes were somewhat moist
> or dirty. At our work it was practically impossible to avoid this; for we had
> to dig anti-tank ditches in the snow.[10]

This is a classical example of, first, the priority given by Germans at all institutional levels to inflicting suffering upon Jews over getting Jews to work pro-

ductively and, second, of the brutality which the Germans structured into the pattern of Jewish existence. As this survivor relates, the Germans set the Jews to a task, which inevitably soiled them, for which they were as a rule whipped, which undoubtedly further impaired their productivity. Thus, when the Jews did their assigned work, the Germans, moved by their curious logic, beat them for doing it.

With the approach of the eastern front, the Germans evacuated the camp, probably on January 20.[11] This was not the first death march for these women, who had already survived the one that had brought them there from Auschwitz. Of the approximately 970 Jewish women who began the Schlesiersee evacuation march, lasting eight or nine days and covering only sixty miles along their circuitous route to Grünberg, about 150 died along the way. Of these, perhaps 20 fell dead from starvation and exhaustion, which is not surprising given the debilitation that they had suffered at Auschwitz and Schlesiersee. The other 130 who did not survive the march were shot by the Germans along the way. On this march, their German keepers immediately killed anyone who was too exhausted to carry on.[12] A Polish laborer, who had worked for a German farmer since 1940, was a witness to one mass execution. The guards of the march, who he says were older German army soldiers— not SS men, not zealous young Nazis—ordered the villagers to put some horse-drawn carts at their disposal. This Polish witness drove one of them: "In front of the school sat totally exhausted women. They were dressed in rags, most of them without shoes, their heads were covered with blankets. . . . [The soldiers] dragged them from their carts, mostly by the hair, while shooting constantly."[13]

The Grünberg camp was founded in either 1941 or 1942 as a forced labor camp for Jewish women. It was situated southwest of Breslau in today's Poland, near the city of Grünberg, and became a satellite camp of Gross-Rosen in the middle of 1944. Little more is known of it. In the summer of 1944 its population was approximately 900 Jewish women aged sixteen to thirty, many of whom came from the eastern part of Upper Silesia. The women labored primarily in a private German textile firm that was located near the camp. The arrival of the death march from Schlesiersee momentarily doubled Grünberg's population to around 1,800. With the Red Army approaching, the camp had to be evacuated immediately.[14] So, having had hardly a chance to catch their breath, the arrivals from Schlesiersee, now accompanied by their fellow sufferers from Grünberg, set off again only a day or two later, on January 29, 1945. The Germans divided the prisoners into two groups with different destinations. One group of guards set off with between 1,000 and 1,100 prisoners for Helmbrechts, a satellite camp of Flossenbürg in the Upper Franconia region of Bavaria, while another contingent of Germans headed with the remaining prisoners for Bergen-Belsen, north of Hannover.[15] One survivor recalls an aspect of the latter march: "On the way many collapsed from exhaustion, or in the morning could not rise any more. These prisoners were killed by their guards on the spot. . . . In our group rode also a horse-drawn cart. During the journey weak prisoners were put on the horse-drawn cart. The half-dead were later driven to the forest and there shot. Every time a cart became full, it was diverted into the forest. According to my estimate only about 30% of our group reached Bergen-Belsen."[16] The march to Bergen-Belsen, a distance of over 250 miles as the crow flies, lasted one month. The prisoners covered almost the entire distance on foot, sleeping mainly in unheated barns. Along the way, a large though indeterminate number of prisoners died or were shot by the Germans.[17]

Upon departing Grünberg, the Germans piled the sickest Jews on a horse-drawn cart and assigned them to the group heading to Helmbrechts. The others walked. The Grünberg prisoners were in better condition than the contingent which had begun the odyssey in Schlesiersee. The Schlesiersee women, in addition to their grave physical debilitation, lacked the most essential gear: "Almost all of us had no decent footwear; a great number had to walk barefoot or had their feet wrapped in rags. During the time of the march, the ground was throughout covered with snow."[18] Some trudged along barefoot.[19] The march to Helmbrechts covered about three hundred miles. It was the middle of the winter.

Of the 1,000 to 1,100 who set out on this march, 621 arrived in Helmbrechts almost five weeks later. The Germans had deposited around 230, including the sick, at other camps, and a few had escaped. Between 150 and 250 women did not survive the journey,[20] in part because of the brutal conditions: "After several days without food or drink—we spent the nights outdoors in the snow, the conditions were extremely bad—many died from exhaustion. Every morning when we got up, many remained lying lifeless on the ground."[21] Yet most of those who perished appear to have been shot by the Germans, often for having lagged behind. The Germans shot fifty women during one massacre.[22] In addition to the killings, this death march had the usual assortment of German violence and torment: brutal beatings, inadequate food, appalling clothing and shelter, and general terror.

Upon arriving in Helmbrechts on March 6, just two months before the Germans' total military collapse and unconditional surrender, the 621 Jewish women were in terrible general health. Dysentery afflicted many of them, as did frostbite. Some had come down with noma, a gangrene condition which produces a grisly condition and appearance. The mouth's mucous membrane as well as the flesh of the cheeks decay to the point where the jawbones become exposed and visible.[23]

The five weeks that these Jewish women spent in Helmbrechts before embarking on yet another death march were weeks of continuing privation and suffering. In the most significant ways—namely in matters pertaining to survival—their German captors treated them differently from the non-Jewish prisoners whose arrival in the camp predated theirs.

THE HELMBRECHTS CAMP, a satellite camp (*Aussenlager*) of the Flossen-bürg camp, was founded in the summer of 1944. The town of Helmbrechts is about ten miles southwest of Hof in Upper Franconia, very close to the point of intersection between Czechoslovakia and what was to become East Germany and West Germany. The camp itself was not very large, and it was situated on a main street at the edge of the town, affording the townspeople—like so many others throughout Germany—opportunities to survey what was taking place inside. It had eleven single-story wooden buildings. The four that served as barracks for the prisoners were surrounded by barbed wire, which was not electrified.[24]

The camp's contingent of guards was small. Fifty-four are known to have served in Helmbrechts. They arrived at different times, often in the company of new prisoners, and appear by and large to have remained at the camp until its end, departing along with the death march. The guards were split evenly by sex: twenty-seven men and twenty-seven women. The men had virtually no contact with the Jewish prisoners, since as a rule they remained outside the prisoner compound, which the Jewish prisoners, unlike the non-Jewish prisoners, never left. The male guards' main task was to accompany the non-Jewish prisoners to work. The women guards were the mistresses of the prisoners' camp section. They determined the quality of daily life within the camp, especially for the Jewish prisoners, who were under their gaze twenty-four hours a day. The camp's commander was a man, Alois Dörr. The women personnel had their own head guard, who was subordinate to Dörr.

Little is known of the guards' biographies. Of the fifty-four guards, only two have existing personnel files, and their autobiographical reporting in postwar legal testimony is meager. On the face of it, they should not have been a particularly threatening lot—by German standards. The twenty-seven male guards came from two groups. The larger consisted of older Germans who were no longer fit for military service and who generally had no SS or Nazi Party affiliation. The smaller was made up of younger ethnic Germans (about eight to ten) from eastern Europe, at least three of whom had either joined or been drafted into SS fighting units. A few of the men seem to have been veterans of the camp system. The birthdays of twenty guards are known. Their mean age was a ripe forty-two and a half years in December

1944. The oldest man serving in the camp was almost fifty-five. Seven of the twenty, fully 35 percent, were in their fifties, and twelve of them, namely 60 percent, were over forty. Only three of them were younger than thirty, the youngest being twenty years old. Their paths to becoming Helmbrechts' jailers were variable and haphazard, by no means suggesting a selection process based on any criteria relevant to the guarding, torturing, and killing of Germany's designated enemies, particularly its Jewish ones. Of the twenty-seven men known to have served in the camp, two—the commander and one other—had SS membership. These two and one other were the only members of the Nazi Party.[25] By institutional affiliation, therefore, they were almost completely a non-Nazi group.

Hartmuth Reich, born in 1900 and a World War I veteran, explains how he and a comrade made it to Helmbrechts. As the father of many children, he received a military deferment until 1944, when, Germany's situation becoming more desperate, he was drafted into a ranger unit and received brief military training in Paris. For his and his wife's taste, he was too far away from home: "At the various requests of my wife, I was ordered back to Würzburg in August 1944 and remained there until shortly before Christmas." It is worth noting that his wife tried to get him a transfer and was eventually successful. "In Würzburg I became acquainted with my compatriot from Hof, Eberhard Vogel. He too was the father of many children." Together, they were sent to the Sachsenhausen camp. In January 1945, a group of one hundred rangers, men likely to have been of similar military bearing as Reich, were transferred to Flossenbürg in order, as he tells it, to guard prisoners who were being sent out to work. They stayed there until sometime between the middle of February and March. "In order to be nearer to our families, we volunteered for the satellite camp, Helmbrechts." Reich belonged neither to the Nazi Party nor to the SS.[26]

A second path to Helmbrechts began in Romania, the home of Martin Wirth, who at the age of twenty was the youngest male guard in the camp. In 1943, Wirth, after brief military training, was drafted into the SS fighting division "Prinz-Eugen." Because of a heart condition, he was declared unfit for combat and was therefore given guard duty. In the summer of 1944, he was sent to Flossenbürg, and a few months later to Helmbrechts. Initially meant to be a combat soldier—in an SS division that functioned not much differently than an army division—this ethnic German was set, owing to a fortuitous physical disability, on a road he likely never imagined taking, and did not choose, yet would end up relishing.[27]

Another guard's career path landing him at Helmbrechts hardly suggests that he was a man who sought a position in the service of Nazism's most sensitive ideological enterprise, or who was cut from an ideological warrior's cloth. Born in Cologne in 1905, Gerhard Hauer was called up to the army in 1940, only to be released after eight weeks owing to a heart condition. Neither a Party nor an SS member, he worked, subsequent to his return to civilian life, first for a food wholesaler, then, after the firm was destroyed in an air raid, for an agricultural cooperative, and then in a factory. In February 1944 he was recalled to the army, and completed an eight-week training course in the Netherlands, followed by a stint stationed in Münster. He was then transferred to Lublin, where he underwent further military training. With the approach of the Red Army, he was assigned to the evacuation of a nearby camp for women. He and thirty to forty other soldiers brought some of the women to Flossenbürg, where for three or four weeks he supervised work commandos. Hauer and a few other soldiers were then sent to Helmbrechts; they were the first male guards of the camp.[28]

The biographies of these men were typical for the male guards in Helmbrechts and for a large class of men who staffed camps, who—contrary to the prevailing, greatly mythological image of camp guards—were not specially chosen and trained, unusually fervent Nazis. Two elements of these three men's biographies, common to many though not to all of their brethren, were particularly significant. These men had been deemed earlier to be unfit for military duty, and they ended up in Helmbrechts not according to some well-conceived administrative plan that found them to be the right people for the job, but quite obviously mainly by chance, because they happened to have been in a certain place at a certain time. With the exception of the SS man, Michael Ritter, and Commandant Dörr, no evidence exists to suggest that any of the male guards in Helmbrechts were especially suitable for this ideological duty. And there is no reason to believe that any of them, Dörr aside, ended up there because of any qualities they had displayed that would have made them appear to higher authorities as men fit to torture and slaughter Jews. By and large, these were ordinary, working-class Germans.

The backgrounds of the twenty-seven women guards differed from those of the men, and are easily summarized. They were considerably younger and were exclusively German. They ranged in age from twenty to forty-five, yet their mean age was only slightly over twenty-eight years, fourteen years younger than that of the men. Twelve of them, 45 percent, were under twenty-five, and only one was over forty. Although they were formally in the SS, the available biographies indicate that they entered the SS late in the war, between June and December 1944, so their membership consisted of little more than wearing SS uniforms. Half say they were conscripted and half volunteered, though their given reasons for volunteering suggest that they saw guarding "foreigners" as preferable to working in factories, which almost all of them had been doing up to that time.[29] Their resemblance to real SS men was close to nil. The head woman guard referred to them in her testimony as "SS" guards, with ironical quotation marks around "SS." These women were working-class Germans who were not Nazi Party members, who late in the war ended up becoming camp guards. The sense of belonging to an elite order, and the military and intensive ideological training characterizing the SS, was not part of their makeup.[30]

Relations among the guards were excellent. Although the women were considerably younger than the men, and despite the general subordinate status of women in German society, the men and women regarded each other as rough equals. As one of the men recalls: "Between the female guards and the male members of the camp, there was no superior and subordinate relationship. Untouched by such a relation were in any case the close friendships between certain women and men; well known were the affairs between Dörr and Helga Hegel, between Hirsch and Marianne, between Riedl and Emma Schneider, between Koslowski and Ida, between Wagner and Schäfer, between Kemnitz and Irena."[31] A striking number of enduring romantic relationships developed among the guards living in the shadow of the camp's cruelty and misery, which they themselves produced. It is also noteworthy that at least three of the ethnic Germans—who appear to have been accepted by the others as Germans—were engaged in such love affairs. Obviously, the Germans talked much among themselves, about all of the subjects that co-workers, friends, and lovers discuss. They, of course, had their institutional and personal intrigues, most notably the one between the woman who was initially the head guard and the woman who eventually replaced her, who, significantly, was also Dörr's lover. Nevertheless, harmony seemed to prevail among them, especially among the women: "The relations among us women guards had been very good." A casualness appears to have been the rule among the guards and also with regard to their vocation. The wives and even the children of some of the male guards visited them in the camp.[32] Family members of some of the guards, even one guard's child, were present during one of the most brutal displays of torture that the camp ever witnessed.[33] The openness of the guards about the treatment of the prisoners, their evident lack of shame concerning their lives, and the harmonious relations among them in the face of the brutal treatment to which they subjected the Jewish prisoners (described below) all suggest strongly that no dissension existed among them over the cruel and lethal conditions that they themselves created and enforced. A consensus must have reigned that their community, a community of cruelty, was just and appropriate. In their postwar testimony, they are practically devoid of sympathy for the plight of the victims, even when one of them describes the brutal handiwork of another guard.

It is difficult to know how to assess the influence of Dörr upon camp life. Camp commanders had it within their power to ameliorate conditions, as some did.[34] Dörr was not among them. An old Nazi, who joined the Party in December 1932 and who was admitted to the SS on January 28, 1933, right before the takeover of power, Dörr was an exacting superior and cruel to the prisoners. His attitude to his job is variously described by underlings and prisoners. Some describe him as a passionate Jew-hater. One prisoner recounts that before beating a Jewish woman, he lashed her with a taunt: " 'What are you up to, you little kike [*du Jüdle*].' "[35] Of the camp's male personnel, only Dörr entered the camp, and even he was always accompanied by a woman guard. However much his cruelty may have inspired the women, his supervision of them was not considerable. They were, moreover, not in fear of him: "Dörr treated us very decently."[36] The women guards, these progeny of the German nation, roamed the camp freely and had tremendous leeway to treat the prisoners as they wished. They were brutal.

The Germans made love in barracks next to enormous privation and incessant cruelty. What did they talk about when their heads rested quietly on their pillows, when they were smoking their cigarettes in those relaxing moments after their physical needs had been met? Did one relate to another accounts of a particularly amusing beating that she or he had administered or observed, of the rush of power that engulfed her when the righteous adrenaline of Jew-beating caused her body to pulse with energy? It appears unlikely that these Germans lamented their vicious assaults on the Jews, that they spoke in pity-filled tones of the squalor, pain, and sickness into which they had plunged the Jews, only to awaken the next day and voluntarily mete out another dose of misery. They certainly gave no evidence of such a stance either at the time or afterwards. This community of Germans, many of whom had paired off in intimate relationships, flourished side by side with the hell for Jews, which these same Germans created and enthusiastically policed. The Germans had absolute power over the Jews, yet the position of domination, the structural relationship, does not explain their treatment of the Jewish women.

HELMBRECHTS HOUSED WOMEN prisoners who worked in the Neumeyer armaments firm. The camp's first 179 women prisoners arrived on July 19, 1944. The camp's facilities, including its barracks, were constructed during the first few months of its existence. For the first month, the women slept in the factory. Four additional transports brought the prisoner population to between 670 and 680 women, most of whom were non-Jewish Polish and Russian "protective custody" prisoners (*Schutzhäftlinge*). About twenty-five German women were also incarcerated, most for consorting (*Umgangs*) with prisoners of war or foreign workers, and some for defaming (*Beleidigung*) Hitler or aiding Jews (*Judenbegünstigung*).[37]

The living conditions of Helmbrechts' non-Jewish prisoners, although hard and brutal, were, by camp norms, relatively good. The women worked twelve-hour shifts and lived on meager food, which was nevertheless more generous than the typical camp fare. They received for breakfast coffee and bread, for lunch either potato or turnip soup, which occasionally contained pieces of meat; and for supper a small portion of bread, supplemented by margarine and either sausage or cheese. Those on shifts in the factory enjoyed an additional sandwich during their break. Whatever state of hunger their rations left them in, and however spare those rations may have been, the food was nevertheless sufficiently nourishing to maintain the prisoners in passable health.[38] Former German prisoners of the camp have testified to this: "Food consisted for the most part of turnips, potatoes, and sometimes also pieces of meat. For us in the factory, the food was in my estimation adequate."[39] With the exception of three whom the Germans killed after they escaped and were captured, it appears that *no non-Jewish women* died in Helmbrechts.[40] This, by Jewish norms, shocking longevity occurred despite severe punishments for the stealing of food or materials (punishment sometimes included the denial of all food for two days), and beatings for real or imagined violations of the rules. The medical care that the non-Jewish women received helped maintain their health, and it was a hallmark of the substantially better quality of their lives (compared to those of the Jews) in this camp. Until the end of February, a prisoner doctor and two aides tended their medical needs in the prisoner infirmary. A private doctor from the town of Helmbrechts treated the seriously ill. His prescriptions were filled in the town's pharmacy. The Germans tended even to the non-Jewish prisoners' dental problems, bringing them to a local dentist.[41]

The Jewish prisoners never received the services of a doctor, despite the far graver state of their health. A doctor visited them only once, shortly after their arrival in the camp, because the camp authorities feared that some epidemic might break out. The doctor inspected the Jews and concluded that an epidemic was not impending, whereupon, without treating even one of the gravely ill, he left—never to see them again. The Germans provided the Jews with none of the medicines that the non-Jewish prisoners could draw upon in their infirmary. The Jews had their own "infirmary," which by no recognizable standards could be called an infirmary; it was nothing more than one-half of one of the two Jewish barracks, namely the area where all of the seriously ill lay together.[42]

Upon arriving in Helmbrechts, the debilitated Jewish women were deloused and assigned to two barracks reserved exclusively for their use, where they remained segregated from the other prisoners. In order to be deloused, the Jews had to undress and stand completely naked for hours outside their barracks, exposed to the early March temperature. Eventually, each trudged by the delousing station, where a woman guard dunked every piece of clothing into the fluid, returning them to the prisoner soaking wet. "It was not permitted to wring out the dripping clothes. Each of us then had to put on at once whatever dripping garment was handed to her, and to proceed immediately to the barracks. They were unheated. The clothes had to dry on the body."[43] Just as the doctor had inspected the Jewish prisoners not for the sake of their health—allowing the Jews' wounds to fester, and their illnesses to remain untreated—but in order to safeguard the well-being of non-Jews, so too did the Germans delouse the Jews without a thought for the women's fate, the delousing having been a prophylaxis for all of the non-Jews in the camp and in the region. A survivor, who relates the details of the delousing, sums up its real effects: "As a consequence of this procedure, several of the women prisoners died."

The Jewish prisoners were discriminated against in every conceivable manner. Their physical separation in their own barracks bespoke a complete social and symbolic division of the Jewish and non-Jewish prisoners in this small camp. While the Germans did not even provide the Jewish prisoners with enough beds (planks) and straw to accommodate them, they replaced the non-Jews' worn straw before holidays. Some of the Jews had to sleep directly on the buildings' cold floors.[44] The inadequacy and general squalor of their living conditions degraded and debilitated them, particularly in the one barracks where the sickest among them lay. At night, the Germans locked the barracks of the Jews and non-Jews alike from without, making the latrines inaccessible. Buckets within the barracks were used as a substitute. Yet in the Jewish barracks, they were of insufficient volume, so that they overflowed, soiling the floor and the straw. Moreover, since many of the Jewish prisoners suffered from dysentery, they were often unable even to reach the buckets. The Jewish barracks stank terribly. As if the permanent stench were not in itself a sufficient form of punishment, the camp's guards beat the Jewish women daily, including the seriously ill, ostensibly for the soiling of their barracks.[45] Yet they would not provide the Jews with the additional buckets that would have altered the conditions producing these "punishments." The Germans also punished the Jews by forcing them to stand outside in the freezing cold for hours: "Punitive roll calls occurred as a rule when the barracks had become unclean during the night. This, however, could not be avoided because the receptacles that had been placed there for the night were simply not sufficient for all the prisoners." As this former prisoner relates, during such punishment roll calls of the Jews, "many women prisoners collapsed into unconsciousness. Some in fact died."[46] Her account captures the essence of the life conditions that the Germans here and elsewhere created for Jews. They "punished" Jews for doing things which the Germans themselves guaranteed that the Jews could not avoid doing.

Unlike the non-Jews, the Jewish prisoners wore rags, and many had no shoes. The commander of the camp chose not to issue the Jews adequate clothing and footwear, despite the supplies that lay unused in the camp's storerooms. The food that the Germans allotted the Jews was a pittance of the normal rations. They gave the Jews food only once a day, at noontime. It was usually soup and of a quality so poor that the camp's non-Jews bestowed upon it a special name, "Jew-soup" (*Judensuppe*). Often the Germans did not provide enough for all of the Jews, so some went away deprived of a day's one chance (however meager) for nourishment.[47] The Jews, gripped by constant, acute hunger and aware that the Germans routinely prepared an insufficient quantity of food for them, were often unruly while waiting in line for the daily "Jew-soup." The former chief woman guard of the camp tells of one such incident, and of her own brutal response to the Jews' understandable conduct: "In Helmbrecht[s] shortly after the Grünberg transport arrived, the girls plunged a little prematurely into the food that was ready for them. Food disposition was always rough because of the inhuman hunger of these women. We caught eight of them at this time and I ordered as punishment for them standing in the yard (being taken in only at night) without food for three days. It was extremely cold at this time and I believe it snowed."[48] The discord induced by food distribution gave the German guards another excuse to transform a moment of sustenance into a source of misery: "At mealtime there was often a row. We always feared to fetch the food because blows were always dealt to us."[49] Even the prospect of receiving food—thoughts of which preoccupied Jews obsessively, because food under German rule was the single greatest daily want of Jews and the most important ingredient in the daunting survival struggle—was greeted by Helmbrechts' Jews with mixed emotions.

Although the Germans had marched the Jews to Helmbrechts ostensibly for work, they (unlike the camp's non-Jewish prisoners) remained unutilized. The armaments firm had no places for them. But that was immaterial, because the Germans had already weakened most of the Jews beyond the point where they could work productively.[50]

The guards of the camp were brutal to all of the prisoners. Non-Jewish prisoners tell of beatings that they suffered.[51] Their violations of camp rules could bring down upon them the full fury of a guard. Yet they themselves recognized and, after the war, remark upon the vastly greater sufferings of the Jewish inmates, owing both to the general conditions of their lives in the camp and to the cruelties which the camp's personnel perpetrated upon them. One former Russian prisoner recalls: "The Jewish population was mistreated worse than we and they received little, very little to eat. No Russian woman died of hunger. If we did not abide by the rules of the camp, we were denied the little food we would receive. The Jewesses in the camp were beaten until they lost consciousness. When they regained consciousness, their clothes were ripped off them and they had to stand naked outdoors until 7 o'clock."[52] A former German prisoner portrays the condition of the Jewish women in a concurring manner, implying all along that the situation of the non-Jews was enormously different and better. The Jews

> were squeezed into very small barracks; they had to sleep on icy floors. Everything was taken from them. They had to weather the winter months dressed only in shirts. We were situated near the barracks and could not sleep for all the wailing, howling, and moaning. It was a terrible torture [*Martyrium*]. The food for the Jews was still worse; nothing but turnips once a day. If these poor women concealed but a small thing of their possessions, such as a beloved keepsake, photographs, etc., they were beaten bloody by the SS women with truncheons, undressed, and forced to stand long days barefoot on thick gravel in the bitter cold. Their legs were swollen like butter barrels; the ones in the poorest condition collapsed from pain. After a short while more Jews arrived.[53]

The German women personnel sought to strip the Jews of all vestiges of humanity. They ignored their basic survival needs. They beat them bloody and senseless at a whim. They forbade them from possessing the smallest personal item, the tiniest marker of a personal identity.[54] In every way, the Germans treated the non-Jewish prisoners differently, in a manner acknowledging, if only grudgingly, the humanity which they, the Germans, shared with the non-Jews. There was strict segregation of the Jews and non-Jews, with an absolute prohibition of talk between them.[55] The Germans permitted the non-Jews to possess personal belongings, and provided them with nourishment to maintain them at sufficient strength for productive factory labor. The beatings that the non-Jews received from the German women guards did not approach in severity the ferocious, crippling assaults that they routinely inflicted upon the Jewish women. The Russian prisoners, who were conceived to be the lowest among the non-Jewish "subhumans," lived a life of comparative luxury. The measure of this, always a reliable measure during the Nazi period, was the mortality rate. Over the course of a number of months, not one Russian prisoner died in Helmbrechts from starvation or starvation-related ailments.[56] In the brief time that they were in Helmbrechts, but five weeks, forty-four Jews died, which, assuming that the rate would have remained constant (although it would likely have increased), would project roughly to a 70 percent yearly mortality rate.[57] This differential treatment occurred even though it was not ordered from above. The camp's personnel were themselves responsible for it.

The corpses of twenty-two of the Jewish women whom the Germans killed in Helmbrechts

The photo above shows the bodies of the emaciated dead Jewish women when they were disinterred by the Americans on April 18, 1945, five days after the camp's evacuation.

The Jews' interlude in Helmbrechts, with the symbolic and practical division between Jews and non-Jews, and with the ongoing destruction of the Jews, in body and spirit, was a prelude to the Helmbrechts death march, which began on April 13, 1945, less than four weeks before the war's end, and when the German military situation had for a long time been obviously hopeless, beyond salvation. Dörr appears to have made the decision on his own authority to evacuate the camp, although the details of the decision making, the chronology of the evacuation of the camp itself, and the exact orders Dörr gave to his staff are all murky. Before their departure, he addressed some of the camp's staff, explaining to them that they would divide the prisoners into three groups, each one being delegated a contingent of both men and women guards. The groups were to march to some destination, which he did not specify. The very ill were to be transported. Although it is not clear what orders he gave for the disposition of prisoners in the marching columns who became too weak to continue, he did say that they should not be left behind alive and he certainly did not forbid the guards from shooting them.[58]

The Germans' spirits could not have been buoyant as they contemplated the road ahead. They were setting out on a journey but a step ahead of a conquering army, of their effective pursuers. The world which they had inhabited for the last twelve years, one which had seen the heady days of continental conquest and of the seemingly possible fulfillment of the thousand-year promise, was with their every step being pulverized further. A new dispensation of unknown character was about to be imposed upon them. The Germans were on the verge of becoming powerless people at the mercy of their enemies, some of whom had suffered previously unimaginable devastation, misery, and cruelties at the Germans' hands. It was possible, with the war lost and with their own capture imminent, that the Germans would realize that their political cultural norms no longer applied, that all prisoners would finally become equal in the Germans' eyes. But they did not. This is one of the remarkable aspects of the death marches, including the Helmbrechts death march.

Prior to departure, Dörr ordered the camp's unused supplies of clothing to be distributed, but only to the non-Jewish prisoners. Even before this discriminatory allocation, the Jews, then covered in rags, possessed clothing that was inferior to that of the non-Jewish prisoners, and were therefore more exposed to the elements. Now the vulnerability of the Jews had increased further in comparison to that of the non-Jews. The relative ill health and generally greater physical weakness of the Jews rendered this favoritism all the more damaging to their prospects of survival. As if this bias were not deadly enough on its own, the Germans discriminated further, giving the non-Jews a ration of bread with some sausage and margarine. It appears that the Germans gave the Jews nothing.[59]

So under these general circumstances with orders not precisely specified, these Germans set out with about 580 Jewish prisoners and about 590 non-Jewish prisoners. Approximately equal in number, the Jews and non-Jews were to experience nothing but inequality along the way. An estimated forty-seven Germans—twenty-two men and twenty-five women—escorted the prisoners on their way. The male guards bore rifles, having received extra ammunition for the march, and the women carried rods.[60]

As in so many other phases of the Germans' terror and destructiveness during the Nazi period, the Germans' treatment of Jews during this march—and typically in other death marches as well—differed fundamentally from that meted out to non-Jewish prisoners, even though all prisoners were in the same structural relationship vis-à-vis the Germans—namely, powerless, defenseless, bereft of rights and protections, subject to the Germans' absolute domination and hostage to their whims.[61] The non-Jews were made up of the same two distinct groups that had been in Helmbrechts. The first, composing the overwhelming majority, consisted of all the non-German prisoners, mainly Russian and Polish women. The Germans kept them on the march for only the first few days, leaving them behind when departing the Zwotau camp (in Svatava) on the seventh day. The testimony suggests that perhaps not even one among them died while on the march, and certainly almost all were deposited in a nearby camp in (by the standards of the time) decent health. The second group of non-Jews contained the twenty-five German prisoners of the camp. They remained on the march until the end, but functionally only partly as prisoners; they served also as jailers. The Helmbrechts' guards shifted them from within the prisoner columns to its sides, from jailed to jailers, where, at least part of the time during the march, they helped ensure, in their new deputized capacity, that no Jews escaped: "It is true that we German prisoners had to walk alongside the marching column in order to keep an eye on the other prisoners."[62] German prisoners who had been incarcerated for their own actions, for having as individuals violated the regime's precepts, remained in their jailers' eyes Germans, members of the *Volk*, blood relations. As such, the German prisoners were so elevated above the Jews, whose only crime was birth, that they were fit to be deputized in the incremental, ambulatory slaughter of the Jews. So, although an equal number of Jews and non-Jews emerged from the abandoned camp of Helmbrechts, the Germans either soon detached the non-Jews from the march (having suffered infinitesimally compared to the Jews) or transformed them into the Jews' captors. The Helmbrechts march turned out to be a *death* march for Jews and only for Jews.

The march proceeded in three distinct groups, each with its own contingent of guards. There were also "sick wagons" on which the weakest of the Jews (one Jewish survivor says between 180 and 200) rode prostrate and were packed in like so many sardines.[63] On average, they covered about nine miles a day, with typical days covering anywhere from five to more than thirteen miles.[64] The march's route was relatively direct.

Just as in the camps, the Germans transformed every aspect of existence during the march into a source of torment or death for the Jews. Just as in the camps, the suffering was almost always unnecessary. The general conditions of life on the march—the marching, the clothing, eating, and sleeping—suggest that the purpose of the march in the minds of the guards, no matter what the higher authorities conceived it to have been, was to degrade, injure, immiserate, and kill Jews. The Germans accompanying the march consciously and consistently made choices that could have been calculated to produce only these ends.

Hof

Helmbrechts

Schwarzenbach
an der Saale — *Saale River*

Neuhausen

Aš

Svatava

Ohře River

Karlovy Vary
(Karlsbad)

Čistá

Dvorek

Mariánské
Lázně

Bayreuth

Chodavá
Planá

Flossenbürg

German–
Czechoslovakia
Border, Pre-1938

Stráž

Radbuza River

Plzeň

Otava River

Nuremberg

GERMANY

Vlkanov

CZECHOSLOVAKIA

Maxov

German–
Czechoslovakia
Border, April 1945

Ondřejovice

Regensburg

Rejštejn

Prachatice

miles   25

kilometers   40

Kvilda

Volary

Vltava River

**Helmbrechts
Death March: 195 miles**

Danube River

Passau

© Mark Stein Studios, 1995

AUSTRIA

The Jews departed Helmbrechts in deplorable health and were denied available extra clothing and food. During the march, the Germans systematically prevented them from receiving adequate provisions of either one. Normally, they gave the Jews some food only once a day, sometimes at midday, sometimes in the evening (after reaching the point for their overnight stay), sometimes not at all. The food was utterly inadequate, consisting some days of a little bread, or a little soup, or a meager portion of potatoes. The testimony about the quality of the women's nourishment and physical condition—from Jewish survivors, the better-fed German prisoners, bystanders, and even guards—is extensive, sickening, and given almost in a single voice: The Germans were giving the Jewish women virtually nothing to eat, and hunger was literally consuming them. They were starving to death. The women were so hungry that, when coming across a pile of animal fodder, they "pounced upon" it and consumed it with abandon, even though the fodder was rotting and obviously unfit to be fed even to animals.[65] The Jewish women's privation was such that they were also driven regularly to eat grass.[66] On the final two days of the death march, when the women who had managed to survive to that point were holding on to life but tenuously, they put in a full day's march, while receiving only contemptible nourishment. On Thursday, May 3, the march's penultimate day, at noontime, "the women received," according to the testimony of the head German woman guard, "one glass of watery soup, after which they did not receive anything until Friday noon and it merely consisted of three small potatoes and half a glass of milk."[67] These final "meals" (and this is true of the rations during the entire death march) were obviously insufficient to keep these women healthy, or even to keep many of them alive.

Why did the Germans not provide the Jewish women with more than starvation rations? It was not because of the chaos and general food shortage of the time, or the frequent unwillingness of local German citizens to spare food for Jewish "subhumans." Had there been an abundance of food, had the Jews been walking through the Garden of Eden itself, the German guards would not have permitted the Jews to sate their hunger, to nourish and fortify their bodies against the ravages of starvation and its diseases. As it was, the German guards actively and vigorously prevented the Jews from receiving the additional food that *was* available and that was freely offered to them. They did this throughout the march.

On the first day of the march, the Germans showed their determination to transform the Jews into ambulatory skeletons and then corpses. Already the Jews were so weak that they were faltering, and many had to be supported by others in order to continue. Just a few miles outside Helmbrechts, in Ahornberg, German civilians responded to the supplications of the Jews for food and water, only to meet the interdiction of the guards. On the eighth day of the march, part of the column paused for a while in the town of Sangerberg, during which time the Jews communicated to the townspeople standing nearby that they were suffering from hunger: "A few women from Sangerberg tried to pass to the prisoners some bread. At once, however, the nearby SS women prevented it. A male guard threatened one of the women who wanted to distribute food that he would shoot her if she should try again to pass food to the prisoners. In two cases, one guard struck with his rifle butt prisoners who wanted to accept foodstuffs. A female guard cast bread, which had been intended for the prisoners, to chickens."[68] On the previous day, the Germans had given the Jews no food whatsoever after a full day's march and, owing to their hunger and their exposure from sleeping outdoors in the cold (the reason for which is described below), a dozen women had died during the night.

This was the backdrop for the scene which saw the German guards *choosing* to distribute bread not to the starving women but to chickens.

The guards' attempts to limit the nutrition received by the Jews continued with success throughout the march. On its sixteenth day, after a twelve-mile march, they allowed the Jews to have some soup that the people of Althütten had prepared, but forbade them from receiving any other food. On the twenty-first day of the march, when the Americans were closing in on them and the end was imminent, the guards still refused to allow townspeople, this time from Volary, to feed the Jews. The women guards beat any Jew who tried to accept the offerings.[69]

The Jewish women suffered throughout not only from hunger but also from persistent thirst and certain dehydration. The Germans rarely permitted them to drink, despite the ready availability of water: "Whenever we came to rivers, the guards forced us to go on without allowing us to drink."[70] The guards themselves acknowledged that the Jewish women were on the verge of starvation, that they, the guards, could not have made the march on so little food and water, and that they, the guards, nevertheless made no effort to procure any additional food and water for the Jews. The head woman guard, Hegel, recounts: "I never once procured additional meals for the women, although it would have been in my power to do so."[71]

After a long day's march, during which the Germans did not allow the debilitated women sufficient pauses for rest, they reached the day's end point and their night's place of repose. But night—that opportunity for restorative sleep—was a Janus-faced respite from the wearying way, fraught with its own perils for the Jews. For these Jewish travelers, the best accommodations turned out to be unheated barns, which were highly preferable to the Germans' frequently chosen alternative for them: sleeping outside under April skies. In addition to the physical suffering of spending the night under these conditions, the women were tormented by the persistent cacophony of cries and moans that starving, diseased, wounded, and freezing people make. The overnight environment was such that some women typically did not rise when the morning came, having died of the cold and their other ailments.[72]

Similar to the Germans' staunch refusals to permit the Jews to receive available additional food and water was the choice made by Dörr on several occasions to force the Jews to spend the night outside, even though indoor quarters were available. Upon arriving in Čistá at the end of the march's seventh day, the town's Mayor proposed to accommodate the Jewish women in the hall that had been prepared with bedding for a large group of women auxiliaries of the German army who had been expected but had not shown up. Dörr refused the offer, compelling the Jewish women to sleep exposed on an athletic field. Townspeople remember that this night was very cold, that the women were utterly exhausted and emaciated, and that they moaned the night away. There was hoarfrost. By morning, twelve women had died from exposure.[73] Dörr denied available indoor accommodations to the Jewish women at least three other times during the march.[74]

It is difficult to convey the misery of these women as they dragged themselves, often shoeless, along frozen roads, one pain-filled step promising but another, one pain-filled day yielding seemingly inevitably but another. The women had no known destination, no end point in sight. Every step required the marshaling of their energies, for they were at best listless, in their emaciated and diseased conditions. Every dawn saw them awake to gnawing hunger, swollen and pus-filled feet, limbs that no longer functioned, and open wounds that would not heal. They knew that an entire day's march stood before them, during which they would be given by their tormentors few opportunities to rest. Perhaps, when evening finally came, they would consume a few morsels of food. They would then end the day in shivering, pain-filled half-sleep, only to awaken to the repetition of another day's and night's cycle of horrors. Such was a "normal" day. Of course, some days presented special hardships, such as the need to climb hundreds of meters, to plant their inadequately protected or bare feet on snow-covered ground, to suffer air attacks from Allied planes, or to grow used to new wounds.

Conditions on the march were such that they could have found their way into Dante's imagination as a path for those journeying from one circle down to the next. Nevertheless, as if the dangers to the Jews' lives owing to malnutrition, exhaustion, and the elements were not sufficient—as if this journey to hell on earth were unsatisfyingly nightmarish—the Germans saw to it that its material conditions were but a portion of the torment that they would force the Jewish women to endure. The horrors were augmented by the regular application of the tried-and-true means of German expression: the rod and the rifle.

The women guards were not outfitted with rods for no reason, and the men carried rifles, with handy rifle butts, not only for emergencies. Acting according to the unarticulated norm, "A rod in hand must be a rod applied," the German guards beat the Jewish women freely and mercilessly. Once again, the testimony on this point comes from all vantage points and with no essential ambiguity.

Beatings, "naturally," began on the day of evacuation. As was often the case in the hellish world which the Germans had constructed for Jews, beginnings and moments of transition were occasions for symbolic and physical cruelty, as if to announce to the victims how abject their status and condition would be. "On April 13, 1945, during the preparations for the evacuation, I saw Willi Rust beat many sick Jews with a wooden plank."[75] The keepers of the social dead frequently feel compelled to reaffirm the status quo lest the social dead conclude that substantive change in their social position and quality of life is in the offing.[76]

The Germans beat the Jews for any reason and for no reason whatsoever. They beat them for being sick. They beat them for moving too sluggishly— a riposte to their slowness unlikely to improve their already greatly impaired ability to keep pace.[77] It has already been mentioned that when townspeople tried to give food to the Jews, the guards responded by beating not the townspeople but the Jews. When Jews tried to better their situation, however innocuously, however understandably, the Germans bludgeoned them viciously for their efforts: ". . . I stopped once to pick up a rotten potato peel. A guard came over and beat me on the head. He did this with the butt of his rifle, causing a wound on my head which started to bleed, and I never received any medical treatment whatsoever. The dirty rag which I had to put around my head soon caused the wound to become infected."[78] The guards, male and female, virtually without exception, all beat the wretched Jews. One survivor remembers: "All of the women guards had rods and clubs, which they, at their pleasure, would put to use at the drop of a hat."[79] This was substantiated by Hegel shortly after her capture by the Americans: "All the 'SS' women guards carried rods and all of them beat the girls."[80] Another woman guard confesses: "I beat the women often and hard. I used for that purpose my hands and sometimes also an implement of one sort or another. Between Zwotau [Svatava] and Wallern [Volary], I beat a girl quite brutally, in consequence of which she died the next day."[81] A rambling account by this guard of some of the cruelties that came to mind when asked by her interrogator to describe some "particulars from incidents during the march" provides a glimpse of the march and of the German guards' character:

> Jensen, Koslowski, Wagner, and Riedl beat to death three or four girls because they had thrown themselves on a heap of rotten beet roots. . . .[82] Every evening I heard Koslowski speak of the number of girls he had shot during the day. I do not know how many they were altogether, but usually it involved two to four every day. Koslowski told me once that Wagner had helped him in the killing of some women. I saw Dörr beat repeatedly with extreme brutality. I recall that once a girl collapsed immediately under his blows. Schmidt, Schäfer, and Reitsch were very brutal in their treatment of the girls. I did not see it myself, but it was in general talked about among the guards. Once I saw also Hegel, too, beat a girl brutally with a rod. I do not, however, know what had become of that girl, since I had to leave at that time.[83]

Including herself, this custodian of the Jews incriminates ten of the march's forty-one German guard contingent by name.

As her account indicates, Jewish women died as a consequence not only of the march's intentionally induced privations or even of the heartless and vicious beatings. The Germans also shot Jewish women liberally. Some executions were ordered by Dörr or by Hegel, the chief woman guard. But each German had discretion to kill Jews as he or she saw fit (although only the men possessed rifles). Hegel gives an overview of the killing:

> Who was to be shot was in reality decided by each guard himself, however, the leaders in each column possessed the power to command the guards under them to abstain from shooting the prisoners—this did not occur. Duerr [sic] never gave the command that no one was to be shot although he had the power to do so. I do not know the exact number that were shot every day but to my knowledge it was on an average of six to ten every day. These women were shot simply because they were too weak to go on—they committed no crime whatsoever.[84]

The German guards knew that the march could not go on forever, but at no point did they resolve to stop the slaughter, eagerly killing Jewish women until the last moment. Indeed, the concluding scenes of this death march featured not contrition but several emblematic acts on the part of the Germans, in addition to their continuing willful denial of food to the Jews.

It was May 4 and the trap was closing, leaving the Germans with virtually no place to turn without running into enemy forces. Realizing that their capture was imminent, they decided to abandon the Jewish women, though they planned to do so only after sending them over the border into the part of Czechoslovakia which the Germans called the "Protectorate." The Germans marched the still ambulatory Jews towards Prachatice, then a German border town about nine miles northeast of Volary, and loaded some of the sickest Jews onto carts pulled by a tractor by which they were to reach the same destination. While under way, an American plane attacked the vehicles, killing a pregnant woman guard (the father was one of the male guards) and wounding two of the other women guards.

The subsequent events are a bit murky, for the testimony presents a conflicting and indistinct record. That the Germans killed a significant number of Jews is indisputable, though exactly how and when is not so clear. When the plane had departed and the damage to German life and limb became apparent, some of the guards worked themselves into a frenzy. Spontaneously, they shot their rifles into the mass of prostrate Jews. The helpless Jews had done nothing.

The chaos created by the air attack had been used by some of the Jews to flee. The surviving Jews riding on the carts were by and large too weak to avail themselves of this opportunity to steal their freedom, to cheat their hangmen. Unable now to continue on foot as they would have had to, the Germans incarcerated them overnight in the barn of a local peasant. These Jews had the bad luck to be under the watch of three of the most savage killers among the male guards, who proceeded now to perpetrate two additional massacres. During one, they took the lives of twelve Jews. The court judgment gives the following account of the second one, which occurred the day after the air attack, the day on which the rest of Helmbrechts' surviving Jews were being set free. These ethnic German guards removed the Jewish women from the barn, marched them through a wood, always uphill, as if to sap them of their meager remaining strength. During the half hour of unremitting climbing, the women began to fade. The three guards shot whoever could not continue the ascent, one by one, until fourteen of the seventeen women were dead. They finally allowed the three who were still standing to go free. All of this occurred on May 5, the day before the entire area came under American army occupation.[85]

The ambulatory Jews who had not fled during the air attack, unlike those who had been riding on the carts, continued the march to Prachatice. Along the way, one guard shot one of the Jewish women through the head. On the following day, the Germans set the Jewish women walking from Prachatice, unaccompanied, towards the Czech border, which was about a mile away. The Jews wandered across the political and moral demarcation line and were taken in by Czech villagers. Their excruciating journey was over.

Only a portion of the sickest Jews had been riding on the ill-fated carts to Prachatice. The rest, the majority, were liberated by American forces in Volary. They had remained there because, upon learning of the air attack, the Germans who had stayed behind in order to guard these Jews had declined to put themselves at similar risk by accompanying the Jews to the border. Between May 3 and May 5, twenty of the Jewish women died in Volary. Two more died on the day of the American arrival and of their liberation, May 6, and four more failed to survive the ensuing days, the medical care notwithstanding.[86] Their condition was so abject, so unbelievable, that the examining physician wrote: "My first glance at these individuals was one of extreme shock not ever believing that a human being can be degraded, can be starved, can be so skinny and even live under such circumstances." The horrifying, detailed description of Jewish survivors to be found towards the beginning of this chapter is about these women.

Thus, the Helmbrechts death march ended for the Jews in a variety of ways: At least two separate massacres claimed at least twenty-six lives, a single shot ended the life of another, some fled to freedom under the cover of an American air attack, the majority were released by being sent off into

Czechoslovakia, and the sickest were abandoned by the Germans to die where they lay in Volary.[87] Up to the moment of Nazism's last breaths, the eloquent discrimination between Jews and non-Jews continued: Alois Dörr, hater and glorying genocidal killer of Jews, ended his relationship with Helmbrechts' German prisoners solicitously, by procuring identity papers for them from the German District Office in Prachatice.[88]

The Helmbrechts death march began and ended in slaughter. The Germans shot or beat to death ten Jews on the first day of the march and twenty-seven on its last two days. How many Jews died on the twenty-two days of the march (and during the ensuing few days) cannot be determined exactly. The figure accepted by the Federal Republic of Germany's court was 178: 129 from starvation, disease, and exhaustion, and 49 from beatings and shootings.[89] It is likely that the death toll was significantly higher, around 275.[90] Even according to the court's niggardly estimate, 30 percent of the Jews died in slightly over three weeks. According to the American physician who examined some of the survivors, 50 percent of them would have died within twenty-four hours of his arrival had they not been rescued and been treated to intensive lifesaving measures.[91] It is safe to assume that within a few days almost all of them would have died. For marches like this one, it makes no sense to speak of a "death rate" (usually calculated annually) in any meaningful way. This march was simply a "death march," in effect a German march of extermination, which (even using the court's low figures) likely would have killed its entire Jewish contingent had it lasted two months, a speed of decimation exceeding all German institutions, including all camps, save the camps devoted explicitly to extermination.

14

MARCHING TO WHAT END?

HOW SHOULD THE events of the Helmbrechts death march and of death marches in general be understood? Why did the Germans from Helmbrechts lead the Jewish women on this bizarre march to nowhere? Why did they stay with the Jews and continue until the final moments to kill and torture them, even though the war was clearly lost and their meanderings clearly would not have promoted Germany's fortunes in any way? Why did they not abandon this seemingly senseless enterprise, instead risking their own capture? How did all of this make sense to them?

The circumstances of the march, the Germans' treatment of the prisoners, and their own words suggest that the death march, marching the Jews to death, was an end in itself. Yet the question remains: What did the Germans understand themselves to be doing?

It is not clear what precisely the Germans' orders were, though some things about them can be said. Dörr did evacuate the camp under standing orders to do so when the Americans approached. His initial destination of Dachau was unreachable, since it had been captured by the Americans. During the march, Dörr therefore got the destination of his orders changed to Austria. He must also have had the unremarkable order to avoid capture. Although there is conflicting testimony about the instructions that Dörr *initially* gave his contingent of guards regarding how they should treat women who could no longer march, it appears likely that he did tell them to shoot all stragglers.[1] He also issued a prohibition on contact between the Jewish women and the townspeople. Once under way, Dörr and the German guard contingent had no regular connection to any command structure. They had no prescribed route, so they had to feel their way towards some undetermined destination. They did not even possess a map.[2] Whatever their general orders might have been, these Germans were, as a matter of fact and practicality, on their own. As one guard states: "Throughout the march, the guards were unaware of where we were supposed to march to."[3] The guards had to improvise constantly with the changing conditions. They were the ones who were deciding what to do with their prisoners, how to treat them, how to feed them, whether the Jews would live or die.

The German personnel therefore lacked clarity about almost all aspects of their orders. There is one notable, crucial exception. They learned on the second day of the march that they were under *explicit orders* from the highest authority *not to kill the Jews*. They were under binding orders to treat the Jewish women humanely.

On the march's second day, an SS lieutenant, who was a courier from Himmler, found their column and communicated to Dörr a directive from Himmler regarding the prisoners. This courier first learned from Dörr how many prisoners he and his guards had already killed (it is unknown what Dörr told him), and then he informed Dörr that Himmler had *expressly forbidden* that any more Jews be killed. Himmler was negotiating with the Americans and did not want continuing killings to undermine his efforts. The courier further commanded the SS women to dispose of their rods. If ever in danger of capture, the Germans were to destroy the camp's records.[4] They were also *not* to kill the Jews but to release them in the woods.

Himmler's orders were then communicated to the death march's German personnel. One male guard tells of Himmler's emissary himself doing the talking: "We, the guards, had to assemble and this lieutenant announced to us that he was an adjutant of Himmler's. He further said that negotiations were being conducted with the American troops and the prisoners must be treated humanely. This lieutenant then proceeded to announce that Himmler had issued an order that prisoners should not be shot anymore. He also prohibited the guards from carrying wooden canes, as was our practice."[5] Some disagreement exists over whether the lieutenant or Dörr himself addressed the German guards.[6] The main points of what was said, however, are clear: The Germans were *forbidden* from killing any more Jews.

Even had they not received Himmler's explicit, binding order to treat the Jews decently, the Germans' actions can in no sense be seen as being the consequence of any set of rational, reasonable considerations. They were marching to death women who could hardly walk; they were withholding food from women who were so emaciated that observers were astonished that the women were still alive; they were forcing women clothed in rags and bereft of protective body fat to sleep outside in winter conditions. They were cudgeling people who could barely raise an arm in self-protection. The notion that they were transporting these women to some spot where they could be put to work was ludicrous; the Jewish women had been so weakened even before leaving Helmbrechts that they had been incapable of working while in the camp. After the privations and brutalities of the march, those who survived were half-dead. Even had the Germans not been contravening a binding order not to kill the Jews and to treat them humanely, the Germans' multifarious cruel and lethal actions can be seen as having been an expression only of their own inner desires. In light of Himmler's order, their killing and cruelty was also in violation of their duty. These Germans chose, against orders, authority, and all reason, to act as they did. They were voluntaristic actors.

Their voluntarism did not produce uniformly lethal and cruel action. The German guards treated the few German prisoners among them well, and even employed them to guard the Jewish women. In Svatava, seven days into the march, they left behind all of the non-Jewish prisoners except for the few Germans. As one guard comments about the favored non-Jews, "these very prisoners were in a comparatively good physical condition. They were able to walk."[7] It was precisely the prisoners whom the Germans left behind who were healthy, who could have been workers had the Germans really had any intention (and realistic chance) of rescuing workers for the tottering Reich. The Germans' torturing and killing was not diffuse; their actions were not the expression of sadistic or generally brutalized personalities that seek gratification on any potential victim. Their cruelty and lust to kill was victim specific, reserved and centered upon the Jews. They chose to torture and kill only when they had *Jewish* victims.

How must they have conceived of the Jews, of their chosen victims, for them to act as they did? As photographs of them (such as the ones on the next two pages) taken days after their liberation show, the Jews were no manifest threat to the Germans. The Jewish women could hardly move.

How could any person have looked upon these pitiable, sick Jewish women without feeling sympathy for them, without feeling horror at the abject physical condition into which they had been plunged? The average weight of ninety-three survivors, recorded by the examining American doctor, was ninety pounds. Twenty-nine women weighed eighty pounds or less. Five of the women weighed sixty-five pounds or less.[8] They were barely living skeletons.

Despite all of this, no evidence supports the notion that the Germans felt sympathy for the Jews. And much evidence—almost every facet of their actions—argues that sympathy for these Jewish women was an emotion foreign to them. What numbed these Germans so to the human suffering of these people? What impelled them to treat the Jews cruelly, so cruelly that many interpreters find it hard to believe—and have therefore ruled out the possibility *a priori*—that ordinary people could have perpetrated such "inhuman" cruelty willingly? It took some powerful motivation for them to have done this. This motivation—the Germans' conceptions of the Jews and of this march's purpose—did not remain completely unarticulated. A few of their revealing utterances have survived and come down to us.

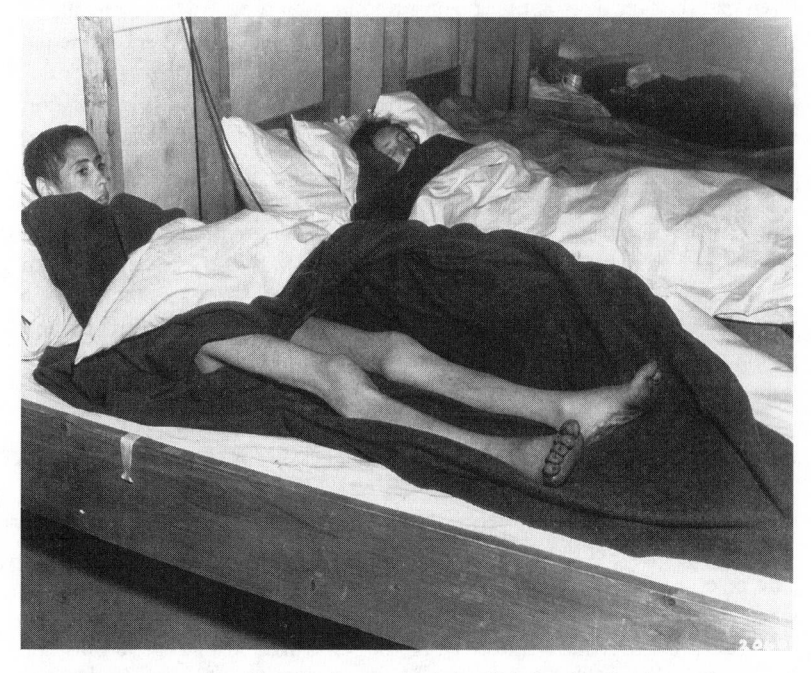

A seventeen-year-old girl, who survived the Helmbrechts death march, on May 8, 1945

As was mentioned in the previous chapter, one of the guards, Koslowski, continually boasted to other Germans of the Jews whom he killed during the march.[9] That the boasting continued here throughout reflected the moral assent to the killings that pervaded the social community which the German guards formed. Words spoken not just to comrades but also to victims by their executioners immediately before or while they wield the ax can divulge much about motivation, for these are moments of self-expression, often of unusual candor. One survivor recalls one of the cold, bitter nights of the march, when a perpetrator chose to attack his victim with self-satisfied irony as introduction to the searing pain of his blows: "When on the way we stayed in a barn for the night, a large number of dead women lay in the barn. One woman screamed that she was freezing. This SS man ordered the woman to lie down on the corpses, saying, 'Now you will be warm.' He beat the victim so long until she expired."[10] The only kind of warmth a Jew could expect from this man was the cold grave. The crematorium was unavailable.

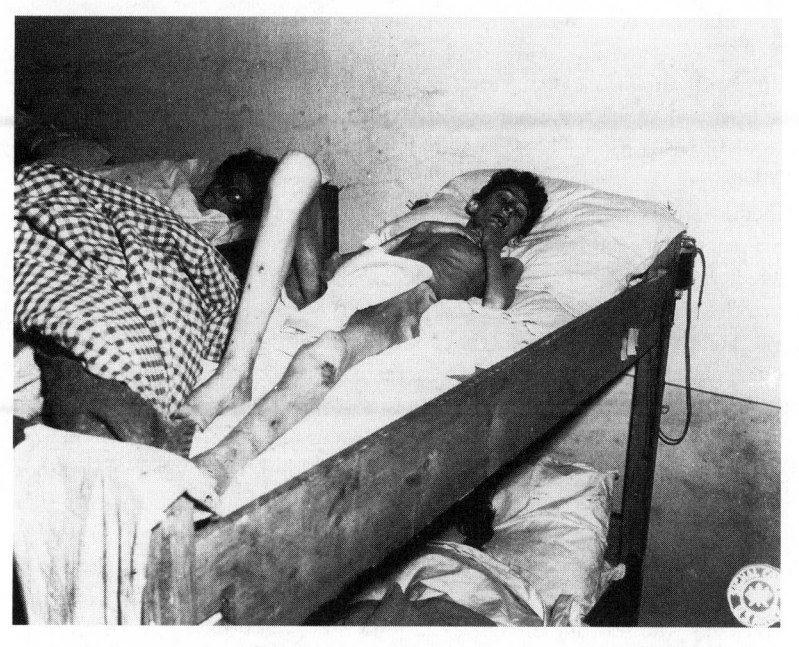

A thirty-two-year-old Hungarian Jewish survivor of the Helmbrechts death march on May 8, 1945. The American physician recorded that she "has the appearance of a seventy-five-year-old woman and presents a picture of extreme emaciation with dehydration and weakness. There is extreme edema of feet with ulceration of toes and marked stomatitis." Before the war, she had earned a doctorate in French.

Another revealing statement came from Dörr himself. During the march, the corpses of the Jews were sometimes buried, and sometimes left in the open to rot. A former German prisoner recounts one of the times that they did bury the Jewish victims. She had noticed that one or two of the women still "showed signs of life," and told Dörr "that he could not bury people who were still alive. Whereupon he answered literally: They will perish anyhow.

The more Jews perish, the better! They are anyhow about to die."[11] The inhumanity of burying people alive did unsettle this German prisoner but not Dörr—or, it seems, a large number of the German perpetrators during these genocidal years, who would sometimes in the killing operations fail to make an effort to ensure that the Jews whom they were burying were indeed all dead.[12] With his pronouncement, Dörr both expressed explicitly his attitude towards the Jews and unveiled his conception of this march and their enterprise: The more dead Jews, the merrier.

The actions of the German guards after the first of two air-raid attacks during this march were very much in the spirit of this ethos. In the confusion during the aftermath of the attack, some German army personnel had taken at least two of the wounded prisoners to an army hospital, where they were receiving treatment. The death march's guards made the effort to track down the women, prevented further medical care from being applied, and forced them, wounds notwithstanding, to rejoin the march. The German guards explained that for Jews there was to be no hospital care, there was to be no help.[13] Medical care violated the very essence of the death march. It was the death march's antithesis.

Some variation existed in the actions of the guards, some exceptions stood out against the numbing norm of general brutality, but the deviations from the standard themselves indicate how widespread the brutality was and, by implication, highlight the voluntarism of the perpetrators. The Jews on this march, like the suffering Jews in general, were astute empiricists. They understood the Germans who failed to act cruelly to be exceptional and noteworthy. The Jewish women once appealed to one older guard: " 'Let us live; you do not belong to this society.' "[14] This guard did not belong to this "society," a society of Jew-killers *par excellence*. He was one of the "older" guards, one of those Germans who was old enough to have been bred not only on Nazi German culture: "The older men of the guard unit were for the most part good-natured and did not beat or otherwise torment us. The younger SS men were far more brutal [*schon brutaler*]."[15] The younger guards were unrelenting.

The better guards were a distinct minority, and it was only among the men that they were to be found.[16] The women guards acted with hostility, brutality, and cruelty to the Jews. There was no exception.[17] Because they were operating under virtually no supervision (since both Dörr and the head woman guard were absent from the column during the daily marching, as a rule having gone ahead on bicycles to handle unending logistical matters), the guards were their own masters. A few took advantage of the laxity of command and supervision to flee their posts, to take leave of the death march. On the second day of the march, six of the women guards fled from the march. Why did the others not do the same? The Reich was finished; the end was already in sight. Getting away was easy, particularly for those among them who came from the local area. Similarly, why did they not let Jews who tried to flee get away? Why did they always kill the Jews whom they took into the woods instead of giving them their freedom, even though they were unsupervised? During the march, one guard did explicitly refuse to kill. This was openly discussed among the guards. Nothing appears to have happened to him.[18] Why did the others not refuse?

It bears emphasis that the women guards were without exception brutal to the Jews. Both in Helmbrechts (the male guards generally did not have much contact with the women) and on the march, the prisoners speak more of the cruelty of the women, and have nothing good to say about them. Given the testimony of the survivors, given the absence of evidence indicating that the guards were ever ordered on the march to be cruel to the prisoners—and many of the guards themselves have testified about the march—the assertion by the head woman guard that "all the 'SS' women guards carried rods and all of them beat the girls" should be taken as the final and conclusive word on their deeds and their voluntarism.

THE SIX-MONTH ordeal of the Jews which began in the Gross-Rosen satellite camp Schlesiersee and ended with the American doctor's examination and lifesaving emergency medical intervention defies or seems to defy comprehension in more than one sense. Even discounting all that these women had suffered prior to the six-month closing scene of this German-choreographed destructive drama—in other words, had the Jews begun this journey as pictures of health, instead of in an already frail and malnourished state—then it would still be difficult to comprehend how they survived, physically, psychologically, and emotionally, these six months of endless wandering, endless privations, endless cruelty and beatings, endless fear, and, most of all, endless starvation. It is simply hard, from the comfort of our chairs, to understand the pain and suffering that they endured, to imagine what each miserable hour of their ordeal was like. It is also hard to understand the Germans' purpose in conducting these marches, because marching the Jews around with no apparent purpose and killing them in increments violated any substantively rational foundation for policy. Finally, in light of the misery of the Jews' existence, it is hard to understand how people could willfully subject others to such treatment, let alone revel in it. The character of these Jews' six months of meanderings, which so defies the expectations of our common sense, was typical for Jews at the end of the war. The purposelessness of their movements, the privations, the misery, and the deaths constituted their everyday existence, constituted the everyday world constructed for them by their German keepers. Indeed, the Helmbrechts march, for all of its seeming extremeness, for all of its seeming incomprehensibility, is itself one of the most illustrative episodes of the Holocaust and provides a lens of perhaps unsurpassed clarity through which to view death marches.

The Helmbrechts death march was characterized by a number of features that should have been unusually propitious for producing decent treatment of Jews. Indeed, if one were to imagine the conditions that would most likely have led Germans to treat Jews well, this march in many ways came as close to approximating them as could have been expected in the Germany that had given itself to Nazism.

The end of the war was imminent. Whatever the personal or institutional incentives were that may have once existed for Germans' slavish devotion to orders, they no longer had any force in light of the momentary extinction of the regime. The old rules would presently no longer apply. The Germans had no reason to believe, under the as yet undefined, but certainly radically different incoming dispensation in the post-Nazi world, that the Jews would be seen and treated as different from other peoples, that they would be conceived of as "subhuman," let alone as "subhumanity's" most abject and hated element—in fact, given the prevailing conception that the Jews were the power behind both capitalism and Bolshevism, that they pulled the strings that made the Allies dance, these Germans had every reason to believe precisely the opposite, namely that the Jews would be powerful, favored, and privileged. These considerations applied, of course, to all German personnel shepherding death marches (or garrisoning camps) in the last months of the war and not just to the Helmbrechts' Germans. They should have informed the Germans' actions, had their conduct been conditioned by such kinds of considerations at all.

The German guards on this march (this was true of many others as well) operated virtually unsupervised, even by their commanding officer, so their actions went unmonitored by potentially punishing authority. They therefore had enormous discretion to act as they themselves desired. They could have easily escaped from the march, particularly since they were moving mainly through Germany itself—where they did not have to fear the local population—and through the very region which a number of them called home. Thus, had they been opposed to the mistreatment and killing of Jews, these Germans had great "structural" incentives and opportunities to treat them decently, or simply to flee their posts. Most striking and perhaps most significant, the Germans conducting this march also had explicit orders from Himmler not to kill the Jews and to treat them humanely, specific orders even to denude themselves of their implements of torture. These orders in themselves should have been decisive in shaping their conduct, producing humane conditions and treatment for the Jews on this march.

Turning to the victims, it would be hard to imagine a more unthreatening group of people. They were women, and women retained in European culture a certain immunity in military matters, if only because they were deemed less martial and threatening. Their debilitated physical condition, moreover, was such that no rational person, no person not in the grip of some powerfully distorting cognitive framework, could have seen them as threatening. So no objective reason of security or self-defense existed to warrant treating these women as a danger.

Just as the victims were among the least threatening people imaginable, the guards of this march should have been, by a number of measures, not appreciably more likely to be draconian than large sections of the German population. They were mainly non-SS, not clearly distinguishable from some haphazardly selected group of Germans. (Those in the SS, moreover, had had little additional ideological training.) The Jews were therefore not being guarded by people any more ideologized, any more in the grip of eliminationist antisemitism, than was the norm in Germany at the time. By their actions, moreover, the guards demonstrated that they were not *generally* brutal, that dispensing pain and suffering was not an invariable character trait of theirs, for they treated non-Jewish prisoners far better, some of them even well. Nothing, therefore, supports the belief that the Jews were being guarded by people who were inwardly, psychologically compelled to brutalize and kill any people who fell under their domination. Much evidence argues to the contrary.

Yet these conditions, singly and in sum total, unusually propitious by German standards for the decent treatment of Jews, produced precisely the opposite. The character of the Helmbrechts death march suggests why other death marches and other German institutions housing Jews were also lethal, brutal, and replete with willful cruelty. Although they were usually characterized by conditions far less favorable to the well-being of Jews, it was not the conditions that moved the Germans in institutions of killing to act as they did. The Helmbrechts death march demonstrates that the *conditions* themselves, that the structural "imperatives" of the institution, that even the content of the orders under which the Germans operated could all be varied, with little effect upon the treatment of the Jews. All of these factors, therefore, clearly had little to do with producing the Germans' brutality. Situational factors were not what caused the Germans to act as they did. The Helmbrechts death march is *crucial* for our understanding because it demonstrates that—so long as Nazi German society was intact—given the Germans' exterminationist antisemitism, Germans could not easily be induced to treat Jews decently after the years of eliminationist persecution and slaughter.

DURING THE THIRD death march period, from the end of 1944 to May 1945, hundreds of death marches similar to the ones departing Schlesiersee and Helmbrechts wended their way, often senselessly, through the ever-shrinking German dominion. An extensive, though not exhaustive, survey suggests certain patterns and recurrent features of death marches which mirror those of the ones discussed here.[19]

The death marches of the third period, whatever their many commonalities, composed a chaotic phenomenon, with sometimes significant variations in their character.[20] Authority was fracturing increasingly within Germany, and central control of the marches was conspicuously lacking; thus, it is no surprise that the Germans guarding the marches conducted them in varying manners. It is therefore all the more noteworthy that—despite the lack of centralized command, and in the unruly conditions of the war's denouement, when the institutionalized patterns of action in so many spheres broke down—the Germans guiding the marches generally acted in adherence to the basic, genocidal tenets of the German ethos during its Nazi period.

The disparities among the death marches were such that it would be hard to construct a persuasive model of them. The orders that the German commanders and the guards received about the purpose of the marches, their destinations, and the manner in which they were to transport and conduct the marches differed. Some marches saw the Germans treat non-Jews and Jews with approximately equal brutality, though in no case known to me did the Germans bestow preferential treatment on Jews. Yet, in general, the marches were death marches above all for Jews, and the Germans' actions towards them were in the main brutal and homicidal. In some camps, including Auschwitz and many of its satellite camps, the Germans abandoned Jews whom they deemed unable to take part in the march, leaving them to die or to be liberated, as fate would have it.[21] Yet, generally, the Germans killed totally incapacitated Jews (and sometimes non-Jews) either before evacuating the ambulatory prisoners from a camp or during the march, when their ability to keep up with the columns of dragging prisoners faltered. The prisoners mainly traveled on foot, though they sometimes rode in carts and even by train.

Foremost among the many little-known aspects of death marches are the identities of the guards. Typically, they were drawn from the personnel of the evacuating camps; as such, many were by vocation camp guards, members of the SS Death's Heads. Yet many were not. SS men were among them, as were many non-SS men, who belonged to civil defense forces and to different kinds of military or police units. The available, scattered evidence suggests that the guards' ages and backgrounds ran the gamut of physically able adults. Sometimes, as in the Helmbrechts march, ordinary German women alongside ordinary German men contributed to the ambulatory torture; ethnic Germans who had thrown their lot in with the Reich also stood side by side with their native-born German brethren as the victims collapsed at their feet.

As on the Helmbrechts march, the victims and their escorts traveled through territory that was sometimes unfriendly (as in Poland and Czechoslovakia) and sometimes friendly to the Germans. Most of the marches at the very end of the war took place on German soil. The German populace by the tens of thousands saw the forlorn columns of broken, often visibly wounded skeletons staggering through their towns and villages. Sometimes they acted with pity. More frequently, they looked upon these "subhumans" with hostility and moral disgust. They jeered. They threw stones. The extirpation of these "subhumans," even during these final hours of Nazism, was apparently not anathema to them. Civilian Germans are known to have aided the guards in recapturing escaped prisoners.[22] When the spirit moved them, German civilians also participated in the slaughter of the prisoners, which they themselves sometimes initiated.[23]

Noting these differences, the overwhelming fact remains that for Jews, these marches were death marches of the Helmbrechts kind. The same ceaseless Jewish agony could be recounted for so many other marches. The Jews suffered discriminatory treatment of all kinds in this final period of the war.[24] The Germans chose to kill them more frequently;[25] the German repertoire of cruelty was practiced more on them; Jews received the necessities of life in smaller and qualitatively impoverished quantities; the Germans, in some cases, would send them on the debilitating marches from camps where they allowed non-Jewish prisoners to remain.[26] Of course, the withholding of available food and water from the prisoners was an eloquent, if mute, announcement, almost incontestable in meaning, of the guards' understanding of the marches' purpose, of what the German guards hoped would happen to those under their care: "We passed through some German town. We asked for food. At first they thought that we were German refugees. The SS man who accompanied us shouted: 'Don't give them [anything] to eat, it's Jews they are.' And so I got no food. German children began to throw stones at us."[27] This occurred on the road between Neusalz and Bergen-Belsen. The German children, knowing nothing of Jews but what they learned from their society, understood how they were to act.

It was not only the treatment that the Germans accorded Jews in face-to-face relations which suggests death and suffering to have been their purpose. The absolute senselessness of the marches and the aimlessness of the routes that they followed also suggest that the marches, with their daily, hourly yield of debilitation and death, were their own reason for being. Many did follow relatively direct routes to their destinations. Yet many did not. One march, from Flossenbürg to Regensburg, a distance of 50 miles, set out on March 27. The march route took the following course.[28]

Flossenbürg
to Regensburg
Death March,
April 1945:
250 miles

Chemnitz

Lengenfeld

Auerbach

Plauen

Johanngeorgenstadt

Chomutov

Helmbrechts

Saale River

Ohře River

Karlovy Vary
(Karlsbad)

GERMANY

Mariánské
Lázně

Flossenbürg

German–
Czechoslovakia
Border, Pre-1938

Plzeň

Radbuza River

Náab River

Ohava River

Nuremberg

CZECHOSLOVAKIA

German–
Czechoslovakia
Border, April 1945

0   miles   25
0   kilometers   40

Regensburg

Regen River

Danube River

© Mark Stein Studios, 1995

The prisoners, under way for three weeks, covered 250 miles, five times the real distance. Averaging more than 20 miles a day, it is no wonder that few survived the ordeal.[29]

Viewing the maps of some other death march routes should be sufficient to convince anyone that the meanderings could have had no end other than to keep the prisoners marching. And the effects were calculable—and calculated.

The Germans in charge of the marches, who, cut off from headquarters, were almost always on their own while under way, were under no compulsion to trek aimlessly; they could have chosen to remain in one place, feed their

0 miles 25
0 kilometers 40

Dresden ●

● Gera

Chemnitz ●

Berga ●----●
Zwickau

Lengenfeld ●

Saale River

Plauen ●   ● Auerbach

Chomutov ●

Helmbrechts ●

● Kraslice

Ohře River

Karlovy Vary ●
(Karlsbad)

N
W-E
S

G E R M A N Y

Mariánské ●
Lázně

CZECHOSLOVAKIA

Flossenbürg ●

German–
Czechoslovakia
Border, Pre-1938

● Plzeň

Radbuza River

Otava River

**Berga to Plauen
Death March,
April 1945:
170 miles**

German–
Czechoslovakia
Border, April 1945

© Mark Stein Studios, 1995

prisoners, and deliver them to the Allies, who, no matter what, were bound to reach them in a few days or weeks. As far as is known, this never occurred.[30] The death marches were not means of transport; the marching transports were means of death.

Finally, the fidelity of the Germans to their genocidal enterprise was so great as seeming to defy comprehension. Their world was disintegrating around them, yet they persisted in genocidal killing until the end. A survivor of a march from the Dora-Mittelbau camp indicts not only the guards but also the German bystanders who had no need to involve themselves in this matter:

> One night we stopped near the town of Gardelegen. We lay down in a field and several Germans went to consult about what they should do. They returned with a lot of young people from the Hitler Youth and with members of the police force from the town. They chased us all into a large barn. Since

Neuengamme to Sandbostel Death March, April 1945: 215 miles

© Mark Stein Studios, 1995

we were 5,000–6,000 people, the wall of the barn collapsed from the pressure of the mass of people, and many of us fled. The Germans poured out petrol and set the barn on fire. Several thousand people were burned alive. Those of us who had managed to escape, lay down in the nearby wood and heard the heart-rending screams of the victims. This was on April 13. One day later the place was conquered by Eisenhower's army. When the Americans got there, the bodies were still burning.[31]

The Germans started marches in the final days of the war from many camps. Flossenbürg, Sachsenhausen, Neuengamme, Magdeburg, Mauthausen, Ravensbrück, and satellite camps of Dachau all disgorged prisoners on journeys with no effective destination.[32] What could their German jailers possibly have been thinking that they were accomplishing? Germany's final death march, which was perhaps the last and fitting gasp of Nazism, set out on the night of May 7, when virtually all of Germany was already occupied, and less than twenty-four hours before its official surrender.[33]

Jewish survivors report with virtual unanimity German cruelties and killings until the very end.[34] They leave no doubt that the Germans were seething with hatred for their victims; the Germans were not emotionally neutral executors of superior orders, or cognitively and emotionally neutral bureaucrats indifferent to the nature of their deeds. The Germans chose to act as they did with no effectual supervision, guided only by their own comprehension of the world, by their own notions of justice, and in contradistinction to their own interests in avoiding capture with blood on their hands. Their trueness to meting out suffering and death was not an imposed behavior; it came from within, an expression of their innermost selves.[35]

One of the burned victims of Gardelegen in the position in which he died

In the governmental, institutional, logistical, and emotional chaos of the last months and weeks of the war, it is no surprise that an incoherent phenomenon like the death march would have become a central institution of Germany during the Nazi period. The marches were ostensibly intended to move prisoners *qua* workers to new work locations so that they could continue to produce for the Reich. As the discussion of Jewish "work" has demonstrated, the Germans' invocation of "work" was not necessarily or primarily referring to productive labor, "work" for Jews having been understood in the German linguistic community for what it was: just another means of slaughter, a slow and sometimes satisfying one for the Germans. Similarly, the marches did not, in fact, serve any real productive purposes—how many of

Bodies of Gardelegen victims who attempted to burrow under the barn's doors

the guards could have fought, how many trains could have moved troops or supplies?—regardless of the German verbal homage to the victims' labor power. Just as the Germans in camps knew that economic productivity was not the reason that they compelled the Jews to perform non-instrumental labor—such as in Buchenwald, where "work consisted of carrying sacks of wet salt back and forth"[36]—and that the Jews were not confined in that or any other camp primarily to do work, the guards of Helmbrechts and of other death marches knew that their Jews were not being marched around because of some productive potential within them that was to be reaped for Germany. Whatever hallucinatory notions those who ordered the death marches may have had about using the prisoners for work, the ordinary Germans guarding the Helmbrechts and other marches could have been under no illusions, when facing these walking corpses, that their task was to husband them as valuable productive resources. Ideologized or not, every person recognizes such weakened people as incapable of physical labor. No person in possession of his senses could have believed that the marches served any utilitarian purpose save the victims' further punishment, suffering, and deaths. When it came to Jews, Germans—from the lowest of ranks to Hitler himself—understood what they with their actions were seeking to accomplish.

Indeed, every aspect of the Germans' actions violated a premise of the marchers' future labor productivity. The Germans who had most to say about the treatment of the Jews and their fate were these ordinary Germans who guarded the Jews and other prisoners. And they acted in a manner that leaves no plausible conclusion about their understanding of what intention they believed the death marches served, other than the one voiced by one of the guards from the Helmbrechts death march while reflecting on its sense and purpose: "If I were asked whether the purpose of the march was, more or less, that the Jewish prisoners should gradually be driven to death, I must say that one could indeed have this feeling. I have no proof of this, but the manner in which this transport was carried out speaks for it."[37] The death marches were but the continuation of the work of the concentration and extermination camps, the work of Hitler, the work of all Germans who contributed to this innocent people's destruction.[38]

These German guards of Schlesiersee, Helmbrechts, and the other death marches, these ordinary Germans, knew that they were continuing the work that had begun and had been to a great extent already accomplished in the camp system and in the other institutions of killing: to exterminate the Jewish people.

In naming them "death marches," the victims were not engaging in mere rhetorical flourish or simply characterizing them according to the high death rates. The entire manner in which the Germans conducted them suggested to the Jews that they intended death. To the very end, the ordinary Germans who perpetrated the Holocaust willfully, faithfully, and zealously slaughtered Jews. They did so even when they were risking their own capture. They did so even when they had received a command from no less a personage than Himmler that they desist from their killing.

PART VI

Eliminationist Antisemitism, Ordinary Germans, Willing Executioners

We had fed the heart on fantasies,
The heart's grown brutal from the fare
WILLIAM BUTLER YEATS, "MEDITATIONS IN TIME
OF CIVIL WAR"

If for years, for decades, one preaches that the Slavic race is an inferior race, that the Jews are not human beings at all, then the inevitable end result must be such an explosion.
SS GENERAL ERICH VON DEM BACH–ZELEWSKI AT THE NUREMBERG
MAJOR WAR CRIMINALS TRIALS EXPLAINING THE RELATIONSHIP
BETWEEN NAZI IDEOLOGY AND THE CRIMES THAT GERMANS
PERPETRATED, INCLUDING THE *EINSATZGRUPPEN*'S GENOCIDAL
SLAUGHTER IN THE SOVIET UNION

Death is a master from Germany.
PAUL CELAN, "DEATH FUGUE"

15

EXPLAINING

THE PERPETRATORS' ACTIONS:

ASSESSING THE COMPETING

EXPLANATIONS

THIS BOOK ENDEAVORS to place the perpetrators at the center of the study of the Holocaust and to explain their actions. It seeks to answer a number of questions about them, principally the following three: Did the perpetrators of the Holocaust kill willingly? If so, what motivated them to kill and brutalize Jews? How was this motivation engendered?

The answering of these questions began with an investigation of the evolution of eliminationist antisemitism in modern Germany which demonstrated the persistence of a widespread, profound German cultural animus towards Jews that evolved from an early nineteenth-century eliminationist form to the more deadly twentieth-century incarnation. The ensuing analysis of the overall course of the Germans' anti-Jewish policy showed that the policy, which was always an expression of eliminationist antisemitism, evolved in conjunction with the real opportunities for "solving" the "Jewish Problem." Only when the Germans gained control of the majority of European Jews and when, owing to the war, external constraints disappeared, could the Germans finally act upon Hitler's pre-existing exterminationist intention—and they did. Then, following a general account of the paradigmatic institution of killing, the camp, came the empirical heart of the study: a more thorough investigation and evaluation of three types of killing institutions. The discussion of the institutions of killing detailed the perpetrators' actions, chronicled their deeds, and highlighted their general voluntarism, enthusiasm, and cruelty in performing their assigned and self-appointed tasks.

In light of what these investigations have demonstrated, it is now possible to begin a more methodical, integrated analysis of the perpetrators, by drawing together the lessons from the cases, by providing a systematic account of the perpetrators' actions, and by undertaking a more considered evaluation of various explanations of the perpetration of the Holocaust, both the conventional ones in the literature and my own. Whatever this analysis shows, its conclusions have far-reaching implications for how this period should be understood, an aspect of which is touched upon in the Epilogue.

EACH INSTITUTION OF killing—police battalions, "work" camps, and death marches—were chosen for study precisely because, in different ways, they provide a difficult test for my explanation. Their study, moreover, unearths particularly important aspects of the Holocaust that have not been until now sufficiently discussed. The findings from the cases also indicate that four categories of action were generally to be found among the perpetrators of the Holocaust.

THE PERPETRATORS' ACTIONS

Ordered by Authority

		Yes	No
Cruelty	Yes	Organized and "Structured" Cruelty	"Excesses" Such as Torture
	No	Killing Operations and Individual Killings	"Acts of Initiative" Such as Individually Initiated Killings

Each of the four types of action was an ordinary, typical, even a regularly occurring constituent feature of the perpetrators' treatment of Jews. First, Germans routinely took initiative in killing Jews, both by customarily carrying out their orders with dedication and inventiveness and, frequently, by taking it upon themselves to kill Jews even when they had no orders to do so, or could have left it to others. This individual initiative, this killing beyond the call of their orders, is in need of explanation. Second, the perpetrators' actions undertaken under direct superior orders—which included most of what they did that contributed to the slaying of Jews—is as demanding of explanation as those that they initiated themselves. This study, particularly of police battalions, demonstrates that the Germans' opportunities to extract themselves from killing operations render "following orders" a more complex psychological and motivational problem than has been generally acknowledged.

The third and fourth types of action, which were different kinds of cruelty, were each a well-nigh continuous feature of the perpetrators' treatment of Jews. The third, authoritative cruelty, took two forms. The Germans who were both making and implementing decisions structured institutions that housed Jews so that they would produce immense Jewish suffering, which, no matter what the material scarcity of the times may have been, was objectively unnecessary. In the case of the "work" institutions, the Germans' brutalizing of Jews was in complete violation of the institutions' formal purpose. A second sort of authoritative cruelty was another common feature of the Holocaust, namely when officers and even non-commissioned officers organized groups of their men to torture Jews.

The fourth type of action was the individually initiated German cruelty. It was so routine, so part of quotidian existence, particularly in institutions with extended intimate contact between Germans and Jews, that as an action to be explained, it must be conceived of as being on a par, in frequency and importance, with the killing itself. Such voluntaristic cruelty was the grammar of German expression in camps of all kinds, including "work" camps, taking its most mundane form in the reflexive beatings Germans administered to Jews with their ever-present whips and rods. As one survivor of the Józefów massacre and of years of living under and hiding from the Germans put it, when speaking of the collective Jewish experience at the hands of Germans, "the Germans always came to us with whips and dogs."[1] The cruelty, it must be emphasized, had no instrumental purpose save Jewish suffering and German satisfaction. The Germans often gave this cruelty symbolic form, from the physically painless, such as mocking the Jews and cutting off Jewish beards, to the excruciatingly painful and deadly, such as the beating of Jewish men selected for their bearded Jewish appearance and the burning to death of people in synagogues. This cruelty, which expressed, moreover, a symbolic quality transparent to all, is also in need of explanation.

The nature of the existing evidence, of course, does not permit us to know what each perpetrator did. Yet the following can still be said: Every perpetrator contributed to the program of extermination (this is a definitional matter), and very few opted out of such duties in the institutions which are known to have given them the choice. In institutions where intimate contact existed between Germans and Jews, namely where the opportunity to be brutal existed, German cruelty was nearly universal. This was true of camps in general, whether they were concentration camps, "work" camps, or ghettos.

The abundant testimony of survivors is clear on this point, and it is supported even by admissions of the perpetrators themselves. This cruelty, moreover, was almost always voluntaristic, which means that all those who inflicted it took initiative in the brutalizing of Jews. Finally, the killing operations were characterized by widespread German dedication and zeal, without which the genocide would never have proceeded so smoothly. Thus, with the exception of those who had little or no opportunity (owing to an absence of intimate contact) to brutalize Jews, either all or at least the vast majority of perpetrators engaged in the various actions discussed here.

Explaining these four generalized actions must be done while taking into account a number of other factors. The gruesomeness of killing operations for all those in police battalions, particularly when they themselves conducted mass slaughters with gunfire, should have provided great incentive for the men to excuse themselves from further killing operations. Even when the Germans were not bespattered by the blood or the flying body matter of the victims, the Jews' cries of extreme pain and anguish should also have provided great incentive for the perpetrators to refrain from inflicting such pain upon them further. Yet the extraordinary, horrific nature of the campaign of extermination against the Jews, which constituted the phenomenological reality of the perpetrators, appears to have deterred few from treating Jews in the customary German manner of these years.

In some institutions more than others, and in some circumstances within an institution, role templates—that is, the latitude the actors had in deciding for themselves how they were to act—were quite loose, quite permissive. Put differently, Germans sometimes had opportunities, sometimes substantial opportunities, to "exit," both from killing institutions and from certain activities within those institutions. They rarely availed themselves of them. They also had opportunities for "voice," if only to express whatever dissatisfaction they might have had, either to their superiors or, especially, to their comrades. Untainted evidence of such dissent is paltry, almost non-existent. Any explanation of their actions must account for the perpetrators' failure to "exit" and their failure to express dissent.

The character of the perpetrators' non-killing actions was also not trivial, and indeed in some ways extraordinary. Their celebrations, their willingness to have their wives live among them as they slaughtered Jews by the thousands, their eagerness to preserve the memories of their genocidal deeds by means of photographs which they took and posed for with evident pride and willingly exhibited and made available to their comrades, not to mention the boasting of cruelties that took place among them—all these at once provide insight into the killers' motivations and are distinguishing features of this genocide. All of them need to be explained.

THE CONVENTIONAL EXPLANATIONS cannot account for the findings of this study, for the evidence from the cases presented here. They are belied by the actions of the perpetrators, glaringly and irrefutably. The notions that the perpetrators contributed to genocide because they were coerced, because they were unthinking, obedient executors of state orders, because of social psychological pressure, because of the prospects of personal advancement, or because they did not comprehend or feel responsible for what they were doing, owing to the putative fragmentation of tasks, can each be demonstrated in quick order to be untenable. These conventional explanations cannot account for the perpetrators' killing activities, which, it must be emphasized, are generally *the only type of action that they directly address.* The other perpetrator actions that have been specified and described here, especially the endemic cruelty, the conventional explanations all but ignore. Even the most cursory glance shows that they are inadequate for explaining these actions. The conventional explanations' enormous shortcomings, moreover, are not only empirical. They suffer from common conceptual and theoretical failings.

Any explanation which relies upon the notion that the perpetrators operated under external compulsion, or even under an erroneous presumption on their part that they had no choice but to kill, can be dismissed immediately. Evidence from police battalions has already been presented regarding the opportunities that Germans had to refuse to kill. More generally, it can be said with certitude that never in the history of the Holocaust was a German, SS man or otherwise, killed, sent to a concentration camp, jailed, or punished in any serious way for refusing to kill Jews. How can we be sure of this?[2]

In light of the incessant, rote assertions of German postwar trial defendants that refusal brought dire consequences, it is in itself telling that after the legal investigations of many tens of thousands of Germans, there were only fourteen cases in which it was claimed that the punishment for refusing to carry out an execution order (not only of Jews) was either death (nine cases), imprisonment in a concentration camp (four cases), or transfer to a military penal unit (one case). Moreover, not one of these cases has been able to withstand scrutiny. Two separate comprehensive studies of the possibility for Germans to refuse execution orders have each demonstrated these claims to be false.[3] One of the studies concludes unequivocally: "In no case could it be proven that the refusal to kill resulted in an injury to life and limb."[4]

Because the records of the SS and police courts show that no one was ever executed or sent to a concentration camp for refusing to kill Jews, because Himmler's personal role in confirming death sentences for SS men precluded the possibility of summary executions, and, most of all, because no one has ever produced even one verified case of a man having been killed or sent to a concentration camp for not carrying out an execution order—despite the enormous effort made to unearth such cases (the defense at Nuremberg was allowed into the SS internment camps to seek out instances) and the enormous incentive that all perpetrators had for providing such evidence— we can conclude only that the likelihood of any SS man ever having suffered such punishment for refusing to kill Jews is small.[5] The abundance and strength of the evidence, in fact, justify the conclusion that it never happened.

Unable to produce for the courts even one example to substantiate their assertions, many of the German killers have resorted to the argument that, regardless of the true state of affairs, they had sincerely believed that refusing to carry out an execution order was suicidal, and that they had simply acted on this belief; if their knowledge was faulty, they were not to blame.[6]

This postwar assertion is also false because it was well known certainly among many of the German executioners that they did not have to kill and that they were even permitted to transfer out of their killing units. This has already been discussed at length with regard to Police Battalion 101 and other police battalions. In at least nine of them—and we simply do not know about most of the others—the men knew that they did not have to kill. There is similar evidence for the other major peripatetic killing institution, the *Einsatzgruppen*, for concentration camps, and for other institutions of killing.[7] There was a written order by Himmler which allowed men in the *Einsatzgruppen* who so wished to transfer, in the words of a member of *Einsatzgruppe A*, "for other work back home."[8] Himmler issued this order after the difficulties that some men had had during the initial period of slaughter. The evidence suggests that formal orders permitting the men of police units to avoid killing also existed, which means that the knowledge that refusing to kill was possible was still more widespread than in the nine battalions for which there is positive evidence. A member of Police Battalion 67 testifies "that we were repeatedly, in my opinion monthly, instructed that, in accordance with a Himmler Order, nobody can order us to shoot anyone."[9] Himmler, the *Einsatzgruppen* officers, and many police commanders apparently believed that only those who were dedicated and up to the task would be asked to kill Jews.[10]

There were, moreover, instances when Germans successfully requested transfers from institutions of killing. This has already been documented for police battalions; it also occurred in the *Einsatzgruppen*. The commander of *Einsatzgruppe D*, the then SS Colonel Otto Ohlendorf, declared during his trial at Nuremberg: "I had sufficient occasion to see how many men of my

Gruppe did not agree to this order in their inner opinion. Thus, I forbade the participation in these executions on the part of some of these men and I sent some back to Germany."[11] A lieutenant, serving in *Einsatzgruppe D* as an adjutant, corroborated that such transfers occurred frequently in the *Einsatzgruppen,* and that the executioners knew that they could transfer because the "commanding officer himself announced to the Gruppe that particular individuals were unfit for the performance of such tasks and therefore were to be released."[12] A similar situation prevailed in *Einsatzgruppe C,* where its commander, SS General Max Thomas, had given an explicit order to his subordinates that anyone who could not bring himself to kill the Jews, either for reasons of conscience or weakness, should be sent back to Germany or assigned to other work. Thomas did, in fact, send a number of people home.[13]

The evidence that no German was ever killed or incarcerated for having refused to kill Jews is conclusive. It is also incontestable that the knowledge that they did not have to kill, if they preferred not to, was *extremely widespread* among the killers, as the discussion of police battalions and what is known about the *Einsatzgruppen* and other institutions of killing affirm. The courts of the Federal Republic of Germany have steadfastly and rightly rejected claims on the part of the perpetrators that they had genuinely believed that they had had no choice but to kill. The courts have rejected this not only because it was widely known among the killers that they did not have to kill but also because of the ordinary, minimal steps—such as appealing to a superior or applying for a transfer—that anyone who was opposed to the killing could have taken without subjecting himself to danger. The evidence suggests that the perpetrators almost never took these steps.

Because the killers, at least a very large number of them, did not have to kill, any explanation which is incompatible with the killers' possibility of choice must, in light of this evidence, be ruled out. Germans could say "no" to mass murder. They chose to say "yes."

A second conventional line of explanation depends on the notion that people in general, and particularly Germans, are strongly if not ineluctably prone to obeying orders, regardless of their content. The perpetrators, in this view, were blind followers of orders, unwavering servants of authority, and acted because of this moral and psychological imperative to obey. Articulated and unarticulated, fully elaborated and half-conscious notions about obedience shape much discussion of the Holocaust and its perpetrators.

Regarding Germany during the Nazi period and its crimes, the argument is made, often reflexively as though it were an axiomatic truth, that Germans are particularly obedient to state authority. This argument cannot be sustained. The very people, Germans, who supposedly were slavishly devoted to the cult of the state and to obedience for obedience's sake, were the same people, Germans, who battled in the streets of Weimar in defiance of existing state authority and often in order to overthrow it.[14] In light of this, it can hardly be maintained that Nazis or Germans regarded all state orders as sacred commands and believed that they were to be carried out unconditionally, regardless of their content.

This, not its opposite, is the obvious conclusion, given that millions of Germans were in open rebellion against the authority of Weimar. The legal order and state authority of the Weimar Republic was disdained, openly mocked, and routinely violated by an enormous number of Germans spanning the political spectrum, by ordinary citizens and state officials alike. Germans' *conditional* regard for authority should be the truism. Germans should not be caricatured; like other peoples, they have regard for authority if they hold it to be legitimate, and for orders that they deem to be legitimate. They too weigh an order's source and its meaning when deciding if and how to carry it out. Orders deemed in violation of moral norms—especially of fundamental moral norms—in fact, can do much to undermine the legitimacy of the regime from which they emanate—as the order to massacre community after community, tens of thousands of defenseless men, women, and children, would have in the eyes of anyone who believed the victims' deaths to be unjust.

Indeed, Germans of all ranks, even the most Nazified, disobeyed orders that they opposed, that they deemed illegitimate. Generals who willingly contributed to the extermination of Soviet Jews conspired against Hitler.[15] Army soldiers, on their own, participated in the killing of Jews without orders to do so, or in disobedience of orders to keep their distance from the massacres.[16] Sometimes Germans were insubordinate in order to satisfy their lust to kill Jews. The men of Police Battalion 101 violated their commander's, indeed their beloved commander's, injunction not to be cruel. To recall the opening section of this book, one of the officers in Police Battalion 101, a zealous executioner of Jews, Captain Wolfgang Hoffmann, once forcefully set in writing his refusal to obey a superior order that he deemed morally objectionable. The man who led the members of his company in gruesome, prolific genocidal slaughter refused to allow them to sign a declaration which implied that they might steal from Poles, for the signing would have been an acknowledgment that they could conceivably violate the "honor" of a German soldier.[17] This one letter provides more insight into the Germans' genocidal mind-set and into their capacity to make moral decisions and to act upon them than do reams of the perpetrators' self-serving postwar testimony. The Germans who marched the emaciated and sick Jewish women from Helmbrechts provide another telling example of the Germans' capacity and practice of disobeying orders of which they disapproved. These Germans continued to kill the Jewish women despite an explicit order from Himmler, announced to them by his personal courier, to cease killing. Many more instances—from German military and police institutions, as well as from German society itself, including the frequent labor strikes, the vociferous protests against various governmental religious policies, and the widespread vocal opposition to the so-called Euthanasia program—of German disobedience of authority during the Nazi period occurred. The more that the actual actions of Germans are investigated, including those of the perpetrators, the more fanciful assertions become about blind German obedience, and the clearer it becomes that this is a moral alibi that ought to be exposed and discarded.[18]

Arguments holding that Germans inflexibly obey authority—namely that they reflexively obey any order, regardless of its content—are untenable. By extension, so are the claims by Stanley Milgram and many others that humans in general are blindly obedient to authority.[19] All "obedience," all "crimes of obedience" (and this refers only to situations in which coercion is not applied or threatened), depend upon the existence of a propitious social and political context, in which the actors deem the authority to issue commands legitimate and the commands themselves not to be a gross transgression of sacred values and the overarching moral order.[20] Otherwise, people seek ways, granted with differential success, not to violate their deepest moral beliefs and not to undertake such grievous acts.

The third of the conventional explanations maintains that the perpetrators were induced to contribute to mass murder by the social psychological pressure engendered by situational factors and by their peers.[21] Pressure to conform was indeed to be found among the perpetrators, as in the case of Germans staffing "work" and concentration camps who hit or feigned at hitting Jews when and only when in the presence of other Germans. Lieutenant Buchmann of Police Battalion 101, despite his evident disapproval of the killing, seems to have been sufficiently pressured at one time that he took part in a killing operation. Nevertheless, the evidence suggests overwhelmingly that this peer and institutional pressure was not of fundamental importance for bringing the perpetrators to mass slaughter, and would not have been sufficient had it been the main motivational pillar of the undertaking.

The notion that peer pressure, namely the desire either not to let down one's comrades or not to incur their censure, could move individuals to undertake actions that they oppose, even abhor, is plausible even for the German perpetrators, but only as an account of the participation of some *individuals* in the perpetration of the Holocaust. It cannot be operative for more than a few individuals in a group, especially over a long period of time. If a large segment of a group, not to mention the vast majority of its members, opposes or abhors an act, then the social psychological pressure would work to *prevent,* not to encourage, individuals to undertake the act. If indeed Germans had disapproved of the mass slaughter, then peer pressure would not have induced people to kill against their will, but would have sustained their individual and collective resolve to avoid killing.[22] At best, and in all probability rightly, the actions of only some small minority of the perpetrators can be accounted for by positing the existence of social psychological pressure to conform. The explanation is self-contradictory when applied to the actions of *entire groups* of Germans.[23] Its explanatory capacity, therefore, is greatly limited. The kindred psychological argumentation of these second and third conventional lines of reasoning—that Germans in particular and humans in general are prone to obey orders, and that social psychological pressure was sufficient to induce them to kill—are untenable. As is shown, in part, by the choice of some to opt out of the genocidal killing, Germans were indeed *capable* of saying "no."

The fourth of the conventional explanations holds that the perpetrators, like petty bureaucrats, pursued their self-interest (conceptualized of as career advancement or personal enrichment) in total disregard of other considerations. This explanation has been advanced to account for the acts taken by Germans in positions of responsibility in institutions that were involved in the making or executing of German policy towards Jews. Whatever its (extremely) remote plausibility in explaining these perpetrators' actions, it is untenable as an explanation of the foot soldiers' actions in this war against the Jews. Most of the men of police battalions, as well as many other perpetrators, had no bureaucratic or career interests to advance by their involvement. They were not bucking for promotions, meaningless promotions, for these were older conscripts who would soon return to their private middle-, lower-middle-, and working-class lives. Also, few of them stood to enrich themselves, and the evidence does not suggest that any but a few did.[24] As a source of motivation to commit mass murder, this "self-interest" argument fails to accord with even the basic facts.[25] With some exceptions, the perpetrators did not have any career or material personal incentives to continue killing, to make them not to want to say "no" to mass murder.

The fifth of the conventional explanations posits that the perpetrators' tasks were so fragmented that they either did not comprehend the real significance of their individual actions or, if they did, that the alleged fragmentation then allowed them to displace responsibility onto others. As a general explanation of the perpetrators' actions—of the Germans, for example, who were shooting Jews face to face, after having been told explicitly of the order for the total annihilation of the Jewish people—this line of reasoning is fanciful. It is a fanciful account even of the actions of the so-called desk murderers, for which this explanation is, without evidence, often proposed. Since it is clear that tens of thousands of Germans who understood all too well what they were doing were willing to kill Jews, there is no need to concoct an (empirically unsustainable) alibi of incomprehension to explain why some others did not understand quite what it was that they were doing or did not realize that they had the responsibility to say "no." Most of them understood perfectly well, and there is no reason to believe that those who did not would have acted otherwise had they had more knowledge.

None of the five conventional explanations can adequately account even for the Germans' killing of Jews under orders. Whatever their enormous failings in explaining the act of killing under orders, they have at least a surface plausibility regarding this category of action. In accounting, however, for the other types of perpetrators' actions, the conventional explanations do not have even this semblance of credibility. In fact, their adherents almost universally fail to address directly, explicitly, or systematically the perpetrators' actions other than killing under orders.

The initiative that perpetrators routinely showed in their cruel and lethal actions towards the Jews, the zeal that characterized the Germans carrying out the retributive and exterminatory policy against European Jewry, cannot be accounted for by the conventional explanations. Each one asserts or assumes that the Germans were in principle opposed (or would have been had they not, supposedly, been rendered "indifferent," numbed by their institutional circumstances) to the mass slaughter of Jews, to a genocidal program. Raul Hilberg, who can be seen as an exemplar of this sort of thinking, asks: "Just how did the German bureaucracy overcome its moral scruples?"[26] He assumes that "the German bureaucracy" naturally had "moral scruples" regarding the treatment of Jews which with difficulty had to be surmounted in order for the persecution of the Jews to proceed. Hilberg and the other adherents of such explanations purport to present reasons why such putative disapproval and opposition could be overcome (or why such "indifference" could be produced) and why Germans would act against their inner wishes and kill Jews. Explanations proceeding in this manner cannot account for Germans taking initiative, doing more than they had to, or volunteering for killing duty when no such volunteering was necessary—all of which occurred routinely. Such explanations cannot account for the instances in which Germans killed Jews in violation of orders not to do so. Such explanations cannot account for the overall, indeed incredible, smoothness that characterized the execution of this far-flung program which was dependent upon so many people, people who, either through sabotage or foot-dragging, could have produced innumerable mishaps and poorly executed tasks.[27]

The initiative in killing, the devotion to their Nazi calling is matched, perhaps surpassed, by the cruelty which the perpetrators visited upon their victims. A constant and pervasive cruelty marked the Germans' treatment of Jews, especially in camps and ghettos. The Germans were cruel not only in that they incarcerated the Jews within wretched enclosures under a harsh regime designed to cause pain and suffering and then killed them in gruesome ways. Their cruelty was also personal, direct, and immediate. With their ubiquitous and ever-present whips and rods, with their bare hands, with their boots, the Germans pummeled Jews, lacerated their flesh, trampled them underfoot, and forced them to perform bizarre and self-abasing acts. The scene in Białystok in which a member of Police Battalion 309 urinated on a Jew in public in the presence of a German general is emblematic. To this ordinary German, Jews were excrement to be treated accordingly. One of the German physicians at Auschwitz, Heinz Thilo, described the camp as "*anus mundi*," the anus of the world,[28] the orifice through which the Germans were eliminating the putative social-biological excrement of humanity: the Jews.

"Cruelty has a human heart," begins one of William Blake's great poems.[29] The record of human history is replete with large-scale, organized, sanctioned cruelties. Slave hunters and slave owners, tyrannical regimes, colonial predators, ecclesiastical inquisitors, and police interrogators have tortured and tormented in order to maintain and increase their power, to amass riches, and to extract confessions. Yet in the long annals of human barbarism, the cruelties practiced by Germans upon Jews during the Nazi period stand out by their scope, variety, inventiveness, and, above all, by their wantonness. Orlando Patterson, in his magisterial work *Slavery and Social Death*, discusses fifty-eight slave societies which he studied closely. He finds that in nearly 80 percent of these societies the masters generally treated the slaves well and only in roughly 20 percent "badly or brutally." He further reports that though in 29 percent of these societies there were no legal restraints upon them, the masters nevertheless generally treated their slaves well.[30] And it would appear that even in the distinct minority of societies in which masters acted brutally towards their slaves, the treatment was seldom as constant, as limitless, as varied, or as purposefully contrived as the brutality that prevailed in the German-run camps and ghettos. The universe of death and torment into which the Germans hurled the Jews finds its closest approximation in the portrayals of hell contained in religious teachings and in the art of Dante or Hieronymus Bosch. "By comparison" to what he was witnessing at Auschwitz, wrote one of the German physicians in the camp, Johann Paul Kremer, "Dante's *Inferno* seems to me to be almost a comedy."[31]

To the German overlords, the Jew was not a slave whom they occasionally whipped in order to make him work to the limit of his physical strength but whose body, being a valuable commodity, they preserved in sound condition. He was not a political subversive whom the Germans tortured in order to extract from him the secrets of the underground to which he belonged. He was not a suspected heretic whom the Germans placed on the rack in order to make him confess to his deviant beliefs. The very being, the very sight of the Jews, regardless of their conduct, aroused in the German overlords the impulse to violence.

The Germans' voluntaristic cruelty, the Germans' beatings that were the "invariable daily fare" for the Jews living in camps, the Germans' "sport" practiced upon the Jews, the Germans' symbolic cruelty perpetrated upon the Jews, were an integral and typical feature of the Germans' actions. The Germans often used Jews as playthings, compelling them, like circus animals, to perform antics—antics that debased the Jews and amused their tormentors.

Germans force Jews to leap-frog in Minsk Mazowiecki.

Of their treatment at the hands of the Germans, the Jews could say, paraphrasing King Lear, "As flies to wanton boys are we to the Germans, they kill and torture us for their sport." In Poland, the Germans' sport began with their arrival in 1939. According to one Jewish survivor, "life quickly became unbearable. Beatings were routine. They [the Germans] sacked and plundered. They raided neighboring villages, and after each trip the notorious gray execution lists covered the walls. They incited displaced Poles to loot Jewish homes. They rounded us up for all kinds of sadistic performances, and prophesied that they would be here a full year, during which time we would not have five minutes' peace—easily the grossest understatement of the war."[32] Such brutality was as a rule voluntaristic, performed for no master other than a German's own passions. Among the Germans who ruled directly over the doomed Jewish denizens of the empire of torment and death, cruelty became normative and well-nigh universal. The minority of Germans who inwardly shrank from being cruel felt compelled to dissemble brutality in order to conform to the prevailing ethos. Jewish survivors provide evidence of a few Germans who beat Jews only when observed by other Germans, and beat them so as to inflict minimal injury and pain. This is eloquent testimony that the other Germans could have done so but rather *chose* to brutalize the Jews, whether they were being observed or not. Chaim Kaplan, the brilliant diarist of the Warsaw ghetto, took pains to describe those few instances when, of the many Germans from various institutions whom he observed or learned about in Warsaw, any departed from the standard brutal and cruel practices. One non-murderous foreman knew that if he did not explicitly declare his humanity, then the Jews, based on their vast, painful experience, would assume him to be like all the other brutes. He told a friend of Kaplan's: " 'Don't be afraid of me. I am not tainted with hatred for the Jews.' " Kaplan recounts another instance when some German soldiers courteously asked to be included in a sporting match that some Jews were playing. The Germans' friendly participation was astonishing. In Kaplan's words: "It was a miracle."[33] Any survey of the life of camps and ghettos shows how rare it was for a German to act humanely. As Erich Goldhagen writes, "these 'Good Germans,' as they were called, seemed like lonely sober figures in the midst of a macabre, orgiastic carnival. Their common decency seemed as rare and wondrous as the conduct of saintly men in ordinary times. The Jews recounted the deeds of such individuals as one recounts the lives of saints, with awe and wonderment, and legends were spun around their names."[34] The Germans, namely the vast majority of the perpetrators, whose actions made the rare instances of decent conduct seem like a miracle, could not have condemned the final goal of the "Final Solution," to which their cruelty contributed significantly. German cruelty towards Jews—which as a rule was gratuitous and had no instrumental, pragmatic purpose save the satisfaction and pleasure of the perpetrators[35]—defies any explanation which holds that the actors disapproved of their own actions.

The cruelty that Germans inflicted on Jews which flowed from superior authority—whether of the systemic, structured kind, embedded in every fiber of camp life, or of the impromptu, on-the-spot, organized variety—provides insight into the perpetrators' temper of mind. Such cruelty demonstrated to the perpetrators, and to an enormous number of other Germans who knew of it, that the enterprise that they supported could not possibly be "lawful"—as a "lawful" execution, even a wholesale one, of deadly foes might somehow appear to be—in any but some perverted sense. The cruelty demonstrated that Germany's treatment of the Jews could in no traditional way be moral, certainly not in any "Christian" sense of the term. Only in the framework of the new Nazi German morality could the perpetrators have believed themselves to be engaged in just action. This systemic cruelty, moreover, gave lie to the feeble, transparently inadequate rationales for the killing of the Jews that were sometimes uttered at the time, and have been repeated uncritically since by the perpetrators and some interpreters. It gives lie to the perpetrators' postwar assertions that they were obliged to follow orders either because orders are to be followed or because they were in no position to evaluate the morality and legality of the orders. The systemic cruelty demonstrated to all Germans involved that their countrymen were treating Jews as they did, not because of any military necessity, not because German civilians were dying in bombing raids (the systemic cruelty, as did much of the genocidal slaughter, preceded the devastating aerial attacks), not for any traditional justification for killing an enemy, but because of a set of beliefs that defined the Jews in a way that demanded Jewish suffering as retribution, a set of beliefs which inhered as profound a hatred as one people has likely ever harbored for another.

AN EXPLANATION of the perpetrators' actions must minimally be able to account for the empirical evidence, namely for the four kinds of action that have been shown here to have been typical. None of the conventional explanations can explain why the Germans did not take advantage of their ready opportunities either to avoid killing or to ameliorate Jewish suffering. None can explain why, by and large, the Germans did the opposite, producing unnecessary Jewish suffering and carrying out their lethal tasks with zeal and, for many, apparent eagerness. The conventional explanations fail on this count. An explanation must also meet a variety of conceptual, theoretical, and comparative demands, which the conventional ones also cannot do.

Because each of the conventional explanations explicitly or implicitly posits universal human traits, the conventional explanations should hold true for any people who might find themselves in the perpetrators' shoes. But this is obviously and demonstrably false. The variation in treatment that victims received was greatly dependent upon the identity and attitudes of their keepers. This was illustrated when the camps set up for Jews by the Slovakian Ministry of the Interior replaced the guard personnel: "The camps were guarded by Hlinka Guards, but because of their hostile attitude toward the camp inmates, the Jews pleaded with the Slovakian authorities to have them replaced. As a result, the Hlinka Guards were replaced by the Slovakian gendarmerie, and the situation in the camps improved."[36] The guards had to be changed precisely because their hatred of Jews so governed their actions that if the goal was to ameliorate the conditions of the camp, then it was more effective to substitute for them less hostile guards than to try to induce these vicious antisemites to act more humanely.

Since the conventional explanations ignore the identity of the perpetrators, they assert additionally, by implication, that had, say, the Italian government ordered such a genocide, then—whether because of the alleged universal obedience to authority, the putative overwhelming power of situational pressure, or the hypothesized invariable pursuit of personal interests— ordinary Italians would have slaughtered and brutalized Jewish men, women, and children more or less as the Germans did. This fanciful notion is falsified by the actual historical record. Italians, even the Italian military, by and large disobeyed Mussolini's orders for the deportation of Jews to what they knew would have been death at the Germans' hands.[37] Because it is indisputable that not all people in similar structural situations—either as guards in a camp or as executors of other genocidal orders—did act or would have acted as the Germans did, "universal" psychological and social psychological factors could not possibly have moved the perpetrators to act as they did. So the question is: What were the particularities of mid-twentieth-century Germans,[38] of German politics, society, and culture, that prepared Germans to do what Italians would not?

Another conceptual problem, even greater than denying the relevance of the perpetrators' identity, besets the conventional explanations. It is their common neglect of the *victims'* identity. This can be highlighted by posing a series of hypotheticals. Would the perpetrators have carried out an order to kill the entire Danish people, their own Nordic cousins, just as they did the Jews? Would they have exterminated, root and branch, all the people of Munich? Would they have killed, under Hitler's orders, their own families? Conceding that the vast number of Germans who contributed to the persecution and slaughter of Jews would not have obeyed such orders—and I cannot imagine any German historian or, for that matter, any honest contemporary asserting the contrary—means that the perpetrators' *conception of the victims* was a critical source of their willingness to kill them. This recognition necessitates, then, a specification of those attributes that Germans imputed to Jews that led them to see the Jews as fit for, if not requiring, total annihilation.[39]

The smoothness of the Germans' implementation of the extermination program is another of its extraordinary features. Bureaucracies, administrations charged with executing policies, and subordinates who must carry out the orders of (distant) superiors can all sabotage, cripple, or slow down policies that they dislike or oppose. Large-scale undertakings, moreover, need more than minimal compliance on the part of those implementing them if they are to proceed apace and not just creep along. This is particularly so for an undertaking like continent-wide genocide that requires ingenuity and initiative at many of its junctures from institutions and individuals subjected to many distracting demands and competing goals and, as if this were not demanding enough, that often must move forward at breakneck speed. Such an undertaking depends upon people applying themselves with energy, energy that derives generally from enthusiasm for the project. From where did so many ordinary Germans derive this genocidal drive and energy?

In addition to accounting for the diverse actions which the cases have specified, an explanation of the perpetration of the Holocaust must account for the specific identities of both the perpetrators and the victims. It must also account for the varied persons, institutions, and settings of the perpetration. It must identify features common to the perpetrators that would explain both why such relatively uniform action and why *these particular* discrete actions would emerge in varied settings among a large number of heterogeneous individuals. It must explain the smoothness of the overall operation. It must also achieve the following. It needs to integrate the various levels of analysis, namely the remarkable convergence of the overall policy, the frequently uncoordinated local implementation of it, including the character of institutions of killing, and the actions of individuals. This is most striking in the domain of Jewish "work." Typically, until now, macro analysis of Nazism and the Holocaust has been generally disjointed from the meso and micro analyses.[40] An explanation must further account for the genocide in a comparative perspective—which the conventional explanations typically do not even address and for which they are inadequate. Crucially, an explanation must supply the motivational mainspring that is adequate to all of these demands. Finally, it must explain the genesis of this motivation.

The conventional explanations are incapable of satisfying even the most limited of these explanatory demands. No matter how inventive, ingenious, or tortuous the reasoning, one cannot construct an even remotely plausible-sounding patchwork explanation of the basic facts of the perpetration of the Holocaust by employing one of the conventional explanations to account for one feature of the Holocaust, a second for another, a third for yet another, and so on—especially because some of the Germans' actions defy all of the conventional explanations. In addition to these enormous empirical shortcomings that, on their own, disqualify the conventional explanations, the conventional explanations also suffer from fatal conceptual inadequacies.

The conventional views are abstract, ahistorical explanations,[41] one of them having been conceived in a social psychological laboratory. Indeed, the conventional explanations are so abstract and universal in character that they by implication posit that the task of explaining (1) the willingness of Germans (2) to slaughter (3) the entire Jewish people is no different from the task of explaining how (1) any person can be brought (2) to do anything that he does not want to do (3) to any object, whether that object is a person or a thing. The conventional explanations do not account for the historic specificity of the perpetrators themselves and of the society that nurtured them, for the explicit, extraordinary character of the perpetrators' actions, or for the identity of the victims. The structure of the conventional explanations is such that they deem all of these features of the Holocaust, including that it was genocide, to have been epiphenomenal and therefore irrelevant to its explanation. The authors of the conventional explanations, when presenting their views, could choose not to mention that the perpetrators were German, that the deeds included mass slaughter and systematic brutality, and that the victims were Jews, and these omissions would not change the character and force of their explanations. The conventional explanations proceed as if it can be assumed that an ordinary person's participation in genocide and an ordinary person's willingness to enforce a governmental tax policy a little too strictly are phenomena that are not different in kind. Coercion, obedience to authority, social psychological pressure, self-interest, and displacement of responsibility onto others are explanations, according to their own logic, that are applicable equally and as unproblematically to the perpetrators of the Holocaust as they are to explaining, say, why bureaucrats today would help to implement a policy regarding air quality that they might think is misguided.

The conceptual inadequacies of the conventional explanations are profound. The conventional explanations do not acknowledge, indeed they deny, the humanity of the perpetrators, namely that they were agents, moral beings capable of making moral choices. They do not acknowledge the "inhumanity" of the deeds as being anything other than epiphenomenal to the underlying phenomenon to be explained. They do not acknowledge the humanity of the victims, for, according to the conventional explanations, it does not matter that the objects of the perpetrators' actions were people (rather than animals or things), people with their particular identities.

All the conventional explanations must be rejected in favor of an explanation, first, that can meet the explanatory demands that have just been enumerated, which include the task of accounting for the perpetrators' actions, the identity of the perpetrators, and the identity of the victims and, second, that recognizes the agency of the perpetrators, the particular, extraordinary nature of the perpetrators' actions, and the humanity of the victims.[42] The one explanation adequate to these tasks holds that a demonological antisemitism, of the virulent racial variety, was the common structure of the perpetrators' cognition and of German society in general. The German perpetrators, in this view, were assenting mass executioners, men and women who, true to their own eliminationist antisemitic beliefs, faithful to their cultural antisemitic credo, considered the slaughter to be just.

That the perpetrators' own convictions moved them to kill was acknowledged by the commanders of the *Einsatzgruppen* in what may be the most significant and illuminating testimony given after the war, testimony that, surprisingly, has been all but neglected. Reinhard Maurach's expert legal brief for the defense submitted at the Nuremberg *Einsatzgruppen* trial presented the court with the simple truth: the *Einsatzkommandos* had genuinely believed that Bolshevism, with which Germany was locked in apocalyptic battle, "was a Jewish invention and was only serving the interests of Jewry." He made the argument that this provided subjective justification for the Germans' extermination of the Jews, since Germans, perpetrators and non-perpetrators alike, rightly or wrongly, had believed that the preservation of Germany had depended on it. In presenting this argument, Maurach explained the source of their beliefs: ". . . it cannot be doubted that National Socialism had succeeded to the fullest extent in convincing public opinion and furthermore *the overwhelming majority of the German people* of the identity of bolshevism and Jewry [my emphasis]." Maurach, like the perpetrators themselves in this immediate postwar period, was still in the grip of this ideology, so he proceeded to defend these beliefs as being correct. What the Germans saw of the Jews in the Soviet Union, namely their dominance of Party, state, and security institutions, "confirm[ed] the correctness of the National Socialist ideology." The malevolent power of the Jews was, in Maurach's view, so obviously great that it even succeeded in converting the small group of non-antisemites within the army into antisemites. At the end of the brief, Maurach summarized the dual sources that had engendered the perpetrators' belief that the Jews had to be killed: "The defendants, according to the National Socialist theory as well as due to their own conception and experience, were obsessed with a psychological delusion based on a fallacious idea concerning the identity of the aims of bolshevism and the political role of Jewry in eastern Europe. This conception was apt . . . to bring the defendants to the conviction that the attack against the future existence of the German Reich and people was to be expected mainly from the Jewish population in the occupied Russian territories."[43] Maurach leaves no doubt. The perpetrators really believed these delusions.

Otto Ohlendorf, the former commander of *Einsatzgruppe D*, confirmed that Maurach had aptly characterized their beliefs when he candidly articulated in a 1947 letter, smuggled out from prison to his wife, the views that had moved him and thousands of others to slaughter Jews. Jewry, even after the war, he wrote, "has continued to sow hate; and it reaps hate again. . . . How else could one see it as anything but the work of demons who wage their battle against us?"[44] Ohlendorf was anything but a sadist and was otherwise known as an unusually decent man, even as an "idealist" within the Nazi movement, who believed in its vision of a harmonious utopia. Yet with regard to the Jews, this highly educated man shared the demonological view of Jews common to German society, and thus asks earnestly and rhetorically: "How else could one see it as anything but the work of demons?"[45] The perpetrators, like Ohlendorf, believed that the Jews had left them no choice. There can be no doubt that their beliefs about Jews were of a sufficiently virulent kind and intensity to have led them to accept the genocide as an appropriate "solution," if not the only "final solution to the Jewish Problem."[46] How did such beliefs produce all of the distinctive features of the Holocaust?

Germans' beliefs about Jews, which were different from their beliefs about the Danes or Bavarians, rendered the Jews, unlike the Danish people or the denizens of Munich, *fit* and *necessary* to annihilate. That such beliefs could motivate the total annihilation of the Jewish people cannot be doubted. The logic is illustrated and was explicitly stated in the German press for all Germans to read and contemplate: "In the case of the Jews there are not merely a few criminals (as in every other people), but all of Jewry rose from criminal roots, and in its very nature it is criminal. The Jews are no people like other people, but a pseudo-people welded together by hereditary criminality [*eine zu einem Scheinvolk zusammengeschlossene Erbkriminalität*]. . . . The annihilation of Jewry is no loss to humanity, but just as useful as capital punishment or protective custody against other criminals."[47] How would such beliefs explain the range of Germans' actions? How does the notion that the perpetrators harbored such beliefs hold up when the choices that they made are examined?

Such beliefs led them collectively and each one individually to choose to carry out genocidal orders, instead of to opt to avoid killing, or to remove themselves altogether from institutions of killing. For those who believed that Jewry was locked in an apocalyptic battle with Germandom, to annihilate Jewry appeared just and necessary. Letting such a mortal threat persist, fester, and build was to let down one's countrymen, to betray one's loved ones. A popular children's book—*The Poisoned Mushroom*, which was an illustrated, vicious account of the perfidies of the Jews who, like poisoned mushrooms, appear good but are fatal—expressed to the children of Germany this sentiment and logic in its final chapter title, namely the necessity of expurgating the world of Jews: "Without a solution to the Jewish Problem/ No salvation of humanity!"[48]

Germans' belief in the justice of the enterprise caused them regularly to take initiative in exterminating Jews, by devoting themselves to their assigned tasks with the ardor of true believers, or by killing Jews when they had no explicit orders to do so. It explains not only why Germans did not refuse to kill but also why many, such as the men of police battalions, volunteered for killing operations. The eagerness to kill Jews that was to be found among so many ordinary Germans was highlighted during one of Police Battalion 101's killing operations. It became known one evening in mid-November 1942 that they were to slaughter Jews the following day in Łuków. "On that evening an entertainment unit of Berlin policemen, serving as so-called welfare providers for the front, were our guests. This entertainment unit consisted of musicians and artists of the spoken word. The members of this unit had also learned of the forthcoming shooting of the Jews and indeed offered, even pleaded emphatically for permission to participate in the execution of these Jews. This strange request was granted by the battalion."[49] These German entertainers, whose official duties had nothing to do with the killing of Jews, did not have to be pressured, ordered, or coerced to kill Jews. In accord with the general voluntaristic spirit of the enterprise, they themselves pleaded for the opportunity to kill Jews. Their desire to slaughter Jews, moreover, was not treated as a pathology or an aberration; the next day these entertainers made up the majority of the executioners. They, like so many German perpetrators, whether they were explicit volunteers or not, easily and with alacrity became executioners of Jews.

Germans' belief in the justice of the extermination of the Jews also explains the general voluntaristic *manner* of Germans' participation in the destruction of European Jewry, captured by one survivor who blames the Germans not for having carried out orders, because "we never expected individual Germans to disobey orders." It was the Germans' voluntarism, expressed in so many different ways, which made them so deadly and which produced this man's evaluation of them: "Their record is fatal because, above and beyond the orders, they individually and voluntarily, actively and tacitly, endorsed, enjoyed and enlarged the official program [of extermination]."[50]

The Germans' eagerness to kill was manifest in one killing operation after the next, as it was in Uściług on the Ukrainian side of the Polish border. After the Germans had deported to death or shot all Jews whom they easily rounded up, in the words of one survivor, they started

> the hunt for those who had gone into hiding. It was a hunt the likes of which mankind had never seen. Whole families would hide out in skrytkas as we had in Włodzimierz, and they would be hunted down inexorably, relentlessly. Street by street, house by house, inch by inch, from attic to cellar. The Germans became expert at finding these hiding places. When they searched a house, they went tapping the walls, listening for the hollow sound that indicated a double wall. They punched holes in ceilings or floors. . . .

These were no longer limited "actions"; this was total annihilation. Teams of SS men roamed the streets, searching ditches, outhouses, bushes, barns, stables, pigsties. And they caught and killed Jews by the thousands; then by the hundreds; then by tens; and finally one by one.[51]

This "hunt," "the likes of which mankind had never seen," was entirely typical for German ghetto clearings. It also was reminiscent of the "Jew-hunts" conducted both within the ghettos and in the countryside by the ordinary Germans of many police battalions, including Police Battalion 101. The overwhelming impression of those who ever witnessed a German ghetto clearing was that they were observing not men who were brought to their tasks reluctantly, but men driven by the passion, determination, tirelessness, and enthusiasm of religious zealots on a holy, redemptive mission.

Just as many young men have through the ages volunteered to go to war in order to fight for their countries, so too were Germans willing to volunteer to destroy this cognitively created mortal enemy. That the men were assenting executioners also explains why police battalions could permit killing squads to be filled on a voluntary basis. The officers knew that their men stood with them shoulder to shoulder in this Germanic undertaking, so they ran no risks in often relying upon volunteers to perform this grisly duty; the officers were confident, correctly confident, that enough eager men would step forward.

The belief that the Jews had already greatly harmed Germans, and would always work to injure them still more, at least partly explains the tremendous cruelty that Germans inflicted upon Jews. In the words of one former German police official who served in the Cracow region, and who testified that those serving with him "were, with a few exceptions, quite happy to take part in shootings of Jews. They had a ball!," their killing was motivated by "great hatred against the Jews; it was revenge . . . ."[52] The cruelty that Germans perpetrated under orders, both the structured and the spontaneously organized variety, was not apprehended by the vast majority of Germans who worked the institutions of killing as unlawful or immoral. Such cruelty, which had no purpose other than Jewish suffering, did not serve to delegitimize the regime, to undercut the authority of the authorities from whom it issued, as it would have if the Germans had believed that any "rational" justification, any "lawful" measure, any traditional reason of state underlay or ought to underlie the treatment of Jews. The demonological antisemitism also helped to produce cruelty towards Jews on this vast scale; perpetrating such cruelty often became a norm with no exceptions in settings where Germans had regular, intimate contact with the victims. Such beliefs were the necessary cause of such widespread, frequent, thorough, and unmerciful brutality towards the Jews,

for they removed Jews *utterly* from the purview of the ethical code that protected non-Jewish members of society. The lifting of the code's constraints
at the very least *permitted* Germans to treat Jews with cruelty that they would
never have considered visiting upon Germans. German antisemitism also
called for retribution—annihilation being its ultimate form—retribution
which for many Germans meant compelling the Jews to suffer, and which
could be understood by the victims only as a pathology afflicting all Germans:
"The beast within the Nazi is whole, completely healthy—it attacks and
preys upon others; but the man within him is pathologically ill. Nature has
struck him with the illness of sadism, and this disease has penetrated into the
very fiber of his being. There is no Nazi whose soul is not diseased, who is not
tyrannical, sadistic . . ."[53] Germans' beliefs about Jews unleashed indwelling
destructive and ferocious passions that are usually tamed and curbed by civilization. They also provided Germans with a moral rationale and psychological impulse to exercise those passions against Jews.

If the killers had been not antisemites animated by the conviction that the
Jews deserve to die, but unfeeling, blind executors of orders, then they should
have indeed been "coldly uninvolved with their victims."[54] They would have
told themselves that they do not understand why the Jews must die, but if the
infallible Führer in his infinite wisdom had ordered the slaughter, then it
must be for a good reason, some deep undivulged reason of state. Their attitude would then have been akin to that of the cavalrymen of the Light
Brigade. Paraphrasing Tennyson, they would have said, "Ours is not to reason why / Ours is but to do and die."[55]

If Germans had regarded the Jews as mere capital criminals, guilty of a
particularly heinous crime, then they should have been equally "coldly uninvolved" as a modern professional hangman is. The German perpetrators
were, after all, the executioners of an entire nation, whom the German state
had sentenced to death. The modern state's authorized hangman is required
to administer death in a prescribed quasi-clinical manner—swiftly, without
torment, and with minimum pain, to abide, as it were, by the maxim of
Shakespeare's Brutus: "Let's kill him boldly, but not wrathfully."[56] Germans,
who approved of the death sentence, would have been outraged if the execution of a German common murderer were accompanied by tortures or humiliations of the doomed convict. After the abortive attempt to assassinate
Hitler on July 20, 1944, Hitler ordered that the German conspirators be
strangled by piano wire while hanging animal-like from meathooks. When a
film which contained the scene was shown to audiences of the German army,
the viewers were so outraged that they walked out.[57] Although some of the
spectators may have sympathized with the conspirators, all agreed—including those who believed that the conspirators were guilty of the highest crime

and deserved to die—that killing them in so barbarous a manner was unworthy of a "civilized" nation.

Coldly uninvolved were the Germans who killed the mentally ill and the severely handicapped in the so-called Euthanasia program. Most of them were physicians and nurses who dispatched their victims in the dispassionate manner of surgeons, who excise from the body some hideous and hindering excrescence.[58] By contrast, the Germans' killing of the Jews was often wrathful, preceded and attended by cruelty, degradation, mockery, and Mephistophelean laughter. Why? Why did these hangmen of the Jewish people not act as hangmen do? Why did these ordinary Germans turned executioners almost overnight exhibit so much wanton, spontaneous, and unbidden cruelty? The answer to this question lies in their conception of the Jews. In their eyes, *der Jude* is not merely a heinous capital criminal. He is a terrestrial demon, the "plastic demon of the decay of humanity," a phrase which Richard Wagner had coined and whose original German "*der plastische Dämon des verfalls der Menschheit*" has a particularly fear-inspiring and menacing ring.[59] Numberless are the evils of which *der Jude* is guilty. He is the principal author of the disorder, turmoil, and the sanguinary convulsions that have plagued the world. He is cunning and cruel in the extreme. In speaking of him, writers and preachers would let loose a stream of hyperbole, like enraged persons who vent their rage in a crescendo of indiscriminate invectives. "They [the Jews, in this particular instance, the Jewish leaders of sports] are worse than cholera, than lung pest, than syphilis . . . worse than a conflagration, famine, the break of a dam, extreme drought, the worst locust plague, poison gas—worse than all of these because these elements destroy only the German people, those [the Jews], however, Germany itself."[60]

It was an unspoken maxim among the perpetrators that death is not a sufficient punishment for these world-historical malefactors. One must avenge upon them the injuries that they had caused. One must exact from them "*harte Sühne*," severe retribution—they must be made to pay for their innumerable malefactions. For their millennial parasitism, for their looting, robbing, and exploiting, they must be made to perform hard, lethal labor; for having overweeningly used their immense secret power to debase nations and social classes, they must be degraded and made to grovel in the dust; for the physical suffering that they have caused through their machinations, they must be made to pay with their own ceaseless bodily pain. In the ghettos and the camps, on the way to the killing sites, even at the very edge of the mass graves, Germans brutalized Jews, venting upon them the collective rage at the misfortunes that, real and imaginary, had befallen Germany. "It was revenge." Germans' violent anger at the Jews is akin to the passion that drove Ahab to hunt Moby-Dick. Melville's memorable description of Ahab's motives may serve as a fitting motto for the unrelenting, unspeakable, unsurpassable cruelties that Germans visited upon Jews:

All that most maddens and torments; all that stirs up the lees of things; all truth with malice in it; all that cracks the sinews and cakes the brain; all the subtle demonism of life and thought; all evil, to crazy Ahab were visibly personified and made practically assailable in Moby-Dick. He piled upon the whale's white hump the sum of all the general rage and hate felt by his whole race from Adam down; and then, as if his chest had been a mortar, he burst his hot heart's shell upon it.[61]

Although the Germans' brutality remains somewhat unfathomable, German antisemitism helps explain their immense cruelty towards Jews that was almost always voluntaristic, initiated by each individual himself or herself.[62]

The perpetrators' antisemitism thus explains the four significant actions specified by the matrix of authority and cruelty. It explains the Germans' willingness to carry out orders, the initiative they took both in killing and in brutalizing Jews, as well as the general brutality, both institutionally structured and individually produced. It explains the perpetrators' zeal, and why this far-flung operation proceeded so smoothly, for the belief in the necessity and the justice of the genocide provided the energy and the devotion that such operations require. It explains why Germans at every level of the various institutions of killing showed so little consideration for ameliorating the suffering of Jews, which could have been done so easily by those who saw the killing as unstoppable but who wanted to spare the victims unnecessary anguish and pain. It explains why so few of the perpetrators availed themselves of opportunities to avoid killing. It explains why so many people who were not great supporters of the Nazi regime and why even opponents of Nazism contributed to the extermination of the Jews,[63] for, as the discussion here of the development of German antisemitism has shown, Germans' beliefs about the Jews could be distinct from their evaluation of Nazism. Because eliminationist antisemitism was a German cultural cognitive model that predated Nazi political power, a committed anti-Nazi could be a committed, passionate racial antisemite. Killing the Jews was for many a deed done not for Nazism but for Germany.[64]

A consonance between the macro, the meso, and the micro existed, because the same beliefs moved policy makers, infused and shaped the character of the institutions of killing, and motivated the executors of genocidal policy. Of one mind, confronting their common foe, Germans in face-to-face relations with Jews reproduced the thinking of those who shaped overall policy. Unsurprisingly, Germans occasionally took local initiative that seemingly went ahead of the program emanating from the central authorities, for when faced with a "problem" at the local level (a "problem" having been typically little more than Jews living within their reach), the local administrators acted in the spirit of their age and culture.

Animated by common views of Jews and thus by a common guide to action, it is no wonder that so many Germans from different walks of life, from different social backgrounds, under different institutional arrangements and with different opportunity structures, in vastly different settings—in totally organized camps, in the partly routinized, partly wild roundups and shooting operations, in the relatively unsupervised "Jew-hunts" requiring initiative, and in the virtually autonomous conditions of the death marches—engaged in the actions specified here as having been common to the perpetrators. The invisible coordination that common beliefs and values provide meant that an absence of central coordination and the differences that circumstance and setting might otherwise produce in people who were simply responding to situational factors did not result in greatly divergent treatment of Jews. The perpetrators' eliminationist antisemitism, their common structure of cognitions, harnessed to the state-initiated and -coordinated national program of extermination, was such a powerful motivation to action that it diminished enormously the influence of other "structures" and factors in shaping their actions. Since all of the other structures varied, only the common structure of cognition can account for the essential constancy of Germans' actions towards Jews.

Many German actions that would in other circumstances appear to have been unusual, irrational, even bizarre were perfectly sensible and "rational" products of their antisemitism. Germans often preferred to brutalize (or, put differently, could not restrain themselves from brutalizing) Jews, rather than to employ them in an economically productive manner. "Surplus" brutality on a grand scale was the standard feature of Germans' treatment of Jews, of the German-Jewish relationship during the Nazi period. The celebratory atmosphere that sometimes prevailed in institutions of killing, the boasting, the acceptance by the Germans of savage cruelty towards Jews as a norm—in both senses of the word, as commonplace and desirable—were the action correlates of their hatred.[65]

Finally, the genocidal devotion that antisemitism imbued in ordinary Germans gave so many people—who, it might have been thought, were by dint of background and training not unusually fit to become genocidal killers—the resolve to persist in the task despite its evident horror and the visceral revulsion that many felt upon their initiation into it. The licentious brutality of ghetto clearings, the sight of starved, emaciated, visibly ill, and wounded Jews falling dead as they walked or as they were being savaged by their German keepers, the gruesomeness of the mass executions by gunfire—all of these failed to wilt the Germans' determination.

And in those infrequent instances in which any of them did wilt, or when a perpetrator objected to, or was unnerved by, the wantonness of a comrade's manner of killing, by no means should it be understood, without explicit evidence, to indicate principled moral disapproval of the slaughter, to indicate anything other than what it almost always was, an aesthetic revulsion at the ghastliness of the scene. One German perpetrator who was giving commands to others during a killing operation objected to one of the men's method of killing. He describes it thus:

> Meanwhile, Rottenführer Abraham shot the children with a pistol. There were about five of them. These were children whom I would think were aged between two and six years. The way Abraham killed the children was brutal. He got hold of some of the children by the hair, lifted them up from the ground, shot them through the back of their heads and then threw them into the grave. After a while I just could not watch this any more and I told him to stop. What I meant was he should not lift the children up by the hair, he should kill them in a more decent way.[66]

It was not their killing of the children that the German deemed "brutal" but only the manner of killing. He could not bear the sight of it. How unseemly. Presumably, if Abraham had killed the children by forcing them to lie on the ground and firing into their little heads, then that would have been a "decent" mode of execution, one which this German could have watched with equanimity.

The frightfulness, the ghoulishness of the perpetrators' phenomenological reality, except in rare instances, was grossly insufficient to stay the Germans' genocidal hands. As Ohlendorf said, speaking for all the perpetrators: "How else could one see it as anything but the work of demons?" Demons must be destroyed, after all.

IN LIGHT OF THIS discussion, the significance of the common and individual aspects of the institutions of killing presented here can be further highlighted. Police battalions, "work" camps, and death marches, each casts in sharp relief important aspects of the perpetration of the Holocaust and, in different ways, demonstrates both the voluntaristic nature of the perpetrators' actions and the centrality of racial eliminationist antisemitism to their motivation.[67]

The actions of Germans in police battalions raise the question of how Germans not prepared by previous service or background who were operating in an institution that neither indoctrinated them in any substantial or effective way nor put inordinate pressure on them, that indeed offered them the choice not to kill or brutalize Jews, would choose to act. By dint of background, these "ordinary" Germans were among the least likely of adult Ger-

man men to become genocidal killers, and they worked in an unusually voluntaristic institution, yet their actions conformed to what would have been
expected from the most dedicated German antisemites. The makeup of police battalions—as their method of recruitment suggests and as the demographic sample studied here confirms—means that the conclusions drawn
about the overall character of the members' actions can, indeed must be, generalized to *the German people in general*. What these *ordinary* Germans did
also could have been expected of other *ordinary* Germans.

The case of Jewish "work," particularly in those camps ostensibly devoted exclusively to utilizing Jewish labor, examines whether or not eliminationist antisemitism would shape the actors' conduct even when counteracted
by the normally overwhelmingly powerful motivation and logic of economic
rationality, a rationality that by and large characterized the German economy.
This realm of the Germans' treatment of Jews, more than any other, estab-
lishes the enormous power of German antisemitism, for it was able to pervert
institutions and practices that, particularly in wartime circumstances, would
have been expected to continue to function according to impersonal and in-
corruptible dictates of economic productivity. The Germans treated Jews
substantially differently from other subject peoples at all organizational levels—in the general pattern of employing Jewish labor, in the character of the
institutions of Jewish labor, and in the Germans' individual treatment of Jewish workers—violating the Germans' self-interest, which was to produce urgently needed provisions and material for war. That they did so greatly
substantiates the notion that the Jews had a special cognitive status in Germans' minds. Particularly worth noting is that the idea of Jewish work-
shirking parasitism, so important for understanding the Germans' "use" of
Jewish labor, had deep historical roots in Germany. The power of the antisemitic ideology in *producing* German action, in *causing* them to act in an otherwise abnormal manner, is perhaps nowhere better illustrated than in the
realm of "work."

The death marches provide still another perplexing phenomenon and
therefore a stringent test of any explanation. During the chaos and danger of
the waning months, weeks, and days of the war, under conditions far different from the imperial success of 1939–1942, when it had seemed possible that
all of Europe would perpetually march to the Nazified German tune, the
Germans had much to lose by continuing to kill and brutalize Jews. Furthermore, many of the death marches proceeded with minimal or no supervision
of its guard personnel, or control and guidance from central authority. The
Germans who chaperoned the Jews were their own masters. Explanations
which deny the existence and centrality of the perpetrators' demonological
antisemitism would produce the expectation that a diminution or cessation of

the Germans' genocidal actions would have occurred under such changed social psychological conditions and transformed incentive structure. Yet the
dedication and zeal of these Germans—in the case of the Helmbrechts death
march, their unwavering murderousness and brutality towards Jews, *and only
towards Jews*—demonstrates that these were internally motivated killers,
moved by a boundless hatred of Jews. They killed and brutalized Jews even
after having received Himmler's own orders to stop the killing. The Germans' treatment of Jews was autistic, responding, once the genocidal program had been unleashed, to little else save their own internal impulses,
governed principally by their conception of the victims.

Each of these three institutions of killing represents a crucial aspect of
the perpetration of the Holocaust in close to a pure form. Police battalions indicate how broadly antisemitism had infected German society, such that ordinary men became executioners of this sort. Death marches indicate how
deeply the perpetrators had internalized the need to slaughter Jews and how
devoted they were to their task, so that they on their own killed Jews until the
last moment. The subject of work suggests how enormously powerful the antisemitism was, in that it was able to induce the Germans to act in such an
economically self-injurious manner.

One of the remarkable features of the genocide—and this is true for police battalions, "work" camps, death marches, *Einsatzkommandos,* and the
other institutions of killing—is how readily and naturally Germans, perpetrators and non-perpetrators alike, *understood* why they were supposed to kill
Jews. Imagine if any western government today were to let it be known to a
large heterogeneous group of ordinary citizens that it was setting out to kill,
root and branch, another people. Aside from their moral reaction to the information, people would find the announcement simply incomprehensible.
They would react as to the words of a madman. Antisemitism in Germany
was such that when Germans, participants or bystanders, learned that the
Jews were to be killed, they evinced not surprise, not incredulity, but comprehension. Whatever their moral or utilitarian stances towards the killing
were, the annihilation of the Jews *made sense to them.*

The most noteworthy aspect of the perpetrators' testimony about the
moment when they learned of the expected or ongoing destruction of the
Jews, and of their own intended roles in it, is their failure to have evinced incomprehensibility and surprise, to have posed questions, whether to commanders or among themselves, about why this was to be done, and to have
expressed outrage at having to do the bidding of madmen. One Jewish survivor recalls his own thoughts of October 1942 while ensconced in a hideout
in Hrubieszów, a city southeast of Lublin, as the killing and hunting proceeded around him: "I was struck repeatedly by how incredible it all was—

total strangers remorselessly hunting down people who had done nothing whatever to hurt them. The world was mad."[68] Jews, but not Germans, had such thoughts. So deeply and widely had this genocidal-potential anti-semitism penetrated German society that upon learning of Hitler's wishes, Germans really comprehended them. A member of *Sonderkommando 4a*, in a September 1942 letter to his wife ("My dear Soska"), speaking not only for himself but for his comrades, for German soldiers in general, expressed as clearly and unequivocally as could be the beliefs that produced this general comprehension and endorsement.

> We are fighting this war today for the very existence [*Sein oder Nichtsein*] of our *Volk*. Thank God that you in the homeland do not feel too much of it. The bombing raids, however, have shown what the enemy has in store for us if he had the power. Those at the front experience it at every turn. My com-rades literally are fighting for the existence of our *Volk*. They are doing the same that the enemy would do [to us]. I believe that you understand me. Be-cause this war in our view is a Jewish war, the Jews are primarily bearing the brunt of it. In Russia, wherever there is a German soldier, the Jews are no more.[69]

Germans did not merely understand themselves to be carrying out what were considered to be the crazy plans of a criminal madman; rather, they really comprehended why such radical action (their fears of failure and Jewish re-venge notwithstanding) had to be undertaken, why, in order to safeguard the existence of the *Volk*, the extermination of the Jews was to be a German na-tional project.

The perpetrators' belief in the unalterably demonic character of the Jews also led their commanders rightly to expect that their patently absurd asser-tions (which they proffered genuinely) about Jewish responsibility for bomb-ing raids and partisan attacks would be comprehensible and reasonable to their men and would bolster their resolve. The idea of slaughtering all the Jewish children of Poland in revenge or in retaliation for the British and American bombing of German cities would have struck any rational mind, any non-Nazified mind, as insane. Not, however, the ordinary Germans who served in Police Battalion 101 and other units. To their minds, it was a logi-cal argument, the nexus between the Jews of impoverished, provincial towns in the heart of Poland and the bombing of Berlin and Hamburg having been perfectly comprehensible. For, having been imbued with a demonological an-tisemitism, these ordinary Germans believed that behind the bombing of German cities stood that global ogre, variously called "World Jewry" (*das Weltjudentum*) or "the Jew" (*der Jude*), and that the Jews of Poland and of

Józefów were tentacles of that ogre. In lopping off that tentacle, these Germans would contribute to the destruction of that monstrous force, that source of many evils, which was raining bombs on their cities. Major Trapp, in urging his men to conjure up before their minds' eyes images of "our women and children in our homeland" who died in bombing raids, so that they would overcome whatever inhibitions they might have had to slaughter Jewish children, assumed as a matter of course that his men would readily understand and take his advice. These ordinary Germans needed no further explanation. For the advice was based on the "common-sense" view of Jewry that was common to them. Indeed, no men came forth to ask, "What is the connection between the Jewish children of Józefów and the Anglo-American bombing of German cities?" The connection appears to have been "self-evident" to all.[70]

German commanders' knowledge of their men's thoroughgoing antisemitism also led them to permit their men to avoid killing duties that they could not bring themselves to perform, yet to be confident that only a few would avail themselves of this option. Such laxness was, for the same reason, endorsed by Himmler.[71] Similarly, this knowledge gave them the confidence necessary often to allow the men—in "Jew-hunts," ghetto clearings, "work" camps, and in death marches—to undertake their tasks with little or no supervision. The perpetrators' belief in the justice of the enterprise ensured that few dallied at their tasks or deserted their posts, even at the end of the war. Eduard Strauch, the former commander of *Einsatzkommando 2*, spoke not only for his men but also for the perpetrators in general when, in an April 1943 lecture to a conference in Minsk, he expressed his indignation that anyone would doubt the eagerness of the killers, even if the killing was "hard and unpleasant." "Gentlemen . . . we are convinced that someone must carry out these tasks. I can state with pride that my men . . . are proud to act out of conviction and fidelity to their *Führer.*"[72] At all institutional levels, the perpetrators were "tuned in" to the genocidal enterprise, and this was known to Himmler, Strauch, to other commanders, and, with exceptions, to all Germans involved.

The perpetrators of the Holocaust took pride in their accomplishments, in their genocidal vocation, to which they were dedicated. They expressed this again and again in their actions, in the endless stream of choices that they made to tread the killing fields—and while they were there. They also expressed this in their words and actions while not on their killing forays. If they had indeed in principle disapproved of the genocide, then why would they have taken obviously approving photographs of their killing operations and their lives while executioners—and then circulate them and permit copies to be made for others?[73] The following photograph of a German soldier killing a Jewish mother and child was sent home through the mail. On the back of it was penned: "Ukraine 1942, Jewish Aktion, Ivangorod."

Why would the perpetrators have their wives and girlfriends, even their children, on hand to bear witness to their slaughters and cruelties? Why would they have celebrations to mark significant massacres, killings, or events? Why would they not talk among themselves—if they had been so disapproving—and express their dissatisfaction with their duties? Why would they talk among themselves not to lament their fate and that of their victims, but to boast of their self-conceived heroics?

The moment that aspects, especially the social aspects, of the perpetrators' lives come into focus other than the simple act of killing, the false images of the Germans as one-dimensional men in situations that abstract them away from their social relations become harder to maintain. Even though the full character of the perpetrators' social and cultural existence is hard to recover, the unreal images of them as isolated, frightened, thoughtless beings performing their tasks reluctantly are erroneous.[74] The German executioners, like other people, consistently made choices about how they would act, choices that consistently produced immense Jewish suffering and mortality. They individually made those choices as contented members of an assenting genocidal community, in which the killing of Jews was normative and often celebrated.

THE GERMANS' SLAUGHTER OF THE JEWS IN COMPARATIVE PERSPECTIVE

There are several comparisons for which an explanation must be adequate. The first is internal to the genocide, namely of the different personnel, institutions, and settings of the Germans' perpetration of the Holocaust, and of the essentially common actions that were produced even when these factors varied. This first comparison is a central subject of this study and has just been discussed at length, so this section addresses the other three types of comparison. The second comparison—which, for the reasons stated in the Introduction, has not been a central subject of this study—broadens the investigation of the perpetrators from a concentration on Germans to include the actions of members of other nationalities towards Jews. The third comparison juxtaposes the Germans' strikingly different treatment of the Jews and of other subject and devalued peoples, which, because it is so instructive, has already been touched upon at various points. The fourth comparison focuses on the features of the Holocaust that distinguish it from other genocides and large-scale killing programs.

In front of a photographer, a German soldier takes aim at a Jewish mother and child during the slaughter of the Jews of Ivangorod, Ukraine, in 1942.

In comparing the character of Germans' and non-Germans' treatment of Jews, there are two tasks. The first is to establish whether or not there were other national groups that in similar circumstances did not treat or would not have treated Jews as the Germans did. Had a battalion of ordinary Danes or that of ordinary Italians—composed of men of background and training similar to that of the ordinary Germans of Police Battalion 101 and of many other police battalions—somehow have found themselves in the Lublin region and received the same orders from their government *with the same opportunity to have exempted themselves,* would they have slaughtered, deported, and hunted down, with the same efficacy and brutality, Jewish men, women, and children, as these ordinary Germans did? Would Danish or Italian guards have treated Jewish workers in work camps and installations in the Germans' incessantly brutal, lethal manner that ran so counter to economic rationality? Would Danish or Italian men and women guarding marching columns of emaciated, sick, and starving Jewish women have denied them available clothing and shelter, beaten them mercilessly, and withheld available food from them? The notion that ordinary Danes or Italians would have acted as the ordinary Germans did strains credulity beyond the breaking point. It is also falsified by the actual historical record. The Danes saved their country's Jews, and before that resisted the imposition of antisemitic measures by the Germans. More generally, the Danes showed every inclination to treat the Jews of Denmark as human beings and as members of the Danish national community. The Italians, as has already been mentioned, even the Italian military (in Croatia), by and large disobeyed Mussolini's orders for the deportation of Jews to what they knew would be death at the Germans' hands.[75] The refusal or the unwillingness of others to do what Germans did demonstrates that the Germans were not ordinary *men,* namely transhistorical, acultural beings, but that there was something particular about them, something particular about their political cultural parentage, that shaped their views of the victims, such that they could willingly, even eagerly, have brutalized and killed Jews, convinced of the rightness of their actions and of the larger enterprise.

Once the primary task of establishing the differences between Germans and non-Germans is completed, the secondary and important task of investigating those non-Germans who aided the Germans in their persecution and slaughter of Jews can begin. There are two possible outcomes here. That some non-Germans did act similarly suggests either that we must uncover what they had in common with the German perpetrators or that we must recognize that there might be more than one path to becoming a perpetrator of mass slaughter. After all, there were enormous differences between the circumstances of the Germans' lives and actions and those of, say, the Ukrainians who served in German institutions. The Germans had defeated, repressed, and dehumanized Ukrainians, and there were pressures operating on the Ukrainians that did not exist for the Germans. The leniency and solicitude that the commander of Police Battalion 101 and other German commanders showed for those among their men who could not bring themselves to kill or to continue killing was unlikely to have characterized the Germans' conduct towards their eastern European minions, which was generally draconian.

Nevertheless, the circumstances and character of the non-Germans who helped to kill Jews should be investigated in depth. We currently know still much less about them than about the German perpetrators. The most important national groups who aided the Germans in slaughtering Jews were the Ukrainians, Latvians, and Lithuanians, about whom two things can be said. They came from cultures that were profoundly antisemitic,[76] and the knowledge that we have, little as it is, of the men who actually aided the Germans suggests that many of them were animated by vehement hatred of Jews.[77] Much work remains to be done on these people. Before conclusions are drawn about the sources of their participation—and also what their actions tell us about the German perpetrators—careful analysis of the (often enormously different) contexts of their actions, as well as of the similarities and differences in their views of the victims, should be undertaken.[78]

The crucial comparative strategy in assessing the sources of the actions of Germans and non-Germans towards Jews is to establish first whether or not there was something not purely structural about the perpetration of the deed. (That is, did the *identities* of the perpetrators or of the victims matter in any way?) Because there were other peoples who did not treat Jews as Germans did and because, as I have shown, it is clear that the actions of the German perpetrators cannot be explained by non-cognitive structural features, when investigating different (national) groups of perpetrators, it is necessary to eschew explanations that in a reductionist fashion attribute complex and highly variable actions to structural factors or allegedly universalistic social psychological processes; the task, then, is to specify what combination of cognitive and situational factors brought the perpetrators, whatever their identities were, to contribute to the Holocaust in all of the ways that they did. This I have done for the German perpetrators. When undertaking analogous investigations for the non-German perpetrators, it must be kept in mind that different influences might have moved different groups of perpetrators. Whatever such studies would yield, the main purpose of comparing the German perpetrators to those from other national groups who aided the Germans remains the illumination of the sources of the Germans' actions, because, as I maintained in the Introduction, the Germans were the prime movers, and the central and only indispensable perpetrators of the Holocaust.

Just as Germans' cognitions and values, particularly Germans' conception of the victims, explain their treatment of the Jews, they should also shed light on their treatment of non-Jewish peoples as well, which is yet another important comparative demand.[79] Without suggesting that the following is an in-depth and comprehensive analysis of this vast subject, a sketch of the comparative cognitive logic of the German ideology concerning two other groups provides a framework for such a treatment. A schematization of the dominant beliefs in Germany, beliefs that predated significant murderous or barbarous acts, which can be found in Appendix 2, regarding three groups of people—Jews, the mentally ill, and Slavs (who suffered immeasurably at the Germans' hands), illustrates two things: the tight connection between Germans' prior belief and their actions—in other words, that belief governed action—and the comparative explanatory power of the specific content of German antisemitism for the Germans' treatment of Jews.

Essentially, the Jews were seen as a biologically programmed people of great power, dedicated to destroying Germany, who by constitution and deed forfeited the protection of traditional morality. Security dictated that they had to be killed, and morality permitted (even lauded) such action. The mentally ill and severely handicapped were conceived of as biological cripples threatening the organic health of the German people. For those who thoroughly accepted the Nazi biologized view of existence, these people were at best useless eaters, at worst sources of racial disease. This view was contested in Germany, as was the applicability of traditional morality to them. For the most Nazified, these people needed to be killed, but in a painless manner. For many Germans, this was a violation of deeply held convictions, hence the widespread protest.[80] The Slavs, seen as racially inferior, were considered fit to be beasts of burden. The threat that they posed to Germany was understood to be a social Darwinian competition for land and resources. The treatment that the Germans would accord to the Slavs was utilitarian (only the utility of the Germans was to be at issue). Germans were to subjugate and exploit them physically to the extent that the economy could usefully employ them. This meant killing the leadership, treating all opposition ruthlessly, and reducing the rest to an uneducated Helot-like status. Those who were of the right physiognomy, the indicator of exalted racial stock, would be Germanized. This, of course, could never happen to a Jew, no matter how he or she might look.

Since the Nazi leadership's own cognitions about these groups by and large mirrored those elucidated here (though somewhat less uniformly when it came to the mentally ill), this account explains the determinants of the leadership's intentions and policies *and* of the success that it had in implementing them. The German ideology governed the Germans' treatment not only of Jews but also of other peoples.

More generally, the Nazi view of humanity, much of which had penetrated and found assent in wide portions of German society, informed the

Germans' manner of treatment of conquered and subject peoples. This view divided human beings into a hierarchy of races, race being understood in biological terms. The Nordic peoples—tall, blond, blue-eyed—were at the apex. Below them were various western European racial strains. Below them were southern Europeans. Below them, already far down, were Slavs. Still below them were Asian peoples. At the bottom, somewhere near the boundary separating human beings and primates, were Blacks.[81] Although all sorts of hazy notions informed the conceptualization of the continuum, it was essentially a continuum of putative capacity, with valued attributes, such as intelligence, to be found in diminishing quantity the lower a people's position was in the hierarchy. Corresponding quite well with this conceptualization—and obviously derived from it—was the Germans' treatment of conquered countries. The Nordic Scandinavians received the finest and most lenient treatment. The western Europeans, treated less well, still fared better than did southern Europeans. So powerful was this delusionary ideology that the Germans treated the Slavic peoples with an enormous brutality and murderousness that greatly harmed the German war effort by arousing enmity where sometimes they had initially found a willingness to cooperate. As the discussion of Jewish "work" has shown, the German people's differentiated manner of treating the different foreign workers in their midst, and not only those remaining in the conquered countries, also reproduced this racial hierarchy.

This hierarchy of humanity also suggests the singular position occupied by the Jews in Germans' imaginations. Jews were not even accorded a place on the continuum. As one 1936 children's book put it:

> *The Devil is the father of the Jew.*
> *When God created the world,*
> *He invented the races:*
> *The Indians, the Negroes, the Chinese*
> *And also the wicked creature called the Jew.*[82]

Walter Buch, the supreme judge of the Nazi Party, made clear in a 1938 contribution to the esteemed journal *Deutsche Justiz* that this "wicked creature" should not be seen as having kinship even with "inferior" races: "The National Socialist has recognized [that] the Jew is not a human being."[83] Jews belonged not to the hierarchy of the human race, but to a race *sui generis*, an "anti-race" (*Gegenrasse*). The term "subhuman" (*Untermensch*), used loosely by Germans, was applied to the allegedly inferior "races," such as Slavs, as a description of their putative diminished capacity. The Jews were deemed to be "subhuman" not because Germans believed them to be of such inferior capabilities. In fact, Germans considered the Jews to be greatly capable, in the sense of being highly intelligent and able foes. According to Hitler, "the mental qualities of the Jew have been schooled in the course of many centuries. Today he passes as 'smart,' and this in a certain sense he has been at all times."[84] The clever Jew, devilishly conniving to harm and cheat Germans, whether as a Machiavellian international financier or as a local merchant, was a prominent figure in the German mental landscape; the Jews' putative capacity to live parasitically off honest German labor was the strategy and achievement of a dangerous foe. The "subhumanity" of the Jews was of a character different from that of all other "subhumans": the Jews were understood to be morally depraved, and their depravity was so vast that Himmler could say in 1938, to a conference of SS generals, that the Jews were the "primary matter of everything negative" (*Urstoff alles Negativen*).[85] Germans' belief that the Jews combined great intelligence and cunning on the one hand, and implacable malevolence on the other, made the Jews seem to them the deadliest of foes, to be dealt with as no other people, as a people whom the Germans ultimately had to annihilate.

The distinctive quality of Germans' cognitions and values, principally the character of their antisemitism—in addition to having produced different German treatment of Jews and of other devalued peoples—also imparted to the Holocaust features not to be found in other genocides. This comparative investigation indicates that a number of the Holocaust's distinctive features stand out.

Although there are exceptions (the Khmer Rouge genocide in Cambodia is a partial example), almost all other large-scale mass slaughters occurred in the context of some preexisting realistic conflict (territorial, class, ethnic, or religious);[86] the Jews of Germany, it need hardly be emphasized, wanted nothing more than to be good Germans; the Jews of eastern Europe felt no prior enmity towards Germans, if anything the opposite, since large segments of eastern European Jewry were Germanophile.[87] The Germans' characterization of the Jews and their beliefs about them were absolutely fantastical, the sorts of beliefs that ordinarily only madmen have of others. When it came to Jews, the proneness to wild, "magical thinking"—by the Nazi leadership and the perpetrators—and their incapacity for "reality testing" generally distinguishes them from the perpetrators of other mass slaughters.

The geographic scope of the Germans' exterminationist drive against the Jews has no parallel, certainly not in the twentieth century. The Germans sought to uncover and kill Jews everywhere that they could, outside their country and the territories that they controlled, ultimately throughout the world. Not just its spatial reach but the comprehensiveness of the Germans' extermination of the Jews is also distinctive. Every last Jew, every Jewish child, had to die. Hitler had articulated the logic behind this already in the

Estimated Number of Jews Murdered During the Holocaust

(1945 borders are shown)

Arctic Ocean

Norwegian Sea

North Atlantic Ocean

FINLAND
7

NORWAY
762

SWEDEN

Helsinki

Leningrad

Oslo

Stockholm

ESTONIA
1,500–2,000

Moscow

North Sea

DENMARK
60

Copenhagen

Baltic Sea

Riga

LATVIA
70,000–71,500

Dublin

IRELAND

UNITED KINGDOM

NETHERLANDS
100,000

Berlin

LITHUANIA
140,000–143,000

Minsk

SOVIET UNION
1,000,000–1,100,000

London

English Channel

BELGIUM
28,900

GERMANY
134,500–141,500

POLAND
2,900,000–3,000,000

Warsaw

Kiev

Paris

Prague

Cracow

Lublin

LUXEMBOURG
1,950

BOHEMIA AND MORAVIA
78,150

CZECHOSLOVAKIA

SLOVAKIA
68,000–71,000

FRANCE
77,320

Vienna

AUSTRIA
50,000

Budapest

Odessa

SWITZERLAND

HUNGARY
550,000–569,000

ROMANIA
271,000–287,000

Zagreb

Belgrade

Bucharest

Black Sea

Marseilles

YUGOSLAVIA
56,200–63,300

BULGARIA
0

PORTUGAL

Madrid

ITALY
7,680

Rome

Adriatic Sea

Sofia

Istanbul

SPAIN

ALBANIA

TURKEY

Mediterranean

GREECE
60,000–67,000

Athens

Aegean Sea

Sea

0 miles 400
0 kilometers 600

N
W E
S

© Mark Stein Studios, 1995

early 1920s: "This is the point: even if not one synagogue, not one Jewish school, the Old Testament and the Bible had not existed, the Jewish spirit would still be there and have its effect. From the beginning it has been there and no Jew, not one, that does not embody it."[88] People of Jewish ancestry who by deed had renounced their Jewishness by converting to Christianity, or even those who had never had any Jewish identity (having been the baptized children of Jewish ancestors), people who, in other words, did not consider themselves to be Jewish, the Germans treated as Jews, for they too were of Jewish blood and therefore spirit. Even though the Germans considered Poles to be subhuman, these same Germans stole children of Polish parents, characterized by approved Germanic racial physiognomy, and brought them up as Germans to be incorporated into the master race.[89] The Turks, to cite but one of many possible examples from other genocides, let many Armenian children live who were young enough to forget their heritage and who therefore could be brought up safely as Turks and Moslems. The Turks also sometimes spared Armenian women who would convert to Islam.[90]

Finally, the quantity and quality of personalized brutality and cruelty that the Germans perpetrated upon Jews was also distinctive. This has been highlighted through comparisons with the Germans' treatment of other subject peoples. It could also be demonstrated through comparisons with other genocides and concentration camp systems.[91]

These distinctive features of the Holocaust grew organically from the demonizing German racial antisemitism, an antisemitism that produced the will for *comprehensive* killing of Jews *in all lands* despite the absence of any *objective prior conflict* with Jews; that, because of its *fantastical* construction of Jewry, demanded, unlike in other genocides, the *total* extermination of the Jews, so that no "germ-cell" would remain to spawn this eternal enemy anew; that energized the Germans' campaign of annihilation such that they could coordinate and persist in this enormous, *continent-wide* project; and that imbued the perpetrators with a rage, a lust for vengeance, that unleashed the *unprecedented cruelty*.

For people to kill another large group of people, the ethical and emotional constraints that normally inhibit them from adopting such a radical measure must be lifted. Something profound must happen to people before they will become willing perpetrators of enormous mass slaughter. The more that the range and character of the German perpetrators' actions become known, the less the notion appears tenable that they were not tuned in to the Hitlerian view of the world.

This brief comparative treatment suggests that the cognitive explanation of the perpetration of the Holocaust does fulfill the criteria of a powerful explanation. It achieves still more than accounting for the difficult-to-fathom actions of the perpetrators, for the comparative aspects internal to the Nazi genocide of Jews, and for the variance in action towards Jews of Germans and the members of other national groups, such as Danes and Italians. By being additionally sufficient both for explaining the Germans' treatment of non-Jewish subject peoples and for accounting for the distinctive comparative features of the Holocaust vis-à-vis other genocides, the cognitive explanation demonstrates itself to be compatible with kindred explanations of other comparable phenomena.

16

ELIMINATIONIST ANTISEMITISM
AS GENOCIDAL MOTIVATION

THAT THE PERPETRATORS approved of the mass slaughter, that they willingly gave assent to their own participation in the slaughter, is certain. That their approval derived in the main from their own conception of Jews is all but certain, for no other source of motivation can plausibly account for their actions. This means that had they not been antisemites, and antisemites of a particular kind, then they would not have taken part in the extermination, and Hitler's campaign against the Jews would have unfolded substantially differently from how it did. The perpetrators' antisemitism, and hence their motivation to kill, was, furthermore, not derived from some other non-ideational source. It is not an intervening variable, but an independent one. It is not reducible to any other factor.

This, it must be emphasized, is not a monocausal account of the perpetration of the Holocaust. Many factors were necessary for Hitler and others to have conceived the genocidal program, for them to have risen to the position from which they could implement it, for its undertaking to have become a realistic possibility, and for it then to have been carried out. Most of these elements are well understood. This book has focused on one of a number of the causes of the Holocaust, the least well-understood one, namely the crucial motivational element which moved the German men and women, without whom it would and could not have occurred, to devote their bodies, souls, and ingenuity to the enterprise. With regard to the *motivational* cause of the Holocaust, for the vast majority of perpetrators, a monocausal explanation does suffice.

When focusing on only the motivational cause of the Holocaust, the following can be said. The claim here is that this virulent brand of German racial antisemitism was in *this historical instance* causally sufficient to provide not only the Nazi leadership in its decision making but also the perpetrators with the requisite motivation to participate willingly in the extermination of the Jews. This does not necessarily mean that some other set of factors (independent of or conjoined with the regnant German antisemitism) could not conceivably have induced Germans to slaughter Jews. It merely means that it simply did not happen.

To be sure, some of the mechanisms specified by the conventional explanations were at work, shaping the actions of some *individuals*. It cannot be doubted that individual Germans became perpetrators despite a principled disapproval of the extermination. After all, not all perpetrators were offered the opportunity to refuse to kill and not all were serving under a commander as kindly as Police Battalion 101's "Papa" Trapp. It is also likely that disapproving individuals, finding themselves in an *atmosphere of general approval*, would, because of group pressure, commit acts which they had considered to be crimes, perhaps finding comforting rationalizations to assuage their consciences. It cannot be ruled out that some individuals, who were themselves not beholden to virulent German antisemitism, would have been moved to kill by a cynicism that set the value of some coveted advantage, material or otherwise, higher than that of the lives of innocent people. A presumption of coercion, social psychological pressure from assenting comrades, and the occasional opportunities for personal advancement, in different measures, were at times real enough; yet they cannot explain, for all the reasons already adduced, the actions in *all* of their varieties of the perpetrators *as a class*, but only some actions of some individuals who might have killed despite their disapproval, or of others who might have needed but a push to overcome reluctance, whatever its source. Nevertheless, none of these factors influenced the general course of the perpetration of the Holocaust fundamentally. Had these particular non-ideological factors—to the extent that they even existed—not been present, then the Holocaust would still have proceeded apace. And it must be emphasized that for analytical purposes these factors are not very significant; all the ordinary, representative Germans who were not under coercion, who had no career or material advantage to gain from killing, who formed the assenting majority that might have created pressure for dissenting individuals, and who nevertheless killed, all these ordinary, representative Germans show that these non-ideological factors were mainly irrelevant to the perpetration of the Holocaust.[1] They show that racial eliminationist antisemitism was a sufficient cause, a sufficiently potent motivator, to lead Germans to kill Jews willingly; absent these other tertiary factors, the perpetrators would have acted more or less as they did—once mobilized by Hitler in this national undertaking.

A second claim is equally strong. Not only was German antisemitism in this historical instance a sufficient cause, but it was also a *necessary* cause for such broad German participation in the persecution and mass slaughter of Jews, *and* for Germans to have treated Jews in all the heartless, harsh, and cruel ways that they did. Had ordinary Germans not shared their leadership's eliminationist ideals, then they would have reacted to the ever-intensifying assault on their Jewish countrymen and brethren with at least as much opposition and non-cooperation as they did to their government's attacks on Christianity and to the so-called Euthanasia program. As has already been discussed, especially with regard to religious policies, the Nazis backed down when faced with serious, widespread popular opposition. Had the Nazis been faced with a German populace who saw Jews as ordinary human beings, and German Jews as their brothers and sisters, then it is hard to imagine that the Nazis would have proceeded, or would have been able to proceed, with the extermination of the Jews. If they somehow had been able to go forward, then the probability that the assault would have unfolded as it did, and that Germans would have killed so many Jews, is extremely low. The probability that it would have produced so much German cruelty and exterminatory zeal is zero. A German population roused against the elimination and extermination of the Jews most likely would have stayed the regime's hand.

More generally, it can be said that certain kinds of dehumanizing beliefs[2] about people, or the attribution of extreme malevolence to them, are necessary and *can* be sufficient to induce others to take part in the genocidal slaughter of the dehumanized people, if they are given proper opportunity and coordination, typically by a state.[3] Yet such beliefs alone are not on their own always sufficient to produce a genocide, for other inhibiting factors may be operative, such as an ethical code and a moral sensibility which prohibit killing of this sort. Such beliefs constitute the enabling conditions necessary for a state to mobilize large groups of people to take part in genocidal slaughter. A hypothetical exception to the necessary existence of such genocidal beliefs is when coercion on a massive scale might be applied (by the state) to people compelled to become perpetrators. Although this could undoubtedly cause individuals to kill, it seems to me unlikely ever to succeed in making tens of thousands murder hundreds of thousands or millions over a prolonged time. Moreover, as far as I know, it has never happened—not in Cambodia, Turkey, Burundi, Rwanda, or the Soviet Union, to name prominent twentieth-century places of genocide.[4] The Nazi leadership, like other genocidal elites, never applied, and most likely would not have been willing to apply, the vast amount of coercion that it would have needed to move tens of thousands of non-antisemitic Germans to kill millions of Jews. The Nazis, knowing that ordinary Germans shared their convictions, had no need to do so.

The Holocaust was a *sui generis* event that has a historically specific explanation. The explanation specifies the enabling conditions created by the long-incubating, pervasive, virulent, racist, eliminationist antisemitism of German culture, which was mobilized by a criminal regime beholden to an eliminationist, genocidal ideology, and which was given shape and energized by a leader, Hitler, who was adored by the vast majority of the German people, a leader who was known to be committed wholeheartedly to the unfolding, brutal eliminationist program. During the Nazi period, the eliminationist antisemitism provided the motivational source for the German leadership and for rank-and-file Germans to kill the Jews. It also was the motivational source of the other non-killing actions of the perpetrators that were integral to the Holocaust.

It is precisely because antisemitism alone did not produce the Holocaust that it is not essential to establish the differences between antisemitism in Germany and elsewhere.[5] Whatever the antisemitic traditions were in other European countries, it was only in Germany that an openly and rabidly antisemitic movement came to power—indeed was elected to power—that was bent upon turning antisemitic fantasy into state-organized genocidal slaughter. This alone ensured that German antisemitism would have qualitatively different consequences from the antisemitisms of other countries, and substantiates the *Sonderweg* thesis: that Germany developed along a singular path, setting it apart from other western countries. So whatever the extent and intensity of antisemitism was among, say, the Poles or the French, their antisemitism is not important for *explaining* the Germans' genocide of the Jews; it might help to explain the Polish or French people's reactions to the German genocidal onslaught, but that is not an issue under consideration here.[6] Even if, for explanatory purposes, it is not essential to discuss German antisemitism comparatively, it is still worth stating that the antisemitism of no other European country came close to combining *all* of the following features of German antisemitism (indeed, virtually every other country fell short on *each* dimension). No other country's antisemitism was at once so widespread as to have been a cultural axiom, was so firmly wedded to racism, had as its foundation such a pernicious image of Jews that deemed them to be a mortal threat to the *Volk*, and was so deadly in content, producing, even in the nineteenth century, such frequent and explicit calls for the extermination of the Jews, calls which expressed the logic of the racist eliminationist antisemitism that prevailed in Germany. The unmatched volume and the vitriolic and murderous substance of German antisemitic literature of the nineteenth and twentieth centuries alone indicate that German antisemitism was *sui generis*.

This is a historically specific explanation, yet it has implications for our understanding of other genocides and suggests why a greater number of genocides have not occurred; even though severe conflicts and war have characterized group relations throughout history and today, a genocidal ideology and genocidal opportunities must be simultaneously present if people are to be motivated and able to exterminate other groups of people. The genocidal ideology has generally been absent, and even when it has been present and has motivated people to kill others, the *content* of the ideology, which always includes an account of the putative nature of the victims, has led other perpetrators to treat their victims in ways that have differed significantly from the comprehensively and singularly brutal deadly German assault upon the Jews.

IT IS BECAUSE factors other than exterminationist antisemitism shaped the Germans' actions that the character of the interaction of the various influences, including strategic and material constraints, needs to be understood. This, as was detailed earlier, can be seen at the policy level in the evolution of the Germans' eliminationist policies into exterminationist ones as the opportunities and constraints became more favorable for a "final solution."

Whatever the constancy of Hitler's and other leading Nazis' eliminationist *ideals* was, the Germans' anti-Jewish *intentions* and *policy* had three distinct phases.[7] Each was characterized by different practical opportunities for "solving" the "Jewish Problem" that derived—this was true both of the possibilities and the constraints—from Germany's geostrategic situation, namely from its position on the European continent and its relations with other countries.

The first phase lasted from 1933 until the outbreak of the war. The Germans implemented the utterly radical policies of turning the Jews into socially dead beings and of forcing most of them to flee from their homes and country. They did so by perpetrating ceaseless verbal and sporadic yet ferocious physical violence upon Jews, by depriving them of civil and legal protections and rights, and by progressively excluding them from virtually all spheres of social, economic, and cultural life. At a time when most of Europe's Jews were beyond the Germans' reach—rendering a lethal "solution" to the "Jewish Problem" unfeasible—and when a comparatively weak Germany was pursuing dangerous foreign policy goals and arming in preparation for the coming war, these were the most final "solutions" that were practicable, the only ones that they could prudently adopt.

The second phase lasted from the beginning of the war until early 1941. The conquest of Poland and then of France and the prospective defeat or peace with Britain created new opportunities for the Germans, yet fundamental constraints remained. They now had over two million, not mere hundreds of thousands, of European Jews under their control, so they could entertain some "solution" to the "Jewish Problem" more effective than anything possible while Germany remained confined to its 1939 borders. Yet killing these Jews was still not opportune, because a good part of the putative wellspring of Jewry remained out of reach in the Soviet Union, and because the uneasy non-aggression pact with the "Jewish-Bolshevik" Soviet Union could have been expected to disintegrate prematurely, to the detriment of the Germans, should they then have begun the genocidal killing of Jews under the gaze of the Soviet troops stationed in the heart of Poland. Still, during this period the Germans fashioned more apocalyptic plans and began to implement them. By the beginning of this phase, the Germans had made it clear that the Jews' lives were worthless and forfeit; that anything, literally anything, could be done to them. The Germans proceeded to sever the Jews from the economy of German-occupied Poland, to ghettoize them under inhuman, deadly conditions, which produced starvation and a high mortality rate. All Jews were *"vogelfrei,"* outlaws who were fair game. Germans could and did kill Jews at a whim. The groundwork had clearly already been laid for the Germans to exterminate them or to devise some surrogate quasi-genocidal fate for them.

Under these more propitious circumstances, the Nazis contemplated more radical "solutions"—bloodless equivalents of genocide. They began to explore the possibility of removing this good portion of all of European Jewry living under their dominion to some god-forsaken territory, where they could discard, immure, and leave the Jews to wither and expire. In November 1939, at a meeting devoted to expulsions, Hans Frank, the German Governor of Poland, expressed the underlying exterminationist motive that was already operative in and constitutive of the relocation schemes: ". . . We won't waste much more time on the Jews. It's great to get to grips with the Jewish race at last. The more that die the better."[8] During this second phase, the Germans pursued the most radical "solutions" that were practicable and prudent. Their proto-genocidal policies for handling Jews within their dominion gave a new lethality to their Jewish policies. Their bloodlessly genocidal eliminationist "solution" of vast deportations, however, did prove to be chimerical—the only major German initiative against the Jews that did—but to no great disappointment on the part of the Nazi leadership, for the impending conquest of the Soviet Union rendered such deportations undesirable, by offering them at last the opportunity for a truly final and irrevocable "solution."

The third phase began with the planning of the attack on the Soviet Union and the invasion itself. It was only during this phase that killing the Jews whom the Germans could actually reach would prove to be, from their hallucinatory perspective, an effective and not a counterproductive policy. It was only then that a "final solution" by systematic killing was practical. It was only then that the Germans no longer had major political and military constraints hindering them from pursuing such a policy. It is no surprise, therefore, that immediately upon launching the assault on the Soviet Union, Germans began to implement Hitler's decision, already cast, to exterminate all of European Jewry. During this phase, with the exception of some tactical attempts to use Jews to gain concessions from the Allies, every German measure affecting the Jews either led to their immediate deaths, was a means that would hasten or contribute eventually to their deaths, or was a temporary surrogate for death.[9] With the absence of any but comparatively minor logistical constraints upon their eliminationist desires, the eliminationist compulsion in the form of the slaughter of the Jews came to take priority over every other goal. The Germans continued with it in the form of mass shootings and death marches until, literally, the final day of the war.

Most striking about the Germans' anti-Jewish policy is that in each of the three phases, its major thrust was *the maximum feasible eliminationist option possible* given the existing opportunities and constraints. There was no *unintended* cumulative radicalization of policy because of bureaucratic politics or for any other reason.[10] The extent and virulence of the verbal violence assaulting the Jews from their own countrymen have no parallel in modern history. The rapid enactment of discriminating, debilitating, and dehumanizing legislation also has no parallel in modern history. The speed with which this group of prosperous, economically and culturally relatively well-integrated citizens were stripped of their rights and, with the approval of the vast majority of people in their society, turned into social lepers has no parallel in modern history. Our knowledge of the genocidal measures that followed tends to obscure how radical the Germans' treatment of Jews was during the 1930s. All of these measures, the turning of Jews into socially dead beings, and the policies that sought to compel them, 500,000 people, to emigrate from Germany constituted an utterly "radical" campaign, the likes of which western Europe had not seen for centuries. Those who argue that a radicalization of German policy towards the Jews occurred only in the 1940s minimize the radical nature of the anti-Jewish policy of the 1930s (which was noted as such by contemporaries) and miss the underlying continuity among the three phases of the anti-Jewish policy.

Indeed, the Germans' anti-Jewish policy evolved in a logical manner— always flowing from the eliminationist ideology—in consonance with the creation of new eliminationist opportunities, opportunities which Hitler was happy to exploit, promptly and eagerly, to their limits. Holding Hitler back in the first two phases were the practical limits on policy, limits imposed by Germany's constrained capacity to "solve" the "Jewish Problem"—independent of any other considerations—and by the existence of other considerations, the prudential ones regarding Germany's military and geo-political situation.[11] On October 25, 1941, a few months after Hitler's genocidal onslaught had begun, Hitler reminded Himmler and Heydrich—during a long disquisition that began with a reference to his January 1939 prophecy that the war would end with the elimination of the Jews—of what they already knew: that, having often operated under severe constraints, he had been content to wait for the right moment to pursue his apocalyptic ideals: "I am compelled to accumulate within me a tremendous amount; that does not, however, mean that what I take note of, but to which I do not react immediately, becomes extinguished in me. It is entered into a ledger; one day the book is brought out. Vis-à-vis the Jews as well, I had to remain for long inactive. It is pointless artificially to cause oneself additional difficulties; the cleverer one proceeds, the better."[12] Hitler was presenting himself as the prudent politician that he often was, biding his time, waiting for a propitious moment to strike. He had for long been "inactive" with regard to the Jews. The word "inactive" (*tatenlos*) here could have meant only "abstinence from mass killing," since for eight years Hitler had been very active indeed against the Jews, persecuting them, degrading them, burning their synagogues, expelling them from Germany, herding them into ghettos, and even killing them sporadically. For him, all these measures had amounted to inaction, for they all fell short of the one act that was adequate to the necessary task, adequate to the threat. The patiently longed-for final act that, for Hitler, qualified as real "action" was the physical annihilation of the Jews.[13]

In no sense was Hitler's monumental, indeed world-historical, decision—driven as it was by his fervent hatred of Jews—to exterminate European Jewry an historical accident, as some have argued, that took place because other options were closed off to him or because of something as ephemeral as Hitler's moods. Killing was not undertaken by Hitler reluctantly. Killing, biological purgation, was for Hitler a natural, preferred method of solving problems. Indeed, killing was Hitler's reflex. He slaughtered those in his own movement whom he saw as a challenge. He killed his political enemies. He killed Germany's mentally ill. Already in 1929, he publicly toyed with the idea of killing all German children born with physical defects, which he numbered in a murderously megalomaniacal moment of fantasy at 700,000 to 800,000 a year.[14] Surely, death was the most fitting penalty for the Jews. A demonic nation deserves nothing less than death.

Indeed, it is hard to imagine Hitler and the German leadership having settled for any other "solution" once they attacked the Soviet Union. The argument that only circumstances of one sort or another *created* Hitler's and the Germans' *motive* to opt for a genocidal "solution" ignores, for no good reason, Hitler's oft-stated and self-understood intention to exterminate the Jews. This argument also implies, counterfactually, that had these putative motivation-engendering circumstances not been brought about—had Hitler's allegedly volatile moods not allegedly swung, had the Germans been able to "resettle" millions of Jews—then Hitler and the others would have preferred some other "solution" and then millions of additional Jews would have survived the war. This counterfactual reasoning is highly implausible.[15] It would have necessitated that during this *Vernichtungskrieg*, this avowed war of total destruction, some circumstances would have led the Germans to spare their "anti-Christ," the Jews, even though Hitler and Himmler were planning to dispossess and kill millions of, in their view, the far less threatening Slavs (before the attack on the Soviet Union, Himmler once set the expected body count for that country at thirty million), when creating the planned "Germanic Eden" of eastern Europe.[16]

Hitler, on January 25, 1942, after affirming that "the absolute extermination" of the Jews was the appropriate policy, himself pointed out to Himmler, the head of his Chancery, Hans Lammers, and General Kurt Zeitzler how nonsensical it would have been not to be killing the Jews: "Why should I look upon a Jew with eyes other than [if he were] a Russian prisoner [of war]? In the POW camps many are dying, because we have been driven by the Jews into this situation. What can I do about it? Why did the Jews instigate this war?"[17] In addition to the general implausibility of the counterfactual notion that Hitler and Himmler preferred or would have preferred a non-genocidal course once they had unleashed their forces against the Soviet Union, the facts do not support such speculative reasoning. Once the extermination program began, the Germans conceiving and implementing the mass slaughter did not consider any other "solution" to be preferable;[18] they did not lament that the "Jewish Problem" could not be solved through emigration or "resettlement." All indications suggest that they understood the genocidal slaughter as the natural and therefore appropriate means to dispose of the Jews now that such an option had become practicable.

The idea that death and death alone is the only fitting punishment for Jews was publicly articulated by Hitler at the beginning of his political career on August 13, 1920, in a speech entirely devoted to antisemitism, "Why Are We Antisemites?" In the middle of that speech, the still politically obscure Hitler suddenly digressed to the subject of the death sentence and why it ought to be applied to the Jews. Healthy elements of a nation, he declared, know that "criminals guilty of crimes against the nation, i.e., parasites on the national community," cannot be tolerated, that under certain circumstances they must be punished only with death, since imprisonment lacks the quality of irrevocableness. "The heaviest bolt is not heavy enough and the securest prison is not secure enough that *a few million* could not in the end open it. Only one bolt cannot be opened—*and that is death* [my emphasis]."[19] This was not a casual utterance, but reflected an idea and resolve that had already ripened and taken root in Hitler's mind.

In the discussion that ensued with members of the audience about the above-mentioned speech, Hitler revealed that he had contemplated the question of how the "Jewish Problem" is to be solved. He resolved to be thoroughgoing. "We have, however, decided that we shall not come with ifs, ands, or buts, but when the matter comes to a solution, it will be done thoroughly."[20] In the speech proper, Hitler spelled out, with a candid explicitness that he prudently would not repeat in public after he had achieved national prominence, what he meant by the phrase "it will be done thoroughly." It meant that putting the entire Jewish nation to death—or, as Hitler himself had stated publicly a few months earlier in another speech, "to seize the Evil [the Jews] by the roots and to exterminate it root and branch"—would be the most just and effective punishment, the only enduring "solution." Mere imprisonment would be too clement a penalty for such world-historical criminals and one, moreover, fraught with danger, since the Jews could one day emerge from their prisons and resume their evil ways. Hitler's maniacal conception of the Jews, his consuming hatred of them, and his natural murderous propensity rendered him incapable of becoming reconciled permanently to any "solution of the Jewish Problem" save that of extinction.

The road to Auschwitz was not twisted. Conceived by Hitler's apocalyptically bent mind as an urgent, though future, project, its completion had to wait until conditions were right. The instant that they were, Hitler commissioned his architects, Himmler and Heydrich, to work from his vague blueprint in designing and engineering the road. They, in turn, easily enlisted ordinary Germans by the tens of thousands, who built and paved it with an immense dedication born of great hatred for the Jews whom they drove down that road. When the road's construction was completed, Hitler, the architects, and their willing helpers looked upon it not as an undesirable construction, but with satisfaction. In no sense did they regard it as a road chosen only because other, preferable venues had proven to be dead ends. They held it to be the best, safest, and speediest of all possible roads, the only one that led to a destination from which the satanic Jews are absolutely sure never to return.

THE INTERACTION of a variety of influences on the Germans' treatment of Jews on all institutional levels can be seen also, in a manner still more complex than in the evolution of the Germans' general eliminationist assault on the Jews, in the realm of Jewish "work." In the area of Jewish "work," as with the anti-Jewish policy, despite enormous material obstacles and constraints (in this case, urgent economic need), the power of German eliminationist antisemitism was the force that drove the Germans to override other considerations, even if the pattern of German actions that emerged at first seems hard to fathom.

There can be no doubt that the objective economic needs were the principal cause of Germans putting Jews to work. But the rational *need* did not produce anything resembling a rational German *response*, and the two should not be confused. The need could be translated into labor only in a distorted, atrophied way, because it came into conflict with far more powerful ideological dictates. The creation of a special Jewish economy, which was by and large separated from the general economy, produced an enormous drop in overall Jewish productivity and did substantial damage to the economic health of war-engulfed Germany. The Lublin camps are particularly noteworthy because they existed in a context of the Germans' general work mobilization of continental Europe, and after orders had been given by Himmler to treat non-German workers better. They show that the ideological foundations of Germany during the Nazi period rendered it constitutionally incapable of creating the conditions for the decent treatment and the rational use of Jewish labor power. Because of the Germans' fantastical beliefs about Jewish evil, the Jews *had* to be segregated, *had* to be removed from the general economy, in which they should have been integrated had the Germans wanted to utilize their talents, skills, and labor in an economically rational manner. The policies that brought millions of other laborers to Germany, both people from the West and "subhumans" from the East, and that led to over thirty thousand of them fleeing their German masters every month in 1943,[21] could not have been duplicated for Jews. Any policy which held out at this time the mere possibility, however unintended, of large numbers of Jews roaming around the countryside unchecked was unimaginable in Germany. The Jews had to be incarcerated in the only places deemed fitting, in leper-like colonies where disease and death festered. This produced even more deleterious economic results. And this Jewish economy was itself absolutely irrationally organized and run, and woefully unproductive. In war-ravaged Europe, the Germans found it difficult to bring to these bizarre and eerie colonies on the figurative frontier of humanity the plant, equipment, and conditions of work that were necessary for any rational kind of production to occur. Furthermore, it was itself destroyed in large chunks at a time when the Germans decided, for extra-economic reasons, to kill some group or community of Jews. The realm of politics and the realm of social relations, in this matter, worked hand in glove towards the same end. The political-ideological imperative to separate the Jews from Germans, to punish the Jews, and to kill them, together with the manifold forms of crippling and fatal abuse to which the Jews' "foremen" subjected their "workers" in face-to-face relations, prevented the Germans from meeting their pressing economic needs. The objective economic need existed. The Germans were ideologically and psychologically unfit to respond to it. If the Germans had used all the Jews as slaves, which they could easily have done, then they would have extracted great economic profit from them. But they did not do so. They were like slave masters who, driven by frenzied delusions, murdered most of their slaves and treated the small percentage whom they did put to work so recklessly and cruelly that they crippled the slaves' capacity for work.

Economic irrationality and cruelty and debilitation were embedded in the organizational, material, and psychological constitution of the German institutions (including the overseers) of Jewish "work." It is not just, as others have correctly maintained, that extermination had political priority over economics and work, as if the leadership had willfully made a choice between alternative possibilities.[22] During its Nazi period, Germany developed along a path, according to the logic of its animating beliefs, that made it, probably by 1941 and certainly by 1943, generally *incapable* of the rational economic use of Jews, except, at times, on a local basis. The Germans were so beholden to the barbarous implications of their ideology that even when they tried to apply the normal linguistic and practical forms of work to Jews, they generally failed, except in crippled and crippling approximations. The power of German antisemitism to derail rationality in the economy, the realm of modern industrial society where rationality is most consistently sought, and which for non-Jews was highly rationally organized, demonstrates that with regard to the Jews, the Germans' ideology had created for them a cognitive map singular in nature, leading them in directions that they themselves would have considered false and dangerous—at odds with reality and rationality—for peoples other than Jews.[23]

Just as antisemitism operated in conjunction with other factors on the levels of policy and of institutional practice, so too did it at times on the individual level. On the individual level, it is clear that although German antisemitism was sufficient to motivate the perpetrators, it did not produce completely uniform practices. Other factors of belief and personality naturally gave variation to individual action. The degree of enthusiasm that Germans brought to their dealings with Jews as well as the cruelty that they showed did vary, undoubtedly because of the perpetrators' different degrees of inhibitions, their characters, and, especially in the case of cruelty, their taste for barbarism, the pleasure that they took in the suffering of Jews, their sadism. The norm in Police Battalion 101 was that the men carried out their eliminationist tasks willingly and skillfully, yet, as one of the battalion's lieutenants, fully aware of the base-line exemplary performance of his compatriots, says, there were men "who particularly distinguished themselves on missions. This was true in this respect also for Jewish actions."[24] Even by the high standard that the genocidal cohort that was Police Battalion 101 set, some, indeed many, of the men distinguished themselves. Similarly, virtually all Germans in concentration camps brutalized Jews. That was the common feature. Some brutalized Jews more frequently, vigorously, or inventively than others. That was the variance which, in light of the Holocaust's constituent feature of near universal cruelty, is really but a nuance of action in need of explanation. It is also no surprise that a small number of people refrained from killing or brutalizing Jews. In Germany, some people dissented from the prevailing Nazified conception of Jews, and others, even if they shared this view, still adhered to a restraining ethical standard at odds with the disinhibiting one of the new dispensation. Minority cognitions of these sorts gave such people, but a tiny percentage of Germans, the impetus to help hide Jews in Germany[25] and, in the killing fields, made such people unwilling to take part in the genocide. The existing opportunities to avoid killing permitted these same people to realize their wishes. Hence the *small* group of refusers.

THE VIRULENT, racial antisemitism, in motivating Germans to push the eliminationist program forward on the macro, meso, and micro levels, must be understood to have been moving people who were operating under constraints, both external ones and those created by competing goals. This was true of Hitler and of the lowliest guard in a "work" camp. These ameliorating circumstances notwithstanding, the eliminationist antisemitism was powerful enough to have set Hitler and the German nation on an exterminationist course, powerful enough to have overridden economic rationality so thoroughly, powerful enough to have produced in so many people such individual voluntarism, zeal, and cruelty. The eliminationist antisemitism, with its hurricane-force potential, resided ultimately in the heart of German political culture, in German society itself.

Because the "Jewish Problem" was openly assigned high political priority and discussed continuously in the public sphere, there can be no doubt that the German people understood the purpose and the radicality of the anti-Jewish measures unfolding before their eyes during the 1930s. How could they not? "Jews are our misfortune"[26] was shouted from every rooftop in Germany. "Jew perish," no mere hyperbolic metaphorical flourish, could be heard and seen around Germany in the 1930s.

In Düsseldorf, an execration painted on the wall of a synagogue: "Jew perish"

The perpetrators, from Hitler to the lowliest officials, were openly proud of their actions, of their achievements; during the 1930s, they proclaimed and carried them out in full view and with the general approval of the *Volk*.

If ordinary Germans did not concur with Melita Maschmann's Nazified conception of Jews as a corporate "active force for evil" whose "wickedness was directed against the prosperity, unity and prestige of the German nation," if Germans did not share her abhorrence and demonology of Jews, then what did they believe? Did they believe that Jews were ordinary human beings, but simply of another religion? Did they believe perhaps that Jews harbored some objectionable qualities, but nothing remotely resembling the perniciousness that the beloved Hitler and the Nazis, as an article of faith, incessantly and emphatically attributed to them? Did they identify with the Jews as innocent victims of a deluded regime? Did they see all of the groups and numerous people in German society who aided the persecution as being deluded? If Germans had dissented from Hitler's conception of Jews, from the characterization of Jews as a powerful evil that is racially destined to harm and destroy the German *Volk*, if Germans had been moved by some other more benevolent conception of Jews, then what is the evidence for it? The Gestapo and its informers pursued people who expressed their divergence from Nazi antisemitism with a zeal that has led the foremost expert on the Gestapo to conclude that all such cases were reported and investigated. Yet in all of Lower Franconia, a region with 840,663 people (in 1939)—a region in which, as in all regions of Germany, Germans expressed an enormous amount of dissent on a broad range of Nazi policies, including on the treatment of foreigners— during *twelve years* of Nazi rule, only *fifty-two* such cases, four per year, came to the attention of the Gestapo! In the still much larger jurisdiction of Munich between 1933 and 1944, only *seventy* people were tried for remarks critical of the eliminationist project. The number of remarks was so small as to have been "almost insignificant."[27]

At no point during the Nazi period did significant portions, or even identifiable minorities, of the German people express either dissent from the dominant elaboration of the nature of Jews or principled disapproval of the eliminationist goals and measures that the German government and so many Germans pursued. After the war, many Germans and many scholars have asserted otherwise, but have provided little real evidence to support their claims.

How many German churchmen in the 1930s did not believe that the Jews were pernicious? Where is the *evidence* to support the contention that a significant number of them rejected the eliminationist antisemitic view of Jews?

How many German generals, the supposed guardians of traditional German honor and moral rectitude, did not want to cleanse Germany of Jews? Himmler, in fact, once discussed the extermination of the Jews in a speech before a good portion of the leadership of the armed forces—three hundred generals and staff officers gathered in Posen on January 25, 1944. The genocide was hardly news to the military leaders for, by then, the Germans had killed millions of Jews, and the army had been a full partner in the slaughter of Soviet Jewry. Himmler, knowing the army leadership well—which, as the abundant and irrefutable evidence shows, was in "fundamental agreement" with the extermination of the Jews[28]—spoke openly as someone does before an approving crowd. Indeed, when Himmler announced that Germany was wiping the Jews off the face of the earth, the military leaders broke into applause. The applause was not scattered; it was well-nigh unanimous. A dissenting general looked about him to see how many in the audience abstained from applauding. He counted five.[29]

What is the evidence for the belief that these men and their brethren saw the Jews as fellow Germans deserving full rights? Even many of those who hated the Nazis and plotted to kill Hitler were eliminationist antisemites.

How many jurists, how many in the medical community, how many in other professions held the ubiquitous, public antisemitism, with its hallucinatory elements, to be sheer nonsense? Where is the evidence?

How many of the over eight million members of the Nazi Party, and how many other ordinary Germans thought that Hitler's obsessive antisemitism were the ravings of a madman—and therefore that Hitler was a madman— that the eliminationist measures and the societal attack upon Jews of the 1930s were criminal, that all those measures ought to have been reversed and the Jews restored to their prior places in German society? Where is the evidence?

To be sure, not all churchmen, generals, jurists, and others wanted to exterminate the Jews. Some wanted to deport them, a few wanted to sterilize them, and some would have been content to deprive the Jews "only" of fundamental rights. Nevertheless, underlying all of these views was an eliminationist ideal. Where is the *evidence* for any other conclusion?

The words of one man, Pastor Walter Höchstädter, who in the summer of 1944 was a hospital chaplain in France, cast into sharp relief the powerful hold that the antisemitic cognitive model had on the rest of Germany, even typically on those who opposed aspects of the eliminationist program. Höchstädter secretly printed his indicting protest and sent one thousand copies through the military mail to soldiers at the front:

> We live in an age which is raging throughout with mad ideas and demons, no less than the Middle Ages. Our allegedly "enlightened" age, instead of indulging in an orgy of crazed witch-hunting, feasts itself in an orgy of maniacal Jew-hatred. Today the Jew-hating madness, which had already raged frightfully in the Middle Ages, has entered upon its acute stage. This, the Church, the community of Jesus Christ, must acknowledge. If she does not do it, then she will have failed, just as she had failed then, during the time of the witch-hunts. Today, the blood of millions of slaughtered Jews, of men, women, and children, cries to heaven. The Church is not permitted to be silent. She is not permitted to say that the settlement of the Jewish Problem is a matter for the state, the right to perform this function having been granted to it by Romans 13. The Church is also not permitted to say that in our time just punishment is being carried out upon the Jews for their sins. . . . There is no such thing as a moderate Christian antisemitism. Even when it is set forth seemingly convincingly by means of reasonable arguments (say, national ones) or even with scientific (read pseudo-scientific) arguments. The witch craze also was once scientifically justified by leading authorities of the theological, legal, and medical faculties. The battle against Jewry proceeds from the same muddy source from which the witch craze once proceeded. Contemporary mankind has not overcome its proclivity to look for a "scapegoat." Therefore it searches for all kinds of guilty parties—the Jews, the Freemasons and supra-state powers. This is the background of the hymns of hate of our time.
>
> . . . Who gives us the right to lay the blame solely on the Jews? A Christian is forbidden to do this. A Christian is not allowed to be an antisemite,

and he is not allowed to be a moderate antisemite. The objection that, without the [defensive] reaction of "moderate" antisemitism, the Jewification of the life of the *Volk* [*Verjudung des Volkslebens*] would become a horrible danger originates from an unbelieving and purely secular outlook, which Christians ought to overcome.

. . . The Church ought to live of love. Woe to her if she does not do that! Woe to her if by her silence and by all sorts of dubious excuses she becomes jointly guilty of the world's outbursts of hatred! Woe to her if she adopts words and slogans that originate in the sphere of hatred . . .[30]

In the annals of the history of Germany during its Nazi period, Höchstädter's letter, in its explicit and thoroughgoing rejection of the eliminationist antisemitic model, is an exceedingly rare and luminous document. Nearly all of the few protests and petitions of Germans that lamented or objected to their nation's treatment of the Jews were themselves imbued with antisemitism, an antisemitism that was irrational in its beliefs and harsh in its practical proposals, yet which can seem moderate when compared with the lethal variety practiced by the Nazis and by all of the ordinary Germans who aided them. Virtually all objectors to the physical violence that Germans inflicted on Jews assumed as a matter of course that a "Jewish Problem" did indeed exist, that the Jews were an evildoing tribe that had harmed Germany, and that a "solution" must be found whereby their corrosive presence would be greatly reduced and their influence eliminated. Such "dissenters" still wanted a "solution," one that was "civilized," bloodless, and orderly, not violent and cruel, as was the one that the Nazis had adopted. They wanted to curtail the putative power of the Jews, to exclude them from many spheres of social life, to prohibit them from holding public office, and to impose other restrictions that would render them powerless to harm Germans. Antisemitism ought to be "decent," "moderate," "spiritual," "ethical," "salutary," as befits a civilized nation. The Bishop of Linz, Johannes Maria Gfoellner, in a pastoral letter circulated in 1933, exhorted the Nazis thus: "If National Socialism . . . wants to incorporate only this spiritual and ethical form of antisemitism into its program, there is nothing to stop it."[31] "Be decent, moderate, spiritual, ethical antisemites, eliminate the Jews, but do not slaughter them" was the spoken or unspoken maxim that informed nearly all of the relatively few German objections to the countrymen's systematic slaughter of the Jews.

The obscure Pastor Höchstädter was dismayed by this brand of "moderation." To him, the Germans' persecution of the Jews sprang from the same troubled mental source from which the medieval witch craze had sprung. The accusations which Germans inside and outside the Church leveled at the Jews were hallucinatory delusions. Höchstädter emphatically rejects the view that existed in the churches and in anti-Nazi circles that what is needed is a "moderate" and "salutary" antisemitism. Antisemitism in any form, he states with a simplicity and clarity that was all but singular during the Nazi period, is a radical evil, a tissue of vicious falsehoods. Therein lies the extreme rarity of Höchstädter's appeal. I know of very few statements by opponents of the Nazis that condemned the wild antisemitic beliefs which were ubiquitous in Germany as wholly false, as devoid of essential truth, as frenzied, monstrous obsessions, in the manner that Höchstädter did in his anguished letter. He calls upon the clergy to come to their senses, to awaken from their delusions, to break their silence in the face of the millionfold slaughter of the Jews. "Therefore Be Sober" reads the admonition with which Höchstädter entitled his appeal.

How singularly sober, how "abnormal," how forlorn Höchstädter's *cri de coeur* appears when set beside the antisemitic utterances of bishops, ecclesiastical leaders, and other renowned members of the Church—when set beside the statement of Martin Niemöller, the celebrated anti-Nazi clergyman, that the Jews poison everything that they take up; beside Bishop Dibelius' recorded hope that the Jewish community, with its low birth rate, would die out and thus free Germany of its injurious presence; beside Bishop Wurm's assurance that he does not dispute with "a single word" the right of the state to combat Jewry as a dangerous element which corrodes "the religious, moral, literary, economic, and political spheres;"[32] beside Bishop August Marahrens' statement (made after the war in August 1945 in the course of his confession of guilt for not having spoken up for the Jews) that although a number of them had brought "a great disaster" (*ein schweres Unheil*) upon the German people, the Jews should not have been attacked in so "inhumane a manner."[33] So besotted were he and all those who shared his sort of "ethical" antisemitism that even after the war the good bishop appeared to imply that a more humane castigation would have been sufficient. Particularly glaring is the contrast between Höchstädter's appeal and the collective declaration of the National Church leaders of the Evangelical churches of Mecklenburg, Thuringia, Saxony, Nassau-Hesse, Schleswig-Holstein, Anhalt, and Lübeck urging that all Jewish converts to Christianity be expelled from the Church, that the "severest measures against the Jews be adopted," and that "they be banished from German lands."[34] Given the Germans' full-scale slaughter of Soviet Jews that was already under way, this proclamation is a unique document in the history of Christendom—an ecclesiastical imprimatur of genocide. Even if these leading men of God had not known that the deportees were destined to be slaughtered (which is highly unlikely since knowledge of the mass killings was already enormously widespread, including among other Church leaders), their proclamation would still be a rare and perhaps unique document in the modern history of the Christian churches—an ecclesiastical appeal to a tyrannous, enormously brutal state to treat an entire people with even greater brutality, to proceed against that people without any mitigation. For the churchmen were not only acquiescing in the persecution of the Jews; they were, on their own initiative, urging their government to adopt not merely "severe measures" but the "severest measures," by which they could have meant only measures even more severe than those to which the Jews had hitherto been subjected, measures which were bound to deepen the Jews' degradation and increase their suffering. The corporate voice of a significant part of the Protestant Church leadership of Germany was scarcely distinguishable from that of the Nazis. It was no doubt ecclesiastical sentiments such as these that Höchstädter had in mind when he included in his appeal the warning sentence "Woe to her [to the Church] if she adopts words and slogans that originate in the sphere of hatred."[35]

In the eyes of posterity, contemplating the darkness that was Germany during the Nazi period, Höchstädter's letter, recalling *The Merchant of Venice*, shines forth like a bright beam: "How far that little candle throws his beams! / So shines a good deed in a naughty world."[36] But in the vast antisemitic darkness that had descended upon Germany, enveloping even the churches, the appeal of Höchstädter was like a tiny, brief flame of reason and humanity, kindled in secret in a remote corner of occupied France, flickering invisibly.

The loneliness of Höchstädter's principled dissent indicates how important it is for us to focus on the Christian churches when trying to understand the nature of antisemitism in Germany during the Nazi period. The churches and the clergy of which they were composed are particularly instructive on this issue because they composed a large network of non-Nazi institutions, and because a large body of evidence has been preserved about their stance towards Jews during the Germans' persecution and slaughter of them. Moreover, Christianity's moral doctrines and complex traditions regarding Jews make this evidence particularly illuminating and telling.

The Christian churches have borne an ancient animus against Jews, regarding them as a guilt-laden people who not only rejected the divinity of Jesus but also crucified him. The churches were also institutions that believed themselves to be bound by a divine ordinance to preach and practice compassion, to foster love, to relieve suffering, and to condemn crime, wanton cruelty, and mass murder. For all these reasons, the attitude of the churches serves as a crucial test case for evaluating the ubiquity and depth of eliminationist antisemitism in Germany. If the ecclesiastical men, whose vocation was to preach love and to be the custodians of compassion, pity, and morality, acquiesced or looked with favor upon and supported the elimination of the Jews from German society, then this would be further and particularly persuasive proof of the ubiquity of eliminationist antisemitism in German society, an antisemitism so strong that it not only inhibited the natural flow of the feeling of pity but also overruled the moral imperatives of the creed to speak out on behalf of those who have fallen among murderers. As studies of the churches have shown, it cannot be doubted that antisemitism did succeed in turning the Christian community—its leaders, its clergy, and its rank and file—against its most fundamental traditions. The foremost historian of the German Protestant Church during this period, Wolfgang Gerlach, entitled his book *When the Witnesses Were Silent*. Similarly, Guenther Lewy ends his treatment of the German Catholic Church and the "Jewish Problem," whose leadership's attitudes towards the eliminationist enterprise were only somewhat more critical than that of the Protestant leadership, by quoting the question posed by the young girl to her priest in Max Frisch's *Andorra*: "Where were you, Father Benedict, when they took away our brother like a beast to the slaughter, like a beast to the slaughter, where were you?"[37]

The churches welcomed the Nazis' ascendancy to power, for they were deeply conservative institutions which, like most other German conservative bodies and associations, expected the Nazis to deliver Germany from what they deemed to have been the spiritual and political mire that was the Weimar Republic, with its libertine culture, democratic "disorder," its powerful Socialist and Communist parties which preached atheism and which threatened to rob the churches of their power and influence. The churches expected that the Nazis would establish an authoritarian regime that would reclaim the wrongly dishonored virtues of unquestioning obedience and submission to authority, restore the cultivation of traditional moral values, and enforce adherence to them. The Nazi Party was, to be sure, not wholly faultless in the eyes of the Christians. Indeed, it exhibited disquieting tendencies. Some of its ideologues were manifestly anti-Christian. Others urged a nebulous version of Teutonic paganism. And the Party's support of Christianity embodied in its program was framed in vague, puzzlingly qualified terms. These unwholesome facets of the Nazis the churches tended to interpret with the sort of wishful optimism that was to be found among many people who welcomed Nazism while disliking certain of its aspects—as transient excrescences upon the body of the Party which Hitler, in his wisdom and benevolence towards religion, would slough off as so many alien accretions.

The Nazis' ferocious antisemitism was not a feature of their movement to which the churches objected. On the contrary, they appreciated it, for they too were antisemitic. They too believed in the necessity of curtailing and eliminating the putative power of the Jews. For decades, nearly all the opinions, utterances, and pronouncements about Jews issuing from German ecclesiastical organs or clergymen of all ranks were informed by a deep hostility to Jews. The hostility was for the most part extra-religious, secular in character—an echo of the temporal enmity to Jews that coursed through German society. It did not spring merely from theological sources; it was not merely a latter-day reiteration of the perennial and deep-rooted Christian condemnation of the Jews as a "reprehensible people," as the crucifiers of Jesus, and as the stiff-necked spurners of the Christian revelation. Conjoined with that ancient accusation, and greatly overshadowing it, was the modern indictment of the Jews as the principal driving force behind the relentless tide of modernity that was steadily eroding hallowed and time-honored values and traditions. They held the Jews to be promoters of mammonism, of "soulless capitalism," of materialism, of liberalism, and, above all, of that skeptical and iconoclastic temper that was seen as the bane of the age. Reflecting the current trend of secular antisemitism, the "modern" Christian denigrators of Jews preached that the wickedness of the Jews derives not from their religion, but from their racial instincts, from immutable inborn destructive drives which cause them to act like cankerous weeds in blossoming gardens. Thus, even in the Christian churches, racist antisemitism overlay and, to a large extent, replaced the traditional religious enmity to Jews; the denunciations of the Jews that Christian clergymen broadcasted had become scarcely distinguishable from the diatribes that the militantly secular, racist antisemites delivered. This was especially the case in Protestant Church circles, where such antisemitic opinions were rampant. One Protestant Church organ bearing, with unintended irony, the name "Life and Light" would, in the words of a contemporary observer, "again and again describe the Jews with great zeal as a foreign body of which the German people must rid itself, as a dangerous adversary against whom one must wage a struggle to the last extreme."[38] Even a pastor who urged moderation in speaking of and treating the Jews nevertheless concurred in the common belief that they were a deadly affliction. "It is indisputable: the Jews have become for us a national plague which we must ward off."[39]

Indeed, the "indisputable" was seldom disputed. These antisemitic sentiments were not confined to a minority within the Protestant churches; they were well-nigh universal. Dissent was rare. To question them took intellectual courage. Who would dare to appear in the frowned-upon role of a defender of that detestable Jewish race whose maleficent character was held to be a self-evident truth? One churchman recalls in his memoirs that antisemitism was so widespread in clerical circles that "explicit objection [to antisemitism] could not be ventured."[40]

Throughout the period of Nazi rule, as the government and people of Germany were subjecting the Jews of Germany and those of the conquered

countries to an increasingly severe persecution that culminated in their physical annihilation, the German Protestant and Catholic churches, their governing bodies, their bishops, and most of their theologians watched the
suffering that Germans inflicted on the Jews in silence. No explicit public
word of sympathy for the Jews, no explicit public condemnation or protest
against their persecution issued from any of the authoritative figures within
the churches or from any of their ecclesiastical offices. Only a few lowly pastors and priests spoke out or, rather, cried out forlornly their sympathy with
the Jews and, with it, their bitter reproach of the Church authorities for their
silence. Of all the Protestant bishops of Germany, one (Bishop Wurm), in a
confidential letter to Hitler, protested the slaughter of the Jews. The other
bishops were almost as impassive in private as they were in public, and at least
one (Martin Sasse of Thuringia) published a pamphlet, bristling with virulent antisemitism, that explicitly justified the burning of the synagogues and
large scale anti-Jewish violence.

In sum, in the face of the persecution and annihilation of the Jews, the
churches, Protestant and Catholic, as corporate bodies exhibited an apparent,
striking impassiveness. Moreover, in the ranks of the clergy at all levels, numerous voices could be heard vilifying the Jews in Nazi-like terms, hurling
imprecations at them, and acclaiming their persecution at the hands of their
country's government. No serious historian would dispute the anti-Nazi theologian Karl Barth's verdict contained in his parting letter before leaving
Germany in 1935: "For the millions that suffer unjustly, the Confessing
Church does not yet have a heart."[41] To which it could be added, "and would
not exhibit a heart during the entire Nazi era."

The impassiveness of the Protestant and Catholic churches, their official
public silence is thrown into particularly sharp relief by the very few, scattered, impassioned, yet barely audible and utterly ineffectual voices of reproach and protest that were raised within their precincts by lowly isolated
figures. Perhaps the most impassioned, the bluntest, the most detailed and
most damning of the protests against the silence of the Christian churches
came from the pen of a comparatively obscure officer of one of its auxiliary
organizations, the chair of the Evangelical Welfare Service of the Berlin-
Zehlendorf district, Marga Meusel. It consisted of a lengthy memorandum
prepared for the synod of the Protestant Confessing Church which met at
Steglitz between September 26 and 29, 1935. Meusel supplemented the
memorandum with additions which she completed on May 8, 1936. She had
been prompted to make these additions by the worsening plight of the Jews
that resulted from the Nuremberg Laws. The memorandum vividly describes
the manner in which the Jews have been persecuted, giving examples of the
indignities, torments, and brutalities to which Germans subjected them. It

shows that even German children, nourished in this antisemitic culture, had taken to defaming and abusing Jews. "It is Christian children that do it, and Christian parents, teachers, and clergymen who allow it to happen." With clarity and directness, Meusel contends that "it is not an exaggeration when one speaks of the attempt to annihilate the Jews." In the presence of this fury of hate and immense suffering, the Church stands idle and mute. "What should one reply to the desperate and bitter questions and accusations? Why does the Church do nothing? Why does it allow unspeakable injustice to occur?" Particularly telling was Meusel's denunciation of the Church's warm welcome of Nazi rule, the Church's avowal of fealty to Hitler's regime. She quotes and concurs with the verdict of a Swedish report "that the Germans have a new God, and it is The Race, and to this God they bring human sacrifices." "How can it again and again profess joyous loyalty to the National Socialist state?" wonders Meusel. Alluding to the Nazi doctrine that decreed humaneness to be a base and contemptible sentiment, she asks: "Does it mean that all that is incompatible with humaneness, which is so disdained today, is compatible with Christianity?" In dire words of surpassing accusatory harshness, Meusel warns the Church: "What shall we one day answer to the question, where is thy brother Abel? The only answer that will be left to us as well as to the Confessing Church is the answer of Cain."

The German churches provide a crucial case in the study of the breadth, character, and power of modern German eliminationist antisemitism, because their leadership and membership could have been expected, for a variety of reasons, to have been among the people in Germany most resistant to it. The churches retained a large measure of their institutional independence, they contained many people who regarding other matters harbored non-Nazi and anti-Nazi sympathies, and their governing doctrines and humanistic traditions clashed glaringly with central precepts of the eliminationist project. The abundant evidence about their leadership's and membership's conceptions of Jews and stances towards the eliminationist persecution merely confirms and, because it is a crucial case, further strengthens greatly the conclusion that among the German people, the Nazified conception of Jews and support for the eliminationist project was extremely widespread, a virtual axiom.

Not only the churches and their leadership but also, as was shown in Chapter 3, virtually the entire German elite—intellectual, professional, religious, political, and military—embraced eliminationist antisemitism wholeheartedly as its own. The German elite and ordinary Germans alike failed to express dissent from the Nazi conception of Jewry in 1933, 1938, 1941, and 1944, although the nature and status of the Jews was one of the most relentlessly discussed subjects in the German public sphere. No evidence suggests that any but an insignificant scattering of Germans harbored opposition to the eliminationist program, save for its most brutally wanton aspects. Even violent anti-Nazi diatribes typically did not dwell on the eliminationist anti-semitism or measures as reasons for hating and opposing the Nazis.[42] Germans not only failed to indicate that they believed the (by non-Nazi standards) criminal treatment of the Jews to be unjust. They not only failed to lend help to their beleaguered countrymen, let alone foreign Jews. But even worse for the Jews, so many Germans also willingly aided the eliminationist enterprise. They did so by taking initiative to further it, by attacking Jews verbally and physically, or by hastening the process of excluding and isolating them from German society and thereby accelerating the process of turning Jews into socially dead beings and German Jewry into a leprous community.

It is often said that the German people were "indifferent" to the fate of the Jews.[43] Those who claim this typically ignore the vast number of ordinary Germans who contributed to the eliminationist program, even to its exterminationist aspects, and those many more Germans who at one time or another demonstrated their concurrence with the prevailing cultural cognitive model of the Jews or showed enthusiasm for their country's anti-Jewish measures, such as the approximately 100,000 people in Nuremberg alone, who, with obvious approval, attended a rally on the day after *Kristallnacht* which celebrated the night's events. Those who postulate that "indifference" governed the German people proceed as if all these Germans, who either openly assented to or were complicit in the eliminationist program, were a trivial number of people, and as if we learn from these Germans' actions nothing about the character of the German people in general. Ignoring, for the moment, these fundamental, unsurmountable empirical and analytical problems in asserting that Germans were "indifferent" to their national project of persecuting and exterminating the Jews, the invocation of "indifference" suffers from fatal conceptual problems as well.

Before the concept of "indifference" should be used, at least two issues must be addressed. The first is its meaning. How could Germans have been "indifferent"—in the sense of having no views or predilections on the matter, in the sense of feeling no emotions, of being utterly neutral, morally and in every other way—to the mass slaughter of thousands of people, including children, which the people themselves or their countrymen were helping to perpetrate in their name? Similarly, how could Germans have been "indifferent" to all of the earlier eliminationist measures, including the forcible wresting from their own neighborhoods of people (Jews) who had lived there for generations? The public vitriol against Jews was so ubiquitous in Germany during its Nazi period that it was as impossible for Germans to have had no views about Jews or about the elimination of Jews from German society as it was for Whites in the American South during the heyday of the civil rights movement to have had no views about Blacks or about the desirability of desegregation. "Indifference" was a virtual psychological impossibility.[44]

If, however, somehow "indifference" existed, if somehow many Germans had no views about Jews and no views about the justice of what their countrymen were doing to the Jews, then this cognitive state still must be elucidated, which would not obviate the problems of using the concept, but lead to the second issue. Germans, like others, were not indiscriminately "indifferent" to all matters. So why would they have been "indifferent" to the slaughter of Jews but not to many other occurrences that, on the face of it, should have been less likely to have stirred them from a state of total neutrality than would the eliminationist measures that culminated in mass murder? The structure and content of cognition and value and the nature of social relations that would produce "indifference" (if indeed it ever obtained) to such radical and unnerving measures as the anti-Jewish program in all its facets must be explicated if the concept is to have any meaning—if it is to be more than a label to be slapped on the German people, a label which prevents considered analysis of the difficult issues.

The psychologically implausible attitude of "indifference" should not be projected onto the Germans who lived through (let alone those who contributed to) the process of turning the Jews into the social dead, who all over Germany stood by with curiosity and watched the synagogues burn on *Kristallnacht* (let alone those who applauded that night's events), who observed their countrymen deport their Jewish neighbors (let alone those who jeered them), and who witnessed or heard about the exterminatory slaughter. Instead, it would be better to recall from W. H. Auden lines that could have been written for the millions of Germans who watched the events unfold:

> *Intellectual disgrace*
> *stares from every human face,*
> *and the seas of pity lie*
> *locked and frozen in each eye.*[45]

Indeed, the evidence indicates not Germans' "indifference," but their pitilessness.[46] It is oxymoronic to suggest that those who stood with curiosity gazing upon the annihilative infernos of *Kristallnacht*, like the "thousands, probably tens of thousands of Frankfurters,"[47] looked upon the destruction with "indifference." People generally flee scenes and events that they consider to be horrific, criminal, or dangerous. Yet Germans flocked to watch the assaults on the Jews and their buildings, just as spectators once flocked to medieval executions and as children flock to a circus. The evidence for the putative, general German "indifference," as far as I can tell, is typically little more than the absence of (recorded) expression with regard to some anti-Jewish measure. Absent any evidence to indicate otherwise, such silence far more likely indicated tacit approval of measures which we understand to have been criminal, but which "indifferent" Germans obviously did not.

After all, there is usually a natural flow of sympathy for people who suffer great wrongs. As Thomas Hobbes' exposition of pity underscores, the Germans should have felt great compassion for the Jews: "Pity is imagination or fiction of future calamity to ourselves, proceeding from the sense of another man's calamity. But when it lighteth on such as we think have not deserved the same, the compassion is greater, because there then appeareth more probability, that the same may happen to us; for the evil that happeneth to an innocent man may happen to every man."[48] What in Germans blocked the natural flow of compassion? Something must have. Would Germans not have been overcome with pity, would they have been "indifferent," would they have been so silent, if they had been witnessing the forced deportation of thousands of non-Jewish Germans? Apparently, they did not conjure up this "fiction of future calamity" to themselves when this happened to Jews. Apparently, they did not believe themselves to have been watching Hobbes' "innocent" men.

At the same time that Germans quietly or with open approval watched their countrymen persecute, immiserate, and kill the Jews, many of these same Germans were expressing dissent from a wide variety of governmental policies. For these other policies, including the so-called Euthanasia program and often the treatment of "inferior" races of foreigners as well, many Germans were anything but indifferent. They were possessed of a divergent cognitive map, a will to oppose these policies, a will that moved them to work actively to block or subvert them, even in matters that could have resulted in punishment as harsh as any that they would have received for having aided Jews. Tomes have been written on discontent and resistance in Germany during the Nazi period, filled copiously with examples of each, yet virtually nothing has come to light to lend credence to, let alone substantiate, the belief that Germans departed from essential features of the Nazi conception of Jews, viewed the persecution of the Jews as immoral, and judged the regime as a consequence to be criminal.[49]

This is not surprising, for no alternative, institutionally supported public image of the Jews portraying them as human beings was available on which Germans could have drawn. In fact, every significant institution in Germany supported a malevolent image of Jews, and virtually every one of them actively contributed to the eliminationist program, many even to the extermination itself. Again, it must be asked of those who hold that a large number of Germans were not governed by eliminationist antisemitism to *explain* and *show* from where and how—from what institutions, from what church sermons, from what literature, from what schoolbooks—these Germans were supposed to have derived a positive image of Jews. Against this view stands the entire public conversation in Germany during the Nazi period and the overwhelming majority of it before Nazism, as well as the confession of one former *Einsatzkommando* executioner that he and his countrymen were all antisemites. He explains why: ". . . it was hammered into us, during years of propaganda, again and again, that the Jews were the ruin of every *Volk* in the midst of which they appear, and that peace would reign in Europe only then, when the Jewish race is exterminated. No one could entirely escape this propaganda . . ."[50]—which was but the loudest part of the general societal conversation about Jews. The antisemitism of Germans was already so poisonously pernicious before this intensive public barrage of the regime that one Jewish refugee, who left Germany well before the worst isolationist and eliminationist measures, ended his account of the first months of Germany's existence during its Nazi period by explaining with theoretical perspicacity: "I left Hitler's Germany so that I could again become a human being."[51] Another Jew, one who remained, summarized the stance of the German people towards the socially dead Jews definitively: "One shunned us like lepers."[52]

In light of the ubiquitous demonizing, racial antisemitism in the public sphere, in their communities, and among their countrymen, given, just as crucially, the long history of an intense, culturally borne antipathy and hatred of Jews, and given the long support *prior to Nazism* of major German political, social, and cultural institutions for the eliminationist antisemitic worldview, it is hard to justify, either theoretically or empirically, any conclusion but that a near universal acceptance of the central aspects of the Nazi image of Jews characterized the German people. Eliminationist antisemitism was so widespread and deeply rooted that even in the first years after the Second World War, when all Germans could see the horrors that their antisemitism and racism had produced (as well as its consequences for Germany, namely Germany's lost independence and condemnation by the rest of the world), survey data as well as the testimony of Jews in Germany show that an enormous number of Germans remained profoundly antisemitic.[53]

Just as the evidence is overwhelming that eliminationist antisemitism was ubiquitous in Germany during the Nazi period, it is equally clear that it did not spring forth out of nowhere and materialize first on January 30, 1933, fully formed. The great success of the German eliminationist program of the 1930s and 1940s was, therefore, owing in the main to the preexisting, demonological, racially based, eliminationist antisemitism of the German people, which Hitler essentially unleashed, even if he also continually inflamed it. As early as 1920 Hitler publicly identified that this was the character and potential of antisemitism in Germany, as he himself at the time explained in his August 13 speech to an enthusiastically approving audience. Hitler declared that the "broad masses" of Germans possess an "instinctive" (*instinkt-mässig*) antisemitism. His task consists in "waking, whipping up, and inflaming" that "emotional" (*gefühlsmässig*) antisemitism of the people until "it decides to join the movement which is ready to draw from it the [necessary] consequence."[54] With these prophetic words, Hitler displayed his acute insight into the nature of the German people and into the way in which their "instinctive" antisemitism would be activated by him for the necessary consequences, which he made clear elsewhere in the speech would be, circumstances permitting, the death sentence.

That what Hitler and the Nazis actually did was to unshackle and thereby activate Germans' pre-existing, pent-up antisemitism can be seen, from among numerous other episodes, in a letter from the Office of the Evangelical Church in Kassel to its national Executive Committee that indicts both the Church and ordinary Germans for their newly liberated eliminationist ardor in persecuting Christians who were born as Jews:

> At the Evangelical Church one must level the grave reproach that it did not stop the persecution of the children of her faith [the baptised Jews]—indeed that from the pulpits she implored [God's] blessing for the work of those who worked against the children of her faith—and at the majority of the Evangelical faithful the reproach must be leveled that they consciously waged this struggle against their own brothers in faith—and that both Church and Church members drove away from their community, from their churches, people with whom they were united in worship, as one drives away mangy dogs from one's door.[55]

This widespread assault by ordinary Germans and their moral pastors alike on *converts* is telling. It reveals that they were governed by a racial conception of Jews, the power of which was sufficient to move them to deny and ignore the fundamental Christian doctrine of salvation through baptism. Perhaps more significant still, it occurred in the first months of Nazi rule (the letter is from May 1933), before the Nazis had had much of an opportunity to "indoctrinate" anyone. It was long-existing cultural beliefs that these Germans willfully acted upon, now that the political dispensation had become permissive, even encouraging.

The cultural cognitive model of Jews that governed Germany during its Nazi period had deep historical roots, in Weimar and before, and was but an intensified variant of the one that had taken its modern form in the nineteenth century. Although continually evolving during the modern era in its manifest content, the model maintained stability in its bedrock conception of Jews as beings immutably different from Germans: malevolent, extremely powerful, and a permanent threat to the well-being of German society. Throughout, this conception of Jews was woven into the social and moral fabric of society, imbuing it with cultural and political centrality and a tenacious permanency. Indeed, this model of Jews had for long been almost as much a part of German culture as the ubiquitous, virtually unquestioned belief in the qualities of the revered German *Volk*. Naturally, during the Nazi period, when a wildly popular leader worked the existing hallucinatory views of Jews relentlessly and expertly, a further intensification of this antisemitism occurred.[56]

It needs to be emphasized that the eliminationist antisemitic ideology was multipotential in action. The indeterminate issue was which of the rough, functionally substitutable "solutions" to the "Jewish Problem" would the Nazi leadership choose, and which would be deemed acceptable by what parts of the German people. That "solutions" of various kinds and of various degrees of radicality were compatible with the regnant German cultural cognitive model of Jews is obvious, since Hitler and his followers opted for different eliminationist policies at different stages of their rule, even though their conception of Jews remained unchanged. The logical compatibility of different "solutions" with the "Jewish Problem" can be seen clearly in the theologian Gerhard Kittel's 1933 public lecture, which was discussed earlier, on the advisability and feasibility of four eliminationist options for "solving" the "Jewish Problem": extermination, separating the Jews from other peoples by giving them their own state, the Jews' disappearance through total assimilation, and effective large-scale ghettoization.[57] In his lecture, Kittel made explicit the logical relationship and kindred nature of such different "solutions," and articulated openly and transparently the thought process that eliminationist antisemites went through when formulating their "solutions"—even if all antisemites, because they were governed by different considerations (including ethical ones), did not settle upon the same option. These "solutions" were but variations—of different degrees of acceptability, radicality, and finality—flowing from the principles and goals of eliminationist antisemitism.

Even though the elminationist antisemitic ideology was multipotential in action, it strongly tended, given the Germans' twentieth-century conception of the Jews, to metastasize into its most extreme, exterminationist variant, promising a commensurate political "solution" to the putative "problem." The elective affinity between a person subscribing to a racially based, virulent eliminationist antisemitism and a person concluding that an exterminationist "solution" was desirable could already be seen in the latter part of the pre-genocidal nineteenth century. Fully two-thirds of the prominent antisemitic polemicists proposing "solutions" to the "Jewish Problem," who were examined in one study, agitated during this period explicitly for a genocidal assault against the Jews.[58] The beliefs that promoted the Nazis' steps to eliminate German Jewish citizens first from influence in German society and then from the society itself—aside from some cases where the material interests of Germans were severely harmed—produced enthusiastic support among the German population for the eliminationist measures. Indeed, every major feature of the evolving eliminationist program, from verbal violence to ghettoization to the killing itself, was willingly abetted by an enormous number of ordinary Germans and failed to produce significant dissatisfaction and (principled) dissent within the general German populace. The dire diagnosis and prognosis for Germany—should the Germans not succeed in eradicating the putative Jewish illness from the German body social—engendered both the exclusionary measures, eventually seen as but temporary and insufficient, and the exterminatory impulse. These beliefs justified extermination as the Germans' appropriate final treatment for the putative social pathology of Jewry. As one physician who worked for a time in Auschwitz explains, the nexus between belief and action—between Germans' antisemitism and their willing slaughter of the Jews, who were considered by Germans to be, in his words, the "arch enemies of Germany"—was exceedingly close. "The step," as this man trenchantly puts it, from the monstrous accusations leveled at the Jews, "to their annihilation is only a millimeter long."

Returning to the dimensional analysis adopted here for analyzing antisemitism, it cannot be doubted that Germans considered the source of the Jews' perniciousness to be racial and the perniciousness to be extreme. For the perpetrators, antisemitism was obviously completely manifest, having been, at the time of their genocidal actions, central in their mental and emotional world. For ordinary Germans, particularly in the 1930s, the same antisemitism was far less manifest. Ordinary Germans did not leap to mass extermination on their own, or generally even urge it—although they harbored such virulent, eliminationist beliefs, upon which many did act in other, non-lethal ways. This is not surprising, the exterminationist potential within them notwithstanding. A number of factors in all probability prevented them from doing so. They included Germans' knowledge that they could confidently leave the "solution" of the "Jewish Problem" to Hitler and the Nazi government, which was openly devoting itself to it—and making great strides towards achieving their goals. After all, the most virulent, committed antisemites in human history were steering the helm of state. The relative latency of German antisemitism, owing to an absence of regular contact with Jews and to the national focus on rebuilding German strength at home and abroad, and the absence of appropriate conditions—including a relevant precedent, sufficient German military strength, and the simple fact that the vast majority of European Jewry was beyond the Germans' grasp—meant that most people, on their own, could simply not have made the moral and imaginative leap necessary to consider and advocate mass slaughter on this scale, no matter their ready willingness to follow when others finally showed the way. The best that Germans could have hoped for during the 1930s, given these conditions, was to remove the Jews from German public life and to place them at arm's length, eliminating their putative corrosive presence through emigration. Hitler was already working towards this goal with heart and soul, so many Germans sat by, satisfied that their government was doing the best that any government conceivably could. Many others applauded the policies and actively urged them forward.

The same virulent, eliminationist antisemitism thus at once failed to produce widespread German calls for the extermination of the Jews and was able to move the same Germans *under propitious circumstances* to kill Jews willingly and often eagerly. This is not as curious as it might at first seem. That latent antisemitism can be *activated* explains this seeming paradox of German society during the Nazi period. The willingness, for example, of Americans to fight Japanese in the event of a war, a far more "normal" and probable eventuality than genocide, was similarly not a burning conversational topic in the United States in the 1930s. If today evidence were sought of the then ordinary Americans' pre-existing willingness to bear arms against Japan, similarly too little would be uncovered to persuade the skeptic. Yet when the circumstances presented themselves, Americans willingly fought, fully believing in the justice of their cause. The perpetrators of the Holocaust underwent the same process—even if the substance of the beliefs and the morality was enormously different, even if, unlike Americans' realistic understanding of their conflict with Japan, the German perpetrators' understanding of their enemy was hallucinatory. The analytical point is that the American soldiers' moral evaluation of *their* undertaking against Japan was not fundamentally different from the moral stance of American civilians, or from what the soldiers themselves had undoubtedly believed before the possibility of war with Japan had even loomed on the horizon—that is, had they before the war ever considered what a proper response to Japanese attack and imperial conquest should be. Similarly, the antisemitism of the perpetrators and of the vast majority of the German people was, for all practical purposes, identical in content, identical in the evaluation of the nature and severity of the Jewish threat. Ordinary Germans became willing perpetrators because their pre-existing antisemitism, the common currency of German society—which one forthright liberal Catholic attested to in 1927 by writing, "the average citizen in Germany is a latent antisemite"[59]—became *activated* in two senses, of becoming more manifest, more central to its bearers, and of having its lethal potential realized, turned into action. For this to happen, changed circumstances and the intervention of the German state were crucial.

Hitler leaped across the moral chasm that ordinary Germans on their own could not cross. He also engineered the conditions that enabled the exterminationist version of the eliminationist ideology to become a practical guide for action. By bringing people harboring an eliminationist mind-set with exterminationist potential into institutions of killing, by sanctioning their actions with the orders, hence the blessings, of a charismatic, beloved leader, the German state was able, easily, to enlist ordinary Germans in the program of extermination, even though, prior to its implementation, most of them had certainly never imagined that they would be mass executioners. After the years of turmoil, disorder, and privations that Germans believed the Jews to have caused their country, Hitler was offering Germans a true "final solution." They latched themselves onto Hitler's exterminationist wagon, working in concert to realize his vision and promise, which was compatible with their own worldview, with their deepest moral dictates.[60]

The symbiosis between Hitler's passionately held and pursued aim of extinguishing Jewish power by whatever means and the German people's racial eliminationist view of Jews together produced the conditions and the drive to undertake the eliminationist policies of the 1930s and 1940s.[61] On this issue, Hitler and the Nazi leadership knew that the German people were of like mind. In a telling exchange during the high-level November 12, 1938, meeting on "The Jewish Problem" convened by Göring after *Kristallnacht*, Heydrich explained to Göring why controlling the Jews of Germany was easier without the creation of ghettos, which, because the Jews would be living only among Jews, would, according to the Nazis' hallucinatory view, "remain the eternal hideout for crimes and above all [a breeding ground] for epidemics and similar things." Heydrich had a better solution which was to rely on the antisemitic German people: "Today it is so that the German population . . . forces Jews to congregate in [certain] blocks or houses. The control of the Jew through the watchful eye of the entire population is better than if you have the Jews in the thousands and but thousands in one quarter of a city where I, using uniformed officials, cannot establish control of their daily life."[62] Heydrich knew that when it came to the Jews, the German people served as his police force and that they were a more effective force in policing the Jews ultimately than the Gestapo.

Heydrich and the Nazi leadership were not in the habit of deluding themselves about the German people. They were well aware that the people did not support them on many issues. For example, although the Nazis were profoundly anti-Christian and would have destroyed Christianity after the war, they knew that until that time, they would remain hamstrung by the German people. According to Goebbels, who himself expected that after military victory they would undertake the dismantling of the churches, the anti-Christian measures undertaken by Martin Bormann, the Secretary of the Party, which were still relatively mild, were, because of their unpopularity, causing "more harm than good." Goebbels noted in his diary the contrast between the people's reaction to these measures and to the assault on the Jews. With the persecution and extermination of the Jews, the regime ran no risk of causing a second front to form at home, though he feared that that would be the result should the regime move forcefully against the churches. Goebbels' diary entry further substantiates two notions discussed earlier, namely that had the German people and the Christian leadership opposed the elimination and extermination of the Jews, then they could have stopped the regime and, second, that Hitler and the Nazis, when faced with constraints, repeatedly deferred the implementation of their programmatic goals until the right conditions appeared. Goebbels—in the privacy of his diary and therefore reflecting his sincere belief—also provides the answer to the question of why the German people granted the regime a free hand with regard to the Jews, but not with regard to churches. It was the concordance of their views: "All Germans are at present against the Jews."[63]

This symbiosis between Hitler and the German people's racist eliminationist view of Jews also produced the consonance that has, in a variety of areas, been demonstrated here, among the macro, meso, and micro levels of action—of overall policy, institutional structure, and individual action. Initiative in persecuting and eliminating Jews, if having come mainly from the person of Hitler, the state, and the Party, also came from individuals and groups in all spheres and levels of society, so that, if in fits and starts, an ever-increasing exclusion of Jews from society, accompanied by increasing levels of violence, characterized the evolutionary direction of Germany. This was apparent to everyone.[64] Hitler and the Nazis were obviously the driving force behind the persecution and eventual slaughter of Jewry, yet the German people's own prior antisemitism created the *necessary enabling condition* for the eliminationist program to unfold, of which they, with sadly few exceptions, approved in principle, if not wholeheartedly.[65]

The beliefs, principally the cultural cognitive model of Jews, that underlay this participation and approval of the general eliminationist program were the same ones that underlay the extermination. Prior to the initiation of the genocidal program, they were the common property of ordinary Germans, perpetrators and non-perpetrators alike, the perpetrators having been but ordinary Germans who brought the common German ideational property to their task.[66] That it was the common German ideational property is testified to by a German Jew who in May 1942 recorded in his diary the reason why virtually all Germans shunned him, which clearly, in summary form, also expressed the content of German beliefs about Jews: "It was, after all, no surprise. Because for nearly ten years the inferiority and harmfulness of the Jews has been emphasized in every newspaper, morning and evening, in every radio broadcast and on many posters, etc., without a voice in favor of the Jews being permitted to be raised."[67] Genocide was immanent in the conversation of Germany society. It was immanent in its language and emotion. It was immanent in the structure of cognition.[68] And it was immanent in the society's proto-genocidal practice of the 1930s. Under the proper circumstances, eliminationist antisemitism metastasized into its most virulent exterminationist form, and ordinary Germans became willing genocidal killers.

The autonomous power of the eliminationist antisemitism, once given free rein, to shape the Germans' actions, to induce Germans voluntarily on their own initiative to act barbarously towards Jews, was such that Germans who were not even formally engaged in the persecution and extermination of the Jews routinely assaulted Jews physically, not to mention verbally. One memoirist describes a paradigmatic occurrence. Young soldiers, veterans of the western front, arrived in Łosice, a town of eight thousand people in the Lublin region of Poland. They initially acted courteously. Then they learned that the vast majority of the town's denizens were Jews, "and immediately they were transformed. Their *Sie* turned to *du*; they made us polish their boots and clubbed us for not tipping our hats promptly."[69] Nothing had changed. The Germans beheld people who looked exactly as they had before, people who acted no differently. Yet everything had changed, for the Germans had gained knowledge of the identity of these people and, like their countrymen all over eastern Europe, immediately became "transformed," using the demeaning *"du"* form of address, instead of the normal, respectful *"Sie,"* exacting symbolic obeisance, and beating the innocent people.

So profound and near universal was the antisemitism during the Nazi period that to the Jewish victims it appeared as if its hold on Germans could be captured and conveyed only in organic terms: "A poison of diseased hatred permeates the blood of the Nazis."[70] Once activated, Germans' profound hatred of Jews, which had in the 1930s by necessity lain relatively dormant, so possessed them that it appeared to exude from their every pore. Kaplan, the keen diarist of the Warsaw ghetto, observed many Germans from September 1939 until March 1940 when he penned his evaluation derived from their actions and words.

The gigantic catastrophe which has descended on Polish Jewry has no parallel, even in the darkest periods of Jewish history. First, in the depth of hatred. This is not just hatred whose source is in a party platform, and which was invented for political purposes. It is a hatred of emotion, whose source is some psychopathic malady. In its outward manifestations it functions as physiological hatred, which imagines the object of hatred to be unclean in body, a leper who has no place within the camp.

The [German] masses have absorbed this sort of qualitative hatred. . . . They have absorbed their masters' teachings in a concrete, corporeal form. The Jew is filthy; the Jew is a swindler and an evildoer; the Jew is the enemy of Germany, who undermines its existence; the Jew was the prime mover in the Versailles Treaty, which reduced Germany to nothing; the Jew is Satan, who sows dissension between one nation and another, arousing them to bloodshed in order to profit from their destruction. These are easily understood concepts whose effect in day-to-day life can be felt immediately.[71]

Significantly, this characterization and the previous description of the young German soldiers in Łosice are each based on the words and acts of Germans—of SS men, policemen, soldiers, administrators, and those working in the economy—*before* the formal genocidal program of systematic killing had begun. It is the masses, the ordinary Germans, not the Nazi ideologues and theoreticians, whom Kaplan exposes. The causal link between the Germans' beliefs and actions is palpable, so that the Jews feel the effect of their "concepts" "in day-to-day life." In the more than two and a half years of subsequent concentrated observation of the Germans in Warsaw, Kaplan saw no reason to alter this evaluation.

THE BELIEFS ABOUT Jews that underlay the German people's participation and approval of the eliminationist policies of the 1930s, and that led ordinary Germans in Łosice and Warsaw prior to the initiation of a formal program of genocide to act so barbarously, were the beliefs that prepared ordinary Germans—as it did the men of Police Battalion 3—to concur with what an officer of the battalion said while addressing his men in Minsk, before the first enormous massacre that they were to perpetrate, namely that "no suffering should accrue to noble German blood in the process of destroying this subhumanity." These ordinary Germans saw the world in such a manner that the slaughter of thousands of Jews was seen as an obvious necessity that produced concern only for the well-being of "noble German blood." Their beliefs about Jews prepared these representative Germans to hear the officer's accompanying offer to be excused if they were not up to the task, yet to choose to slaughter Jewish men, women, and children willingly.[72]

These were the beliefs that engendered in ordinary Germans the lethal racial fantasies which led them to write to loved ones and friends of the genocidal exploits of their nation and its representative men. A member of Police Battalion 105 wrote to his wife on August 7, 1941, from the Soviet Union, in explicit and approving terms, of the total annihilation of the Jews, and then added; "Dear H., don't lose sleep over it, it has to be." Having borne witness to continual, ongoing genocidal killing, and written openly and with the obvious expectation of his wife's general understanding (whatever misgivings she might have had notwithstanding), this man could write to her again one month later that he was "proud" to be a German soldier, because "I can take part up here and have many adventures." These were the beliefs that led him, now filled with pride in the German national accomplishments on their genocidal march through the Soviet Union, to take photographs (he did not specify of what), as did legions of other Germans, so that he would have a document of his time, which would be "extremely interesting for our children."[73] These same beliefs led an air force sergeant, Herbert Habermalz, to write in June 1943, candidly and proudly, of what he considered to be a German national accomplishment—the final, utter destruction of the largest Jewish population in Europe, the Warsaw ghetto, which once housed almost 450,000 Jews: "We flew several circles above the city. And with great satisfaction we could recognize the complete extermination of the Jewish Ghetto. There our folks did really a fantastic job. There is no house which has not been totally destroyed."[74] Habermalz, as did many German soldiers, sent this and other letters to his former place of employment, a firm producing farm equipment. These letter writers knew that employers often circulated the letters' contents to their workers, in order to solidify between the workers and their brethren at the front a sense of common purpose in the pursuit of the war. Habermalz, governed by exterminationist beliefs about Jews—beliefs which he apparently believed, no doubt correctly, that his co-workers shared—wanted to convey to those at home his thrill at having had such a rare and satisfying visual overview of this "fantastic" genocidal job.

These were the beliefs that prepared officers of Police Regiment 25 to boast, like so many other Germans engaged in the slaughter, and to believe themselves "to have accomplished feats of heroism by these killings." These were the beliefs that led so many ordinary Germans to kill for pleasure and to do so not while trying to hide their deeds but in full view of others, even of women, girlfriends and wives, some of whom, like those in Stanisławów, used to laugh as their men picked off Jews from their balconies, like so many ducks in a shooting gallery.[75] These same beliefs moved the men of Police Battalion 61's First Company, who guarded the Warsaw ghetto and eagerly shot Jews attempting to sneak in or out of the ghetto during 1941–1942, to create a recreational shrine to their slaughter of Jews. These German reservists turned a room in their quarters into a bar, adorned its walls with antisemitic caricatures and sayings, and hung over the bar itself a large, internally illuminated Star of David. Lest some of their heroics go unnoticed, by the door to the bar was a running tabulation of the number of Jews whom the company's men shot. After successful kills, these Germans were in the habit of rewarding themselves by holding special "victory celebrations" (*Siegesfeiern*).[76]

The beliefs about Jews that governed the German people's assent and contributions to the eliminationist program of the 1930s were the beliefs that prepared the men of Police Battalion 101 and so many other Germans to be eager killers who volunteered again and again for their "Jew-hunts," and to call Międzyrzec, a city in which they conducted repeated roundups, killings, and deportations—playing on its name with obvious reference to its many thousands of Jews—*"Menschenschreck,"* or "human horror."[77] These were the beliefs that led Germans, in the words of Herbert Hummel, the Bureau Chief of the Warsaw District, to have "welcomed thankfully" the 1941 "shoot-to-kill order," which authorized them to kill any Jews found outside ghettos.[78] These same beliefs moved the men of another police unit, ordinary Germans, to shoot Jews whom they found even "without express orders, completely voluntarily." One of the men explains: "I must admit that we felt a certain joy when we would seize a Jew whom one could kill. I cannot remember an instance when a policeman had to be ordered to an execution. The shootings were, to my knowledge, always carried out on a voluntary basis; one could have gained the impression that various policemen got a big kick out of it." Why the "joy," why the eager voluntarism? Obviously, because of these ordinary Germans' beliefs about the Jews, which this man summarizes definitively: "The Jew was not acknowledged by us to be a human being."[79] With this simple observation and admission, this former executioner uncovers from below the shrouds of obfuscation the mainspring of the Holocaust.

These were the beliefs that led so many ordinary Germans who degraded, brutalized, and tortured Jews in camps and elsewhere—the cruelty in the camps having been near universal—to *choose* to do so. They did not choose (like the tiny minority who showed that restraint was possible) not to hit, or, if under supervision, to hit in a manner that would do the least damage, but instead regularly chose to terrorize, to inflict pain, and to maim. These were the beliefs that prepared the men of Police Battalion 309, ordinary Germans, not to hate, but to esteem the captain who had led them in their orgy of killing and synagogue-burning in Białystok in a manner similar to the glowing evaluations of "Papa" Trapp given by the men of Police Battalion 101, esteem which echoed the sentiments of men in many other killing institutions towards their commanders. This captain, according to his men, "was entirely humane [*sic*] and as a superior beyond reproach."[80] After all, in the transvaluated world of Germany during the Nazi period, ordinary Germans deemed the killing of Jews to be a beneficent act for humanity. These were the beliefs that led Germans often to mark and celebrate Jewish holidays, such as Yom Kippur, with killing operations,[81] and for a member of Police Battalion 9, who was attached to *Einsatzkommando 11a*, to compose two poems, one for Christmas 1941 and the other for a social evening, ten days later, that celebrated their deeds in the Soviet Union. He managed to work into his verse, for the enjoyment of all, a reference to the "skull-cracking blows" (*Nüssknacken*) that they had undoubtedly delivered with relish to their Jewish victims.[82]

These were the beliefs that led Germans to take joy, make merry, and celebrate their genocide of the Jews, such as with the party (*Abschlussfeier*) thrown upon the closing down of the Chełmno extermination camp in April 1943 to reward its German staff for a job well done. By then, the Germans had killed over 145,000 Jews in Chełmno.[83] The German perpetrators' rejoicing proudly in their mass annihilation of the Jews occurred also at the conclusion of the more concentrated slaughter of twelve thousand Jews on the "Blood Sunday" of October 12, 1941, in Stanisławów, where the Germans there threw a victory celebration.[84] Yet another such celebration was organized in August 1941, during the heady days in the midst of the Germans' campaign of extermination of Latvian Jewry. On the occasion of their slaughter of the Jews of Cēsis, the local German security police and members of the German military assembled to eat and drink at what they dubbed a "death banquet [*Totenmahl*] for the Jews." During their festivities, the celebrants drank repeated toasts to the extermination of the Jews.[85]

While the perpetrators' routine symbolic degradation of their Jewish victims, their celebrations of their killings, and their photographic mementos of their genocidal achievements and milestones all attest to this transvaluation of values, perhaps nothing demonstrates this more sharply than the farewell given by a man who should have been a moral conscience for Germany. Like the leaders of a good portion of the Protestant Evangelical Church of Germany, who in a proclamation declared the Jews to be "born enemies of the world and the Reich," incapable of being saved by baptism, and responsible for the war, and who, having accepted the logic of their racial, demonological antisemitism, gave their explicit ecclesiastical authorization for the implementation of the "severest measures" against the Jews while the genocidal program was well under way, Cardinal Adolf Bertram of Breslau once appears to have explicitly expressed his own understanding of the extermination of the Jews, except for those who had converted to Christianity. The beliefs that led the German people to support the eliminationist program and the perpetrators to carry it out were the beliefs that moved Bertram—who, like the entire Catholic and Protestant ecclesiastical leadership, was fully cog-

454   HITLER'S WILLING EXECUTIONERS

nizant of the extermination of the Jews and of the antisemitic attitudes of his parishioners—to pay final homage to the man who was the mass murderer of the Jewish people and who had for twelve years served as the beacon of the German nation. Upon learning of Hitler's death, Cardinal Bertram in the first days of May 1945 ordered that in all the churches of his archdiocese a special requiem, namely "a solemn requiem mass be held in commemoration of the Führer . . ."[86] so that his and Hitler's flock could pray to the Almighty, in accord with the requiem's liturgy, that the Almighty's son, Hitler, be admitted to paradise.[87]

The beliefs that were already the common property of the German people upon Hitler's assumption of power and which led the German people to assent and contribute to the eliminationist measures of the 1930s were the beliefs that prepared not just the Germans who by circumstances, chance, or choice ended up as perpetrators but also the vast majority of the German people to understand, assent to, and, when possible, do their part to further the extermination, root and branch, of the Jewish people. The inescapable truth is that, regarding Jews, German political culture had evolved to the point where an enormous number of ordinary, representative Germans became—and most of the rest of their fellow Germans were fit to be—Hitler's willing executioners.

Epilogue

THE NAZI
GERMAN REVOLUTION

THIS STUDY OF the Holocaust and its perpetrators assigns to their beliefs paramount importance. It reverses the Marxian dictum, in holding that consciousness determined being. Its conclusion that the eliminationist antisemitic German political culture, the genesis of which must be and is explicable historically, was the prime mover of both the Nazi leadership and ordinary Germans in the persecution and extermination of the Jews, and therefore was the Holocaust's principal cause, may at once be hard to believe for many and commonsensical to others. The evidence that so many ordinary people did maintain at the center of their worldview palpably absurd beliefs about Jews like those that Hitler articulated in *Mein Kampf* is overwhelming. And the evidence has been available for years, indeed available to any observer in Germany during the 1930s. But because the beliefs have seemed to us to be so ridiculous, indeed worthy of the ravings of madmen, the truth that they were the common property of the German people has been and will likely continue to be hard to accept by many who are beholden to our common-sense view of the world, or who find the implications of this truth too disquieting.

Germany during the Nazi period was inhabited by people animated by beliefs about Jews that made them willing to become consenting mass executioners. The study of the perpetrators, especially of police battalions, who were a representative cross section of German men—and therefore are indicative of what ordinary Germans were like regarding Jews—compels us, precisely because they were representative of Germans, to draw this conclusion about the German people. Being ordinary in the Germany that gave itself to Nazism was to have been a member of an extraordinary, lethal political culture. That German political culture was producing such voluntaristic killers suggests, in turn, that perhaps this was a society that had undergone other important and fundamental changes, particularly cognitive and moral ones. The study of the Holocaust's perpetrators thus provides a window through which German society can be viewed and examined in a new light. It demands that important features of the society be conceived anew. It suggests further that the Nazis were the most profound revolutionaries of modern times and that the revolution that they wrought during their but brief suzerainty in Germany was the most extreme and thoroughgoing in the annals of western civilization. It was, above all, a cognitive-moral revolution which reversed processes that had been shaping Europe for centuries. This book is ultimately not only about the perpetrators of the Holocaust. Because the perpetrators of the Holocaust were Germany's representative citizens, this book is about Germany during the Nazi period and before, its people and its culture.[1]

The Nazi German revolution, like all revolutions, had two fundamental, related thrusts: a destructive enterprise, which was a thoroughgoing revolt against civilization, and a constructive enterprise, which was a singular attempt to make a new man, a new body social, and a new Nazified order in Europe and beyond. It was an unusual revolution in that, domestically, it was being realized—the repression of the political left in the first few years notwithstanding—without massive coercion and violence. The revolution was primarily the transformation of consciousness—the inculcation in the Germans of a new ethos. By and large, it was a peaceful revolution willingly acquiesced to by the German people. Domestically, the Nazi German revolution was, on the whole, consensual.

While it was consensual at home, the Nazi German revolution was the most brutal and barbarous revolution of modern western history for those who would be excluded from the new Germany and Europe, namely the tens of millions whom the Germans marked for subjugation, enslavement, and extermination. The essential nature of the revolution—how it was transforming the mental and moral substance of the German people and how it was destroying, to use Himmler's formulation, the "human substance" of non-Germans—was to be discerned in Germany's emblematic institution during its Nazi period: the camp.

THE CAMP WAS NOT merely the paradigmatic institution for the Germans' violent domination, exploitation, and slaughter of those whom they designated as enemies, for the Germans' most uninhibited self-expression of mastery, and for the Germans' molding of their victims according to their "subhuman" image of them. The camp's essence was not reducible to these particular features (which were discussed in Chapter 5), because the camp was above all else a revolutionary institution, one that Germans actively put to ends that they understood to be radically transformative.

The revolution was one of *sensibility and practice*. As a world of unrestrained impulses and cruelty, the camp system allowed for the expression of the new Nazi moral dispensation, one which was in its essential features the antithesis of Christian morality and Enlightenment humanism—"those, stupid, false, and unhealthy ideals of humanity," as Göring called them.[2] The camp system denied in practice the Christian and Enlightenment belief in the moral equality of human beings. In the Nazi German cosmology, some humans, by reason of their biology, ought to be killed; others were fit for slavery, and they too could be killed if the Germans deemed them to be superfluous. The camp system was predicated upon the existence of superiors and inferiors, of masters and slaves. Both its theory and practice mocked the Christian admonition to love one's brother, to feel pity for the downtrodden, to be guided by empathy. Instead, the ethos of the camp preached and was animated by the hatred of others, banished pity from its discourse and practice, and inculcated not an empathetic emotional reverberation for the suffering of others, but a hardened disdain, if not a gleeful enjoyment of it.

Suffering and torture in the German camp world was, therefore, not incidental, episodic, or a violation of rules, but central, ceaseless, and normative. Gazing upon a suffering or recently slaughtered Jew or, for that matter, a suffering Russian or Pole, did not elicit and, according to the moral life of the camp, should not have elicited sympathy, but was indeed greeted, as it ought to have been according to the Nazi German morality, by German hardness and satisfaction in having furthered the reconstructive destructive vision for the new Germany and the new German-ruled Europe.

The ideal guiding the Germans' treatment of the most hated of the camp world's prisoners, the Jews, was that it ought to be a world of unremitting suffering which would end in their deaths. A Jew's life ought to be a worldly hell, always in torment, always in physical pain, with no comfort available. It is worth emphasizing that this was a profound alteration, a revolutionary alteration, in sensibility occurring in mid-twentieth-century Europe. So brutal was the German revolutionary practice that Chaim Kaplan was already struck by it in late 1939—before the formal program of extermination had begun:

> The horrible persecutions of the Middle Ages are as nothing in face of the
> terrible troubles in which the Nazis enmesh us. In primitive times, methods

of torture were also primitive. The oppressors of the Middle Ages knew only two alternatives: life or death. As long as a man lived, even if he were a Jew, they let him live. He also had an opportunity to live out his days by choosing conversion or exile. The Nazi inquisition, however, is different. They take a Jew's life by throttling his livelihood, by "legal" limitations, by cruel edicts, by such sadistic tortures that even a tyrant of the Middle Ages would have been ashamed to publicize them. It was part of the concept of that generation to burn a sinning soul, but it was not their habit to torture a man because he was born "in sin," according to the hangman's ideas.[3]

The regression to barbarism, the logic of modern German antisemitism, and the tasks to which the Nazi leadership put it were such that Kaplan and, presumably, many other Jews would have preferred to live not in this German twentieth century, with its exemplary institution of the camp, but under some benighted medieval tyrant.

The second goal for which the Germans employed the camp world was the *revolutionary transformation of society* in a manner that denied basic premises of European civilization. The Nazi German revolution sought to reconstitute and reshape the European social landscape according to its racial biological principles, by killing millions of people deemed, according to its racial fantasies, dangerous or expendable, and thereby to increase the proportion of the "superior races" and strengthen the overall biological stock of humanity and, complementing this, to reduce the danger to the "superior races" by the more numerous "inferior" ones. The ethos of the vast, regressive reconstructive enterprise that Nazism envisaged for a German-dominated Europe was frequently declaimed by Himmler, who was spearheading the revolution: "Whether nations live in prosperity or starve to death interest me only insofar as we need them as slaves for our *Kultur*, otherwise it is of no interest to me."[4] Eastern Europe would become a German colony populated by German settlers and Slavic slaves.[5]

The camp world was revolutionary because it was the main instrument for the Germans' fundamental reshaping of the social and human landscape of Europe. The camp world and the *system* of German society which it composed was understood to have been guided by principles which stood on its head the body of principles that had previously informed the public morality and (the many exceptions notwithstanding) the conduct of German and European society. The establishment of this new world would have meant the end of western civilization as it was known, which would have included and been symbolized by the destruction of Christianity itself.[6] The camp system was also revolutionary because it was itself already a microcosm of that world, the social model that was to be imposed on a large part of Europe and the moral model that was to become the foundation for the European society which the Germans were forging. Indeed, the ever-growing camp system was the embryo of the new Germanic Europe, which essentially would have become a large concentration camp, with the German people as its guards and the remaining European peoples (with the exception of the "racially" privileged) as its corpses, slaves, and inmates.

Already in the fall of 1940, Hans Frank, the German Governor of Poland outlined clearly this vision of Europe, though he spoke directly only of his jurisdictional area of Poland. "We think here in imperial terms, in the most grandiose style of all times. The imperialism that we develop is incomparable with those miserable attempts that previous weak German governments have undertaken in Africa." Frank reported to his audience that "the *Führer* has further said explicitly" that Poland is (in Frank's paraphrase) "destined" to be a "gigantic work camp, where everything that means power and independence is in the hands of the Germans." No Pole would receive higher education, and "none may rise to a rank higher than foreman." In Hitler's and Frank's view, the Polish state would never be restored. The Poles would be permanently "subjugated" to the master race. Frank's elaboration upon this vision of the concentration camp as the model for Poland was not done in secret but expressed in two speeches to the heads of the departments of his administration. Frank was imparting the governing ethos to the people who were governing Poland.[7]

The camp system was a defining feature of German society during its Nazi period, and the camp was the society's emblematic institution. It was the institution that most prominently set Germany apart from other European countries, that to a large extent gave it its distinctive murderous character. The camp system was also the largest and most important institutional innovation of Nazism, forming an entire new subsystem of society. The first few camps of 1933, set up shortly after Hitler's ascension to power, laid the foundation for this new system of society, which continually expanded geographically in the number of its installations (reaching over ten thousand) and in the size of its population. The camp system was the greatest growth institution during this period of German history, and it would only have increased in size and importance had Germany not been defeated. Finally, it was defining and emblematic because manifold features of camps represented and symbolized distinctive central aspects of Germany during its Nazi period. The camp system was the site where the Nazi German world was most unreservedly, most unabashedly being created. Nazi ideology, which cannot be doubted to have been the source of and the driving force behind the murderous and transformative German policies under Hitler, was most fully expressed in the camp world. The type of society and values which Nazi ideology called for, which the German educational system was inculcating in Germany's young, and which Hitler and Himmler made clear they were working to create, was realized first and found its closest empirical referent in the camp world. Thus, it was in the camps that the essential features of the Nazi German revolution and the revolution's new German man, the character of its refashioned body social, and the nature of the intended European order could most clearly be seen.

The camp world taught its victims firsthand lessons and therefore teaches us secondhand lessons about the essential nature of Germany during the Nazi period. The camp system exposes not just Nazism's but also Germany's true face. The notion that Germany during the Nazi period was an "ordinary," "normal" society which had the misfortune to have been governed by evil and ruthless rulers who, using the institutions of modern societies, moved people to commit acts that they abhorred, is in its essence false. Germany during the Nazi period was a society which was in important ways fundamentally different from ours today, operating according to a different ontology and cosmology, inhabited by people whose general understanding of important realms of social existence was not "ordinary" by our standards. The notion, for example, that an individual's defining characteristics were derived from his race and that the world was divided into distinct races—whose respective capacities and moral worth were biologically determined and widely variable—was, if not quite an axiom of German society during the Nazi period, then an extremely widespread belief. That the world ought to be organized or reorganized according to this conception of an immutable hierarchy of races was an accepted norm. The possibility of peaceful coexistence among the races was not a central part of the cognitive landscape of the society. Instead, races were believed to be inexorably competing and warring until one or another triumphed or was vanquished. Life within the camp system demonstrated how radically ordinary Germans would implement the racist, destructive set of beliefs and values that was the country's formal and informal public ideology. The camp—Germany's distinguishing, distinctive, indeed, perhaps, central institution—was the training ground for the masterly conduct of the ordinary new German "superman," and it revealed his nature. The camp reveals that Himmler's *Kultur* had, to a great extent, already become the *Kultur* of Germany.

The ever-expanding camp world was the principal site of central aspects of the Nazi German revolution. The Germans' mass murder, their reintroduction of slavery on the European continent, their adoption of free license to treat "subhumans" however they wished without any restraints—all suggest that the camp was the emblematic institution of Germany during its Nazi period and the paradigm for the Thousand Year Reich. The camp world reveals the essence of the Germany that gave itself to Nazism, no less than the perpetrators reveal the slaughter and barbarism that ordinary Germans were willing to perpetrate in order to save Germany and the German people from the ultimate danger—DER JUDE.

Afterword

IN ALL THE COUNTRIES in which this book has appeared, it has attracted considerable scholarly and popular attention and provoked intense discussion. Nowhere has the reaction been as far-reaching, long-lasting, intense, and impassioned as in Germany. Shortly after the book's first U.S. publication at the end of March 1996, months before it appeared in German, it became the object of a heated, prolonged discussion, which included a barrage of vitriolic attacks upon the book and me personally. These articles by both journalists and academics consisted almost wholly of denunciations and misrepresentations of the book's contents, including the almost axiomatic accusation that I was charging Germans with "collective guilt," that the book's argument attributes to Germans an unchanging "national character," that it impermissibly generalizes about Germans of the time, and that it puts forward a monocausal explanation of the Holocaust. The critics presented no serious argument and no evidence to support their contentions on these and other points. They did not do so because such arguments and evidence do not exist.

Others in Germany rose to defend the book and to point out, correctly, that its disparagers were not discussing the book's findings, arguments, and conclusions, but rather were raising a series of false issues, in what one commentator called a "discourse of avoidance" (*Vermeidungsdiskurs*).

The almost four-month-long heated discussion of this book prior to its German publication in August had a surrealistic quality. The German public, subjected to a continuous barrage of impassioned rhetoric in print, on radio, and on television about the most sensitive and charged period in their history, with all kinds of claims and counterclaims being hurled at them, were not able to check to see which assertions were true. The license which all too many journalists and academics took to invent notions that could be calculated to lead the German public to scorn the book before it ever hit the German market was shocking. Many people urged me to react immediately, to refute the misrepresentations and distortions, lest the German public reject the book irrevocably.

I refused. It made no sense to take part in an unreal discussion about a book that people could not read. I also believed that the storm would be weathered, and that when German readers finally had the opportunity to judge for themselves, many would find merit in my work. A letter from a Nuremberg woman at the beginning of August bore this out. She began: "I am honestly sorry for the letter I sent to you last May!" That earlier, scathing letter, she informed me, was based upon what she had gleaned from the initial attacks on my book, especially upon the belief that it was about the "idea of national character," which she "hated." She explained: "I did not expect scholars of the Holocaust to represent the content of 'Hitler's Willing Executioners' in a misleading way." She then procured a copy (of the English edition) and, "to put it mildly, I was surprised about what I found. This was not the book I had expected. I think it should be obvious to anyone who reads your book, that these scholars twisted your words or criticized mistakes that are either very far-fetched or non-existent." She continued: "I learned a lot by reading your book (and by following this hypocritical debate) and it caused a very positive discussion among my fellow students, as well as among the adults I am teaching. So far I have not come across anyone who knew the real nature of your arguments and thought them absurd, nor anyone who was not disturbed by the historical facts that you described (apart from one whose grandfather had been a member of the SS—he has had a hard time, though, ever since I introduced your book in his class)." Her letter may turn out to be the definitive commentary on and explanation of the course of the book's reception in Germany.

To coincide with the book's German publication, I was invited at the beginning of August to compose a lengthy reply to the German critics in the influential weekly newspaper *Die Zeit*, which had been running a series of more measured responses to the book from different intellectuals lasting nine weeks. This allowed me to address the many untruths that had been put forward and to challenge people finally to address the book's themes and findings. This published reply and the appearance on the market of the German translation, which included a special Foreword (reprinted here as Appendix 3) that clarified many of the same issues, were met by a flood of new responses, which, by and large, were more tempered and responsible. The critics could no longer credibly maintain their initial baseless charges.

Four weeks later, I went to Germany for ten days in order to discuss the book in a variety of venues, including six panel discussions with scholars and commentators, many of which were televised regionally and even nationally. Many of the panelists praised the book for filling important gaps in our knowledge about the Holocaust and accepted its fundamental arguments. Even the most bitter critics, most of whom had been specially invited to sit on one or another of the panels, conceded many points once we engaged in direct discussion before a public that was now familiar with the book's contents. Still, it was remarkable how little these critics dealt directly with the book's findings and conclusions. Doing so, after all, would have made clear that I have raised new questions, provided new information, and supplied answers—all things that these critics could not bear to acknowledge.

Shortly after my arrival in Germany, something else became clear. The German public, in keeping with the letter writer from Nuremberg and her acquaintances, was rejecting the previous "wisdom" of the opinion makers, although many had undoubtedly initially accepted these views. To the evident surprise of a great number of people, the public was embracing the book. The large audiences attending the panel discussions were overwhelmingly on the side of the book and not in agreement with its critics. They listened to the respective arguments and the quality of the evidence that was adduced, and they made their own judgments. Their applause, which was frequent and vigorous, was almost always in support of the book's point of view. The interest in Germany was intense. Not only were tickets for the various panel discussions snapped up (for example, all 2,400 seats in the Munich Philharmonic Hall were quickly sold and the newspapers wrote that the organizers could have filled the Olympic Stadium), but it was reported that the book was also *the* subject of general discussion. It was the topic of the day. To my surprise, it has since become the number one bestseller in Germany and in Austria.

By the end of my trip, the German media, which initially had been generally hostile, was declaring both the visit and the book to be huge successes, so much so that leading liberal and conservative newspapers in their concluding comments on the trip used the same term "*Triumphzug*" (a triumphal procession) to describe it. I had entertained the hope that the book would be well received in Germany once people were exposed to its arguments, yet the warmth and breadth of the responses far exceeded my expectations.

Fifty years after the end of the war, many Germans want to have an honest reckoning with the past. They are not satisfied with the myths and misleading perspectives that have dominated public discussion of the Holocaust and given comfort and alibis to so many. Upon learning of the book's real contents, they understood that the new questions, ideas, and shifts in perspective that it offers are valid. They immediately realized that old ones had to be discarded, that many of the issues central to the Holocaust had not been addressed, and that much about their own understanding of the past had to be questioned and likely had to be revised. This is true regardless of whether or not individuals accept all of my conclusions. Many in Germany have, of course, never really accepted the unrealistic dominant view of the perpetration of the Holocaust—that a small band of Nazis terrorized all other, disapproving Germans into acquiescing or even participating in the persecution and extermination of the Jews—but they did not have the information available to them to contest it effectively. Even to raise many of the book's issues, whether in private or public, has until now been difficult.

Since the book's publication, a fairly broad consensus seems to have developed in Germany that the discussion which it launched is not only necessary but also long overdue, and that, no matter what conclusions individuals may draw, it will produce only good. Many, even some who disagree with my conclusions, have said as much. Ultimately, this is why the book has resonated so positively in Germany and why much of the public has rebelled against those opinion leaders who tried to quash the discussion. People are sick of the myths and the alibis.

The reception that this book has received tells us a great deal about what is positive in Germany today. For Germans to confront this horrific part of their past is unpleasant in the extreme. That so many are willing to do so is yet another indication of how radically transformed democratic Germany has become in the second half of the twentieth century.

Daniel Jonah Goldhagen
Cambridge, Massachusetts
November 1996

APPENDIX 1

A NOTE ON METHOD

As important as it is to lay bare the general and theoretical considerations that guide this book's inquiry, it is equally necessary to specify other considerations of method that have given shape to this investigation of the perpetrators.

Because the scope of what we do not know of the perpetrators and of the Holocaust is so large, and because of the consequent need to be selective, this book covers only some of the institutions of killing. It makes no pretense of providing a comprehensive history of the Holocaust. Its cases derive not from considerations of narrative fluency and comprehensiveness, but of their appropriateness for answering certain questions, for testing certain hypotheses. The book's intent is primarily explanatory and theoretical. Narrative and description, important as they are for specifying the perpetrators' actions and the settings for their actions properly, are here subordinate to the explanatory goals.

The hypothesis that I believed most likely to be borne out, upon embarking on the empirical research for this study, was that the perpetrators were motivated to take part in the lethal persecution of the Jews because of their beliefs about the victims, and that various German institutions were therefore easily able to harness the perpetrators' pre-existing antisemitism once Hitler gave the order to undertake the extermination. I therefore chose to investigate institutions and particular cases of those institutions which would in a variety of ways isolate the influence of antisemitism in order to assess its causal efficacy. Should the hypothesis be erroneous, then the cases chosen here would have clearly confounded it. The three institutions analyzed in depth are police battalions, "work" camps, and death marches, each of which, as it happens, has been greatly neglected.

A further consideration informed the choice of cases and samples. Two different target populations are the object of this study: the population of perpetrators and the German people themselves. This is a study of the perpetrators of the Holocaust and simultaneously of Germany during the Nazi period, its people and political culture. Thus, the institutions treated here are intended to do double analytical duty. They should permit the motivations of the perpetrators in those particular institutions to be uncovered, and also allow for generalizing both to the perpetrators as a group and to the second target group of this study, the German people. Much of what is said here about methods therefore pertains both to the perpetrators and to the larger population of Germans.

This study subjects the competing hypotheses discussed earlier to empirical scrutiny, drawing on a variety of cases, including, occasionally, comparative material from non-German actors and other genocides. It draws on my research on a large number of different kinds of units and institutions engaged in the Holocaust: over thirty-five police battalions involved in mass killings; all eighteen *Einsatzkommandos*, which were the killing squads set up for the extermination of Soviet Jewry; a number of different ghettos and concentration camps; "work" camps; Auschwitz and the other death camps; and a dozen death marches that took place in the waning days of the war.[1] So even though the case chapters are devoted to only a few police battalions, "work" camps, and death marches, my conclusions are buttressed by a still more extensive fund of knowledge. The chapters of Part VI, which bring together the lessons learned from the cases, selectively draws on material from other cases. An effort, though, has been made not to poach from other cases, for the temptation to pick and choose propitious material from a large number of cases should be resisted so as to avoid bias in the conclusions. My research has been guided by the belief that examining the men (and women) working in different kinds of institutions with different kinds of tasks would provide a comparative perspective on the perpetrators that would yield insights unobtainable by focusing on one kind of institution.[2]

Of the many units I have researched, the ones I decided to study most intensively tended to share a number of characteristics, although not every unit shared each one. Chief among them were units in which it could be proven conclusively that the men knew that they did not have to kill. As long as the threat of coercion might have existed, it would be hard to assess whether or not other motivations were operative. I also concentrated on units that were engaged in repeated face-to-face killings, where they confronted their victims and were parties to unspeakably gruesome scenes of spattered blood, bone, and brain matter, over an extended period of time because, for a variety of reasons, the actions of people who were *vocational* killers *of this sort* rather than episodic ones make greater explanatory demands. Of the units that satisfied the first two criteria, I focused a great deal of attention on those that were also made up of the men who seemed by their backgrounds to be the *least* likely candidates for becoming willing executioners. This is one reason for the emphasis on police battalions, many of which were composed of "ordinary" Germans. It is these people, and not Hitler's most fanatical followers, whose actions are most difficult to explain and therefore test most severely any explanation. So any explanation has to be able to account for their participation, and if it can do so for them, then it is likely to explain the actions of Hitler's more zealous acolytes, who presumably would have been far more willing than less enthusiastic followers to carry out a given policy whatever it was.

A number of police battalions satisfy all the criteria. Surprisingly, these units, until two recent books,[3] have hardly even been mentioned in the literature on Nazi genocide, and until I began my research (before these books appeared), I too was unaware of the scope of their actions and, naturally, their significance for understanding this period of German society and politics. Many police battalions were units of men drawn haphazardly into them (they were drafted), who had no special ideological training, no particular military background, who were often older, in their mid-thirties, and who were family men—not the pliable eighteen-year-olds that armies love to mold. Furthermore, these units ended up in killing operations not by design, but by chance. In sending these men to kill, the regime proceeded as if any German was fit to be a mass executioner. All of this is treated in great detail in Part III.

The rationale for studying "work" camps was to subject the operative hypothesis to its toughest test. Institutions devoted to economic production, whose calling card is rationality, should have been the least susceptible to the influence of a pre-existing ideology—in this case, to antisemitism. If it turned out that the functioning of "work" camps could be explained only by taking into account the existence of antisemitism among the responsible Germans, then this would be powerful evidence for the primary importance of antisemitism in explaining the Germans' actions. Naturally, were this hypothesis not borne out in this case, then it would have to be jettisoned, qualified, or complemented by other ones. The camps studied most intensively were those around Lublin during a later phase of the Holocaust when the Germans were permitting Jews to remain alive in Poland ostensibly *only* to extract labor from them. This was the time and these were the circumstances when "work" camps should have been most purely for work, and so, in studying them, it should be easiest to isolate the capacity of German antisemitism to undermine, if indeed it did, the rational operation of institutions of labor.

The death marches of 1945, when Germans marched Jews around the European and German countryside in flight from allied armies, among other things, allow the perpetrators' actions to be examined at a time when, because they were under virtually no supervision, they could choose most freely to act as they wished, and when, because Germany was imminently to become a defeated, occupied, and perhaps punished country, killing and brutalizing Jews actually imperiled their captors. The death marches permit the perpetrators' actions and motivations under conditions of virtual autonomy and, consequently, the degree of their devotion to the mass slaughter to be assessed. Under these conditions, those not devoted to the suffering and deaths of Jews should have desisted from harming them. The death marches therefore subject the hypothesis that the perpetrators were motivated by their own antisemitism, by their attendant belief in the justice of the slaughter of the Jews, to a different kind of difficult test.

The cases chosen here can be conceived of as different kinds of "crucial cases," namely cases chosen on the basis of explanatory variables that are most likely to confound my proposed explanation. They are therefore also the cases which would most firmly lend credence to that explanation, if it can account for them.[4] The cases have the further virtue of allowing for the isolation of the various factors that could plausibly explain the perpetrators' actions and thereby permit for a necessary degree of analytical clarity.

I decided to study selected entire institutions and their personnel, rather than take some scientific sample of perpetrators from a larger number of institutions (though for the purposes of studying the backgrounds of the perpetrators, samples were taken from different institutions). The perpetrators, I reasoned, could not be understood, their actions could not be explained, if wrested from their institutional contexts. It makes little sense to view them as individuals disembedded from their immediate social relations. Without studying the units in which they operated, too little would be learned about the character of their lives for a proper assessment of their motivations. Institutions of killing (such as police battalions, *Einsatzkommandos*, camps of different kinds, and death marches) differed from each other, as did different units within each type of institution, in a host of ways. Studying some scientific sample of individuals from many units would efface the institutional, material, and social psychological circumstances of the Holocaust's perpetration.

A second reason for choosing entire units is that not enough is known about the actions of most individuals in order to make it sensible to base a study on such a methodology. While a fair amount can be unearthed about the overall character and *patterns of action* in given institutions of killing, no such robust knowledge can be acquired about the vast majority of individuals who would form the sample of such a research strategy. The perpetrators about whom much is known are an unrepresentative group of people who were intensively investigated by the Federal Republic of Germany's legal authorities because, generally speaking, they were in command positions or, by their actions, distinguished themselves as having been especially brutal. These people are no doubt of great interest, and the knowledge we have of them is used here, but because they are an unrepresentative group, they cannot provide the basis for answers to the *general* empirical and theoretical questions of this book.

The particular cases from each institution chosen here depended on the criteria mentioned as well as on the availability of sufficient data. A problem in studying the perpetrators is the unevenness of the extant material. Contemporary documents which illuminate in sufficient detail the perpetrators' actions, or anything at all about their motivations, barely exist. About some institutions of killing, including some of the cases discussed here, virtually no contemporary documents of any kind have survived. Therefore, the primary material for this study has been drawn mainly from materials amassed during the Federal Republic of Germany's postwar legal investigations of Nazi crimes, which reside in the German justice system. These investigations are the major, indeed the indispensable, almost sole source for studying the executioners, yet they remain greatly underutilized. They contain the relevant documents that could be found and obtained, and, more important, extensive interrogations of the perpetrators themselves as well as of surviving victims and bystanders.[5] From these interrogations and testimonies, a detailed portrait of life within an institution of killing and of the history of its members' actions can often be constructed.

Since frequently a number of people, sometimes people positioned differently in relation to the execution ditch, give testimony about the same events, the opportunity exists to check and cross-check accounts. This often produces mutual verification and clarity, though at other times it leads to contradictions, which cannot be resolved except logically and according to the judgment of the interpreter.[6] Fortunately, when such unresolvable discrepancies do occur, especially over the number of Jews whom the Germans deported or killed in a given operation, they are generally not especially significant for analytical purposes.[7]

This rich, illuminating postwar testimony is also a problematic source. Aside from memory's natural deficiencies in portraying events often of over twenty years past,[8] the perpetrators have powerful motivations for concealing, evading, dissimulating, and lying. Their testimony is replete with omissions, half-truths, and lies. They, it should not be forgotten, were giving testimony to police interrogators and other legal authorities about crimes which were considered by their own society, the Federal Republic of Germany, and by the world at large to be among the greatest in human history. Many perpetrators had spent the two to three decades prior to their testimony denying to others, whether by silence or prevarication, the degree of their involvement in the genocide. Even when they could not completely hide that they had given their bodies to the slaughter, they in all likelihood denied that they had given to it their souls, their inner will and moral assent. To do otherwise was to declare to family, and friends, to their growing children, to their now disapproving society: "I was a mass murderer and am (or was) proud of it." After years of habitual repression and denial, they found themselves facing the legal authorities, forced to confront their deeds, long buried from the conversation of their daily lives. Is it any surprise that they would not now be eager to declare to their interrogators that they had been mass murderers and that they had approved of their actions, even perhaps enjoyed them? They could also not have been sure that they would not themselves be held accountable for their crimes. Motivations for lying, for not announcing that they were among history's greatest criminals, were powerful indeed. And indeed it is easy to demonstrate that they do lie rampantly, by word and by omission, in order to minimize their physical and cognitive involvement in the mass slaughters. Because of this, the only methodological position that makes sense is to discount *all* self-exculpating testimony that finds no corroboration from other sources.[9]

Attempting to explain the Germans' actions, indeed just writing a history of this period, by relying on their self-exonerating testimony would be akin to writing a history of criminality in America by relying on the statements of criminals as given to police, prosecutors, and before courts. Most criminals assert that they have been wrongly accused of the crimes. They certainly neglect to volunteer information about other criminal acts that they may have engaged in, of which the authorities are ignorant. If they are unable to deny plausibly their material culpability, then they find whatever ways they can to attribute responsibility for the crimes to others. If asked, whether in court or by the news media, then they ordinarily profess, even with great conviction and passion, to abhor the crimes which they, despite their protestations, have committed. When facing the authorities, as well as the general society, criminals

lie about their actions and their motivations. Even after conviction, even after the evidence has been presented which convinces a jury beyond a reasonable doubt that a
person is guilty, criminals habitually proclaim their innocence. Why should we think
that those who were complicit in one of the greatest crimes in human history should
be more honest, more self-incriminating?

To accept the perpetrators' self-exonerations without corroborating evidence
is to guarantee that one will be led down many false paths, paths that preclude one
from ever finding one's way back to the truth. On the other hand, were such self-
exonerations indeed true, a variety of other evidence supporting them should have
come to light. It rarely does. As the chapters treating the perpetrators lay out in
depth, had the perpetrators really disapproved of the mass murder, had they really
been opposed to participating in it, then many ways to express this were available to
them—the spectrum ran from outright refusal to kill, to expressing disapproval and
opposition either symbolically or in discussion with comrades[10]—that entailed few, if
any, costs to the perpetrators.[11]

APPENDIX 2

SCHEMATIZATION OF THE
DOMINANT BELIEFS IN
GERMANY ABOUT JEWS,
THE MENTALLY ILL, AND SLAVS

Source of Their Character
1. Jews: race/biology
2. Mentally ill: biology
3. Slavs: race/biology

Essential Quality
1. Jews: evil/threat
2. Mentally ill: disease
3. Slavs: inferiority

Degree of Perniciousness and Danger
1. Jews: incalculable and extreme
2. Mentally ill: chronic, festering, and somewhat debilitating
3. Slavs: potentially great, yet manageable

Attribution of Motivation and Responsibility
1. Jews: want to destroy Germany, and are responsible for their own malignancy
2. Mentally ill: unfortunate victims, no malignant motives, no responsibility for their condition or for the threat that they pose to the biological health of Germany
3. Slavs: no malignant intention, and no responsibility for their inferior condition

Metaphorical and Logical Implication
1. Jews: "eliminate," permanently only by killing
2. Mentally ill: eradicate or quarantine
3. Slavs: "helotize" (meaning "subjugate" and decimate to whatever extent is utilitarian)

Institutional Support for Images

1. Jews: state—intense and continuous barrage; Church—support for beliefs, no counter-image offered; schools—similar to state; army—no different

2. Mentally ill: state—less direct, continuous, and intense dissemination of biological notions, and no prohibition of counter-images; Church—direct opposition to Nazi ideas on this matter; schools—tended to support these notions; army—silent on the issue

3. Slavs: state—consistent dissemination of beliefs about their "subhumanity," though lacking the intensity, the vituperation, and the virulence of those about the Jews; Church—relative silence on the matter, continued preaching of universal morality (with the exclusion of Jews), and considered Slavs as Christians; schools—similar to state; army—tended to concur with the state, but with dissenting opinions in all ranks

Degree of Penetration of Beliefs

(Two dimensions: breadth/depth)

1. Jews: near universal/deep
2. Mentally ill: restricted to certain groups/among them deep
3. Slavs: widespread/more variation, generally less deeply rooted than Jews

Aesthetic Reaction

1. Jews: offended sense of order and goodness
2. Mentally ill: offended sense of order, but not goodness
3. Slavs: offended neither if kept in their proper place, since they were useful beasts; they were not a moral blight

Ethical Attitude

1. Jews: as non-humans, beyond moral law
2. Mentally ill: mixed—suspension of traditional morality of the sanctity of human life, but to be treated without cruelty and unnecessary suffering
3. Slavs: inconsistent (and often violated) application of watered-down traditional morality

Interaction of Beliefs, Traditional Morality, and Degree of Penetration into Society

1. Jews: no role for traditional morality; nature of Jews invalidates their application; beliefs about Jews were so widespread that this was almost universally accepted

2. Mentally ill: biological metaphor was not so widespread, so traditional morality influenced many; also the mentally ill, unlike the Jews, were not seen as morally culpable

3. Slavs: beliefs about their inferiority were widespread, though traditional morality could still influence people's actions, yet often weakly; beliefs about Slavs were not as central as those about Jews, so the "problems" that they posed were not seen to be as urgent

Result

1. Jews: genocide; opposed by a small minority, usually on ethical or aesthetic grounds (because of the application of "outmoded" and "inapplicable" traditional morality); no trouble finding willing and dedicated killers

2. Mentally ill: "euthanasia" program formally halted because of vigorous opposition; able to find a dedicated group of ideologically attuned medical personnel to staff the killing program

3. Slavs: inconsistent policy with all sorts of major exceptions; absence of genocidal killing, but brutal slaying of all opposition; killers much less likely to be enthusiastic about their job; policy considerations (alliances) able to mold German image of particular Slavic group, because of comparative shallowness of beliefs and also because the Slavs were deemed to be fundamentally not dangerous (as long as they were kept in check) and to be without malignant intentions; intended to be a massive reservoir of slave labor; millions already so employed

APPENDIX 3

FOREWORD TO THE GERMAN EDITION

The following essay appeared in the German edition,
which was published in August 1996.

Given the particular interests with which German readers might approach this book and its theme, a few prefatory words about its purpose, about the nature and focus of its argument, about issues of guilt, and about Germany today might be helpful.

This book shifts the focus of the investigation of the Holocaust away from impersonal institutions and abstract structures back to the actors, back to the human beings who committed the crimes and to the populace from which these men and women came. It eschews the ahistorical, universal social psychological explanations—such as the notions that people obey all authority or that they will do anything because of peer pressure—that are typically, reflexively invoked when accounting for the perpetrators' actions. Instead, it recognizes the individuality and humanity of the actors, that they were people who had beliefs and values about the wisdom of the regime's policies which informed the choices that they made collectively and individually. Indeed, the analysis here is predicated upon the notion that each individual made choices about how to treat Jews. The book also takes seriously the real historical context in which the German perpetrators developed their beliefs and values about the world, beliefs and values that were critical for their understanding of what was right and necessary in the treatment of Jews. For these reasons, it is important to learn as much as possible about the German perpetrators and their views of the victims and their motives, as well as about the views of Jews that more generally existed in their society.

Questions central to the understanding of the Holocaust are posed here that have not received the concerted discussion that they deserve. Two sets of questions can be discerned. The first set is about the perpetrators: What did they believe about Jews? Did they look upon them as a dangerous, evil enemy or as forlorn human beings who were being treated unjustly? Did they believe that their treatment of the Jews was right and necessary? The second set of questions is about Germans during the Nazi period: How many were antisemites? What was the character of their antisemitism? What did they think of the anti-Jewish measures of the 1930s? What did they know about and think of the extermination of Jews?

A striking aspect of the literature on the Holocaust is that, with some exceptions, these central questions about the mentality of the actors are not addressed directly, systematically, and thoroughly. The questions, particularly those about the mentality of the perpetrators, are often barely raised at all and, if raised, answered in a perfunctory manner, without the careful presentation and weighing of evidence that other topics receive. Indeed, any work that fails to answer these questions cannot plausibly claim to explain the perpetration of the Holocaust. This book seeks to do so. It presents new evidence and arguments that challenge much conventional wisdom about this period and its actors.

Hitler's Willing Executioners is at once about the worldviews, actions, and choices of individuals, about the responsibility of each individual as the author of his own actions, and about the political culture from which they derived their views. It shows that a set of beliefs about Jews came to be very widespread in Germany's political cultural life already well before the Nazis came to power and that such beliefs then informed what ordinary Germans, individually and together, were willing to tolerate and to do during the Nazi period. The character and evolution of political cultures are explicable historically. Political cultures evolve and change, as has German political culture during the Federal Republic. Nothing about them is immutable. The argument of this book, therefore, in no sense posits anything about some eternal German "national character"; it is in no sense about any essential, unchangeable psychological dispositions of "the Germans." I reject categorically these notions; my book and its arguments owe nothing to them.

Just as discussing the substance of a society's political culture does not imply or rely upon notions of unchangeable characteristics of that country's people, so too generalizing about the people in a country does not imply or rely upon any notions of ethnicity or "race." The process of generalizing is essential to human thought. Without generalization, we could not make sense of the world and of our experience. We generalize all the time about different groups and societies and when we compare them: "Most Germans today are genuine democrats." "Most whites in the American South before the American Civil War believed that Blacks were by their constitution intellectually and morally inferior, and were fit to be beasts of burden, to be slaves." Most whites in the American South were racists and their racism governed their beliefs about the appropriate status of Blacks and how they were willing to treat them. Both of these generalizations are true. The issue, therefore, is not about the appropriateness of generalization per se but about the veracity and evidentiary basis of generalizations. There is nothing "racist" or improper about asserting that most Germans today are good democrats any more than there is about maintaining that the vast majority of whites in the antebellum South were racists, or that most Germans in the 1930s were antisemites. The appropriateness of any of these generalizations depends on whether or not it is correct—on the quality of the evidentiary foundation and of the analysis used to derive the general conclusions.

This book presents evidence and interprets that evidence to explain why and how the Holocaust occurred, indeed why it could have occurred. It is a work of historical explanation, not of moral evaluation. The book begins from the obvious starting point: the Holocaust emanated from Germany and was therefore principally a German phenomenon. This is a historical fact. An explanation of the Holocaust must obviously ground the Holocaust as a development of German history. It should be recognized, however, that although the Holocaust was a development of German history, it was not the inevitable outcome of that history. Had Hitler and the Nazis never come to power, then the Holocaust would not have happened. Had there not been an economic depression in Germany, then the Nazis, in all likelihood, never would have come to power. Many developments had to occur—developments that were not inevitable—for the Holocaust to happen.

No adequate explanation for the Holocaust can be monocausal. Many factors contributed to creating the conditions necessary for the Holocaust to be both possible and realized. Most of these factors—such as how the Nazis gained power, how they crushed internal opposition, how they conquered Europe, how they created the institutions of killing and organized the slaughter—are well known, so the book does not dwell on them. Instead, it focuses on the motivational element of the Holocaust, and it argues that the *will* to kill Jews was derived, both for Hitler and for those who implemented his murderous plans, principally from a single, common source, namely a virulent antisemitism. How the antisemitism was mobilized and found expression, depended on a host of other factors—material, situational, strategic, and ideological—and these are discussed in depth, especially in the analysis of the evolution of the regime's anti-Jewish policies and of the character of Jewish "work" during the Nazi period. The regime and the perpetrators produced complex and sometimes even seemingly inconsistent policies and actions toward Jews precisely because they were acting upon their antisemitic animus within political, social, and economic contexts that often placed practical restraints upon their actions and because, in formulating and implementing their anti-Jewish policies, they naturally took into account the other practical and ideological goals which they were simultaneously pursuing. Explaining the Holocaust and its every feature requires, therefore, attention to many factors other than antisemitism. Yet whatever the influence of such factors was upon the formation and implementation of the Nazis' antisemitic program, the source of the *will* of the Nazi leadership and of the ordinary Germans who executed the policies to persecute and kill Jews did not derive from these other factors but principally from the actors' common antisemitism.

Although a virulent form of antisemitism, which was the dominant view of Jews in Germany before and during the Nazi period, provided the motivation for Germans to persecute and, when called upon, to kill Jews, had the Nazis never come to power, then that same antisemitism would have remained dormant. The Holocaust occurred in Germany because and only because three factors came together. The most committed, virulent antisemites in human history took state power in Germany and decided to turn private, murderous fantasy into the core of state policy. They did so in a society where their essential views of Jews were widely shared. Had either of these two factors not obtained, then the Holocaust would not have occurred, certainly not as it did. The most virulent hatred, whether it be antisemitism or some other form of racism or prejudice, does not result in systematic slaughter unless a political leadership mobilizes and organizes those who hate into a program of killing. So without the Nazis, and without Hitler, the Holocaust would not have occurred. But without a broad willingness among the ordinary Germans to tolerate, to support, and even, for many, first to contribute to the utterly radical persecution of Jews in the 1930s and then, at least for those who were called upon, to participate in the slaughter of Jews, the regime would never have been able to kill six million Jews. Both the Nazis' assumption of power and the willingness of Germans to support the state's antisemitic policies were necessary factors for the Holocaust to occur. Neither was, on its own, sufficient. Only in Germany did these two factors come together.

This also makes clear why the extent and substance of antisemitism in other countries is not relevant for explaining what happened in Germany and the actions of Germans. Of course, there was antisemitism in France, Poland, and Ukraine. In none of these countries did a regime come to power intent upon exterminating Jews. People's antisemitism alone, when it is not harnessed to a state policy of violent persecution and killing, does not produce genocide. For this reason, a comparative analysis of antisemitism is not necessary for explaining why antisemitism in Germany but not elsewhere had such catastrophic consequences. Because both conditions—an antisemitic populace and a regime bent on the mass annihilation of Jews—were necessary, which means that neither was alone sufficient, to produce the Holocaust, the obvious absence of one of the necessary conditions in other countries (a regime bent on mass murder), means that there is no need, within the scope and for the purposes of this book, to investigate the degree to which the other condition (virulent eliminationist antisemitism) was present. It should be said, however, that the existence of much antisemitism elsewhere in Europe does explain why the Germans found so many people in other countries who were willing and eager to help them kill Jews.

A third factor makes clear that the Holocaust—certainly as a continent-wide program of extermination—could have been produced only by Germany. Only Germany had the military prowess to conquer the European continent and therefore only a German leadership could begin to slaughter Jews with impunity, without fear of the reaction of other countries. For this reason it is unlikely—had some other European country been governed by a Nazi-like leadership that wanted to kill its Jews—that it would have ever enacted such a policy. Even Hitler, a man obsessively devoted to the extirpation of Jewry, moved cautiously against the Jews in the 1930s, when Germany was militarily and diplomatically vulnerable and when a "solution" to the "Jewish Problem" was not yet practical. This does not mean that some local genocidal slaughter of Jews could not conceivably have occurred in another country, merely that it was unlikely given these constraints. As a historical fact, no Nazi-like leadership came to power elsewhere which decided to slaughter its country's Jews, so the virulent anti-semitism that did exist elsewhere did not move its bearers to commit mass murder until the conquering Germans began persecuting and killing the Jews of a given country.

This book is not a comprehensive history of the Holocaust, of Nazi Germany, of modern German political development, or of recent German political culture. There are many features of each that remained unmentioned. Because the book focuses on illuminating the central, dominant aspects of the issues that it does investigate, exceptions and variations are also sometimes not discussed or are treated only briefly. None of this denies that they existed. Many of them, such as virtually every aspect of the resistance to Hitler, are well known. The task of the book is to explain why and how the Holocaust unfolded as it did, to explain the general, central, and dominant features which, in my view, have not been adequately explained.

It is because the task of this investigation is historical explanation, not moral evaluation, that issues of guilt and responsibility are never directly addressed. The book explains why and how people thought and acted as they did, not how we should judge them. I did not discuss this mainly because, whatever the moral significance of this book may be, moral evaluation of this sort has no place in the explanatory enterprise. Addressing the moral issues, I thought, would lead only to confusion about the book's purpose and its conclusions. I also have no particular professional competence for writing about these issues, so I was eager to leave them, on the one hand, to those with greater expertise—such as moral philosophers—and, on the other hand, to each reader to judge for himself or herself according to each one's own moral framework. It is clear, though, now that this book is being published for the German public, for whom issues of guilt and responsibility are so charged, that a few words about my own views on the subject are necessary.

I reject categorically the notion of collective guilt. The thrust of the charge of collective guilt is that a person—regardless of that person's actions—is guilty merely by dint of his or her membership in a collectivity, in this case as members of the German populace. Not collective groups but only individuals are to be deemed guilty and only for their own individual deeds. The concept of guilt should be applied to an individual only when that person has committed a crime, for the term when used in this fashion carries with it all the connotations of legal guilt, namely guilt of a crime. In the Federal Republic of Germany and in the United States, people are not deemed guilty and therefore legally culpable for thinking certain things, for hating other groups (unless, in the Federal Republic, they express such beliefs publicly), for approving of crimes that others commit, or for the crimes that they might be willing to commit if given the opportunity. The same standard should apply to Germans who lived during the Nazi period, and this is the standard which the justice system in the Federal Republic has applied to crimes committed during the Nazi period. In this book, I do show that individual complicity was more widespread than many have assumed and, if one takes into account all the crimes committed against non-Jews during the Nazi period, then the number of Germans who committed acts which are to be deemed criminal is enormous. Yet it remains that the only people who are to be considered guilty are those who acted in a criminal manner. Indeed, this book goes against much of the literature on the Holocaust in its insistence that we must recognize that individual Germans were not will-less cogs in a machine, were not automatons, but were responsible actors, were capable of making choices, and were ultimately the authors of their own actions. Because the analysis of this book emphasizes that every individual made choices about how to treat Jews, its entire mode of analysis runs directly contrary to, and provides powerful argument against, any notion of collective guilt.

What moral judgments are to be made about Germans—or, for that matter, about Poles, French, and Ukrainians—who were antisemites, who approved of various phases of the persecution of the Jews, or who would have willingly killed or harmed Jews had they found themselves in institutions of killing *but who did not*, is to be left to each individual who wants to render moral judgments, just as each individual today is left to evaluate his or her contemporaries who harbor reprehensible views and tendencies. It goes without saying that any German born after the war, or who was a child during the war, cannot possibly be guilty, and is in no sense responsible for the commission of crimes. Whatever the continuing responsibility may be of Germany and Germans to make amends with the Jews and non-Jews, and their surviving relatives, against whom their countrymen committed crimes, that is distinctly different from holding them responsible for the commission of crimes.

Germany's political culture has obviously changed in the fifty years since the end of World War II, particularly in two related aspects. In the Federal Republic of Germany, the political culture and most individual Germans have become genuinely democratic. Also, its antisemitic component has diminished enormously and is, by and large, changed in character, having lost the central, hallucinatory elements—which attributed to the Jews demonic powers and intentions—that characterized antisemitism during the Nazi period and before. The general, steady decline and changed nature of antisemitism in the Federal Republic, which is reflected unequivocally in the survey data, is explicable historically according to the same framework of analysis used in this book to account for the widespread persistence of antisemitism in Germany before and during the Nazi period.

The loss of the war and the installation of a democratic political system in Germany meant that new democratic beliefs and values replaced the old antidemocratic and antisemitic beliefs and values in the public sphere. Instead of the political and social institutions of society putting forward and supporting antidemocratic and antisemitic views as they did before 1945, the institutions of the Federal Republic have nurtured a view of politics and humanity that rejected and delegitimized the antisemitism of the Nazi period and before. German society gradually underwent change. The young of the Federal Republic have been taught a universalistic creed that all people are created equal instead of one that holds humanity to be composed of a hierarchy of races that are differently abled, owed different moral obligations, and are inexorably in conflict with one another. Since people's fundamental views are, to a great extent, imparted to them by their society and their culture, the creation of a new public political culture in Germany and generational replacement has produced what one would have expected: a decline and a fundamental change in the character of antisemitism.

Since the appearance of the English-language edition of this book, I have often been asked what I hoped to achieve by writing it. The two-fold answer is simple: To improve knowledge of the past by providing a true account and the best interpretation of the Holocaust and of the people who perpetrated it of which I am capable. To allow all people who wish to do so to derive meaning from the past by affording them the opportunity to confront this knowledge openly and honestly.

Daniel Jonah Goldhagen
Cambridge, Massachusetts
July 1996

PSEUDONYMS

Bekemeier, Heinrich
Bentheim, Anton
Brand, Lucia
Brand, Paul
Buchmann, Heinz
Dietrich, Max
Dressler, Alfred
Eisenstein, Oscar
Fischer, Albert
Grafmann, Erwin
Hahn, Irena
Hauer, Gerhard
Hergert, Ernst
Jensen, Walter
Kammer, Arthur
Kemnitz, Simon
Koch, Johann
Koslowski, Wilhelm
Mehler, Conrad
Metzger, Paul

Moering, Hermann
Nehring, Erwin
Papen, Georg
Peters, Oscar
Raeder, Karl
Reich, Hartmuth
Reitsch, Viktoria
Riedl, Siegfried
Ritter, Michael
Rust, Willi
Schäfer, Rita
Schmidt, Irena
Schneider, Emma
Schoenfelder, Dr.
Steinmetz, Heinrich
Vogel, Eberhard
Wagner, Karl
Weber, Alois
Wirth, Martin

ABBREVIATIONS

BAK	Bundesarchiv Koblenz
Buchs	ZStL 205 AR-Z 20/60
Dörr	Investigation and trial of Alois Dörr, StA Hof 2 Js 1325/62
Grünberg	ZStL 410 AR 1750/61
HG	Investigation of H.G. et al., StA Hamburg 141 Js 128/65
HGS	*Holocaust and Genocide Studies*
Hoffmann	Investigation and trial of Wolfgang Hoffmann et al., StA Hamburg 141 Js 1957/62
HSSPF	Higher SS and Police Leader
IMT	*Trials of the Major War Criminals Before the International Military Tribunal*, vols. 1–42
JK	ZStL 206 AR-Z 6/62
KdO	Commander of the Order Police
KR	ZStL 208 AR 967/69
Nazism	J. Noakes and G. Pridham, eds., *Nazism: A History in Documents and Eyewitness Accounts, 1919–1945* (New York: Schocken Books, 1988)
SSPF	SS and Police Leader
SSPF Lublin	Investigation Against the *SSPF* Lublin, ZStL 208 AR-Z 74/60
StA	Office of the State Prosecutor
StAH	Hamburg State Archive
Streckenbach	Indictment Against Streckenbach, ZStL 201 AR-Z 76/59

TWC   *Trials of War Criminals before the Nürnberg Military Tribunals*
               under Control Council Law No. 10. Nürnberg, October 1946–April
               1949, vols. 1–15
VfZ   *Vierteljahrshefte für Zeitgeschichte*
YVS   *Yad Vashem Studies*
ZStL   Zentrale Stelle der Landesjustizverwaltungen zur Aufklärung
               nationalsozialistische Verbrechen in Ludwigsburg

NOTES

Introduction

1. See letter of Jan. 30, 1943, StA Hamburg 147 Js 1957/62, pp. 523–524.

2. They departed from this admittedly vague standard, both in the ordinary language sense of being civilized and in Norbert Elias' social theoretical sense of imposing external and especially internal controls over emotional displays, including outbursts of destructive violence. See *The Civilizing Process*, 2 vols., (New York: Pantheon, 1978).

3. Definitional and substantive issues pertaining to the category of "perpetrators" are discussed in Chapter 5.

4. The literature's neglect of the perpetrators takes more subtle form than a mere failure to focus on them. Through conscious, half-conscious, and unconscious linguistic usage, the perpetrators often, and for some authors, typically, disappear from the page and from the deeds. The use of the passive voice removes the actors from the scene of carnage, from their own acts. It betrays the authors' understanding of the events and forms the public's comprehension of them, an understanding robbed of human agency. See Martin Broszat and Saul Friedländer, "A Controversy about the Historicization of National Socialism," in Peter Baldwin, ed., *Reworking the Past: Hitler, the Holocaust, and the Historians' Debate* (Boston: Beacon Press, 1990), pp. 102–134, for a discussion of this tendency in the work of Martin Broszat, one of the most influential interpreters of the Holocaust and of Germany during the Nazi period.

5. We do not hesitate to refer to the citizens of the United States who fought in Vietnam to achieve the aims of their government as "Americans," and for good reason. The reason is just as good in the case of Germans and the Holocaust. The per-

petrators were Germans as much as the soldiers in Vietnam were Americans, even if not all people in either country supported their nation's efforts. Customary usage for analogous cases, as well as descriptive accuracy and rectitude, not only permit but also mandate the use of "Germans" as the term of choice. Moreover, the Jewish victims conceived of the German perpetrators and referred to them overwhelmingly not as Nazis but as Germans. This usage does not mean that all Germans are included when the term "Germans" is employed (just as the term "Americans" does not implicate every single American), because some Germans opposed and resisted the Nazis as well as the persecution of the Jews. That they did so does not alter the identity of those who were perpetrators, or what we should properly call them.

A real terminological problem exists when discussing "Germans," because "Germans," particularly when contrasted to "Jews," seems to imply that the Jews of Germany were not also Germans. I have, with some misgivings, decided to call Germans simply "Germans" and not to use some cumbersome locution like "non-Jewish Germans." Thus, whenever German Jews are referred to as "Jews," their Germanness is implicit.

6. Many non-Germans contributed to the genocidal slaying of Jews, particularly various formations of eastern European auxiliaries who worked in conjunction with Germans under German supervision. Perhaps the most notable of these were the so-called Trawnikis, the mainly Ukrainian auxiliaries who contributed greatly to the decimation of the Jews living in the *Generalgouvernement*, by being parties to deportations and mass shootings and working in the extermination centers of Treblinka, Bełżec, and Sobibór. The Germans found willing helpers in Lithuania, Latvia, in the various regions of the conquered Soviet Union, in other countries of eastern and central Europe, and in western Europe as well. Generally speaking, these perpetrators have been neglected in the literature on this period. Their comparative study should be undertaken (and is discussed briefly in Chapter 15), yet it is not an integral part of this book, for two reasons. The first, already mentioned, is that the Germans and not the non-Germans were the prime movers and executors of the Holocaust. The second is a practical consideration. This book is already ambitious in scope, so its purview had to be restricted so as to be manageable. The study of non-German perpetrators, which would include a large number of people of many nationalities, is the fitting subject for another project. For a discussion of the disposition of ethnic Germans during the war, see Valdis O. Lumans, *Himmler's Auxiliaries: The Volksdeutsche Mittelstelle and the German National Minorities of Europe, 1933–1945* (Chapel Hill: University of North Carolina Press, 1993); for the contributions of the "Trawnikis," the east European auxiliaries who manned the extermination camps of Bełżec, Treblinka, and Sobibór, and who killed and brutalized tens of thousands of Jews while deporting them from the ghettos of Poland or while shooting them themselves, see Judgment Against Karl Richard Streibel et al., Hamburg 147 Ks 1/72; for the Soviet Union, see Richard Breitman, "Himmler's Police Auxiliaries in the Occupied Soviet Territories," *Simon Wiesenthal Annual* 7 (1994): pp. 23–39.

7. See Clifford Geertz, "Thick Description: Toward an Interpretive Theory of Culture," in *The Interpretation of Cultures: Selected Essays* (New York: Basic Books, 1973), pp. 3–30.

8. This is discussed in Chapter 3.

9. See Hans-Heinrich Wilhelm, "The Holocaust in National-Socialist Rhetoric and Writings: Some Evidence against the Thesis that before 1945 Nothing Was Known about the 'Final Solution,' " *YVS* 16 (1984): pp. 95–127; and Wolfgang Benz, "The Persecution and Extermination of the Jews in the German Consciousness," in John Milfull, ed., *Why Germany? National Socialist Anti-Semitism and the European Context* (Providence: Berg Publishers, 1993), pp. 91–104, esp. 97–98.

10. See, for example, Max Domarus, *Hitler: Speeches and Proclamations, 1932–1945* (London: I. B. Tauris, 1990), vol. 1, p. 41; and C. C. Aronsfeld, *The Text of the Holocaust: A Study of the Nazis' Extermination Propaganda, from 1919–1945* (Marblehead, Mass.: Micah Publications, 1985), pp. 34–36.

11. This is the subject of the "intentionalist-functionalist" debate discussed below. On the motivation for the decision to exterminate European Jewry, see Erich Goldhagen, "Obsession and *Realpolitik* in the 'Final Solution,' " *Patterns of Prejudice* 12, no. 1 (1978): pp. 1–16; and Eberhard Jäckel, *Hitler's World View: A Blueprint for Power* (Cambridge: Harvard University Press, 1981).

12. This was a consequence of Germany's military expansion.

13. This is a major focus of Raul Hilberg, *The Destruction of the European Jews* (New York: New Viewpoints, 1973).

14. Naturally, it is the biographers of Hitler who wrestle most with this question. See, for example, Allan Bullock, *Hitler: A Study in Tyranny* (Harmondsworth: Penguin, 1974); Robert G. L. Waite, *The Psychopathic God: Adolf Hitler* (New York: Signet Books, 1977); Joachim C. Fest, *Hitler* (New York: Vintage, 1975); see also Hitler's own account in Adolf Hitler, *Mein Kampf* (Boston: Houghton Mifflin, 1971). For two treatments of the Nazis' ascent to power, see Karl Dietrich Bracher, *Die Auflösung der Weimarer Republik* (Villingen: Schwarzwald Ring Verlag, 1964); and William Sheridan Allen, *The Nazi Seizure of Power: The Experience of a Single German Town, 1922–1945*, rev. ed. (New York: Franklin Watts, 1984).

15. These are discussed in Chapter 5.

16. The focus on the gassing, to the exclusion of other features of the Holocaust, with the exception of a fair amount of attention that has been devoted to the *Einsatzgruppen*, justified the title of Wolfgang Scheffler's article "The Forgotten Part of the 'Final Solution': The Liquidation of the Ghettos," *Simon Wiesenthal Center Annual* 2 (1985): pp. 31–51.

17. This is a common notion, whose most prominent exponent is Hilberg, *The Destruction of the European Jews*.

18. See Uwe Dietrich Adam's recent discussion, "The Gas Chambers," in François Furet, ed., *Unanswered Questions: Nazi Germany and the Genocide of the Jews* (New York: Schocken Books, 1989), pp. 134–154. He opens the essay appropriately: "Even today certain false ideas and abusive generalizations about the existence, placement, functioning, and 'efficiency' of the gas chambers continue to circulate even in reputable historical works, and these lead to confusion and errors" (p. 134).

19. This is demonstrated by the literature's general, overwhelming failure to discuss the perpetrators in a manner which indicates clearly that many were not SS men; had this been understood, then it would have been emphasized as an important feature of the genocide.

20. It is astonishing how readily available material on this has been ignored; it is not even mentioned in virtually all of the standard works on the Holocaust, including the most recent treatments. This subject is taken up at length during the discussion of police battalions in Part III and in Chapter 15.

21. For the positions of the major protagonists, see Tim Mason, "Intention and Explanation: A Current Controversy about the Interpretation of National Socialism," in Gerhard Hirschfeld and Lothar Kettenacker, eds., *Der "Führerstaat": Mythos und Realität* (Stuttgart: Klett-Cotta, 1981), pp. 23–40; Ian Kershaw, *The Nazi Dictatorship: Problems and Perspectives of Interpretation*, 3d ed. (London: Edward Arnold, 1993), pp. 80–107; and Michael R. Marrus, *The Holocaust in History* (Hanover: University Press of New England, 1987), pp. 31–51.

22. Hans Mommsen, "The Realization of the Unthinkable: The 'Final Solution of the Jewish Question' in the Third Reich," in Gerhard Hirschfeld, ed., *The Policies of Genocide: Jews and Soviet Prisoners of War in Nazi Germany* (London: Allen & Unwin, 1986), pp. 98–99.

23. *Encyclopedia of the Holocaust*, 4 vols., ed. Israel Gutman (New York: Macmillan, 1990), for example, which attempts to summarize and codify the state of knowledge about the Holocaust, and which provides statistics on an enormous array of matters, as far as I can tell, neither addresses the subject nor provides an estimate.

24. This is obviously a widely shared belief among the public that the perpetrators had the choice either to kill or to be killed. Few recent scholarly interpreters have made this assertion so baldly. For one, see Sarah Gordon, *Hitler, Germans and the "Jewish Question"* (Princeton: Princeton University Press, 1984), who says as much about the German army's cooperation in the genocide (p. 283).

25. See Saul Friedländer, *History and Psychoanalysis: An Inquiry into the Possibilities and Limits of Psychohistory* (New York: Holmes & Meier, 1978).

26. See Stanley Milgram, *Obedience to Authority: An Experimental View* (New York: Harper Colophon, 1969). See also Herbert C. Kelman and V. Lee Hamilton, *Crimes of Obedience: Toward A Social Psychology of Authority and Responsibility* (New Haven: Yale University Press, 1989).

27. This propensity is sometimes conceived of as having been historically formed. See Erich Fromm, *Escape from Freedom* (New York: Avon Books, 1965); and G. P. Gooch et al., *The German Mind and Outlook* (London: Chapman & Hall, 1945).

28. See Hannah Arendt, *The Origins of Totalitarianism* (New York: Meridian, 1971). Hans Mommsen, in "The Realization of the Unthinkable," pp. 98–99, 128–129, follows a related line of reasoning, as does Rainer C. Baum, *The Holocaust and the German Elite: Genocide and National Suicide in Germany, 1871–1945* (Totawa, N.J.: Rowman & Littlefield, 1981).

29. The most recent and most considered account of this sort is Christopher R. Browning, *Ordinary Men: Reserve Police Battalion 101 and the Final Solution in Poland* (New York: HarperCollins, 1992). Essentially, this is also Hilberg's position in *The Destruction of the European Jews*. Robert Jay Lifton, who has studied the German doctors at Auschwitz in *The Nazi Doctors: Medical Killing and the Psychology of Genocide* (New York: Basic Books, 1986), provides a psychoanalytic explanation for how professional healers could become killers, how otherwise decent men could perpetrate such evil. It too depends on situational factors and psychological mechanisms, and, its psychoanalytical bearing notwithstanding, falls into this category.

30. Mommsen, "The Realization of the Unthinkable"; Götz Aly and Susanne Heim, *Vordenker der Vernichtung: Auschwitz und die deutschen Pläne für eine neue europäische Ordnung* (Hamburg: Hoffmann und Campe, 1991); also Gordon, *Hitler, Germans and the "Jewish Question,"* p. 312.

31. This explanation is so untenable in the face of what the actual killers were doing, such as shooting defenseless people at point-blank range, that it need be mentioned only because some have seen fit to put it forward. Marrus, an exponent of this view, writes with unwarranted certitude: "As students of the Holocaust have long understood, the extensive division of labor associated with the killing process helped perpetrators diffuse their own responsibility." See *The Holocaust in History*, p. 47. To the (small) extent that this is true, it is a tiny part of the story and not, as Marrus appears to be contending, almost the whole of it.

32. A partial exception is the acknowledgment by Herbert Jäger, *Verbrechen unter totalitärer Herrschaft: Studien zur nationalsozialistischen Gewaltkriminalität* (Olton: Walter-Verlag, 1967), that some percentage of the perpetrators acted out of ideological conviction (pp. 62–64). Jäger, however, does not believe that it was ideological conviction that moved most of the perpetrators (see pp. 76–78). On the whole, as the book's title, "Crimes under Totalitarian Domination," suggests, Jäger accepts the 1950s totalitarian model of Germany during the Nazi period (see pp. 186–208), employing concepts such as "totalitarian mentality" (*totalitäre Geisteshaltung*) (p. 186). This model—wrong in the most fundamental of ways and which continues to obscure for many the substantial freedom and pluralism that actually existed within German society—consistently misdirects Jäger's analysis, which in many ways is rich and insightful. For revisions and critiques of the totalitarian model's applicability to Germany during the Nazi period and of the general issues and debates in classifying Nazism, see Kershaw, *The Nazi Dictatorship*, pp. 17–39. Hans Safrian, in the introduction to his recent study of those who worked under Adolf Eichmann to deport European Jewry to their deaths, has also called into question the historical consensus that antisemitism did not motivate the perpetrators, though he fails to develop this notion much beyond asserting it. See *Die Eichmann-Männer* (Vienna: Europaverlag, 1993), pp. 17–22.

33. Others have of course recognized and emphasized the importance of political ideology and antisemitism for the Nazi *leadership's* decision to undertake the total extermination of the Jews. For a wide-ranging discussion of this issue, see Eberhard Jäckel and Jürgen Rohwer, eds., *Der Mord an den Juden im Zweiten Weltkrieg: Entschlussbildung und Verwirklichung* (Stuttgart: Deutsche Verlags-Anstalt, 1985); Lucy Dawidowicz, *The War Against the Jews, 1933–1945* (New York: Bantam Books, 1975); Gerald Fleming, *Hitler and the Final Solution* (Berkeley: University of California Press, 1984), and Saul Friedländer's introduction to the book; and Klaus Hildebrand, *The Third Reich* (London: Allen & Unwin, 1984). Those who do take this position, however, either have not looked at the perpetrators or have denied that the perpetrators as a group were themselves moved by similar cognitions. Marrus, citing approvingly Hans Mommsen, speaks for the historical consensus in his historiographic *The Holocaust in History*: "Antisemitic indoctrination is plainly an insufficient answer, for we know [*sic*] that many of the officials involved in the administration of mass murder did not come to their tasks displaying intense antisemitism. In some cases, indeed, they appear to have had no history of anti-Jewish

hatred and to have been coldly uninvolved with their victims" (p. 47). Erich Goldhagen is an exception to this general consensus, and although he has not published on the subject, he has emphasized in his course lectures and in our many conversations precisely the point being made here. Thus, while my claim might not sound so novel to some, it actually stands in contradiction to the existing literature.

34. For an overview of a number of cases from the recent and distant past, see Frank Chalk and Kurt Jonassohn, *The History and Sociology of Genocide: Analyses and Case Studies* (New Haven: Yale University Press, 1990).

35. See Cecil Roth, *The Spanish Inquisition* (New York: W. W. Norton, 1964); and Malise Ruthven, *Torture: The Grand Conspiracy* (London: Weidenfeld & Nicolson, 1978). The Spanish in the New World were genocidally murderous towards the indigenous inhabitants, usually in the name of Jesus; see Bartolome de las Casa, *The Devastation of the Indies: A Brief Account* (New York: Seabury Press, 1974).

36. See Clifford Geertz, "Common Sense as a Cultural System," in *Local Knowledge: Further Essays in Interpretive Anthropology* (New York: Basic Books, 1983).

37. The crucial subject of how different starting assumptions bias conclusions by requiring different kinds of falsifying evidence is discussed in Chapter 1. Generally speaking, the fewer data that exist on a given subject, the more prejudicial the assumptions will be. And since interpretations of the issue at hand often depend on readings of the actors' cognitions, for which the data is far from ideal, particular attention must be given to justifying the assumptions being used: incompatible assumptions about, say, the attitudes of Germans may *each* be "unfalsifiable"; data that allows for generalizing with confidence about large groups of Germans is often hard to come by, so most data can be deemed by someone holding a given assumption to be anecdotal and therefore not sufficient to *falsify* the initial assumption.

38. This is obviously hypothetical, yet thinking about it—particularly if the conclusion drawn is that boundaries did exist which the perpetrators would not have crossed—should lead to a consideration of the nature of the limits of their willingness to act.

39. Primo Levi, *The Drowned and the Saved* (New York: Summit Books, 1986), is one who attempts, not entirely successfully, to understand the Germans' cruelty (pp. 105–126).

40. Discussing and delimiting "cruelty" for the phenomena that collectively compose the Holocaust, or, more broadly, the Germans' persecution of European Jewry, is always difficult. The Germans' actions were so "out of this world" that they skew our frames of reference. Killing innocent people might be justly conceived of as being an act of cruelty, as would forcing people who are emaciated and debilitated to perform taxing manual labor. Still, these were ordinary—"normal" in the German context of the times—utilitarian parts of the Germans' jobs, so it makes sense to distinguish them from acts (in this context) of gratuitous cruelty, such as beating, mocking, torturing Jews or forcing them to perform senseless, debilitating labor for the sole purpose of immiserating them further.

41. Jäger, *Verbrechen unter totalitärer Herrschaft*, is aware of these issues, the discussion of which he pioneered in the published literature. See pp. 76–160. For another discussion of this issue, see Hans Buchheim, "Command and Compliance," in

Helmut Krausnick et al., *Anatomy of the SS State* (London: Collins, 1968), pp. 303–396.

42. German cruelty towards Jews occurred not only during the killing operations. This is another reason why cruelty (and the other actions) are best conceptualized as variables analytically distinct from the killing itself.

43. The horror is significant for still another reason. Since Hannah Arendt, a dominant strand of interpretation has assumed or explicitly held that the perpetrators were "affectively neutral," devoid of emotion towards the Jews. All explanations which deny the importance of the identity of the victims at least potentially imply that the perpetrators' views about the victims, whatever they were, were not causally important. As if the wholesale killing of people alone were not sufficient to force the perpetrators to examine their views of their actions, having to confront the horror of their deeds would have made it virtually impossible for them to have no view of the desirability of the slaughter. The notion that the perpetrators were totally neutral towards the Jews is, I am willing to assert, a psychological impossibility. And if not neutral, then what did they think of Jews, what emotions did they bring to the mass slaughters? Whatever these cogitations and emotions were, how did they influence the perpetrators' actions? This line of thinking is meant merely to emphasize the need to investigate as thoroughly as possible the cognitions of the perpetrators, indeed their shared cognitions; for once it is admitted that they could not have been neutral towards their actions and the victims, then their thoughts and feelings must be taken seriously as sources of their actions.

44. See Max Weber, *Economy and Society*, eds. Guenther Roth and Claus Wittich (Berkeley: University of California Press, 1978), pp. 8–9.

45. Categorizing the killings and the killers is difficult. One question to ask in thinking about them is: What would an enabling order such as "Do what you can to kill Jews," which carried no sanctions and promised no rewards, have spurred each German to have done and why? Would he have sat immobile? Would he have worked towards their deaths in a perfunctory manner? Killed with efficiency? Or zealously pursued, with body and soul, the extermination of as many Jews as possible?

46. Obviously, in order to answer the questions guiding this inquiry, it is not enough to explicate the motivations of those who set policy or of those who worked at the pinnacle of the genocidal institutions. The elite's motivations and actions are, of course, important, so it is good that we know already a fair amount about many of them. For a few examples, see Waite, *The Psychopathic God*; Richard Breitman, *The Architect of Genocide: Himmler and the Final Solution* (New York: Alfred A. Knopf, 1991); Matthias Schmidt, *Albert Speer: The End of a Myth* (New York: St. Martin's Press, 1984); and Ruth Bettina Birn, *Die Höheren SS- und Polizeiführer: Himmlers Vertreter im Reich und in den besetzten Gebieten* (Düsseldorf: Droste Verlag, 1986).

47. Anthony Giddens, *The Constitution of Society: Outline of the Theory of Structuration* (Berkeley: University of California Press, 1984), writes: "Structural constraint is not expressed in terms of the implacable causal forms which structural sociologists have in mind when they emphasize so strongly the association of 'structure' with 'constraint'. Structural constraints do not operate independently of the motives and reasons that agents have for what they do. They cannot be compared with the effect of, say, an earthquake which destroys a town and its inhabitants without their in any way being

able to do anything about it. The only moving objects in human social relations are individual agents, who employ resources to make things happen, intentionally or otherwise. The structural properties of social systems do not act, or 'act on', anyone like forces of nature to 'compel' him or her to behave in a particular way" (pp. 180–181).

48. For an example of this kind of reasoning, see Theda Skocpol, *States and Social Revolutions: A Comparative Analysis of France, Russia, and China* (Cambridge: Cambridge University Press, 1979).

49. This recommendation follows in the tradition of Weber's demand for achieving *"Verstehen."* See Weber, *Economy and Society*, pp. 4–24.

50. See Marrus, *The Holocaust in History*, p. 51.

51. Part of the reason that many have failed to understand the killers and the moving forces behind the Holocaust is likely that they have systematically, if not self-consciously, avoided coming to grips with the phenomenological horror of the genocidal killings. Reading most of the "explanations" reveals few gruesome scenes; when presented, they are typically followed by little analysis, the horror remaining unexplored, mute, as the discussion turns to other (often logistical) matters. When ghetto roundups and deportations, mass slaughters, and gassings are mentioned, they are frequently merely recorded as having happened. The horror of specific killing operations is not adequately conveyed, which makes it difficult to comprehend the compass of the horror for the perpetrators, the frequency of their immersion in it, and its cumulative toll on them.

Those who do take into account the horrors are the survivors and the scholars who focus on them. These people, however, have as a rule not concerned themselves with explaining the perpetrators' acts, except impressionistically and in passing. An interesting feature of scholarship on the Holocaust is how little overlap and intersection there has been between those who write about the perpetrators and those who write about the victims. My work is not much of an exception in this respect.

52. Jäger, *Verbrechen unter totalitärer Herrschaft*, is an obvious exception to this, as is, to a lesser extent, Browning, *Ordinary Men*; Hermann Langbein, *Menschen in Auschwitz* (Frankfurt/M: Ullstein, 1980), also takes cognizance of the varieties of the perpetrators' actions.

53. Those who, like Browning in *Ordinary Men*, have failed to integrate their investigations adequately with the two higher levels of analysis.

Chapter 1

1. Gregor Athalwin Ziemer, *Education for Death: the Making of the Nazi* (London: Oxford University Press, 1941), pp. 193–194.

2. See Emile Durkheim, *The Elementary Forms of the Religious Life* (New York: Free Press, 1965); Jacques Soustelle, *Daily Life of the Aztecs* (London: Weidenfeld & Nicolson, 1961), esp. pp. 96–97; and Joshua Trachtenberg, *The Devil and the Jews: The Medieval Conception of the Jew and Its Relation to Modern Anti-Semitism* (Philadelphia: Jewish Publication Society of America, 1983).

3. See Orlando Patterson, *Freedom in the Making of Western Culture*, vol. 1 of *Freedom* (New York: Basic Books, 1991).

4. Even though the various German states had not yet been politically unified, it still makes sense to speak of "Germany" when discussing many (though not all) social, cultural, and political matters, just as it is sensible to talk of "France," despite all of its regional and local variations.

5. Ian Kershaw, *Popular Opinion and Political Dissent in the Third Reich: Bavaria, 1933–1945* (Oxford: Oxford University Press, 1983), p. 370.

6. Dorothy Holland and Naomi Quinn write on this point in "Culture and Cognition," in their edited volume, *Cultural Models in Language and Thought* (Cambridge: Cambridge University Press, 1987), pp. 3–40: "Our cultural understanding of the world is founded on many tacit assumptions. This underlying cultural knowledge is, to use Hutchins' words, 'often transparent to those who use it. Once learned, it becomes what one *sees with*, but seldom what one *sees*.' This 'referential transparency', we note in a previous section, causes cultural knowledge to go unquestioned by its bearer. At the same time, this transparency has posed an absorbing methodological problem for the analyst: how, and from what manner of evidence, to reconstruct the cultural models people use but do not often reflect on or explicitly articulate. The problem has remained central to cognitive anthropology, but approaches to it have changed" (p. 14). This statement is true both of shared cultural assumptions, which are articulated far less than their importance warrants precisely because people see no need to declaim cultural truths, as well as of the underlying cognitive models of thought, of which people are generally not aware.

7. Michael Kater, *The Nazi Party: A Social Profile of Members and Leaders, 1919–1945* (Cambridge: Harvard University Press, 1983), p. 263.

8. Another example might be the opinion of the ordinary English person living in England during the nineteenth century about the inferiority of Blacks and Asians. The extent of such views' expression—especially on the part of ordinary individuals—certainly grossly underrepresented the degree to which they were held. And what small portion of that which was expressed has come down to us?

9. Rom Harré, *Personal Being: A Theory for Individual Psychology* (Cambridge: Harvard University Press, 1984), p. 20. "Conversation" includes all linguistic production, whether oral or written, as well as symbols (which are always linguistically framed and interpreted, and therefore dependent upon the conversation, though at the same time a part of it).

10. Roy D'Andrade, "A Folk Model of the Mind," in Holland and Quinn, eds., *Cultural Models in Language and Thought*, p. 112.

11. See George Lakoff and Zoltán Kövecses, "The Cognitive Model of Anger Inherent in American English," in Holland and Quinn, eds., *Cultural Models in Language and Thought*, pp. 195–221.

12. D'Andrade writes: The "cultural model of *buying* something [is] made up of the *purchaser*, the *seller*, the *merchandise*, the *price*, the *sale*, and the *money*. There are several relationships among these parts; there is the interaction between the *purchaser* and the *seller*, which involves the *communication* to the *buyer* of the *price*, perhaps *bargaining*, the *offer to buy*, the *acceptance of sale*, the *transfer* of ownership of the *merchandise* and the *money*, and so on. This model is needed to understand [and to partake in] not just *buying*, but also such cultural activities and institutions as *lending, renting, leasing, gypping, salesmanship, profit making, stores, ads*, and so on." See "A

Folk Model of the Mind," in Holland and Quinn, eds., *Cultural Models in Language and Thought*, p. 112.

13. Much of Erving Goffman's work consists of uncovering the cognitive models that, unbeknownst to us, structure and smoothly lubricate our face-to-face interactions. See *The Presentation of Self in Everyday Life* (Garden City: Anchor Books, 1959) and *Relations in Public* (New York: Harper Colophon, 1971).

14. See Naomi Quinn, "Convergent evidence for a model of american marriage," in Holland and Quinn, eds., *Cultural Models in Language and Thought*, pp. 173–192.

15. Alexander George's discussion of an "operational code" is a partly successful attempt to conceptualize the building blocks of perception, evaluation, beliefs, and action for politics. See "The 'Operational Code': A Neglected Approach to the Study of Political Leaders and Decision Making," *International Studies Quarterly* 13 (1969): pp. 190–222. Benedict Anderson's exemplary work on nationalism, *Imagined Communities: Reflections on the Origin and Spread of Nationalism* (London: Verso, 1983), illustrates how a new cognitive model, "the nation," was created and, once culturally shared as common sense, came to shape the ways in which people understood the social and political world.

16. John Boswell, in *The Kindness of Strangers: The Abandonment of Children in Western Europe from Late Antiquity to the Renaissance* (New York: Pantheon, 1988), demonstrates this for the historically highly variable treatment of children, and indeed for the very conception of the category of child. See esp. pp. 26–27.

17. This is Harré's argument in *Personal Being*. See also Takeo Doi, *The Anatomy of Dependence* (Tokyo: Kodansha International, 1973), for the radically different character of Japanese psychology and individuality.

18. This has led many to want not to look, and to create accounts of human existence which deny the domain's importance altogether. While such a position may be comforting to some, and bring solace to those wishing for parsimony and seeming methodological power by removing from consideration the most intractable of variables, it creates an artificial and invariably misleading view of the world. For all the difficulty and explanatory frustration it yields, investigating what is in people's heads remains necessary no matter what the current methodological pyrotechnics may be.

19. Kershaw, for example, in *Popular Opinion and Political Dissent in the Third Reich*, makes this distinction when evaluating the German people after *Kristallnacht*: "People's minds were increasingly poisoned against the Jews in at least an abstract way, the conviction was spreading that there *was* a Jewish Question" (p. 272).

20. Or if what is meant is that it is derived not from real-life experiences with Jews, but from culturally current prejudices, nothing is changed, because the beliefs are still used as a guide in relations with Jews.

21. For the nature and consequences of stereotypes, see Gordon W. Allport, *The Nature of Prejudice* (New York: Anchor Books, 1958). The notion of "abstract" antisemitism, and the distinction between it and "real" antisemitism, in fact, captures virtually nothing about the varieties of antisemitism that exist. It only dimly reflects the knowledge that people who are antisemites can also have Jewish acquaintances and "friends," just as many people who are deeply prejudiced against Blacks can maintain that a particular Black person is not such a bad sort. Scholars who employ

a category like "abstract" antisemitism are confusing analytical dimensions, or rather do not recognize that people are capable of making exceptions to general rules, and that the exceptions are, in fact, rare ones, and of only tertiary significance, because the people making the exceptions think of *millions* of real live Jews in the terms laid down by their "abstract" antisemitism.

22. Kershaw, *Popular Opinion and Political Dissent in the Third Reich*, p. 274; to some extent, he is following Michael Müller-Claudius, *Der Antisemitismus und das deutsche Verhängnis* (Frankfurt/M: Verlag Josef Knecht, 1948), pp. 76–78. Any analytical scheme must keep the cognitive and action dimensions distinct, which Müller-Claudius fails to do.

23. For a useful discussion and alternative dimensional analysis of antisemitism, see Helen Fein, "Dimensions of Antisemitism: Attitudes, Collective Accusations, and Actions," in Helen Fein, ed., *The Persisting Question: Sociological Perspectives and Social Contexts of Modern Antisemitism* (Berlin: Walter de Gruyter, 1987), pp. 68–85.

24. For the history of one such image, that of the "Jewish parasite," see Alexander Bein, "Der Jüdische Parasit," *VfZ* 13, no. 2 (1965): pp. 121–149. For a discussion of the logic of metaphors, see George Lakoff and Mark Johnson, *Metaphors We Live By* (Chicago: University of Chicago Press, 1980).

25. This, of course, has been attempted in studies of antisemitism, most notably in T. W. Adorno et al., *The Authoritarian Personality* (New York: Harper & Brothers, 1950).

26. See Trachtenberg, *The Devil and the Jews*; Malcolm Hay, *Europe and the Jews: The Pressure of Christendom over 1900 Years* (Chicago: Academy Chicago Publishers, 1992).

27. This is the crucial distinction in antisemitism, contrary to Langmuir's contention that it is when antisemitism becomes fantasy-based. See Gavan I. Langmuir, "Toward a Definition of Antisemitism," in Fein, ed., *The Persisting Question*, pp. 86–127. Many antisemitisms have become embedded in fantasy, yet, among other things, they issue in different actions and consequences.

28. See Allport's classic study, *The Nature of Prejudice*; for theories about the nature and sources of antisemitism, see Fein, ed., *The Persisting Question*; and Werner Bergmann, ed., *Error Without Trial: Psychological Research on Antisemitism* (Berlin: Walter de Gruyter, 1988).

29. An alternative explanation would have to be that people become antisemites because of economic jealousy and then invent all the fantastical charges leveled at Jews. See, for example, Hillel Levine's study of Polish antisemitism, *Economic Origins of Antisemitism: Poland and Its Jews in the Early Modern Period* (New Haven: Yale University Press, 1991). Why would this occur, and by what mechanism do "objective" economic jealousies metamorphose themselves into unrelated and wild views of Jews? The explanation would have to account for this. Why do other intergroup antipathies, even those with a large component of economic competition, not also produce the array of accusations that are routine among antisemites? I know of no explanation of antisemitism which posits objective conflict as antisemitism's source that answers, or that possesses a theoretical apparatus capable of answering, these questions.

30. For an overview of the subject, see Walter P. Zenner, "Middleman Minority Theories: a Critical Review," in Fein, ed., *The Persisting Question*, pp. 255–276.

31. Bernard Glassman, *Anti-Semitic Stereotypes Without Jews: Images of the Jews in England, 1290–1700* (Detroit: Wayne State University Press, 1975), p. 14.

32. Glassman, *Anti-Semitic Stereotypes Without Jews*, in fact, emphasizes the crucial importance of Christian sermonic material in spreading and sustaining antisemitism in England.

33. For the long list of expulsions of Jews, see Paul E. Grosser and Edwin G. Halperin, *Anti-Semitism: The Causes and Effects of a Prejudice* (Secaucus: Citadel, 1979), pp. 33–38.

34. For a social profile of German Jewry in 1933, see Avraham Barkai, *From Boycott to Annihilation: The Economic Struggle of German Jews, 1933–1943* (Hanover: University Press of New England, 1989), pp. 1–2.

35. Glassman writes about England during the period of expulsion: "Since there were so few Jews in England during this period, the average Englishman was obliged to rely upon what he heard from the pulpit, saw on the stage, and absorbed from the wandering minstrel and storyteller to form his opinions. This oral tradition, which was supplemented by various tracts and pamphlets, was an important source of information about Jews, and there was virtually nothing in society to counterbalance these forces that had the weight of centuries of Christian teachings behind them" (p. 11). The next chapter puts forth the argument that this account of England is far more applicable to Germany during its Nazi period than people imagine.

36. Trachtenberg persuasively argues this in *The Devil and the Jews*.

37. See Allport's discussion of scapegoats in *The Nature of Prejudice*, pp. 235–249.

38. "Antisemitic expression" (or some equivalent) is used to indicate the expression, either verbally or through physical acts, of antisemitism. "Antisemitism" is used to describe the mere existence of antisemitic beliefs. Many people harbor antisemitism, without it being expressed over long periods of time. Often students of antisemitism confuse the two, leading them to mistake the upsurge of *antisemitic expression* for an upsurge of *antisemitism*.

39. This is not to say that through the institutional adoption of antisemitism, particularly in politics, that the beliefs and emotions that move antisemites cannot be infused with a new intensity or molded into somewhat new forms. In fact, this often happens. For such embellishments and even transformations to occur, the existing core of the antisemitic creed must already be in place. Otherwise, the appeals would fall on deaf ears.

40. In eastern Europe and especially in the former Soviet Union, where traditional antisemitic expression had generally been banned under Communism from public institutions and fora, a tidal wave of antisemitic expression welled up from the bosom of society the moment that constraints on public expression were lifted. This development has a number of striking aspects: (1) no relationship exists between the number of Jews in the country and the intensity or character of the antisemitic expression; (2) the fantastical images of the Jews and the hallucinatory accusations directed at them bear many marked similarities to those that were current before Communism made their public expression taboo; (3) antisemitism, its articulated content and its underlying cognitive models, was thus sustained, nourished, and transmitted to new generations by the family and by the other micro-institutions of

society; (4) based on its *expression* under Communism, little evidence suggested the pervasiveness and depth of the antisemitism in these countries that obviously existed. See, for example, *Newsbreak*, Newsletter of the National Conference on Soviet Jewry.

41. Many have labored to demonstrate how our framework of assumptions interprets and creates reality for us. As far as I know, no one has worked to demonstrate how this same framework can be unexpectedly and rapidly tapped in such a way as to produce a radical alteration in sensibility and attendant actions. This has happened in many outbursts of violent persecution, murderousness, and genocide. This happened to Germans. Edward O. Wilson, in *On Human Nature* (Cambridge: Harvard University Press, 1978), pp. 99–120, gives an evolutionary explanation for the sudden outbursts of aggression. This, of course, even if correct for aggression, does not shed light on rapid transformations of belief systems.

42. The most notable example is probably its upsurge at the outbreak of the First World War, when many Marxists discovered that, their internationalism notwithstanding, they had intense national feelings.

43. For a treatment of the relationship between nationalism and antisemitism, see Shmuel Almog, *Nationalism and Antisemitism in Modern Europe, 1815–1945* (London: Pergamon Press, 1990).

44. D'Andrade's study, "A Folk Model of the Mind," in Holland and Quinn, eds., *Cultural Models in Language and Thought*, concludes that the culturally shared cognitive model of the mind can reproduce itself over centuries (p. 138).

Chapter 2

1. See Robert Chazan, "Medieval Anti-Semitism," in David Berger, ed., *History and Hate: The Dimensions of Anti-Semitism* (Philadelphia: Jewish Publication Society, 1986), pp. 53–54.

2. Bernard Glassman, *Anti-Semitic Stereotypes Without Jews: Images of the Jews in England, 1290–1700* (Detroit: Wayne State University Press, 1975), p. 152. He is writing here specifically about England, where antisemitism was actually far less virulent than in the Germanic areas of central Europe.

3. For an account of the elaborate Christian demonology of the Jews and of the endless ills attributed to their doing, see Joshua Trachtenberg, *The Devil and the Jews: The Medieval Conception of the Jew and Its Relation to Modern Anti-Semitism* (Philadelphia: Jewish Publication Society, 1986); for England, see Glassman, *Anti-Semitic Stereotypes Without Jews*, esp. pp. 153–154.

4. See Chazan, "Medieval Anti-Semitism," pp. 61–62.

5. Quoted in Jeremy Cohen, "Robert Chazan's 'Medieval Anti-Semitism': A Note on the Impact of Theology," in Berger, ed., *History and Hate*, p. 69.

6. Cohen writes in "Robert Chazan's 'Medieval Anti-Semitism' ": "From the earliest generations of the Catholic Church, Christian clergymen deemed it a religious duty to polemicise against the Jews. Where the latter posed little or no immediate threat to the Church, or even in the complete absence of Jews, the *Adversus Judaeos* tradition continued to flourish; for the logic of early Christian history dic-

tated the affirmation of Christianity in terms of the negation of Judaism" (pp. 68–69).

7. Trachtenberg, *The Devil and the Jews*, p. 79; and Chazan, "Medieval Anti-Semitism," p. 50.

8. James Parkes, *Antisemitism* (Chicago: Quadrangle Books, 1969), p. 60; see also Jeremy Cohen, *The Friars and the Jews: The Evolution of Medieval Anti-Judaism* (Ithaca: Cornell University Press, 1982), p. 155; and Glassman, *Anti-Semitic Stereotypes Without Jews*, p. 153.

9. Trachtenberg, *The Devil and the Jews*, traces through the centuries central Christian images of Jews, each of which depended on this underlying cognitive model; see esp. pp. 32–43, 124–139, 191–192.

10. Trachtenberg, *The Devil and the Jews*.

11. Quoted in Trachtenberg, *The Devil and the Jews*, p. 18.

12. Trachtenberg, *The Devil and the Jews*, p. 186. For Luther's antisemitism, see Martin Luther, *Von den Jueden und Iren Luegen*, in *Luthers Kampfschriften gegen das Judentum*, ed. Walther Linden (Berlin: Klinkhardt & Biermann, 1936).

13. Cohen, *The Friars and the Jews*, p. 245. Trachtenberg writes: "Little wonder, too, that Jews were accused of the foulest crimes, since Satan was their instigator. Chaucer, in his 'Prioresses Tale,' placed the ultimate blame for the alleged slaughter of a Christian child by a Jew upon 'our firste fo, the Serpent Sathanas, that hath in Iewes herte his waspes nest.' . . . Everyone knew that the devil and the Jews worked together. This explains why it was so easy to condemn the Jews a priori for every conceivable misdeed, even if it made no sense" (*The Devil and the Jews*, pp. 42–43).

14. Cohen, *The Friars and the Jews*, p. 245; for a compilation of European antisemitic violence and expulsions, see Paul E. Grosser and Edwin G. Halperin, *Anti-Semitism: The Causes and Effects of a Prejudice* (Secaucus: Citadel Press, 1979).

15. Trachtenberg, *The Devil and the Jews*, p. 12.

16. Malcolm Hay, *Europe and the Jews: The Pressure of Christendom over 1900 Years* (Chicago: Academy Chicago Publishers, 1992), pp. 68–87.

17. My treatment of antisemitism focuses on its *central tendencies*. It does not present all of the qualifications, nuances, and exceptions that a longer discussion would. For reasons of space, it also does not engage the debates within the literature about the nature of nineteenth-century German antisemitism. Even among the works cited for substantiation, many disagreements exist. My understanding of nineteenth-century antisemitism, because it is informed by my theoretical and methodological positions, emphasizes the underlying continuity of German antisemitism, and asserts its ubiquity, more than any other accounts that I know, with the possible exception of Klemens Felden, "Die Uebernahme des antisemitischen Stereotyps als soziale Norm durch die bürgerliche Gesellschaft Deutschlands (1875–1900)" (Ph.D. diss., Ruprecht-Karl-Universität, Heidelberg, 1963), on which I draw liberally; Rainer Erb and Werner Bergmann, *Die Nachtseite Der Judenemanzipation: Der Widerstand gegen die Integration der Juden in Deutschland, 1780–1860* (Berlin: Metropol, 1989), esp. p. 11; and Paul Lawrence Rose, *Revolutionary Antisemitism in Germany from Kant to Wagner* (Princeton: Princeton University Press, 1990), who, perhaps because his analysis is primarily restricted to a small number of intellectuals and writers, has a different understanding of the nature of the continuity, which, like

the rest of his account of German antisemitism, is not grounded in an analysis of the beliefs of other strata and groups in German society.

18. Felden, "Die Uebernahme des antisemitischen Stereotyps," pp. 18–19.

19. See Eleonore Sterling, *Judenhass: Die Anfänge des politischen Antisemitismus in Deutschland (1815–1850)* (Frankfurt/M: Europäische Verlagsanstalt, 1969), pp. 117 and 126, and on liberals' use of the term, pp. 86–87; and Erb and Bergmann, *Die Nachtseite Der Judenemanzipation*, pp. 48–52. For the history of the concept of race, see Werner Conze, "Rasse," in *Geschichtliche Grundbegriffe: Historisches Lexikon zur politisch-sozialen Sprache Deutschlands*, eds. Otto Brunner, Werner Conze, and Reinhart Koselleck (Stuttgart: Klett-Cotta, 1984), vol. 5, pp. 135–178.

20. See Jacob Katz, *From Prejudice to Destruction: Anti-Semitism, 1700–1933* (Cambridge: Harvard University Press, 1980), pp. 148–49; and David Sorkin, *The Transformation of German Jewry, 1780–1840* (New York: Oxford University Press, 1987), pp. 22–23.

21. Katz, *From Prejudice to Destruction*, pp. 149–151.

22. Quoted in Katz, *From Prejudice to Destruction*, p. 150.

23. Katz concludes: "The alienness of the Jews is a recurrent theme in anti-Jewish polemics." See *From Prejudice to Destruction*, p. 87.

24. Felden, "Die Uebernahme des antisemitischen Stereotyps," pp. 19–20. Rose makes a similar point, though he understands Germans to have conceived of the Jews as both the "*symbol* of everything that obstructs redemption" and the "*actual practical* obstacles to that redemption." See *Revolutionary Antisemitism in Germany from Kant to Wagner*, p. 57.

25. Felden, "Die Uebernahme des antisemitischen Stereotyps"; Sterling, *Judenhass*; and Nicoline Hortzitz, *"Früh-Antisemitismus" in Deutschland (1789–1871/72): Strukturelle Untersuchungen zu Wortschatz, Text und Argumentation* (Tübingen: Max Niemeyer Verlag, 1988), all make this point repeatedly.

26. This was Württemberg; Baden followed in 1809, Frankfurt in 1811, Prussia in 1812, and Mecklenburg, in a limited fashion, in 1813. See Sorkin, *The Transformation of German Jewry, 1780–1840*, p. 29. For a general account of the course of the Jews' emancipation, and how many of the initial emancipatory provisions were later voided, see Werner E. Mosse, "From 'Schutzjuden' to 'Deutsche Staatsbürger Jüdischen Glaubens': The Long and Bumpy Road of Jewish Emancipation in Germany," in Pierre Birnbaum and Ira Katznelson, eds., *Paths of Emancipation: Jews, States, and Citizenship* (Princeton: Princeton University Press, 1995), pp. 59–93; and Reinhard Rürup, "The Tortuous and Thorny Path to Legal Equality: 'Jew Laws' and Emancipatory Legislation in Germany from the Late Eighteenth Century," *Leo Baeck Institute Yearbook* 31 (1986): pp. 3–33.

27. For Bavaria, see James F. Harris, *The People Speak! Anti-Semitism and Emancipation in Nineteenth-Century Bavaria* (Ann Arbor: University of Michigan Press, 1994); for Baden, see Dagmar Herzog, *Intimacy and Exclusion: Religious Politics in Pre-Revolutionary Baden* (Princeton: Princeton University Press, 1996). For an account of the Hep Hep anti-Jewish riots of Würzburg, Frankfurt, and Hamburg, among other places, see Katz, *From Prejudice to Destruction*, pp. 92–104.

28. See Shmuel Almog, *Nationalism and Antisemitism in Modern Europe, 1815–1945* (London: Pergamon Press, 1990), pp. 13–16; and Peter G. J. Pulzer, *The*

Rise of Political Anti-Semitism in Germany and Austria (New York: John Wiley & Sons, 1964), pp. 226–233.

29. See Sterling, *Judenhass*, pp. 105–129; Katz, *From Prejudice to Destruction*, pp. 51–104; and Hortzitz, *"Früh-Antisemitismus" in Deutschland.*

30. Christian Wilhelm Dohm, *Ueber die bürgerliche Verbesserung der Juden* (Berlin: Friedrich Nicolai, 1781).

31. Quoted in Sorkin, *The Transformation of German Jewry, 1780–1840*, p. 25.

32. Quoted in Sorkin, *The Transformation of German Jewry, 1780–1840*, p. 25. In a similar vein, a paean to Joseph II's Austrian Edict of Toleration, which, while maintaining a strict conceptual and legal division between Jews and non-Jews, did remove important disabilities, praised Joseph II: "You make of the Jew a human being . . ." See Rose, *Revolutionary Antisemitism in Germany from Kant to Wagner*, pp. 77–79.

33. Quoted in Sorkin, *The Transformation of German Jewry, 1780–1840*, pp. 30–31.

34. In practice, emancipation proceeded piecemeal in all of the German states, with some granting more rights to the Jews than others, and some later rescinding rights granted during the initial emancipation by the French. Thus, even after the Jews were "emancipated," legally, politically, and socially, they continued to be set off from other Germans as different and inferior. The cultural prejudices continued to be codified in law and practice. See Sorkin, *The Transformation of German Jewry, 1780–1840*, p. 36.

35. Sorkin, *The Transformation of German Jewry, 1780–1840*, p. 23; see also Erb and Bergmann, *Die Nachtseite Der Judenemanzipation*, for a discussion of the "dark side" of emancipation and the arguments that undergirded it (pp. 27–28 and the next three chapters). For a discussion of the reasons of state—derived from Enlightenment notions of the state, modernity, and citizenship—that led different German states to emancipate Jews (even despite their own ministers' acceptance of the prevailing cultural cognitive model about Jews as fundamentally and disagreeably "alien"), see Mosse, "From 'Schutzjuden' to 'Deutsche Staatsbürger Jüdischen Glaubens,' " pp. 68–71, 84–87.

36. See Uriel Tal, *Christians and Jews in Germany: Religion, Politics, and Ideology in the Second Reich, 1870–1914* (Ithaca: Cornell University Press, 1975), pp. 295–298.

37. Rose writes: "The particular danger of many German "pro-Jewish" writings lies in the fact that their virtues are often only the manifest aspect of a general system of argument, of which unseen vices are an integral part. When Dohm set out so laudably his argument for Jewish rights, he did so in terms that implicitly accepted deep-seated German perceptions of Jewish 'alienness.' " See *Revolutionary Antisemitism in Germany from Kant to Wagner*, p. 77.

38. This follows closely a paragraph in Sterling, *Judenhass*, p. 85. At the beginning of the 1840s, a German newspaper summed up the promise of emancipation, the "liberal" vision of a modern Jewry: Through emancipation, "Jewry would perish" and the "very essence of Jewry would be shattered and the ground in which their religion is rooted removed; it will thus wither of itself and the synagogues will turn into Christian prayer houses."

39. Sterling, *Judenhass*, pp. 85–86; see also Alfred D. Low, *Jews in the Eyes of Germans: From the Enlightenment to Imperial Germany* (Philadelphia: Institute for the Study of Human Issues, 1979), pp. 246–247.

40. Felden, "Die Uebernahme des antisemitischen Stereotyps," pp. 109–112; and Katz, *From Prejudice to Destruction*, pp. 257–259, 267–268.

41. Tal, *Christians and Jews in Germany*, p. 296.

42. Felden, "Die Uebernahme des antisemitischen Stereotyps," p. 39; and Sterling, *Judenhass*, pp. 68–87, 117, 126.

43. The material in the last two paragraphs is based on Sterling, *Judenhass*, pp. 143–144, 148–156, 161.

44. See Mosse, "From 'Schutzjuden' to 'Deutsche Staatsbürger Jüdischen Glaubens,' " pp. 68–71.

45. For Christians' views of Jews, see Sterling, *Judenhass*, pp. 48–66.

46. For artisans, see Shulamit Volkov, *The Rise of Popular Antimodernism in Germany: The Urban Master Artisans, 1873–1896* (Princeton: Princeton University Press, 1978), esp. pp. 215–229.

47. Sterling, *Judenhass*, p. 146.

48. Low concludes his study on German antisemitism, which concentrates mainly on the views of the political elite, intellectuals, and writers, with a devastating evaluation of its ubiquity in German society, observing that few Germans avoided "some extended anti-Semitic phase and many . . . never escaped its grip. . . . Numerous Germans remained for life prisoners of their prejudicial notions; others overcame them to some extent; few liberated themselves completely." See *Jews in the Eyes of the Germans*, pp. 413–414.

49. Katz, *From Prejudice to Destruction*, p. 176.

50. Felden, "Die Uebernahme des antisemitischen Stereotyps," pp. 34–35; and Katz, *From Prejudice to Destruction*, pp. 2–3.

51. For a discussion of the petition campaign, see Harris, *The People Speak!*, pp. 123–149, especially 123–126. Sterling points out that the value of the petitions as a guide to the views of Bavarians regarding Jewish rights was contested at the time by supporters of Jewish rights, who asserted that pro-rights petitions had been confiscated by the local authorities. The investigation by the Bavarian government concluded that not all regions or people in Bavaria were against Jewish rights, that many were indeed indifferent, unless their passions were inflamed by priests and other anti-Jewish agitators (*Judenhass*, pp. 160–162). The conclusion of the investigation, even though it held that the populace was not uniformly, poisonously antisemitic, indicates how antisemitic Bavarians were, precisely because agitators could so easily induce them to antisemitic expression.

52. Harris, *The People Speak!*, p. 166.

53. Harris, *The People Speak!*, p. 169.

54. Harris, *The People Speak!*, pp. 128, 132–137, 142.

55. Harris, *The People Speak!*, p. 142.

56. Harris, *The People Speak!*, p. 137.

57. Katz, *From Prejudice to Destruction*, p. 268. In addition to general anti-Jewish movements, Germans mounted many campaigns to outlaw various Jewish practices, most notably *shchitah*, the ritual slaughtering of animals that is necessary for meat to

be kosher. Campaigns against practices considered fundamental to (Orthodox) Jewish existence were symbolic attacks on Jews themselves; they declared that foundational features of Judaism and Jewish life violated morality by putatively causing
animals to suffer needlessly. See Isaac Lewin, Michael Munk, and Jeremiah Berman,
Religious Freedom: The Right to Practice Shchitah (New York: Research Institute for
Post-War Problems of Religious Jewry, 1946).

58. In 1871, 512,000 Jews lived in the German Empire, composing 1.25 percent
of the population. By 1910, the number of Jews had risen to 615,000, yet the Jewish
portion of the by then more populous Germany had dropped to below 1 percent. See
Pulzer, *The Rise of Political Anti-Semitism*, p. 9.

59. Quoted in Hortzitz, *"Früh-Antisemitismus" in Deutschland*, p. 61.

60. Sterling, *Judenhass*, p. 51. The rendering of this "problem" in cosmological
proportions followed from the threat which Germans saw the Jews to be posing to the
moral order of society, an order which, to the Christian-minded, was bound up in the
natural order, thereby making the threat one of global proportions.

61. Felden, "Die Uebernahme des antisemitischen Stereotyps," p. 20.

62. Pulzer, *The Rise of Political Anti-Semitism*, p. 71. The culturally borne notion that the Jews use Christian blood for ritual practices has an impressive pedigree
dating back to the middle ages. See R. Po-chia Hsia, *The Myth of Ritual Murder: Jews
and Magic in Reformation Germany* (New Haven: Yale University Press, 1988).

63. See, for examples, Sterling, *Judenhass*, pp. 144–145; and Felden, "Die Uebernahme des antisemitischen Stereotyps," p. 44.

64. Sterling, *Judenhass*, p. 146.

65. Felden, "Die Uebernahme des antisemitischen Stereotyps," p. 38.

66. See Felden, "Die Uebernahme des antisemitischen Stereotyps," pp. 35–36,
47–71.

67. Quoted in Katz, *From Prejudice to Destruction*, p. 150.

68. For an analysis of the changes, see Felden, "Die Uebernahme des antisemitischen Stereotyps"; Hortztiz, *"Früh-Antisemitismus" in Deutschland*; and Katz, *From
Prejudice to Destruction*.

69. This is based on, among other sources, a reading of the material in Hortzitz,
"Früh-Antisemitismus" in Deutschland; a particularly instructive expression of the
anti-emancipationist sentiment was made by a Baden priest in the 1830s, who said
that he would rather have cholera come to his community than the emancipation of
Jews to his home (Erb and Bergmann, *Die Nachtseite Der Judenemanzipation*, p. 193).

70. Germans' conception of Jews as a "nation" with a specific, noxious "national character" is at the core of Rose's argument in *Revolutionary Antisemitism in
Germany from Kant to Wagner* about the continuity and nature of modern German
antisemitism (see esp. pp. 3–22). Rose, however, understands the predominance of
this conception of the Jews as having become the core of German antisemitism before the time of the Jews' emancipation, without any fundamental subsequent alteration in the nineteenth century save the grafting onto it of the pseudo-scientific
conception of race.

71. Felden, "Die Uebernahme des antisemitischen Stereotyps," p. 41.

72. Felden, "Die Uebernahme des antisemitischen Stereotyps," p. 71.

73. Katz, *From Prejudice to Destruction*, p. 8.

74. Sorkin, *The Transformation of German Jewry, 1780–1840*, p. 28; and Rose, *Revolutionary Antisemitism in Germany from Kant to Wagner*, pp. 12–14.

75. Sterling, *Judenhass*, p. 126. See also Erb and Bergmann, *Die Nachtseite Der Judenemanzipation*, pp. 48–52. They write that at this time, "in the popular press, a 'racism before racism' was present" (p. 50).

76. Quoted in Sterling, *Judenhass*, p. 120.

77. See Felden, "Die Uebernahme des antisemitischen Stereotyps," p. 34, on this point.

78. Steven Aschheim writes, ". . . the historical image of the Jew had never died in Germany and was available for exploitation in appropriate structural crises. Onto the traditional fear and distrust of the Talmud and ghetto Jew was grafted the notion of the modern Jew, characterless and destructive in intent." See *Brothers and Strangers: The East European Jew in German and German Jewish Consciousness, 1800–1923* (Madison: University of Wisconsin Press, 1982), p. 78.

79. See Pulzer, *The Rise of Political Anti-Semitism*, p. 50.

80. Pulzer succinctly, if imprecisely, captures the relationship between what he calls "pre-liberal, backward-looking" and "post-liberal mass-based" antisemitism: "The audience's vague and irrational image of the Jew as the enemy probably did not change much when the orators stopped talking about 'Christ-slayers' and began talking about the laws of blood. The difference lay in the effect achieved. It enabled anti-Semitism to be more elemental and uncompromising. Its logical conclusion was to substitute the gas chamber for the pogrom." See *The Rise of Political Anti-Semitism*, p. 70.

81. For an account of the charges, see Felden, "Die Uebernahme des antisemitischen Stereotyps," pp. 47–70.

82. Felden, "Die Uebernahme des antisemitischen Stereotyps," p. 51. The emphasis on the physiological, racial basis of the Jews' Jewishness became ever more pronounced in the latter part of the nineteenth century. Pictorial depictions of Jews regularly presented them in sinister and demonic forms. See, for example, Eduard Fuchs, *Die Juden in der Karikatur* (Munich: Albert Langen, 1921).

83. Felden, "Die Uebernahme des antisemitischen Stereotyps," p. 66.

84. Quoted in Felden, "Die Uebernahme des antisemitischen Stereotyps," p. 51.

85. See Sterling, *Judenhass*, pp. 113–114, 128–129.

86. Tal writes that "racial anti-Semitism and traditional Christianity, although starting from opposite poles and with no discernible principle of reconciliation, were moved by a common impulse directed either to the conversion or to the extermination of Jews." See *Christians and Jews in Germany*, p. 304. For a discussion of the relationship of various proposals for ridding Germany of Jews, see Rose, *Revolutionary Antisemitism in Germany from Kant to Wagner*, pp. 35–39.

87. Quoted in Sterling, *Judenhass*, p. 121.

88. Felden, "Die Uebernahme des antisemitischen Stereotyps," p. 68.

89. Quoted in Pulzer, *The Rise of Political Anti-Semitism*, p. 50.

90. Felden, "Die Uebernahme des antisemitischen Stereotyps," p. 69. Here he is paraphrasing a number of different writers.

91. See the table that is the final (unnumbered) page of Felden, "Die Uebernahme des antisemitischen Stereotyps." The following analysis of his data is my own.

92. To be sure, the eliminationist mind-set was capable of, and did consider, various courses of action. Eliminationist beliefs, like most others, are *multipotential*, the courses chosen depending on a host of other cognitive and non-cognitive factors. Here I merely wish to establish that the beliefs themselves—prior to and obviously independent of the Nazi state—tended strongly towards a genocidal "solution." For more instances, see Felden, "Die Uebernahme des antisemitischen Stereotyps," pp. 150–151; Hortzitz, *"Früh-Antisemitismus" in Deutschland*, p. 283; and Sterling, *Judenhass*, pp. 113–114.

93. Erb and Bergmann, *Die Nachtseite Der Judenemanzipation*, pp. 26–27.

94. *Deutsche Parteiprogramme*, ed. Wilhelm Mommsen (Munich: Isar Verlag, 1960), vol. 1, p. 84.

95. Mosse, in "From 'Schutzjuden' to 'Deutsche Staatsbürger Jüdischen Glaubens,' " writes that during the 1880s and 1890s, "there can be little doubt that without [the state's] neutrality and [its] maintenance of law and order, where necessary by force, a wave of pogroms would have swept Germany with incalculable results" (p. 90). For a vivid account of a man bursting to assault Jews physically, but who was restrained by the limits imposed by the state, see Erich Goldhagen, "The Mad Count: A Forgotten Portent of the Holocaust," *Midstream 22*, no. 2 (Feb. 1976). Goldhagen writes: "Mere words, however, did not satisfy the Count—he thirsted for action. But the pleasure of striking at Jews physically was denied to him by the Imperial Government which, while condoning barking against Jews, would not tolerate the beating of them. Count Pueckler, therefore, chose to vent his passions through make-believe gestures. At the head of a troop of mounted peasants, whom he had especially arrayed for these occasions, and to the fanfare of trumpets, he would lead cavalry charges against imaginary Jews, striking them down and trampling them under foot. It was a spectacle affording a psychic equivalent for murder. It was also a remarkable prefigurement of the Final Solution" (pp. 61–62).

96. Werner Jochmann, "Structure and Functions of German Anti-Semitism, 1878–1914," in Herbert A. Strauss, ed., *Hostages of Modernization: Studies on Modern Antisemitism, 1870–1933/39* (Berlin: Walter de Gruyter, 1993), pp. 52–53.

97. See Hans Rosenberg, "Anti-Semitism and the 'Great Depression,' 1873–1896," in Strauss, ed., *Hostages of Modernization*, p. 24.

98. Jochmann, "Structure and Functions of German Anti-Semitism," pp. 54–55 and 58.

99. Quoted in Hans-Ulrich Wehler, "Anti-Semitism and Minority Policy," in Strauss, ed., *Hostages of Modernization*, p. 30.

100. See Peter Pulzer, *Jews and the German State: The Political History of a Minority, 1848–1933* (Oxford: Basil Blackwell, 1992), pp. 44–66.

101. Jochmann, "Structure and Functions of German Anti-Semitism," p. 48.

102. See George L. Mosse, *The Crisis of German Ideology: Intellectual Origins of the Third Reich* (New York: Grosset & Dunlap, 1964), pp. 88–107.

103. Jochmann, "Structure and Functions of German Anti-Semitism," p. 58.

104. Wehler, "Anti-Semitism and Minority Policy," p. 30.

105. Felden, "Die Uebernahme des antisemitischen Stereotyps," p. 85.

106. See Pulzer, *Jews and the German State*, pp. 148–167.

107. By 1890, both the National Liberal Party and the Center Party were including antisemitic appeals in their political campaigns. Felden, "Die Uebernahme des antisemitischen Stereotyps," p. 46.

108. The Erfurt Program of Böckel's Anti-Semitic People's Party began with an unequivocal declaration of its identity and central aspiration: "The Anti-Semite Party . . . aims at the repeal, by legal means, of Jewish emancipation, the placing of Jews under an Aliens' Law, and the creation of healthy social legislation." (For the Party's eighteen-point program, see Pulzer, *The Rise of Political Anti-Semitism*, pp. 339–340).

109. Quoted in Pulzer, *The Rise of Political Anti-Semitism*, p. 119.

110. Quoted in Pulzer, *The Rise of Political Anti-Semitism*, p. 120.

111. Pulzer, *The Rise of Political Anti-Semitism*, pp. 121, 123. Of course, the Conservative Party stood for many other things, yet antisemitism in Germany was symbolically and conceptually intertwined with many other aspects of politics, including nationalism.

112. For a discussion of these issues, see Pulzer, *The Rise of Political Anti-Semitism*, pp. 194–197. He points out that even the liberal parties, while not avowedly racist, had quietly come to accept antisemitism because, if nothing else, they realized that many of their supporters were antisemites (pp. 194–195).

113. Pulzer writes: "Insofar as they had impregnated wide sections of the population with anti-Semitic ideas, the anti-Semitic parties had not only succeeded in their object but worked themselves out of a job." See *The Rise of Political Anti-Semitism*, p. 290.

114. This subject is discussed in Chapter 16. See Katz, *From Prejudice to Destruction*, for a comparative treatment of the development of antisemitism in a number of European regions.

115. Erb and Bergmann, *Die Nachtseite Der Judenemanzipation*, agree that almost all Germans during the period of their study (1780–1860) to a greater or lesser degree held the "shared conviction in the perniciousness of the Jews" and that the exterminatory calls grew out of this common cultural model (p. 196).

116. Rosenberg, "Anti-Semitism and the 'Great Depression,' " pp. 19–20.

117. See Low, *Jews in the Eyes of the Germans*, for rich material from written expressions of antisemitism; for pictorial depictions of Jews, see Fuchs, *Die Juden in der Karikatur*.

118. Werner Mosse, "From 'Schutzjuden' to 'Deutsche Staatsbürger Jüdischen Glaubens,' " writes: "In fact, during the decades that followed [emancipation] it became axiomatic—and not without justification—that the bulk of the population, particularly in rural areas where most Jews resided, disliked them and was hostile to their further emancipation" (p. 72).

Chapter 3

1. Klemens Felden, "Die Uebernahme des antisemitischen Stereotyps als soziale Norm durch die bürgerliche Gesellschaft Deutschlands (1875–1900)" (Ph.D. diss., Ruprecht-Karl-Universität, Heidelberg, 1963), p. 47.

2. See Werner Jochmann, "Die Ausbreitung des Antisemitismus in Deutschland, 1914–1923," in *Gesellschaftskrise und Judenfeindschaft in Deutschland, 1870–1945* (Hamburg: Hans Christians Verlag, 1988), p. 99. Alex Bein, *The Jewish Question: Biography of a World Problem* (New York: Herzl Press, 1990), dates the upsurge in the use of the concept "Jewish Problem" to around 1880: "In the large number of writings that appeared at that time, the concept 'Jewish Question' was again primarily used by foes of the Jews, to whom the existence of the Jews and their conduct appeared at least problematic and perhaps even dangerous" (p. 20).

3. Jews' linguistic usage was also constrained by the cognitive and linguistic models of the day, so they too were compelled to include *"Judenfrage"* in their social lexicon as well as in their printed one. "The Jewish Lexicon" of 1929 defined *"Judenfrage"* as "the totality of the problems arising out of the coexistence of the Jews with other peoples." This idiosyncratic, neutral definition denies the Jews' responsibility for the "problems" that the term's cognitive model ascribed to them. Even if the editors of this lexicon would not acknowledge and codify the true meaning of the term, when Jews heard or read the term, they, as members of this society, undoubtedly understood its full implication. See Leonore Siegele-Wenschkewitz, "Aus ein ander setzungen mit einem Stereotyp: Die Judenfrage im Leben Martin Niemöllers," in Ursula Büttner, ed., *Die Deutschen und die Judenverfolgung im Dritten Reich* (Hamburg: Hans Christians Verlag, 1992), p. 293. On the use of the term "Jewish Problem" by Germans and Jews, see Bein, *The Jewish Question*, pp. 18–21.

4. Beginning in the late nineteenth century, Germans began to focus on the eastern European Jews who were living in Germany as revealing the essence of Jewishness. Steven Aschheim writes in *Brothers and Strangers: The East European Jew in German and German Jewish Consciousness, 1800–1923* (Madison: University of Wisconsin Press, 1982): "While the caftan Jew embodied a mysterious past, the cravat Jew symbolized a frightening present" (p. 76). "Race," in their minds, linked the eastern Jews to the German Jews. Thus, the eastern Jews "served as a constant reminder of the mysterious and brooding ghetto presence" and were seen by the antisemites as the "living embodiment of a fundamentally alien, even hostile, culture" (pp. 58–59), reinforcing the Germans' cultural cognitive model about Jews.

5. Peter G. J. Pulzer, *The Rise of Political Anti-Semitism in Germany and Austria* (New York: John Wiley & Sons, 1964), p. 288. In keeping with the usage here, "Jewish Problem" has been substituted for "Jewish Question," which appears in the translation quoted.

6. See Jochmann's treatment of Germans' attacks on German Jews during the war in "Die Ausbreitung des Antisemitismus in Deutschland, 1914–1923," pp. 101–117; and Saul Friedländer, "Political Transformations During the War and Their Effect on the Jewish Question," in Herbert A. Strauss, ed., *Hostages of Modernization: Studies on Modern Antisemitism 1870–1933/39* (Berlin/New York: Walter de Gruyter, 1993), pp. 150–164. The attacks were so vicious, their themes becoming cultural truisms during Weimar, that the Jewish community believed itself compelled to respond with statistical proof that belied the antisemitic charges. See Jacob Segall, *Die deutschen Juden als Soldaten im Kriege, 1914–1918: Eine statistische Studie* (Berlin: Philo-Verlag, 1921).

7. Quoted in Jochmann, "Die Ausbreitung des Antisemitismus in Deutschland, 1914–1923," p. 101.

8. Quoted in Uwe Lohalm, "Völkisch Origins of Early Nazism: Anti-Semitism in Culture and Politics," in Strauss, ed., *Hostages of Modernization*, pp. 178, 192.

9. Lohalm, "Völkisch Origins of Early Nazism," pp. 185–186.

10. The material in this paragraph is drawn from Lohalm, "Völkisch Origins of Early Nazism," pp. 186–189.

11. Heinrich August Winkler, "Anti-Semitism in Weimar Society," in Strauss, ed., *Hostages of Modernization*, pp. 201–202.

12. Quoted in Robert Craft, "Jews and Geniuses," *New York Review of Books* 36, no. 2 (Feb. 16, 1989): p. 36. In 1929, Einstein attested, "when I came to Germany [from Zurich] fifteen years ago, I discovered for the first time that I was a Jew. I owe this discovery more to gentiles than to Jews."

13. Quoted in Lohalm, "Völkisch Origins of Early Nazism," p. 192.

14. Jochmann, "Die Ausbreitung des Antisemitismus in Deutschland, 1914–1923," p. 167. The essay is a devastating assessment of the ubiquitousness of anti-semitism throughout German society during Weimar.

15. Michael Kater, "Everyday Anti-Semitism in Prewar Nazi Germany: The Popular Bases," *YVS* 16 (1984): pp. 129–159, 133–134.

16. See Winkler, "Anti-Semitism in Weimar Society," pp. 196–198. The exception to this was the politically insignificant liberal German People's Party. Even the SPD did little to attack the Nazis' antisemitism. See Donna Harsch, *German Social Democracy and the Rise of Nazism* (Chapel Hill: University of North Carolina Press, 1993), p. 70.

17. Franz Böhm, "Antisemitismus" (lecture of Mar. 12, 1958), cited in Werner Jochmann, "Antisemitismus und Untergang der Weimarer Republik," in *Gesellschaftskrise und Judenfeindschaft in Deutschland, 1870–1945*, p. 193.

18. Max Warburg, letter to Heinrich v. Gleichen of May 28, 1931, quoted in Jochmann, "Antisemitismus und Untergang der Weimarer Republik," p. 192.

19. The Nazi Party program is reproduced in *Nazism*, pp. 14–16.

20. Adolf Hitler, *Mein Kampf* (Boston: Houghton Mifflin, 1971), p. 651.

21. Hitler, *Mein Kampf*, p. 679.

22. It is hard to know, in the mix of the many factors that drew so many Germans to the Nazis, how important the Nazis' antisemitism was for their final electoral success. For analyses of Nazi electoral support, see Jürgen W. Falter, *Hitlers Wähler* (Munich: Verlag C. H. Beck, 1991); Thomas Childers, *The Nazi Voter: The Social Foundations of Fascism in Germany, 1919–1933* (Chapel Hill: University of North Carolina Press, 1983; and Richard F. Hamilton, *Who Voted for Hitler?* (Princeton: Princeton University Press, 1982). While the most powerful proximate causes for the turn to the Nazis were undoubtedly the pressing, spectacular issues of the day—the economic depression, the political chaos, and the institutional breakdown of Weimar—there is no doubt that Hitler's virulent, lethal-sounding antisemitism did not at the very least deter Germans by the millions from throwing their support to him.

23. For election results, see Falter, *Hitlers Wähler*, pp. 31, 36.

24. A number of general analyses of German antisemitism and attitudes towards the persecution of the Jews exist. Naturally, they do not all agree with one another or with the conclusions presented here. The most important secondary analysis is David Bankier, *The Germans and the Final Solution: Public Opinion under Nazism* (Oxford: Blackwell, 1992). It contains far greater empirical support for my positions

than space permits me to offer here, and indeed puts forward aspects of the argument that I am making here, though significant differences remain between Bankier's understanding and mine. The absence from the book, for example, of a theoretical or analytical account of antisemitism or a more general discussion of the nature of cognition, beliefs, and ideologies and their relation to action leads Bankier to interpret the evidence in ways that can be contested. For a sample of the existing literature, see the many publications of Ian Kershaw, including "Antisemitismus und Volksmeinung: Reaktionen auf die Judenverfolgung," in Martin Broszat and Elke Fröhlich, eds., *Bayern in der NS-Zeit* (Munich: R. Oldenbourg Verlag, 1989), vol. 2, pp. 281–348; *Popular Opinion and Political Dissent in the Third Reich: Bavaria, 1933–1945* (Oxford: Oxford University Press, 1983), chaps. 6, 9; "German popular opinion and the 'Jewish Question,' 1939–1943: Some Further Reflections," in Arnold Paucker, ed., *Die Juden im nationalsozialistischen Deutschland: The Jews in Nazi Germany, 1933–1943* (New York: Leo Baeck Institute, 1986), pp. 365–386; see also Otto Dov Kulka and Aron Rodrigue, "The German Population and the Jews in the Third Reich: Recent Publications and Trends in Research on German Society and the 'Jewish Question,' " *YVS* 16 (1984): pp. 421–435; Kater, "Everyday Anti-Semitism in Prewar Nazi Germany"; and Robert Gellately, *The Gestapo and German Society: Enforcing Racial Policy, 1933–1945* (Oxford: Clarendon Press, 1990). Two published documentary sources which are repeatedly used in many of these studies are *Deutschland-Berichte der Sozialdemokratischen Partei Deutschlands (Sopade), 1934–1940*, vols. 1–7 (Salzhausen: Verlag Petra Nettelbeck and Frankfurt/M: Zweitausendeins, 1980) (hereafter cited as *Sopade*); and *Meldungen aus dem Reich, 1938–1945: Die geheimen Lageberichte des Sicherheitsdienstes der SS*, ed. Heinz Boberach, vols. 1–17 (Herrsching: Pawlak Verlag, 1984).

25. Melita Maschmann, *Account Rendered: A Dossier of My Former Self* (London: Abelard-Schuman, 1964), pp. 40–41.

26. Investigating the practically limitless examples of the quality and obsessiveness of the Nazis' racist antisemitism can begin with Hitler's *Mein Kampf*; see also the prominent Nazi theoretician Alfred Rosenberg, *Der Mythus des zwanzigsten Jahrhunderts* (Munich: Hohelichen Verlag, 1944); for a more popular account, see Hans Günther, *Die Rassenkunde des deutschen Volkes* (Munich: Lehmann Verlag, 1935). See also the vicious, lurid, racial antisemitism of Julius Streicher's newspaper, *Der Stürmer*, which at its greatest appeal had a circulation of 800,000, and a readership many times that number; the official Nazi Party newspaper, *Völkischer Beobachter*, was also replete with racial antisemitism. For secondary analyses, see Eberhard Jäckel, *Hitler's World View: A Blueprint for Power* (Cambridge: Harvard University Press, 1981); and Erich Goldhagen, "Obsession and *Realpolitik* in the 'Final Solution,' " *Patterns of Prejudice* 12, no. 1 (1978): pp. 1–16. William L. Combs, *The Voice of the SS: A History of the SS Journal "Das Schwarze Korps"* (New York: Peter Lang, 1986), chronicles the virulent, unrelenting antisemitism of the official organ of the movement's praetorian guard.

27. For a discussion of "social death," see Orlando Patterson, *Slavery and Social Death: A Comparative Study* (Cambridge: Harvard University Press, 1982), esp. pp. 1–14. The "social death" of Jews in Germany during the Nazi period is discussed in Chapter 5.

28. For an account of the assaults of these initial months, see Rudolf Diels, *Lucifer Ante Portas: Zwischen Severing und Heydrich* (Zurich: Interverlag, n.d.).

29. This national boycott had been preceded at the beginning of March by local boycotts in at least twelve German cities. See Gellately, *The Gestapo and German Society*, p. 102.

30. *Why I Left Germany*, by a German Jewish Scientist (London: M. M. Dent & Sons, 1934), pp. 132–133. The author, who was able to read the writing on the wall, fled Germany in 1933. The atmosphere of virtually universal hatred for the Jews left him no hope that conditions for the Jews would improve or even stabilize. Afterwards, he ruminates on how widely shared the moral and actual culpability for the anti-Jewish atmosphere and policies ought to be spread. " 'Are the people as a whole responsible for every crime committed in their name?' I asked myself. A voice within me answered: 'In this case the entire nation is responsible for a government it has brought into power, and which, in a full knowledge of what is happening, the people cheer loudly whenever an act of violence or an injustice has been committed' " (p. 182).

31. Avraham Barkai, *From Boycott to Annihilation: The Economic Struggle of German Jews, 1933–1943* (Hanover: University Press of New England, 1989), p. 17.

32. For a general account of this, see Raul Hilberg, *The Destruction of the European Jews* (New York: New Viewpoints, 1973), pp. 43–105; and Reinhard Rürup, "Das Ende der Emanzipation: die antijüdische Politik in Deutschland von der 'Machtergreifung' bis zum Zweiten Weltkrieg," in Paucker, ed., *Die Juden im nationalsozialistischen Deutschland*, pp. 97–114; for the economic exclusion and strangulation of the Jews, see Barkai, *From Boycott to Annihilation*; for the medical profession, see Michael Kater, *Doctors Under Hitler* (Chapel Hill: University of North Carolina Press, 1989), pp. 177–221.

33. Bankier, *The Germans and the Final Solution*, p. 68; Hilberg, *Destruction of the European Jews*, pp. 56–57.

34. Bankier writes: "Although in general the public recognized the necessity for some solution to the Jewish problem, large sectors found the form of persecution abhorrent." See *The Germans and the Final Solution*, p. 68.

35. Bankier, *The Germans and the Final Solution*, pp. 69–70.

36. Kershaw, *Popular Opinion and Political Dissent in the Third Reich*, pp. 142–143.

37. Cited in Fritz Stern, *Dreams and Delusions: National Socialism in the Drama of the German Past* (New York: Vintage Books, 1987), p. 180.

38. For a listing of the many legal prohibitions and restrictions under which Germans compelled the Jews of Germany to live, see Joseph Walk, ed., *Das Sonderrecht für die Juden im NS-Staat: Eine Sammlung der gesetzlichen Massnahmen und Richtlinien—Inhalt und Bedeutung* (Heidelberg: C. F. Müller Juristischer Verlag, 1981).

39. Gellately, *The Gestapo and German Society*, p. 105.

40. Kater, "Everyday Anti-Semitism in Prewar Nazi Germany," p. 145.

41. Marvin Lowenthal, *The Jews of Germany: A Story of Sixteen Centuries* (Philadelphia: The Jewish Publication Society of America, 1938), p. 411.

42. This characterization is from a Würzburg Jew's 1934 letter of complaint. Quoted in Gellately, *The Gestapo and German Society*, p. 105.

43. *Why I Left Germany,* by a German Jewish Scientist, p. 82.

44. For an account of many of the events described in this paragraph, see Kater, "Everyday Anti-Semitism in Prewar Nazi Germany," pp. 142–150.

45. Quoted in Kater, "Everyday Anti-Semitism in Prewar Nazi Germany," pp. 144–145.

46. Konrad Kwiet and Helmut Eschwege, *Selbstbehauptung und Widerstand: Deutsche Juden im Kampf um Existenz und Menschenwuerde, 1933–1945* (Hamburg: Hans Christians Verlag, 1984), p. 44.

47. Gellately describes the similar effects of similar violence in Franconia, concluding that the Jews in Germany "left the country, especially the rural areas, primarily out of a fear of violence to their persons or property. News of a beating, arrest, or damage to property travels fast in the rural and small-town milieu." See *The Gestapo and German Society*, p. 103.

48. This account follows closely Herbert Schultheis, *Die Reichskristallnacht in Deutschland: Nach Augenzeugenberichten* (Bad Neustadt a.d. Saale: Rötter Druck und Verlag, 1986), pp. 158–159. For a similar story of yet another town, Ober-Seemen, see pp. 159–160.

49. Wolf-Arno Kropat, *Kristallnacht in Hessen: Der Judenpogrom vom November 1938* (Wiesbaden: Kommission für die Geschichte der Juden in Hessen, 1988), p. 245.

50. See Kater, "Everyday Anti-Semitism in Prewar Nazi Germany," p. 148, on this point.

51. These violent urges, however, had specific targets, not merely randomly selected ones. An SA song, frequently sung, expressed the murderous wishes which the SA men harbored for Jews:

> *When Jewish blood spurts from the knife*
> *All is fine and dandy*
> *Blood must flow thick as hail.*

Could anyone in this institution or anyone who only heard this or other blood-thirsty Nazi songs have doubted that these were people, that this was a movement that meant lethal business? How could someone have supported such a movement without sharing the Nazified understanding of the nature of Jews?

52. Kater, "Everyday Anti-Semitism in Prewar Nazi Germany," p. 142.

53. Gellately, *The Gestapo and German Society*, p. 109.

54. For an account of the barring of Jews from bathing facilities, see Kater, "Everyday Anti-Semitism in Prewar Nazi Germany," pp. 156–158; see also *Nazism*, p. 531, for a Bavarian police report about one spontaneous demonstration in 1935 by German bathers demanding that Jews be banished from their pool.

55. This is Kater's conclusion, "Everyday Anti-Semitism in Prewar Nazi Germany," p. 154.

56. Kater, "Everyday Anti-Semitism in Prewar Nazi Germany," pp. 150–154, and *Doctors under Hitler*, pp. 177–221.

57. See, for example, Arye Carmon, "The Impact of Nazi Racial Decrees on the University of Heidelberg," *YVS* 11 (1976), pp. 131–163.

58. Quoted in *The Jews in Nazi Germany: A Handbook of Facts Regarding Their Present Situation* (New York: American Jewish Committee, 1935), pp. 52–53.

59. See Ingo Müller, *Hitler's Justice: The Courts of the Third Reich* (Cambridge: Harvard University Press, 1991), p. 92.

60. Müller's book, *Hitler's Justice*, provides ample evidence in support of this view. Many judges also clearly shared the more general racial biologism that was widespread in Germany, which led them to support the Nazis' lethal eugenics policies (pp. 120–125).

61. Otto Dov Kulka, "Die Nürnberger Rassengesetze und die deutsche Bevölkerung im Lichte geheimer NS-Lage- und Stimmungsberichte," *VfZ* 32 (1984), p. 623.

62. For the text of these laws, see *Nazism*, pp. 535–537. For discussions of the Nuremberg Laws and of Germans' attempts to define a Jew more generally, see Hilberg, *Destruction of the European Jews*, pp. 43–53; and Lothar Gruchmann, " 'Blutschutzgesetz' und Justiz: Zur Entstehung und Auswirkung des Nürnberger Gesetzes vom 15. September 1935," *VfZ* 31 (1983): pp. 418–442.

63. Quoted in Gellately, *The Gestapo and German Society*, pp. 109–110; see also pp. 108–111. Gellately notes that although some middle-class people thought the laws to be somewhat extreme, by and large they received them quite favorably. For a fuller discussion of Germans' reactions, see Kulka, "Die Nürnberger Rassengesetze und die deutsche Bevölkerung im Lichte geheimer NS-Lage- und Stimmungsberichte," pp. 582–624.

64. Klaus Mlynek, ed., *Gestapo Hannover meldet . . . : Polizei- und Regierungsberichte für das mittlere und südliche Niedersachsen zwischen 1933 und 1937* (Hildesheim: Verlag August Lax, 1986), p. 524. This report was prompted by the people's rage following the killing of a Swiss Nazi leader by a Jew.

65. *Sopade*, July 1938, A76.

66. *Sopade*, July 1938, A78.

67. Bankier, *The Germans and the Final Solution*, pp. 83–85.

68. See Walter H. Pehle, ed., *November 1938: From "Reichskristallnacht" to Genocide* (New York: Berg Publishers, 1991), especially the essays by Wolfgang Benz, Trude Maurer, and Uwe Dietrich Adam; for a regional study, see Kropat, *Kristallnacht in Hessen*.

69. Avraham Barkai, "The Fateful Year 1938: The Continuation and Acceleration of Plunder," in Pehle, ed., *November 1938*, pp. 116–117.

70. Kropat, *Kristallnacht in Hessen*, p. 187.

71. Kropat, *Kristallnacht in Hessen*, p. 66–74, 243–244.

72. Bankier, *The Germans and the Final Solution*, p. 86. One Communist underground leaflet explained: "Catholics were horrified to see that the burning of synagogues was frighteningly similar to the attacks of the Hitler gangs against the bishops' manses in Rothenburg, Vienna, and Munich."

73. Kropat, *Kristallnacht in Hessen*, p. 243.

74. Bernt Engelmann, *In Hitler's Germany: Everyday Life in the Third Reich* (New York: Schocken Books, 1986), p. 138.

75. Kershaw, *Popular Opinion and Political Dissent in the Third Reich*, pp. 267–271; Bankier, *The Germans and the Final Solution*, pp. 85–88; and Gellately, *The Gestapo and German Society*, p. 122.

76. Kershaw writes: "A widespread hostility to the Jews, uncritical approval of the anti-Semitic decrees of the government, but sharp condemnation of the pogrom

because of its material destruction and the tasteless hooligan character of the 'action' perpetrated by 'gutter elements' characterized the reactions of considerable sections of the population. Even many anti-Semites, including Party members, found the pogrom itself distasteful while approving of the root cause of it and of its consequences." See *Popular Opinion and Political Dissent in the Third Reich*, p. 269.

77. See Barkai, *From Boycott to Annihilation*, p. 136.

78. Bankier, *The Germans and the Final Solution*, p. 87.

79. Hermann Glaser, "Die Mehrheit hätte ohne Gefahr von Repressionen fernbleiben können," in Jörg Wollenberg, ed., *"Niemand war dabei und keiner hat's gewusst": Die deutsche Öffentlichkeit und die Judenverfolgung 1933–1945* (Munich: Piper, 1989), pp. 26–27.

80. Alfons Heck, *The Burden of Hitler's Legacy* (Frederick, Colo.: Renaissance House, 1988), p. 62.

81. Kershaw, *Popular Opinion and Political Dissent in the Third Reich*, p. 147.

82. Maschmann, *Account Rendered*, p. 56.

83. This is Erich Goldhagen's term.

84. See Bankier, *The Germans and the Final Solution*, pp. 77–78. For the legal treatment of "race defilement" in one region of Germany, see Hans Robinsohn, *Justiz als politische Verfolgung: Die Rechtsprechung in "Rassenschandefällen" beim Landgericht Hamburg, 1936–1943* (Stuttgart: Deutsche Verlags-Anstalt, 1977).

85. The account of this paragraph closely follows Bankier, *The Germans and the Final Solution*, pp. 122–123.

86. Even if some might have formally abjured "racism" as being against the universalist teachings of the Church, they accepted the central tenet of the "racist" view (which had inherent eliminationist implications), namely that the Jews could not be redeemed.

87. Bankier, *The Germans and the Final Solution*, p. 122. See also Guenter Lewy, *The Catholic Church and Nazi Germany* (New York: McGraw-Hill, 1964), pp. 285–286; and Richard Gutteridge, *The German Evangelical Church and the Jews, 1879–1950* (New York: Harper & Row, 1976), p. 233.

88. Bankier, *The Germans and the Final Solution*, p. 122.

89. This is, of course, excepting the continued existence of Jews exempted because of mixed marriages or because of mixed parentage, those in concentration camps within German borders, and the eventual return of tens of thousands of Jews at the end of the war via the death marches (which are treated in Chapters 13 and 14).

90. Anna Haag, *Das Glück zu Leben* (Stuttgart: Bonz, 1967), entry for Oct. 5, 1942. It is difficult to understand why Bankier, who also recounts this episode, concludes that "incidents of this sort substantiate the contention that day-to-day contact with a virulent, antisemitic atmosphere progressively dulled people's sensitivity to the plight of their Jewish neighbours" (*The Germans and the Final Solution*, p. 130). The incident, like so many others, provides evidence not of dulled sensitivity, but of the nature of the Germans' deeply held beliefs and their willingness to express them. That any but a small number of Germans ever possessed "sensitivity to the plight of their Jewish neighbors" during the Nazi period is an assumption which cannot be substantiated, and which, in my reading of it, is undermined by the empirical evidence which Bankier presents throughout his book.

91. Gerhard Schoenberner, ed., *Wir Haben es Gesehen: Augenzeugenberichte über Terror und Judenverfolgung im Dritten Reich* (Hamburg: Rütten & Loening Verlag, 1962), p. 300.

92. Bankier, *The Germans and the Final Solution*, p. 135.

93. Karl Ley, *Wir Glauben Ihnen: Tagebuchaufzeichnungen und Erinnerungen eines Lehrers aus dunkler Zeit* (Siegen-Volnsberg: Rebenhain-Verlag, 1973), p. 115.

94. Ruth Andreas-Friedrich, *Berlin Underground, 1938–1945* (New York: Paragon House, 1989), p. 83. Kershaw writes: "Evidence about knowledge of the fate of the Jews is, therefore, overwhelming in indicating that the availability of that knowledge was widespread." See "German Popular Opinion and the 'Jewish Question,' 1939–1943," p. 380. For a November 1942 internal report of the Nazi Party Chancellery on the news that abounded in Germany about the slaughter of Jews, see Peter Longerich, ed., *Die Ermordung der Europäischen Juden: Eine umfassende Dokumenation des Holocaust, 1941–1945* (Munich: Piper, 1989), pp. 433–434. The notion that few in Germany knew of their country's systematic slaughter of Jews is clearly contravened by much evidence, which makes it all the more surprising that this myth continues to be believed and propagated. For a treatment of this subject, see Hans-Heinrich Wilhelm, "The Holocaust in National-Socialist Rhetoric and Writings: Some Evidence against the Thesis that before 1945 Nothing Was Known about the 'Final Solution,' " *YVS* 16 (1984): pp. 95–127; and Wolfgang Benz, "The Persecution and Extermination of the Jews in the German Consciousness," in John Milfull, ed., *Why Germany? National Socialist Anti-Semitism and the European Context* (Providence: Berg Publishers, 1993), pp. 91–104, esp. 97–98; for a contrary view, see Hans Mommsen, "What did the Germans Know about the Genocide of the Jews?," in Pehle, ed., *November 1938*, pp. 187–221.

95. Marlis Steinert, *Hitlers Krieg und die Deutschen: Stimmung und Haltung der deutschen Bevölkerung im Zweiten Weltkrieg* (Düsseldorf: Econ Verlag, 1970), pp. 238–239; and Bankier, *The Germans and the Final Solution*, pp. 133–137, where he also discusses some cases in which Germans expressed sympathy for the Jews. Bankier sees many of the Germans as having been "indifferent"—"deliberately indifferent," as he emphasizes—"to a criminal act" (p. 137). As I discuss at length in Chapter 16, the concept of "indifference" is undertheorized and inappropriately applied to Germans during the Nazi period, who could not but have had views about and attitudes towards the many aspects of the persecution of the Jews, including their deportation.

96. While Catholics in general abandoned Jewish converts to Catholicism, much of the highest Church leadership remained faithful to the doctrine of baptism. See Lewy, *The Catholic Church and Nazi Germany*, pp. 284–287.

97. Quoted in Lewy, *The Catholic Church and Nazi Germany*, p. 163; see pp. 162–166 for further evidence that the Catholic Church adopted and preached the idiom of race (even if it continued to defend the primacy of God's divine law over the racial laws of humanity).

98. *Sopade*, Jan. 1936, A18.

99. *Sopade*, Jan. 1936, A17.

100. Kershaw writes: "The feeling that there *was* a 'Jewish Question', that the Jews *were* another race, and that they deserved whatever measures had been taken to counter their undue influence, and should be excluded from Germany altogether had

[by 1938–1939] spread ominously." See "German Popular Opinion and the 'Jewish Question,' 1939–1943," p. 370. See Bankier's discussion of German workers' anti-semitism, in *The Germans and the Final Solution*, pp. 89–95. His account of workers is more differentiated than the brief one presented here, yet his conclusion supports my own: "It is small wonder that workers reacted to antisemitic measures in the same way as other sectors of German society. More surprising is what also emerges . . . from . . . *Sopade* surveys: that the Nazi regime did succeed in getting significant portions of the working class to identify with Jew-hatred and even to endorse antisemitic policy" (p. 94).

101. Gutteridge, *The German Evangelical Church and the Jews, 1879–1950*, pp. 35, 39. Even in apology, after the war, the profound antisemitism could not always be suppressed. Bishop August Marahrens preached: "In matters of belief we may have been far removed from the Jews, a succession of Jews may have caused grievous harm to our people, but they ought not to have been attacked in inhuman fashion" (p. 300). (The grammatical construction is worth commenting upon: the *Jews* do the Germans harm, yet the perpetrators, namely "we" or "the Germans," drop from the clause describing the inhumanity which the Jews suffered.) The cultural cognitive model of Jews does not disappear quickly. For excerpts of the antisemitic 1948 Council of Brethren of the Evangelical Church of Germany's "Word on the Jewish Question" (. . . "In crucifying the Messiah, Israel has rejected its election and vocation [as the Chosen People] . . ."), see Julius H. Schoeps, *Leiden an Deutschland: Vom antisemitischen Wahn und der Last der Erinnerung* (Munich: Piper, 1990), p. 62.

102. Wolfgang Gerlach, *Als die Zeugen schwiegen: Bekennende Kirche und die Juden*, 2d ed. (Berlin: Institut Kirche und Judentum, 1993), pp. 30ff.

103. Klaus Gotto and Konrad Repgen, eds., *Die Katholiken und das Dritte Reich* (Mainz: Matthias-Grünewald-Verlag, 1990), p. 199.

104. Quoted in Gerlach, *Als die Zeugen schwiegen*, pp. 32–33.

105. Werner Jochmann, "Antijüdische Tradition im deutschen Protestantismus und nationalsozialistische Judenverfolgung," in *Gesellschaftskrise und Judenfeind-schaft in Deutschland, 1870–1945*, p. 272. Jochmann writes that in the years preceding Hitler's assumption of power, Protestant antisemitism was so great that "all appeals of Jews to the Christian conscience were ineffectual." When a rabbi from Kiel, for example, appealed in May 1932 to the local Ecclesiastical Office for some cooperation in working against the ever-intensifying, already powerful antisemitism, his letter did not even receive a reply (pp. 272–273).

106. Quoted in Gerlach, *Als die Zeugen schwiegen*, p. 42.

107. Wolfgang Gerlach, "Zwischen Kreuz und Davidstern: Bekennende Kirche in ihrer Stellung zum Judentum im Dritten Reich" (Ph.D. diss., Evang-Theologischen Fackultät der Universität Hamburg, 1970), endnotes, p. 11.

108. Gerlach, *Als die Zeugen schwiegen*, p. 43.

109. Quoted in Schoeps, *Leiden an Deutschland*, p. 58.

110. Friedrich Heer, *God's First Love* (Worcester: Trinity Press, 1967), p. 324.

111. Bernd Nellessen, "Die schweigende Kirche: Katholiken und Judenverfolgung," in Büttner, ed., *Die Deutschen und die Judenverfolgung im Dritten Reich*, p. 265.

112. Quoted in Lewy, *The Catholic Church and Nazi Germany*, p. 294.

113. Nellessen, "Die schweigende Kirche," p. 261.

114. Lewy, *The Catholic Church and Nazi Germany*, pp. 291–292; Gutteridge, *The German Evangelical Church and the Jews*, esp. pp. 153, 267–313; and J. S. Conway, *The Nazi Persecution of the Churches, 1933–1945* (New York: Basic Books, 1968), pp. 261–267.

115. Saul Friedländer, *Pius XII and the Third Reich: A Documentation* (New York: Alfred A. Knopf, 1966), p. 115.

116. Lewy, *The Catholic Church and Nazi Germany*, p. 282. The Church complained only that complying with the law was overtaxing priests, who received no offsetting remuneration.

117. Heer, *God's First Love*, p. 323.

118. For Protestants, see Johan M. Snoek, *The Grey Book: A Collection of Protests Against Anti-Semitism and the Persecution of Jews Issued by Non-Roman Catholic Churches and Church Leaders During Hitler[']s Rule* (Assen: Van Gorcum, 1969); for Catholics, see Lewy, *The Catholic Church and Nazi Germany*, p. 293; for France, see Michael R. Marrus and Robert O. Paxton, *Vichy France and the Jews* (New York: Schocken Books, 1983), pp. 262, 270–275.

119. Not one German Catholic was excommunicated either while or after committing crimes as great as any in human history. See Heer, *God's First Love*, p. 323.

120. See Schoeps, *Leiden an Deutschland*, p. 60.

121. Stewart W. Herman, *It's Your Souls We Want* (New York: Harper & Brothers, 1943), p. 234. Herman also mentions explicitly the slaughter of Lithuanian and Latvian Jewry.

122. Gerhard Schäfer, ed., *Landesbischof D. Wurm und der Nationalsozialistische Staat, 1940–1945: Eine Dokumentation* (Stuttgart: Calwer Verlag, 1968), p. 158.

123. *Kirchliches Jahrbuch für die Evangelische Kirche in Deutschland, 1933–1944* (Gütersloh: C. Bertelsmann Verlag, 1948), p. 481. Their racism was explicit: "Since the crucifixion of Christ to the present day, the Jews have fought against Christianity or abused and falsified it for the attainment of their selfish aims. Christian baptism does not alter at all the racial character of the Jew, his affiliation to his people, or his biological being." This does not mean that all members of the Church hierarchy conceived of the Jews in racial terms; on this point, differences existed within the churches, and undoubtedly, much confusion and vagueness characterized their views as the old dominant type of antisemitism was eroded by the new cultural model. See Gutteridge, *The German Evangelical Church and the Jews*, pp. 35–90, for a discussion of this issue. While essential points of congruence and identity existed between the two worldviews—hence the great attraction of Nazism to the Christian establishment and laity—fundamental disagreements also existed, disagreements which were repressed, denied, skirted, or harmonized in a variety of ways.

124. Some would undoubtedly argue that these men did not know of the extermination, and point to their statement that the Jews should be banished from the German domain as an indication that this was not an endorsement of genocide. The notion that they were ignorant of the ongoing killing is difficult to accept, given how widespread the knowledge of mass extermination already was, and given the many channels of information that were available to the Church leaders, which made them often among the best-informed people in the country. By the time of their proclamation, word of the systematic slaughter of Jews was out in Germany. The Germans

had already killed hundreds of thousands of Jews in the Soviet Union (the direction in which the Church leaders, employing the Nazi euphemism of the day, would "banish" the Jews). Millions of German soldiers in the Soviet Union knew of the genocide, since so many of the killings had been perpetrated out in the open, in the midst of army personnel, and since the army itself had been a full partner in the killings. The extermination was also known to the army's legion of priests and pastors, who undoubtedly reported back to their superiors. Bishop Wurm, who was in constant contact with other bishops, makes it indisputable that knowledge of the killings had reached Church leaders. In the context of Hitler's repeated, open declaration of his exterminatory intent, moreover, it is highly unlikely that Church leaders of this stature would have used, in a carefully crafted collective proclamation, the phrase "severest measures" if they had not meant extermination. The subsequent phrase "banished from German lands" in this context was but a euphemism for killing of the sort that was in standard usage, and understood by all Germans involved in the genocide. The camouflaging language rules of the regime dictated that the genocide not be called what it was in public and even in most official correspondence. So phrases like "resettlement," "sent to the East," became the ordinary code words and synonyms for extermination. Since Germany was at war and could not then banish the Jews anywhere, as these churchmen well knew, the only way to banish the Jews was to kill them.

    125. Martin Niemöller, *Here Stand I!* (Chicago: Willett, Clarke & Co., 1937), p. 195. In this sermon, Niemöller also attacks the Nazis (without naming them) by likening them to the Jews! How evil are these Jews? They are responsible, in Niemöller's view, not just for "the blood of Jesus and the blood of all his messengers" but for still much more, namely for "the blood of all the righteous men who were ever murdered because they testified to the holy will of God against tyrannical human will" (p. 197). Niemöller serves as an exemplar of the committed anti-Nazi who was a committed antisemite.

    126. Niemöller, unlike most German antisemites, took an ethical stance that led him to caution against taking retribution on the Jews, which, in his view, justly could be done only by God. After saying this, however, he continued with vituperative condemnation of the Jews who, among other things, would be cursed for eternity for having crucified Jesus. For a discussion of Niemöller's antisemitism, see Gutteridge, *The German Evangelical Church and the Jews*, pp. 100–104.

    127. Quoted in Harmut Ludwig, "Die Opfer unter dem Rad Verbinden: Vor- und Entstehungsgeschichte, Arbeit und Mitarbeiter des 'Büro Pfarrer Grüber' " (Habil., Berlin, 1988), pp. 73–74.

    128. Quoted in Schoeps, *Leiden an Deutschland*, p. 58. In a 1967 letter, Barth confessed "that in personal encounters with living Jews (even Jewish Christians!) I have always, so long as I can remember, had to suppress a totally irrational aversion . . ." Karl Barth, *Letters, 1961–1968* (Grand Rapids: William B. Eerdmans, 1981), p. 262.

    129. Snoek, *The Grey Book*, p. 113.

    130. Jochmann, "Antijüdische Tradition im deutschen Protestantismus und nationalsozialistische Judenverfolgung," pp. 273–74.

    131. Schoeps, *Leiden an Deutschland*, p. 61.

132. Quoted in Gutteridge, *The German Evangelical Church and the Jews*, p. 304. In a 1945 sermon, Niemöller similarly condemned the thoroughgoing antisemitism of the Church. If the fourteen thousand Evangelical pastors in Germany, he said, had recognized "at the beginning of the Jewish persecutions . . . that it was the Lord Jesus Christ Who was being persecuted . . . the number of victims might well have been only some ten thousand" (pp. 303–304). As Niemöller understood, the unwillingness of the Christian leadership to speak out and work on behalf of Jews was not primarily for fear of the regime, but for a more fundamental reason: the men of the cloth did not condemn the eliminationist measures that were being pursued in their own name.

133. Report of Aug. 7, 1944, quoted in Christof Dipper, "The German Resistance and the Jews," *YVS* 16 (1984): p. 79.

134. Quoted in Dipper, "The German Resistance and the Jews," p. 78.

135. Quoted in Dipper, "The German Resistance and the Jews," p. 79.

136. *In der Stunde Null: Die Denkschrift des Freiburger "Bonhoeffer-Kreises,"* ed. Helmut Thielicke (Tübingen: Mohr, 1979), pp. 147–151. For a discussion of the status of this proposal, see Dipper, "The German Resistance and the Jews," p. 77.

137. The characterization of the resistance presented here is substantiated by Dipper, "The German Resistance and the Jews." See esp. pp. 60, 71–72, 75–76, 81, 83–84, 91–92.

138. Kwiet and Eschwege, *Selbstbehauptung und Widerstand*, p. 48. For the extent of working-class antisemitism and support of the eliminationist program, see Bankier, *The Germans and the Final Solution*, pp. 89–95.

139. Bankier, *The Germans and the Final Solution*, notes this phenomenon among the working class, writing that many self-conceived non-Nazis "nevertheless agreed with the drastic curtailment of Jews' rights and their separation from the German nation. Even a good many socialists who disapproved of the Third Reich's brutal methods believed that 'it is not so terrible to treat the Jews in this manner' " (p. 94).

140. See Chapter 11 for a more extensive discussion of this topic.

141. Gellately, *The Gestapo and German Society*, p. 251.

142. Gellately, *The Gestapo and German Society*, pp. 216–252.

143. Gellately, *The Gestapo and German Society*, pp. 226–227.

144. Gellately, *The Gestapo and German Society*, p. 252.

145. Quoted in Gellately, *The Gestapo and German Society*, pp. 248–249.

146. Gellately, *The Gestapo and German Society*, pp. 242–243. He says that it was especially religious Germans who uttered such criticism.

147. Quoted in Gellately, *The Gestapo and German Society*, p. 226.

148. Kershaw, *Popular Opinion and Political Dissent in the Third Reich*, pp. 205–208. See also Jeremy Noakes, "The Oldenburg Crucifix Struggle of November 1936: A Case Study of Opposition in the Third Reich," in Peter D. Stachura, ed., *The Shaping of the Nazi State* (London: Croom Helm, 1978), pp. 210–233. A still more bitter struggle over crucifixes occurred between April and September 1941 in Bavaria, coincident with the beginning of the Germans' genocidal killing of Jews. The struggle ended in a resounding defeat for the regime. See Kershaw, *Popular Opinion and Political Dissent in the Third Reich*, pp. 340–357. The protesters, although

violently opposed to the Nazis' religious policies, made their *ideological support* for the regime's most general goals clear enough, with frequent expressions of their passionate anti-communism and, less frequently, of racism. One anonymous postcard sent to the Bavarian Minister President echoes the axiomatic attribution of blame to the Jews for Bolshevism, while expressing its support for the regime: "The campaign against Jewish Bolshevism is in our eyes a crusade. . . ." It was signed "The Catholics of Bavaria" (Kershaw, *Popular Opinion and Political Dissent in the Third Reich*, p. 356).

149. Bankier, *The Germans and the Final Solution*, p. 17.

150. See Kershaw, *Popular Opinion and Political Dissent in the Third Reich*, pp. 66–110.

151. Kershaw, *Popular Opinion and Political Dissent in the Third Reich*, p. 90.

152. See Bankier, *The Germans and the Final Solution*, pp. 20–26.

153. Kershaw's book, *Popular Opinion and Political Dissent in the Third Reich*, relies heavily on these reports. The reports, reproduced in the seventeen-volume *Meldungen aus dem Reich, 1938–1945*, contain a deluge of statements expressing disagreement with governmental policies and discontent on an enormously wide variety of subjects.

154. Kershaw, *Popular Opinion and Political Dissent in the Third Reich*, p. 8. This and much other evidence indicate that the degree of intimidation that existed for ordinary Germans during the Nazi period has generally been exaggerated.

155. See Henry Friedlander, *The Origins of Nazi Genocide: From Euthanasia to the Final Solution* (Chapel Hill: University of North Carolina Press, 1995), pp. 111ff.; Michael Burleigh, *Death and Deliverance: Euthanasia in Germany c. 1900–1945* (Cambridge: Cambridge University Press, 1994), pp. 162–180; Kershaw, *Popular Opinion and Political Dissent in the Third Reich*, pp. 334–340; Lewy, *The Catholic Church and Nazi Germany*, pp. 263–267; and Ernst Klee *"Euthanasie" im NS-Staat: Die "Vernichtung lebensunwerten Lebens"* (Frankfurt/M: Fischer Verlag, 1983), pp. 294–345. The regime's killing of "life unworthy of living," though formally suspended, did continue with greater concealment in a program known as "Aktion 14f13." Still, Germans' moral opposition to and political protest against these murders led to the sparing of many Germans' lives.

156. Germans' opposition to the killing of the mentally ill and the handicapped was, of course, a consequence of their rejection of important aspects of Nazi biological racism. As far as these Germans were concerned, the victims were German people, possessing the right to life and to decent care that such membership brought. This is a salient example of the inability of the Nazi regime to *transform* Germans' deeply rooted beliefs and values and to get them to acquiesce in a policy merely because the state deemed it to be appropriate and necessary. This example alone belies the "brainwashing" thesis regarding antisemitism that is popular among interpreters of this period.

157. See Nathan Stoltzfus, "Dissent in Nazi Germany," *The Atlantic Monthly* 270, no. 3 (September 1992): pp. 86–94.

158. For a discussion of the substantial influence of public opinion on the regime's policies, see Bankier, *The Germans and the Final Solution*, pp. 10–13.

159. Bankier also makes this point in *The Germans and the Final Solution*, p. 27.

160. See Ian Kershaw, *The "Hitler Myth"* (Oxford: Clarendon Press, 1987), esp. p. 147.

161. Kershaw, *Popular Opinion and Political Dissent in the Third Reich*, pp. 176–177. Similarly, he concludes that widespread Protestant abhorrence of the Nazis' anti-Christian character and policies went hand in hand with enthusiastic support of many of the national political goals which they shared with the Nazis (p. 184). Kershaw also concludes that vocal middle-class discontent with policies of the regime was perfectly compatible with, indeed was often accompanied by, enthusiastic support for Nazism (pp. 131, 139).

162. A major, if not the major, source for such statements of discontent, namely the Social Democratic Party's reports on Germany (*Sopade*), should be read with circumspection for two related reasons. The Party's agents were obviously eager and ideologically disposed to finding among the German people—especially among the working class—evidence of dissent from the Nazi regime and its policies. It is even more likely that the writers of the reports were prone to make the interpretive mistakes, discussed presently in the text, that historians of the period have made when trying to make sense of Germans' criticism of the eliminationist enterprise, such as it was. They were likely to misinterpret criticism of specific policies as being synonymous with a rejection of antisemitism and of the eliminationist goals in general. If historians, with schooled analytical and interpretive skills, have made this mistake, then it is no surprise that these hopeful Social Democratic reporters would also err in this manner. Therefore, the general evaluative and interpretive judgments to this effect that can be found in the reports should be seen to be far less reliable than the particular episodes that the agents report, on which they presumably based their evaluations. These positive general evaluations and interpretations have already been filtered through their distorting lenses, lenses which held that the draconian Nazi terror dictatorship was repressing the majority of the German people. The individual episodes that the agents report—the less interpretively tainted, "raw" data—generally conform to one of the forms discussed presently in the text, and therefore do not substantiate the overly eager positive general interpretations that the Social Democrats occasionally offered that cast doubt on Germans' antisemitism. It should be noted that these reports also contain much to suggest explicitly that antisemitism was rife among the German people, including general statements to this effect. Some of this has been presented earlier in the chapter.

163. See, for examples, Hans Mommsen and Dieter Obst, "Die Reaktion der deutschen Bevölkerung auf die Verfolgung der Juden, 1933–1945," in Hans Mommsen and Susanne Willems, eds., *Herrschaftsalltag im Dritten Reich: Studien und Texte* (Düsseldorf: Schwann, 1988), pp. 378–381.

164. Mlynek, ed., *Gestapo Hannover meldet . . .* , p. 411.

165. Analogous criticism was voiced against the brand of antisemitism that *Der Stürmer* purveyed in every issue. Regular protests against its quasi-pornographic, lurid antisemitic accounts and caricatures came from the most inveterate antisemites and Nazis of all ranks, because they found *Der Stürmer*'s antisemitism obscene and concluded that it was endangering the moral health of Germans, especially of German youth. *Das Schwarze Korps*, the official organ of the SS, the most ideologically radical of all Nazi papers and naturally also a virulently antisemitic one, in June 1935 upbraided *Der Stürmer* in an article entitled "The Antisemitism That Causes Us Harm." Even the commandant of Auschwitz, Rudolf Höss, who presided over the

mass murder of hundreds of thousands of Jews, was repelled by the character of its antisemitism. Clearly, the objection to aspects of Nazi antisemitic expression or policy did not logically or, as a matter of fact, generally mean a rejection of eliminationist antisemitism itself. See *Kommandant in Auschwitz: Autobiographische Aufzeichnungen des Rudolf Höss*, ed. Martin Broszat (Munich: Deutscher Taschenbuch Verlag, 1963), p. 112.

166. Heinz Boberach, "Quellen für die Einstellung der deutschen Bevölkerung und die Judenverfolgung, 1933–1945," in Büttner, ed., *Die Deutschen und die Judenverfolgung im Dritten Reich*, p. 38.

167. It was not unknown, after bombing raids, for Germans to assault Jews whom they came upon in the street. See Ursula Büttner, "Die deutsche Bevölkerung und die Juden Verfolgung, 1933–1945," in Büttner, ed., *Die Deutschen und die Judenverfolgung im Dritten Reich*, p. 78.

168. *Sopade*, Feb. 1938, A67.

169. For some general ethical statements by the German Catholic leadership against killing, see Burkhard van Schewick, "Katholische Kirche und nationalsozialistische Rassenpolitik," in Gotto and Repgen, eds., *Die Katholiken und das Dritte Reich*, p. 168; and Lewy, *The Catholic Church and Nazi Germany*, pp. 291–292.

170. Schäfer, ed., *Landesbischof D. Wurm und der Nationalsozialistische Staat, 1940–1945*, p. 162.

171. Schäfer, ed., *Landesbischof D. Wurm und der Nationalsozialistische Staat, 1940–1945*, p. 312. Wurm's confessional statements, it should be emphasized, were not merely artful constructs concocted for the sensibilities of his audience. They represented his true beliefs. See Gutteridge, *The German Evangelical Church and the Jews 1879–1950*, pp. 186–187, 246.

172. Nur. Doc. 1816-PS, *IMT*, vol. 28, p. 518; see also pp. 499–500.

173. For an overview, summary, and examples of the sources and data on the Germans' attitudes towards Jews and their persecution, see Boberach, "Quellen für die Einstellung der deutschen Bevölkerung und die Judenverfolgung, 1933–1945," pp. 31–49. Space does not permit me to analyze in greater detail the statements of Germans that have been interpreted by many to mean that Germans were not antisemites or did not approve of the eliminationist program. Most such criticisms can easily be shown to have been of the non-principled sort that I have just summarized, examples of which I have already discussed in this chapter (during the treatment, for example, of *Kristallnacht*, the churches, and the resistance to Hitler). In fact, as I have shown with these examples, the comparatively rare misgivings that Germans did express so often betray them to have been eliminationist antisemites.

174. For a discussion of some such people, see Wolfgang Benz, "Überleben im Untergrund, 1943–1945," in Wolfgang Benz, ed., *Die Juden in Deutschland, 1933–1945: Leben unter nationalsozialistischer Herrschaft* (Munich: Verlag C. H. Beck, 1988), pp. 660–700. Karl Ley, a schoolteacher, who inscribed into his diary his opposition to the eliminationist persecution of the Jews, knew himself to be so isolated in his views that he recorded, at the late date of December 15, 1941, that he had just discovered that he was not all alone in his opposition; someone else finally expressed her own condemnation of the persecution. See *Wir Glauben Ihnen*, p. 116.

175. Boberach's interpretation that the evidence on the German public's antisemitism indicates less widespread antisemitism than my reading of it runs afoul of

this striking difference in Germans' utterances regarding non-Jewish foreigners and Jews, which he himself notes in the concluding paragraph of his essay on the subject. See "Quellen für die Einstellung der deutschen Bevölkerung und die Judenverfolgung, 1933–1945," p. 44. For some examples when Germans' did express sympathy, see Konrad Kwiet, "Nach dem Pogrom: Stufen der Ausgrenzung," in Benz, ed., *Die Juden in Deutschland, 1933–1945*, pp. 619–625.

176. For an illustrative compendium, see C. C. Aronsfeld, *The Text of the Holocaust: A Study of the Nazis' Extermination Propaganda, from 1919–1945* (Marblehead, Mass.: Micah Publications, 1985).

177. For a discussion of injury done to people's dignity, see James C. Scott, *Domination and the Arts of Resistance: Hidden Transcripts* (New Haven: Yale University Press, 1990), pp. 112–115.

178. Since J. L. Austin's discussion of "speech acts" in *How to Do Things with Words* (Cambridge: Harvard University Press, 1962), the sharp distinction between "speaking" and "acting" has been broken down. Speech, especially speech which intends to persuade or to do harm, is action as much as raising one's hand in anger is. Thus, verbal violence, with its acknowledged capacity to do great harm, is really to be seen as on a continuum with physical acts of violence. In fact, certain violent promises (such as a known murderer's threat to kill someone) would undoubtedly be seen as being more harmful than certain acts of physical violence.

179. "Die Unlösbarkeit der Judenfrage," quoted in Ludger Heid, "Die Juden sind unser Unglück!: Der moderne Antisemitismus in Kaiserreich und Weimarer Republik," in Christina von Braun and Ludger Heid, eds., *Der ewige Judenhass: Christlicher Antijudaismus, Deutschnationale Judenfeindlichkeit, Rassistischer Antisemitismus* (Stuttgart: Burg Verlag, 1990), p. 128.

180. Ludwig Lewisohn, "The Assault on Civilization," in Pierre van Paassen and James Waterman Wise, eds., *Nazism: An Assault on Civilization* (New York: Harrison Smith and Robert Haas, 1934), pp. 156–157.

181. Dorothy Thompson, "The Record of Persecution," in van Paassen and Wise, eds., *Nazism*, p. 12. The British newspaper *The Times* made some similar observations in November 1935: "Unless some attempt is made in high quarters to check the ferocity of the anti-Semitic fanatics," the Jews "will be condemned, as it were, to run round blindly in circles until they die. This is the process to which the term 'cold pogrom' has been applied." Quoted in Gellately, *The Gestapo and German Society*, pp. 108–109. See Heer, *God's First Love*, p. 323, for another prediction of the Jews' extermination.

182. Quoted in Gerd Korman, ed., *Hunter and Hunted: Human History of the Holocaust* (New York: Viking, 1973), p. 89.

183. For discussions of Kittel's lecture, see Robert P. Ericksen, *Theologians Under Hitler: Gerhard Kittel, Paul Althaus and Emanuel Hirsch* (New Haven: Yale University Press, 1985), pp. 55–58; and Ino Arndt, "Machtübernahme und Judenboykott in der Sicht evangelischer Sonntagsblätter," *Miscellanea: Festschrift für Helmut Krausnick zum 75. Geburtstag* (Stuttgart: Deutsche Verlags-Anstalt, 1980), pp. 27–29.

184. Quoted in Gerlach, *Als die Zeugen schwiegen*, p. 112.

185. Even Bankier, *The Germans and the Final Solution*, who recognizes the widespread nature of racist antisemitism in Germany and its eliminationist conclusions, writes: "The Nazis' exhortations to endorse their solution to the Jewish question thus failed" (p. 156).

186. See Kershaw, *Popular Opinion and Political Dissent in the Third Reich*, p. 370.

187. Heck, *The Burden of Hitler's Legacy*, p. 87.

Chapter 4

1. Because this chapter presents a new interpretation of known developments and of existing data, I do not feel obliged to cite in great detail the primary sources, the contending positions of others, or even arguments (and the data) that could be adduced against my line of interpretation. They are well known in the literature. The notes to this chapter thus provide minimal references to the works that contain information on the events discussed here—even if these works' interpretations often conflict with my own.

2. For Hitler's enormous popularity and the legitimacy that it helped engender for the regime, see Ian Kershaw, *The "Hitler Myth"* (Oxford: Clarendon Press, 1987), esp. p. 258.

3. For a summary of the various positions that have been taken on this topic, as well as a judicious evaluation, see Ian Kershaw, *The Nazi Dictatorship: Problems and Perspectives of Interpretation*, 3d ed. (London: Edward Arnold, 1993), pp. 59–79.

4. For treatments of this subject, see Edward N. Peterson, *The Limits of Hitler's Power* (Princeton: Princeton University Press, 1969), and Dieter Rebentisch, *Führerstaat und Verwaltung im Zweiten Weltkrieg* (Wiesbaden: F. Steiner Verlag, 1989).

5. For persuasive accounts supporting this conclusion, see David Bankier, "Hitler and the Policy-Making Process in the Jewish Question," *HGS* 3, no. 1 (1988): pp. 1–20; see also Avraham Barkai, *From Boycott to Annihilation: The Economic Struggle of German Jews, 1933–1943* (Hanover: University Press of New England, 1989), on the development of Jewish policy in the 1930s, and Christopher R. Browning, "Beyond 'Intentionalism' and 'Functionalism': The Decision for the Final Solution Reconsidered," *The Path to Genocide: Essays on Launching the Final Solution* (Cambridge: Cambridge University Press, 1992), esp. pp. 120–121, on the 1939 to 1942 period.

6. Reginald H. Phelps, "Hitlers 'Gundlegende' Rede über den Antisemitismus," *VfZ* 16, no. 4 (1968): p. 417. It is worth noting that the word that Hitler used for "removal" is *"Entfernung,"* which also means, euphemistically, "liquidation," as in killing. Hitler sarcastically said that they would "grant" the Jews the right to live (as if this needed to be said) and would happily let them live among other nations.

7. See Eberhard Jäckel, ed., *Hitler: Sämtliche Aufzeichnungen 1905–1924* (Stuttgart: Deutsche Verlags-Anstalt, 1980), pp. 119–120. Hitler's words have been preserved in notes taken at the meeting by an agent of the intelligence service of the police.

8. The concept of "social death" is taken from Orlando Patterson, *Slavery and Social Death: A Comparative Study* (Cambridge: Harvard University Press, 1982), esp. pp. 1–14. The character of the social death of Jews is discussed in the next chapter.

9. Barkai, *From Boycott to Annihilation*, p. 25.

10. Barkai shows convincingly that the arguments which maintain that the anti-Jewish measures proceeded in fits and starts, and that they were often pushed along by pressure created at the local level, are untenable. Instead, the major elements of the anti-Jewish legal, social, cultural, and economic measures were decided upon in Berlin, and were being applied and tightened throughout the 1930s, proceeding at a consistent, if not always entirely even, pace. See *From Boycott to Annihilation*, esp. pp. 56–58, 125–133. For Hitler's role in this, see Bankier, "Hitler and the Policy-Making Process on the Jewish Question."

11. Barkai, *From Boycott to Annihilation*, pp. 25–26.

12. See Barkai, *From Boycott to Annihilation*, pp. 54–108, 116–133.

13. For a compilation, see Joseph Walk, ed., *Das Sonderrecht für die Juden im NS-Staat: Eine Sammlung der gesetzlichen Massnahmen und Richtlinien—Inhalt und Bedeutung* (Heidelberg: C. F. Müller Juristischer Verlag, 1981).

14. For a discussion of these matters, see Raul Hilberg, *The Destruction of the European Jews* (New York: New Viewpoints, 1973), pp. 43–53; and Lothar Gruchmann, " 'Blutschutzgesetz' und Justiz: Zur Entstehung und Auswirkung des Nürnberger Gesetzes vom 15. September 1935," *VfZ* 31 (1983): pp. 418–442.

15. *Nazism*, p. 1109.

16. See Philip Friedman, "The Jewish Badge and the Yellow Star in the Nazi Era," in *Roads to Extinction: Essays on the Holocaust* (Philadelphia: Jewish Publication Society, 1980), pp. 11–33.

17. Barkai, *From Boycott to Annihilation*, pp. 142–143.

18. Quoted in Richard Breitman, *The Architect of Genocide: Himmler and the Final Solution* (New York: Alfred A. Knopf, 1991), p. 154.

19. See Adolf Hitler, *Mein Kampf* (Boston: Houghton Mifflin, 1971), pp. 621–625 for Hitler's views on how the Jews mobilize the other great powers against Germany.

20. For opposing interpretations, see Karl A. Schleunes, *The Twisted Road to Auschwitz: Nazi Policy Toward German Jews, 1933–1939* (Urbana: University of Illinois Press, 1990); Uwe Dietrich Adam, *Judenpolitik im Dritten Reich* (Düsseldorf: Droste Verlag, 1972); and Hans Mommsen, "The Realization of the Unthinkable: the 'Final Solution of the Jewish Question' in the Third Reich," in Gerhard Hirschfeld, ed., *The Policies of Genocide: Jews and Soviet Prisoners of War in Nazi Germany* (London: Allen & Unwin, 1986).

21. For accounts of *Kristallnacht*, see Walter H. Pehle, ed., *November 1938: From "Reichskristallnacht" to Genocide* (New York: Berg Publishers, 1991); and Herbert Schultheis, *Die Reichskristallnacht in Deutschland: Nach Augenzeugenberichten* (Bad Neustadt a.d. Saale: Rötter Druck und Verlag, 1986).

22. Given the immediate announcement of such intentions and Hitler's January 30, 1939, speech (discussed below), it may well have been that *Kristallnacht* was understood to have initiated the new, more deadly eliminationist phase.

23. *Das Schwarze Korps*, Nov. 24, 1938, quoted in Breitman, *The Architect of Genocide*, p. 58.

24. Nur. Doc. 1816-PS, *IMT*, vol. 28, pp. 538–539.

25. Genocidal thinking was clearly in the air, especially that which the SS breathed. Breitman has shown that within the SS, the turning to the explicitly exter-

minationist variant for "solving" the "Jewish Problem" was already under way before the war. See *The Architect of Genocide*, pp. 55–65.

26. Mr. Ogilvie-Forbes to Lord Halifax, Foreign Secretary, on Nov. 17, 1938, quoted in C. C. Aronsfeld, *The Text of the Holocaust: A Study of the Nazis' Extermination Propaganda, from 1919–1945* (Marblehead, Mass.: Micah Publications, 1985), p. 78, n. 280.

27. On January 21, 1939, Hitler told the Czech Foreign Minister the same thing. See Werner Jochmann, "Zum Gedenken an die Deportation der deutschen Juden," in *Gesellschaftskrise und Judenfeindschaft in Deutschland, 1870–1945* (Hamburg: Hans Christians Verlag, 1988), p. 256.

28. *Nazism*, p. 1049.

29. Jochmann, "Zum Gedenken an die Deportation der deutschen Juden," in *Gesellschaftskrise und Judenfeindschaft in Deutschland, 1870–1945*, p. 256.

30. For an account of the so-called Euthanasia program, see Ernst Klee, *"Euthanasie" im NS-Staat: Die "Vernichtung lebensunwerten Lebens"* (Frankfurt/M: Fischer Verlag, 1983).

31. Robert N. Proctor, *Racial Hygiene: Medicine under the Nazis* (Cambridge: Harvard University Press, 1988), pp. 177–185; see pp. 95–117 on the regime's sterilization of around four hundred thousand people deemed unfit to propagate.

32. Werner Jochmann, ed., *Adolf Hitler: Monologe im Führer-Hauptquartier, 1941–1944* (Hamburg: Albrecht Knaus Verlag, 1980), p. 293.

33. As implausible as it is, this seems to be the belief of all those who maintain that Hitler first developed the desire to exterminate European Jewry sometime in 1941.

34. For accounts of these years, see Browning, "Nazi Resettlement Policy and the Search for a Solution to the Jewish Question, 1939–1941," in *The Path to Genocide*, pp. 3–27; Breitman, *The Architect of Genocide*, pp. 116–144; and Philippe Burrin, *Hitler and the Jews: The Genesis of the Holocaust* (London: Edward Arnold, 1994), pp. 65–92.

35. See Ian Kershaw, "Improvised Genocide? The Emergence of the 'Final Solution' in the 'Warthegau,' " *Transactions of the Royal Historical Society*, 6th ser., no. 2 (1992): pp. 56ff.; and Browning, "Nazi Resettlement Policy."

36. See Helmut Heiber, ed., "Der Generalplan Ost," *VfZ* 6 (1958): pp. 281–325; and Browning, "Nazi Resettlement Policy."

37. *Nazism*, p. 1050; and Christopher R. Browning, *The Final Solution and the German Foreign Office: A Study of Referat D III of Abteilung Deutschland, 1940–1943* (New York: Holmes & Meier, 1978), p. 38.

38. Jochmann, ed., *Adolf Hitler*, p. 41.

39. For Hitler's geostrategic considerations during these years, see Klaus Hildebrand, *The Foreign Policy of the Third Reich* (Berkeley: University of California Press, 1973), pp. 91–104; Norman Rich, *Hitler's War Aims: Ideology, the Nazi State, and the Course of Expansion* (New York: Norton, 1973) vol. 1, pp. 157–164; for a contrary view, see Gerhard L. Weinberg, "Hitler and England, 1933–1945: Pretense and Reality," *German Studies Review* 8 (1985): pp. 299–309.

40. Nur. Doc. 3363-PS, quoted in *Nazism*, p. 1051.

41. See Hilberg, *The Destruction of the European Jews*, pp. 144–156; Helge Grabitz and Wolfgang Scheffler, *Letzte Spuren: Ghetto Warschau, SS-Arbeitslager*

Trawniki, Aktion Erntefest (Berlin: Edition Hentrich, 1988), pp. 283–284; and "Ghetto," *Encyclopedia of the Holocaust*, ed. Israel Gutman (New York: Macmillan, 1990), pp. 579–582. For a dissenting view, see Browning, "Nazi Ghettoization Policy in Poland, 1939–1941," in *The Path to Genocide*, pp. 28–56.

42. See Hilberg, *The Destruction of the European Jews*, pp. 125–174; Czesław Madajczyk, *Die Okkupationspolitik Nazideutschlands in Polen, 1939–1945* (Berlin: Akademie-Verlag Berlin, 1987) pp. 365–371; Browning, "Nazi Resettlement Policy," pp. 8ff.; and "Denkschrift Himmlers über die Behandlung der Fremdvölkischen im Osten (Mai 1940)," *VfZ* 5, no. 2 (1957): p. 197.

43. Hilberg, *The Destruction of the European Jews*, p. 149. (The final sentence is my translation.)

44. Seyss-Inquart report, Nov. 20, 1939, Nur. Doc. 2278-PS, in *IMT*, vol. 30, p. 95. The quotation from the report is a paraphrase of the District Governor's words. For discussions of these issues, see Philip Friedman, "The Lublin Reservation and the Madagascar Plan: Two Aspects of Nazi Jewish Policy During the Second World War," in *Roads to Extinction*, pp. 34–58; Jonny Moser, "Nisko: The First Experiment in Deportation," *Simon Wiesenthal Center Annual* 2 (1985): pp. 1–30; Leni Yahil, "Madagascar—Phantom of a Solution for the Jewish Question," in Bela Vago and George L. Mosse, eds., *Jews and Non-Jews in Eastern Europe, 1918–1945* (New York: John Wiley & Sons, 1974), pp. 315–334.

45. Browning, "Nazi Resettlement Policy," is certainly correct that this period should not be seen as an interlude (pp. 26–27), yet his interpretation of the period's significance is to be doubted.

46. Isaiah Trunk, *Judenrat: The Jewish Councils in Eastern Europe under Nazi Occupation* (New York: Stein & Day, 1977), writes: "Nowhere in the ghettos was it possible to sustain life on the allotted rations. Not only were the normal rations infinitesimal—many ghettos, as mentioned, received no food whatsoever for long stretches of time, and large quantities of supplies unfit for human consumption were delivered" (p. 104). For an overview of the conditions in ghettos, which were already deadly, see pp. 149–155.

47. It is probably also not a coincidence that March and April 1941 saw the ghettoization of the Jews of the *Generalgouvernement*, as a preparatory phase for Barbarossa and for the systematic onslaught against the Jews that was to begin at the same time. For the pattern of ghettoization, see Grabitz and Scheffler, *Letzte Spuren*, pp. 283–284.

48. There is enormous controversy over when Hitler took the decision to slaughter Soviet Jewry and all of European Jewry. Richard Breitman also dates Hitler's decision as having occurred during this period. See *The Architect of Genocide*, pp. 153–166, 247–248, and his subsequent article "Plans for the Final Solution in Early 1941," *German Studies Review* 17, no. 3 (Oct. 1994): pp. 483–493, for additional evidence that the decision to exterminate European Jewry had been taken by early 1941. For some of the now extensive discussion of this issue and dissent from the position presented here, see Browning, *The Path to Genocide*, esp. "Beyond 'Intentionalism' and 'Functionalism' " and "The Decision Concerning the Final Solution," in *Fateful Months: Essays on the Emergence of the Final Solution* (New York: Holmes & Meier, 1985), pp. 8–38; and Christopher R. Browning, "The Euphoria of Victory and the Final Solution: Summer–Fall 1941," *German Studies Review* 17, no. 3 (Oct. 1994), pp. 473–481; and Burrin, *Hitler and the Jews*, esp. pp. 115–131.

49. Breitman, "Plans for the Final Solution in Early 1941," pp. 11–12. Breitman argues persuasively that this "Final Solution project" could not have been anything but the program of systematic extermination which began that summer and fall (pp. 11–17).

50. Max Domarus, *Hitler: Reden und Proklamationen, 1932–1945* (Munich: Süddeutscher Verlag, 1965), vol. 4, p. 1663.

51. That was at the anniversary celebration of the Beer Hall Putsch, where Hitler reminded his listeners: "I have . . . again and again stated my view that the hour would come when we shall remove this people [the Jews] from the ranks of our nation" (quoted in Eberhard Jäckel, *Hitler's World View: A Blueprint for Power* [Cambridge: Harvard University Press, 1981], p. 62).

52. As far as I know, no one has pointed out the change in locution in Hitler's repetition of his January 30, 1939, "prophecy," or its significance. In still later references to the initial speech, he repeated the notion that he would have the last laugh, appearing to be particularly peeved that people had not believed him when he had declared his intention to annihilate the Jews in the event of war. For his November 8, 1942, speech, see Aronsfeld, *The Text of the Holocaust*, p. 36.

53. For the agreement, see Brauchitsch Directive, April 28, 1941, Nur. Doc. NOKW-2080; Walter Schellenberg, 11/26/45, 3710-PS; and Otto Ohlendorf, 4/24/47, NO-2890; for the army's thoroughgoing complicity in the slaughter of Soviet Jewry, see Helmut Krausnick and Hans-Heinrich Wilhelm, *Die Truppe des Weltanschauungskrieges: Die Einsatzgruppen der Sicherheitspolizei und des SD, 1938–1942* (Stuttgart: Deutsche Verlags-Anstalt, 1981), pp. 205–278; and the many publications of Jürgen Förster, including "The Wehrmacht and the War of Extermination Against the Soviet Union," *YVS* 14 (1981): pp. 7–34.

54. There is much conflicting testimony about who attended and what transpired on the different occasions. For a summary of some of the material, see Indictment Against Streckenbach, ZStL 201 AR-Z 76/59 (hereafter cited as Streckenbach), pp. 178–191; for the positions of the two main protagonists in this debate, see Krausnick and Wilhelm, *Die Truppe des Weltanschauungskrieges*, pp. 150–172, and "Hitler und die Befehle an die Einsatzgruppen im Sommer 1941," in Eberhard Jäckel and Jürgen Rohwer, eds., *Der Mord an den Juden im Zweiten Weltkrieg: Entschlussbildung und Verwirklichung* (Stuttgart: Deutsche Verlags-Anstalt, 1985), pp. 88–106; and Alfred Streim, *Die Behandlung sowjetischer Kriegsgefangener im Fall Barbarossa* (Heidelberg: C. F. Müller Juristischer Verlag, 1981), pp. 74–93; "Zur Eröffnung des allgemeinen Judenvernichtungsbefehls gegenüber den Einsatzgruppen," in Jäckel and Rohwer, eds., *Der Mord an den Juden im Zweiten Weltkrieg*, pp. 107–119, and "The Tasks of the SS Einsatzgruppen," *Simon Wiesenthal Center Annual* 4 (1987): pp. 309–328; for the exchange between Krausnick and Streim, see *Simon Wiesenthal Center Annual* 6 (1989): pp. 311–347; for a different attempt to synthesize the inconsistent material, see Browning, "Beyond 'Intentionalism' and 'Functionalism,' " pp. 99–111; for Burrin's reading of the evidence, see *Hitler and the Jews*, pp. 90–113.

55. This was codified in Heydrich's July 2, 1941, written order to the *HSSPF.* See *Nazism*, pp. 1091–1092. In keeping with the general practice of not putting into writing explicit orders for the extermination of Jews, preferring to pass the orders on

orally, this order referred only to those killings that were more related to seeming military necessity.

56. The issue of what orders were given to the *Einsatzgruppen*, by whom, and when, has become highly contentious among scholars. The many arguments and facts necessary for a full discussion of alternative interpretations cannot possibly be addressed here. See note 54 above for references to the debate, and note 74 below for references to new evidence.

57. Indictment, Streckenbach, p. 261.

58. See Walter Blume, ZStL 207 AR-Z 15/58, vol. 4, p. 981. He says that operational details were not given to them at the time, so that they did not know how they were to carry out their orders. They expected to receive the instructions later.

59. "Official Transcript of the American Military Tribunal No. 2-A in the Matter of the United States of America Against Otto Ohlendorf et al., defendants sitting at Nuernberg Germany on 15 September 1947," pp. 633, 526.

60. *Einsatzbefehl* No. 1, June 29, 1941, and *Einsatzbefehl* No. 2, July 1, 1941; Heydrich also suggested this in his July 2, 1941, order to the *HSSPF* in the Soviet Union.

61. Member of *Einsatzgruppe A*, quoted in Ernst Klee, Willi Dressen, and Volker Riess, eds., *"The Good Old Days": The Holocaust as Seen by Its Perpetrators and Bystanders* (New York: Free Press, 1988), p. 81.

62. Alfred Filbert, Streckenbach, vol. 11, pp. 7571–7572; see also his statement in Streckenbach, vol. 6, pp. 1580–1585.

63. The pattern of *Einsatzgruppen* killing in the first few weeks is haphazard. Some *Einsatzkommandos* perpetrated significantly larger massacres than others. Even a single *Einsatzkommando* sometimes treated the Jews of different cities and towns substantially differently. The means of killing, whether employing local auxiliaries or doing the killing themselves, also varied. The logistics and techniques of killing differed across *Einsatzkommandos*. Finally, the time of escalation to very large slaughters and the wholesale inclusion of Jewish women and children also varied. I see no way to account for all of the variation unless the *Einsatzgruppen* leaders or the *HSSPF*, under whose jurisdiction they operated, had discretion over the manner of implementing an already announced general extermination order. That they must have had such discretion makes the notion still more plausible that initially they were to habituate their men to killing, and, after this had been done, to proceed with a step-wise escalation of the slaughter. That such attempts at habituating the men occurred elsewhere, such as in Galicia in November 1941—when there is no doubt whatsoever that an order for total extermination had already been given—shows that the *Einsatzkommandos'* failure to kill all Jews at once does not constitute evidence that Hitler had not yet given a comprehensive extermination order. Similarly, even after the Europe-wide extermination program was under way, the Germans did not immediately kill the Jews of every country, region, and community—just as they did not immediately kill all the Jews of the Soviet Union. To expect them to have done so either in the Soviet Union or in the rest of Europe is unrealistic. For the initial habituating killing in Nadvornaya, Galicia, see Judgment Against Hans Krüger et al., Schwurgericht Münster 5 Ks 4/65, pp. 137–194, esp. 143. For overviews of the killing operations of the *Einsatzgruppen*, see Krausnick and Wilhelm, *Die Truppe des*

Weltanschauungskrieges, pp. 173–205, 533–539; and *The Einsatzgruppen Reports: Selections from the Dispatches of the Nazi Death Squads' Campaign Against the Jews in Occupied Territories of the Soviet Union, July 1941–January 1943*, ed. Yitzhak Arad, Shmuel Krakowski, and Shmuel Spector (New York: Holocaust Library, 1989).

64. On the issue of manpower, see Browning, "Beyond 'Intentionalism' and 'Functionalism,' " pp. 101–106; and Yehoshua Büchler, "*Kommandostab Reichsführer-SS:* Himmler's Personal Murder Brigades in 1941," *HGS* 1, no. 1 (1986): pp. 11–25.

65. Indictment Against A.H., StA Frankfurt/M 4 Js 1928/60, p. 15.

66. They discovered, among other things, that shooting was ultimately not a preferable means of killing, because it was too gruesome and psychologically burdensome for the men. Hence the transition to gassing as the primary means of slaughter. See Judgment Against Friedrich Pradel and Harry Wentritt, Hannover, 2 Ks 2/65, p. 33; and Mathias Beer, "Die Entwicklung der Gaswagen Beim Mord an den Juden," *VfZ* 35, no. 3 (1987): pp. 403–417.

67. For an account of such a staged "pogrom" in Grzymalow, Ukraine, when the SS armed Ukrainians and sent them on a rampage through the town, see Judgment Against Daniel Nerling, Stuttgart 2 Ks 1/67, p. 17; for the extensive German-directed "pogroms" in Latvia, see Judgment Against Viktor Arajs, Hamburg (37) 5/76, pp. 16–26, 72–107, 145; and Indictment Against Viktor Arajs, Hamburg 141 Js 534/60, pp. 22–25, 73–89.

68. For an overview of the *Einsatzgruppen* killings, see Krausnick and Wilhelm, *Die Truppe der Weltanschauungskrieges*, pp. 173–205, 533–539. On Kovno, see pp. 205–209; on Lemberg, see pp. 186–187.

69. The Białystok killing is treated at length in Chapter 6 below. For Lutsk, see Alfred Streim, "Das Sonderkommando 4a der Einsatzgruppe C und die mit diesem Kommando eingesetzten Einheiten während des Russland-Feldzuges in der Zeit vom 22. 6. 1941 bis zum Sommer 1943," ZStL 11 (4) AR-Z 269/60, "Abschlussbericht," pp. 153–158. The *Einsatzgruppen* "Operational Situational Report USSR No. 24," July 16, 1941, states *incorrectly* that Ukrainians did the shooting (*Einsatzgruppen Reports*, p. 32). The information contained in these reports is often misleading or incomplete. Although they remain an invaluable source, Burrin, *Hitler and the Jews*, is wrong in maintaining "that these reports are generally complete and precise" (p. 105). In composing them, the Germans often had purposes other than the truth guiding them. Paul Zapp, the commander of *Einsatzkommando 11a*, testified at his trial that the *Einsatzkommando* commanders had received instructions to disguise their genocidal operations in their operational reports because of the danger that they might fall into enemy hands (from Erich Goldhagen's notes of Zapp's testimony on Feb. 17, 1970, during the trial of Zapp and other members of *Einsatzkommando 11a*). In this Lutsk killing, the Germans wanted to present the slaughter as being Ukrainian revenge for the crimes that the Jews had allegedly perpetrated against Ukrainians, so the Germans substituted for the facts the fiction that Ukrainians had done the killing. Those who rely on the situational reports, as Burrin and Browning ("Beyond 'Intentionalism' and 'Functionalism' ") do, without immersing themselves in the more complete materials in the records of the postwar legal investigations, interpret the events based on the Germans' willfully and substantially distorted record of what transpired.

70. Breitman, *The Architect of Genocide*, pp. 190–196.

71. For the logistics of this, see Browning, "Beyond 'Intentionalism' and 'Functionalism,' " pp. 106–111.

72. My conclusion is based on extensive (though not exhaustive) reading in the investigation and trial materials at ZStL of *all* the *Einsatzgruppen*, including the voluminous investigation and trial of Kuno Callsen and other members of *Sonderkommando 4a*, ZStL 204 AR-Z 269/60, which contains over fifty volumes and ten thousand pages of materials. But for considerations of space, I would have included a separate chapter here on the *Einsatzgruppen*. An exception to the general conclusion stated here occurred in *Einsatzkommando 8*. After the war, some of its men told of their anger upon learning in mid-July that they would also have to kill Jewish women and children. The new task of the new operational phase was what had disturbed them. But even here it was clear to them that from the beginning they had been carrying out an explicitly genocidal order by killing the Jewish men. See Judgment Against Karl Strohhammer, Landgericht Frankfurt 4 Ks 1/65, p. 10.

73. W.G., Streckenbach, vol. 11, p. 7578. His account and Filbert's, discussed above, confirm one another.

74. It is surprising that no one has yet adduced this crucial evidence, which is in some ways far more significant than the testimony of the *Einsatzgruppen* leaders, on which others have relied exclusively. For but a small *sampling* of the additional substantiating evidence on this point, see: for *Einsatzgruppe A*, W.M., Streckenbach, vol. 7, p. 7088; for *Einsatzkommando 8*, C.R., Streckenbach, vol. 7, p. 7064, and Judgment Against Strohhammer, Landgericht Frankfurt 4 Ks 1/65, p. 9; for *Einsatzgruppe C*, K.H., Streckenbach, vol. 8, p. 7135; for *Sonderkommando 4b*, H.S., Streckenbach, vol. 18, pp. 8659–8660; for *Sonderkommando 11a*, K.N., Streckenbach, vol. 12, p. 7775. It is particularly significant that the commander of Police Battalion 309 (discussed in Chapter 6) announced to his company commanders, *before the attack on the Soviet Union*, that Hitler had given an order (*Führerbefehl*) for all of the Jews in the Soviet Union to be exterminated—men, women, and children. At least one of the company commanders soon thereafter announced the order to his assembled men. See Judgment Against Buchs et al., Wuppertal, 12 Ks 1/67, pp. 29–30; H.G., ZStL 205 AR-Z 20/60 (hereafter cited as "Buchs"), pp. 363–364; A.A., Buchs, p. 1339R; and E.M., Buchs, p. 1813R. Thus, even before the attack, knowledge of the genocidal decision had already been communicated beyond the restricted circle of the *Einsatzgruppen*. Whatever plausible or implausible (in my view, implausible) motivations have been imputed to the *Einsatzgruppen* commanders for their alleged postwar fabrication of an initial general extermination order, such motives cannot plausibly be ascribed to their subordinates, whose dominant motivation has always been to deny their knowledge of the genocidal character of their activities. Many men from the *Einsatzkommandos*, including commanders, deny—incredibly and against all the evidence—that they ever knew of any genocidal intent or that they killed Jews.

75. "Abschlussbericht," ZStL 202 AR-Z 82/61, vol. 5, pp. 795–843. The shared (though differently elaborated) argument of Browning, "Beyond 'Intentionalism' and 'Functionalism' " (p. 102), and Burrin, *Hitler and the Jews* (pp. 105–106, 113), that in the first weeks, in Browning's words, "the overwhelming majority" of the *Einsatzkommando* victims were "the Jewish male leadership and intelligentsia"—which,

according to the argument, conformed to Heydrich's July 2 order—is untenable. It is belied glaringly by the deeds of the *Einsatzkommandos* (and of police battalions), and by the detailed accounts given by their men describing who and how they killed, and also their understanding of their task. The Germans often were rounding up and killing Jewish men, plain and simple, not the Jewish leadership and intelligentsia (which is an elastic and virtually meaningless category that should be taken about as seriously as a guide to reality as the many other deceptive locutions that the Germans used regarding the annihilation of European Jewry). That the Germans may have sometimes restricted their initial killing to the "elite" is not the significant fact (since their killing operations were not yet everywhere comprehensive anyway). That they routinely killed "non-elite" Jewish men is crucial, however, for it reveals the genocidal scope of their orders. Browning and Burrin have been misled by taking the purposely deceptive locutions of the *Einsatzgruppen*'s reports literally. See, for example, for *Einsatzkommando 8*, the testimony of K.K., ZStL 202 AR-Z 81/59, where he discusses in detail their rounding up of the Jews of Białystok at the beginning of July (vol. 6, pp. 1228–1229). For an example from *Sonderkommando 4a*, see Judgment Against Kuno Callsen et al., ZStL 204 AR-Z 269/60, pp. 161–162. Even the very first *Einsatzkommando* killing of June 24 in Garsden was of *all* the Jewish men whom they could find. See F.M., ZStL 207 AR-Z 15/58, vol. 2, p. 457. Such early *indiscriminate* genocidal slaughters of Jews was perpetrated not only by *Einsatzkommandos* but also by police battalions. In Białystok, on July 13, a few days after the massacre by *Einsatzkommando 8*, Police Battalion 316 and Police Battalion 322 implemented the standing order, which their regimental commander had issued two days earlier, to round up and shoot the male Jews of the region between the ages of seventeen and forty-five. They netted three thousand or more in Białystok. Burrin, *Hitler and the Jews*, against the evidence of the character of this and other enormous killing operations, accepts the Germans' camouflaging language—namely that this order mandated that they should kill the Jews in this age range *who were looters*—as if this were what the order had really meant (p. 111). The German court trying this case dismissed the notion that the order pertained to looters as "an obvious sham justification, a transparent camouflage of the true purpose of the killing order." See Judgment Against Hermann Kraiker et al., Schwurgericht Bochum 15 Ks 1/66, pp. 144–178, esp. 153–155; and Indictment Against Hermann Kraiker et al., Dortmund 45 Js 2/61, pp. 106–108. This order does not show what Burrin believes it to show, but precisely the opposite, namely that there was an extermination plan. Police Battalion 307's slaughter of six thousand to ten thousand Jews in Brest-Litovsk in the first half of July is another example of out-and-out genocidal killing. Browning and Burrin's line of argumentation also does not take into account the wholesale slaughter of thousands that the Germans perpetrated (some with local aid) in the Baltics (including women and children) and in Ukraine. Many of these killings, even large ones, such as in Krottingen, did not make it into the *Einsatzgruppen*'s Operational Situation Reports. Browning and Burrin present them as "pogroms" and pass over them quickly in their analyses, even though the Germans actively organized, aided, supervised, and even participated in the killing operations. A Lithuanian, P.L., for example, describes the Germans' announcement that the Jews, including women and children, were to be killed, and then the commission of the deed in Krottingen by

Lithuanians under German supervision (ZStL 207 AR-Z 15/58, pp. 2744–2745). The scope and comprehensiveness of the German-organized killing in the Baltics indicates that the Germans were, in the *first few weeks* of the attack on the Soviet Union, already carrying out the genocidal policy which Hitler's prior decision had initiated. For substantiation of this, see ZStL 207 AR-Z 15/58.

76. The notion that Hitler would have begun systematically to slaughter Jews on a grand scale, and then stopped, defies everything we know about Hitler's psychology, his style of conducting war (which is how he conceived of his conflict with the Jews), not to mention his understanding of how to neutralize the putative Jewish menace. Therefore, Hitler's decision to slaughter Soviet Jewry was the crucial historical moment.

77. Breitman, "Plans for the Final Solution in Early 1941," shows that in early 1941 an extermination program for all of European Jewry—and not just Soviet Jewry—had already been ordered and was being prepared. Browning, "Beyond 'Intentionalism,' " also sees the contemporaneity of the decisions, yet he dates them at mid-July (p. 113).

78. For a reconstruction of the events, see Browning, "Beyond 'Intentionalism,' " pp. 111–120. He believes the change to have been not operational, but strategic.

79. Ohlendorf's fear was more that the men would become brutalized and rendered unfit for civilized society. While this was not the case for the overwhelming majority, some did find having so much blood on their hands nerve-wracking. For an example, see Daniel Goldhagen, "The 'Cowardly' Executioner: On Disobedience in the SS," *Patterns of Prejudice* 12, no. 1 (1978): pp. 1–16.

80. On the Germans' use of gas vans in the field, see Eugen Kogon, Hermann Langbein, and Adalbert Rückerl, eds., *Nazi Mass Murder: A Documentary History of the Use of Poison Gas* (New Haven: Yale University Press, 1993), pp. 52–72.

81. In fact, the Germans continued to shoot Jews *en masse* throughout the war. It is not at all obvious that gassing was a more "efficient" means of slaughtering Jews than shooting was. There were many instances in which shooting was clearly more efficient. The Germans preferred gassing for reasons other than some genocidal economic calculus. Understanding this suggests that, contrary to both scholarly and popular treatments of the Holocaust, gassing was really epiphenomenal to the Germans' slaughter of Jews. It was a more convenient means, but not an essential development. Had the Germans never invented the gas chamber, then they might well have killed almost as many Jews. The will was primary, the means secondary.

82. See Browning, "Beyond 'Intentionalism' and 'Functionalism,' " pp. 111–120.

83. For a discussion of this issue, see Czesław Madajczyk, "Concentration Camps as a Tool of Oppression in Nazi-Occupied Europe," in *The Nazi Concentration Camps: Structure and Aims, The Image of the Prisoner, The Jews in the Camps* (Jerusalem: Yad Vashem, 1984), pp. 55–57.

84. For the minutes of the meeting, see *Nazism*, pp. 1127–1135. Who can doubt that had the Germans won the European war and succeeded in slaying all of European Jewry, then Hitler would have commissioned Himmler to draw up plans for the annihilation of the remaining Jews of the world, chiefly those in North America? According to the logic of those who write as if intentions do not exist until evidence of actual concrete plans and preparations can be found, it would have to be *assumed* that

Hitler certainly had no wish to exterminate the rest of world Jewry even when the Wannsee Conference codified his plan to annihilate European Jewry.

85. The topics in this paragraph are treated at length in Part IV.

86. Randolf L. Braham, *The Politics of Genocide: The Holocaust in Hungary* (New York: Columbia University Press, 1981), vol. 2, pp. 792–793.

87. See Part V.

88. Quoted in Jäckel, *Hitler's World View*, pp. 65–66.

89. For different interpretations, which place emphasis on "Hitler's fluctuating moods," see Browning, "Beyond 'Intentionalism' and 'Functionalism,' " pp. 120–121; and Burrin, *Hitler and the Jews*, pp. 133–147.

90. Letter to Adolf Gremlich of Sept. 16, 1919, quoted in Ernst Deurlein, "Hitlers Eintritt in die NSDAP und die Reichswehr," *VfZ* 7 (1959): pp. 203–205.

91. It is noteworthy that Hitler used the word "prophecy." A prophecy is not a mere wish; it is a divining of a likely future. Goebbels and others also saw it as having been a *prophecy* and not empty bravado. After a meeting with Hitler on August 19, 1941, Goebbels referred explicitly back to the "prophecy," recording in his diary that it "is being fulfilled in these weeks and months with a definiteness that strikes one as almost uncanny. In the East, the Jews must pay the price, in Germany they have already paid it in part and will have to pay still more in the future" (in Martin Broszat, "Hitler und die Genesis der 'Endlösung': Aus Anlass der Thesen von David Irving," *VfZ* 25, no. 4 [1977]: pp. 749–750).

92. I can think of no other instance in history in which a national leader proclaimed an intention with regard to a matter of this magnitude with such evident conviction and, true to his word, carried out his intention, and *then* historians assert that his words should not be taken literally, that he had had no intention of doing what he announced for the whole world to hear (an announcement to which he later repeatedly and emphatically referred). This interpretive turn regarding Hitler is indeed a curious matter. Perhaps there would be some shred of a justification for maintaining this curious position if the deed had been out of character for the man. Yet Hitler was an enormously murderous man—in thought, in speech, and in deed. His character was to dream of killing his enemies and to try to turn his dreams into reality.

93. Lothar Gruchmann, "Euthanasie und Justiz im Dritten Reich," *VfZ* 20, no. 3 (1972): p. 238. Indeed, Hitler had stated clearly, as early as 1931, that he saw war as an opportunity for a final reckoning, saying that, should the Jews produce another war, the war would result unexpectedly for the Jews. He would "crush" "World Jewry." See Edouard Calic, *Ohne Maske: Hitler-Breiting Geheimgespräche 1931* (Frankfurt: Societäts-Verlag, 1968), pp. 94–95.

Chapter 5

1. The definition of "perpetrator" roughly corresponds to the definition used by the courts of the Federal Republic of Germany for determining whether or not someone was liable for "complicity" in the murder of Jews. For a concise discussion of this issue, see Judgment Against Wolfgang Hoffmann et al., Landgericht Ham-

burg (50) 20/66, p. 243. The focus here is on the Germans' persecution, torture, and slaughter of Jews, and not on their maltreatment and killing of other people. A number of reasons lie behind this decision. Whatever the Germans' other brutalities, killings, and crimes, the Jews were central to the prevailing German worldview, to the development of German politics, to the construction of the death factories of Auschwitz, Treblinka, Bełżec, Sobibór, and Chełmno, as was no other victim group. In fact, no other people occupied nearly as central an ideational place in the public and private lives of Germans, or in their continent-wide murderous enterprises. A second reason for treating the Jews separately is, as the ensuing discussion shows, that the Germans consistently treated them differently and worse than other peoples. The Jews were *sui generis* in the Germans' eyes, and so it makes good analytical sense to treat them similarly here, though elucidative comparisons with other victim groups are periodically presented.

2. Exceptions must be made for individuals in the German institutions that housed Jews who refrained from the general brutality that characterized them, such as guards who were kind to Jews or those who really had nothing to do with Jews, such as some cooks. See Ernst Klee, Willi Dressen, and Volker Riess, eds., *"The Good Old Days": The Holocaust as Seen by Its Perpetrators and Bystanders* (New York: Free Press, 1988), p. xxi, for a different conception of "perpetrator."

3. The main reason for an expansive definition has been given. A corollary benefit of the definition is that it captures an essential element of Germany and the Holocaust—to wit, that so many people were involved, connected to, and knowledgeable about the mass slaughter. A more narrow definition of "perpetrator" would create too great a distinction between those who, say, were in *Einsatzkommando* execution squads and those who stood guard in ghettos or manned deportation trains. After all, Germans moved easily from one role to the next. For the vast majority, chance, not acts of volition, determined who among a group of socially indistinguishable Germans would or would not find himself in an institution of killing. Definitions are inevitably "persuasive," so care must be taken that the manner of a definition's persuasion is desirable and defensible.

4. I know of no serious account of the Holocaust that fails to devote concerted attention to the gas chambers, yet many treat the mass shooting of Jews and other significant aspects of the Holocaust's perpetration either in a perfunctory manner (with the exception of the *Einsatzgruppen* killings in the Soviet Union) or not at all. Even Raul Hilberg, *The Destruction of the European Jews* (New York: New Viewpoints, 1973), slights such killings (see, for example, his section on the deportations from Poland, pp. 308–345). The Germans killed somewhere between 40 and 50 percent of their Jewish victims by means other than gassing, and more Germans were involved in these killings in a greater variety of contexts than in those carried out in the gas chambers. For estimates, see *Encyclopedia of the Holocaust*, ed. Israel Gutman (New York: Macmillan, 1990), pp. 461–463, 1799; and Wolfgang Benz, *Dimension des Völkermords: Die Zahl der jüdischen Opfer des Nationalsozialismus* (Munich: R. Oldenbourg Verlag, 1991), p. 17. The imbalance of attention devoted to the gas chambers needs to be corrected.

5. See, as representative of the vast literature on the camps, the over-seven-hundred-page conference volume *The Nazi Concentration Camps: Structure and*

Aims, The Image of the Prisoner, The Jews in the Camps (Jerusalem: Yad Vashem, 1984), from which very little can be learned about the perpetrators (with the exception of Robert Jay Lifton's contribution on the doctors in Auschwitz). The recent volume, Yisrael Gutman and Michael Berenbaum, eds., *Anatomy of the Auschwitz Death Camp* (Bloomington: Indiana University Press, 1994), does have a section on the perpetrators, yet it contains only a sociological profile of the camp's personnel, another essay on the doctors, and separate essays on the commandant, Rudolf Höss, and on Josef Mengele. Aside from the demographic and personnel data, the volume contains scant information about the perpetrators, let alone sustained analysis of their actions and motivations. A few important exceptions to the neglect of the perpetrators in the camps exist, including Adalbert Rückerl, *Nationalsozialistische Vernichtungslager im Spiegel deutscher Strafprozesse: Belzec, Sobibor, Treblinka, Chelmno* (Munich: Deutscher Taschenbuch Verlag, 1977); and Hermann Langbein, *Menschen in Auschwitz* (Frankfurt/M: Ullstein, 1980), pp. 311–522.

6. For an account of the institutions of killing, see Heinz Artzt, *Mörder in Uniform: Nazi-Verbrecher-Organisationen* (Rastatt: Verlag Arthur Moewig, 1987); see also Richard Henkys, *Die Nationalsozialistischen Gewaltverbrechen: Geschichte und Gericht* (Stuttgart: Kreuz Verlag, 1964); for a treatment of those who worked in Eichmann's office, see Hans Safrian, *Die Eichmann-Männer* (Vienna: Europaverlag, 1993), and in the foreign office, see Christopher R. Browning, *The Final Solution and the German Foreign Office: A Study of Referat D III of Abteilung Deutschland, 1940–43* (New York: Holmes & Meier, 1978).

7. Helmut Krausnick and Hans-Heinrich Wilhelm, *Die Truppe des Weltanschauungskrieges: Die Einsatzgruppen der Sicherheitspolizei und des SD, 1938–1942* (Stuttgart: Deutsche Verlags-Anstalt, 1981). For an earlier, briefer treatment, see Alfred Streim, "Zum Beispiel: Die Verbrechen der *Einsatzgruppen* in der Sowjetunion," in Adalbert Rückerl, ed., *NS-Prozesse: Nach 25 Jahren Strafverfolgung* (Karlsruhe: Verlag C. F. Müller, 1971), pp. 65–106.

8. See, for example, Yisrael Gutman, *The Jews of Warsaw, 1939–1943: Ghetto, Underground, Revolt* (Bloomington: Indiana University Press, 1989). This is a fine study of the Warsaw ghetto, yet from it little can be learned of its German keepers.

9. The recently published *Encyclopedia of the Holocaust* has no entry for police battalions and but a brief and unilluminating entry for the Order Police. They are barely mentioned in such standard works about the Holocaust as Hilberg, *The Destruction of the European Jews*; Lucy S. Dawidowicz, *The War Against the Jews, 1933–1945* (New York: Bantam Books, 1975); or Leni Yahil's recent mammoth work, *The Holocaust: The Fate of European Jewry, 1932–1945* (New York: Oxford University Press, 1990). Yitzhak Arad, *Belzec, Sobibor, Treblinka: The Operation Reinhard Death Camps* (Bloomington: Indiana University Press, 1987), discusses police battalions only sporadically and in passing, even though the success of *Aktion Reinhard* was greatly owing to their participation. Christopher R. Browning, *Ordinary Men: Reserve Police Battalion 101 and the Final Solution in Poland* (New York: HarperCollins, 1992), has contributed greatly to our knowledge of the genocidal activities of police battalions, though, because its primary focus is on one battalion, it too does not provide a systematic or comprehensive account. A smattering of other, less substantial material has also recently been published.

10. In recent years, some good publications have appeared, including Ulrich Herbert, *Fremdarbeiter: Politik und Praxis des 'Ausländer-Einsatzes' in der Kriegswirtschaft des Dritten Reiches* (Berlin: Verlag J. H. W. Dietz Nachf.: 1985); Ulrich Herbert, ed., *Europa und der "Reichseinsatz": Ausländische Zivilarbeiter, Kriegsgefangene und KZ-Häftlinge in Deutschland, 1938–1945* (Essen: Klartext Verlag, 1991); *Das Daimler-Benz Buch: Ein Rüstungskonzern im "Tausendjährigen Reich" und Danach*, ed. der Hamburger Stiftung für Sozialgeschichte des 20. Jahrhunderts (Nordlingen: ECHO, 1988); and Klaus-Jörg Siegfried, *Das Leben der Zwangsarbeiter im Volkswagenwerk, 1939–1945* (Frankfurt/M: Campus Verlag, 1988).

11. See Krausnick and Wilhelm, *Die Truppe des Weltanschauungskrieges*; Omer Bartov, *The Eastern Front, 1941–1945: German Troops and the Barbarization of Warfare* (London: Macmillan, 1985); Ernst Klee and Willi Dressen, eds., *"Gott mit uns": Der deutsche Vernichtungskrieg im Osten, 1939–1945* (Frankfurt/M: S. Fischer Verlag, 1989); Theo J. Schulte, *The German Army and Nazi Policies in Occupied Russia* (Oxford: Berg Publishers, 1989); Jürgen Förster, "Das Unternehmen 'Barbarossa' als Eroberungs- und Vernichtungskrieg," im Militärgeschichtlichen Forschungsamt, *Das Deutsche Reich und die Zweite Weltkrieg*, vol. 4 (Stuttgart: Deutsche Verlags-Anstalt, 1983), pp. 413–447; Alfred Streim, *Sowjetische Gefangene in Hitlers Vernichtungskrieg: Berichte und Dokumente, 1941–1945* (Heidelberg: C. F. Müller Juristischer Verlag); and Christian Streit, *Keine Kameraden: Die Wehrmacht und die sowjetischen Kriegsgefangenen, 1941–1945* (Stuttgart: Deutsche Verlags-Anstalt, 1978).

12. We need to learn more about the people who joined the SS, what their lives in its various branches were like, what their views of the world were, and the like. We need a "thick description" of them. For two existing major works on the subject, see Bernd Wegner, *The Waffen-SS: Organization, Ideology and Function* (Oxford: Basil Blackwell, 1990); and Herbert F. Ziegler, *Nazi Germany's New Aristocracy: The SS Leadership, 1925–1939* (Princeton: Princeton University Press, 1989).

13. Early in my research, I decided that deriving a good estimate of the number of people who were perpetrators would consume more time than I could profitably devote to it, given my other research objectives. Still, I am confident in asserting that the number was huge. By far the best resource for developing such an estimate is the Zentrale Stelle der Landesjustizverwaltungen zur Aufklärung nationalsozialistischer Verbrechen in Ludwigsburg (ZStL), which has coordinated and been the clearinghouse for investigations and prosecutions of Nazi crimes since its founding at the end of 1958. Its name catalogue section (*Namenskartei*) of the main card catalogue (*Zentralkartei*) contains 640,903 cards (as of December 20, 1994) for those people who have been mentioned or have given testimony in investigations. The unit catalogue (*Einheitskartei*), which contains the names of people who were or were suspected of having been members of an institution of killing, has 333,082 cards covering the 4,105 units and agencies that the legal authorities have pursued. Tabulating the number of people who were actually involved in the various institutions would be a lengthy task, because the number of cards in the "unit catalogue" is not a perfect guide to the number of people who served in each institution, or who altogether worked in the institutions of killing. Many of the lists are (often woefully) incomplete; yet they also include duplicates, non-German perpetrators, and the names of people who were not members of the institutions (just being mentioned in someone's

testimony gains an entry for an individual). Moreover, some of the institutions and the people in them were involved or suspected of having been involved in crimes other than the killing of Jews (such as in the so-called Euthanasia program). Even if the substantial problems associated with deciding how to classify individuals or groups of individuals did not exist (owing to various kinds of indeterminacy), simply ascertaining how many people belonged to each of the genocidal institutions would be a laborious, time-consuming task. And there are clearly a large number of institutions that have never been investigated at all.

14. Herbert, *Fremdarbeiter*, p. 271.

15. Gudrun Schwarz, *Die nationalsozialistischen Lager* (Frankfurt/M: Campus Verlag, 1990), p. 221. For example, it is not known how many ghettos existed in Belorussia or in Ukraine (p. 132). It should be noted that the camps varied enormously in size, from the vast Auschwitz complex to those in which the Germans incarcerated but a few dozen people.

16. See Schwarz, *Die nationalsozialistischen Lager*, pp. 221–222, for a summary of the number of camps in each of the different categories.

17. Aleksander Lasik, "Historical-Sociological Profile of the Auschwitz SS," in Gutman and Berenbaum, eds., *Anatomy of the Auschwitz Death Camp*, p. 274. Lasik shows that a significant minority of them were ethnic Germans (pp. 279–281) who had thrown their lot in with Nazism.

18. Wolfgang Sofsky, *Die Ordnung des Terrors: Das Konzentrationslager* (Frankfurt/M: Fischer Verlag, 1993), pp. 341–342, nn. 20, 18.

19. Sofsky, *Die Ordnung des Terrors*, p. 121.

20. See Krausnick and Wilhelm, *Die Truppe des Weltanschauungskrieges*, for a discussion of their initial strength (p. 147).

21. This is a low estimate because it is highly likely that still more police battalions participated in the genocidal killings, and because the average strength of five hundred used for this calculation is likely to be low (many battalions had more men, and personnel rotations took place). This subject and the sources for the estimate are discussed in Chapter 9.

22. Yehoshua Büchler, "*Kommandostab Reichsführer-SS:* Himmler's Personal Murder Brigades in 1941," *HGS* 1, no. 1 (1986): p. 20. Büchler estimates that they killed at least one hundred thousand Jews. If anything, this is a conservative figure.

23. See Orlando Patterson, *Slavery and Social Death: A Comparative Study* (Cambridge: Harvard University Press, 1982), esp. pp. 1–14. "Social death" is to be distinguished from being "civilly dead," namely when people are not granted or lose certain civil rights, such as the right to vote. Social death is a qualitatively different phenomenon.

24. For two typologies of camps, see Schwarz, *Die nationalsozialistischen Lager*, pp. 70–73; and Aharon Weiss, "Categories of Camps—Their Character and Role in the Execution of the 'Final Solution of the Jewish Question,' " in *The Nazi Concentration Camps*, pp. 121–127.

25. See Falk Pingel, *Häftlinge unter SS-Herrschaft: Widerstand, Seblstbehauptung und Vernichtung im Konzentrationslager* (Hamburg: Hoffmann und Campe, 1978), pp. 30–35, for the early history of camps.

26. Schwarz, *Die nationalsozialistischen Lager*, p. 72.

27. Schwarz, *Die nationalsozialistischen Lager*, p. 222. Some of them were undoubtedly quite small and relatively inconspicuous.

28. For a discussion of this, see Daniel Bell, *The Cultural Contradictions of Capitalism* (New York: Basic Books, 1978).

29. For representative examples, see Konnilyn G. Feig, *Hitler's Death Camps: The Sanity of Madness* (New York: Holmes & Meier, 1981), and the essays in *The Nazi Concentration Camps*. Sofsky, *Die Ordnung des Terrors*, is an exception to seeing the camps in such instrumental terms, yet the book's analytical attempt is greatly flawed because, among other reasons, it wrests consideration of the camps from their proper context of German society and generally treats them as if they were isolated islands.

30. For a general account, see Eugen Kogon, Hermann Langbein, and Adalbert Rückerl, eds., *Nazi Mass Murder: A Documentary History of the Use of Poison Gas* (New Haven: Yale University Press, 1993), pp. 73–204; for the memoir of a Jewish survivor who worked in the extermination facilities of Auschwitz, see Filip Müller, *Eyewitness Auschwitz: Three Years in the Gas Chambers* (New York: Stein & Day, 1979).

31. Pingel, *Häftlinge unter SS-Herrschaft*, p. 186.

32. This is why using the term "concentration camp" as the generic term for camps is misleading, unless it is explicitly stated that the term encompasses the other kinds of camps. See Chapters 10 and 11 for a treatment of the themes mentioned here.

33. See Sofsky, *Die Ordnung des Terrors*, p. 135, for a chart representing this. The chart is problematic both in its placement of Jews (as I discuss in Chapter 15, they were not mere "subhumans") and in its characterization of the "life-death" continuum, which was not a continuum, but an array of widely discrete and changing values.

34. For a discussion of this subject, see Pingel, *Häftlinge unter SS-Herrschaft*, pp. 91–96, 133–134.

35. For general analyses, see Joel E. Dimsdale, ed., *Survivors, Victims, and Perpetrators: Essays on the Nazi Holocaust* (Washington: Hemisphere, 1980), chaps. 4–10; for an analysis of the condition and social life of prisoners in Auschwitz, see Langbein, *Menschen in Auschwitz*, pp. 83–128.

Chapter 6

1. No general history of the Order Police during the Nazi period has yet been written, not even one that treats the institution's history aside from its participation in mass murder. Karl-Heinz Heller, "The Reshaping and Political Conditioning of the German Order Police, 1935–1945: A Study of Techniques Used in the Nazi State to Conform" (Ph.D. diss., University of Cincinnati, 1970), focuses on the indoctrination of the Order Police. The volume *Zur Geschichte der Ordnungspolizei, 1936–1945*, containing Georg Tessin, "Die Stäbe und Truppeneinheiten der Ordnungspolizei," and Hans-Joachim Neufeldt, "Entstehung und Organisation des Hauptamtes Ordnungspolizei," is inadequate as an historical work.

2. BAK R19/395 (8/20/40), p. 171.

3. ZStL 206 AR-Z 6/62 (hereafter cited as JK), p. 1949.

4. Police battalions had varying designations depending on their membership. The ones composed mainly of career policemen were designated "police battalions"; those composed mainly of reservists were called "reserve police battalions"; newly created formations were called "police training battalions" during their training period. Among them distinctions were also made according to the age of each battalion's members. Battalions initially with older men were numbered 301 to 325 and were known as *"Wachtmeisterbataillonen."* (Police battalions numbered under 200 were generally reserve police battalions, though a number of the 300-level ones were as well.) It should be noted, though, that from the beginning the manpower composition of battalions often defied their official designations; as the war proceeded, these formal distinctions grew ever more meaningless, owing to changing membership. I have decided to refer to them all generically as "police battalions."

5. BAK R19/395 (8/20/40), p. 175.

6. A report with the findings of the inspection of three police battalions in May of 1940 (BAK R19/265, pp. 168–169) reflects the neglect that the Order Police found itself suffering. See also BAK R19/265 (5/9/40), p. 153.

7. BAK R19/395 (11/20/41), pp. 180–183.

8. See, for example, Tessin, "Die Stäbe und Truppeneinheiten der Ordnungspolizei," pp. 14–15.

9. BAK R19/311 (6/26/40), p. 165.

10. BAK R19/265 (5/23/40), p. 168. Similarly, in May 1940, five police battalions (including number 65 from Recklinghausen, and 67 from Essen) had only two-thirds to four-fifths of the reserves that they needed. The inspection report explained that "in general, the recruitment situation for police reserves is very strained." See BAK R19/265, p. 157.

11. See BAK R19/265 (12/22/37), pp. 91ff.

12. BAK R19/265 (5/9/40), pp. 150–151.

13. See, for example, one representative ideological course for the men of the *Einzeldienst*, BAK R19/308 (3/6/40), pp. 36–43. As this order indicates, the training for police battalions stocked with non-reservists differed slightly. A subsequent order of January 14, 1941, presented more detailed instructions for ideological training, including the page numbers of the pamphlets that were to be used for the discussion of each subject. This order illustrates how paltry the education was, and how unlikely it was that the schooling would have a lasting effect on the men. For the entire ideological training, only sixty-five pages of material were detailed (with an added unspecified number of pages from two pamphlets about the peasantry). A number of topics had fewer than four pages of written material. Under the category of "The Jewish Problem in Germany," only two pages of material (one from each of two different pamphlets) were specified, hardly sufficient to alter a person's views of Jews. See BAK R19/308 (12/20/40), p. 100.

14. See the discussion of their ideological training in Christopher R. Browning, *Ordinary Men: Reserve Police Battalion 101 and the Final Solution in Poland* (New York: HarperCollins, 1992), pp. 176–184. He discusses in more detail the material regarding Jews that was presented to the men. Although he judges the indoctrination

to have been more substantial and effective than I do, he too concludes that this material was not instrumental in moving the men to take part in genocidal killing (p. 184).

15. See BAK R19/308 (2/8/41), pp. 267–268. It is fair to suppose, with the frequent dispersal of a battalion's men over a region and with all of the demands, problems, and distractions of the field, that the instructional meetings worked out far less well than even these orders imply. See also BAK R19/308 (6/2/40), pp. 250–254; for the instructions on the ideological education of the men in the *Einzeldienst*, see pp. 252–253.

16. For the role of Party membership in promotion, see BAK R19/311 (6/18/40), pp. 145–147, 149.

17. The material that exists on police battalions is scattered throughout Germany's justice system. Virtually nothing of value on their killing operations is in the Bundesarchiv Koblenz. I have endeavored to uncover all the material on police battalions at the ZStL, which, though considerable, is by no means comprehensive. Just compiling a listing of the legal investigations which have dealt with police battalion crimes was a difficult task. I cannot claim to have mastered the material on police battalions, because I had to start from square one on material that is dauntingly voluminous. Indeed, I would be surprised if I have not overlooked some of what the ZStL possesses. I have read through investigations that have dealt with over thirty-five police battalions. On some, like Police Battalion 101, I have read thousands of pages; on others, but a few hundred. The quality, not just the quantity, of the pages is, moreover, very uneven. About some battalions scant information (even about the outline of their activities) is available; about others a great deal exists, although rich detail about the actions of the Germans in them is generally lacking even for the best-documented battalions. So the analysis here is not comprehensive, though it draws on an extensive empirical base. The role of police battalions in the Holocaust deserves to be the subject of a large book.

18. See Ruth Bettina Birn, *Die Höheren SS- und Polizeiführer: Himmlers Vertreter im Reich und in den besetzten Gebieten* (Düsseldorf: Droste Verlag, 1986); and ZStL 204 AR-Z 13/60, vol. 4, pp. 397–399.

19. See Helmut Krausnick and Hans-Heinrich Wilhelm, *Die Truppe des Weltanschauungskrieges: Die Einsatzgruppen der Sicherheitspolizei und des SD, 1938–1942* (Stuttgart: Deutsche Verlags-Anstalt, 1981), p. 46; Alfred Streim, "Das Sonderkommando 4a der Einsatzgruppe C und die mit diesem Kommando eingesetzten Einheiten während des Russland-Feldzuges in der Zeit vom 22. 6. 1941 bis zum Sommer 1943," ZStL 11 (4) AR-Z 269/60, "Abschlussbericht," p. 36; and Tessin, "Die Stäbe und Truppeneinheinten der Ordnungspolizei," p. 96.

20. ZStL 204 AR-Z 13/60, vol. 4, pp. 402–403.

21. ZStL 202 AR 2484/67, pp. 2397–2506. More than these eleven police battalions operated in the occupied Soviet Union. For example, Police Battalions 11, 65 (discussed below), and 91 were active there.

22. The battalion commander, Major Weis, convened his officers before the attack and informed them of Hitler's orders to kill all Soviet commissars and annihilate Soviet Jewry. The commander of First Company, Captain H.B., communicated this to his men before the onslaught. Other company officers may have done the same, though the testimony does not reveal this. See ZStL 205 AR-Z 20/60 (hereafter cited as Buchs), A.A., Buchs, p. 1339r; J.B., Buchs, p. 1416, and J.B., ZStL 202

AR 2701/65, vol. 1, p. 101; K.H., Buchs, p. 1565r; H.G., Buchs, pp. 363–364, and H.G., ZStL 202 AR 2701/65, vol. 1, p. 96; R.H., Buchs, p. 681; and the self-contradictory testimony of E.M., Buchs, pp. 1813r, 2794–2795, 764; also Judgment Against Buchs et al., Wuppertal, 12 Ks 1/67 (hereafter cited as Judgment, Buchs), pp. 29–30, 62. It is worth noting that Browning, *Ordinary Men*, fails to mention this most fundamental fact in his account of the battalion (pp. 11–12). It flatly contradicts his assertion (discussed here in Chapter 4, note 70) that no explicit genocidal order had already been given.

23. E.Z., Buchs, p. 1749.

24. See the statements of two survivors, S.J., Buchs, p. 1823; and J.S., Buchs, p. 1830.

25. Judgment, Buchs, p. 43.

26. Judgment, Buchs, p. 42; and J.J., Buchs, p. 1828r.

27. Judgment, Buchs, p. 44.

28. See A.B., Buchs, p. 2875, and T.C., Buchs, pp. 2877–2878.

29. Judgment, Buchs, pp. 51–52. Browning's contention that this slaughter "was the work of an individual commander who correctly intuited and anticipated the wishes of his Führer" is difficult to accept. See *Ordinary Men*, p. 12. Does this mean that Major Weis took it upon himself to initiate the slaughter of many hundreds of Jews? Saying that he "intuited and anticipated" Hitler's wish implies that Weis did not receive the order to slaughter Soviet Jews, although he clearly did—a fact of which the men, even the rank and file, of this battalion were aware and to which they testify. (See note 22 above.) They even had to carry out the killing operation in the face of strenuous objections from the military, which had jurisdictional priority in this area. Also, the Germans perpetrated similar licentious slaughters in many cities on captured Soviet territory. "Intuition" played no causative role in them. Additionally, Browning's discussion of this killing operation, including the characterization of it as having begun as a "pogrom" which then "quickly escalat[ed] into more systematic mass murder" (p. 12), might suggest the mistaken notion that the killing of these Jews was not planned from the beginning of the operation.

30. Judgment, Buchs, pp. 52–54.

31. For the spontaneity of the Germans' burning of the synagogue, see E.M., Buchs, pp. 1814r–1815.

32. H.S., Buchs, p. 1764.

33. The court estimates the number to have been at least seven hundred (Judgment, Buchs, p. 57). The Indictment puts it at a minimum of eight hundred (Buchs, p. 113). Jewish sources place the number at around two thousand. A survivor estimates that 90 percent of the victims were men and 10 percent were women and children. See J.S., Buchs, p. 1830; also, see I.A., Buchs, p. 1835.

34. Judgment, Buchs, pp. 56–58. The Germans forced at least two Jews, a man and a woman, into the building after it was already ablaze (See L.L., Buchs, p. 1775).

35. Judgment, Buchs, p. 59. The latter's wish was to a great extent fulfilled. The fire spread from the synagogue to nearby buildings. The Germans allowed much of the Jewish portion of the city to burn down, with more Jews perishing in these flames. They also prevented firefighters from extinguishing the flames, which spread to other dwellings in the Jewish district in which additional men, women, and children burned to death (Judgment, Buchs, p. 59; and E.Z., Buchs, pp. 1748r–1749).

36. See, for example, J.B., Buchs, p. 1415. Browning's statement that they and other men of 300-level battalions were "volunteers" (*Ordinary Men*, p. 10) can be misunderstood. Typically, men were called up to duty, or anticipated that they would be and opted for this police duty over other military or security services duty. So they should not be called "volunteers" without qualification. For this police battalion, see, for example, H.H., JK, p. 1091; and A.A., JK, p. 1339r. In light of Browning's treatment of Police Battalion 101, which is discussed here in the next two chapters, it is worth noting that these Germans' commentaries—expressing joy at the sight of the genocidal fire—are curiously absent from his account of this slaughter. See *Ordinary Men*, pp. 11–12.

37. Judgment, Buchs, p. 60.

38. To my knowledge, Police Battalion 65 has not been discussed in the literature on the Holocaust. The source for it is JK.

39. Many testimonies and surviving photographs document the savagery and openness of these killings. For a few examples, see Ernst Klee, Willi Dressen, and Volker Riess, eds., *"The Good Old Days": The Holocaust as Seen by Its Perpetrators and Bystanders* (New York: Free Press, 1991) pp. 28–37.

40. P.K., JK, pp. 945–946.

41. Verfügung, JK, pp. 2120–2124.

42. For a summary of the testimony and of much of what is known about the killings in Šiauliai, see "Sachverhaltsdarstellung," JK, pp. 1212–1214. G.T. describes one killing in which he helped bring the Jews to the killing pits (JK, pp. 1487–1488).

43. The Lithuanians probably identified the Jews, since this was the typical pattern (as the Germans themselves did not know who the Jews were). Also, the company's sergeant major told one reservist that they had had to carry out the executions themselves because the Lithuanians had proven themselves to be too brutish (*grausam*) in their manner of killing (H.H., JK, p. 1152).

44. J.F., JK, p. 849.

45. H.K., JK, p. 733. K. says that the Šiauliai killings were done by the professional policemen among them, as were most of the killings during the fall (pp. 732–733). He says that this man, W., died shortly thereafter during the battles around Cholm. Whether or not he actually killed again is unknown.

46. J.F., JK, p. 849. These posters were, however, inaccurate, for Jews remained in Šiauliai for some time to come. Nevertheless, they expressed a yearning for the announced end, the total purging from the city of Jews.

47. Claims have, of course, been made by individual men in this battalion that they were coerced or that they refused to kill. One that is noteworthy asserts that, after having refused to participate in the killing in Šiauliai, the man was told by his sergeant that he had better think it over by evening. The sergeant called the man to him before evening and, learning that the man still refused, told him that he at least could bring the Jews to the killing site. The man says that he did not believe he could refuse this order. This account, unlike most others, sounds truthful, for the man tells his interrogator that he can ask the sergeant himself, who will confirm his story. He says that after this killing in Šiauliai, he participated in no others. If the story is indeed true, it is particularly noteworthy in that this man gives no hint that others in the battalion shared his attitude or attempted to refuse to participate in the killings.

For material relevant to the issue of coercion, see G.T., JK, pp. 1487–1488; H.M., JK, p. 773; and Verfügung, JK, pp. 2196, 2209–2210, 2212–2214, 2138–2139.

48. For a summary of what is known of these killings, see Verfügung, JK, pp. 2120–2171.

49. H.K., JK, p. 733.

50. Verfügung, JK, pp. 2168–2170. H.H. reports having seen a sign, "Luga Jew-free!" (*Luga Judenfrei!*) (JK, p. 1152).

51. Verfügung, JK, p. 2157.

52. Verfügung, JK, pp. 2159–2162.

53. Verfügung, JK, pp. 2166–2168.

54. Given the demonology about Jews undergirding their actions, these Germans appear to have been ready, if not eager, to believe that Jews were ubiquitous, so that they required but meager proof in order to conclude that someone was a Jew. Sometimes, a suspicion was sufficient, as an episode from this battalion's stock of memories, this one from a reservist, illustrates: "From the town of Iwanowskaja I can report as an eyewitness that S., who was then a reservist, beat to death a prisoner of war or a deserter only because the name Abraham appeared in his papers. At the end, an army officer appeared on the scene; however, he came too late" (E.L., JK, p. 783). Naturally, nothing happened to this brutal killer, who, because of repeated exploits, became known for his sadism. This man was the father of nine children born between 1924 and 1940.

55. In the value-inverted world of Germany during the Nazi period, naming a genocidal undertaking after someone—in this case, the assassinated Reinhard Heydrich—was to honor him.

56. For an account of *Aktion Reinhard*, see Yitzhak Arad, *Belzec, Sobibor, Treblinka: The Operation Reinhard Death Camps* (Bloomington: Indiana University Press, 1987); for the Lublin District, see Dieter Pohl, *Von der "Judenpolitik" zum Judenmord: Der Distrikt Lublin des Generalgouvernements, 1939–1944* (Frankfurt/M: Peter Lang, 1993).

57. Indictment Against K.R., ZStL 208 AR 967/69 (hereafter cited as KR), pp. 53–55.

58. For the two different chains of command, see Indictment, KR, pp. 19–22.

59. R.E., KR, pp. 36–37.

60. R.E., KR, p. 37.

61. Indictment, KR, pp. 85–86.

62. Indictment, KR, p. 89.

63. Indictment, KR, p. 103; R.E., KR, p. 39.

64. See Indictment, KR, pp. 104–105; and Browning, *Ordinary Men*, p. 132.

65. The history, manpower composition, and essential features of the third battalion of Police Regiment 25, Police Battalion 67, do not diverge from those of the other two battalions in any significant way that would contradict the thrust of the analysis. See ZStL 202 AR-Z 5/63.

66. JK, pp. 2075–2076.

67. H.K., JK, p. 732.

68. Verfügung, JK, p. 2202.

69. See, for example, Verfügung, JK, p. 2240.

70. A.W., JK, p. 1089.

71. The assertion by the perpetrators that they did not have any idea that "resettlement" meant killing, and that when they deported Jews (even when they themselves accompanied the Jews to the death camps), they were unaware that the Jews were slated for death, is spurious, though widespread. The evidence to the contrary (aside from common sense), is voluminous. For a definitive statement on the subject, see, for example, Indictment, KR, p. 90; the former clerk of the *KdO* Lublin staff testifies: "By 'evacuation' one understood the evacuation of Jews to camps or ghettos. From rumors and hearsay, I knew at that time that the Jews who came into a camp were in some way killed there. Details of this were, however, unknown to me. Of gassing in particular I heard something only later" (R.E., KR, p. 35).

72. J.F., JK, p. 1086.

73. Verfügung, JK, pp. 2199–2202. One participant says that before and during the killing, the killers received Schnapps. The use of alcohol during executions is difficult to verify or disprove. The men in killing institutions often put forward conflicting claims on this point. It cannot be doubted that there were times when Germans consumed alcohol before or during killing operations, not to mention after their work was done.

The killing was discussed frequently among the men, although we know little of what they said. One of the perpetrators, a thirty-three-year old reservist from Dortmund, drafted in August 1939, relates the following about the killings around Cracow:

> Among the men, it was always said that Third Company divided itself for the operations against the Jewish people in the following manner:
> First Platoon: Shovel holes [*Löcher schaufeln*].
> Second Platoon: "Mow them down" [*"Legt um"*].
> Third Platoon: Cover them up and plant trees [*Schaufelt zu und pflanzt Bäume*]."

This is, of course, a fanciful description of what happened. Since the different platoons rotated duties, the Germans almost never dug the graves themselves (either having local auxiliaries or the Jews themselves do it), and they certainly did not plant trees over the graves. Still, from this story three things emerge: the Germans talked about the killings enough for lore to develop around them; they tried to give some form to their killing activities (which were frequent) that would integrate them better into the normal routines of non-killing days; in their talk about the killings, they crowned them with the fanciful creation of life and beauty: the planting of trees, which unwittingly betrays their lack of disapproval of the genocidal killing, and their *common* (note that this was the lore about Third Company) conception of the killing as a regenerative, redemptive, and beautifying enterprise. See H.K., JK, p. 734.

74. Verfügung, JK, pp. 2207–2209. It must be noted that this killer maintains that he and his comrades all disapproved of the killing, and that they had been threatened by their battalion commander should they refuse to do their duty. See Appendix 1 for a discussion of why such claims must be discounted.

75. See Verfügung, JK, p. 2207. The occasional testimony about the posting of killing operations on bulletin boards discusses it as if it had been nothing more remarkable than the posting of ordinary guard duty.

76. Verfügung, JK, pp. 2260, 2269–2275.

77. See Shmuel Krakowski, *The War of the Doomed: Jewish Armed Resistance in Poland, 1942–1944* (New York: Holmes & Meier, 1984). The Germans were often aided by local Poles who led them, with information and as guides, to the hideouts of Jews.

78. Verfügung, JK, pp. 2277–2287.

79. Verfügung, JK, pp. 2078–2079, 2288–2299.

80. The men of police battalions contributed to the slaughter of a large portion of the Jews whom the *Einsatzgruppen* killed, numbering over one million. They also helped perpetrate the slaughter of a good portion of the Jews in the *Generalgouvernement*, numbering around two million, as well as Jews from other areas of Europe. See the chart listing some major police battalion killings in Chapter 9.

Chapter 7

1. The major sources for Police Battalion 101 are the two separate legal investigations, Investigation of Wolfgang Hoffmann et al., StA Hamburg 141 Js 1957/62 (hereafter cited as Hoffmann), and Investigation of H.G. et al., StA Hamburg 141 Js 128/65 (hereafter cited as HG). A smattering of material is also to be found in the Hamburg State Archive (hereafter cited as StAH).

Christopher R. Browning, *Ordinary Men: Reserve Police Battalion 101 and the Final Solution in Poland* (New York: HarperCollins, 1992), which presents a more comprehensive and, in many ways, an admirably constructed account of the battalion's deeds, precludes the necessity of reciting here many facts and events that are not directly pertinent to the task at hand. It also lifts the obligation of presenting here every last item of material which might be construed (even if erroneously) to cast doubt on my understanding of the battalion, for such material can easily be found in Browning's book. I disagree with essential features of Browning's portrait of the battalion, with many of his explanations and interpretations of particular events, even with some of his assertions of fact, and especially with his overall interpretation and explanation of the men's actions. Some of the book's major problems have been laid out in Daniel Jonah Goldhagen, review of *Ordinary Men*, by Christopher R. Browning, *New Republic* 207, nos. 3 and 4 (1992): pp. 49–52. Most important, the unsubstantiated, self-exculpating claims of the battalion men to opposition, reluctance, and refusal, which have been rejected here for methodological reasons (see Appendix 1), permeate *Ordinary Men* and, since Browning appears to have generally accepted them uncritically, they inform and therefore substantially impair his understanding of the battalion. Other substantial, systematic problems include: the book's routine equation of what the men say during their testimony, with what they remember, with what actually happened (this is related to the credulousness of the men's assertions to have opposed the killings); the frequent absence or misinterpretation of evidence that suggests the general voluntarism and approval of the men in the battalion for their genocidal activities; the consistent playing down of the men's critical faculties; and an insufficient comparative perspective of other police battalions and institutions of killing more generally.

2. For a summary of its history, see Judgment Against Hoffmann et al., Hoffmann, pp. 8–10.

3. See B.P., Hoffmann, pp. 1912–1914. Details about this period are not abundant. See Browning's treatment of the battalion's early life in *Ordinary Men*, pp. 38–44.

4. Judgment, Hoffmann, pp. 24–26; B.P., Hoffmann, pp. 1930–1931; H.K., Hoffmann, p. 2246; also Browning, *Ordinary Men*, pp. 42–43. There is a murky story about Lieutenant Gnade having refused to allow his men to participate in the killing of the Jews from one of the transports, and hightailing it back to Hamburg. This outright refusal, if indeed it occurred, is interesting because insubordination of this sort would have been witnessed by a sizable contingent of Police Battalion 101. Also, Gnade was later to become a zealous killer, who performed with extreme ardor and brutality towards the victims during the battalion's extended killing spree in Poland.

5. See Indictment Against Hoffmann et al., Hoffmann, pp. 209–213 for the garrison locations of each company and its platoons in Poland; for a more detailed accounting, see Vermerk, Hoffmann, pp. 2817–2843.

6. Judgment, Hoffmann, pp. 24–25.

7. The data for this section were collected in the following manner. An inventory of those serving in Police Battalion 101 during its genocidal stay in Poland was built up from different sources. The main one is the June 20, 1942, roster of the battalion, which lists the men who were in the battalion when it embarked for Poland. This was supplemented by further names and data that are to be found in the transcripts of the two investigations (Hoffmann and HG) of the battalion's crimes, as well as the information contained in the card files of the ZStL. The list of names, with birthdays and places of birth, was submitted to the Berlin Document Center in order to determine the Nazi institutional membership of the men. The additional data that existed on their Party cards and in their SS files were also recorded.

8. With changing membership, more than 500 served in the battalion during its genocidal activities, a fact of some importance that Browning fails to mention. How many more than 500, or the 550 that I have tallied, is unknown.

9. Very little information exists on their educational levels. In Germany at the time, occupation and education correlate well, since occupations typically required precise educational qualifications. Like most other contemporaneous Germans, a paltry percentage of this battalion was likely to have studied at a university. Few probably had completed the *Abitur*. The overwhelming majority were likely to have had eight years of schooling, at which point they either entered the work force directly as unskilled laborers or enrolled in a training and apprentice program for a specified vocation in business or as a skilled laborer.

10. The categorization employed here follows the one used by Michael Kater, *The Nazi Party: A Social Profile of Members and Leaders, 1919–1945* (Cambridge: Harvard University Press, 1983), from which the occupational profile and the figures for Germany (for the summer of 1933) are drawn (p. 241). The one difference is that here the two categories "Skilled (craft) workers" and "Other skilled workers" are collapsed into one category, "Skilled workers." Since the data on the men were often sketchy, I have undoubtedly made a few contestable decisions in categorizing individuals. Even if these decisions were reversed, the resulting differences would not be

significant, especially since the purpose of this breakdown is to establish an overall social profile of the battalion.

11. Browning's sample is restricted to 210, namely the men who were interrogated by the investigating legal authorities, which leads to a significant skewing of his figures. Moreover, his failure to compare the battalion's occupational structure to that of Germany as a whole leads him to portray the social composition of the battalion erroneously. It is inaccurate to characterize the men of Police Battalion 101 as having come from "the lower orders of German society." Though by no means mirroring the occupational structure of Germany exactly, they still formed some representative cross section of the population. He also fails to discuss their SS membership, except in the cases of the officers and the NCOs. See *Ordinary Men*, pp. 45–48 and p. 199, n. 26.

12. They were young (their average age was twenty-two), active policemen who appear to have been marginal in the battalion's life. Little is known about them.

13. O.I., for example, had previously been released from the Wehrmacht because he was judged to be too old, being born in 1896. Within a fortnight, the Order Police had snapped him up into the police reserve (Hoffmann, pp. 2055–2060, 3053–3054). See also the testimony of H.Ri., who had previously been declared unfit for service while with the *Afrikakorps* (HG, pp. 476–478); and H.Re., HG, pp. 620–629.

14. See Indictment, Hoffmann, pp. 246–248; and H.F., HG, pp. 441–450. G.H. was drafted in May 1942 and had two weeks of training before joining Police Battalion 101 (HG, pp. 536–542).

15. One man, B.D., was temporarily persecuted in 1933, presumably for his activity in his trade union and the Social Democratic Party. He had been a union member since 1923, and resumed membership after the war (Judgment, Hoffmann, pp. 19–20). E.S. had previously been declared unreliable by the Gestapo (Berlin Document Center).

16. Judgment, Hoffmann, pp. 27–28; and Hoffmann, pp. 489–507.

17. Julius Wohlauf, Hoffmann, p. 2880; H.B., Hoffmann, p. 3355; and A.K., Hoffmann, p. 3356.

18. F.B., Hoffmann, p. 2091.

19. He adds: "That evening, Schnapps was given out; in just about every room was a bottle. We were 8 men to a room, so that each was allotted 2–3 Schnapps, from which one could not get drunk. . . ." (F.B., Hoffmann, p. 3692). Browning mentions this assertion about whips, yet immediately casts doubt on its veracity, saying, "No one else, however, remembered whips." (He also fails to mention that the man telling of the whips at Józefów begins his assertion emphatically: "I can still remember clearly . . .") See *Ordinary Men*, p. 56. This discussion of the whips points to important interpretive issues that systematically differentiate my interpretation of this battalion from Browning's. The bearing and use of whips is precisely the sort of detail that the members of the battalion would be biased against presenting; the image of men going to round up women and children armed with ox hide whips is one that is hard to square with the claim that they were acting reluctantly or unwillingly, which is the way that these men try to depict themselves, and which Browning accepts. Presenting the men's *silence* about a subject like their own brutality as an indication of their best attempts to "remember," moreover, suggests that their accounts are a re-

flection of what really happened, rather than what they have chosen to present to a disapproving audience. This problematic mode of interpretation is frequently to be found in Browning's book when he discusses subjects that suggest the men's voluntarism and brutality. That we know the Germans in Police Battalion 101 to have carried whips in one of the deportations from Międzyrzec, and to have used them liberally, which Browning himself includes in his account (p. 108), lends credence to the assertion that they also used whips in Józefów (and probably elsewhere), namely from the beginning of their genocidal operations.

20. F.K., Hoffmann, p. 2482.

21. See, for example, O.S., Hoffmann, p. 4577. A.Z. reports that Gnade, in the Second Company meeting that followed the full-battalion assembly, gave the same justification (HG, p. 275). But it was a transparent fabrication, for at the time there was no organized partisan activity worth mentioning. See B.P., Hoffmann, p. 1919; A.S., Hoffmann, pp. 745–750; and A.K., Hoffmann, p. 2430. A.K. mentions that their anti-partisan activities started only after they had already completed the majority of their slaughtering of Jews.

22. F.E., HG, p. 874; see also his testimony, Hoffmann, p. 1356. Many have commented on Trapp's evident unease with the genocidal order. One man recalls having seen him "crying like a child" at his command post during the killing (E.G., HG, p. 383). Another recounts his emotional sparing of a bleeding ten-year-old Jewish girl (O.S., Hoffmann, pp. 1954–1955).

23. This justification was repeated again and again by the perpetrators of the Holocaust. After the war, the perpetrators—*Einsatzkommandos*, the men of police battalions, and others—routinely utter such nonsense, even though their killing began when Germany reigned supreme and hardly a bomb was being dropped on it.

24. A.W. asserts that Trapp also mentioned the boycott of German goods, which Jews had tried to organize in the United States during the 1930s, with limited success. "The forthcoming mission is a retaliatory measure *[Vergeltungsmassnahme]* for these machinations" (Hoffmann, pp. 2039–2040). This statement was absurd, for by this time the United States, like much of the world, was at war with Germany—though much of the blame for this was laid at the door of the Jews.

25. See, for example, O.S., Hoffmann, p. 4577.

26. O.S., Hoffmann, p. 1953; see also his testimony, Hoffmann, p. 4577. A few state that Trapp first asked for volunteers for the firing squad. A.B. says that more men volunteered than were necessary (Hoffmann, p. 440).

27. For the affection and regard that the men showed Trapp, see Judgment, Hoffmann, p. 28; W.N., Hoffmann, p. 3927; and H.H., Hoffmann, p. 318. The last one was a member of the KdS Radzyn who, despite having not even been a member of Police Battalion 101, was aware of Trapp's standing in his men's eyes.

28. O.S., Hoffmann, p. 1953; see also his testimony, Hoffmann, p. 4577.

29. A.W., Hoffmann, p. 4592; see also his statements, Hoffmann, pp. 2041–2042, 3298, in which he emphasizes that Trapp's offer covered not only the men's participation in the execution squads but also in the other activities, such as driving the Jews from their houses to the market square.

30. See Browning's discussion of the testimony in *Ordinary Men*, p. 194, n. 3 (to chap. 1), and esp. p. 200, n. 9. I do not understand why he says (p. 200, n. 9) that

Weber also "understood" the offer to have been made to the older reservists, when Weber explicitly states the opposite (A.W., Hoffmann, p. 4592).

31. For a sampling of the extensive testimony on this, see W.G., Hoffmann, p. 4362; E.G., Hoffmann, p. 2502; and B.G., Hoffmann, p. 2019.

32. Judgment, Hoffmann, p. 35; and W.G., Hoffmann, p. 2147.

33. E.H., Hoffmann, p. 2716. See also W.G., Hoffmann, p. 2147; and E.G., Hoffmann, p. 1639.

34. E.G., Hoffmann, p. 1639; see also his testimony on p. 2502.

35. E.H., Hoffmann, p. 2716.

36. B.G., Hoffmann, p. 2019; see also F.B., Hoffmann, p. 2091; A.W., Hoffmann, pp. 2041, 2044–2045; F.V., Hoffmann, p. 1539; and H.J., HG, p. 415.

37. See Browning's discussion of the contradictory testimony on the shooting of infants in *Ordinary Men*, p. 59. I see no reason to cast doubt on the testimony of those who assert that the battalion's men did kill infants. The man who Browning says "claimed" that children were also shot is actually quite emphatic on the point: "I remember having entered houses that had already been searched many times and then found in them sick people and infants who had been shot to death" (F.B., Hoffmann, p. 1579). Even one of the men whom Browning quotes to support the notion that they did not shoot infants during the roundup phase says only that "almost all the men" refrained from killing the infants at that time. Undoubtedly, some of the men did shy away from killing small children during the Józefów roundup. Others did not.

38. E.H., Hoffmann, p. 2717.

39. Similarly, H.K. maintains that he had told his men, before the initial roundup, to do their utmost not to shoot Jews on the spot, but to get them all, the sick with the support of the healthy, to the marketplace. He says that the shooting of the specified groups did not agree with him. He adds that, "as if by tacit agreement, the shooting of infants and small children was renounced *[verzichtet]* by all the people," and that in their area of the ghetto no infants and children were lying in the streets among the dead (Hoffmann, pp. 2716–2717). It is difficult to know the truthfulness of these assertions. If true, then he ran the risk of rebuke for not following orders. He gives no hint of this. If true, then it was likely only a visceral inhibition to the killing of children and babies that prevented these Germans from littering the streets with them, and not some aversion to the killing of Jews in general, which they did do. The Germans also subsequently shot these same children. One other man does assert that he left an old woman and a child in their home in Józefów, who were nonetheless killed by a sergeant who subsequently found them. He says he was berated by the sergeant afterwards (H.K., Hoffmann, p. 2270). There is no way to evaluate the truthfulness of this self-exonerating claim.

40. E.H., Hoffmann, p. 2717.

41. Lt. H.B., Hoffmann, pp. 821–822; Indictment, Hoffmann, pp. 216, 225; see also Browning's discussion of the evidence in *Ordinary Men*, p. 201, n. 31. The detail accompanying them was led by Lieutenant Buchmann, who had refused to participate in the killing. For an account of this, see below. A.W. relates an incident which indicates the discretion available to Trapp. Before the systematic shooting began, the manager of a sawmill showed up with a list of twenty-five Jews who

worked for him. Trapp acceded to his request, and turned the Jews over to him so that they could continue working for the time being (Hoffmann, p. 2042).

42. E.H., HG, p. 956. See also his statement, HG, p. 507.

43. Like Trapp, Dr. Schoenfelder appeared to have been somewhat disturbed by their killing assignment. See F.E., HG, p. 874. That physicians, whatever their distaste for the enterprise, would have lent themselves to genocidal slaughter is hardly remarkable for Germany during the Nazi period, a society in which virtually every profession became corrupted. For the complicity of physicians in mass slaughter, see Robert Jay Lifton, *The Nazi Doctors: Medical Killing and the Psychology of Genocide* (New York: Basic Books, 1986); and Ernst Klee *"Euthanasie" im NS-Staat: Die "Vernichtung lebensunwerten Lebens"* (Frankfurt/M: Fischer Verlag, 1983).

44. Lt. K.D., Hoffmann, p. 4337.

45. E.G., Hoffmann, p. 2504.

46. Indictment, Hoffmann, pp. 281–282.

47. See Lt. K.D., Hoffmann, p. 4337, who was in First Company, for a description of his platoon's procedure; also W.G., Hoffmann, pp. 2148–2149. My account of the logistics of the entire killing operation is extremely abbreviated. See Browning's reconstruction in *Ordinary Men*, p. 60–69.

48. For an account of this, see A.Z., HG, pp. 276–277.

49. Lt. K.D., Hoffmann, p. 4337.

50. E.H., Hoffmann, p. 2719. At least some of the men were instructed on how to avoid the problem of spattering body matter: "If one held [the rifle] too high, the whole upper skull flew off. As a result, bits of brain as well as of bones flew about the area. The order was then issued to set the point of the bayonet on the neck. As a rule it did not happen afterwards" (M.D., Hoffmann, p. 2538). Even then, it sometimes happened. The gruesomeness was unavoidable.

51. A.B., Hoffmann, p. 4348.

52. "We did not shoot the Jews always on the same spot, but changed the place every time" (W.G., Hoffmann, p. 2149). See also E.H., Hoffmann, p. 2718.

53. Judgment, Hoffmann, pp. 54–55; and E.H., Hoffmann, p. 2720.

54. E.G., Hoffmann, p. 4344.

55. Lt. K.D., Hoffmann, p. 4338. In their subsequent killings, the Germans typically left it to Polish Mayors to dispose of Jewish bodies (see A.B., Hoffmann, p. 442). It is also worth noting that in Józefów the Poles were given free run to loot the ghetto after the roundups (see E.H., Hoffmann, p. 2717). While destroying this Jewish community, the Germans were oblivious to accumulating booty for the German *Volk*, though it appears that many of the executioners individually took valuables left by those whom they killed (A.B., Hoffmann, p. 441). As economic gain was not a motivation, but an often greatly welcomed byproduct of the real motivation for killing the Jews, it was possible for the Germans to be oblivious to collecting the loot, or simply not to devote time to it, while moving on to other tasks. Similarly, the Germans did not force the Jews to undress before shooting them, and thereby forfeited the Jews' clothing to the graves (W.G., Hoffmann, p. 2148).

56. R.B., Hoffmann, p. 2534; and F.B., Hoffmann, pp. 2951, 4357; see also F.V., Hoffmann, p. 1540.

57. A.B., Hoffmann, pp. 2518–2520; see also his testimony on p. 4354.

58. E.H., Hoffmann, p. 2720; it seems that Hergert took it upon himself to relieve men who were being affected by the strain of killing. One of his men recounts: "I myself participated in ten killings during which I had to kill men and women. I simply could not shoot men and women anymore, a fact which drew the attention of my group leader, Hergert, who noticed that I repeatedly shot past them. For that reason he replaced me. Other comrades were also sooner or later replaced, because they simply could not endure it" (W.G., Hoffmann, p. 2149). In other testimony, he says that the number of Jews that he shot was six to eight (Hoffmann, p. 4362).

59. F.B., Hoffmann, pp. 2092–2093; W.I., Hoffmann, p. 2237; A.B., Hoffmann, pp. 2691–2692, 4348; and B.D., Hoffmann, p. 1876. The men involved were older men. F.B. tells of a request to be excused by two of his comrades that was first put to the company commander, Wohlauf, who he says threatened to shoot them. These two men were later among those excused by Sergeant Kammer. F.B.'s admission that he killed and his assertion that Wohlauf's threat was directed not at him, but at two others, lend credence to the account. Still, it is curious. The company commander is supposed to have threatened men for wanting to be excused (in contravention to the policy laid down by the battalion commander), and yet a lowly sergeant serving under him excused these same men and others.

60. E.G., Hoffmann, p. 1640; see also his testimony on p. 2505.

61. M.D., Hoffmann, p. 2539; and E.G., Hoffmann, p. 2505. August Zorn tells of the event that led him to ask to be excused. The Jew whom he had selected was very old, so the two of them fell behind the others. By the time they arrived at the execution spot, his comrades had already killed their Jews. Upon seeing the dead, the old Jew threw himself on the ground, whereupon Zorn shot him. Zorn was unnerved and aimed too high, hitting him in the skull. "The shot tore off the rear of the upper part of the skull, exposing the brain of my Jew. Fragments of the upper part of the skull flew into the face of the platoon commander, Sergeant Steinmetz." Zorn says he threw up and asked his sergeant to be excused, and was given the duty of guarding Jews for the rest of the operation (HG, p. 277; see also his testimony, Hoffmann, p. 3367).

62. See Lt. H.B., Hoffmann, pp. 2437–2440. The details of this man's refusal and its consequences are discussed presently.

63. For a more extensive discussion of claims of refusal, see Browning, *Ordinary Men*, pp. 64–69.

64. That Captain Hoffmann was by disposition less accommodating makes little difference, since he rarely went to the killing operations himself, giving subordinates a free hand to run them as they pleased; moreover, in the other companies a relatively easygoing attitude towards participation in the killings was rarely taken advantage of by the men.

65. H.E., Hoffmann, p. 2167.

66. W.G., Hoffmann, p. 4362; see also J.R., Hoffmann, p. 1809.

67. A.S., Hoffmann, p. 747.

68. Browning discusses these subjects at length. See *Ordinary Men*, pp. 69, 71–77, which includes his analysis of their reaction, from which I dissent in many large and small matters, as is discussed in detail below. For example, his attribution of "shame" to them (p. 69)—an emotion, in cases like this, dependent upon the sense that one has committed a moral transgression—does not have an evidentiary basis in

the source material. "Visceral disgust," yes; "shame," no. His explanation for the general absence of what one sorely waits to read, namely that an ethical or principled opposition to the killing motivated their refusals and disgust, is hardly believable: "Given the educational level of these reserve policemen, one should not expect a sophisticated articulation of abstract principles" (p. 74). A person does not have to be a Kantian philosopher to condemn the wholesale slaughter of unarmed, unthreatening civilians, men, women, and children, as a moral abomination. Browning acknowledges that it is difficult to know how many men who were assigned to the execution squads asked to be excused from the killing, yet his estimation that between 10 and 20 percent of the men did so appears to be stretching the evidence. He says, for example, that Sergeant Hergert "admitted excusing as many as five from his squad of forty or fifty men" (p. 74). This sergeant actually places the number at "about 2–5 men" (E.H., Hoffmann, p. 2720). Two out of forty or fifty looks less like the 10 percent, let alone the 20 percent, that Browning contends excused themselves. Still other reasons to dissent from his presentation and interpretation of the material in these pages exist.

69. One killer, who asked to be excused after shooting Jews for a while, explains: "Because there were also women and children among the victims, I could not continue after a while" (W.I., Hoffmann, p. 2237). Sergeant Hergert confirms that the reason given to him for requests to be excused was the difficulty the men were having in shooting women and children (E.H., Hoffmann, p. 2720). Shooting Jews in general was not problematic for them. Old Jewish men were fair game. In this first killing operation, they were having particular difficulty in overcoming the taboo that had been inculcated into them that women and children were owed certain protections. Yet only a small percentage of them found even this difficulty too much to surmount.

70. See E.G., Hoffmann, p. 2505; F.K. Hoffmann, p. 2483; G.K., Hoffmann, p. 2634; A.Z., HG, p. 277; M.D., Hoffmann, p. 2539; and G.M., HG, pp. 168–69.

71. H.K., HG, p. 363. He says that during the entire execution he had nothing to do. His assertion should be qualified in light of one incident, of which he may not have known. In the middle of the night, one of the men, apparently so disturbed by his own participation, shot through the roof of their quarters (K.M., Hoffmann, p. 2546).

72. W.G., Hoffmann, p. 2149.

73. The evidence does not indicate that they did not participate in subsequent killing operations. That many killed a number of Jews before asking to be excused also suggests that their desire to be relieved from the gruesome duty was based not on ethical opposition, but on a visceral inability to continue, for had they thought the slaughter to be a crime, given the easy opportunity (and, for some, repeated offers) that they had to avoid killing, it is hard to understand why they did not opt out earlier.

74. F.B., Hoffmann, p. 1581; and H.B., Hoffmann, pp. 889–890. A sketchy incident that is to have taken place in Aleksandrów, a small village near Józefów, is reported by two of the men. After assembling the Jews, Trapp let them go free and returned with his men to Biłgoraj. See F.B., Hoffmann, pp. 2093–2094; and K.G., Hoffmann, p. 2194. Browning discusses this in *Ordinary Men*, pp. 69–70.

75. On the presence of Hamburg Jews, see F.V., Hoffmann, p. 973; and E.H., Hoffmann, p. 2722.

76. Judgment, Hoffmann, p. 72; see also A.B., Hoffmann, p. 2698–2699; E.H., Hoffmann, p. 2722.

77. For a general account of the killing, see Judgment, Hoffmann, pp. 72ff.; Indictment, Hoffmann, pp. 338–379; and E.H., Hoffmann, pp. 2722–2728.

78. In German, "Hiwi" is a shortened form of "Hilfswilliger," meaning "willing helper." It is used to describe all manner of subordinates who do what is generally unpleasant work. During the war, "Hiwi" became a generic term for eastern European minions of the Germans. See "Hilfswillige," *Encyclopedia of the Holocaust*, ed. Israel Gutman (New York: Macmillan, 1990), pp. 659–660.

79. Browning cites the testimony of one man who says that most of the small children and infants were not killed during the roundup (*Ordinary Men*, p. 80). This is not convincing. It is noteworthy that others do not comment that they did not carry out the clear orders from Gnade to kill those who were difficult to bring to the assembly point. Had they indeed abjured from killing the less mobile or recalcitrant Jews (of which, it appears, there were many), then we surely would have more testimony on this point. E.H., for example, during his detailed testimony (he reports, among other things, having spoken to some German-speaking Jews in the Jewish district), tells of Gnade's "order to shoot the elderly, infirm, and infants, again on the spot." He says nothing more about the order, which implies that it was carried out (Hoffmann, p. 2722). The testimony of W.H., the man cited by the court in the Judgment (p. 72), is definitive on this point: "All the sick, infirm, and infants had already been killed by the first clearing commando. . . . In these 20 houses I saw about 25 to 30 dead. They were lying within and in front of the houses" (Hoffmann, p. 2211, cited in Indictment, Hoffmann, p. 359).

80. It is, to say the least, unlikely that the photographer was creating a photographic record to indict himself and his comrades. He never claimed that this had been his purpose. It seems fair to conclude that he was happily documenting his and his friends' deadly exploits.

81. E.H., Hoffmann, p. 2723; and J.P., Hoffmann, p. 2750.

82. F.P., HG, p. 241.

83. J.P., Hoffmann, pp. 2749–2750; and E.H., Hoffmann, p. 2723.

84. The notion that this was a purely pragmatic response to the difficulty that the Germans had with the first batch of Jews that they marched to the execution staging ground (see Browning, *Ordinary Men*, pp. 80–81) is hard to believe. I know of no other time that Germans constructed and employed such a (ridiculous) marching aid (which, not surprisingly, proved to be a dismal failure).

85. A.B., Hoffmann, p. 2700. A long account of his is reproduced in Browning, *Ordinary Men*, p. 81. For other accounts of the march, see E.H., Hoffmann, p. 2723; and W.Z., Hoffmann, p. 2624.

86. See Indictment, Hoffmann, pp. 346–347; J.P, Hoffmann, p. 2750; H.B., HG, p. 98; and A.Z., HG, p. 282.

87. A.Z., HG, p. 282.

88. This account is taken from Indictment, Hoffmann, p. 347. The testimony that I have seen contained within the investigatory record indicates that some of the

men did flank the Jews and force them to run the final stretch to the killing site. Though it stands to reason that violent verbal as well as physical encouragement by the Germans was necessary to get the Jews to run to their own executions, neither testimony states this. See W.Z., Hoffmann, p. 2625; and G.K., Hoffmann, p. 2638. I have included the Indictment's account because in all other matters it has shown itself to be reliable.

89. F.P., HG, pp. 241–242. See also his testimony, Hoffmann, p. 4571.

90. F.P., HG, p. 240; and J.P., Hoffmann, pp. 2749–2750.

91. Indictment, Hoffmann, pp. 347–348; and E.H., Hoffmann, pp. 2724–2726.

92. F.P., Hoffmann, p. 4571; E.H., Hoffmann, p. 2725.

93. The SS officer in charge of the Hiwis was heard to shout at Gnade, "Your fucking police *[Scheisspolizisten]* aren't even shooting," which spurred Gnade to order his men to take up the killing (E.H., Hoffmann, pp. 2725–2726).

94. E.H., Hoffmann, pp. 2726–2727.

95. F.P., HG, p. 242.

96. E.H., Hoffmann, p. 2722; see also Indictment, Hoffmann, p. 341.

97. For Browning's very different analysis of the significance of the Łomazy mass slaughter, see *Ordinary Men*, pp. 84–87.

98. With the exception of a few men who are said to have slinked off from the killing site, all of the men of this company made their fair contribution to the mass slaughter. See E.H., Hoffmann, p. 2727. The shirkers obviously could have avoided killing with the tacit consent of their superiors. Browning identifies by name two men as having avoided shooting Jews, yet the only evidence for this are their own assertions. One claims that he purposely did not shoot a fleeing Jew and avoided the wrath of Gnade only because none of the others squealed on him and Gnade was too drunk to pursue the matter properly. See *Ordinary Men*, p. 86. But this man's testimony is demonstrably unreliable and self-serving, as his interrogator pointed out twice during his testimony (P.M., HG, p. 209). Browning also credits this man with having slipped away from the executions at Józefów (p. 65). Browning's use of this testimony is discussed in more depth in Chapter 8, note 65.

Browning ventures that the apparent failure of this killing operation's leaders explicitly to offer the men the choice to excuse themselves from the massacre made the killing *easier* for the men and helps explain why virtually everyone killed. Because the men did not have the "burden of choice," according to Browning's interpretation, they could just naturally follow their orders and therefore were not torn by the conflicts that the "burden of choice" at Józefów had created for them. See *Ordinary Men*, pp. 84–85. This interpretation—which has no evidentiary basis—skirts a far more obvious, straightforward, and likely explanation of the men's fine performance of their tasks, an explanation which is supported by the character of all of their later killing operations, as well as the histories of other police battalions and the *Einsatzkommandos*. By the time of the Łomazy slaughter, the shock of the first killing operation had dissipated, and with it the source of their distemper. Inured to the unpleasantness of the genocidal duties, they carried out their duties well, not because they had no choice (at least formally), but because they saw no reason to do otherwise. As for Józefów, no basis exists for the belief that those who opposed the killings, especially those who found them ethically abhorrent, had to kill. The explicit offer of choice in Józefów and the absence of such an explicit offer in Łomazy (it is, however, by no means clear that the Józefów offer was not a standing offer) are not what explains the revulsion of some of the men to their initial, personalized, face-to-face slaughter of unarmed men, women, and children, and then, by the time of the Łomazy massacre, their acclimation to the same task. (It was a task which they, as suggested by the absence of ethical statements in their own testimony, did not oppose out of principle.) Are we really to believe that if Gnade had presented the men with the choice to keep their distance, then (1) many men would have excused themselves from the Łomazy operation, and (2) the ones who did not would have reacted to this massacre in a manner similar to Józefów, namely with revulsion? It should not be forgotten, Browning's figures notwithstanding, that not very many men availed themselves of Trapp's Józefów offer in the first place.

99. A.B., Hoffmann, p. 4448.

100. All photographs of Police Battalion 101 that are described here but not shown cannot be published because of an interpretation that a local official has made of the privacy laws of the Federal Republic of Germany. These photographs, and many others that are extremely revealing, are contained in the volume of photographs in the Hoffmann investigation.

101. For many of the killing operations, doubt exists as to how many Jews the Germans killed or deported. In constructing these tables, I have decided to present the minimum estimates that agree with those in Browning's Tables 1 and 2, found in *Ordinary Men*, app. One exception is the number of Jews whom they killed on the "Jew-hunts." Browning estimates that they killed one thousand Jews. My impression is that the number must be higher, though it is hard to know.

102. During the roundup itself, they slaughtered close to one thousand.

103. A.B., Hoffmann, pp. 442–443.

104. A.B., Hoffmann, p. 443.

105. The men of Police Battalion 101 were instructed by their company commanders about the *Schiessbefehl*. See Indictment, Hoffmann, pp. 272–273; F.B., Hoffmann, p. 2103; and A.Z., HG, pp. 274–275.

106. A.K., Hoffmann, p. 1183.

107. E.N., Hoffmann, p. 1693; and B.P., Hoffmann, p. 1917. This is also evident just from reading the perpetrators' testimony. For a list of those who have testified about the search-and-destroy missions, see Browning, *Ordinary Men*, p. 211, n. 20.

108. A.B., Hoffmann, p. 2708.

109. M.D., Hoffmann, p. 3321.

110. B.P., Hoffmann, p. 1917.

111. F.B., Hoffmann, p. 404; and B.D., Hoffmann, p. 2535.

112. H.B., Hoffmann, p. 3066.

113. H.B., Hoffmann, p. 3215. According to this man, B. was quite cruel, both to Jews and to Poles, and that he liked to flaunt his SS insignia on his uniform. "He treated them with chicanery whenever it was possible" (Hoffmann, p. 3066).

114. E.N., Hoffmann, p. 1695. He adds that he remembers that they assigned Poles the task to raze *(einebnen)* the bunkers and to bury the victims. He estimates that at that location they destroyed ten to twelve bunkers in this manner and killed between fifty and one hundred Jews.

115. E.N., Hoffmann, p. 1693.

116. For some of the testimony given by many of the men on this point, see Hoffmann, pp. 2532–2547. This topic is taken up in greater detail in Chapter 8.

117. Judgment, Hoffmann, pp. 143–144.

118. P.H., of First Company, relates: "I myself recall several combings through the woods *[Walddurchkämmungen]* carried out by the company during which the Jew-hunt *(Juden Jagd)* was conducted. We also employed the expression 'Jew-hunt' " (Hoffmann, p. 1653). See also the testimony of C.A., who refers to them as the "so-called Jew-hunt operations *[Judenjagdeinsätze]*" (Hoffmann, p. 3544). He was a member of Second Company. F.S. (HG, p. 306) and G.M. (HG, p. 169) of Second Company also acknowledge the term. Of course, the imagery of a hunt is very different from that of soldiers going into combat. "Hunt" could mean two things or both: the hunting of animals or of outlaws; the Germans describe the Jews repeatedly as having been "outlawed" *(vogelfrei)*.

119. A.B., Hoffmann, p. 442. He says this in the context of describing the repeated killing operations that his platoon undertook in the small towns, villages, or estates of the region around Parczew, during which his comrades would each time shoot ten to forty Jews either in their homes or on the locale's outskirts.

120. W.H., Hoffmann, p. 3566.

Chapter 8

1. For one account of the selection principle, see H.B., Hoffmann, pp. 825–826. Christopher R. Browning, *Ordinary Men: Reserve Police Battalion 101 and the Final Solution in Poland* (New York: HarperCollins, 1992), may be right that in choosing the most marginal inhabitants of the village, Trapp sought to harm relations with Poles as little as possible (p. 101). Still, such thinking depends upon a cognitive orientation at odds with the one that produced these men's actions towards Jews. His characterization of Trapp's decision to slaughter innocent Jews as "an ingenious way to meet it [the quota] without further aggravating relations with the local population" needs to be rethought. Just as these perpetrators were not "ordinary men," but rather "ordinary Germans" of the time, this was not "ordinary ingenuity," but "Nazi" or "German" "ingenuity."

2. A.H., Hoffmann, p. 285.

3. Trapp report to Police Regiment 25, Sept. 26, 1942, Hoffmann, p. 2550.

4. For accounts of these events, see Trapp report to Police Regiment 25, Sept. 26, 1942, Hoffmann, pp. 2548–2550; A.H., Hoffmann, pp. 284–285; F.B., Hoffmann, pp. 1589–1590; H.B., Hoffmann, pp. 825–826; G.W., Hoffmann, p. 1733; F.B., Hoffmann, pp. 2097–2098; H.K., Hoffmann, pp. 2255–2256; H.S., HG, pp. 648–649; and H.B., HG, pp. 464–465; see also Browning's more detailed reconstruction of the events in *Ordinary Men*, pp. 100–102.

5. H.E., Hoffmann, p. 2174.

6. G.W., Hoffmann, p. 1733.

7. H.E., Hoffmann, p. 2179.

8. F.B., Hoffmann, p. 2105. One Second Company member reports that they also shot Poles while on their multipurpose patrols. The circumstances and reasons for killing them he leaves unmentioned (F.P., Hoffmann, p. 4572). B.P. relates that the

men of Police Battalion 101 frequently killed Poles who hid or were suspected of hiding Jews (Hoffmann, pp. 1919, 1925). This is not surprising, given that this was a policy of the ruthless German occupation. It is instructive that only two men from this battalion own up to such killings, even though it must have been common knowledge among them. Browning also makes this point (*Ordinary Men*, p. 157), yet he does not draw the obvious conclusion that these men are also concealing a great deal of their killing and brutalizing of Jews.

9. Julius Wohlauf, Hoffmann, pp. 750–751; and E.R., HG, pp. 609–610. For Lieutenant Brand's wife, see Lieutenant H.B., Hoffmann, p. 2440.

10. F.B., Hoffmann, p. 1583.

11. J.F., Hoffmann, p. 2232; for the *Gendarmerie's* involvement, see G.G., Hoffmann, p. 2183.

12. For the nurses, see F.M., Hoffmann, pp. 2560–2561; for the wives, see the statement of one of the wives, I.L., Hoffmann, p. 1293. That German Red Cross nurses also observed the scene at the market square is known because they complained about the killing of the children, who had done nothing more than stand up at the market square. The perpetrators apparently had no hesitation in letting these women, these agents of healing and succor, observe the mass slaughter.

13. H.E., Hoffmann, p. 2172.

14. E.R., HG, p. 610. H.E., who was on vacation during this killing operation, was told by members of his company of both the brutality of the operation and of Wohlauf's wife's participation: "In this connection the comrades were particularly angry that the wife of Captain Wohlauf was in Międzyrzec and watched the 'action' at close hand" (Hoffmann, p. 2171).

15. F.B., Hoffmann, p. 2099; for another man's account, see F.B., Hoffmann, p. 1582; also, H.B., Hoffmann, pp. 2440, 3357; and A.K., Hoffmann, p. 3357.

16. Browning attributes to them the emotion of "shame"—a powerful, painful emotion that would have been produced (in this context) by a consciousness of their guilt, of having committed grave moral violations—for which no testimony or evidence exists. See Daniel Jonah Goldhagen, review of *Ordinary Men*, by Christopher R. Browning, *New Republic* 207, nos. 3 and 4 (1992), for criticism of this attribution (p. 51). Missing from Browning's interpretation of Frau Wohlauf's stint with Police Battalion 101 and the episode under discussion (see *Ordinary Men*, pp. 91–93) is the testimony cited presently of Lieutenant Brand's wife, which makes it clear that the source of the men's objections was not shame. One of the perpetrators does mention a sense of shame in another context, during a particularly licentious killing episode in the ghetto "hospital" in Kónskowola, when his comrades started shooting "indiscriminately" upon entering the room housing forty to fifty sick and emaciated Jews. Some of the Jews toppled from the upper bunks, making the scene unusually ghastly. "This way of acting disgusted me to such an extent, and I was ashamed to such a degree, that I turned around at once and left the room again" (F.V., Hoffmann, p. 1542). Note, though, that this man's shame resulted from "this way of acting," from the wantonness of his comrades, not from the killing itself, to which his presence was intended to contribute. He wanted them to kill in a manner befitting good, upstanding Germans.

17. L.B., HG, p. 596.

18. B.P., Hoffmann, p. 1917; and E.N., Hoffmann, p. 1693.

19. For a summary of some of the overwhelming evidence that the extermination of the Jews was common knowledge throughout the *Generalgouvernement*, see Judgment Against Johannes von Dollen et al., Hannover 11 Ks 1/75, pp. 42–45, here 42–43; for an account of how public, even boastful, the German killers of the Jews of Hrubieszów were, see Indictment Against Max Stöbner et al., StA Hildesheim 9 Js 204/67, pp. 121–132.

20. Quoted in Indictment, KR, p. 90.

21. L.B., HG, p. 598. It is interesting that she describes this man as, at the time, having sounded to her "cynical" and not "immoral" or "criminal." Her husband, it is worth noting, was not an opponent of the extermination (see H.E., Hoffmann, p. 2172). Browning fails to relate this stunning account to his analysis of the men's reaction to Wohlauf's wife's participation in the Międzyrzec operation. This account suggests, moreover, that a spirit of approval for the genocidal killing existed in the battalion. Otherwise, an ordinary policeman would not have approached his officer in such a manner.

22. See Orlando Patterson, *Slavery and Social Death: A Comparative Study* (Cambridge: Harvard University Press, 1982), for a discussion of the general dishonoring of slaves (esp. pp. 10–12).

23. The man conveniently claims that he did not actually cut off the Jew's beard, and that he was only posing. The truthfulness of his assertion is less an issue than his willful, proud taking of the symbolic pose and memorializing of it. Whatever he actually did, his (and presumably his family's) memento was his shearing off of a Jew's beard, an act denoting his mastery over this symbol of Jewry. Note also his gratuitous comment about the need for the Jew to work. This deep-rooted German cultural notion that the Jews do not work, which is discussed in ensuing chapters, was prominent enough in this German's view of Jews that he scrawls a reference to it on this unrelated photographic image.

24. For a discussion of the significance of the marking of slaves, see the section called "The Rituals and Marks of Enslavement," in Patterson, *Slavery and Social Death*, pp. 51–62.

25. H.F., Hoffmann, p. 2161. He was in Second Company. Inexplicably, Browning fails to present this crucial evidence, which suggests strongly that the men of Police Battalion 101 were quite at ease with, and approving of, their genocidal operations.

26. For a compilation of the platoon's activities, see Vermerk, Hoffmann, pp. 2839–2840.

27. G.M., Hoffmann, p. 3275.

28. G.M., Hoffmann, p. 3279.

29. See H.E., Hoffmann, pp. 2165–2179.

30. See, for example, H.E., Hoffmann, p. 2170–2171.

31. As is explained in Appendix 1, the routine protests by the men of Police Battalion 101 that they had been opposed to the killing must be discounted for methodological reasons. It is noteworthy that the protestations are typically not cast in the clear terms of principled disapproval. One peruses the testimony in vain for declarations of their recognition at the time that Jews were human beings, and that the

racism and antisemitism that was the then official doctrine was anathema to and rejected by them. One waits to read expressions of sympathy for the suffering of the victims. When caught up in a moment of self-exculpation, a perpetrator might say in a ritualistic, unfeeling manner that he was "incensed" *(empört)* by the killings. It is all too apparent from the testimony that the men were more angered at Wohlauf's wife having been at the huge killing operation in Międzyrzec than they were at the genocidal operation itself. Of *her* transgression they speak with genuine passion.

There are but a handful of men who make statements that even suggest that they might have been principled opponents of the genocidal killings. Only one expresses clear moral condemnation: "I thought that it was a great obscenity *[Schweinerei]*. I was embittered that we had turned into bastards *[Schweinen]* and murderers, especially since we had been trained in the barracks to be decent human beings" (A.B., Hoffmann, p. 4355). Even though there is no way to know if this is what he really thought at the time—for it was easy to assert such condemnation after the war—it is striking and revealing that the others do not make principled denunciations of the genocide. The statement by another man who claims to have been an opponent of the killings is still more instructive. He explains: "Since I was a great friend of the Jews, the task was hateful to me" (H.W., Hoffmann, p. 1947). Whether this is true or not, the formulation exposes all the others. This man believes himself compelled to explain something that should be obvious (namely that mass murder is wrong), by saying that what made him opposed to it was his "great" friendship for Jews, the clear implications being that great regard for the Jews was not the norm and that his attitude and stance were exceptional. Indeed, although it does not necessarily imply this logically, in the context in which it was uttered, his statement nevertheless strongly implies what he knew to be true, namely that those who were not great friends of the Jews approved of the extermination. And neither he nor anyone else in the battalion ever asserts in their testimony that their comrades saw the Jews favorably or merely neutrally. For the very few other such statements, all of which suggest the exceptional status of the person testifying, see Browning, *Ordinary Men*, p. 75.

32. E.H., HG, p. 511. Browning interprets this merriment to indicate the "callousness" and "dulled" "sensitivities" of the men who opposed the slaughter, as if some mere deadening process would be sufficient to produce such mirth in men who are unhappily carrying out what they consider to be the crime of mass murder (see *Ordinary Men*, p. 128). A far more plausible interpretation exists. These men were not merely callous and insensitive. They were all joking about deeds of which they obviously approved and in which they obviously enjoyed taking part.

33. A.B., Hoffmann, p. 799.

34. See the discussion in Appendix 1 on the significance of the absence of certain kinds of evidence.

35. H.B., Hoffmann, pp. 2439–2440.

36. He says: ". . . I do not wish, however, that on account of my testimony anyone of my superiors or subordinates should be incriminated or otherwise disadvantaged" (H.B., Hoffmann, p. 2439).

37. H.E., Hoffmann, p. 2172. He says about Lieutenant Brand, for example: "I recollect that Lieutenant Brand also had in no way made objections against the operations against the Jews *[Judeneinsätze]*."

38. See Browning's account of this episode in *Ordinary Men*, pp. 111–113.

39. M.D., Hoffmann, p. 2536.

40. H.B., Hoffmann, pp. 3356–3357. I have omitted the clause "I think it is possible" because in literal form it does not make sense grammatically or historically; Buchmann's statement is declarative. People, he says, were given other tasks. Moreover, he knew that some men, including himself, had been excused from killing operations.

41. E.G., Hoffmann, p. 2534; see also Hoffmann, pp. 2532–2547, where a number of battalion members speak to this issue. In the memories of the men, there is some confusion and disagreement over whether volunteers were asked for at various times or whether it was simply made clear to them that anyone could ask to be excused. This is reflected in E.G.'s slightly ambiguous testimony. The confusion, which is not restricted to him, probably arises from the absence of any effective difference between the two possibilities. Testifying over twenty years later, the men remember that they did not have to kill. Whether this was communicated to them at a given killing by a request for volunteers, or whether it was made clear to them that they could stop if they did not feel up to killing, does not matter; either way, they knew that their participation was voluntary. The details of the procedures by which they could avoid killing made such comparatively little impression on them for two interrelated reasons. Solidarity with the Jews was not a motivation of theirs, so when the possibility of exempting themselves from the killing was presented to them, the offer assumed no great significance, especially moral significance, in their minds. Also, a climate of ideological unanimity in approval of the killing would have made it unlikely that other battalion members would greet any avoidance of the task with the suspicion that the opposition to the killing was a principled one, so contemplating the social consequences of asking out was also not memorable.

42. B.D., Hoffmann, p. 2535; see also Sergeant A.B., Hoffmann, p. 2693.

43. A.Z., HG, p. 246.

44. See Browning, *Ordinary Men*, p. 185, for a conflicting interpretation of the meaning of "cowardice." Chief among the problems with his interpretation is the assertion, for which no evidence exists, that a plea of "weakness" was a mask for the person's "goodness," namely for his moral opposition to the deed. Moreover, since the testimony quoted above is the man's *postwar* account, not a contemporaneous one that he might have given to his comrades, the man would have had every motivation *not* to hide his alleged "goodness." Obviously, he means "coward" and not "opponent." This is made all the clearer by the man's account that immediately precedes his statement about cowardice. He says that during the Józefów killing, he eventually asked to be excused because he no longer felt up to it, owing to the "bone fragments and also brain matter" that were flying about everywhere. He does not say, even though his testimony was given after the war, that he asked to be excused because he thought the killing to be a crime (B.D., Hoffmann, pp. 2534–2535). It is also worth asking whether or not the fear of being called a "coward" would have been sufficient motivation for a person to undertake these gruesome killings, if he had indeed considered them to be a monstrous crime, especially if there were many men in the battalion who shared his view. The psychological devastation that committing such crimes would wreak upon such individuals would be substantial. Yet evidence to this effect is notably absent.

45. E.G., Hoffmann, p. 2533; see also his testimony on p. 4400.

46. A.B., Hoffmann, p. 2532. Sergeant Bentheim takes exception to A.B.'s formulation that enough men, if not more than enough, always volunteered. He does agree with A.B., however, that volunteers were always sought, and "that as executioners only volunteers were employed and none was commandeered" (Hoffmann, pp. 2537–2538). This, of course, suggests that enough men did volunteer.

47. For Grafmann's disgust, see E.G., Hoffmann, p. 2505; for others, see F.K. Hoffmann, p. 2483; G.K., Hoffmann, p. 2634; A.Z., HG, p. 277; and M.D., Hoffmann, p. 2539.

48. See J.S., ZStL AR-Z 24/63, pp. 1370–1371, on the volunteering in Mounted Police Third Squadron; Abschlussbericht, ZStL 202 AR-Z 82/61, p. 55, for Police Battalion 307; Verfügung, ZStL 208 AR-Z 23/63, vol. 3, for Police Battalion 41. Similar evidence exists for other police battalions. This subject is discussed further in Chapter 9.

49. A.W., Hoffmann, p. 4592.

50. H.B., Hoffmann, p. 822.

51. Indictment, Hoffmann, p. 246b.

52. StAH, Polizeibehörde 1, Akte 1185.

53. Kommando der Schutzpolizei, "Abschrift," 12/31/42, StAH, Polizeibehörde 1, Akte 1185.

54. H.R., HG, p. 624. This is discussed immediately below.

55. For examples, see F.S., HG, pp. 300–309; F.B., HG, 961; and P.F., Hoffmann, p. 2242.

56. Lt. K.D., Hoffmann, p. 4339.

57. H.R., HG, p. 624. He was in a particularly good position to have a transfer request granted because an existing provision stipulated that men with many children, the possessor of an hereditary farm *(Erbhof)*, or the last bearer of a family name *(letzte Namensträger)* would be given fighting duty only if they voluntarily chose to accept it. See A.W., Hoffmann, p. 3303. This is but another sign of the solicitousness of the regime for its men.

58. A.H., Hoffmann, p. 281.

59. *Mezrich Zamlbuch*, ed. Yosef Horn (Buenos Aires: 1952), pp. 476, 561. Browning's account does not use survivor testimony, discounting its value. Browning argues that the brutality of the men in Police Battalion 101 was instrumental, induced by the need of an undermanned contingent to move thousands of Jews against their will (p. 95). Survivor testimony belies this interpretation of the perpetrators' brutality, as well as the perpetrators' carefully constructed, sanitized accounts of their own deeds. The subject of the perpetrators' cruelty is addressed more systematically in Chapter 15.

60. E.K., Hoffmann, p. 157. Note that he too was a torturer (see H.B., Hoffmann, pp. 1048–1050), and that his seeming sympathy for the Jews is entirely manufactured, which does not invalidate his description of what the men of Police Battalion 101 did.

61. A.B., Hoffmann, p. 441. As I have discussed in my review of *Ordinary Men*, Browning presents and portrays this admonition by Trapp improperly (p. 87). It was not, as he suggests (in part, by leaving out its first sentence), a prophylactic prohibi-

tion uttered by Trapp before the Józefów massacre that supposedly set a "tone" of restraint for that killing operation (a "tone" that was supposedly far different from the one supposedly set by the cruel Gnade at Łomazy). In fact, it set no tone for that operation (or subsequent ones), but was a *response* to the men's cruelty that Trapp had witnessed in Józefów. Here Browning is attempting to make the case that the personality of the officer in charge of a given operation significantly influenced the actions of the men. I see no evidentiary basis for this conclusion. Trapp's statement, contra Browning, belies the notion. Moreover, the men's wanton cruelty at Międzyrzec was later perpetrated under Trapp's command.

62. William Shakespeare, *Julius Caeser*, 2.1.180.

63. A.B., Hoffmann, p. 799.

64. See Browning's chapter devoted to Hoffmann in *Ordinary Men*, pp. 114–120.

65. Browning's assertion that "a minority of perhaps ten percent—and certainly no more than twenty percent—did not" become killers (*Ordinary Men*, p. 159) is not supported by the evidence. His initial extrapolation that at the Józefów killing, between 10 and 20 percent of those assigned to killing details excused themselves, as was discussed earlier, is itself highly suspect. Even if this extrapolation were correct (and the men actually excused themselves from killing for principled reasons and not, as the evidence suggests, because of weak stomachs), the evidence does not indicate that these men (or others) continued to refuse to serve in subsequent operations as executioners by shooting Jews. (The significance of their contributions to the genocidal operations in ways other than shooting the Jews also needs to be addressed.) The testimony, discussed above, of one of the men, Erwin Grafmann—who, because he became disgusted at the flying body matter, excused himself from the Józefów killing after he had killed at least ten Jews, and who admits that he later *volunteered* for search-and-destroy missions (Hoffmann, pp. 2505, 2533, 4400)—speaks to this point, though it is absent from *Ordinary Men*. There is no reason to believe that some of his fellow retirees from the Józefów slaughter did not do the same. In fact, had 10 to 20 percent of the men consistently avoided contributing their fair share to the genocide, then we would undoubtedly have a fair amount of testimony on the subject, for it would have produced a noticeable division within the battalion.

Similarly, Browning's discussion of the putative ways in which men managed to avoid going "on the 'Jew hunts' or participat[ing] in firing squads" (*Ordinary Men*, p. 129) is problematic. With this section, he seeks not only to present analysis but also to suggest that such strategies were actually employed by those (presumably, 10 to 20 percent) who opposed the killing. Browning constantly plays up the reluctance and opposition of the men which he manages to read into the material, so this particular analysis, like others where he addresses the subject, accepts and presents uncritically the men's self-reported attempts to avoid killing and instances of success, as if they were facts. As if this were not problematic enough, he misportrays the testimony of one man, who credits (in Browning's words) "his early and open opposition to the battalion's Jewish actions with sparing him from further involvement." Browning proceeds to quote this man's story (which may or may not be a tall tale) and concludes that after he made clear his opposition to the killing, he "was never assigned to a firing squad" (p. 129). The man's testimony contains elements that Browning neglects to mention. The impression to be gained from Browning is that this man "spared" himself "from further involvement," especially since Browning is discussing the three lines of action that the men allegedly used to avoid going on "Jew-hunts" or participating in firing squads. Even though this man denies actually having shot any Jews, he tells of ten such "Jew-hunts" which (though he does not say so explicitly) he clearly went on. He was hardly spared "from further involvement." At most, he managed to avoid shooting Jews on the search-and-destroy missions in which he participated, not owing to his reputation as an opponent, but by his reluctance to jump to the fore to shoot (especially since others eagerly did so). He recounts in chilling detail an episode from one "Jew-hunt," which was discussed above. He and about thirty others, traveling through the countryside on bicycles, came upon the bunker of hidden Jews which they sought out upon a Polish informant's information: "Today I still remember exactly that we were already right before the bunker when a five-year-old boy came out crawling. He was immediately grabbed by a policeman and led aside. This policeman set the pistol to his neck and shot him. He was an active policeman *[Beamter]* who was employed in our unit as a medical orderly. He was the only medical orderly in our platoon." With grenades and shots to the head, the men on this patrol killed an estimated one hundred Jews, whom they then left to rot (see A.B., Hoffmann, pp. 442–443). The man's own testimony squarely contradicts Browning's assertion that his alleged "early and open opposition" spared "him from further involvement." Browning's assertions notwithstanding, few cases, few convincing cases, of refusals or evasions exist in the evidentiary record. One of his star "evaders," invoked both for Józefów and Łomazy (*Ordinary Men*, p. 65—he is the man who " 'slipped off' "—and p. 86), gives testimony so contrary to the events of the Łomazy killing (testimony in which he distances himself from the scene of the crime) that his interrogator twice points out to him that his testimony is not to be believed: "Herr Metzger, your statements do not sound credible. They also contradict the statements of your former comrades. It is above all not conceivable that you stood guard in the courtyard until the afternoon, particularly since the Jews had been carted off from there towards noon. Also, your description of your observations is not true. According to the investigations and eyewitness accounts conducted thus far, it has been established that all members of Second Company were deployed in the immediate proximity of the pit already by the beginning of the killings" (P.M., HG, pp. 208–209). The interrogator's challenge to this man's self-serving testimony comes immediately after the episode that Browning cites (p. 86).

66. E.B., HG, p. 960; see also the previous note for an incident recounted by A.B. when a medical corpsman shot a five-year-old Jewish child on a "Jew-hunt" (Hoffmann, p. 443).

67. A.B., Hoffmann, p. 4355.

68. A copy of the citation, dated Jan. 14, 1943, is in Hoffmann, p. 2671.

69. *KdO* Lublin, SS and Police Regiment 25, "Order of the Day!," Sept. 24, 1943, ZStL Ord. 365A4, p. 243.

70. Of them, only C.M.'s explicitly mentions the Jews (Indictment, Hoffmann, p. 330).

Chapter 9

1. *KdO* Lublin, Police Regiment 25, "Regimental Order No. 40," Sept. 24, 1942, ZStL Ord. 365w, p. 155.

2. ZStL Ord. 365w, pp. 171–172. Mounted Police Third Squadron copy.

3. For example, a "soccer championship" game was announced for Sunday, June 7, 1942, at 10 a.m.: "On the playing field behind the soldiers' barracks, a soccer championship game will be played between the SS and Police Sports Club and the Wehrmacht 'Blue-White' [team]." See Command Lublin, "Command Order No. 60," June 5, 1942, ZStL Ord. 365w, p. 19. For another report of competitive success "at this year's district championship in light athletics," see Police Regiment Lublin [25], "Regimental Order No. 26," June 18, 1942, ZStL Ord. 365w, p. 30. One of the regiment's own took second place in the 100-meter dash. He ran it in 12.5 seconds.

4. The men of the Order Police, at least in 1944, must have been eager movie-goers, for they were told that the Wehrmacht movies are oversubscribed on Saturday and Sunday evenings, so they should try whenever possible to attend the Monday or Wednesday showings. *KdO* Lublin, "Regimental Order of the Day No. 5," Feb. 4, 1944, ZStL Ord. 365A4, p. 248.

5. Police Regiment Lublin [25], "Regimental Order No. 27," June 25, 1942, ZStL Ord. 365w, pp. 38–39.

6. "Regimental Order No. 43," Oct. 15, 1942, ZStL Ord. 365w, p. 166.

7. "Regimental Order No. 37," Sept. 4, 1943, ZStL Ord. 365w, p. 162.

8. *KdO* Lublin, Dept. 1a, "Regimental Order of the Day No. 2," Jan. 14, 1944, ZStL Ord. 365A4, p. 214.

9. *KdO* Lublin, Dept. 1a, "Regimental Order of the Day No. 2," Jan. 14, 1944, ZStL Ord. 365A4, p. 214. See also "Regimental Order No. 39," Sept. 17, 1942, which urged the men to keep their quarters clean and to stop the "grossly negligent destruction of state property (toilets, windowpanes, etc.)" (ZStL Ord. 365w, p. 145).

10. See, for example, Raul Hilberg, *The Destruction of the European Jews* (New York: New Viewpoints, 1973); Helmut Krausnick and Hans-Heinrich Wilhelm, *Die Truppe des Weltanschauungskrieges: Die Einsatzgruppen der Sicherheitspolizei und des SD, 1938–1942* (Stuttgart: Deutsche Verlags-Anstalt, 1981), and Lucy S. Dawidowicz, *The War Against the Jews, 1933–1945* (New York: Bantam Books, 1975). Little mention is made of any aspects of their lives aside from the killing and their other operational tasks. This is also the case in Christopher R. Browning, *Ordinary Men: Reserve Police Battalion 101 and the Final Solution in Poland* (New York: HarperCollins, 1992), which neglects the truly "ordinary" aspects of their lives as killers. An exception to this general situation is Robert Jay Lifton, *The Nazi Doctors: Medical Killing and the Psychology of Genocide* (New York: Basic Books, 1986), which is a study of a small, atypical group of perpetrators: the doctors in Auschwitz; see also Tom Segev, *Soldiers of Evil: The Commanders of the Nazi Concentration Camps* (New York: McGraw-Hill, 1987); and Ernst Klee *"Euthanasie" im NS-Staat: Die "Vernichtung lebensunwerten Lebens"* (Frankfurt/M: Fischer Verlag, 1983).

11. R.E., KR, p. 34.

12. E.H., HG, p. 507.

13. H.F., Hoffmann, p. 1389. The cabinetmaker who was in charge of the bowling alley's construction in Międzyrzec also built tables, chairs, and bunks for their quarters, and bicycle stands. Until April 1943, he was permitted to employ Jewish craftsmen.

14. The times for church services were routinely announced to the men. Command Lublin, "Command Order No. 60," of June 5, 1942, for instance, communicated to them that on Sunday, June 7, Catholic services would be held by the army, once at 9 a.m. in one church, and again at 7:15 p.m. in a different church, noting "that at both services there would be opportunities for receiving the sacraments" (ZStL Ord. 365w, p. 19).

15. For examples, see Judgment Against Hermann Kraiker et al., Schwurgericht Bochum 15 Ks 1/66, p. 154; and BAK R19/324 (8/11/41).

16. *KdO* Lublin, Polizei-Regiment-25, "Regimental Order No. 34," Aug. 14, 1942, ZStL Ord. 365w, p. 122.

17. Quoted in Lifton, *The Nazi Doctors*, p. 16.

18. "Regimental Order No. 43," Oct. 15, 1942, ZStL Ord. 365w, p. 166.

19. *KdO* Lublin, SS and Police Regiment 25, "Regimental Order of the Day No. 24," June 11, 1943, ZStL, Ord. 365A4, p. 174. Also see *KdO* Lublin, Polizei-Regiment-25, "Regimental Order No. 34," Aug. 14, 1942, ZStL, Ord. 365w, p. 122; and *Befehlshaber der Ordnungspolizei* Lublin, "Regimental Order of the Day No. 1," Jan. 7, 1944, ZStL, Ord. 365A4, p. 242.

20. F.P., HG, p. 244.

21. One of the men of Police Battalion 101 got a dog, whose name was Ajax (H.K., Hoffmann, p. 2259).

22. Virtually nothing has been written on the Nazis' bizarre attitudes towards animals. My knowledge of the subject is greatly indebted to Erich Goldhagen, who has devoted a chapter to the subject in a forthcoming book. For photographs of the animals in the camp zoo of Treblinka, see Ernst Klee, Willi Dressen, and Volker Riess, eds., *"The Good Old Days": The Holocaust as Seen by Its Perpetrators and Bystanders* (New York: Free Press, 1988), pp. 226–227.

23. Command Lublin, "Command Order No. 69," June 26, 1942, ZStL, Ord. 365w, p. 40.

24. At least, none that I have come across in my extensive research. Also, the widespread use of other units of the Order Police, like the *Gendarmerie*, who were often employed in the destruction of the Jews of the cities that they were garrisoning, strongly suggests that the regime saw just about any German in its employ as being fit to contribute to the genocide.

25. As far as I know, no one has published a list of any kind about police battalion killings. This list, which was compiled from materials in ZStL with a few supplements from the *Encyclopedia of the Holocaust*, 4 vols., ed. Israel Gutman (New York: Macmillan, 1990), is not comprehensive, but illustrative. It should be noted that often a number of battalions participated in the same large mass shooting or deportation. The list is intended not to indicate how many Jews all the police battalions killed, but to present the large killing operations and also the number of deaths in which each police battalion was complicit during those operations. (Most of the battalions carried out many other large and small killing operations.) The issue is what

the men of each police battalion had to face. All of the summary figures for police battalions in the discussion of their activities include two units of the Order Police that were not, strictly speaking, police battalions: Motorized Gendarme Battalion and Mounted Police Third Squadron, which in their composition and killing activities were indistinguishable from police battalions. Both operated in the Lublin region and other areas of the *Generalgouvernement*. Like Police Battalions 65 and 101, they were a part of Police Regiment 25. Police Reserve Company Cologne is also included.

26. For example, see Abschlussbericht, ZStL 202 AR-Z 82/61, pp. 13–16, for Police Battalion 307.

27. Omer Bartov, *The Eastern Front, 1941–1945: German Troops and the Barbarization of Warfare* (London: Macmillan, 1985), has made this argument for the German army in the Soviet Union.

28. The exception to this, of course, is the wild killing forays that resulted when the Germans unleashed Ukrainians, Lithuanians, and Latvians upon the Jews during the early days of the invasion of the Soviet Union. Although the Germans incited and organized the killings, and sometimes participated themselves in the executions, by and large, the Germans kept to the side and observed and contemplated the wanton spectacles that others created according to their design.

29. These numbers are low estimates. The actual number that were stocked with many reservists is likely to have been higher, because for some of the police battalions, membership composition is unknown to me.

30. It is also unequivocal that some of the men of still another police battalion, Police Battalion 9, divided up among the *Einsatzkommandos*, also knew that they did not have to kill, since certainly in some, if not all, of the *Einsatzkommandos*, those manning them had been given the option not to kill. This is discussed in Chapter 15. In order to err on the side of underestimation, this battalion has been left out of the calculations.

31. See, for example, P.K., ZStL 208 AR-Z 5/63, p. 503; for the *Einsatzgruppen*, see Klee, Dressen, and Riess, *"The Good Old Days,"* p. 82.

32. O.P., Hoffmann, pp. 3191–3192.

33. A number of men of Police Battalion 309, responsible for the butchery, shooting, and burning of Białystok, describe their company commander, Captain B., in glowing terms. "He was fatherly," is the evaluation of one (E.B., Buchs, p. 1148). "He was to us fatherly," echoed another (A.E., Buchs, p. 1158). See also W.G., Buchs, p. 1384.

34. Although it is not known how many men refused to kill, the impression of all who have studied the matter is that the number was small. The evidence is so scattered that it would take a research effort of many months just to get a handle on the claims. Of the claims that have been made, it is easy to show that many of them are fabrications. For discussions of the subject, see Herbert Jäger, *Verbrechen unter totalitärer Herrschaft: Studien zur nationalsozialistischen Gewaltkriminalität* (Olton: Walter-Verlag, 1967), pp. 79–160; Kurt Hinrichsen, "Befehlsnotstand," in Adalbert Rückerl, ed., *NS-Prozesse: Nach 25 Jahren Strafverfolgung* (Karlsruhe: Verlag C. F. Müller, 1971), pp. 131–161; Daniel Goldhagen, "The 'Cowardly' Executioner: On Disobedience in the SS," *Patterns of Prejudice* 19, no. 2 (1985): pp. 19–32; and David H. Kitterman, "Those Who Said 'No!': Germans Who Refused to Execute Civilians

During World War II," *German Studies Review* 11, no. 2 (May 1988): pp. 241–254. The issue of the perpetrators' capacity to refuse to kill is discussed in more depth in Chapter 15.

35. A similar evaluation of him can be found in Indictment, Hoffmann, p. 327.

36. E.G., Hoffmann, p. 2505.

37. E.G., Hoffmann, p. 4344.

38. E.G., Hoffmann, p. 2505.

39. E.G., Hoffmann, p. 4344.

40. A.B., Hoffmann, p. 6222r.

41. J.S., ZStL 208 AR-Z 24/63, p. 1371. He was a member of Mounted Police Third Squadron. Browning, *Ordinary Men*, asserts (after commenting that some of the men of Police Battalion 101 used language in their testimony that "reflected the Nazi stereotype") that "the comments of other policemen reflected a different sensibility that recognized the Jews as victimized human beings: they were dressed in rags and half starved" (p. 152). Such a statement constitutes anything but proof that the Germans recognized the Jews' humanity, let alone conceived of them as "victimized human beings." The most vicious antisemites could make the same factual observation about the Jews' condition, as does one of the most brutal women guards of the Helmbrechts death march, cited in Chapter 13. Moreover, as evidence in support of this assertion, Browning cites the statement, such as it is, of only one man. The testimony of Police Battalion 101's men, running thousands of pages, is, in fact, remarkably devoid of these Germans' recognition of the Jews' humanity. If the material were approached with the reasonable belief that the publicly, incessantly proclaimed conception of the Jews in Germany during the Nazi period was shared by these men, then their testimony could not possibly even begin to persuade anyone otherwise. Browning, who argues earnestly that many did see the Jews as "victimized human beings," can muster little evidence to support such a claim. What better proof could there be that such a case cannot be made?

Chapter 10

1. Götz Aly and Susanne Heim, "The Economics of the Final Solution: A Case Study from the General Government," in *Simon Wiesenthal Center Annual* 5 (1988): p. 3.

2. Aly and Heim, "The Economics of the Final Solution," and Susanne Heim and Götz Aly, "Die Oekonomie der 'Endlösung': Menschenvernichtung und wirtschaftliche Neuordnung," in *Sozialpolitik und Judenvernichtung: Gibt es eine Oekonomie der Endlösung?* (Berlin: Rotbuch Verlag, 1987), pp. 11–90; included among those who take an analogous position is Hans Mommsen, "The Realization of the Unthinkable: the 'Final Solution of the Jewish Question' in the Third Reich," in Gerhard Hirschfeld, ed., *The Policies of Genocide: Jews and Soviet Prisoners of War in Nazi Germany* (London: Allen & Unwin, 1986), pp. 119–127, as does much of the Marxian scholarship on this period. Others have dissented vigorously from this erroneous view (see note 19 below for references), yet even they, in their attempts to unearth its meaning and significance, have failed to penetrate central aspects of the obfuscating features of Jewish "work" during the Nazi period.

3. As with many motives, these were only partly understood by the many and varied actors. See Anthony Giddens, *The Constitution of Society: Outline of the Theory of Structuration* (Berkeley: University of California Press, 1984), for a discussion of why actors cannot always account for their motives (p. 6).

4. See, for examples, Max Weber, *The Protestant Ethic and the Spirit of Capitalism* (New York, Charles Scribner's Sons, 1958); and Karl Marx, "The German Ideology," in Robert C. Tucker, ed., *The Marx–Engels Reader*, 2d ed. (New York: W. W. Norton, 1978), pp. 146–200.

5. For France, see Stephen Wilson, *Ideology and Experience: Antisemitism in France at the Time of the Dreyfus Affair* (Rutherford: Fairleigh Dickinson University Press, 1982), pp. 265ff., 626.

6. Martin Luther, *Von den Jueden und Iren Luegen*, quoted in Raul Hilberg, *The Destruction of the European Jews* (New York: New Viewpoints, 1973), p. 9.

7. See James F. Harris, *The People Speak! Anti-Semitism and Emancipation in Nineteenth-Century Bavaria* (Ann Arbor: University of Michigan Press, 1994), p. 134.

8. Klemens Felden, "Die Uebernahme des antisemitischen Stereotyps als soziale Norm durch die bürgerliche Gesellschaft Deutschlands (1875–1900)" (Ph.D. diss., Ruprecht-Karl-Universität, Heidelberg, 1963), p. 20. See also pp. 34–36.

9. Quoted in Nicoline Hortzitz, *"Früh-Antisemitismus" in Deutschland (1789–1871/72): Strukturelle Untersuchungen zu Wortschatz, Text und Argumentation* (Tübingen: Max Niemeyer Verlag, 1988), p. 248; see pp. 182–184, 245–255, 312 for additional examples.

10. See, for example, Maria Zelzer, *Weg und Schicksal der Stuttgarter Juden: Ein Gedenkbuch* (Stuttgart: Ernst Klett Verlag, 1964), p. 178.

11. Adolf Hitler, *Mein Kampf* (Boston: Houghton Mifflin, 1971), pp. 304, 314. The cognitive framework underlying the cultural designation of an activity as "work" undoubtedly generally includes some notion that it must be socially sanctioned and that by and large it is beneficial to society. Since society exists and reproduces itself largely as a consequence of work, it is difficult for virulent antisemites to see the Jews—by definition, anti-social beings—as doing honest work. Similarly, it is difficult for such antisemites to conceive of Jews as being anything but congenital liars, as have antisemites from Luther ("About the Jews and Their Lies") to Hitler, who, after quoting Schopenhauer approvingly, wrote, "Existence impels the Jew to lie, and to lie perpetually . . ." (*Mein Kampf*, p. 305).

12. Hitler, *Mein Kampf*, pp. 496–497. In *Mein Kampf*, Hitler elaborates on the theme of Jewish work-shirking parasitism only briefly in comparison to the attention he gave to it in his August 13, 1920, speech devoted wholly to the nature and danger of the Jews. See Reginald H. Phelps, "Hitlers 'Grundlegende' Rede über den Antisemitismus," *VfZ* 16, no. 4 (1968): pp. 390–420.

13. Frank adds a few sentences later: "Since the Jews moved away from Jerusalem there has been nothing for them except an existence as parasites: that has now come to an end." From Frank's *Work Diary*, quoted in *Documents on the Holocaust: Selected Sources on the Destruction of the Jews of Germany and Austria, Poland, and the Soviet Union* (Jerusalem: Yad Vashem and Pergamon Press, 1987), pp. 246–247. Similarly, on September 12, 1941, *Einsatzgruppe C* reported with astonishment finding "an oddity," namely Jewish farming communities in Ukraine where Jews worked "not only as the managers but also as agricultural laborers." How did

they understand this unexpected phenomenon of Jews doing honest, physical labor? "As far as we could find out they are Jews of low intelligence who had been found unsuitable for important tasks and 'exiled' to the country by the political leaders" (*The Einsatzgruppen Reports: Selections from the Dispatches of the Nazi Death Squads' Campaign Against the Jews in Occupied Territories of the Soviet Union, July 1941–January 1943*, ed. Yitzhak Arad, Shmuel Krakowski, and Shmuel Spector [New York: Holocaust Library, 1989], pp. 131–132).

14. For an analysis of this theme, see Alexander Bein, "Der Jüdische Parasit," *VfZ* 13, no. 2 (1965): pp. 121–149.

15. Max Weber, *Economy and Society*, ed. Guenther Roth and Claus Wittich (Berkeley: University of California Press, 1978), vol. 1, pp. 24–26.

16. Nur. Doc. 032-M, *IMT*, vol. 38, p. 130. English translation quoted in "Propaganda in Education," *Shoah* 3, nos. 2–3 (Fall/Winter 1982–1983): p. 31.

17. Eugen Kogon, *The Theory and Practice of Hell* (New York: Berkeley Medallion Books, 1968), p. 90. Kogon adds: "Often much of the labor was unnecessary or poorly planned and had to be done over two or three times. Whole buildings had to be reconstructed, since their foundations sometimes collapsed, for lack of proper planning." Note that Kogon emphasizes that the guards treated Jews and non-Jews differently.

18. George E. Berkley, *Vienna and Its Jews: The Tragedy of Success, 1880–1980s* (Cambridge: Abt Books, 1988), p. 259. See also Herbert Rosenkranz, *Verfolgung und Selbstbehauptung: Die Juden in Oesterreich, 1938–1945* (Vienna: Herold, 1978), pp. 22–23.

19. For accounts of the contours of German labor policies, I rely heavily on the work of Ulrich Herbert, esp. *Fremdarbeiter: Politik und Praxis des "Ausländer-Einsatzes" in der Kriegswirtschaft des Dritten Reiches* (Berlin: Verlag J. H. W. Dietz Nachf.: 1985); "Arbeit und Vernichtung: Ökonomisches Interesse und Primat der 'Weltanschauung' im Nationalsozialismus," in Dan Diner, ed., *Ist der Nationalsozialismus Geschichte? Zu Historisierung und Historikerstreit* (Frankfurt/M: Fischer Verlag 1987), pp. 198–236; and "Der 'Ausländereinsatz': Fremdarbeiter und Kriegsgefangene in Deutschland, 1939–1945—ein Überblick," in *Herrenmensch und Arbeitsvölker: Ausländische Arbeiter und Deutsche, 1939–1945* (Berlin: Rotbuch Verlag, 1986), pp. 13–54; and Falk Pingel, *Häftlinge unter SS-Herrschaft: Widerstand, Selbstbehauptung und Vernichtung im Konzentrationslager* (Hamburg: Hoffmann und Campe, 1978).

20. For an account of the process, see Avraham Barkai, *From Boycott to Annihilation: The Economic Struggle of German Jews, 1933–1943* (Hanover: University Press of New England, 1989), pp. 57, 110–124.

21. See Albert Speer, *The Slave State: Heinrich Himmler's Masterplan for SS Supremacy* (London: Weidenfeld & Nicolson, 1981), pp. 5–6.

22. Ulrich Herbert, *A History of Foreign Labor in Germany, 1880–1980: Seasonal Workers/Forced Laborers/Guest Workers* (Ann Arbor: University of Michigan Press, 1990), pp. 131–139; Herbert, *Fremdarbeiter*, p. 96; and Herbert, "Der 'Ausländereinsatz,' " p. 23.

23. See *Nazism*, p. 1059.

24. Yisrael Gutman, *The Jews of Warsaw, 1939–1943: Ghetto, Underground, Revolt* (Bloomington: Indiana University Press, 1989), p. 73. By December 1940, Jew-

ish employment levels were a fraction of prewar levels, 12 percent in industry and 16 percent in commerce. The ghetto had virtually no capital, and the Germans were unwilling to pay its craftsmen, who were begging for work and wages sufficient to cover just food expenses. "The 'shops' in the ghetto expanded to a limited degree only at the end of 1941 and in the spring of 1942, particularly in response to reports and rumors of the impending deportation and events in a number of other cities and ghettos. But even at this stage, the number of 'shop' workers reached only four thousand" (pp. 74–75). In December 1941, only sixty-five thousand of the four hundred thousand or so ghetto inhabitants were employed (p. 77). There were some local exceptions to this in some of the major ghettos, such as Łódź, which is described below. Certain German commanders recognized that they had an interest in making their ghettos productive, in order to prolong the ghettos' lives and thereby their own comfortable positions.

25. *Faschismus—Getto—Massenmord: Dokumentation über Ausrottung und Widerstand der Juden in Polen während des zweiten Weltkrieges* (Frankfurt/M.: Röderberg-Verlag, n.d.), p. 112; *Nazism*, p. 1066; Gutman, *The Jews of Warsaw*, p. 60; and Lucy S. Dawidowicz, *The War Against the Jews, 1933–1945* (New York: Bantam Books, 1975), pp. 280–291.

26. *Nazism*, p. 1067. Poles, of course, had far more opportunity to supplement their diets; Jews were sequestered in the ghetto, venturing out in search of food at the risk of death.

27. See the daily nutrition which one Jew's ration card recorded for January to August 1941 in *Faschismus—Getto—Massenmord*, p. 136. This person received on average but two hundred calories a day worth of food.

28. Gutman, *The Jews of Warsaw*, pp. 62–65; *Nazism*, p. 1070; and *Faschismus—Getto—Massenmord*, p. 138. This is compared to 360 deaths in August 1939 out of a population of 360,000, which was .01 percent of the population. See *Faschismus—Getto—Massenmord*, p. 140.

29. See Gutman, *The Jews of Warsaw*, pp. 62–65; and Herbert, *A History of Foreign Labor in Germany*, p. 177.

30. In 1940 and 1941, the Germans did make some effort to extract economic product from the Jews of Poland, yet they continued to practice the politics of starvation and disease upon the Jews. The Germans' paradoxical attitudes and policies towards Jewish "work" can be seen here. See Gutman, *The Jews of Warsaw*, p. 73–74.

31. Herbert, "Arbeit und Vernichtung," p. 213.

32. See Speer, *The Slave State*, pp. 281–282.

33. Nur. Doc. 1201-PS; for a general account of the treatment of Soviet POWs, see Alfred Streim, *Die Behandlung sowjetischer Kriegsgefangener im "Fall Barbarossa": Eine Dokumentation* (Heidelberg: C. F. Müller Juristischer Verlag, 1981).

34. Herbert, "Der 'Ausländereinsatz,' " p. 17.

35. On Soviet POWs, see Christian Streit, *Keine Kameraden: Die Wehrmacht und die sowjetischen Kriegsgefangenen, 1941–1945* (Stuttgart: Deutsche Verlags-Anstalt, 1978), pp. 191–216, 238–288; on employing Soviet citizens in general, see Herbert, *A History of Foreign Labor in Germany*, pp. 143–146; on the economic consequences of killing the Jews, see Hilberg, *The Destruction of the European Jews*, pp. 332–345.

36. For accounts of them, see Konnilyn G. Feig, *Hitler's Death Camps* (New York: Holmes & Meier, 1981).

37. See Czesław Madajczyk, "Concentration Camps as a Tool of Oppression in Nazi-Occupied Europe," in *The Nazi Concentration Camps: Structure and Aims, The Image of the Prisoner, The Jews in the Camps* (Jerusalem: Yad Vashem, 1984), pp. 54–55. For a further discussion of camp mortality, see the following chapter.

38. "Lodz," *Encyclopedia of the Holocaust*, ed. Israel Gutman (New York: Macmillan, 1990), pp. 904–908; and Dawidowicz, *The War Against the Jews*, pp. 188, 196–197, 393–398.

39. Hilberg, *The Destruction of the European Jews*, p. 327.

40. For an account of *Erntefest*, see Yitzhak Arad, *Belzec, Sobibor, Treblinka: The Operation Reinhard Death Camps* (Bloomington: Indiana University Press, 1987), pp. 365–369.

41. Herbert, "Arbeit und Vernichtung," pp. 222–223. For Speer's account of this, see *The Slave State*, pp. 22–25.

42. The breakdown of those killed and those used for "work" comes from Herbert, "Arbeit und Vernichtung," p. 232. Randolf L. Braham, *The Politics of Genocide: The Holocaust in Hungary* (New York: Columbia University Press, 1994), vol. 2, p. 792, accepts the estimation of Rudolf Höss, *Kommandant in Auschwitz: Autobiographische Aufzeichnungen*, ed. Martin Broszat (Munich: Deutscher Taschenbuch Verlag, 1987), that the Germans gassed close to 400,000 of the 435,000 in Auschwitz (p. 167).

43. Yisrael Gutman describes the fate of a number of transports from Hungary, out of which the Germans chose only a handful (seven people from one; nineteen from another; five from a third) to live, gassing all the rest immediately. See "Social Stratification in the Concentration Camps," in *The Nazi Concentration Camps*, pp. 143–176, here p. 148.

44. Herbert, *A History of Foreign Labor in Germany*, pp. 154–156.

45. Nur. Docs. 3663-PS and 3666-PS, *Nazi Conspiracy and Aggression*, (Washington: United States Government Printing Office, 1946), vol. 6, pp. 401–403. See Hilberg, *The Destruction of the European Jews*, pp. 232–234, for a discussion of this exchange.

46. See, for example, Nur. Doc. L-61, *Nazi Conspiracy and Aggression*, vol. 7, pp. 816–817. The Germans' policies towards other "inferior" peoples were also influenced by their racist ideology, and therefore violated economic maxims—but to a far lesser, though varying, degree. See Herbert, *A History of Foreign Labor in Germany*, p. 190.

Chapter 11

1. The complex and confusing Nazi taxonomy and nomenclature for camps, as was discussed in Chapter 5, is not followed here, since for Jews their categories did not mean very much. The term "work camp" is employed when the primary formal function of the camp for Jews was work, regardless of what the Germans called the camp. For a description of the "work" camps in the Lublin District, see Indictment Against Georg Lothar Hoffmann et al., ZStL 208 AR-Z 268/59, pp. 316–329.

2. "Majdanek," *Encyclopedia of the Holocaust*, ed. Israel Gutman (New York: Macmillan, 1990), p. 939.

3. Konnilyn G. Feig, *Hitler's Death Camps* (New York: Holmes & Meier, 1981), p. 322.

4. This memoirist uses "work" ironically, in keeping with the Germans' own usage and practice.

5. Joseph Schupack, *Tote Jahre: Eine jüdische Leidensgeschichte* (Tübingen: Katzmann, 1984), p. 138.

6. Quoted in Edward Gryń and Zofia Murawska, *Majdanek Concentration Camp* (Lublin: Wydawnictwo Lubelskie, 1966), pp. 34–35.

7. Another survivor relates that after a few days in the camp, "we were set to haul stones. The work was frequently completely unnecessary and, in my opinion, was primarily intended to keep the prisoners busy and humiliate them. The whole treatment was altogether extremely inhumane." H.A., in ZStL 407 AR-Z 297/60, p. 1418.

8. For Majdanek, see Judgment Against Hermann Hackmann et al., Landgericht Düsseldorf 8 Ks 1/75, 2 vols.; Indictment Against Hermann Hackmann et al., ZSt Köln 130 (24) Js 200/62(Z); "Majdanek," *Encyclopedia of the Holocaust*, pp. 937–940; Eugen Kogon, Hermann Langbein, and Adalbert Rückerl, eds., *Nazi Mass Murder: A Documentary History of the Use of Poison Gas* (New Haven: Yale University Press, 1993), pp. 174–177; and Heiner Lichtenstein, *Majdanek: Reportage eines Prozesses* (Frankfurt/M: Europäische Verlagsanstalt, 1979).

9. These two camps have not yet been discussed in the literature on Nazism and the Holocaust, aside from fleeting references and an occasional brief mention in a memoir. The one exception known to me is Shmuel Krakowski's account of the life of Polish Jewish POWs in Lipowa in *The War of the Doomed: Jewish Armed Resistance in Poland, 1942–1944* (New York: Holmes & Meier, 1984), pp. 260–271; he focuses only on the POWs (although, surprisingly, he gives no account of the prisoners' ceremonial status-transformation, discussed below), and therefore conveys little else about the camp and its routine. The material used here is drawn from the legal investigation against the *SSPF* Lublin, ZStL 208 AR-Z 74/60 (hereafter cited as *SSPF* Lublin).

10. For accounts of the camp, see Aktenvermerk, *SSPF* Lublin, pp. 8364–8377 and Indictment Against M., *SSPF* Lublin, pp. 11266–11279; for its early history, see p. 8372.

11. Indictment Against M., *SSPF* Lublin, pp. 11267–11268; and Aktenvermerk, *SSPF* Lublin, p. 8372. Krakowski, *The War of the Doomed*, gives slightly different figures (p. 261).

12. Indictment Against M., *SSPF* Lublin, p. 11279.

13. It is difficult to ascertain the number of Jews in the camp during its history. See Aktenvermerk, *SSPF* Lublin, pp. 8375–8377, for a discussion of the camp's likely population; and Indictment Against M., *SSPF* Lublin, pp. 11277–11278, for the combined population figures of the Lipowa camp and of two other camps (*Flughafenlager* and Sawmill Pulawy) under its economic jurisdiction.

14. Aktenvermerk, *SSPF* Lublin, pp. 8380–8381.

15. Aktenvermerk, *SSPF* Lublin, p. 8382.

16. Indictment Against M., *SSPF* Lublin, p. 11275.

17. Nur. Docs. NO-555 and NO-063, in "U.S. v. Pohl et al.," *TWC*, vol. 5, pp. 536–545.

18. Enno Georg, *Die Wirtschaftlichen Unternehmungen der SS* (Stuttgart: Deutsche Verlags-Anstalt, 1963), pp. 61, 96.

19. Indictment Against M., *SSPF* Lublin, pp. 11280–11281.

20. Aktenvermerk, *SSPF* Lublin, pp. 8442–8443.

21. For a general discussion of the Germans' deadly actions, see Aktenvermerk, *SSPF* Lublin, pp. 8425–8428, 8442–8471.

22. See Aktenvermerk, *SSPF* Lublin, pp. 8425–8429; and J.E., *SSPF* Lublin, p. 4030. One former prisoner reports that the Ukrainian guards also constructed a "beating-gauntlet" *("Prügel-Spalier")* through which the laboring Jews had to run (Aktenvermerk, *SSPF* Lublin, p. 8418).

23. It bears repeating that many other "remarkable" events may have taken place, and in all likelihood did, to which no witnesses willing to discuss them survived.

24. See Shmuel Krakowski, "The Fate of Jewish Prisoners of War in the September 1939 Campaign," *YVS* 12 (1977): pp. 297–333.

25. M.K., *SSPF* Lublin, p. 7194. For a general account of the treatment of new prisoners in camps, see Wolfgang Sofsky, *Die Ordnung des Terrors: Das Konzentrationslager* (Frankfurt/M: Fischer Verlag, 1993), pp. 98–103.

26. For two examples, see J.Z., *SSPF* Lublin, p. 7188; and P.O., *SSPF* Lublin, p. 7191.

27. See Orlando Patterson, *Slavery and Social Death: A Comparative Study* (Cambridge: Harvard University Press, 1982), pp. 51–62. This section discusses "The Rituals and Marks of Enslavement."

28. Still, the POWs ended up receiving better treatment than the Jews from Lublin. In the opinion of one survivor, it was because "we were organized militarily and wore uniforms" (J.E., *SSPF* Lublin, p. 4029). For a general discussion of Jewish POWs in Lipowa, see Krakowski, *The War of the Doomed*, pp. 260–271.

29. J.E., *SSPF* Lublin, p. 4031. E. also describes Dressler in a scene characteristic of Germans of this period in Poland, riding like a lord through the ghetto. One day, Dressler spied a woman on Warschawska Street and from his horse shot her dead on the spot.

30. Aktenvermerk, *SSPF* Lublin, p. 8412–8418.

31. For summaries of what the legal investigation of Lipowa uncovered concerning each guard, see Aktenvermerk, *SSPF* Lublin, pp. 8400–8412.

32. Aktenvermerk, *SSPF* Lublin, pp. 8404–8405.

33. See Aktenvermerk, *SSPF* Lublin, pp. 8404–8406. One of the men once refused the commandant's order to hang a Jew (suffering no ill consequences).

34. See Vorbemerkung, *SSPF* Lublin, p. 10394, for a discussion of its various names. Although it was called *Flughafen*, no airport ever existed on its location.

35. For the general history, see Vorbemerkung, *SSPF* Lublin, pp. 10397–10402.

36. Vorbemerkung, *SSPF* Lublin, p. 10403.

37. Vorbemerkung, *SSPF* Lublin, p. 10413.

38. Vorbemerkung, *SSPF* Lublin, p. 10396. The survivors had all been prisoners in the Clothing Works.

39. A.F., *SSPF* Lublin, p. 6681; and Vorbemerkung, *SSPF* Lublin, pp. 10410–10411.

40. Unless otherwise indicated, the following information is based on A.F., *SSPF* Lublin, pp. 6680–6688.

41. The information that I have come across on this subject is meager. Of the Jews who were part of the camp, the name of only one is known—and his, only phonetically. See Vorbemerkung, *SSPF* Lublin, pp. 10400, 10410–10411, 10418–10428. One obvious consequence of this is that every victim must be referred to anonymously, as "the Jew," denuding each of the individuality that should be borne in mind when seeking to fathom the crimes perpetrated against them.

42. For biographical information and a characterization of him, see *SSPF* Lublin, pp. 10502–10508.

43. He is confident that the man died, although he is not certain because Dietrich sent Fischer away before he could make a conclusive determination.

44. *SSPF* Lublin, p. 10517.

45. See *SSPF* Lublin, p. 10507, for more testimony on this point.

46. Little is known of life in the men's camp, since no survivors could be found. It is safe to assume that the conditions there were similar to those in the women's camp.

47. Vorbemerkung, *SSPF* Lublin, pp. 10412–10413. The figures here are based primarily on estimates of former guards and prisoners.

48. Vorbemerkung, *SSPF* Lublin, p. 10430.

49. Vorbemerkung, *SSPF* Lublin, pp. 10402–10403.

50. For the economic side of *Aktion Reinhard*, see "U.S. v. Pohl et al.," *TWC*, vol. 5, pp. 692–763; and Vorbemerkung, *SSPF* Lublin, pp. 10402–10403.

51. Vorbemerkung, *SSPF* Lublin, pp. 10439–10440.

52. Vorbemerkung, *SSPF* Lublin, pp. 10439–10440.

53. S.R., quoted in Vorbemerkung, *SSPF* Lublin, p. 10446.

54. Vorbemerkung, *SSPF* Lublin, pp. 10447–10448.

55. Vorbemerkung, *SSPF* Lublin, p. 10447.

56. A.F., *SSPF* Lublin, p. 6683.

57. Vorbemerkung, *SSPF* Lublin, pp. 10431–10433.

58. Nur. Docs. NO-059 and NO-062, in "U.S. v. Pohl et al.," *TWC*, vol. 5, pp. 725–731.

59. Vorbemerkung, *SSPF* Lublin, p. 10447.

60. Vorbemerkung, *SSPF* Lublin, p. 10440.

61. It was precisely because the Jews had become so debilitated and had been moved away from plant and machinery (which the Osti enterprises did not have the capital to replace) that the Osti enterprises failed in the fall of 1943, owing to a lack of profit. See Raul Hilberg, *The Destruction of the European Jews* (New York: New Viewpoints, 1973), p. 340. This was the case despite its negligible labor costs. See Nur. Doc. NO-1271, in "U.S. v. Pohl et al.," *TWC*, vol. 5, pp. 512–528, for the Osti's own auditing report of June 21, 1944; see particularly pp. 519–520 for the Osti's account of the history of the *Flughafenlager*'s iron foundry—a story of colossal economic irrationality. The brush factory was one of the enterprises that does seem to have been, in the economically most narrow sense, viable.

62. The infirmary was a locus of death during both periods in the camp's existence. G., perhaps the most feared German in the camp, would routinely clear out the

sick, who would then be shot or sent to Majdanek for gassing. S.R., who was a nurse during the first period and was married to the Jewish doctor who ran the infirmary, explains that as a consequence of these "selections," they began to treat anybody but the sickest of Jews on an ambulatory basis, sending them, despite their illnesses, to "work." *SSPF* Lublin, pp. 10525–10526.

63. Vorbemerkung, *SSPF* Lublin, p. 10441.

64. For a suggestive discussion of the purpose and function of public spectacles of this kind, see Michel Foucault, *Discipline and Punish: The Birth of the Prison* (New York: Vintage Books, 1979), esp. pp. 42–54.

65. E.T., *SSPF* Lublin, p. 10973.

66. Vorbemerkung, *SSPF* Lublin, pp. 10444–10445.

67. A young Orthodox Jew in Majdanek, who had declared that he would gladly work double shifts were he allowed to rest on the Sabbath, was hiding one Saturday under the floorboards of the latrine. "He was, however, found and then hanged in the early morning on the roll call square before us all. If I remember correctly, the 'Oberkapo' was in charge of stringing him up. He was an ethnic German who was especially nasty. When the young Jew was already hanging on the gallows, the Oberkapo climbed up on a ladder and urinated on the suspended man" (H.A., ZStL 407 AR-Z 297/60, p. 1418).

68. Vorbemerkung, *SSPF* Lublin, pp. 10445–10446.

69. E.T., *SSPF* Lublin, p. 10970.

70. E.T., *SSPF* Lublin, pp. 3414–3415.

71. One survivor recalls such an instance. For no apparent cause, he compelled an eighteen- to twenty-year-old Jewish woman to disrobe, and then beat her to death with his whip while other Jewish women in the shoemaker's shop looked on (*SSPF* Lublin, p. 10545).

72. Vorbemerkung, *SSPF* Lublin, p. 10443. Atypically, some Germans appear to have raped Jewish women in this camp.

73. For Wirth's biography, see Robert Wistrich, *Wer war wer im Dritten Reich? Ein biographisches Lexikon* (Frankfurt/M.: Fischer Taschenbuch Verlag, 1987), pp. 379–380. Wirth's time in the Clothing Works is not mentioned in the biography.

74. Vorbemerkung, *SSPF* Lublin, p. 10443.

75. For a suggestive discussion of the symbolism of doors, see Peter Armour, *The Door of Purgatory: A Study of Multiple Symbolism in Dante's Purgatorio* (Oxford: Clarendon Press, 1983), esp. pp. 100–118.

76. J.E., *SSPF* Lublin, pp. 5237–5238.

77. One survivor reports having been told that the boy shot both of his parents (C.P., *SSPF* Lublin, p. 9410).

78. There was once one other child. Wirth is reported to have let one newborn stay alive for some time, instead of disposing of it in the usual manner, by sending it to the crematorium in Majdanek (Vorbemerkung, *SSPF* Lublin, p. 10441).

79. Vorbemerkung, *SSPF* Lublin, pp. 10440–10442. There was one prisoner-organized Jewish wedding in Treblinka which some of the SS men attended, but it was a small affair that bore little resemblance to the one in the Clothing Works. See Yitzhak Arad, *Belzec, Sobibor, Treblinka: The Operation Reinhard Death Camps* (Bloomington: Indiana University Press, 1987), p. 236.

80. Vorbemerkung, *SSPF Lublin*, pp. 10441–10442. See also *IMT*, vol. 20, pp. 492–495. The day of the wedding did not pass without an ominous event, as if the Germans, despite themselves, felt compelled to mar any Jewish enjoyment. The spectacle of a public hanging of two Jews was the day's second ceremony. As the history of the camps show, and Wirth was well familiar with the camps, such deception was not necessary for the Germans to gain prisoner compliance; the prisoners were willing to work even if they could expect nothing more than to remain alive for the duration of the task. Nevertheless, the Germans did try to assuage Jewish fears in a number of camps. See Arad, *Belzec, Sobibor, Treblinka*, pp. 226–236.

81. E.T., *SSPF* Lublin, p. 3414.

82. For a general account of life and "work" in the camps, see Feig, *Hitler's Death Camps*; for Auschwitz, see Hermann Langbein, *Menschen in Auschwitz* (Frankfurt/M: Ullstein, 1980); for Buchenwald, see Eugon Kogon, *The Theory and Practice of Hell* (New York: Berkeley Medallion Books, 1968); for Mauthausen, see Benjamin Eckstein, "Jews in the Mauthausen Concentration Camp," in *The Nazi Concentration Camps: Structure and Aims, The Image of the Prisoner, The Jews in the Camps* (Jerusalem: Yad Vashem, 1984), pp. 257–271; for Płaszów, see Judgment Against Franz Josef Müller, Mosback Ks 2/61, Judgment Against Kurt Heinrich, Hannover 11 Ks 2/76, and Malvina Graf, *The Kraków Ghetto and the Płaszów Camp Remembered* (Tallahassee: Florida State University Press, 1989), pp. 86–140; for Budzyń and Kraśnik, see *SSPF* Lublin, esp. vol. 46; and for Poniatowa and Trawniki, see ZStL 208 AR-Z 268/59.

83. "Estimated Jewish Losses in the Holocaust," *Encyclopedia of the Holocaust*, pp. 1797–1802. In some countries, the Germans did treat Gypsies similarly to Jews, exterminating over 200,000 of them systematically. Despite general similarities, the Germans' policies towards the two peoples differed in important ways. See "Gypsies," *Encyclopedia of the Holocaust*, pp. 634–638; and Donald Kenrick and Grattan Puxon, *The Destiny of Europe's Gypsies* (New York: Basic Books, 1972).

84. Danuta Czech, ed., *Kalendarium der Ereignisse im Konzentrationslager Auschwitz-Birkenau, 1939–1945* (Reinbek: Rowohlt Verlag, 1989), entry for Oct. 5, 1942; and Falk Pingel, *Häftlinge unter SS-Herrschaft: Widerstand, Selbstbehauptung und Vernichtung im Konzentrationslager* (Hamburg: Hoffmann und Campe, 1978), p. 140.

85. See "Forced Labor," *Encyclopedia of the Holocaust*, p. 501; and Albert Speer, *The Slave State: Heinrich Himmler's Masterplan for SS Supremacy* (London: Weidenfeld & Nicolson, 1981), pp. 281–282.

86. The radically different position of Jews within the work economy shows up in attempts to create a useful periodization of the history of German camps. Pingel's sensible design illustrates this well. He divides the concentration camp system's history into three periods. During the years 1933–1936, he calls them "special camps for political enemies." He dubs the period 1936–1941 "the first sacrifices for armaments and war." The final period, 1942–1944, he calls "armaments production and mass annihilation." For the Jews, this last period was the time of Auschwitz, Chełmno, Treblinka, Bełżec, and Sobibór, the time of maximum feasible slaughter. For non-Jewish camp prisoners, these years were defined by work mobilization. The camp system during these years thus housed two functionally distinct systems, one for the extermination of Jews, and another for the economic exploitation overwhelmingly of non-

Jews. Pingel's third period, "armaments production and mass annihilation," is really a concatenation of two different, functionally separate, though spatially overlapping systems. See Pingel, *Häftlinge unter SS-Herrschaft*, Inhalt (contents).

87. Pingel, *Häftlinge unter SS-Herrschaft*, p. 186. Sofsky makes sweeping pronouncements about camp labor having been not a form of slavery, but a means of killing the prisoners. This is simply not true for most non-Jewish prisoners, as these statistics and the mobilization of millions of non-Jews for real labor, inside and outside the camp system, show. Sofsky bases his generalizations about the treatment of prisoners on the conditions in the relatively small number of camps that were part of the formal "concentration camp" system, and not on the more general utilization of foreign labor in other camps and broadly in the economy. His characterization is incorrect even for the "concentration camps" and wildly so for the broader treatment of foreign workers. Essentially, Sofsky—guided by a faulty interpretive framework that forces him to underplay systematically and greatly the significantly different fates of the various prisoner groups—has wrongly ascribed the real character of Jews' "work" (death) to the character of other prisoners' work. See *Die Ordnung des Terrors*, pp. 193–225, esp. 215–219. This is also true of his account of non-instrumental labor (pp. 199, 219). Hermann Langbein draws on his intimate knowledge of Auschwitz and other camps in concluding: "The Jews were always on the lowest rung of this hierarchy. They were to be allocated to the heaviest work, indeed it was often forbidden as a matter of principle to assign someone who was forced to wear the Star of David on his zebra-striped uniform to a good unit . . ." ("Work in the Concentration Camp System," *Dachau Review* 1, p. 107).

88. For an account of conditions in Mauthausen, see Feig, *Hitler's Death Camps*, pp. 116–128. Many have argued—from the Nazis themselves, to their postwar apologists, to contemporary scholars—that Jewish deaths were a consequence of the privations of the war, particularly food shortages. This example from Mauthausen is but one that reveals the fallaciousness of this position. The Germans were perfectly able to control conditions in order to alter substantially and quickly the death rates among their subjects. They could do so with a purpose and precision that differentiated among groups within the same institution, as the Mauthausen example shows. The Germans, in a manner parallel to the change in Mauthausen, reduced the overall death rate in the entire German concentration camp system from 10 percent in December 1942 to 2.8 percent in May 1943 (Nur. Doc. 1469-PS, in "U.S. v. Pohl et al.," *TWC*, vol. 5, p. 381), after the reorientation of concentration camp labor towards production was decided upon. The Germans accomplished this despite a large increase in the system's prisoner population. This reduction took place at a time when food supplies were less abundant than they had been when the Jews of Warsaw and the rest of Europe were dying of starvation, allegedly, as some would have it, because there was no food for them. Pingel discusses the various measures that Himmler, Oswald Pohl, and the concentration camp administration took during 1943 and 1944 to improve the life expectancy of non-Jewish concentration camp prisoners. See *Häftlinge unter SS-Herrschaft*, pp. 133–134, 181–187.

89. Pingel, *Häftlinge unter SS-Herrschaft*, p. 140.

90. See Yisrael Gutman, "Social Stratification in the Concentration Camps," in *The Nazi Concentration Camps*, pp. 169–173.

91. For a summary of the differences in treatment generally, see Pingel, *Häftlinge unter SS-Herrschaft*, pp. 92–93. This does not mean that some non-Jews, particularly Russians, ended up side by side with Jews, especially in such projects. This, however, was the exception for non-Jewish foreign workers, not the rule.

92. Herbert, *A History of Foreign Labor in Germany*, pp. 164–165; also "Der 'Ausländereinsatz,' " pp. 37–38. With over seven million foreigners being employed in Germany, there was, naturally, variation from place to place. The ability of the lowest people in the hierarchy to influence the conditions and quality of the subject people's lives could also be seen in the camps—for instance, when, on one rare occasion, brutal guards were replaced by more humane ones in the camps for Jews, causing the lives of the Jews to change radically for the better. See, for an example, Aharon Weiss, "Categories of Camps—Their Character and Role in the Execution of the 'Final Solution of the Jewish Question,' " in *The Nazi Concentration Camps*, p. 129. What was true for the unsupervised peasant in Germany, king of his own castle, was also true for the totalitarian institution of the camp—namely that the small people mattered greatly, whatever the nature of the regime may have been.

93. See Nur. Doc. 205-PS, in *Nazi Conspiracy and Aggression* (Washington: United States Government Printing Office, 1946), pp. 218–222; and Herbert, "Der 'Ausländereinsatz,' " pp. 34–35. The educative attempt's main theme was that all European peoples, including Russians, were fighting Bolshevism together: "The foreign workers employed within the Reich are to be treated in such a manner that their reliability is retained and expedited. . . . Everyone even the primitive man, has a fine perception for justice! Consequently every unjust treatment must have a very bad effect. Injustices, insults, trickery, mistreatment, etc. must be discontinued. Punishment by beating is forbidden." See Nur. Doc. 205-PS, in *Nazi Conspiracy and Aggression*, vol. 3, p. 219. It is ludicrous to imagine that the Nazis would have undertaken a similar public campaign to urge the humane treatment of the Jews, with slogans such as "Jews as fellow Europeans" or "We are not fighting Jews, but the idea of Judaism."

94. See the documents collected in "Dokumentation: Ausgrenzung—Deutsche, Behörden und Ausländer," in *Herrenmensch und Arbeitsvölker: Ausländische Arbeiter und Deutsche, 1939–1945* (Berlin: Rotbuch Verlag, 1986), pp. 131–141, esp. 136–138; see also Herbert, "Der 'Ausländereinsatz,' " pp. 36–37, and *Fremdarbeiter*, pp. 201–205. Herbert comments that the Germans' hierarchical treatment of the various peoples "corresponded to the prejudices of the larger part of the population as well." See "Der 'Ausländereinsatz,' " p. 36.

95. The initial treatment of the Russians was monstrous. See Herbert, "Der 'Ausländereinsatz,' " pp. 31–34; for the deadly conditions to which the Germans subjected the 600,000 Italian POWs who refused to fight for the Germans after Mussolini's fall, see pp. 35–36.

96. *Meldungen aus dem Reich, 1938–1945: Die geheimen Lageberichte des Sicherheitsdienstes der SS*, ed. Heinz Boberach (Herrsching: Pawlak Verlag, 1984), vol. 13, p. 5131.

97. *Meldungen aus dem Reich*, vol. 13, p. 5134.

98. *Meldungen aus dem Reich*, vol. 11, pp. 4235–4237.

99. Robert Gellately, *The Gestapo and German Society: Enforcing Racial Policy, 1933–1945* (Oxford: Clarendon Press, 1990), pp. 226–227.

100. See *Meldungen aus dem Reich*, vol. 10, pp. 3978–3979; and Herbert, "Der 'Ausländereinsatz,' " pp. 31, 37–39.

101. Gellately, *The Gestapo and German Society*, p. 234.

102. See, for example, Joachim Lehmann, "Zwangsarbeiter in der deutschen Landwirtschaft, 1939 bis 1945," in Ulrich Herbert, ed., *Europa und der "Reichsein-satz": Ausländische Zivilarbeiter, Kriegsgefangene und KZ-Häftlinge in Deutschland, 1938–1945* (Essen: Klartext Verlag, 1991), pp. 127–139, 132–136. This flexibility on the individual level parallels the one on the level of policy that permitted the Germans to bring Soviet POWs and civilians to to Germany after the initial prohibition.

103. See Herbert, *A History of Foreign Labor in Germany*, p. 190.

104. *Nazism*, p. 1065.

105. Substantiation of this paragraph's assertions concerning Poles can be found in Jochen August, "Erinnern an Deutschland: Berichte polnischer Zwangsar-beiter," in *Herrenmensch und Arbeitsvölker*, pp. 109–129. This article's material demonstrates (without this being the intent or conclusion of its author) that although Germans displayed great racism, and although they treated the Poles badly and fre-quently brutally, their handling of Poles was qualitatively different and better, by le-gions, than Jews could have ever hoped for. The lives of the Poles were generally harsh, but they remained, unmistakably, the lives of human beings, and not of puta-tive bacilli-carrying, socially dead beings condemned to death. For Russians, see *Mel-dungen aus dem Reich*, vol. 11, pp. 4235–4237, and vol. 13, pp. 5128–5136.

106. Herbert, "Arbeit und Vernichtung," p. 225.

107. Herbert, "Der 'Ausländereinsatz,' " p. 35.

108. The Germans' rationality in their treatment of Poles and other eastern Eu-ropean peoples was also to some extent also circumscribed by their racism and by their general propensity to violence. Nevertheless, the Germans managed to main-tain much more of a utilitarian attitude when employing these peoples.

Chapter 12

1. Karl Jäger, the commander of *Einsatzkommando 3*, himself proposed this in his famous report, reproduced in Ernst Klee, Willi Dressen, and Volker Riess, eds., *"The Good Old Days": The Holocaust as Seen by Its Perpetrators and Bystanders* (New York: Free Press, 1988), p. 56.

2. For an analysis of the efforts that certain German officials expended in order to pursue, ultimately temporarily, this sort of local rationality in the Warsaw and Łódź ghettos, see Christopher R. Browning, "Nazi Ghettoization Policy in Poland, 1939–1941," in *The Path to Genocide: Essays on the Final Solution* (Cambridge: Cam-bridge University Press, 1992), pp. 28–56.

3. Quoted in Albert Speer, *The Slave State: Heinrich Himmler's Masterplan for SS Supremacy* (London: Weidenfeld & Nicolson, 1981), p. 20.

4. The German army, in desperate need of military hardware and supplies, was a general exception to this, as were some economic enterprises. See Raul Hilberg, *The Destruction of the European Jews* (New York: New Viewpoints, 1973), pp. 332–345.

5. Nur. Doc. 3257-PS, in *Nazi Conspiracy and Aggression* (Washington: United States Government Printing Office, 1946), vol. 5, pp. 994–997.

6. *Nazism*, p. 1131. See also *Eichmann Interrogated: Transcripts from the Archives of the Israeli Police*, ed. Jochen von Lang (Toronto: Lester & Orpen Dennys, 1983), p. 91.

7. Nur. Doc. NO-1611, in "U.S. v. Pohl et al.," *TWC*, vol. 5, pp. 616–617.

Chapter 13

1. See "Death Marches," *Encyclopedia of the Holocaust*, ed. Israel Gutman (New York: Macmillan, 1990), p. 350. The general treatments of death marches consist of three articles and two books. Shmuel Krakowski, "The Death Marches in the Period of the Evacuation of the Camps," in *The Nazi Concentration Camps: Structure and Aims, The Image of the Prisoner, The Jews in the Camps* (Jerusalem: Yad Vashem, 1984), pp. 475–489; Yehuda Bauer, "The Death-Marches, January–May, 1945," in Michael R. Marrus, ed., *The Nazi Holocaust: Historical Articles on the Destruction of European Jews* (Westport: Meckler, 1989), vol. 9, pp. 491–511; Livia Rothkirchen, "The Final Solution in Its Last Stages," *YVS* 8 (1970): pp. 7–29; Irena Malá and Ludmila Kubátová, *Pochody Smrti* (Prague: Nakladatelství politické literatury, 1965); and Zygmunt Zonik, *Anus Belli: Ewakuacja I Wyzwolenie Hitlerowskich Obozów Koncentracyjnych* (Warsaw: Panstwowe Wydawnictwo Navkave, 1988). Malá and Kubátová's book is little more than a series of brief summaries of the various death marches. Zonik's is more useful, though it is of somewhat diminished value for the purposes of this study since it does not consistently reveal the identities of the victims, and it fails to treat the individual marches in sufficient detail.

Any discussion of the death marches should begin with a number of caveats. Little systematic research has been published on them, so our understanding of their overall scope, courses, and character is at best approximate. Part of the difficulty lies in the virtual absence of documentary evidence on their many aspects. Little is known of the orders that governed them or of the organizational structure in which they functioned. It is often difficult to ascertain how many people were on a march (not to mention their breakdown by nationality), how many survived, and how many died in what manner along the way. The institutional affiliations and backgrounds of the guards, who were generally German, are usually left to guesswork. Most significantly, the details of their treatment of the victims are frequently not available.

2. This periodization is used neither by Krakowski, "The Death Marches in the Period of the Evacuation of the Camps," nor by Bauer, "The Death-Marches, January–May, 1945."

3. For a brief account of death marches before this period, see Krakowski, "The Death Marches in the Period of the Evacuation of the Camps," pp. 476–477. For an account of a death march on December 1, 1939, during which the Germans marched several thousand Polish Jews from Chełm to the border with the Soviet Union on the Bug river, killing in the process, among just one of the columns, between five hundred and six hundred Jews, see Ermittlungsbericht, ZStL 208 AR-Z 91/61, pp. 2076–2082.

4. Martin Broszat, "The Concentration Camps, 1933–1945," in Helmut Krausnick et al., *Anatomy of the SS State* (London: Collins, 1968), p. 248, and "Death Marches," *Encyclopedia of the Holocaust*, p. 354, state that 250,000 died; Bauer, "The

Death-Marches, January–May, 1945," writing of those who died on death marches and also in the camps during this final phase, believes the figure to be much higher— "50 percent at least, if not considerably more" (p. 492). See Bauer's discussion (pp. 492–494) of the difficulty in establishing how many prisoners were then in the camp system and on death marches.

5. The majority of them were, however, Jews. See Malá and Kubátová, *Pochody Smrti*, p. 311.

6. A.C., StA Hof 2 Js 1325/62, Beiakte J. Upon finding the women, the Americans began an investigation in order to determine what had happened to them. They interviewed and interrogated survivors and some of the perpetrators whom they had captured. The testimony of these guards, given during the immediate aftermath of a shocking defeat, is characterized by an unusual candor (generally absent from testimony given fifteen to twenty-five years later), and it concurs remarkably well with the testimony of survivors.

7. The Helmbrechts death march, the second and more extensively treated of the two cases, has been chosen because (as is made clear later) it is a case that allows many of the crucial analytical issues to be distinguished. It is, moreover, unusually rich in its empirical material. Although it had its idiosyncratic aspects, its typicality with respect to the Germans' treatment of prisoners cannot be doubted, as the subsequent discussion demonstrates. In general, the quality of the materials existing on death marches in the ZStL is greatly inferior to those about other institutions of killing. They were, so to speak, moving targets, and the identities of their personnel was often not known. It may be that the death marches also did not garner as much attention from the legal authorities because they were neither spatially fixed nor often part of an identifiable command structure. The chaos at the end of the war has obscured much about the marches. The material on which the main case discussed here is based is drawn primarily from the investigation and trial of the commander of Helmbrechts, Alois Dörr, the records of which are contained in StA Hof 2 Js 1325/62 (hereafter cited as Dörr); some of the material is cited in ZStL's collection on the Helmbrechts investigation, ZStL 410 AR 1750/61.

8. Schlussvermerk, ZStL 410 AR 1750/61 (hereafter cited as Grünberg), pp. 630–633. Little is known about this camp. Not until 1969 did the Arolsen International Tracing Center establish that the camp had indeed existed. It was located not in the town of Schlesiersee, but in the neighboring town of Przybyszów (pp. 630–631). Little is known also about its guard contingent, which was about twenty strong and seems to have been drawn mainly from army soldiers who had been deemed no longer fit for front-line duty. Complementing them were a few women guards and the camp's administration (eight people have been named), which was drawn from the police (pp. 634–635).

9. B.B., ZStL 410 AR 1750/61, p. 63. She adds that the number of sick was very large, yet she knows of no cases of women being shot in this camp. On this point, see Schlussvermerk, Grünberg, p. 637. Any number of women did die, however, from German-generated malnutrition, exhaustion, and disease, and from their keepers' brutality.

10. Z.H., ZStL 410 AR 1750/61, p. 90.

11. Schlussvermerk, Grünberg, pp. 637–638.

12. B.B., ZStL 410 AR 1750/61, p. 63.

13. F.D., Grünberg, pp. 544–545. The Germans had been drinking, and as he drove them to their next destination after the massacre, they offered to share their Schnapps with him. These older Germans who acted cruelly towards helpless Jewish women were comradely to this Pole.

14. Schlussvermerk, Grünberg, pp. 648–649.

15. For a discussion of the numbers on each march, see Grünberg, pp. 647–648. Little is known about the Germans who guarded the marches (p. 649).

16. H.W., Grünberg, p. 467.

17. It is not clear whether this woman's estimate refers to the entire march's population or only to some smaller group of the march to which she belonged. Either way, the death rate was enormous. See H.W., Grünberg, p. 467. For the few details known about this march, see Schlussvermerk, Grünberg, pp. 661–665.

18. S.K., Dörr, vol. 4, p. 605.

19. Grünberg, p. 650.

20. See Schlussvermerk, Grünberg, pp. 654, 660–661, for an accounting of the fate of this march's prisoners. Thirty-four from one group of 160 sick died during the following month.

21. C.L., Grünberg, p. 401.

22. S.K., Dörr, p. 605; C.L., Grünberg, p. 401; B.B., ZStL 410 AR 1750/61, pp. 63–64; and M.S., ZStL 410 AR 1750/61, p. 84; see also Schlussvermerk, Grünberg, p. 657. B.B. recalls that the guards selected seventy to be shot, of which twenty managed to flee.

23. Judgment, Dörr, p. 23.

24. Judgment, Dörr, pp. 6–8.

25. Another tried repeatedly to enter the Party but had been declared unfit for it. It is possible that two others were members; the records are indeterminate.

26. H.R., Dörr, Zeugen, pp. 1109–1119; it is worth noting that E.V. does not appear on the compiled (incomplete) roster of guards.

27. M.W., Dörr, Zeugen, pp. 1142–1149.

28. G.H., Dörr, vol. 4, p. 628. P.L. was with him, after also having been in Lublin. He was drafted first in April 1944 to a ranger unit (*Landesschützeneinheit*) (Dörr, vol. 3, pp. 610–631).

29. Of course, the self-reporting of the motivation for volunteering for guard duty on the part of those who were not conscripted is hard to evaluate. For examples, see O.K., Dörr, Zeugen; and R.S., Dörr, vol. 3, p. 556.

30. Of the twelve for whom data exist, eight had no formal training whatsoever, three had brief training (lasting about two weeks), and one does not say. Those who served, as almost all did, in Ravensbrück (generally, for a few weeks, though one was there for six months) before heading for Helmbrechts were undoubtedly socialized informally into the community of cruelty by the camp's old hands. See H.P., Dörr, Zeugen; and O.K., Dörr, Zeugen.

31. W.J., Dörr, Zeugen, p. 1068; see also Judgment, Dörr, pp. 12–13.

32. See, for example, W.J., Dörr, Zeugen, p. 1068; and P.K., ZStL 410 AR 1750/61, p. 690.

33. P.K., ZStL 410 AR 1750/61, p. 690; and E.v.W, Zeugen, pp. 1320–1322.

34. See Hermann Langbein, *Menschen in Auschwitz* (Frankfurt/M: Ullstein, 1980), on the improvement of the conditions in Auschwitz after Arthur Liebehenschel replaced Rudolf Höss as commandant (pp. 59–64).

35. E.V., Dörr, Zeugen, p. 1137. For a contrary view, see W.J., Dörr, Zeugen, p. 1068.

36. Statement of E.M., 10/20/64, Dörr, pp. 506–512.

37. Judgment, Dörr, pp. 6–8.

38. Judgment, Dörr, pp. 10–11.

39. M.R., Dörr, Zeugen, p. 1237; see also M.S., Dörr, Zeugen, p. 1251.

40. For a discussion of the brutal torture and slaughter of the Russian woman doctor and her two compatriots after their temporary escape from the camp, see Judgment, Dörr, pp. 14–22.

41. Judgment, Dörr, pp. 10–12; and A.G., Dörr, Zeugen, p. 1194.

42. Judgment, Dörr, pp. 24–25.

43. S.K., Dörr, vol. 4, p. 606; see also E.M., Dörr, vol. 3, p. 515.

44. M.F., Dörr, vol. 4, p. 623; and S.K., Dörr, vol. 4, pp. 605–606. One non-Jewish prisoner, who herself suffered greatly in the camp, puts it only slightly hyperbolically: "The Jewesses had neither beds nor covers." See L.D., Dörr, vol. 1, p. 195.

45. For accounts of the camp's barracks, see Judgment, Dörr, p. 25; and A.G., Dörr, Zeugen, p. 1195.

46. S.K., Dörr, vol. 4, p. 607. Punishment roll calls, at which the Germans forced Jews to stand for hours, often naked, without shoes, often in the snow, are commented upon by Jewish and non-Jewish survivors. This testimony is from a Russian: "I have seen that the Jewesses had to stand all day in the snow without food and without any clothes or shoes. I have seen that they were then beaten by the female SS guards with [their] hands or billy clubs when they did not stand still." See L.D., Dörr, vol. 1, p. 195; and M.H., Dörr, vol. 1, p. 194.

47. Judgment, Dörr, p. 26; and A.G., Dörr, Zeugen, p. 1194. The former head woman guard of Helmbrechts affirms that the Jews were fed less than the non-Jews (H.H., Dörr, vol. 3, p. 600).

48. H.H., Dörr, Beiakte J.

49. R.K., Dörr, Zeugen, p. 1224. She notes that the former Auschwitz prisoners among them were particularly famished. See also A.K., Dörr, vol. 1, p. 103.

50. Judgment, Dörr, pp. 25–26.

51. See, for example, the statement of the Russian woman, S.K., Dörr, vol. 1, p. 205; and N.K., Dörr, vol. 1, p. 203. For a general description of the cruelties, see Judgment, Dörr, pp. 11–12.

52. M.H., Dörr, vol. 1, p. 194.

53. V.D., Dörr, vol. 4, p. 701.

54. A number of former prisoners recall the sufferings of one Jewish woman. Her "crime" was having in her possession a photograph. She was forced to stand in the snow, hair shorn. See S.K., Dörr, vol. 4, p. 607; and R.K., Dörr, Zeugen, p. 1224.

55. L.D., Dörr, vol. 1, p. 195; and S.K., Dörr, vol. 4, p. 606.

56. M.H., Dörr, vol. 1, p. 194.

57. Judgment, Dörr, p. 26.

58. Judgment, Dörr, pp. 27–29.

59. Judgment, Dörr, p. 29.

60. Judgment, Dörr, pp. 28, 30.

61. A summary of each day of the march is contained in Judgment, Dörr, pp. 30–89.

62. M.R., Dörr, Zeugen, p. 1240.

63. A.K., Dörr, vol. 1, p. 101; and Judgment, Dörr, p. 210; for a fuller discussion of the "sick wagons," see below.

64. These figures are based on those contained in Judgment, Dörr, pp. 30–89.

65. E.M., Dörr, vol. 3, p. 516; B.B., ZStL 410 AR 1750/61, p. 64; and Judgment, Dörr, pp. 50, 60–61, 208–209.

66. M.S., ZStL 410 AR 1750/61, p. 82. For more testimony on the quantity and quality of the march's provisions for the Jews, see H.H., Dörr, Beiakte J; and Judgment, Dörr, pp. 208–209.

67. H.H., Dörr, Beiakte J.

68. Judgment, Dörr, p. 57.

69. Judgment, Dörr, pp. 70–71, 194–195.

70. M.S., ZStL 410 AR 1750/61, vol. 1, p. 82; See also B.B., ZStL 410 AR 1750/61, vol. 1, p. 64.

71. H.H., Dörr, Beiakte J; and C.S., ZStL 410 AR 1750/61, p. 72.

72. See Judgment, Dörr, pp. 30–89, for descriptions of the general conditions of the march.

73. Judgment, Dörr, pp. 55–56, 149–150.

74. Judgment, Dörr, pp. 148–152.

75. N.K., Dörr, vol. 1, p. 203.

76. A similar such incident was recounted above, during the discussion of Lipowa Camp. For a general discussion of this point, see Orlando Patterson, *Slavery and Social Death: A Comparative Study* (Cambridge: Harvard University Press, 1982), pp. 51–62.

77. One guard cudgeled women who "were so weak that they could not walk erect; they crawled on all fours" (Judgment, Dörr, pp. 38–39).

78. M.R., Dörr, Beiakte J.

79. M.S., ZStL 410 AR 1750/61, p. 82.

80. H.H., Dörr, Beiakte J. Note her ironic use of "SS."

81. C.S., ZStL 410 AR 1750/61, p. 72; for another example, see M.S., ZStL 410 AR 1750/61, p. 82.

82. The head woman guard remembers a group of five beating these women. She agrees that W., R., and K. were there, maintaining that S. and Z. were present as well. She does not mention J. in connection with this incident. She adds: "Duerr [*sic*] and I both witnessed this and neither of us made any attempt to stop the beating" (H.H., Dörr, Beiakte J).

83. C.S., ZStL 410 AR 1750/61, p. 72.

84. H.H., Dörr, Beiakte J.

85. Judgment, Dörr, pp. 73–75.

86. Judgment, Dörr, pp. 73–74, 77.

87. Judgment, Dörr, pp. 73–74.

88. Judgment, Dörr, pp. 73, 197.

89. Judgment, Dörr, pp. 77–79.

90. Those who took part in the march estimate that there were fewer survivors. Some say that only slightly more than 300 survived, which would mean that around 275 died on the march. This number corresponds with the estimates of daily deaths given by guards and former prisoners alike. They should know, since roll calls were taken every morning, which revealed the number of deaths during the previous night. On this point, see M.R., Dörr, vol. 2, p. 404.

91. A.C., Dörr, Beiakte J.

Chapter 14

1. The evidence on this point is contradictory. See G.H., Dörr, vol. 4, p. 637; H.H., Dörr, Beiakte J; and Judgment, Dörr, p. 29.

2. Judgment, Dörr, p. 54.

3. G.H., Dörr, vol. 4, p. 639. Also see C.S., Grünberg, who says that towards the end of the march she had no idea where they were supposed to be taking the Jewish women (p. 71).

4. Dörr did indeed burn their papers. See Judgment, Dörr, p. 49; and V.D., Dörr, vol. 4, p. 702.

5. M.R., Dörr, vol. 2, pp. 403–404. The need to give an order to treat people "humanely" itself indicates the existing German norms of treating Jews.

6. It is possible that this confusion exists because they both might have spoken. See M.R., Dörr, vol. 2, pp. 403–404; and Judgment, Dörr, pp. 48–49. It seems that Dörr chose not to transmit every item of Himmler's order to his staff, including the order that they let the Jews go free when the Americans were closing in on them.

7. M.R., Dörr, vol. 2, p. 403.

8. The weights were recorded by Captain W.W. of the U.S. Army Medical Corps on May 11, 1945. A copy is contained in Dörr.

9. C.S., Grünberg, p. 72.

10. S.S., Dörr, vol. 1, p. 117.

11. G.v.E., Dörr, Zeugen, p. 1183.

12. This happened at Police Battalion 101's slaughter in Łomazy. See Indictment, Hoffmann, pp. 347–348; and E.H., Hoffmann, pp. 2724–2726.

13. Judgment, Dörr, pp. 212–213.

14. M.S., Dörr, Zeugen, p. 1256. She does not even hint that the Jewish women's evaluation of the society of guards was inaccurate.

15. S.K., Dörr, vol. 4, p. 610.

16. Just because they did not glory in cruelty does not mean that they disapproved of the general treatment of Jews. Although displays of cruelty indicated the actors' approval, it does not logically follow that the absence of cruelty meant disapproval. And in fact, we know of zealous executioners of Jews who believed that the killers should not act with licentious brutality.

17. Judgment, Dörr, p. 82.

18. G.v.E., Dörr, vol. 2, p. 350.

19. In addition to the literature listed in Chapter 13, note 1, and the accounts of death marches that are given in dozens of memoirs, I have read the detailed materials from the Federal Republic's legal investigations of twelve death marches.

20. This is also true of the treatment of prisoners within camps in the last days of the war. Yehuda Bauer, "The Death-Marches, January–May, 1945," in Michael R. Marrus, ed., *The Nazi Holocaust: Historical Articles on the Destruction of European Jews* (Westport: Meckler, 1989), vol. 9, asserts that they should be seen as separate phenomena (p. 495). The justification for such a distinction is not clear to me.

21. Many of them subsequently died, owing to their injured health and the unavailability of medical care and even food. For Auschwitz, see Hermann Langbein, *Menschen in Auschwitz* (Frankfurt/M: Ullstein, 1980), pp. 525–529.

22. This happened, for example, on the death march from the Sonnenberg camp, in April or May 1945. See Judgment Against Ottomar Böhme and Josef Brüsseler, Marburg 6 Ks 1/68, p. 11.

23. Obviously, it is difficult to characterize the thoughts and emotions of the huge number of bystanders as they watched the walking skeletons, plunged into their condition in the name of Germany, file by them during these days of uncertainty and dread. How many Germans had what attitudes towards the prisoners? How many Germans tried to lessen their suffering by offering them food and water? How many contributed to their misery, either by spitting venom at them, by pelting them with projectiles, by searching them out when they escaped, or by killing them with their own hands? The sense of Shmuel Krakowski, "The Death Marches in the Period of the Evacuation of the Camps," in *The Nazi Concentration Camps: Structure and Aims, The Image of the Prisoner, The Jews in the Camps* (Jerusalem: Yad Vashem, 1984), who has used the survivors' testimonies in Yad Vashem which contain material on seventy different death marches during March and April 1945, is that the populace, without prompting or supervision from any authority, acted in a manner overwhelmingly in keeping with treatment that might have been prescribed by Nazi pedagogues (p. 484). Zygmunt Zonik, *Anus Belli: Ewakuacja I Wyzwolenie Hitlerowskich Obozów Koncentracyjnych* (Warsaw: Panstwowe Wydawnictwo Navkave, 1988), concludes that although some Germans tried to help the prisoners, the vast majority did not, cursing them as they passed and, with some frequency, exhorting their escorts to kill them (pp. 198–199). The material with which I am familiar suggests the same conclusions.

24. Henry Orenstein and a friend ripped off their yellow badges and passed as Poles on an exclusively Polish death march that was debilitating enough to produce an astronomical death rate. Orenstein recounts in his memoir, *I Shall Live: Surviving Against All Odds, 1939–1945* (New York: Touchstone, 1989), his sense of the protection which his new Polish identity afforded him despite the desperate conditions:

Strangely, even though it was now clear that the march was going to be a murderous affair, I still felt far safer than I ever had in the camp. Here they didn't know I was a Jew, and if they were going to kill me it would be only because I couldn't walk, not simply because I was a Jew. . . . Having lived for so many years under the gun, when any one of the guards had the clear and unquestioned right to murder me at any moment, at a whim, even for fun, even though I had done nothing to provoke it, for the sole reason that I was born a Jew, I had grown to yearn to have my right to live judged by some other criterion, any other—even by whether or not I was able to walk. . . . The odds seemed good that the SS would not kill so many people, especially since as far as they knew there were no Jews among us (p. 243).

Orenstein underestimated the murderousness of the Germans, yet his sense of new-found ontological security remains telling.

25. The ability and willingness of the guards to discriminate among prisoners cannot be overemphasized. A more extreme version of the preferred status that the Helmbrechts guards bestowed upon the German prisoners by enlisting them as jailers of the Jews was in evidence on the Janinagrube march. There the guards tried to enlist the German prisoners as executioners, arming them and encouraging them to take part in a shooting massacre of hundreds of Jews. See Judgment Against Heinrich Niemeier, Hannover 11 Ks 1/77, pp. 20–22, 92–97. See also the Lieberose death march, on which the German guards shot large numbers of Jews yet did not shoot one of the German prisoners. These guards, moreover, were under no supervision; their commander had declined to join the march. See Indictment of E.R. and W.K., StA Fulda 3 Js 800/63, pp. 48–56.

26. Buchenwald was such a case. See Krakowski, "The Death Marches in the Period of the Evacuation of the Camps," pp. 484–485. It should be emphasized that the Germans by no means treated those left in the camp with solicitude—far from it.

27. Krakowski, "The Death Marches in the Period of the Evacuation of the Camps," p. 489. The Janinagrube death march was another instance in which the Germans intervened to stop people who attempted to feed the Jews. The march, composed almost exclusively of Jews, had hooked up with a death march of thousands from Auschwitz and its satellite camps. Upon departing Auschwitz, the Janinagrube Jews received one piece of bread with preserves to be split between two of them. The usual shooting of stragglers prevailed in the mid-winter conditions of January. After a few days, the commander disappeared together with the provision wagon. Some of the SS men, together with some preferred prisoners (*Funktionshäftlinge*) went to procure food from local peasants, because the Germans too now had no food. Other SS men prevented the Jews from receiving any of the food. One former prisoner remembers their hunger: "During the evacuation march we received no food. The Polish population in Silesia gave us, in a few localities on its own initiative, bread and milk. It occurred that the SS guards wantonly kicked over the milk jugs." Fortunately for some of the Jews, the Poles sometimes managed to slip them food, despite the Germans' efforts to prevent them from doing so. See Indictment Against Heinrich Niemeier, StA Hannover 11 Js 5/73, p. 23; and Judgment, Hannover 11 Ks 1/77, pp. 16–20. For additional cases in which Germans denied available food and water to prisoners, see Bauer, "The Death-Marches, January–May, 1945," pp. 500, 503; and Krakowski, "The Death Marches in the Period of the Evacuation of the Camps," pp. 478–479, 484.

28. For maps of many other such seemingly aimless death marches, see Irena Malá and Ludmila Kubátová, *Pochody Smrti* (Prague: Nakladatelství politické literatury, 1965).

29. Bauer, "The Death-Marches, January–May, 1945," p. 499.

30. Bauer makes this point in "The Death-Marches, January–May, 1945," p. 497.

31. Quoted in Krakowski, "The Death Marches in the Period of the Evacuation of the Camps," p. 485.

32. Krakowski, "The Death Marches in the Period of the Evacuation of the Camps," p. 485.

33. Krakowski, "The Death Marches in the Period of the Evacuation of the Camps," p. 486.

34. Krakowski, "The Death Marches in the Period of the Evacuation of the Camps," p. 489.

35. Although Bauer is wrong about the perpetrators when he writes that generally the Germans' killing was "ice-cold" (*Eiskalt*), he is correct in saying that the Germans were anything but cool, detached killers on the death marches (although this was not, as he says, a reversion to the 1930s SA style of action). See "The Death-Marches, January–May, 1945," p. 502. To give but one additional example, on the Janinagrube death march, one German used to do an "Indian dance," openly joyful of his accomplishment after killing a Jew. One survivor had the distinct impression that this guard and another were engaged in an ongoing killing competition. See Judgment, Hannover 11 Ks 1/77, pp. 26–27, 63.

36. Quoted in Dieter Vaupel, *Spuren die nicht vergehen: Eine Studie über Zwangsarbeit und Entschädigung* (Kassel: Verlag Gesamthochschulbibliothek Kassel, 1990), pp. 112–113. Such scenes occurred in the last year of the war, during the height of German labor mobilization.

37. S.R., Dörr, vol. 3, p. 570. It is noteworthy that he chooses to speak of the Jews in this context and does not mention the non-Jewish prisoners who set out with them from Helmbrechts.

38. Bauer also makes this point in "The Death-Marches, January–May, 1945," p. 499. It was not just the guards assigned to death marches who killed Jews to the very end. It came naturally to those who were not charged with any responsibilities regarding Jews to kill Jews upon whom they stumbled. On the way home from Hungary, a "repair company" (*Werkstattkompanie*) of the SS Division "Das Reich" came upon small groups of unarmed and obviously unthreatening Jews on two occasions. After torturing some of them, the Germans killed all the Jews—including one First World War veteran with an Iron Cross, and a beautiful twenty-year-old whom they shot, as she requested, while standing with her face to the sun. See Judgment Against Reiter et al., München I, 116 Ks 1/67, pp. 10–14, 28–29.

Chapter 15

1. Rachel Luchfeld, interview by author, Sept. 8, 1995. It should be noted that she could not say for sure that the men of Police Battalion 101 carried whips during their killing operation in Józefów, because she survived in hiding and therefore did not see the Germans. Her parents, who had concealed themselves in another hiding place in the same room, were discovered, and the Germans killed them on the spot. She heard the yelling and the shots.

2. The following section reproduces a portion of Daniel Goldhagen, "The 'Cowardly' Executioner: On Disobedience in the SS," *Patterns of Prejudice* 19, no. 2 (1985): pp. 20–21.

3. Herbert Jäger, *Verbrechen unter totalitärer Herrschaft: Studien zur national-sozialistischen Gewaltkriminalität* (Olton: Walter-Verlag, 1967), pp. 79–160; and Kurt Hinrichsen, "Befehlsnotstand," in Adalbert Rückerl, ed., *NS-Prozesse: Nach 25 Jahren Strafverfolgung* (Karlsruhe: Verlag C. F. Müller, 1971), pp. 131–161. Hinrichsen's article is based on an unpublished, more comprehensive study, *Zum Problem des sog. Befehlsnotstandes in NSG-Verfahrens* (1964), that he did under the auspices of the ZStL as an expert opinion for the trials taking place in the Federal Republic's courts. See also David H. Kitterman, "Those Who Said 'No!': Germans Who Refused to Execute Civilians During World War II," *German Studies Review* 11, no. 2 (May 1988): pp. 241–254. Kitterman's treatment of the subject and his statistical compilations are marred by his apparent general willingness to accept the perpetrators' (obviously self-serving) accounts of their actions and motivations at face value.

4. Jäger, *Verbrechen unter totalitärer Herrschaft*, p. 120.

5. For a more detailed discussion of these issues, see Hinrichsen, "Befehlsnotstand," pp. 143–146, 149–153, 156–157. Not even one of the seventy-seven people convicted by the SS and police courts of disobedience involved the refusal to carry out an order to kill Jews. Moreover, not one SS judge has ever been found who adjudicated a case in which the accused was charged with refusing to kill Jews.

6. This defense argument is known as "putative coercion by superior orders" (*putativer Befehlsnotstand*).

7. For the *Einsatzkommandos* in general, see, for example, Indictment Against Alfred Filbert et al., ZStL 202 AR 72/60, pp. 83–84, 162–163; for *Einsatzgruppe C*, see Albert Hartl, ZStL 207 AR-Z 15/58, pp. 1840–1845; for *Einsatzgruppe D*, see H.S., ZStL 213 AR 1902/66, pp. 95–96. For Sachsenhausen, see ZStL Sammelband 363, pp. 15–17; for the security police in Tarnopol, see Indictment Against Paul Raebel et al., StA Stuttgart 12 Js 1403/61, pp. 117–118.

8. Ernst Klee, Willi Dressen, and Volker Riess, eds., *"The Good Old Days": The Holocaust as Seen by Its Perpetrators and Bystanders* (New York: Free Press, 1988), p. 82.

9. P.K., ZStL 208 AR-Z 5/63, p. 503; see also Vermerk, ZStL 208/2 AR-Z 1176/62, p. 732.

10. See Goldhagen, "The 'Cowardly' Executioner," p. 31, n. 11.

11. "Official Transcript of the American Military Tribunal No. 2-A in the Matter of the United States of America Against Otto Ohlendorf et al., defendants sitting at Nuernberg Germany on 15 September 1947," p. 593.

12. Jäger, *Verbrechen unter totalitärer Herrschaft*, p. 147.

13. This testimony comes from Albert Hartl, the personnel chief of *Einsatzgruppe C*, ZStL 207 AR-Z 15/58, p. 1840; see also Robert M. W. Kempner, *SS im Kreuzverhör* (Munich: Rütten & Loening Verlag, 1964), p. 82. Why were the SS and security institutions so lenient, given that their leadership conceived of the Jews as Germany's and humanity's greatest foe, as a malignant race determined to destroy all other races? Himmler himself provided the probable explanation when he said that the extermination of the Jews "could only be carried out by . . . the staunchest

individuals . . . [by] fanatical, deeply committed National Socialists." "Thus," Himmler explained on another occasion, "if a man thinks that he cannot be answerable for obeying an order . . . [and] you think: his nerve has gone, he's weak. Then you can say: Good, retire on a pension." As the cases discussed earlier demonstrate and Himmler's words confirm, a German's failure to perform his duty because of weakness was permissible. It disqualified him from being a Nazi superman, but it did not make him a criminal. See Hans Buchheim, "Command and Compliance," in Helmut Krausnick et al., *Anatomy of the SS State* (London: Collins, 1968), p. 366; Nur. Doc. 1919-PS, in *Nazi Conspiracy and Aggression* (Washington: United States Government Printing Office, 1946), vol. 4, p. 567; and Hinrichsen, "Befehlsnotstand," p. 161.

14. See Robert G. L. Waite, *Vanguard of Nazism: The Free Corps Movement in Postwar Germany, 1918–1923* (New York: W. W. Norton, 1969), for an account of a movement that was later to supply many shock troops who would serve Hitler. For a local account of the open defiance and violence against Weimar, see William Sheridan Allen, *The Nazi Seizure of Power: The Experience of a Single German Town, 1922–1945*, rev. ed. (New York: Franklin Watts, 1984), pp. 23–147.

15. This paradoxical action started at the highest levels, with the army's Chief of Staff, General Franz Halder, under whose auspices the army became a full partner in the extermination of Soviet Jewry. Halder, a dedicated foe of Hitler, himself considered assassinating him. See Helmuth Groscurth, *Tagebücher eines Abwehroffiziers, 1938–1940* (Stuttgart: Deutsche Verlags-Anstalt, 1970), private diary, entry of Nov. 1, 1939.

16. For examples, see Nur. Doc. 3257-PS, *IMT,* vol. 32, pp. 73–74; and Helmut Krausnick and Hans-Heinrich Wilhelm, *Die Truppe des Weltanschauungskrieges: Die Einsatzgruppen der Sicherheitspolizei und des SD, 1938–1942* (Stuttgart: Deutsche Verlags-Anstalt, 1981), p. 229. For that matter, the army lobbied hard against the order to kill Soviet commissars (the real agents of Bolshevism) but not against the order to kill Soviet Jews (the fictive source of Bolshevism). The resistance to the Commissar Order stemmed from the belief among army field commanders that it was strengthening resistance among Soviet troops. See Jürgen Förster, "Hitler's War Aims Against the Soviet Union and the German Military Leaders," *Militärhistorisk Tidskrift* 183 (1979): pp. 88–89; and Hans-Adolf Jacobsen, "The *Kommissarbefehl* and Mass Executions of Soviet Russian Prisoners of War" in Krausnick et al., *Anatomy of the SS State*, pp. 505–535, 521–523.

17. Letter of Jan. 30, 1943, Hoffmann, pp. 523–524. For a discussion of the contents of the letter, see the opening sections of the Introduction. Browning devotes a small chapter to Hoffmann and mentions the letter, but he inexplicably neglects to discuss and interpret in any detail the crucial contents of a document that reveals the mind of a genocidal killer (who was, moreover, central to the life of this police battalion), a document which divulges his *contemporaneous* judgment concerning the minds and motives of his men. Surely, this document is as deserving of analysis as the postwar self-exonerations of the killers. See the account of this letter and of the subsequent events in Christopher R. Browning, *Ordinary Men: Reserve Police Battalion 101 and the Final Solution in Poland* (New York: HarperCollins, 1992), pp. 119–120.

18. See, for example, Richard Evans, "In Pursuit of the *Untertanengeist*: Crime, Law and Social Order in Germany History," in *Rethinking German History: Nineteenth-Century Germany and the Origins of the Third Reich* (London: Allen & Unwin, 1987), pp. 156–187. It is astonishing that people can continue to assert that Germans obey authority unthinkingly, given the abundant evidence of disobedience and flouting of authority of many kinds during Weimar, not to mention the revolutions and insurrections that have occurred in modern German history.

19. Stanley Milgram, *Obedience to Authority: An Experimental View* (New York: Harper Colophon, 1969). Milgram's own experiment undermines the notion that his findings are relevant to an explanation of the perpetrators' actions—though Milgram does not draw this conclusion. By varying the conditions of his experiment, he discovered that the more the people who administered the shocks confronted the apparent pain of the person being shocked, the more frequently they were willing to defy the authority of the Yale University experimenter, so that fully 70 percent refused to administer shocks when they themselves had to place the victim's hand on the shock plate (pp. 33–36). Don Mixon, after redoing Milgram's experiment using role-playing, persuasively reinterprets the experiment to be not about obedience to authority at all but about trust. See "Instead of Deception," *Journal for the Theory of Social Behaviour* 2, no. 2 (1972): pp. 145–177.

20. See Herbert C. Kelman and V. Lee Hamilton, *Crimes of Obedience: Toward a Social Psychology of Authority and Responsibility* (New Haven: Yale University Press, 1989). The authors cover the issues pertinent to this topic. Their analysis, however, is flawed, especially with regard to the perpetrators of the Holocaust, because it depends upon the notion that the actors recognize their actions to be crimes.

21. This case has been put forward most recently and forcefully by Browning in *Ordinary Men*, esp. pp. 159–189.

22. Browning, *Ordinary Men*, argues that most of the men of Police Battalion 101 really did not want to kill Jews but that, since the job had to be done, each man felt himself to be under pressure not to leave the unpleasant task to others (pp. 184–185). This interpretation is psychologically implausible in light of what the perpetrators were being asked to do, namely to slaughter men, women, and children whom the perpetrators, in this view, would have considered to be completely innocent victims. There are limits to what people will do for their compatriots. Even more problematic for this line of argument is that there is virtually nothing in the material on Police Battalion 101—either in the men's words or in their actions—to support it. When the testimony of Germans in other police battalions and other institutions of killing is surveyed, the untenability of this interpretation becomes still clearer. In my extensive reading of the perpetrators' testimony, I have never once come across a German's assertion that the men serving in his killing institution were opposed to the slaughter but that they had all felt obliged not to leave the unpleasant duty for the others to perform. If this situation had obtained, either in Police Battalion 101 or in other institutions of killing, then an abundance of explicit testimony would exist that would make it obvious.

23. The explanation could be true for an entire group of people only if each is laboring under the misconception that the others held views contrary to his own. This would necessitate a degree of atomization of the kind that Hannah Arendt

imagined in *The Origins of Totalitarianism* (New York: Meridian Books, 1971) to have existed in Germany during the Nazi period. According to her, totalitarian domination destroys not just the public realm. It "destroys private life as well. It bases itself on loneliness, on the experience of not belonging to the world at all, which is among the most radical and desperate experiences of man" (p. 475). Contrary to Arendt's assertions, the perpetrators were not such atomized, lonely beings. They decidedly belonged to their world and had plenty of opportunities, which they obviously used, to discuss and reflect upon their exploits.

24. For a few cases, including that of Karl Koch, who was executed by the Nazis for his thievery, see Tom Segev, *Soldiers of Evil: The Commanders of Nazi Concentration Camps* (New York: McGraw-Hill, 1987), pp. 142ff., 210.

25. To some extent the plausibility of this proposed explanation depends upon a person's own understanding of the cynicism of people. Scholars who believe that for a promotion or for a few marks, these Germans were willing to slaughter Jews by the thousands should also believe that for tenure at a university or even for a small raise, virtually all of their colleagues today, and they themselves, would mow down innocent people by the thousands. Similarly, physicians should subscribe to the notion that virtually all of their colleagues would gladly, eagerly give lethal injections to thousands at the prospect of bettering their own institutional positions.

26. Raul Hilberg, *The Destruction of the European Jews* (New York: New Viewpoints, 1973), p. 649.

27. See Hilberg, *The Destruction of the European Jews*, pp. 643–649, for a discussion of the smoothness of the killing operation, although it was on the whole, undermanned. I disagree with much of Hilberg's interpretation, yet his conclusion regarding the unfolding of the genocide cannot be disputed: "No moral problem proved insurmountable. When all participating personnel were put to the test, there were very few lingerers and almost no deserters. The old moral order did not break through anywhere along the line. That is a phenomenon of the greatest magnitude" (p. 649).

28. Quoted in Robert J. Lifton, *The Nazi Doctors: Medical Killing and the Psychology of Genocide* (New York: Basic Books, 1986), p. 147.

29. William Blake, "A Divine Image," *Songs of Experience.*

30. Orlando Patterson, *Slavery and Social Death: A Comparative Study* (Cambridge: Harvard University Press, 1982), p. 198.

31. Quoted in Hermann Langbein, *Menschen in Auschwitz* (Frankfurt/M: Ullstein, 1980), p. 389.

32. Oskar Pinkus, *The House of Ashes* (Cleveland: World Publishing Co., 1964), pp. 24–25.

33. Chaim A. Kaplan, *The Warsaw Diary of Chaim A. Kaplan*, ed. Abraham I. Katsh (New York: Collier Books, 1973), pp. 155–156. As do so many other survivors, Henry Orenstein, in *I Shall Live: Surviving Against All Odds, 1939–1945* (New York: Touchstone, 1989), took note of the exceptional decent German: "A new young man from the Gestapo arrived in Hrubieszów. He was a simpleton, with a horse-like laugh, but at least he never harmed anyone; he was the only member of the Gestapo no one was afraid of " (p. 131). Perhaps the "simpleton's" good nature is what made him the exception to the general cruelty.

34. Erich Goldhagen, "The Mind and Spirit of East European Jewry During the Holocaust," *The Beiner-Citrin Memorial Lecture* (Cambridge: Harvard College Library, 1979), pp. 8–9.

35. Browning's view that the Germans' brutality was a utilitarian response to objective difficulties, such as the undermanning of ghetto-clearing operations (*Ordinary Men*, p. 95), and Raul Hilberg's related view that it was "most often" an "expression of impatience" during the routinized killing operations (*Perpetrators Victims Bystanders: The Jewish Catastrophe, 1933–1945* [New York: Asher Books, 1992], p. 54) are untenable. No doubt, each did occur, but to explain the Germans' practically limitless record of cruelty—so much of which occurred not during killing operations but during their quotidian contact with Jews inside and outside the camps—by appealing to pragmatism or impatience is to ignore and misunderstand a constituent feature of the Holocaust, the non-pragmatic nature of which, even and especially during killing operations, is testified to over and over again and virtually without exception in the many diaries of the victims written during the Holocaust and in the vast memoir literature of the survivors.

36. Aharon Weiss, "Categories of Camps—Their Character and Role in the Execution of the 'Final Solution of the Jewish Question,' " in *The Nazi Concentration Camps: Structure and Aims, The Image of the Prisoner, The Jews in the Camps* (Jerusalem: Yad Vashem, 1984), p. 129.

37. See Susan Zuccotti, *The Italians and the Holocaust: Persecution, Rescue, Survival* (New York: Basic Books, 1987); and Daniel Carpi, "The Rescue of Jews in the Italian Zone of Occupied Croatia," *Rescue Attempts During the Holocaust: Proceedings of the Second Yad Vashem International Conference*, ed. Yisrael Gutman and Efraim Zuroff (Jerusalem: "Ahva" Cooperative Press, 1977), pp. 465–506.

38. By no means should this be understood to imply that a *timeless* German character exists. The character structure and the common cognitive models of Germans have developed and evolved historically and, especially since the loss of the Second World War, have changed dramatically.

39. Similarly, the attributes that Germans imputed to other peoples which permitted them to treat those peoples as they did—to kill, to enslave, and to brutalize them—also need to be specified. This topic is addressed in the next chapter.

40. For a discussion of this general theme in the social sciences, see Jeffrey C. Alexander et al., eds., *The Micro-Macro Link* (Berkeley: University of California Press, 1987).

41. One exception is possibly (depending on how it is cast) the explanation that maintains that Germans were prone to obey authority.

42. Furthermore, if a single explanatory fact, particularly one that provides the common motivational element, can be found which accounts for the vast majority of the phenomena under study, then such an approach is preferable to some strained patchwork explanation.

43. Dr. Reinhard Maurach, "Expert Legal Opinion Presented on Behalf of the Defense," "U.S. v. Ohlendorf et al.," *TWC*, vol. 4., pp. 339–355, here pp. 351, 350, 353, 354. Maurach's brief vacillates throughout between maintaining that the perpetrators' beliefs about Jews were erroneous and asserting that they were based in reality. But he leaves no doubt that the perpetrators' beliefs were genuine.

44. Otto Ohlendorf, letter of Aug. 7, 1947, copy in my possession. That Maurach accurately represented the *Einsatzkommandos'* beliefs about Jewry's enmity towards Germany finds ample support in the perpetrators' own testimony not only in the Nuremberg *Einsatzgruppen* trial but also in subsequent investigations. See, for example, W.K., ZStL 207 AR-Z 15/58, pp. 2453–2454.

45. For an analysis of this complex figure, see Daniel Jonah Goldhagen, "The 'Humanist' as a Mass Murderer: The Mind and Deeds of SS General Otto Ohlendorf" (B.A. thesis, Harvard College, 1982).

46. This explanation should be accepted not only because (as is shown below) it meets the standard of accounting for the perpetrators' actions *better* than any rival explanation—leaving us no choice but to adopt it—but also because it meets the tougher standard of being able to account for the various phenomena (the inevitable exceptions notwithstanding) extraordinarily well. It is also theoretically and historically grounded, which lends it that much more credibility.

47. *Deutscher Wochendienst*, Apr. 2, 1943, Nur. Doc. NG-4713, quoted in Hilberg, *The Destruction of the European Jews*, p. 656.

48. Ernst Hiemer, *Der Giftpilz* (Nuremberg: Verlag Der Stürmer, 1938), p. 62.

49. H.G., HG, p. 456.

50. Pinkus, *The House of Ashes*, p. 119. He lived in the town of Łosice immediately north of the region that Police Battalion 101 helped to decimate.

51. Orenstein, *I Shall Live*, pp. 86–87.

52. Quoted in Klee, Dressen, and Riess, eds., *"The Good Old Days,"* p. 76. The man also mentions the great opportunities for collecting booty, but this was clearly a nice bonus for the men and not the source of either their hatred of Jews or their joy in killing them.

53. Kaplan, *Warsaw Diary*, p. 87. Kaplan's use of "Nazis" should be read as "Germans," for throughout the diary he describes all the Germans whom he knew or learned about—many of whom were not "Nazis" by institutional affiliation—as Nazis. It is significant that he considered Germans in general to have been Nazis.

54. This is Michael R. Marrus' characterization of them in *The Holocaust in History* (Hanover: University Press of New England, 1987), p. 47.

55. These lines of poetry were also quoted in the Judgment of the Nuremberg *Einsatzgruppen* trial, which rejected the self-exculpatory arguments of the defendants. See "U.S. v. Ohlendorf et al.," pp. 483–488.

56. William Shakespeare, *Julius Caesar*, 2.1.172.

57. See John Wheeler-Bennett, *The Nemesis of Power: The German Army in Politics, 1918–1945* (New York: St. Martin's Press, 1953), pp. 683–684; and Allen Dulles, *Germany's Underground* (New York: The Macmillan Co., 1947), p. 83.

58. For the search for a "humane" method of killing the mentally ill and severely handicapped, see Henry Friedlander, *The Origins of Nazi Genocide: From Euthanasia to the Final Solution* (Chapel Hill: University of North Carolina Press, 1995), p. 86.

59. Alfred Rosenberg, *Die Protokolle der Weisen von Zion und die jüdische Weltpolitik* (Munich: Deutsche Volksverlag, 1933), p. 132.

60. Bruno Malitz, *Die Leibesuebungen in der nationalsozialistischen Idee* (Munich: Verlag Frz. Eher Nacht., 1934), p. 45.

61. Herman Melville, *Moby-Dick* (Harmondsworth: Penguin, 1972), p. 283.

62. As much as the Germans' antisemitism was the basis of their profound hatred of the Jews and the psychological impulse to make them suffer, it obviously does not explain people's capacity for cruelty in the first place or the gratification many derive from it. The Germans' cruelty towards the Jews was so immense that it remains hard to fathom.

63. The tenacious adherence to the cultural cognitive model of Jews can be seen in a letter from an "ordinary" German army soldier written in June 1943, by which time the war had been going badly for Germany for a while. He writes that no one cares anymore about the Nazi regime. How does he know? "Among us comrades we can say anything. The time of fanaticism and intolerance of other opinions is over . . ." he reports, and the changes consist of general sobering, "and gradually one begins to think more clearly and more soberly. If we want to win the war, then we must become more reasonable and we ought not to repel the whole world, grandiloquently and boastfully. You yourself have noticed it during roll call that today one speaks differently from three years ago. . . ." So this man describes a new general critical attitude towards the regime, a new realization that they must find a way to live more harmoniously with others, and a total freedom of expression of these views, among his comrades. But with regard to the Jews, they remain Nazis: "It is true that we must win the war in order not to be exposed to the vengeance of the Jews, but the dreams of world domination are gone. . . ." Quoted in *Das andere Gesicht des Krieges: deutsche Feldpostbriefe, 1939–1945*, ed. Ortwin Buchbender and Reinhold Sterz (Munich: C. H. Beck, 1982), pp. 117–118. The virulent, obsessive antisemitism contained in these letters from ordinary soldiers, collected in this volume, brings to life the utterly fantastic, demonological vision that they had of Jews.

64. It is, therefore, no surprise that adherence to the cultural beliefs and support for Nazism could remain distinct, and that those who opposed Nazism on other grounds could march in lockstep with it against the Jews. This dimensional independence was as true for Germany during its Nazi period as it is in Germany or the United States today, where die-hard opponents of the party in power might nonetheless support, even enthusiastically support, certain policies of that same party.

65. The perpetrators' celebrations and boasting should surprise no one, since soldiers commonly celebrate great victories and boast of their heroics; the victories against Jewry were, after all, epochal victories to the demonological antisemite. Except for the immense cruelty, all of the Germans' actions could have been anticipated had people taken the extent and nature of German antisemitism seriously and considered its effects when harnessed to a governmental program of extermination. Of course, it is easy to say retrospectively that certain actions and outcomes could have been foretold. Nevertheless, in the case of celebrations, the somewhat comparable cases of victorious soldiers could have served as a guide.

66. Quoted in Klee, Dressen, and Riess, eds., *"The Good Old Days,"* p. 197.

67. In the presentation of each institution of killing, one or two central cases have been discussed in depth in order to provide the detailed description necessary to convey the character of the institution and its members' actions. This was supplemented by a broader discussion of each of the institutions of killing, which demonstrated that the essential aspects of the cases treated in depth were also general features of the given killing institution. These killing institutions were chosen for

study precisely because they, in different ways, should have put to the severest test the notion that racial eliminationist antisemitism motivated the perpetrators to kill Jews and that this antisemitism was powerful enough to override other considerations that should have tempered the exterminationist drive.

68. Orenstein, *I Shall Live*, p. 112.

69. Letter of Karl Kretschmer, Sept. 27, 1942, ZStL 204 AR-Z 269/60, Sonderband KA, p. 13.

70. German commanders' references to Jews' putative responsibility for the bombing of Germany, for partisan warfare, for the harming of the German economy, etc., were not offered as explanations (as if these alleged Jewish actions had been the cause) for the genocide, which included the Germans' slaughter of all Jewish children. Rather, commanders mentioned them, even casually, as but telling instances of the Jews' putative maleficence and machinations, which were meant to remind their men of the Jews' essential evil and of the mortal threat that the Jews were believed to pose to Germany.

71. See note 13 above.

72. Quoted in Krausnick and Wilhelm, *Die Truppe des Weltanschauugskrieges*, p. 557.

73. For the case of one SS man, an unusually brutal killer of Jews, who was convicted by an SS and Police Court of, among other things, taking photographs of killing operations and showing them to his wife and friends, see Klee, Dressen, and Riess, eds., *"The Good Old Days,"* pp. 196–207, esp. 202. The court, however, explicitly lauds him for his "real hatred of the Jews [that] was [the] driving motivation of the accused" (p. 201).

74. The person most responsible for promulgating this image is, of course, Hannah Arendt. See *Eichmann in Jerusalem: A Report on the Banality of Evil* (New York: Viking Press, 1968), and *The Origins of Totalitarianism*. Even Browning's enormously more nuanced account in *Ordinary Men* sometimes lapses into such tones (for examples, see pp. 74, 185).

75. In evaluating the various factors that contributed to the survival rate of Italian Jews, which was the highest of any country (except heroic Denmark) that was occupied by the Germans, Zuccotti, *The Italians and the Holocaust*, writes: "Clearly, the immediate factors favorable to Jewish rescue during the Holocaust must be placed in the context of the customs and traditions of individual countries. The most pertinent tradition, of course, is the existence or absence of anti-Semitism. For many reasons, modern Italy lacked an anti-Semitic tradition" (p. 278); see also Carpi, "The Rescue of Jews in the Italian Zone of Occupied Croatia," pp. 465–506. For an account of the Danes' rescue of the Danish Jews, see Leni Yahil, *The Rescue of Danish Jewry: Test of a Democracy* (Philadelphia: Jewish Publication Society of America, 1969). For a general discussion of the crucial influence that a country's antisemitism had for the survival of its Jews under German occupation, see Helen Fein, *Accounting for Genocide: National Responses and Jewish Victimization During the Holocaust* (New York: Free Press, 1979), esp. p. 82.

76. One Lithuanian recorded in her diary: "All Lithuanians and especially the intelligentsia, with a small number of exceptions, are united in their hatred of the Jews . . . I do not believe my eyes and ears; I shudder at the force of the blind ha-

tred . . ." Quoted in Mendl Sudarski, Uriyah Katzenelbogen, and Y. Gisin, eds., *Lite* (New York: Futuro Press, 1951), p. 1666. See also L. Garfunkel, *Kovna Hay'hudit B'khurbanah* (Jerusalem: Yad Vashem, 1959); Peter J. Potichny and Howard Aster, eds., *Ukrainian-Jewish Relations in Historical Perspective*, 2d ed. (Edmonton: CIUS, 1990); B. F. Sabrin, ed., *Alliance for Murder: The Nazi-Ukrainian Nationalist Partnership in Genocide* (New York: Sarpedon, 1991); and Shmuel Spector, *The Holocaust and Volhynian Jews, 1941–1944* (Jerusalem: Yad Vashem, 1990).

77. See, for example, Judgment Against Viktor Arajs, Hamburg (37) 5/76; Indictment Against Viktor Arajs, Hamburg 141 Js 534/60; and Judgment Against Karl Richard Streibel et al., Hamburg 147 Ks 1/72.

78. It is remarkable how little is known about the perpetrators of other genocides. A review of the literature reveals little about their identities, the character of their lives as killers, or their motivations. For an example, see Frank Chalk and Kurt Jonassohn, *The History and Sociology of Genocide: Analyses and Case Studies* (New Haven: Yale University Press, 1990).

79. This is an instructive comparison, since, among other things, it affords us the opportunity to examine the differences in Germans' actions towards people of different "races" and nationalities in structurally similar situations, especially in camps. Such an investigation reinforces the conclusion that structural and situational variables cannot account for the variance in the Germans' actions, because if there is no variation in the independent variable (the structure remains constant), then that variable cannot account for variation in the dependent variable (the different treatment of different groups of victims); this comparison strongly buttresses the conclusion that structural and situational causes were not paramount in engendering the Germans' willingness to kill and brutalize Jews. Even Wolfgang Sofsky, who argues forcefully in *Die Ordnung des Terrors: Das Konzentrationslager* (Frankfurt/M: Fischer Verlag, 1993) for a structural interpretation of the actions of concentration camp guards, must acknowledge that the guards' treatment of different prisoner groups varied enormously (pp. 137–151). This, of course, casts doubt on his structural perspective, though he fails to draw the appropriate conclusions. For an overview of the Nazis' assaults on non-Jews, see Michael Berenbaum, ed., *A Mosaic of Victims: Non-Jews Persecuted and Murdered by the Nazis* (New York: New York University Press, 1990).

80. Significantly, the medical and scientific elite were more susceptible to these notions about the infirm than was the peasant. See Robert Proctor, *Racial Hygiene: Medicine under the Nazis* (Cambridge: Harvard University Press, 1988). Those who argue that the killers were of simple mental capacity, that they were the unthinking members typifying all societies who, it is alleged, could easily be nudged to brutality, have to write off this intellectual elite (and those with Ph.D.s in the *Sicherheitsdienst* [SD]) as "super"-Nazis in order to explain how intelligent people could have perpetrated these crimes. Why see them as super-Nazis? They were an intellectual elite who, using pseudo-scientific reasoning, elaborated upon and brought the common German ideational strains to a logical conclusion. They merely gave gutter beliefs—which ran not only through the gutter but also through bourgeois German homes and German universities—scientific form and, hence, drew practical implications that left, if anything, less room for variation. Those who deny the shared

Nazified outlook of the perpetrators give one kind of explanation for the supposed simple souls, another for the super-Nazis, and declare by fiat that everyone in between was of another attitude towards the systematic slaughter of designated groups. It makes much more sense to look for the common, unifying threads that made Germans from all stations and walks of life assenting agents of death.

81. For central aspects of Nazi race theory, see Hans Günther, *Rassenkunde des deutschen Volkes* (Munich: Lehmanns Verlag, 1935); also Hans Jürgen Lutzhöft, *Der Nordische Gedanke in Deutschland, 1920–1940* (Stuttgart: Ernst Klett Verlag, 1971).

82. Christa Kamenetsky, *Children's Literature in Hitler's Germany: The Cultural Policy of National Socialism* (Athens, Ohio: Ohio University Press, 1984), p. 166.

83. Max Weinreich, *Hitler's Professors: The Part of Scholarship in Germany's Crimes Against the Jewish People* (New York: YIVO, 1946), p. 89, n. 204.

84. Adolf Hitler, *Mein Kampf* (Boston: Houghton Mifflin, 1971), p. 300.

85. Josef Ackermann, *Heinrich Himmler Als Ideologe* (Göttingen: Musterschmidt, 1970), p. 160.

86. This is true of the Turkish slaughter of the Armenians, the slaughter of the Indonesian Communists, the Burundian Tutsi slaughter of the Hutus, Stalin's slaughter of the Kulaks and his genocidal measures in Ukraine, the Pakistanis' slaughter of Bengalis in Bangladesh, to name but a few. For accounts of these and other genocidal killings, see Frank Chalk and Kurt Jonassohn, *The History and Sociology of Genocide: Analyses and Case Studies* (New Haven: Yale University Press, 1990); Leo Kuper, *Genocide: Its Political Use in the Twentieth Century* (New Haven: Yale University Press, 1981); and Robert Conquest, *Harvest of Sorrow: Soviet Collectivization and the Terror-Famine* (New York: Oxford University Press, 1986). Although objective conflicts did exist, this, of course, neither justifies the genocidal measures nor casts any responsibility on the victims for the acts of the killers.

87. Soviet Jews, before they realized that these Germans were like no Germans they had ever known, initially greeted the advancing German army obligingly and without hostility. A German armaments inspector remarked upon this in his report to General Georg Thomas, explaining "that [the Jews] hated the German administration and army inwardly is obvious and cannot be surprising . . ." (Nur. Doc. 3257-PS, *IMT*, vol. 32, p. 73). Such were the distorting lenses of German antisemitism.

88. Quoted in Steven E. Aschheim, " 'The Jew Within': The Myth of 'Judaization' in Germany," in Jehuda Reinharz and Walter Schatzberg, *The Jewish Response to German Culture: From the Enlightenment to the Second World War* (Hanover: University Press of New England, 1985), p. 240.

89. See Georg Lilienthal, *Der "Lebensborn e.V.": Ein Instrument nationalsozialistischer Rassenpolitik* (Stuttgart: Gustav Fischer Verlag, 1985), pp. 218–234.

90. See Kuper, *Genocide*, p. 110.

91. To be sure, the Gulag's conditions were often lethal and its guards treated the prisoners in a brutal and murderous manner, yet the cruelty of the guards did not even begin to approach that which the Germans inflicted on Jews. See Robert Conquest, *The Great Terror: A Reassessment* (New York: Oxford University Press, 1990), pp. 308–340, for an account; this is also borne out by Aleksandr Solzhenitsyn, *The Gulag Archipelago, 1918–1956: An Experiment in Literary Investigation* (New York: Harper & Row, 1974).

Chapter 16

1. The analytical issue is simple: If a person has a prior willingness to act, then a presumption that a punishment exists for inaction does not explain the action. For this individual, the presumption of punishment—assuming that he gives it any thought—is irrelevant to the voluntaristic action. The same holds for material advantage. If a person is willing to do something for free, then the offer of reward may be a nice bonus, but it does not explain the person's voluntaristic act.

2. It is not enough merely to dehumanize people, for slaves, who are dehumanized in many cultures to an extraordinary extent, are typically not killed. For killing to ensue, a particular set of beliefs are necessary which typically includes the conviction that the dehumanized group is a source of grave danger.

3. Without receiving institutional support and direction, such beliefs do not produce violence more sustained than that of riots or pogroms. Similarly, states often restrain the violent impulses that such beliefs engender in people, as the German state did in the nineteenth century. Otto Stobbe, a historian of German Jewry in the middle ages, reflected in 1866 on how little the underlying German hatred of Jews had changed since the middle ages: "Even though the latest legislation, in many places, has pronounced the complete emancipation of the Jews, much is lacking still for its full realization. And if the State did not protect the Jew against gross injustice, Jewry today would still be exposed to persecution and abuse by the mob." Quoted in Guido Kisch, *The Jews in Medieval Germany: A Study of Their Legal and Social Status* (Chicago: University of Chicago Press, 1949), p. x.

4. For treatments of prominent cases of genocide, see Frank Chalk and Kurt Jonassohn, *The History and Sociology of Genocide: Analyses and Case Studies* (New Haven: Yale University Press, 1990).

5. See Jacob Katz, *From Prejudice to Destruction: Anti-Semitism, 1700–1933* (Cambridge: Harvard University Press, 1980), for a comparative treatment of the development of antisemitism in a number of European areas.

6. This has been borne out by Helen Fein, *Accounting for Genocide: National Responses and Jewish Victimization During the Holocaust* (New York: Free Press, 1979), who has shown that across occupied Europe, the degree of each country's prewar antisemitism explains a great deal of the variance in the Germans' success in killing the Jews of different countries (see pp. 64–92). It should be added that the capacity of Germans to influence or block the regime was so much greater than that of the peoples of occupied Europe.

7. The periodization changes slightly depending on whether it marks the *intentions* or the *policies*. The periodization given here focuses on policy. If it were to be made according to Hitler's intentions, then *Kristallnacht* might delimit the beginning of the second phase; Hitler's *decision* to annihilate the Jews would mark the beginning of the third phase. Eberhard Jäckel, *Hitler's World View: A Blueprint for Power* (Cambridge: Harvard University Press, 1981), delimits similar phases, although his understanding of their genesis and character differs fundamentally (p. 61).

8. *Nazism*, p. 1055.

9. On the Nazis' use of Jews in negotiations for material or political advantage, see Yehuda Bauer, *Jews for Sale? Nazi-Jewish Negotiations, 1933–1945* (New Haven:

Yale University Press, 1994). Bauer notes that as temporary, tactical exceptions, these initiatives did not ultimately run counter to the Nazis' intention of destroying Jewry completely.

10. See David Bankier, "Hitler and the Policy-Making Process on the Jewish Question," *HGS* 3, no. 1 (1988): pp. 1–20, esp. pp. 16–17.

11. The central role of geo-strategic considerations in fashioning the eliminationist policy was at the heart of the June 3, 1940, memorandum from the head of the German Foreign Office's Jewish desk, Franz Rademacher, to his superior, Martin Luther, on the disposition of the Jews. It is characterized by the axiomatic belief in the power of Jews to manipulate foreign powers (in this case, the United States) and therefore in the strategic value in holding so many Jews hostage, both of which influenced Hitler's strategic thinking. Rademacher stated here explicitly the shared understanding of the dual and intertwined aims of the war: imperialistic expansion of Germany and "liberation of the world from the chains of Jewry and free masonry. . . ." For a long excerpt from this memorandum, see Christopher R. Browning, *The Final Solution and the German Foreign Office: A Study of Referat D III of Abteilung Deutschland, 1940–1943* (New York: Holmes & Meier, 1978), pp. 36–37.

12. Werner Jochmann, ed., *Adolf Hitler: Monologe im Führer-Hauptquartier, 1941–1944* (Hamburg: Albrecht Knaus Verlag, 1980), p. 108.

13. Goebbels, in a June 1944 speech in Nuremberg, boasted that the Nazis had not made their ultimate intentions known publicly, and, by implication, confirmed that they had had to wait for the opportune moment to put their intentions into practice: "It would have been very unwise if we had given exact explanations to the Jews, prior to the Seizure of Power, of what we intended to do with them. . . . It was quite good that [they] did not take the National-Socialist movement quite as seriously as it actually deserved. . . ." Quoted in Hans-Heinrich Wilhelm, "The Holocaust in National-Socialist Rhetoric and Writings: Some Evidence against the Thesis that before 1945 Nothing Was Known about the 'Final Solution,' " *YVS* 16 (1984): p. 112, n. 23.

14. *Völkischer Beobachter*, Aug. 7, 1929, quoted in Erich Goldhagen, "Obsession and Realpolitik in the 'Final Solution,' " *Patterns of Prejudice* 12, no. 1 (Jan.–Feb. 1978): p. 10. Shortly after assuming power in 1933, Hitler expressed in a policy meeting the notion that they should kill the mentally ill. See Michael Burleigh, *Death and Deliverance: Euthanasia in Germany c. 1900–1945* (Cambridge: Cambridge University Press, 1994), p. 97.

15. Had the Germans, say, in 1940, deported the Jews living under their dominion to Lublin, Madagascar, or some other place, there is nothing to suggest that they would have continued to let these Jews live. The decision to slaughter Soviet Jewry, root and branch, a decision organic to the Nazi worldview, would undoubtedly have been applied to Jews whom the Germans had previously moved to some "reservation," just as the Germans did, in fact, apply it to ghettoized Polish Jews and to French Jews, and expected to apply it to English and Turkish Jews. Indeed, had Hitler been so inclined during the spring, summer, and fall of 1941, as the prospective new master of Europe and the vast Russian landmass stretching to the Pacific, he could easily have revived the previously considered plans for deporting the Jews of Poland and Europe to some isolated, sealed colony, plans which he could have expected to implement in a leisurely manner at the proper time. Yet he did not do this.

16. For Himmler's murderous statement, which he made in a speech, see the testimony of SS General Erich von dem Bach-Zelewski, *IMT*, vol. 4, p. 482. For a general account of the Germans' murderous plans in eastern Europe, see Ihor Kamenetsky, *Secret Nazi Plans for Eastern Europe: A Study of Lebensraum Policies* (New York: Bookman Associates, 1961); and Robert Gibbons, "Allgemeine Richtlinien für die politische und wirtschaftliche Verwaltung der besetzten Ostgebiete," *VfZ* 24 (1977): pp. 252–261.

17. Jochmann, ed., *Adolf Hitler*, p. 229.

18. There were rare exceptions, like General Franz von Rocques. During the first days of the slaughter of Soviet Jewry, he told General Wilhelm von Leeb (who, without dissent, recorded the suggestion in his diary) that the mass shooting of Jews would not be successful. "The surest way to solve [the Jewish Problem]," he ventured, "would be to sterilize all Jewish males." Here is an instance in which, although there was obviously no disagreement over the Hitlerian understanding of the "Jewish Problem," there was a desire for a functionally equivalent, if pragmatically and aesthetically (in their eyes) superior, "solution." See Helmut Krausnick and Hans-Heinrich Wilhelm, *Die Truppe des Weltanschauungskrieges: Die Einsatzgruppen der Sicherheitspolizei und des SD, 1938–1942* (Stuttgart: Deutsche Verlags-Anstalt, 1981), pp. 207–208.

19. Reginald H. Phelps, "Hitlers 'Grundlegende' Rede über den Antisemitismus," *VfZ* 16, no. 4 (1968): p. 412. Hitler added that the Jews were against the death penalty because they knew that it should be applied to them.

20. Phelps, "Hitlers 'Grundlegende' Rede über den Antisemitismus," p. 418.

21. An approximate average of escaping foreign workers for the months of February through August and December 1943 is 33,000, with an unbroken increase from February of slightly over 20,000 to December of 46,000. Most of the escapees were captured quickly. See Ulrich Herbert, "Der 'Ausländereinsatz': Fremdarbeiter und Kriegsgefangene in Deutschland, 1939–1945—ein Überblick," in *Herrenmensch und Arbeitsvölker: Ausländische Arbeiter und Deutsche, 1939–1945* (Berlin: Rotbuch Verlag, 1986), p. 41.

22. See Falk Pingel, *Häftlinge unter SS-Herrschaft: Widerstand, Selbstbehauptung und Vernichtung im Konzentrationslager* (Hamburg: Hoffmann und Campe, 1978), pp. 118–179; and Ulrich Herbert, "Arbeit und Vernichtung: Ökonomisches Interesse und Primat der 'Weltanschauung' im Nationalsozialismus," in Dan Diner, ed., *Ist der Nationalsozialismus Geschichte? Zu Historisierung und Historikerstreit* (Frankfurt/M: Fischer, 1987), pp. 198–236.

23. How, at least in this instance, should the power of eliminationist antisemitism, when operating in interaction with other German aspirations and constraints, be evaluated? In light of the entire set of conflicting German goals, among which economic production was secondary, it is fair to say that overall, in the means-ends, instrumental sense of rationality, the Germans acted in a more or less rational manner. They managed to kill millions of Jews; they extracted some production out of them without letting the production confound their primary aim of extermination; and they made the Jews suffer to previously unimaginable degrees along the way. Their policies were inconsistent and, even from their point of view, certainly could have been far more intelligently formulated and implemented. But overall, in

light of their values and their incompatible needs, the Germans did not do a bad job. The Germans themselves generally judged their endeavor a success. They managed to harness "work" to the cart of death, an extraordinary feat and a testament to their worldview, its antisemitism, and its power to pervert them.

24. K.D., Hoffmann, p. 2677.

25. For a discussion of such cases, see Wolfgang Benz, "Überleben im Untergrund, 1943–1945," in Wolfgang Benz, ed., *Die Juden in Deutschland, 1933–1945: Leben unter nationalsozialistischer Herrschaft* (Munich: Verlag C. H. Beck, 1988), pp. 660–700.

26. This was the famous antisemitic cry coined by Heinrich von Treitschke, the most prominent of the disaffected liberal intellectuals who embraced antisemitism. He was writing in 1879, yet he expressed the transcendent appeal of antisemitism in Germany that was to endure for almost three-quarters of a century when noting that even "from among men who would scornfully reject every notion of clerical intolerance or national arrogance, one hears today unanimously: 'The Jews are our misfortune!' " (quoted in Alfred D. Low, *Jews in the Eyes of Germans: From the Enlightenment to Imperial Germany* [Philadelphia: Institute for the Study of Human Issues, 1979], p. 372).

27. Robert Gellately, *The Gestapo and German Society: Enforcing Racial Policy, 1933–1945* (Oxford: Clarendon Press, 1990), pp. 205–206, 58. Even among this paltry number of critical remarks, some did not contest the prevalent conception of Jews or the justice of the eliminationist program, but instead questioned the wisdom of the measures given the speakers' expectations that the Jews would take revenge on Germany (see pp. 208–209). Others could be construed as critical in this manner only by liberal interpretation. Almost half of the Munich cases were dropped, so flimsy must they have been (p. 206). Gellately concludes that the dearth of remarks critical of German policy towards the Jews "is an indication of the extent to which citizens accommodated themselves to the official line." I see no reason to conclude that they were merely "accommodating" themselves, in the sense of adapting themselves to circumstances over which, in this case, they had little control—especially since Germans failed to be critical throughout the history of the eliminationist persecution, regardless of the policies then being pursued or the changing circumstances and fortunes of Germany. As I have been arguing all along, the record suggests that not accommodation, but ideological congruity characterized the Germans' acceptance and support for the eliminationist enterprise. If mere "accommodation" had indeed occurred, then why, to ask the not-frequently-enough-posed comparative question, did Germans "accommodate" themselves in this sphere but not in other analogous ones?

28. Manfred Messerschmidt, "Harte Sühne am Judentum: Befehlslage und Wissen in der deutschen Wehrmacht" in Jörg Wollenberg, ed., *"Niemand war dabei und keiner hat's gewusst": Die deutsche Öffentlichkeit und die Judenverfolgung 1933–1945* (Munich: Piper, 1989), p. 123.

29. Kunrat von Hammerstein, *Spähtrupp* (Stuttgart: Henry Goverts Verlag, 1963), p. 192.

30. Quoted in Wolfgang Gerlach, *Als die Zeugen schwiegen: Bekennende Kirche und die Juden*, 2d ed. (Berlin: Institut Kirche und Judentum, 1993), pp. 372–373.

31. Quoted in Friedrich Heer, *God's First Love* (Worcester: Trinity Press, 1967), p. 272.

32. Quoted in Gerlach, *Als die Zeugen schwiegen*, p. 244.

33. Quoted in Gerlach, *Als die Zeugen schwiegen*, p. 376.

34. *Kirchliches Jahrbuch Für Die Evangelische Kirche in Deutschland, 1933–1944* (Gütersloh: C. Bertelsmann Verlag, 1948), p. 481.

35. Quoted in Gerlach, *Als die Zeugen schwiegen*, p. 372.

36. William Shakespeare, *The Merchant of Venice*, 5.1. 90–91.

37. Guenter Lewy, *The Catholic Church and Nazi Germany* (New York: McGraw-Hill, 1964), p. 308.

38. Quoted in Gerlach, *Als die Zeugen schwiegen*, p. 31.

39. Quoted in Gerlach, *Als die Zeugen schwiegen*, p. 29.

40. Quoted in Gerlach, *Als die Zeugen schwiegen*, p. 29. This judgment about the ubiquity and nature of antisemitism in the Protestant churches echoes Gerlach's conclusion.

41. Quoted in Gerlach, *Als die Zeugen schwiegen*, p. 153.

42. See, for example, Johannes Steiner, ed., *Prophetien wider das Dritte Reich* (Munich: Verlag Dr. Schell und Dr. Steiner, 1946).

43. See Otto Dov Kulka and Aron Rodrigue, "The German Population and the Jews in the Third Reich: Recent Publications and Trends in Research on German Society and the 'Jewish Question,' " in *YVS* 16 (1984): pp. 421–435; and Ian Kershaw, "German Popular Opinion and the 'Jewish Question,' 1939–1943: Some Further Reflections," in Arnold Paucker, ed., *Die Juden im nationalsozialistischen Deutschland: The Jews in Nazi Germany, 1933–1945* (New York: Leo Baeck Institute, 1986), pp. 365–386; David Bankier, *The Germans and the Final Solution: Public Opinion under Nazism* (Oxford: Basil Blackwell, 1992), p. 137; and Hans Mommsen and Dieter Obst, "Die Reaktion der deutschen Bevölkerung auf die Verfolgung der Juden, 1933–1945," in Hans Mommsen and Susanne Willems, eds., *Herrschaftsalltag im Dritten Reich: Studien und Texte* (Düsseldorf: Schwann, 1988), pp. 374–421, esp. p. 406, where they even say that there was "widespread moral indifference."

44. For a different understanding of "indifference," see Michael Herzfeld, *The Social Production of Indifference: Exploring the Symbolic Roots of Western Bureaucracy* (New York: Berg Publishers, 1992).

45. W. H. Auden, "In Memory of W. B. Yeats," *Another Time: Poems* (New York: Random House, 1940).

46. The German word that was used by contemporaries to describe the attitude of the populace towards the persecution of the Jews is *"teilnahmslos,"* typically translated as "indifference" or "apathetic." Ian Kershaw, "The Persecution of the Jews and German Popular Opinion in the Third Reich," *Leo Baeck Yearbook* 26 (1981), for example, quoting a *Sopade* report, writes about Baden: "Although some 'sharply rejected' the persecution, the majority of the population remained 'completely apathetic' [*absolut teilnahmslos*]" (p. 330). This does not convey the sense of the German accurately. *"Teilnahmslos"* is better rendered in English as "unsympathetic." The Germans here were "completely unsympathetic," which captures the meaning of people's emotions in the face of great suffering. They *lacked* sympathy, which was the source and mechanism of their seeming "apathy" or "indifference." *"Teilnahmslos"* does not mean "indifferent" in the sense that the word *"gleichgültig"* does, in the sense of a lack of concern, of the absence of caring one way or the other. Although a person can be *"teilnahmslos,"*

namely without compassion, to the suffering of another, he cannot be *"teilnahmslos"* to the success of another. *"Teilnahmslos"* bespeaks callousness, and something must make people callous, since it is not the naturally occurring response to such horrors.

47. Wolfgang Wippermann, *Das Leben in Frankfurt zur NS-Zeit: Die national-sozialistische Judenverfolgung* (Frankfurt/M: Kramer, 1986), vol. 1, p. 104.

48. Thomas Hobbes, "Of the Passions of the Mind," *The Elements of Law: Natural and Politic* (London: Frank Cass & Co., 1969), p. 40.

49. As I have argued, the burden of proof rightly falls on those who maintain that a large portion of the Germans did not subscribe to Nazi-like antisemitism, to what has been described here as the cultural cognitive model of Jews. In reading works that assert this view, it is indeed striking how little or non-existent the *evidence* is that they present to support the claim that Germans' beliefs about Jews differed from the incessantly trumpeted Nazi one.

50. E.C., ZStL 204 AR-Z 269/60, vol. 2, p. 471. This man had been so beholden to the Nazified view of the world that in this 1962 interrogation he could say that their views about Jews had found substantiation in "much of what we experienced in Russia" (as well as in the Morgenthau Plan).

51. *Why I Left Germany*, by a German Jewish Scientist (London: M. M. Dent & Sons, 1934), p. 214.

52. Quoted in Harmut Ludwig, "Die Opfer unter dem Rad Verbinden: Vor- und Entstehungsgeschichte, Arbeit und Mitarbeiter des Büro Pfarrer Grüber" (habilitation diss., Berlin, 1988), p. 76, n. 208.

53. A survey done by American occupation authorities at the end of 1946 revealed that fully 61 percent of Germans were willing to express views that classified them as racists or antisemites. Another 19 percent received the classification of nationalists. The report describes the depressing situation: "To sum up: four in ten Germans are so strongly imbued with anti-semitism that it is very doubtful that they would object to overt action against the Jews, though all of them might themselves not participate in such actions. . . . Less than two in ten could probably be counted on to resist such overt behavior." This was a year and a half after the defeat of Nazism! These figures, moreover, undoubtedly greatly *understate* the degree of antisemitism that existed in Germany. It is well known that surveys tend to understate the extent of prejudice that people have. In this case, these views could potentially have landed people in trouble, since the country was being governed by the Allies and antisemitic expression could have been seen as risky. Moreover, the surveys were conducted in person by Americans from the Military Government, which would have reduced still further the willingness of Germans to reveal their racism and antisemitism. (Indeed, a test showed that when Germans conducted these surveys, the percentage of Germans who were willing to express favorable views of Nazism—compared to when Americans asked the same questions—rose by over 10 percent.) See Frank Stern, *The Whitewhashing of the Yellow Badge: Antisemitism and Philosemitism in Postwar Germany* (Oxford: Pergamon Press, 1992), pp. 106–157, here p. 124; Anna J. Merritt and Richard L. Merritt, *Public Opinion in Occupied Germany: The OMGUS Surveys, 1945–1949* (Urbana: University of Illinois Press, 1970), pp. 5–8, 146–148.

This is not to say that antisemitism in Germany did not greatly dissipate and change its character in the Federal Republic (although Germany continues to this day to remain infected by antisemitism). It did so for a number of reasons. Essentially, after the war, Germans were reeducated. The public conversation in Germany ceased being antisemitic; in fact, antisemitic expression became illegal. Germans, moreover, were subjected to counter-images of Jews, first under Allied occupation and then when they regained sovereignty. Young Germans were not brought up and educated in a publicly antisemitic culture. The Nazified view of Jews, because it was so at odds with reality, was also fragile; its hallucinatory components were difficult to maintain without institutional reinforcement. As Germans became democrats, as they reintegrated themselves into the western world and began to look upon the persecution of the Jews more with the eyes of the rest of the world, as they came to see the Holocaust as the greatest crime in European history, it became ever more difficult for them to maintain a demonized image of Jews, even if many Germans continued not to like Jews. That absurd beliefs can rapidly dissipate is well known. The change in Whites' consciousness about the nature of Blacks and their appropriate place in American society underwent a sea change in the American South between 1960 and, say, 1980. Just as no one would point to the beliefs of non-racist White southerners today as evidence that their counterparts in the 1950s had not been racists, no one should point to the extent and character of antisemitism in Germany in the 1960s or 1970s as evidence that Germans were not eliminationist antisemites in 1940.

54. Phelps, "Hitlers 'Grundlegende' Rede über den Antisemitismus," p. 417.

55. Quoted in Gerlach, *Als die Zeugen schwiegen*, p. 46.

56. Yet it must be emphasized that in no sense did the Nazis "brainwash" the German people; the Nazis' enormous efforts notwithstanding, they failed in their efforts to "indoctrinate" Germans on a host of other issues, so the notion that overnight they could induce Germans to accept a hallucinatory, demonized image of Jews which was contrary to what Germans had previously believed is simply absurd. Germans' prior beliefs were crucial for determining which elements of the Nazi eschatology they would accept and follow.

57. See Robert P. Ericksen, *Theologians under Hitler: Gerhard Kittel, Paul Althaus and Emanuel Hirsch* (New Haven: Yale University Press, 1985), pp. 55–56.

58. See the table that is the final (unnumbered) page of Klemens Felden, "Die Uebernahme des antisemitischen Stereotyps als soziale Norm durch die bürgerliche Gesellschaft Deutschlands (1875–1900)" (Ph.D. diss., Ruprecht-Karl-Universität, Heidelberg, 1963).

59. Theodor Haecker, "Zur Europäischen Judenfrage," *Hochland* 24, no. 2 (Apr–Sept 1927), p. 618. He added, "We do not want to conceal this fact from ourselves."

60. That Hitler could do so with the extermination of the Jews and not with the so-called Euthanasia program shows that Germans would not follow Hitler in violation of their deepest moral dictates, of their sense of what was acceptable and desirable. For a discussion of the differential constancy of the German people's devotion to Hitler's different causes, see Ian Kershaw, *The "Hitler Myth"* (Oxford: Clarendon Press, 1987).

61. Werner Jochmann also takes this position in "Die deutsche Bevölkerung und die nationalsozialistische Judenpolitik bis zur Verkündung der Nürnberger Gesetze," in *Gesellschaftskrise und Judenfeindschaft in Deutschland, 1870–1945* (Ham-

burg: Hans Christians Verlag, 1988): "There was thus a fundamental concord [*Grundkonsens*] between the people and the leadership," which was the necessary condition that enabled Hitler to proceed quickly with the persecution of the Jews without encountering opposition (p. 237).

62. Nur. Doc. 1816-PS, *IMT*, vol. 28, p. 534. Ursula Büttner, "Die deutsche Bevölkerung und die Juden Verfolgung, 1933–1945," in Ursula Büttner, ed., *Die Deutschen und die Judenverfolgung im Dritten Reich* (Hamburg: Hans Christians Verlag, 1992), also makes this point (p. 77).

63. Quoted in Georg Denzler and Volker Fabricius, *Die Kirchen im Dritten Reich: Christen und Nazis Hand in Hand?* (Frankfurt/M: Fischer, 1985), vol. 1, p. 95.

64. Bankier, *The Germans and the Final Solution*, writes, ". . . the bulk of Germans endorsed antisemitic policy fully aware that a pure racial community could not be achieved if one were unduly sensitive to morality" (p. 156). His understatement ("unduly sensitive to morality") notwithstanding, it was clear to all that the morality which applied to relations among Germans was wholly suspended when dealing with Jews.

65. Konrad Kwiet and Helmut Eschwege, *Selbstbehauptung und Widerstand: Deutsche Juden im Kampf um Existenz und Menschenwuerde, 1933–1945* (Hamburg: Hans Christians Verlag, 1984), also make this point (p. 34).

66. This is excepting, to some extent, SS men who were part of an organization that was obsessively antisemitic. For an account of the centrality of antisemitism in the SS, see Bernd Wegner, *The Waffen-SS: Organization, Ideology and Function* (Oxford: Basil Blackwell, 1990), esp. pp. 48–53.

67. Quoted in Konrad Kwiet, "Nach dem Pogrom: Stufen der Ausgrenzung," in Benz, ed., *Die Juden in Deutschland, 1933–1945*, p. 627.

68. The exterminationist impulse inherent in this antisemitism was observed by Lothrop Stoddard, an American journalist who, during a visit to Germany at the end of 1939, was a witness to its frequent expression: "In Nazi Germany, the resolve to eliminate the Jews is further exacerbated by theories of race. The upshot, in Nazi circles, is a most uncompromising attitude. If this is not oftener expressed, the issue is already decided in principle and that elimination of the Jews will be completed within a relatively short space of time. So, ordinarily, the subject does not arise. But it crops up at unexpected moments. For instance, I have been stunned at a luncheon or dinner with Nazis, where the Jewish question had not been even mentioned, to have somebody raise his glass and casually toast: *Sterben Juden!*—'May the Jews Die!' " Repeatedly and casually did these Germans speak murderous words in the presence of an American journalist. They treated this intended fate of the Jews as a matter of common sense—apparent, understood, and accepted by all—fit to be toasted without any prior discussion. In 1939 (and earlier), the whiff of genocide could be detected in the antisemitic German atmosphere. See Lothrop Stoddard, *Into the Darkness: Nazi Germany Today* (New York: Duell, Sloan & Pearce, 1940), pp. 287–288.

69. Oskar Pinkus, *The House of Ashes* (Cleveland: World Publishing Co., 1964), p. 36.

70. Chaim A. Kaplan, *The Warsaw Diary of Chaim A. Kaplan*, ed. Abraham I. Katsh (New York: Collier Books, 1973), p. 120.

71. Kaplan, *Warsaw Diary*, pp. 129–130. Though recording his own thoughts, Kaplan's views were anything but idiosyncratic. It was considered to be a document of such historical value that Emmanuel Ringelblum, the chronicler of the Warsaw ghetto, "implored" Kaplan to give him the diary for safekeeping. See Abraham Katsh's introduction to the diary, pp. 14–15.

72. Verfügung, ZStL 202 AR 165/61, pp. 401–402.

73. Ludwig Eiber " '. . . ein bisschen die Wahrheit': Briefe eines Bremer Kaufmanns von seinem Einsatz beim Reserve-Polizeibataillon 105 in der Sowjetunion 1941," *1999* 1/91 (1991): pp. 73, 75.

74. Quoted in Alf Lüdtke, "The Appeal of Exterminating 'Others': German Workers and the Limits of Resistance," in Michael Geyer and John W. Boyer, eds., *Resistance Against the Third Reich, 1933–1990* (Chicago: University of Chicago Press, 1994), p. 73. This letter, with its unequivocal statement about the "complete extermination" of Jews, suggests that by this time, knowledge of the extermination in Germany was widespread and casual. Halbermalz assumed that those at home already knew of the genocide, as is indicated by his failure to explain the context of the Germans' razing of the ghetto, which is necessary to know if someone is to make sense of the event itself or, for that matter, to understand (and share in) the satisfaction that it provides.

75. Indictment Against Hans Krüger, ZStL, 208 AR-Z 498/59, pp. 255–256.

76. Judgment Against Br. et al., Dortmund 10 Ks 1/53, in *Justiz und NS-Verbrechen: Sammlung Deutscher Strafurteile Wegen Nationalsozialistischer Tötungsverbrechen, 1945–1966* (Amsterdam: University Press Amsterdam, 1974), vol. 12, p. 332; see also Christopher R. Browning, *Ordinary Men: Reserve Police Battalion 101 and the Final Solution in Poland* (New York: HarperCollins, 1992), p. 41.

77. J.U., Hoffmann, p. 2665; W.H., Hoffmann, p. 2213; and K.S., HG, p. 659.

78. For an account of the meeting of December 16, 1941, at which leading German officials applauded the "shoot-to-kill order," see Hans Frank, *Das Diensttagebuch des deutschen Generalgouverneurs in Polen 1939–1945*, ed. Werner Präg and Wolfgang Jacobmeyer (Stuttgart: Deutsche Verlags-Anstalt, 1975), pp. 452–458.

79. J.S., ZStL, 208 AR-Z 24/63, p. 1371.

80. W.G., Buchs, p. 1384.

81. For examples, see Indictment of Paul Raebel et al., StA Stuttgart 12 Js 1403/61, for two Yom Kippur killing operations in Tarnopol (pp. 129–130); and Judgment Against Hans Krüger et al., Münster 5 Ks 4/65, for a killing operation in Nadvornaya on the first day of Sukkot (pp. 137–194).

82. ZStL 213 AR 1900/66, doc. vol. 4, pp. 668–677. The "poet" also mentioned explicitly the Krimchaks, a two-thousand-year-old group of Crimean Jews whom the Germans slaughtered. The men of *Einsatzkommando 11a*—this includes the *Einsatzkommandos* and the men of Police Battalion 9—were so antisemitic that they "universally" taunted one of the men of Police Battalion 9 who had a Jewish-sounding name and dark hair, by calling him "Jew Eisenstein." They even threatened to kill him because of these features (O.E., ZStL 213 AR 1900/66, p. 1822). What is the likelihood that they disapproved of their country's slaughter of the Jews?

83. Adalbert Rückerl, *Nationalsozialistische Vernichtungslager im Spiegel deutscher Strafprozesse: Belzec, Sobibor, Treblinka, Chelmno* (Munich: Deutscher Taschenbuch Verlag, 1977), pp. 281, 292. The Germans subsequently reopened Chełmno in 1944 for further killing.

84. Indictment Against Hans Krüger et al., ZSt Dortmund 45 Js 53/61, p. 189.

85. Indictment Against A.B., StA Lübeck 2 Js 394/70, p. 148.

86. See Klaus Scholder, "Ein Requiem für Hitler: Kardinal Bertram und der deutsche Episkopat im Dritten Reich," *Frankfurter Allgemeine Zeitung*, Oct. 25, 1980. Scholder writes about the special significance of the "solemn requiem mass": "According to Catholic Church law a solemn requiem mass may be celebrated only for a believing member of the Church and only on an important occasion, and if it is in the public interest of the Church . . ." In a January 1944 letter, Bertram appears, by implication, to have given his own and—claiming to speak for them—the German people's endorsement to the extermination of the Jews, a fate that he (and, according to him, they) would not countenance for baptized Christians. Although Bertram objected "if these fellow Christians now would have to meet a fate similar to that of the Jews," which he explicitly wrote was "extermination," Bertram did not object to the Jews' fate either then or earlier. See Lewy, *The Catholic Church and Nazi Germany*, p. 291. As the discussion of the Church leadership's thoroughgoing antisemitism has shown, Bertram's antisemitism reflected the prevailing norm.

87. Thousands of Catholic priests and Protestant ministers tended to the spiritual needs of the millions of Germans who served in the army, in police units, and in other institutions of killing. Did the Catholics among the perpetrators confess their killing of Jews as sins? Did the millions who witnessed and knew of the wholesale slaughter (especially in the Soviet Union, where the killings took place in the open for all to see) seek counsel from their spiritual guides? What did the men of God tell them? And why, as far as we know, did virtually none of them ever raise a voice against the slaughter of the Jews?

Epilogue

1. Not surprisingly, it was the generation socialized during the Nazi period that became still more rabidly antisemitic than their parents' generation and previous generations were. By all accounts, during the Nazi period the youth of Germany were thoroughly racist and antisemitic, were living, essentially, in a world structured by important cultural cognitive assumptions as fantastically different from our own as those that have governed distant times and places. One former Hitler Youth, Alfons Heck, *The Burden of Hitler's Legacy* (Frederick, Colo.: Renaissance House, 1988), describes the widespread antisemitism, "shared by millions of Germans," which was imparted to them in school during their weekly "racial science" classes. He and the other children "absorbed [their teacher's] demented views as matter-of-factly as if he were teaching arithmetic" (pp. 49–50). Heck, drawing on his own experience, rightly indicts his countrymen: "All children are defenseless receptacles, waiting to be filled with wisdom or venom by their parents and educators. We who were born into Nazism never had a chance unless our parents were brave enough to resist the tide and transmit their opposition to their children. There were few of those. The majority of Germans lined up solidly behind Hitler, once he had proven he could indeed wreak fundamental change" (p. 44). As Heck understands it, ordinary Germans were themselves at least as culpable as the "educators" were for the views of their children. Two revealing accounts of German youth during the Nazi period—one written in 1941, the other composed after the war—have arrived at the same conclusion, which

is expressed in their titles: Gregor Athalwin Ziemer, *Education for Death, the Making of the Nazi* (London: Oxford University Press, 1941); and Geert Platner and Schüler der Gerhart-Hauptmann-Schule in Kassel, eds., *Schule im Dritten Reich: Erziehung zum Tod* ["Schools in the Third Reich: Education for Death"] (Cologne: Pahl-Rugenstein, 1988). For accounts of the racist antisemitic ideas with which German students were inundated, see *The Nazi Primer: Official Handbook for Schooling the Hitler Youth* (New York: Harper & Brothers, 1938), which was the textbook for the seven million fourteen- to eighteen-year-olds in the Hitler Youth. It presents the Jews in an explicit eliminationist manner; Gilmer W. Blackburn, *Education in the Third Reich: Race and History in Nazi Textbooks* (Albany: State University of New York Press, 1985); and Kurt-Ingo Flessau, *Schule der Diktatur: Lehrpläne und Schulbücher des Nationalsozialismus* (Munich: Fischer Verlag, 1977).

2. Quoted in Erich Goldhagen, "Obsession and Realpolitik in the 'Final Solution,' " *Patterns of Prejudice* 12, no. 1 (1978): p. 9.

3. Chaim A. Kaplan, *The Warsaw Diary of Chaim A. Kaplan*, ed. Abraham I. Katsh (New York: Collier Books, 1973), p. 64.

4. Speech of Oct. 1943, Nur. Doc. NO-5001.

5. Did ordinary Germans think that they would give back eastern Europe and live in peace with a German-resuscitated independent Poland and independent Russia? The evidence does not suggest that they expected to be anything but imperial overlords. Jacob Perel, the subject of the film *Europa, Europa*, when asked what he envisaged would happen to him after a German victory (in which he fully believed), responded that he imagined that he would inherit the estate of the SS man who had adopted him and that he would become "a little *Führer*" of the Slavs working for him.

6. Erich Goldhagen, "Obsession and Realpolitik in the 'Final Solution,' " p. 9.

7. Léon Poliakov and Joseph Wulf, eds., *Das Dritte Reich und seine Denker* (Frankfurt/M: Ullstein, 1983), pp. 503–504. Similarly, SS General Friedrich Jeckeln, who was the *HSSPF* Russia-South, when discussing during the summer of 1941 the extermination of the Jews with one of his subordinates, R.R., mentioned that Himmler had said in conversation, in the words of R., that "the Ukrainians should become a people of Helots [*ein Helotenvolk*] that work only for us" (Indictment Against R.R., M.B., and E.K., StA Regensburg I 4 Js 1495/65, p. 36). This was not idle talk. The Germans were actually putting this into practice.

Appendix 1

1. My study of these institutions is based upon, in addition to the secondary literature, the materials from the Federal Republic of Germany's legal investigations and trials housed in the ZStL, which contain interrogations of the perpetrators, statements by survivors and bystanders, as well as all relevant documents that could be found. The materials, of course, are highly variable in quantity and quality even for like cases. Some cases contain dozens of volumes in typescript, totaling thousands of pages and including hundreds of interviews and interrogations. For Police Battalion 101, for example, there were two separate legal investigations, Hoffmann and HG. The transcript of the Hoffmann investigation is in 27 volumes (two of which are of trial testimony) and 4,517 pages. Twelve additional volumes contain generally unilluminating material from the

appeals process. Additionally, an Indictment and a lengthy Judgment from the first trial were produced. Each is a meaty document summarizing the major events and points of the case. A volume of documents is also part of the investigation. The HG investigation is in 13 volumes and 2,284 pages. It never went to trial and no indictment was prepared. In addition, a volume of photographs is part of the Hoffmann investigation. (A few photographs not contained in it are to be found in ZStL.) The Helmbrechts death march investigation, also discussed here, includes 25 volumes, 10 additional Beiakten (A–J), and a series of Zeugen volumes (which reproduce and order much of the testimony of the other volumes), as well as the Judgment against the commander, Dörr, which is contained in vol. 25. These are by no means among the most voluminous investigations. Some investigations, in contrast, are as slim as a single volume. It should also be clear that I have not studied each case mentioned in equivalent depth. For some, I read only as much as I thought necessary, in order to extract the essential features of the case (undoubtedly missing many telling episodes, facts, and evaluations). Others, including the ones cited here, I read thoroughly.

2. For various considerations on the analytical power of the comparative method, see Ivan Vallier, ed., *Comparative Methods in Sociology: Essays on Trends and Applications* (Berkeley: University of California Press, 1973); see also Arend Lijphart, "Comparative Politics and the Comparative Method," *American Political Science Review* 65 (1971): pp. 682–683; and Gary King, Robert O. Keohane, and Sidney Verba, *Designing Social Inquiry: Scientific Inference in Qualitative Research* (Princeton: Princeton University Press, 1994).

3. Christopher R. Browning, *Ordinary Men: Reserve Police Battalion 101 and the Final Solution in Poland* (New York: HarperCollins, 1992); and Heiner Lichtenstein, *Himmlers grüne Helfer: Die Schutz- und Ordnungspolizei im "Dritten Reich"* (Cologne: Bund Verlag, 1990).

4. On crucial cases and the criteria for selecting them, see Harry Eckstein, "Case Study and Theory in Political Science," in *Strategies of Inquiry*, ed. Fred I. Greenstein and Nelson W. Polsby, vol. 7 of *Handbook of Political Science* (Reading, Mass.: Addison-Wesley, 1975), pp. 79–138. For a critique of the notion of a "crucial case," see King, Keohane, and Verba, *Designing Social Inquiry*, pp. 209–212. Because my study draws on a *number* of cases, which could be considered in different ways each to be a "least likely case" to confirm the proposed explanation, the criticism which King, Keohane, and Verba direct at the "crucial case" method does not apply here. Indeed, by choosing a number of cases based on independent variables, the case selection method conforms to their prescriptions.

5. Typically, when a killing operation, location, or institution was being investigated, the investigators would build up, from documents and interrogations, a list of those suspected of having been involved in the crimes. They would then endeavor to track down those people and to interrogate them. They also would contact survivors and, sometimes, bystanders, from whom depositions would be taken. In some investigations, they managed to find and interrogate hundreds of perpetrators. The interrogations might be as brief as a typescript page, or might fill twenty or more pages. Many perpetrators were interrogated on a number of occasions, as cases proceeded and new information was obtained. The interrogations tended to focus on the life history of the institution under investigation (often the investigators began with lit-

tle or virtually no knowledge of what the institution's members had done), on the logistics of the killing operation (particularly, the identity of those present, what the individuals did, and who gave commands), and on the actions of those who were likely to be indicted or already were under indictment. In short, the interrogations focus on establishing what crimes were committed and who committed them. The only crime with which all but the earliest investigations (and they were few and unrevealing) were concerned was murder, because the statute of limitations had expired for all other crimes. So the investigators were generally interested in acts of cruelty only insofar as they were perpetrated by the tiny percentage of perpetrators whom they indicted or believed they might indict, because such acts of cruelty would help to establish a perpetrator's motive; investigators, therefore, generally did not ask about or delve into the cruelties that the vast majority of perpetrators committed. The investigators were, to give another example, also not interested in investigating the lives of the perpetrators while they were in genocidal institutions but were not undertaking killing operations. This neglect includes the character of the perpetrators' social relations. So, although the investigatory materials, especially the interrogations, are the richest, most revealing source for studying the perpetrators, they are biased in the materials that they contain, systematically omitting a variety of materials that would be of great interest to the historian and social scientist alike, and which would have further enriched this study.

6. Such discrepancies are most obviously in evidence when it comes to estimating the number of people whom the Germans killed or deported during a given operation. The numbers are of great historical but of little analytical importance in this context. Whether the Germans killed in one city 1,200, 1,500, or 2,000 Jews had no substantial bearing on the nature of the operation, the phenomenology of the killing, or the perpetrators' psychology. The numerical discrepancies are usually of this order. In the analysis, I present alternative accounts and discussions of the discrepancies only when doing so is of analytical or substantial historical significance. With regard to the number of Jews whom the Germans killed or deported in a given operation, I either present what seems to me to be the most sensible figure or offer the most sensible range of the number of victims. All such numbers should be seen as being estimates; though they are at times imprecise, the imprecision never significantly bears on the analysis of the themes treated here. I have decided not to include or cite every last utterance or reference to every last utterance regarding numbers in the text and the notes, for though such scholarly thoroughness brings admiration for its own sake, it contributes little towards the goal of analysis.

7. The privacy laws of the Federal Republic of Germany oblige researchers not to reveal the names of those mentioned in the legal investigations unless the people have died or their names have already become public. Therefore, pseudonyms are sometimes used for people mentioned in the text and initials are often used for those mentioned only in the notes.

8. For considerations of the deficiencies of postwar reconstructions, see the essays in Saul Friedländer, ed., *Probing the Limits of Representation: Nazism and the "Final Solution"* (Cambridge: Harvard University Press, 1992).

9. Any statement to the effect "We all disapproved" is *self*-exonerating. If someone were to say "I approved of the killing and all the others did not," then his statement would carry much weight.

10. The work of James C. Scott, *Domination and the Arts of Resistance: Hidden Transcripts* (New Haven: Yale University Press, 1985), has very much influenced my own thinking on this subject. It explores the myriad ways in which violently dominated people express their opposition to their condition. These themes are taken up in the case chapters.

11. Believing the perpetrators' self-exonerations would thus be terribly misleading. Rejecting them entails but small costs, because if the self-serving claims were true, then, in the main, the verification demanded would be in evidence. Undoubtedly, some truthful self-exonerations will be dismissed because of this methodological position; this will somewhat bias the view of the perpetrators that is developed. Nevertheless, for the reasons stated—reasons which become very clear and which are buttressed by extensive argument and evidence in the body of the book—I believe that such uncorroborated true statements are few, and that such bias is negligible. Simply put, there is no other sensible methodological choice other than discounting them. If others disagree, then it is incumbent upon them to articulate a superior approach to this difficult material.

ACKNOWLEDGMENTS

Most of my primary research for this book was done over more than a year at the Zentrale Stelle der Landesjustizverwaltungen in Ludwigsburg, where its permanent denizens, prosecutors and staff people alike, did everything possible to facilitate my work and to make me feel welcome. I am thankful for having found myself in such an hospitable atmosphere while working in a foreign country, daily, on such a trying subject. I thank in particular Alfred Streim, who as the director of the Zentrale Stelle sets the tone that engenders the cooperative working environment, and Willi Dressen, who generously extended to me his help and knowledge. Many staff people, especially Herta Doms, Herr Fritschle, and Ute Böhler, showed patience and dedication in helping me find the material that I sought and in providing the intangible support one needs when carrying out such research. Bettina Birn and Volker Riess, while doing their own research, provided comradeship and valuable advice during the course of my stay.

I thank also Eberhard Jäckel for his support during my time in Stuttgart. Helge Grabitz in the Hamburg State Prosecutor's Office, Oberstaatsanwalt Hofmann in the Hof State Prosecutor's Office, Hermann Weiss in the Institut für Zeitgeschichte in Munich, and Genya Markon and Sharon Muller of the United States Holocaust Memorial Museum's Photo Archive each provided me with kind help, for which I am appreciative.

My research was aided by grants from the Fulbright program, the Krupp Foundation, and the Minda de Gunzburg Center for European Studies at Harvard University and its Program for the Study of Germany and Europe. The Whiting Foundation, the Littauer Foundation, and the Simon Wiesenthal Center in Los Angeles also provided financial assistance. To all of these institutions, I am grateful.

I thank particularly the people who collectively compose the Center for European Studies, a most congenial institution to have as an intellectual home. Many of its members deserve thanks for their friendship no less than for the help that they have extended to me. I feel particular gratitude for Stanley Hoffmann, Guido Goldman, and Abby Collins for having made me feel so welcome at the center.

Stanley Hoffmann, Peter Hall, and Sidney Verba, who supervised the dissertation that was the basis of this book, encouraged and assisted my work, and provided the mix of guidance and latitude that was just right for me. Their personal warmth and kindness, together with their strengths as scholars, make them lofty examples for a young scholar. Richard Breitman, Mustafa Emirbayer, Saul Friedländer, and Paul Pierson deserve special thanks for their helpful comments on the manuscript, as does Norma Goldhagen, my mother. I would like to thank *all* of the people at Alfred A. Knopf, in particular Stephanie Koven, Barbara de Wilde, Max Franke, Amy Robbins, Mark Stein, and Brooke Zimmer, who helped in the production of the book and with whom it has been a pleasure to work. I am especially grateful to Carol Janeway, who, with imagination, dedication, and good cheer, has done everything that an author could hope an editor would do, and to Simon Schama for putting me in touch with her.

My greatest debt is to my father, Erich Goldhagen, a man of remarkable intellectual and human qualities. Without his continuous, enriching conversation, his keen insights tossed forward with the ease of casual remarks, and his standard and model of intellectual sobriety and probity, it would not have been possible for me to have made of my talents however much I have. In particular, my understanding of Nazism and of the Holocaust is firmly indebted to his, and the substance of this work is greatly improved because of his unparalleled knowledge and understanding of the people and events of this most difficult-to-fathom period. During my research and writing, he was my constant discussion partner. For these and other reasons, I dedicate this book to him.

INDEX

Italicized page numbers refer to photographs; numbers in **boldface** refer to maps.

Page 92: © Bildarchiv Preussischer Kulturbesitz, Berlin, Germany / Courtesy of
United States Holocaust Memorial Museum (USHMM), Washington, D.C.

93: © Bildarchiv Preussischer Kulturbesitz, Berlin, Germany (Arthur Grimm,
photographer) / Courtesy of USHMM

96: Rijks Instituut Voor Oorlogsdocumentatie, Amsterdam, Netherlands /
Courtesy of USHMM

99: Courtesy of the Leo Baeck Institute, New York, New York / Courtesy of
USHMM

100: © Bildarchiv Preussischer Kulturbesitz, Berlin, Germany / Courtesy of
USHMM

124: National Archives, Washington, D.C. / Courtesy of USHMM

151 (top and bottom): Courtesy of Yad Vashem, Jerusalem, Israel

154: Main Commission for the Investigation of Nazi Crimes, Warsaw, Poland /
Courtesy of USHMM

155 (top): Main Commission for the Investigation of Nazi Crimes, Warsaw,
Poland / Courtesy of USHMM

155 (bottom): Babi Yar Society, Kiev, Ukraine / Courtesy of USHMM

224: Courtesy of ZStL, Ludwigsburg, Germany

225 (top and bottom): Courtesy of ZStL, Ludwigsburg, Germany

226 (top and bottom): Courtesy of ZStL, Ludwigsburg, Germany

236: Courtesy of Staatsanwaltschaft Hamburg, Hamburg, Germany

243 (left and right): Courtesy of Berlin Document Center, Berlin, Germany

245: Courtesy of ZStL, Ludwigsburg, Germany

257: Courtesy of Yad Vashem, Jerusalem, Israel

258: Main Commission for the Investigation of Nazi Crimes, Warsaw, Poland /
Courtesy of USHMM

260 (top and bottom): Courtesy of Yad Vashem, Jerusalem, Israel